Java™ Performance

The Java™ Series

Effective Java Second Edition — Joshua Bloch

Filthy Rich Clients Developing Animated and Graphical Effects for Desktop Java Applications — Chet Haase · Romain Guy — Foreword by James Gosling

The Java Tutorial Fourth Edition A Short Course on the Basics — Sharon Zakhour · Scott Hommel · Jacob Royal · Isaac Rabinovitch · Tom Risser · Mark Hoeber

The Java Programming Language, Fourth Edition — Ken Arnold · James Gosling · David Holmes

The Java EE 5 Tutorial Third Edition

✦ Addison-Wesley

Visit **informit.com/thejavaseries** for a complete list of available publications.

Publications in **The Java™ Series** are supported, endorsed, and written by the creators of Java at Sun Microsystems, Inc. This series is the official source for expert instruction in Java and provides the complete set of tools you'll need to build effective, robust, and portable applications and applets. **The Java™ Series** is an indispensable resource for anyone looking for definitive information on Java technology.

Visit Sun Microsystems Press at **sun.com/books** to view additional titles for developers, programmers, and system administrators working with Java and other Sun technologies.

Java™ Performance

Charlie Hunt
Binu John

✦✦Addison-Wesley

Upper Saddle River, NJ • Boston • Indianapolis • San Francisco
New York • Toronto • Montreal • London • Munich • Paris • Madrid
Capetown • Sydney • Tokyo • Singapore • Mexico City

The publisher offers excellent discounts on this book when ordered in quantity for bulk purchases or special sales, which may include electronic versions and/or custom covers and content particular to your business, training goals, marketing focus, and branding interests. For more information, please contact

U.S. Corporate and Government Sales
(800) 382-3419
corpsales@pearsontechgroup.com

For sales outside the United States, please contact:

International Sales
international@pearson.com

Visit us on the Web: informit.com/aw

Library of Congress Cataloging-in-Publication Data

Hunt, Charlie, 1962-
 Java performance / Charlie Hunt, Binu John.
     p.   cm.
 Includes bibliographical references and index.
 ISBN-13: 978-0-13-714252-1
 ISBN-10: 0-13-714252-8 (pbk. : alk. paper)
 1. Java (Computer program language)   2. Computer programming.   I. John, Binu, 1967-   II. Title.
 QA76.73.J38H845 2012
 005.13'3—dc23   2011031889

ISBN-13: 978-0-13-714252-1
ISBN-10:   0-13-714252-8

Text printed in the United States on recycled paper at Edwards Brothers in Ann Arbor, Michigan.
First printing, September 2011

To the three B's, Barb, Boyd, and Beau – C.H.
To Rita, Rachael, and Kevin – B.J.

Contents

Foreword

Tuning a Java application can be challenging in today's large-scale mission-critical world. There are issues to be aware of in everything from the structure of your algorithms, to their memory allocation patterns, to the way they do disk and file I/O. Almost always, the hardest part is figuring out where the issues are. Even (perhaps especially) seasoned practitioners find that their intuitions are wrong. Performance-killing gremlins hide in the most unlikely places.

As Wikipedia says, "Science (from Latin: *scientia* meaning 'knowledge') is a systematic enterprise that builds and organizes knowledge in the form of testable explanations and predictions about the world." Performance tuning must be approached as an experimental science: To do it properly, you have to construct experiments, perform them, and from the result construct hypotheses.

Fortunately, the Java universe is awash in performance monitoring tools. From standalone applications to profilers built into development environments to tools provided by the operating system. They all need to be applied in a cohesive way to tease out the truth from a sea of noise.

This book is *the* definitive masterclass in performance tuning Java applications. It readably covers a wide variety of tools to monitor and measure performance on a variety of hardware architectures and operating systems. And it covers how to construct experiments, interpret their results, and act on them. If you love all the gory details, this is the book for you.

—James Gosling

Foreword

Today, Java is used at the heart of the world's largest and most critical computing systems. However, when I joined the Java team in 1997 the platform was young and just gaining popularity. People loved the simplicity of the language, the portability of bytecodes, and the safety of garbage collection (versus traditional malloc/free memory management of other systems). However, there was a trade-off for these great features. Java was slow, and this limited the kinds of environments where you could use it.

Over the next few years, we set about trying to fix this. We believed that just because Java applications were portable and safe they didn't have to be slow. There were two major areas where we focused our attention. The first was to simply make the Java platform faster. Great strides were made in the core VM with advanced Just In Time compilation techniques, parallel garbage collection, and advanced lock management. At the same time the class libraries were tweaked and tuned to make them more efficient. All this led to substantial improvements in the ability to use Java for larger, more critical systems.

The second area of focus for us was to teach people how to write fast software in Java. It turned out that although the syntax of the language looked similar to C, the techniques you needed to write efficient programs were quite different. To that end, Jeff Kessleman and I wrote one of the first books on Java performance, which was published back in 2000. Since then, many books have covered this topic, and experienced developers have learned to avoid some of the most common pitfalls that used to befall Java developers.

After the platform began to get faster, and developers learned some of the tricks of writing faster applications, Java transformed into the enterprise-grade software powerhouse it is today. It began to be used for the largest, most important systems anywhere. However, as this started to happen, people began to realize one part was still missing. This missing piece was *observability*. When these systems get larger and larger, how do you know if you're getting all the performance you can get?

In the early days of Java we had primitive profiling tools. While these were useful, they had a huge impact on the runtime performance of the code. Now, modern JVMs come with built-in observability tools that allow you to understand key elements of your system's performance with almost no performance penalty. This means these tools can be left enabled all the time, and you can check on aspects of your application while it's running. This again changes the way people can approach performance.

The authors of *Java™ Performance* bring all these concepts together and update them to account for all the work that's happened in the last decade since Jeff and I published our book. This book you are now reading is the most ambitious book on the topic of Java performance that has ever been written. Inside are a great many techniques for improving the performance of your Java applications. You'll also come to understand the state of the art in JVM technology from the inside out. Curious about how the latest GC algorithms work? It's in here! You'll also learn how to use the latest and greatest observability tools, including those built into the JDK and other important tools bundled into popular operating systems.

It's exciting to see how all these recent advancements continue to push the platform forward, and I can't wait to see what comes next.

—Steve Wilson
VP Engineering, Oracle Corporation
Founding member of the Java Performance team
Coauthor of *Java™ Platform Performance: Strategies and Tactics*

Preface

Welcome to the definitive reference on Java performance tuning!

This book offers Java performance tuning advice for both Java SE and Java EE applications. More specifically, it offers advice in each of the following areas: performance monitoring, profiling, tuning the Java HotSpot VM (referred to as HotSpot VM hereafter), writing effective benchmarks, and Java EE application performance tuning. Although several Java performance books have been written over the years, few have packed the breadth of information found in this book. For example, the topics covered in this book include items such as an introduction into the inner workings of a modern Java Virtual Machine, garbage collection tuning, tuning Java EE applications, and writing effective benchmarks.

This book can be read from cover to cover to gain an in-depth understanding of many Java performance topics. It can also be used as a task reference where you can pick up the text, go to a specific chapter on a given topic of interest, and find answers.

Readers who are fairly new, or consider themselves a novice in the area of Java performance tuning, will likely benefit the most by reading the first four chapters and then proceeding to the topics or chapters that best address the particular Java performance tuning task they are undertaking. More experienced readers, those who have a fundamental understanding of performance tuning approaches and a basic understanding of the internals of the HotSpot VM along with an understanding of the tools to use for monitoring operating system performance and monitoring JVM performance, will find jumping to the chapters that focus on the performance tuning task at hand to be most useful. However, even those with advanced Java performance skills may find the information in the first four chapters useful.

Reading this book cover to cover is not intended to provide an exact formula to follow, or to provide the full and complete knowledge to turn you into an experienced Java performance tuning expert. Some Java performance issues will require specialized expertise to resolve. Much of performance tuning is an art. The more you work on Java performance issues, the better versed you become. Java performance tuning also continues to evolve. For example, the most common Java performance issues observed five years ago were different from the ones observed today. Modern JVMs continue to evolve by integrating more sophisticated optimizations, runtimes, and garbage collectors. So too do underlying hardware platforms and operating systems evolve. This book provides up-to-date information as of the time of its writing. Reading and understanding the material presented in this book should greatly enhance your Java performance skills. It may also allow you to build a foundation of fundamentals needed to become fluent in the art of Java performance tuning. And once you have a solid foundation of the fundamentals you will be able to evolve your performance tuning skills as hardware platforms, operating systems, and JVMs evolve.

Here's what you can expect to find in each chapter.

Chapter 1, "Strategies, Approaches, and Methodologies," presents various different approaches, strategies, and methodologies often used in Java performance tuning efforts. It also proposes a proactive approach to meeting performance and scalability goals for a software application under development through an enhancement to the traditional software development process.

Chapter 2, "Operating System Performance Monitoring," discusses performance monitoring at the operating system level. It presents which operating system statistics are of interest to monitor along with the tools to use to monitor those statistics. The operating systems of Windows, Linux, and Oracle Solaris are covered in this chapter. The performance statistics to monitor on other Unix-based systems, such as Mac OS X, use similar commands, if not the same commands as Linux or Oracle Solaris.

Chapter 3, "JVM Overview," provides a high level overview of the HotSpot VM. It provides some of the fundamental concepts of the architecture and workings of a modern Java Virtual Machine. It establishes a foundation for many of the chapters that follow in the book. Not all the information presented in this chapter is required to resolve every Java performance tuning task. Nor is it exhaustive in providing all the necessary background to solve any Java performance issue. However, it does provide sufficient background to address a large majority of Java performance issues that may require some of the concepts of the internal workings and capabilities of a modern Java Virtual Machine. The information in this chapter is applicable to understanding how to tune the HotSpot VM along with understanding the subject matter of Chapter 7 and how to write effective benchmarks, the topics covered in Chapters 8 and 9.

Chapter 4, "JVM Performance Monitoring," as the title suggests, covers JVM performance monitoring. It presents which JVM statistics are of interest to monitor along with showing tools that can be used to monitor those statistics. It concludes with suggesting tools that can be extended to integrate both JVM level monitoring statistics along with Java application statistics of interest within the same monitoring tool.

Chapter 5, "Java Application Profiling," and Chapter 6, "Java Application Profiling Tips and Tricks," cover profiling. These two chapters can be seen as complementary material to Chapter 2 and Chapter 4, which cover performance monitoring. Performance monitoring is typically used to identify whether a performance issue exists, or provides clues as to where the performance issue exists, that is, in the operating system, JVM, Java application, and so on. Once a performance issue is identified and further isolated with performance monitoring, a profiling activity usually follows. Chapter 5 presents the basics of Java method profiling and Java heap (memory) profiling. This profiling chapter presents free tools for illustrating the concepts behind these types of profiling. The tools shown in this chapter are not intended to suggest they are the only tools that can be used for profiling. Many profiling tools are available both commercially and for free that offer similar capabilities, and some tools offer capabilities beyond what's covered in Chapter 5. Chapter 6 offers several tips and tricks to resolving some of the more commonly observed patterns in profiles that tend to be indicative of particular types of performance problems. The tips and tricks identified in this chapter are not necessarily an exhaustive list but are ones that have been observed frequently by the authors over the course of years of Java performance tuning activities. The source code in many of the examples illustrated in this chapter can be found in Appendix B.

Chapter 7, "Tuning the JVM, Step by Step," covers tuning the HotSpot VM. The topics of tuning the HotSpot VM for startup, memory footprint, response time/latency, and throughput are covered in the chapter. Chapter 7 presents a step-by-step approach to tuning the HotSpot VM covering choices such as which JIT compiler to use, which garbage collector to use, and how to size Java heaps, and also provides an indication when the Java application itself may require some rework to meet the performance goals set forth by application stakeholders. Most readers will likely find Chapter 7 to be the most useful and most referenced chapter in this book.

Chapter 8, "Benchmarking Java Applications," and Chapter 9, "Benchmarking Multi-tiered Applications," present information on how to write effective benchmarks. Often benchmarks are used to help qualify the performance of a Java application by implementing a smaller subset of a larger application's functionality. These two chapters also discuss the art of creating effective Java benchmarks. Chapter 8 covers the more general topics associated with writing effective benchmarks such as exploring some of the optimizations performed by a modern JVM. Chapter 8 also includes information on how to incorporate the use of statistical methods to gain confidence in your benchmarking experiments. Chapter 9 focuses more specifically on writing effective Java EE benchmarks.

For readers who have a specific interest in tuning Java EE applications, Chapter 10, "Web Application Performance," Chapter 11, "Web Services Performance," and Chapter 12, "Java Persistence and Enterprise Java Beans Performance," focus specifically on the areas of Web applications, Web services, persistence, and Enterprise Java Bean performance, respectively. These three chapters present in-depth coverage of the performance issues often observed in Java EE applications and provide suggested advice and/or solutions to common Java EE performance issues.

This book also includes two appendixes. Appendix A, "HotSpot VM Command Line Options of Interest," lists HotSpot VM command line options that are referenced in the book and additional ones that may be of interest when tuning the HotSpot VM. For each command line option, a description of what the command line option does is given along with suggestions on when it is applicable to use them. Appendix B, "Profiling Tips and Tricks Example Source Code," contains the source code used in Chapter 6's examples for reducing lock contention, resizing Java collections, and increasing parallelism.

Acknowledgments

Charlie Hunt

Without the help of so many people this book would not have been possible. First I have to thank my coauthor, Binu John, for his many contributions to this book. Binu wrote all the Java EE material in this book. He is a talented Java performance engineer and a great friend. I also want to thank Greg Doech, our editor, for his patience. It took almost three years to go from a first draft of the book's chapter outline until we handed over a manuscript. Thank you to Paul Hohensee and Dave Keenan for their insight, encouragement, support, and thorough reviews. To Tony Printezis and Tom Rodriguez, thanks for your contributions on the details of the inner workings of the Java HotSpot VM garbage collectors and JIT compilers. And thanks to all the engineers on the Java HotSpot VM runtime team for having detailed documentation on how various pieces of the HotSpot VM fit together. To both James Gosling and Steve Wilson, thanks for making time to write a foreword. Thanks to Peter Kessler for his thorough review of Chapter 7, "Tuning the JVM, Step by Step." Thanks to others who contributed to the quality of this book through their insight and reviews: Darryl Gove, Marty Itzkowitz, Geertjan Wielenga, Monica Beckwith, Alejandro Murillo, Jon Masamitsu, Y. Srinivas Ramkakrishna (aka Ramki), Chuck Rasbold, Kirk Pepperdine, Peter Gratzer, Jeanfrancois Arcand, Joe Bologna, Anders Åstrand, Henrik Löf, and Staffan Friberg. Thanks to Paul Ciciora for stating the obvious, "losing the race" (when the CMS garbage collector can't free enough space to keep up with the young generation promotion rate). Also, thanks to Kirill Soshalskiy, Jerry Driscoll, both of whom I have worked under during the time of writing this book, and to John Pampuch (Director of VM Technologies at Oracle) for their support. A very special thanks to my wife, Barb, and sons, Beau and Boyd, for putting up with a grumpy writer, especially during those times of "writer's cramp."

Binu John

This book has been possible only because of the vision, determination, and perseverance of my coauthor, Charlie Hunt. Not only did he write the sections relating to Java SE but also completed all the additional work necessary to get it ready for publication. I really enjoyed working with him and learned a great deal along the way. Thank you, Charlie. A special thanks goes to Rahul Biswas for providing content relating to EJB and Java persistence and also for his willingness to review multiple drafts and provide valuable feedback. I would like to thank several people who helped improve the quality of the content. Thank you to Scott Oaks and Kim Lichong for their encouragement and valuable insights into various aspects of Java EE performance; Bharath Mundlapudi, Jitendra Kotamraju, and Rama Pulavarthi for their in-depth knowledge of XML and Web services; Mitesh Meswani, Marina Vatkina, and Mahesh Kannan for their help with EJB and Java persistence; and Jeanfrancois Arcand for his explanations, blogs, and comments relating to Web container. I was fortunate to work for managers who were supportive of this work. Thanks to Madhu Konda, Senior Manager during my days at Sun Microsystems; Sef Kloninger, VP of Engineering, Infrastructure, and Operations; and Sridatta Viswanath, Senior VP of Engineering and Operations at Ning, Inc. A special thank you to my children, Rachael and Kevin, and my wonderful wife, Rita, for their support and encouragement during this process.

About the Authors

Charlie Hunt is the JVM Performance Lead Engineer at Oracle. He is responsible for improving the performance of the HotSpot Java Virtual Machine and Java SE class libraries. He has also been involved in improving the performance of both GlassFish Server Open Source Edition and Oracle WebLogic application servers. He wrote his first Java program in 1998 and joined Sun Microsystems, Inc., in 1999 as a Senior Java Architect. He has been working on improving the performance of Java and Java applications ever since. He is a regular speaker on the subject of Java performance at many worldwide conferences including the JavaOne Conference. Charlie holds a Master of Science in Computer Science from the Illinois Institute of Technology and a Bachelor of Science in Computer Science from Iowa State University.

Binu John is a Senior Performance Engineer at Ning, Inc., the world's largest platform for creating social web sites. In his current role, he is focused on improving the performance and scalability of the Ning platform to support millions of page views per month. Before joining Ning, Binu spent more than a decade working on Java performance at Sun Microsystems, Inc. As a member of the Enterprise Java Performance team, he worked on several open source projects including the GlassFish Server Open Source Edition application server, the Open Source Enterprise Service Bus (Open ESB), and Open MQ JMS product. He has been an active contributor in the development of the various industry standard benchmarks such as SPECjms2007 and SPECjEnterprise2010, has published several performance white papers and has previously contributed to the XMLTest and WSTest benchmark projects at java.net. Binu holds Master of Science degrees in Biomedical Engineering and Computer Science from The University of Iowa.

1

Strategies, Approaches, and Methodologies

With Java performance tuning, as with many other activities, you need a plan of action, an approach, or strategy. And, like many other activities, a set of information or background is required in a given domain to be successful. To be successful in a Java performance tuning effort, you need to be beyond the stage of "*I don't know what I don't know*" and into the "*I know what I don't know*" stage or already be in the "*I already know what I need to know*" stage.

If you find yourself a little lost in the definition of these three stages, they are further clarified here:

- **I don't know what I don't know.** Sometimes you are given a task that involves understanding a new problem domain. The first challenge in understanding a new problem domain is to learn as much about the problem as you can because you may know little if anything about the problem domain. In this new problem domain there are many artifacts about the problem domain you do not know, or do not know what is important to know. In other words, you do not know what you need to know about the problem domain. Hence, the phrase, "*I don't know what I don't know.*"

- **I know what I don't know.** Normally when you enter a new problem domain, one that you know little about, you eventually reach a point where you have discovered many different things about the problem domain that are important to know. But you do not know the specific details about those things that are important to know. When you have reached this stage it is called the "*I know what I don't know*" stage.

- **I already know what I need to know.**   At other times you are given a task in a problem domain in which you are familiar or you have developed the necessary skills and knowledge in the area to the point where you are considered a subject matter expert. Or as you learn a new problem domain you reach a point where you feel comfortable working within it, i.e., you have learned the information necessary to be effective in the problem domain. When you have reached this point, you are at the stage of *"I already know what I need to know."*

Given you have either bought this book or are considering buying this book, you probably are not in the *"I already know what I need know"* stage, unless you have a need to keep a good reference close by. If you are in the *"I don't know what I don't know"* stage, this chapter will likely help you identify what you don't know and help you with an approach or strategy to tackle your Java performance issue. Those in the *"I know what I don't know"* stage may also find the information in this chapter useful.

This chapter begins by looking at the traditional forces at play that typically result in a performance tuning effort and suggests a high level process for integrating performance tuning into the software development process. This chapter then looks at two different performance tuning approaches, top down and bottom up.

Forces at Play

It is generally accepted at a high level that the traditional software development process consists of four major phases: analysis, design, coding, and testing. How these phases flow to together is illustrated in Figure 1-1.

Analysis is the first phase of the process where requirements are evaluated, architectural choices are weighed against their advantages and challenges, and high level abstractions are conceived. Design is the phase where, given the high level architecture choices made in the analysis phase along with its high level abstractions, finer grained abstractions are realized and concrete implementations begin their conception. Coding, of course, is the phase where implementation of the design occurs. Following coding is the testing phase where the implementation is tested against the application requirements. It is worth noting that often the testing phase encompasses only functional testing, i.e, does the application do what it is specified to do, does it execute the actions it is specified to execute. Once the testing phase is completed the application is shipped or released to its customer(s).

Many applications developed through these traditional software development phases tend to give little attention to performance or scalability until the application is released, or at the earliest in the testing phase. Wilson and Kesselman in their popular *Java Platform Performance* book [Wilson & Kesselman 2000] introduced an

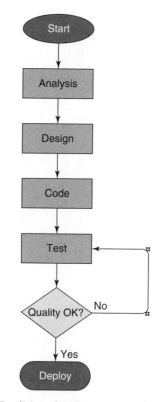

Figure 1-1 Traditional Software Development Process

additional performance phase to complement the traditional software development process. The proposed performance testing phase was added after the testing phase and contained a decision branch of "performance acceptable." If the performance and scalability criteria are met in this phase, the application is deemed ready to be shipped. Otherwise, the work flow results in profiling the application and branches back into one or more of the previous phases. Which particular phase the work flow branches back into depends on the results of the profiling activity. In other words, the output of the profiling activity identifies where the performance issue was introduced. A diagram illustrating Wilson and Kesselman's additional performance phase is shown in Figure 1-2.

To aid in the development of performance criteria to be evaluated in the performance testing phase, Wilson and Kesselman proposed the notion of specifying use cases to meet or address requirements specifically targeting performance in the analysis phase. However, it is often the case an application's requirements document fails to specify performance or scalability requirements. If an application you are working with, or developing, does not specify performance and scalability requirements explicitly you should ask for specific performance and scalability requirements.

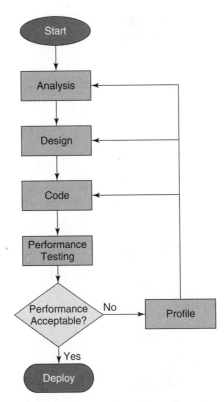

Figure 1-2 Wilson & Kesselman's Performance Process

For example, you should ask for throughput and latency requirements. The following list is an example of the types of questions these requirements should answer:

- What is the expected throughput of the application?
- What is the expected latency between a stimulus and a response to that stimulus?
- How many concurrent users or concurrent tasks shall the application support?
- What is the accepted throughput and latency at the maximum number of concurrent users or concurrent tasks?
- What is the maximum worst case latency?
- What is the frequency of garbage collection induced latencies that will be tolerated?

The requirements and corresponding use cases documented to answer questions such as those listed above should be used to drive the development of benchmarks and performance tests to ensure the application meets the expected performance and scalability. These benchmarks and performance tests should be executed as part of the performance testing phase. As you evaluate use cases, some may be considered high risk, i.e., those that may be difficult to meet. High risk cases should be mitigated well before completion of the analysis phase by implementing prototypes, benchmarks, and micro-benchmarks. This approach allows you to catch painful decisions that are expensive to change once the software development leaves the analysis phase. It has been well documented that the later in the software development cycle a defect, poor design, or poor implementation choice is detected, the more expensive it is to fix it. Mitigating high risk use cases helps avoid those costly mistakes.

Today many applications under development utilize automated build and test procedures. As a result, the enhanced software development process proposed by Wilson and Kesselman can be further improved by integrating automated performance testing as part of the automated build and test activity. The output of an automated performance testing activity could emit notifications, such as sending e-mail to the application stakeholders notifying them of performance results, such as identified performance regressions, identified performance improvements, or status on how well performance criteria is being met. The automated procedures could also file defects in a tracking system and automatically include pertinent performance statistics from the performance tests that fail to meet the application's performance criteria.

Integrating performance testing into automated build processes allows performance regressions to be identified earlier in the software development process by more easily tracking performance at each coding change committed to the source code base.

Another practice worth consideration of integrating into the automated performance testing system is the use of statistical methods and automated statistical analysis. The use of statistical methods improves confidence in your performance testing results. Guidance and advice on the use of statistical methods, which can be challenging for many software developers (and mere mortals for that matter), is presented in the latter part of Chapter 8, "Benchmarking Java Applications."

Two Approaches, Top Down and Bottom Up

There are two commonly accepted approaches to performance analysis: top down or bottom up. Top down, as the term implies, focuses at the top level of the application and drills down the software stack looking for problem areas and optimization opportunities. In contrast, bottom up begins at the lowest level of the software stack, at the CPU level looking at statistics such as CPU cache misses, inefficient use of CPU instructions, and then working up the software stack at what constructs or idioms are used by the application. The top down approach is most commonly used by application developers. The bottom up approach is commonly used by performance specialists in situations where the performance task involves identifying performance differences in an application on differing platform architectures, operating systems, or in the case of Java differing implementations of Java Virtual Machines. As you might expect, each approach finds different types of performance issues.

In the following two subsections, these two approaches are looked at more closely by presenting more specifics about the activities performed within each approach.

Top Down Approach

The top down approach, as mentioned earlier, is likely the most common approach utilized for performance tuning. This approach is also commonly used when you have the ability to change the code at the highest level of the application software stack.

In this approach, you begin by monitoring the application of interest under a load at which a stakeholder observes a performance issue. There are also situations in which an application is continuously monitored and as a result of a change in the application's configuration or a change in the typical load the application experiences a degradation in performance. There may also be situations in which performance and scalability requirements for the application change and the application in its current state cannot meet those new requirements.

Whatever the cause that stimulates the performance tuning activity, monitoring the application while it is running under a load of particular interest is the first step in a top down approach. This monitoring activity may include observing operating system level statistics, Java Virtual Machine (JVM) statistics, Java EE container statistics, and/or application performance instrumentation statistics. Then based on what the monitoring information suggests you begin the next step such as tuning the JVM's garbage collectors, tuning the JVM's command line options, tuning the operating system or profiling the application. Profiling the application may result in making implementation changes to the application, identifying an inefficient implementation of a third-party library, or identifying an inefficient implementation of a class or method in the Java SE class library.

For assistance in knowing what to monitor in a top down approach you can turn to Chapters 2, "Operating System Performance Monitoring," and Chapter 4, "JVM Performance Monitoring." These two chapters document the statistics of interest to monitor and suggest clues as to what values of a given statistic should be cause for further investigation. Then based on what the monitored statistics indicate as something worthy of further investigation, you can turn to other chapters for suggestions on corrective actions. For example, if monitoring operating system statistics suggests high sys CPU utilization, you should profile the application to determine what methods are consuming the highest sys CPU cycles. Instructions on how to use the NetBeans

Profiler and Oracle Solaris Studio Performance Analyzer (formerly known as Sun Studio Performance Analyzer) can be found in Chapter 5, "Java Application Profiling," and Chapter 6, "Java Application Profiling Tips and Tricks." If the monitoring activity and monitored statistic suggests the JVM's garbage collectors require tuning, turn to Chapter 7, "Tuning the JVM, Step by Step." If you are familiar with the general operation and basic workings of the Java HotSpot VM's garbage collectors, consider reading the section on garbage collectors in Chapter 3, "JVM Overview," before reading the chapter on tuning the JVM. If you are monitoring application level statistics, such as those provided by a Java EE container, read the chapters on Java EE performance tuning: Chapter 10, "Web Application Performance"; Chapter 11, "Web Services Performance"; and Chapter 12, "Java Persistence and Enterprise Java Beans Performance," to learn how to resolve performance issues in an enterprise application.

Bottom Up Approach

The bottom up approach is most commonly used by performance specialists when wanting to improve the performance of an application on one platform relative to another where differences exists in the underlying CPU, CPU architecture, or number of CPUs. The bottom up approach is also often used when wanting to improve the performance of an application when it is migrated to support a different operating system. This approach is also frequently used when it is not possible to make a change to the application's source code such as when an application is currently deployed in production environments or in competitive situations where computer systems vendors are vying for the business opportunity to run an application at peak performance.

In the bottom up approach, the gathering of performance statistics and the monitoring activity begin at the lowest level, the CPU. Statistics that are monitored at the CPU level may include the number of CPU instructions required to execute a given workload on the CPU, often referred to as *path length* and the number of CPU cache misses that occur while running the application under load. Other CPU statistics may be of interest, but the number of CPU instructions and the number CPU caches misses tend to be the most commonly observed statistics in a bottom up approach. If an application can perform and scale well under load by executing a fewer number of CPU instructions it will likely execute the application faster. Reducing CPU cache misses also improves an application's performance since a CPU cache miss results in wasted CPU cycles waiting for requested data to be fetched from memory. By reducing CPU cache misses, the application performs better since the CPU spends less time waiting for data to be fetched from memory.

The focus of the bottom up approach is usually to improve the utilization of the CPU without making changes to the application. In cases where the application can be modified, the bottom up approach may result in making changes to the application. These modifications may include a change to the application source code such as moving frequently accessed data near each other so they can be accessed on the same CPU cache line and thus not having to wait to fetch the data from memory. Such a change could reduce CPU cache misses and thereby reduce the amount of time the CPU waits for data to be fetched from memory.

In the context of a Java application executing in a modern Java Virtual Machine that has a sophisticated JIT compiler there may be cause to implement optimizations that would, for example, emit more efficient generated machine code based on memory access patterns exhibited by the application or the specific code paths taken by the application. There may also be settings at the operating system level that may be tuned or modified to allow for improved performance such as changing a CPU scheduling algorithm or the amount time the operating system waits before it migrates an executing application thread to a different CPU hardware thread.

If you find yourself in a situation where a bottom up approach would be useful, you should begin by collecting operating system statistics and JVM statistics. Monitoring these statistics provides hints as to where to focus in the next step. Chapter 2 and Chapter 4 provide information as to what statistics to monitor. From there you decide whether it makes sense to profile the application and the JVM. To profile both the application and the JVM, use a profiling tool that can provide that information. The Oracle Solaris Studio Performance Analyzer tool does this for Oracle Solaris SPARC, Oracle Solaris x86/x64, and Linux x86/x64 operating systems. Other popular tools such as Intel VTune or AMD's CodeAnalyst Performance Analyzer can provide similar information on Windows and Linux. All three tools also have the capability to collect specific CPU counter information such as the number of CPU instructions executed and CPU cache misses along with being able to associate them with specific methods or functions in a Java application of Java Virtual Machine. Using a profiler with these capabilities is essential in a bottom up approach. You can find additional information on how to use the Oracle Solaris Studio Performance Analyzer in Chapter 5 and Chapter 6.

Choosing the Right Platform and Evaluating a System

At times a performance specialist is called upon to improve the performance of an application only to find that the application is being run on an inappropriate CPU architecture or system. CPU architectures and systems have evolved substantially with the introduction of multiple cores per CPU and multiple hardware threads per core (also known as CMT, chip multithreading). As a result, choosing the right platform and CPU architecture for a given application has become more important. In addition, the way in which the performance of a system is evaluated must also be updated or revised as a result of the evolution of CPU architectures. This section looks at some of the differences in CPU architectures available on modern systems and presents some considerations to keep in mind when choosing a system on which to run an application. This section also describes why traditional methods of evaluating a system's performance are invalid when it comes to modern multiple hardware thread per core CPU architectures such as the SPARC T-series family of processors.

Choosing the Right CPU Architecture

The introduction of the SPARC T-series processor brought chip multiprocessing and chip multithreading to Oracle's offering of processors. One of the major design points behind the SPARC T-series processors is to address CPU cache misses by introducing multiple hardware threads per core. The first generation SPARC T-series, UltraSPARC T1, has four hardware threads per core and comes in four, six, or eight cores per CPU. An UltraSPARC T1 processor with eight cores looks like a 32-processor system from an operating system viewpoint. That is, the operating system views each of the four hardware threads per core as a processor. Hence, a system configured with an UltraSPARC T1 having eight cores would be seen as having 32 processors from an operating system.

An important distinction between an UltraSPARC T1 is it has four hardware threads per core. Of the four hardware threads per core, only one of the four threads per core executes on a given clock cycle. However, when a long latency event occurs, such as a CPU cache miss, if there is another runnable hardware thread in the same UltraSPARC T1 core, that hardware thread executes on the next clock cycle. In contrast, other modern CPUs with a single hardware thread per core, or even hyperthreaded cores, will block on long latency events such as CPU cache misses and may waste clock cycles while waiting for a long latency event to be satisfied. In other modern CPUs, if another runnable application thread is ready to run and no other hardware threads are available, a thread context switch must occur before another runnable application thread can execute. Thread context switches generally take hundreds of clock cycles to complete. Hence, on a highly threaded application with many threads ready to execute, the SPARC T-series processors have the capability to execute the application faster as a result of their capability to switch to another runnable thread within a core on the next clock cycle. The capability to have multiple hardware threads per core and switch to a different runnable hardware thread in the same core on the next clock cycle comes at the expense of a CPU with a slower clock rate. In other words, CPUs such as the SPARC T-series processor that have multiple hardware threads tend to execute at a slower clock rate than other modern CPUs that have a single hardware thread per core or do not offer the capability to switch to another runnable hardware thread on a subsequent clock cycle.

> **Tip**
>
> Sun Microsystems evolved the first generation SPARC T-series processor from the UltraSPARC T1 to the UltraSPARC T2 and T3 by adding additional hardware threads per core and the capability for multiple hardware threads per core to execute in a clock cycle. However, for the purposes of this discussion, it is easier to talk about and understand how the UltraSPARC T1 processor differs from other modern CPUs. Once the difference in CPU architecture is understood, it becomes easier to extend the design points behind the UltraSPARC T1 to the UltraSPARC T2 and T3 processors.

When it comes to choosing a computing system, if the target application is expected to have a large number of simultaneous application threads executing concurrently, it is likely this type of application will perform and scale better on a SPARC T-series processor than a smaller number of hardware threads per core type of processor. In contrast, an application that is expected to have a small number of application threads, especially if the number of simultaneous application threads is expected to be less than the total number of hardware threads on a SPARC T-series processor, this application will likely perform better on a higher clock rate, smaller number of hardware threads per core type of processor than a slower clock rate SPARC T-series processor. In short, for a SPARC T-series processor to perform well, it needs a large number of simultaneous application threads to keep the larger number of hardware threads busy to leverage its capability to switch to a different hardware thread on subsequent clock cycles when events such as CPU cache misses occur. In the absence of a large number of simultaneous application threads, the SPARC T-series generally performs like slower clock rate traditional processors. The artifact of requiring a large number of simultaneous application threads to keep the many SPARC T-series hardware threads busy also suggests the traditional manner in which a system's performance is qualified may not represent a system's true performance. This is the topic of the next subsection.

Evaluating a System's Performance

To evaluate the performance of a SPARC T-series, since it has the capability to switch to another runnable hardware thread within a core on the next clock cycle, it must be loaded with a workload having a large number of simultaneous application threads.

A common approach used to qualify or evaluate the performance of a new system has been to place a portion of the expected target load on the system, or execute one or more micro-benchmarks and observe how the system performs or observe the amount of work the application does per some unit of time. However, to evaluate the performance of a SPARC T-series processor, it must be loaded with enough concurrent application threads to keep the large number of hardware threads busy. The workload needs to be large enough for the SPARC T-series to reap the benefit of switching to a different runnable thread on the next clock cycle when long latency events such as CPU cache misses occur. Blocking and waiting for a CPU cache miss to be satisfied takes many CPU cycles, on the order of hundreds of clock cycles. Therefore, to take full advantage of a SPARC T-series processor, the system needs to be loaded with enough concurrent work to where its design point of switching to another runnable hardware thread on the next clock cycle can be realized.

In situations where a subset of a targeted workload is executed by a SPARC T-series processor, it may appear as though the system does not perform very well since all its hardware threads may not be busy. Remember that one of the major design points for the SPARC T-series processors is to address long latency CPU events by allowing other runnable hardware threads to execute on the next clock cycle. In a single hardware thread per core family of processors, long latency events such as a CPU cache miss mean many CPU clock cycles are wasted waiting for data to be fetched from memory. To switch to another runnable application thread, that other runnable application thread and its state information must replace the existing thread and its state information. This not only requires clock cycles to make this context switch, it may also require the CPU cache to fetch different state information for the new runnable application thread.

Hence, when evaluating the performance of a SPARC T-series processor it is important to put enough load on the system to take advantage of the additional hardware threads and its capability to switch to another runnable hardware thread within the same CPU core on the next clock cycle.

Bibliography

Dagastine, David, and Brian Doherty. *Java Platform Performance* presentation. Java-One Conference, San Francisco, CA, 2005.

Wilson, Steve, and Jeff Kesselman. *Java Platform Performance: Strategies and Tactics,* Addison-Wesley, Reading, MA, 2000. ISBN 0-201-70969-4.

Operating System Performance Monitoring

Knowing when an application is not performing as desired or expected is important to an application's capability to meet service level agreement(s) set forth by the application's stakeholders. Hence, knowing what to monitor, where in the software stack to monitor, and what tools to use are critical. This chapter describes what should be monitored at the operating system level and presents operating system tools that can be used to observe an application's performance. Additionally, general guidelines are given to help identify potential performance issues. The operating systems covered in this chapter are Windows, Linux, and Oracle Solaris, also referred to as Solaris hereafter. The monitoring tools presented are not intended to be an exhaustive list of tools or the only means to monitor an application's or a system's performance. Rather, the principles of why and what attributes of a system are important to monitor is the intention. Readers who are running a Java application on an operating system other than those covered should be able to identify the operating system performance statistics to monitor and be able to identify appropriate monitoring tools.

> **Tip**
>
> The first step in isolating a performance issue is to monitor the application's behavior. Monitoring offers clues as to the type or general category of performance issue.

This chapter begins by presenting definitions for performance monitoring, performance profiling, and performance tuning. Then sections that describe operating system statistics of interest to monitor are presented. Both command line and GUI tools that can be used to monitor the performance statistics are included. In addition, guidelines are offered as to what performance statistic values are indicators of potential root causes, or a next step to take in your performance analysis.

Definitions

Three distinct activities are involved when engaging in performance improvement activities: performance monitoring, performance profiling, and performance tuning.

- Performance monitoring is an act of nonintrusively collecting or observing performance data from an operating or running application. Monitoring is usually a preventative or proactive type of action and is usually performed in a production environment, qualification environment, or development environment. Monitoring is also usually the first step in a reactive situation where an application stakeholder has reported a performance issue but has not provided sufficient information or clues as to a potential root cause. In this situation, performance profiling likely follows performance monitoring.

- Performance profiling in contrast to performance monitoring is an act of collecting performance data from an operating or running application that may be intrusive on application responsiveness or throughput. Performance profiling tends to be a reactive type of activity, or an activity in response to a stakeholder reporting a performance issue, and usually has a more narrow focus than performance monitoring. Profiling is rarely done in production environments. It is typically done in qualification, testing, or development environments and is often an act that follows a monitoring activity that indicates some kind of performance issue.

- Performance tuning, in contrast to performance monitoring and performance profiling, is an act of changing tune-ables, source code, or configuration attribute(s) for the purposes of improving application responsiveness or throughput. Performance tuning often follows performance monitoring or performance profiling activities.

CPU Utilization

For an application to reach its highest performance or scalability it needs to not only take full advantage of the CPU cycles available to it but also to utilize them in a manner that is not wasteful. Being able to make efficient use of CPU cycles can be challenging for multithreaded applications running on multiprocessor and multicore systems. Additionally, it is important to note that an application that can saturate CPU resources does not necessarily imply it has reached its maximum performance or scalability. To identify how an application is utilizing CPU cycles, you monitor CPU utilization at the operating system level. CPU utilization on most operating systems is reported in both user CPU utilization and kernel or system (sys) CPU utilization. User CPU utilization is the percent of time the application spends in application code. In contrast, kernel or system CPU utilization is the percent of time the application spends executing operating system kernel code on behalf of the application. High kernel or system CPU utilization can be an indication of shared resource contention or a large number of interactions between I/O devices. The ideal situation for maximum application performance and scalability is to have 0% kernel or system CPU utilization since CPU cycles spent executing in operating system kernel code are CPU cycles that could be utilized by application code. Hence, one of the objectives to achieving maximum application performance and scalability is to reduce kernel or system CPU utilization as much as possible.

For applications that are compute intensive, performance monitoring may go much deeper than observing user CPU utilization and kernel or system utilization. On compute-intensive systems, further monitoring of the number of CPU instructions per CPU clock cycle (also known as IPC, instructions per clock) or the number of CPU clock cycles per CPU instruction (also known as CPI, cycles per instruction) may be required. These two additional metrics are of interest to compute intensive applications because CPU utilization monitoring tools bundled with modern operating systems report CPU utilization and do not report the percentage of CPU clock cycles the CPU has been executing instructions. This means that the operating system tools report a CPU as being utilized even though the CPU may be waiting for data to be fetched from memory. This scenario is commonly referred to as a *stall*. Stalls occur any time the CPU executes an instruction and the data being operated on by the instruction is not readily available in a CPU register or cache. When this occurs, the CPU wastes clock cycles because it must wait for the data to be loaded from memory into a CPU register before the CPU instruction can execute on it. It is common for a CPU to wait (waste) several hundred clock cycles during a stall. Thus the strategy for increasing the performance of a compute intensive application is to reduce the number of stalls or improve the CPU's cache utilization so fewer CPU clock cycles are wasted waiting for data to be fetched from memory. Performance monitoring activities of this kind go beyond the scope of this book and may require the assistance of a performance expert. However, the profiler covered in Chapter 5, "Java Application Profiling," Oracle Solaris Studio Performance Analyzer, has the capability to capture a profile of a Java application including this kind of data.

Each operating system presents user CPU utilization and kernel or system CPU utilization differently. The next several sections describe tools to monitor CPU utilization on Microsoft Windows, Linux, and Solaris operating systems.

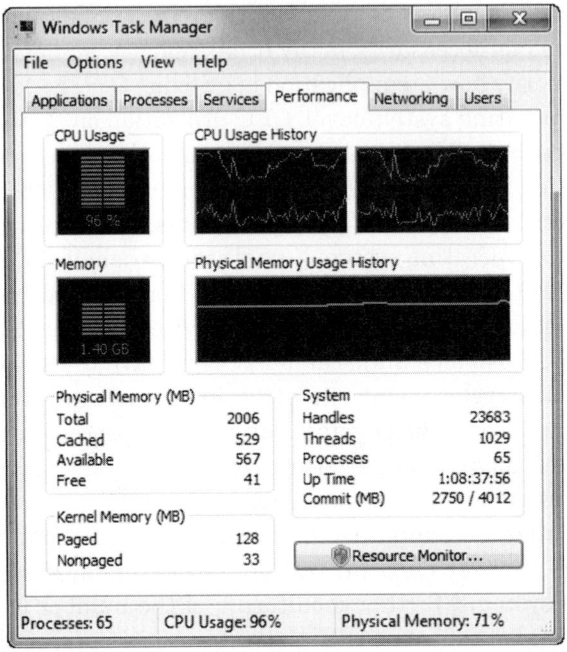

Figure 2-1 Windows Task Manager. The graph lines in the two CPU usage history windows shows both user and kernel/system CPU utilization

Monitoring CPU Utilization on Windows

The commonly used CPU utilization monitoring tool on Windows is Task Manager and Performance Monitor. Both Task Manager and Performance Monitor use a coloring scheme to distinguish between user CPU and kernel or system CPU utilization. Figure 2-1 shows the Windows Task Manager performance monitoring window.

CPU utilization is shown in the upper half of the Windows Task Manager. CPU utilization across all processors is shown in the CPU Usage panel on the upper left. A running history of CPU utilization for each processor is displayed in the CPU Usage History panel on the upper right. The upper line, a green colored line, indicates the combined user and system or kernel CPU utilization. The lower line, a red colored line, indicates the percentage of system or kernel CPU usage. The space between the lower line and upper line represents the percentage of user CPU utilization. Note that to view system or kernel CPU utilization in Window's Task Manager, the Show Kernel Utilization option must be enabled in the View > Show Kernel Utilization menu.

On Windows systems that include the Performance Monitor (perfmon), the default view of the Performance Monitor varies depending on the Windows operating system.

This chapter describes the Performance Monitor view in Windows 7. Note that to run the Windows Performance Monitor you must have membership in either the Administrators, Performance Log Users, or equivalent group.

The Windows Performance Monitor uses a concept of performance objects. Performance objects are categorized into areas such as network, memory, processor, thread, process, network interface, logical disk, and many others. Within each of these categories are specific performance attributes, or counters, that can be selected as performance statistics to monitor. Covering all the performance counters available to monitor is beyond the scope of this chapter. The focus in this chapter is to identify the performance statistics of most interest to monitor and the tools to monitor them.

User CPU utilization and kernel or system CPU utilization can be added to the Performance Monitor by right-clicking in the Performance Monitor's display area and selecting the Add Counters option from the context sensitive menu. User and kernel or system CPU utilization can be monitored by selecting the Processor performance object, and then selecting both % User Time and % Privileged Time counters and clicking the Add button. Windows uses the term "Privileged Time" to represent kernel or system CPU utilization. See Figure 2-2 for an example of the Add Counters screen.

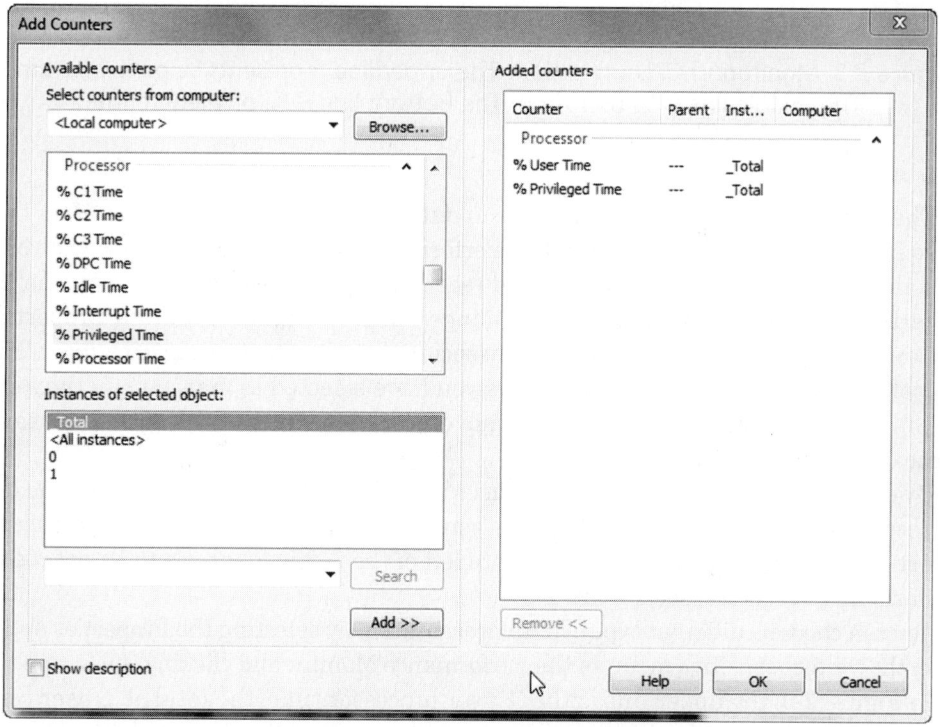

Figure 2-2 Performance Monitor's user time and privileged time

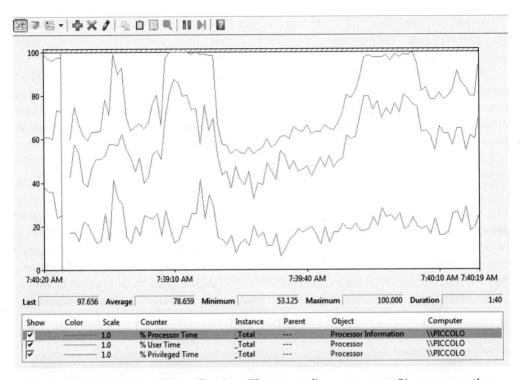

Figure 2-3 Monitoring CPU utilization. The upper line represents % processor time. The middle line is % user time. The bottom line is % privileged time

The Performance Monitor display is updated with the new counters after they have been added. At the bottom of the Performance Monitor, you can see the counters that are currently being monitored (see Figure 2-3). Right-clicking on the list of performance counters allows you to change the performance counters' properties. For example, you can change the color associated with a performance counter. This is useful when the performance counters you have selected to monitor use the same default color. You can also add and remove performance counters from the same context sensitive menu.

By default the Performance Monitor uses a scrolling style window to show the last 60 seconds of performance statistics. The scrolling part of the window is identified by a vertical bar. The values to the immediate left of the vertical bar are the most recent performance statistics, see Figure 2-3.

You can choose a different type of data presentation by selecting the Properties option from the context sensitive menu in the Performance Monitor and clicking the Graph tab.

In Figure 2-3, the upper line is the % user processor time, the total of % user time, and % privileged time. In this example, the monitored application has higher % user time than % privileged time. That relationship is a desired relationship to observe. In other words, it is desirable for an application to spend more time executing application code than executing in operating system kernel code.

Many additional capabilities in the Performance Monitor can be leveraged such as the ability to create a Data Collector Set and generate performance reports. Creating Data Collector Sets, generating performance reports, and other capabilities are beyond the scope of this chapter but may be of interest to further explore as part of your performance monitoring efforts.

Monitoring CPU Utilization with Windows `typeperf`

Windows `typeperf` is a command line tool that can be used to collect operating system performance statistics. `typeperf` can be run in a Windows Command Prompt window, or it can be scripted and run from a bat or cmd file. You specify the performance statistics you want to collect using the Microsoft performance counter names. The Microsoft performance counter names are the same as those used in the Performance Monitor. For example, to collect user and kernel or system CPU utilization you specify the User Time and Privileged Time performance counters. In a Command Prompt window, or in a cmd file, the command looks like

```
typeperf "\Processor(_Total)\% Privileged Time" "\Processor(_Total)\% User
Time"
```

Each performance counter should be enclosed in quotation marks, and the syntax of the performance counter follows the name as you would find it in the Performance Monitor. You can also assemble a list of performance counters in a file and pass the name of the file to the `typeperf` command. For example, you can enter the following performance counters in a file named `cpu-util.txt`:

```
\Processor(_Total)\% Privileged Time
\Processor(_Total)\% User Time
```

Then, invoke the `typeperf` command with the option `-cf` followed by the file name.

```
typeperf -cf cpu-util.txt
```

The following output shows the result of executing the `typeperf` command using three performance counters to capture the total, kernel, or system and user CPU utilization.

```
typeperf "\Processor(_Total)\% User Time" "\Processor(_Total)%
Privileged Time" "\Processor(_Total)% Processor Time"

"(PDH-CSV 4.0)","\\PICCOLO\Processor(_Total)% User
Time","\\PICCOLO\Processor(_Total)% Privileged
Time","\\PICCOLO\Processor(_Total)% Processor Time"
"02/15/2011 11:33:54.079","77.343750","21.875000","99.218750"
"02/15/2011 11:33:55.079","75.000000","21.875000","96.875000"
"02/15/2011 11:33:56.079","58.593750","21.875000","80.468750"
"02/15/2011 11:33:57.079","62.500000","21.093750","83.593750"
"02/15/2011 11:33:58.079","64.062500","15.625000","79.687500"
```

In the preceding output, the first row is a header describing the data to be collected. That is followed by rows of reported data. In each row, there is a date and time stamp indicating when the data was collected along with the values of the performance counters. By default, the `typeperf` reporting interval is one second. The reporting interval can be changed using the `-si` option. The `-si` option accepts a form of *[mm:]ss* where *mm:* is optional minutes and *ss* is the number of seconds. You may consider specifying a larger interval than the default if you intend to monitor over an extended period of time to reduce the amount of data you need to process.

Additional details on the `typeperf` command and its options can be found at http://www.microsoft.com/resources/documentation/windows/xp/all/proddocs/en-us/nt_command_typeperf.mspx?mfr=true.

Monitoring CPU Utilization on Linux

On Linux, CPU utilization can be monitored graphically with the GNOME System Monitor tool, which is launched with the `gnome-system-monitor` command. The GNOME System Monitor tool displays CPU utilization is the upper portion of the display of the Resource tab, as shown in Figure 2-4.

The GNOME System Monitor shown in Figure 2-4 is running on a system with two virtual processors. The number of virtual processors matches the number returned by the Java API `Runtime.availableProcessors()`. A system with a single CPU socket with a quad core processor with hyperthreading disabled will show four CPUs in the GNOME System Monitor and report four virtual processors using the Java API `Runtime.availableProcessors()`.

In the GNOME System Monitor, there is a CPU history area where a line for each virtual processor's CPU utilization is drawn illustrating its CPU utilization over a period of time. The GNOME System Monitor also displays the current CPU utilization for each virtual processor found on the system in a table below the CPU history.

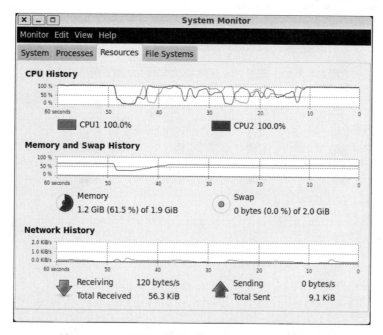

Figure 2-4 GNOME System Monitor on Linux

Another popular graphical tool to monitor CPU utilization on Linux is xosview. Some Linux distributions may not include xosview in their default distribution. But a search of their distribution's software package management facility for xosview will likely find it. One of the additional features of xosview in CPU utilization is further broken down into user CPU, kernel or system CPU, and idle CPU.

Monitoring CPU Utilization on Solaris

On Solaris, CPU utilization can be monitored graphically with the GNOME System Monitor tool. It is launched with the gnome-system-monitor command. An example of the GNOME System Monitor monitoring a system with 32 virtual processors is shown in Figure 2-5.

Another way to graphically observe CPU utilization on Solaris is using an optional tool called cpubar found on the Solaris Performance Tools CD 3.0 (also downloadable at http://www.schneider4me.de/ToolsCD-v3.0.iso.zip). In addition to monitoring CPU utilization, other system attributes can be monitored with cpubar such as kernel thread queue depths, memory paging, and memory scan rate. Figure 2-6 shows cpubar.

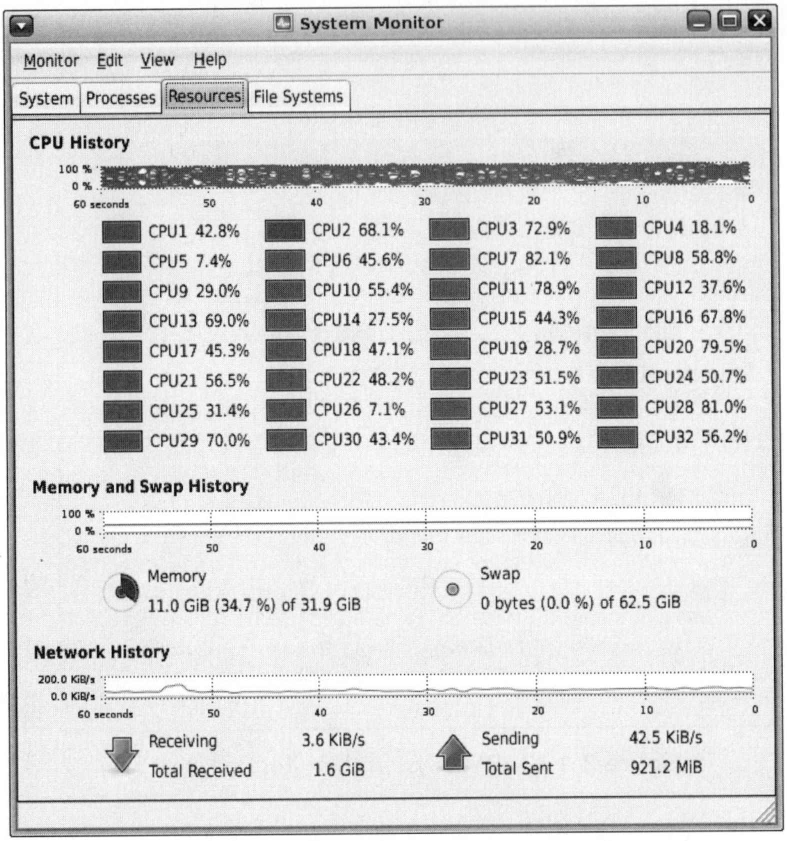

System Monitor

Monitor Edit View Help

System | Processes | Resources | File Systems

CPU History

100 %
0 %
60 seconds   50   40   30   20   10   0

CPU1 42.8%	CPU2 68.1%	CPU3 72.9%	CPU4 18.1%
CPU5 7.4%	CPU6 45.6%	CPU7 82.1%	CPU8 58.8%
CPU9 29.0%	CPU10 55.4%	CPU11 78.9%	CPU12 37.6%
CPU13 69.0%	CPU14 27.5%	CPU15 44.3%	CPU16 67.8%
CPU17 45.3%	CPU18 47.1%	CPU19 28.7%	CPU20 79.5%
CPU21 56.5%	CPU22 48.2%	CPU23 51.5%	CPU24 50.7%
CPU25 31.4%	CPU26 7.1%	CPU27 53.1%	CPU28 81.0%
CPU29 70.0%	CPU30 43.4%	CPU31 50.9%	CPU32 56.2%

Memory and Swap History

100 %
0 %
60 seconds   50   40   30   20   10   0

Memory
11.0 GiB (34.7 %) of 31.9 GiB

Swap
0 bytes (0.0 %) of 62.5 GiB

Network History

200.0 KiB/s
0.0 KiB/s
60 seconds   50   40   30   20   10   0

Receiving   3.6 KiB/s
Total Received   1.6 GiB

Sending   42.5 KiB/s
Total Sent   921.2 MiB

Figure 2-5 GNOME System Monitor on Solaris

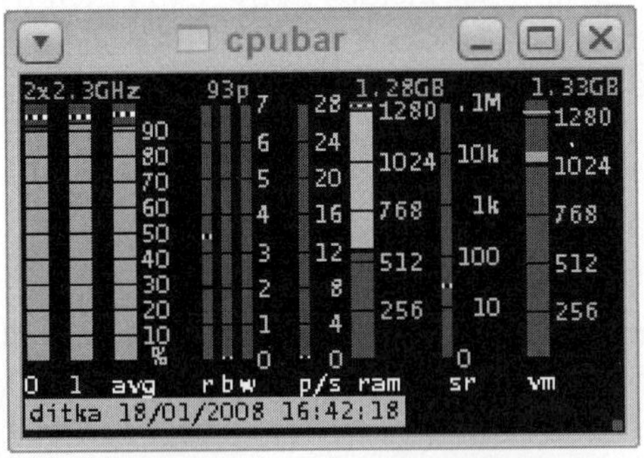

cpubar

2x2.3GHz   93p   1.28GB   1.33GB

ditka 18/01/2008 16:42:18

Figure 2-6 Solaris cpubar uses color to indicate system status. In 0 bar, 1 bar, and avg bar, green represents user CPU utilization, red represents system or kernel CPU utilization, and a blue color is idle. For the r bar, b bar, and w bar, red indicates occupancy, and blue represents emptiness. For the p/s bar, red represents activity; blue represents idle. For the ram bar, red represents the amount of memory committed, yellow represents allocated, and blue represents free/available memory. The sr bar is similar to the p/s bar: red indicates activity; blue represents idle. In the vm bar, red represents committed virtual memory, green represents allocated memory, and blue represents free/available virtual memory.

On multicore and multiprocessor systems the bar with the avg label shows the overall CPU utilization. To the left of the overall CPU utilization bar there is an individual bar for each virtual processor's CPU utilization. The combined colors of green and red show overall CPU utilization. The blue color indicates idle CPU utilization. The green color shows the percentage of user CPU utilization, and a red color shows the percentage of system or kernel CPU utilization. The hyphenated/dashed horizontal bar embedded within the CPU utilization bars represents a running historical average CPU utilization since the system was last booted.

Also shown in Solaris cpubar are additional performance statistics such as kernel thread queue depths, memory paging, amount of memory utilized, page scan rate, and amount of memory utilized by the Solaris VM. The kernel threads' queue depths are found to the right of the CPU utilization bars and have an "r" label, "b" label, and "w" label. Each of the vertical bars above those three labels represents a queue depth. The vertical bar for the "r" label represents the run queue depth. Entries show up in the run queue when there are kernel threads that are ready to run but do not have an available processor to run. In Figure 2-6, the vertical bar above the "r" label indicates there are two kernel threads ready to run and waiting for a CPU to execute. Monitoring the kernel thread's run queue is an important statistic to monitor. How you monitor the kernel thread's run queue is presented in the "CPU Scheduler Run Queue" section later in this chapter. The vertical bar for the "b" label represents the blocked queue. Entries show up in the blocked queue when kernel threads are waiting on resources such as I/O, memory pages, and so on. The vertical bar for the "w" label represents the waiting queue. Entries show up in the waiting queue when a swapped out lightweight process is waiting for resources to finish. The number above the three kernel thread queue vertical bars is the number of kernel threads currently running on the system. In Figure 2-6, 93 kernel threads were running at the time the screenshot was taken.

To the right of the kernel thread queue depths is a vertical bar illustrating the page in/page out activity, that is, the number of memory pages paged in or paged out. This vertical bar has the "p/s" label below it. In Figure 2-6, there was little paging activity at the time the screenshot was taken. Monitoring paging activity is covered in the "Memory Utilization" section later in this chapter.

To the right of the memory paging activity (p/s) vertical bar is a vertical bar illustrating the amount of physical RAM currently being utilized by the system. This vertical bar has the "ram" label below it. A red color shows the amount of memory utilized by the kernel. A yellow color shows the amount of memory utilized by user processes, and blue is the amount of free or available memory. Figure 2-6 shows there was little free memory available at the time the screenshot was taken.

To the right of the physical memory utilization (ram) vertical bar is a vertical bar illustrating the page scanning rate. This vertical bar has an "sr" label below it. As the amount of free physical memory reduces, the system attempts to free up memory by locating pages that have not been used in a long time. It then pages these out to disk. This page scanning activity is reported as scan rate. A high scan rate is an indicator of low physical memory. Monitoring the page scan rate is essential to identifying when a system is swapping. This is presented in more detail in the "Memory Utilization" section of this chapter.

To the right of the page scanning (sr) vertical bar is a bar representing virtual memory usage, or swap usage. This vertical bar has the "vm" label below it. The amount of virtual memory used is colored red. The amount of virtual memory reserved is colored yellow, and the amount of free memory is colored blue. The total amount of virtual memory is displayed at the top of the vertical bar. Figure 2-6 shows 1.33 gigabytes of virtual memory on the system.

Monitoring CPU Utilization on Linux and Solaris with Command Line Tools

Linux and Solaris also provide command line tools to monitor CPU utilization. These command line tools are useful when you want to keep a running textual history of CPU utilization or keep a log of CPU utilization. Linux and Solaris have vmstat, which shows combined CPU utilization across all virtual processors. Both versions of vmstat optionally take a reporting interval, in seconds, as a command line argument. If no reporting interval is given to vmstat, the reported output is a summary of all CPU utilization data collected since the system has last been booted. When a reporting interval is specified, the first row of statistics is a summary of all data collected since the system was last booted. As a result, the first row of data from vmstat is most often ignored.

The display format of vmstat for Linux and Solaris is similar. For example, the following shows vmstat from Linux. The columns of interest for monitoring CPU utilization are shown in bold.

procs		----------memory----------			---swap--		-----io----		--system--		----**cpu**----			
r	b	swpd	free	buff	cache	si	so	bi	bo	in	cs	**us**	**sy**	**id**	wa
4	0	0	959476	340784	1387176	0	0	0	0	1030	8977	**63**	**35**	**1**	0
3	0	0	959444	340784	1387176	0	0	0	0	1014	7981	**62**	**36**	**2**	0
6	0	0	959460	340784	1387176	0	0	0	16	1019	9380	**63**	**36**	**1**	0
1	0	0	958820	340784	1387176	0	0	0	0	1036	9157	**63**	**35**	**2**	0
4	0	0	958500	340784	1387176	0	0	0	29	1012	8582	**62**	**37**	**1**	0

The "us" column shows the percentage of user CPU utilization. The "sy" column shows the percentage of kernel or system CPU utilization. The "id" column shows the percentage of idle or available CPU. The sum of the "us" column and "sy" column should be equal to 100 minus the value in the "id" column, that is, 100 − ("id" column value).

The `vmstat` output from Solaris, shown in the following example, has three columns of CPU utilization interest and has column headings of "us," "sy," and "id" that show user, kernel or system, and idle CPU utilization, respectively.

kthr			memory				page						disk				faults			cpu		
r	b	w	swap	free	re	mf	pi	po	fr	de	sr	f0	s0	s1	s2	in	sy	cs	us	sy	id
0	0	0	672604	141500	10	40	36	6	10	0	20	0	3	0	2	425	1043	491	4	3	93
1	1	0	888460	632992	7	32	97	0	0	0	0	21	0	12		462	1099	429	32	19	49
0	1	0	887848	631772	4	35	128	0	0	0	0	30	0	13		325	575	314	38	13	49
0	1	0	887592	630844	6	26	79	0	0	0	0	40	0	11		324	501	287	36	10	54
1	0	0	887304	630160	5	33	112	0	0	0	0	50	0	16		369	899	367	37	11	52
0	1	0	886920	629092	4	30	101	0	0	0	0	26	0	18		354	707	260	39	14	46

Solaris and Linux also offer a tabular view of CPU utilization for each virtual processor using the command line tool `mpstat`.

> **Tip**
>
> Most Linux distributions require an installation of the sysstat package to use `mpstat`.

Using `mpstat` to observe per virtual processor CPU utilization can be useful in identifying whether an application has threads that tend to consume larger percentages of CPU cycles than other threads or whether application threads tend to utilize the same percentage of CPU cycles. The latter observed behavior usually suggests an application that may scale better. CPU utilization in Solaris `mpstat`, as shown in the following example, is reported in the columns "usr," "sys," "wt," and "idl," where `usr` is the percentage of CPU time spent executing user code, `sys` is the percentage of CPU time spent executing kernel code, `wt` is the percentage of I/O wait time (no longer calculated and always reports 0), and `idl` is percentage of time the CPU was idle.

CPU	minf	mjf	xcal	intr	ithr	csw	icsw	migr	smtx	srw	syscl	usr	sys	wt	idl
0	28	2	0	192	83	92	32	14	2	0	185	78	15	0	7
1	49	1	0	37	1	80	28	16	2	0	139	80	16	0	4
2	28	1	0	20	7	94	34	17	1	0	283	83	12	0	5
3	39	1	2	52	1	99	36	16	3	0	219	74	19	0	7
CPU	minf	mjf	xcal	intr	ithr	csw	icsw	migr	smtx	srw	syscl	usr	sys	wt	idl
0	34	0	2	171	75	78	32	12	1	0	173	90	9	0	2
1	38	1	0	39	1	84	29	13	2	0	153	66	12	0	23
2	28	8	0	21	9	97	31	20	2	0	167	67	13	0	20
3	35	3	1	43	1	98	29	20	3	0	190	52	25	0	23

If no reporting interval is given to `mpstat`, the reported output is a summary of all `mpstat` data collected since the system was last booted. When a reporting interval is given, the first row of statistics is a summary of all data collected since the system was last booted.

Other popular alternatives to `vmstat` on Solaris and Linux can be used to monitor CPU utilization. A couple of the more common ones are `prstat` for Solaris and `top` for Linux.

Linux `top` reports not only CPU utilization but also process statistics and memory utilization. Its display, shown in the following example, has two major parts. The upper section of the display reports overall system statistics, while the lower section reports process level statistics that, by default, are ordered in highest to lowest CPU utilization.

```
top - 14:43:56 up 194 days,  2:53,  4 users,  load average: 8.96, 6.23, 3.96
Tasks: 127 total,   2 running, 125 sleeping,   0 stopped,   0 zombie
Cpu(s): 62.1% us, 26.2% sy,  0.8% ni,  1.7% id,  0.0% wa,  0.0% hi,  9.1% si
Mem:   4090648k total,  3141940k used,   948708k free,   340816k buffers
Swap:  4192956k total,        0k used,  4192956k free,  1387144k cached

  PID USER      PR  NI  VIRT  RES  SHR S %CPU %MEM    TIME+  COMMAND
30156 root      25  10 32168  18m  10m R  2.3  0.5 20:41.96 rhn-applet-gui
30072 root      15   0 16344  12m 2964 S  0.7  0.3 13:08.52 Xvnc
 5830 huntch    16   0  3652 1084  840 R  0.7  0.0  0:00.16 top
    1 root      16   0  3516  560  480 S  0.0  0.0  0:01.62 init
    2 root      RT   0     0    0    0 S  0.0  0.0  0:07.38 migration/0
    3 root      34  19     0    0    0 S  0.0  0.0  0:00.27 ksoftirqd/0
    4 root      RT   0     0    0    0 S  0.0  0.0  0:08.03 migration/1
...
```

Solaris `prstat` shows similar information to Linux `top`. The following example is the default output for `prstat`.

```
  PID USERNAME  SIZE   RSS STATE  PRI NICE      TIME  CPU PROCESS/NLWP
 1807 huntch    356M  269M cpu1    45    0   0:00:37  46% java/40
 1254 huntch    375M  161M run     29    0   0:06:51 2.9% firefox-bin/13
  987 huntch    151M  123M sleep   59    0   0:06:25 2.7% Xorg/1
 1234 huntch    257M  132M sleep   49    0   0:03:52 0.5% soffice.bin/7
...
```

Solaris `prstat` does not show an overall system summary section like `top`. But, like `top`, it does report per process level statistics that are ordered, by default, from highest to lowest CPU utilization.

Both `prstat` and `top` are good tools for providing a high level view of CPU utilization at a per process level. But as the need arises to focus more on per process and per lightweight process CPU utilization, Solaris `prstat` has additional capabilities such as reporting both user and kernel or system CPU utilization along with other microstate information using the `prstat -m` and `-L` options. The `-m` option prints microstate information, and `-L` prints statistics on per lightweight process.

Using the `-m` and `-L` options can be useful when you want to isolate CPU utilization per lightweight process and Java thread. A Java process showing high CPU utilization with `prstat -mL` can be mapped to a Java process and Java thread(s) on Solaris through a sequence of steps using `prstat`, `pstack`, and Java 6's `jstack` command line tool. The following example illustrates how to do this.

The output in the following example, gathered with `prstat -mL 5`, shows process id 3897 has three lightweight process ids consuming about 5% of kernel or system CPU. LWPID 2 is consuming the most at 5.7%.

```
PID USERNAME USR SYS TRP TFL DFL LCK SLP LAT VCX ICX SCL SIG PROC/LWPID
3897 huntch   6.0 5.7 0.1 0.0 0.0 2.6 8.2  78  9K  8K 64K   0 java/2
3897 huntch   4.9 4.8 0.0 0.0 0.0  59 0.0  31  6K  6K 76K   0 java/13
3897 huntch   4.7 4.6 0.0 0.0 0.0  56 0.0  35  5K  6K 72K   0 java/14
3917 huntch   7.4 1.5 0.0 0.0 0.0 3.8  53  34  5K 887 16K   0 java/28
...
```

In the absence of using a profiler, which is covered in detail in Chapter 5, there is a quick way to isolate which Java thread, along with which Java method, is consuming large amounts of CPU as reported by `prstat`, either USR or SYS. A Java, or JVM, process thread stack dump at the Solaris level can be generated using the Solaris command line tool `pstack` and the process id 3897. The `pstack` output in the following example, produced using the command `pstack 3897/2`, shows the lightweight process (lwp) id and thread id that matches LWPID 2 from `prstat`.

```
----------------- lwp# 2 / thread# 2 -----------------
fef085c7 _lwp_cond_signal (81f4200) + 7
feb45f04 __1cNObjectMonitorKExitEpilog6MpnGThread_pnMObjectWaiter__v_
(829f2d4, 806f800, e990d710) + 64
fe6e7e26 __1cNObjectMonitorEexit6MpnGThread__v_ (829f2d4, 806f800) + 4fe
fe6cabcb __1cSObjectSynchronizerJfast_exit6FpnHoopDesc_pnJBasicLock_
pnGThread__v_ (ee802108, fe45bb10, 806f800) + 6b
```

If you convert the thread id value to hexadecimal and use the JDK's `jstack` command you can find the Java thread that corresponds to Solaris thread# 2 by searching for a "nid" label. The thread number, 2 in decimal, is also 2 in hexadecimal. The following output from the JDK's `jstack` command is trimmed but shows that a Java thread with a 0x2 is the "main" Java thread. According to the stack trace produced by `jstack`, the Java thread corresponding to Solaris `pstack`'s LWPID 2 and `prstat`'s LWPID 2 is executing a Java NIO `Selector.select()` method.

```
"main" prio=3 tid=0x0806f800 nid=0x2 runnable [0xfe45b000..0xfe45bd38]
   java.lang.Thread.State: RUNNABLE
        at sun.nio.ch.DevPollArrayWrapper.poll0(Native Method)
        at sun.nio.ch.DevPollArrayWrapper.poll(DevPollArrayWrapper.java:164)
        at sun.nio.ch.DevPollSelectorImpl.doSelect(DevPollSelectorImpl.java:68)
        at sun.nio.ch.SelectorImpl.lockAndDoSelect(SelectorImpl.java:69)
        - locked <0xee809778> (a sun.nio.ch.Util$1)
        - locked <0xee809768> (a java.util.Collections$UnmodifiableSet)
        - locked <0xee802440> (a sun.nio.ch.DevPollSelectorImpl)
        at sun.nio.ch.SelectorImpl.select(SelectorImpl.java:80)
        at com.sun.grizzly.SelectorThread.doSelect(SelectorThread.java:1276)
```

Once a Java thread has been identified and with the stack trace readily available, you can begin to investigate in more detail the methods shown in the stack trace for possible candidates of high kernel or system CPU utilization through a more thorough profiling activity.

CPU Scheduler Run Queue

In addition to CPU utilization, monitoring the CPU scheduler's run queue is important to tell if the system is being saturated with work. The run queue is where lightweight processes are held that are ready to run but are waiting for a CPU where it can execute. When there are more lightweight processes ready to execute than the system's processors can handle, the run queue builds up with entries. A high run queue depth can be an indication a system is saturated with work. A system operating at a run queue depth equal to the number of virtual processors may not experience much user visible performance degradation. The number of virtual processors is the number of hardware threads on the system. It is also the value returned by the Java API, `Runtime.availableProcessors()`. In the event the run queue depth reaches four times the number of virtual processors or greater, the system will have observable sluggish responsiveness.

A general guideline to follow is observing run queue depths over an extended period of time greater than 1 times the number of virtual processors is something to be concerned about but may not require urgent action. Run queue depths at 3 to 4 times, or greater, than the number of virtual processors over an extended time period should be considered an observation that requires immediate attention or action.

There are generally two alternative resolutions to observing high run queue depth. One is to acquire additional CPUs and spread the load across those additional CPUs, or reduce the amount of load put on the processors available. This approach essentially reduces the number of active threads per virtual processor and as a result fewer lightweight processes build up in the run queue.

The other alternative is to profile the applications being run on the system and improve the CPU utilization of those applications. In other words, explore alternative approaches that will result in fewer CPU cycles necessary to run the application such as reducing garbage collection frequency or alternative algorithms that result in fewer CPU instructions to execute the same work. Performance experts often refer to this latter alternative as reducing code path length and better CPU instruction selection. A Java programmer can realize better performance through choosing more efficient algorithms and data structures. The JVM, through a modern JIT compiler, can improve an application's performance by generating code that includes sophisticated optimizations. Since there is little a Java application programmer can do to manipulate a JVM's JIT compiler, the focus for Java developers should be on more efficient alternative algorithms and data structures. Where to focus with alternative algorithms and data structures is identified through profiling activities.

Monitoring Windows CPU Scheduler Run Queue

The run queue depth on Windows is monitored using the \System\Processor Queue Length performance counter. This performance counter can be added to the Performance Monitor by selecting the System > Processor Queue Length performance counter from the Add Counters dialog. Recall from the "Monitoring CPU Utilization on Windows" section earlier in the chapter, the Add Counters dialog is displayed by right-clicking in the Performance Monitor's main window and selecting the Add Counters option from the context sensitive menu.

Figure 2-7 shows the Performance Monitor monitoring a system's run queue depth.

It is important to notice the scale factor in Performance Monitor. In Figure 2-7, the scale factor is 10. This means a run queue depth of 1 is displayed on the chart as 10, 2 as 20, 3 as 30, and so on. Based on a scale factor of 10, the actual run queue depth in Figure 2-7 ranges from 3 to at least 10. The reported run queue depth should be evaluated against the number of virtual processors on the system to determine whether further action is required such as monitoring over a longer period of time or initiating profiling activities.

Windows `typeperf` can also be used to monitor run queue depth. As mentioned in earlier sections, the `typeperf` command accepts Windows performance counter names and prints the collected performance data in a tabular form. The following `typeperf` command monitors run queue depth:

```
typeperf "\System\Processor Queue Length"
```

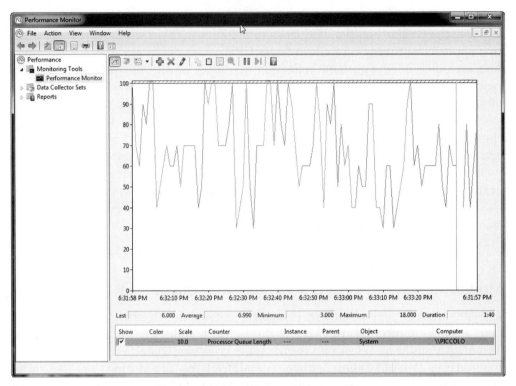

Figure 2-7 Processor queue length

What follows is example output using `typeperf` and the \System\Processor Queue Length performance counter reporting at a 5 second interval rather than a default 1 second.

```
typeperf -si 5 "\System\Processor Queue Length"

"(PDH-CSV 4.0)","\\PICCOLO\System\Processor Queue Length"
"02/26/2011 18:20:53.329","3.000000"
"02/26/2011 18:20:58.344","7.000000"
"02/26/2011 18:21:03.391","9.000000"
"02/26/2011 18:21:08.485","6.000000"
"02/26/2011 18:21:13.516","3.000000"
"02/26/2011 18:21:18.563","3.000000"
"02/26/2011 18:21:23.547","3.000000"
"02/26/2011 18:22:28.610","3.000000"
```

The run queue depth reported by `typeperf` is its actual value. There is no scale factor involved as there is with the Performance Monitor. In the above data, the run

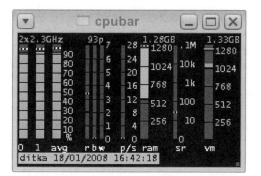

Figure 2-8 Solaris `cpubar` showing run queue depth

queue depth over the reported 35 second interval ranges from 3 to 9. The run queue data suggests the peak of 9 may be short lived. If further monitoring confirms this is the case, no corrective action is needed since this data is from a system that has four virtual processors.

Monitoring Solaris CPU Scheduler Run Queue

On Solaris, a system's run queue depth can be monitored graphically using `cpubar` and via command line using `vmstat`. Solaris `cpubar`, shown in Figure 2-8, shows run queue depth to the right of the CPU utilization bars with the vertical bar above the "r" label. The height of the bar is scaled based on the actual number of entries in the run queue, not a percentage of queue fullness.

The run queue can also be monitored with the `vmstat` command. The first column in `vmstat` reports the run queue depth. The value reported is the number of lightweight processes in the run queue. The following is an example with the run queue column in bold.

kthr			memory		page						disk					faults			cpu		
r	b	w	swap	free	re	mf	pi	po	fr	de	sr	cd	s0	-	-	n	sy	cs	us	sy	id
2	0	0	333273	177562	99	265	0	0	0	0	0	97	0	0	0	1737	14347	1225	28	4	68
4	0	0	330234	174274	69	977	0	0	0	0	0	70	0	0	0	1487	13715	1293	68	3	29
2	0	0	326140	169259	48	303	0	0	0	0	0	85	0	0	0	1746	29014	2394	48	5	47
6	0	0	323751	164876	92	730	0	0	0	0	0	58	0	0	0	1662	48860	3029	67	5	28
5	0	0	321284	160069	38	206	0	0	0	0	0	48	0	0	0	1635	50938	2714	83	5	12

Monitoring Linux CPU Scheduler Run Queue

On Linux a system's run queue depth can be monitored using the `vmstat` command. The first column in `vmstat` reports the run queue depth. The number reported is the actual number of lightweight processes in the run queue. The following is an example with the run queue column in bold.

```
procs ----------memory---------- ---swap-- -----io---- --system-- ----cpu----
 r  b   swpd   free   buff   cache   si   so    bi    bo   in     cs us sy id wa
 4  0      0 959476 340784 1387176    0    0     0     0 1030   8977 63 35  1  0
 3  0      0 959444 340784 1387176    0    0     0     0 1014   7981 62 36  2  0
 6  0      0 959460 340784 1387176    0    0     0    16 1019   9380 63 36  1  0
 1  0      0 958820 340784 1387176    0    0     0     0 1036   9157 63 35  2  0
 4  0      0 958500 340784 1387176    0    0     0    29 1012   8582 62 37  1  0
```

Memory Utilization

In addition to CPU utilization there are attributes of a system's memory that should be monitored, such as paging or swapping activity, locking, and voluntary and involuntary context switching along with thread migration activity.

A Java application or JVM that is swapping or utilizing virtual memory experiences pronounced performance issues. Swapping occurs when there is more memory being consumed by applications running on the system than there is physical memory available. To deal with this potential situation, a system is usually configured with an area called *swap space*. Swap space is typically allocated on a disk in a distinct disk partition. When the amount of physical memory is exhausted by the applications running on the system, the operating system swaps out a portion of an application to swap space on disk. Usually the operating system swaps out a portion of an application that is executing the least frequently so as to not impact the applications or the portions of applications that are the busiest. When a portion of an application is accessed that has been swapped out, that portion of the application must be paged in from the swap space on disk to memory. Swapping in from disk to memory can have a significant impact on an application's responsiveness and throughput.

A JVM's garbage collector performs poorly on systems that are swapping because a large portion of memory is traversed by the garbage collector to reclaim space from objects that are unreachable. If part of the Java heap has been swapped out it must be paged into memory so its contents can be scanned for live objects by the garbage collector. The time it takes to page in any portion of the Java heap into memory can dramatically increase the duration of a garbage collection. If the garbage collection is a "stop the world" type of operation, one that stops all application threads from executing, a system that is swapping during a garbage collection is likely to experience lengthy JVM induced pause times.

If you observe lengthy garbage collections, it is a possibility that the system is swapping. To prove whether the lengthy garbage collection pauses are caused by swapping, you must monitor the system for swapping activity.

Monitoring Memory Utilization on Windows

On Windows systems that include the Performance Monitor, monitoring memory pages per second (\Memory\Pages / second) and available memory bytes (\Memory\ Available MBytes), can identify whether the system is swapping. When the available memory, as reported by the \Memory\Available MBytes counter, is low and you observe paging activity, as reported by the \Memory\Pages / Second counter, the system is likely swapping.

It is easiest to illustrate a Windows system that is swapping using the output from the typeperf command. The following is a typeperf command to report available memory and paging activity at 5 second intervals (the -si specifies the reporting interval).

```
typeperf -si 5 "\Memory\Available Mbytes" "\Memory\Pages/sec"
```

The following output from typeperf is taken from a system that is swapping. The first column of data is the date and time stamp. The second column is the available memory, and the third column is the pages per second.

```
"02/15/2011 15:28:11.737","150.000000","0.941208"
"02/15/2011 15:28:16.799","149.000000","1.857361"
"02/15/2011 15:28:21.815","149.000000","2.996049"
"02/15/2011 15:28:26.831","149.000000","17.687691"
"02/15/2011 15:28:31.909","149.000000","0.929074"
"02/15/2011 15:28:36.940","149.000000","1.919541"
"02/15/2011 15:28:41.956","149.000000","0.991037"
"02/15/2011 15:28:46.971","149.000000","1.977258"
"02/15/2011 15:28:51.002","149.000000","0.969558"
"02/15/2011 15:28:56.065","149.000000","14.120284"
"02/15/2011 15:29:01.127","150.000000","8.470692"
"02/15/2011 15:29:06.174","152.000000","9.552139"
"02/15/2011 15:29:11.174","151.000000","2.000104"
"02/15/2011 15:29:16.174","152.000000","1.999969"
"02/15/2011 15:29:21.174","153.000000","0.999945"
```

Notice the amount of memory available is staying fairly constant around 150 megabytes yet there is consistent paging activity. Since the amount of available memory is staying fairly constant, it is reasonable to assume no new applications are being launched. When an application launches, the amount of available memory is expected to drop, and it is expected to see paging activity since the application must be paged into memory. Therefore, if the system is using a fairly consistent amount of memory and no new applications are launching, yet there is paging activity, it is likely the system is swapping.

It is important to note that a system can report little available memory and report no paging activity. In such a situation, the system is not swapping. It just simply is utilizing most of the physical RAM available on the system. Likewise, a system may be experiencing paging activity, yet have sufficient memory available and as a result not be swapping. The paging activity could be the result of an application being launched.

Monitoring Memory Utilization on Solaris

On Solaris, when available memory becomes low, the kernel's page scanner begins looking for memory pages no longer in use by an application so they can be made available for other applications and processes. If the page scanner is unable to find the memory demanded by the applications and no additional physical memory is available, it begins to swap out the least recently used memory pages to a swap space on disk. The lower the amount of available memory, the higher the page scan rate. In other words, as lower memory is available, the page scanner gets more aggressive with trying to find available memory pages it can reclaim.

Since the page scanner becomes more aggressive as available memory becomes low, identifying a Solaris system that is experiencing swapping requires monitoring a combination of the amount of free memory and page scanner activity. Both available free memory and page scanner activity are reported in Solaris vmstat columns labeled "free" and "sr."

When vmstat, cpubar, or any other Solaris monitoring tool reports a scan rate of 0, regardless of the reported available free memory, no swapping is occurring. However, if the scan rate is nonzero and the trend of reported free memory is decreasing, then swapping is likely occurring. The following example output from Solaris vmstat illustrates a system currently using most of its available physical memory; about 100 megabytes are free, as shown in the "free" column, but it is not swapping since its scan rate, the "sr" column, is 0.

kthr			memory		page							disk				faults			cpu		
r	b	w	swap	**free**	re	mf	pi	po	fr	de	**sr**	cd	f0	s0	–	in	sy	cs	us	sy	id
0	0	0	1641936	**861222**	106	2591	0	3	3	0	**0**	0	0	0	0	4930	24959	10371	60	10	30
0	0	0	1594944	**116940**	37	1718	8	0	0	0	**8**	0	0	0	0	4169	17820	10111	52	5	43
0	0	0	1579952	**103208**	24	521	0	0	0	0	**1**	0	0	0	0	2948	14274	6814	67	4	29
0	0	0	1556244	**107408**	97	1116	3	0	0	0	**11**	0	0	0	0	1336	7662	1576	45	3	52

In contrast, the following example illustrates a system that is experiencing a shortage of available physical memory, dropping pretty rapidly from about 150 Mbytes to 44 Mbytes, and by the time it reaches 17 Mbytes, the scan rate, the "sr" column, is reporting significant activity. Observing this kind of pattern with vmstat is an indication the system may be swapping and its performance will begin to become sluggish if it is not already.

```
 kthr      memory            page                        disk          faults          cpu
 r b w   swap   free  re  mf pi   po    fr de    sr cd f0 s0 --   in    sy    cs us sy id
 1 0 0 499792 154720   1 1697  0    0     0  0     0  0  0  0 12  811   612  1761 90  7  4
 1 0 0 498856  44052   1 3214  0    0     0  0     0  0  0  0 12 1290  2185  3078 66 18 15
 3 0 0 501188  17212   1 1400  2 2092  4911  0 37694  0 53  0 12 5262  3387  1485 52 27 21
 1 0 0 500696  20344  26 2562 13 4265  7553  0  9220  0 66  0 12 1192  3007  2733 71 17 12
 1 0 0 499976  20108   3 3146 24 3032 10009  0 10971  0 63  0  6 1346  1317  3358 78 15  7
 1 0 0 743664  25908  61 1706 70 8882 10017  0 19866  0 78  0 52 1213   595   688 70 12 18
```

Notice in the example, paying attention only to either the "free" or "swap" columns can be misleading and alone do not provide obvious clues that a system may be swapping.

Monitoring Memory Utilization on Linux

On Linux, monitoring for swapping activity can be done using vmstat and observing the free column. There are other ways to monitor for swap activity on Linux such as using the top command or observing the contents of the file /proc/meminfo. Monitoring for swapping activity using Linux vmstat is shown here. The columns in Linux vmstat to monitor are the "si" and "so" columns, which represent the amount of memory paged-in and the amount of memory paged-out. In addition, the "free" column reports the amount of available free memory. The actual units are not as important as observing whether the amount of free memory is low and high paging activity is occurring at the same time. Observing the pattern just described in these statistics is an indication that the system maybe experiencing swapping activity. The following is an example of a system that is experiencing no swapping activity; since there is no paging activity as shown in the "si" and "so" columns and the amount of free memory is not very low.

```
procs -----------memory---------- ---swap-- -----io---- --system-- -----cpu------
 r  b   swpd    free   buff   cache   si   so   bi   bo    in    cs us sy  id wa st
 2  0      0 9383948 265684 1879740    0    0    0     0     1     1  0  0 100  0  0
 3  0      0 9383948 265684 1879740    0    0    0    11  1012   529 14  0  86  0  0
 3  0      0 9383916 265684 1879740    0    0    0     0  1021  5105 20  0  80  0  0
 3  0      0 9383932 265684 1879740    0    0    0    13  1014   259 19  0  81  0  0
 3  0      0 9383932 265684 1879740    0    0    0     7  1018  4952 20  0  80  0  0
```

However, the following `vmstat` output from a Linux system illustrates a system that is experiencing swapping.

```
procs -----------memory---------- ----swap--- -----io---- --system-- -----cpu------
 r  b   swpd    free    buff  cache    si    so    bi    bo   in    cs us sy id wa st
 1  0      0 9500784 265744 1879752     0     0     0     0 1015   228  0  6 94  0  0
 1  0      0 8750540 265744 1879752     0     0     0     2 1011   216  0  6 94  0  0
 1  0      0 2999792 265744 1879752     0     0     0     2 1012   218  0  6 94  0  0
 2  0      0  155964 185204 1370300     0     0     0     0 1009   215  0  9 90  0  0
 2  0   9816  155636  24160  815332     0  1963     0  2000 1040   238  0 13 87  0  0
 0  2 218420  165152    384   18964     0 41490     0 41498 1247   286  0  6 88  5  0
 0  6 494504  157028    396   18280    45 55217    67 55219 1363   278  0  1 79 21  0
 0  7 799972  159508    408   18356    70 61094   145 61095 1585   337  0  1 72 27  0
 0  8 1084136 155592    416   18512    65 56833    90 56836 1359   292  0  1 75 24  0
 0  3 1248428 174292    500   23420   563 32858  1689 32869 1391   550  0  0 83 17  0
 1  1 1287616 163312    624   28800 13901  7838 15010  7838 2710  6765  1  0 93  6  0
 1  0 1407744 163508    648   29688 18218 24026 18358 24054 3154  2465  1  1 92  6  0
 0  2 1467764 159484    648   28380 19386 12053 19395 12118 2893  2746  2  1 91  5  0
```

Notice the pattern in this example. Where free memory initially decreases, there is little paging activity shown in either the "si" column or "so" column. But as free memory reaches values in the 155,000 − 175,000 range, page-out activity picks up as shown in the "so" column. Once the page-out activity begins to plateau, the page-in activity begins and increases rather quickly as shown in the "si" column. In general what is happening is the system has an application, or set of applications, that placed significant memory allocation and/or memory access pressure on the system. As the amount of physical memory started to become exhausted, the system began to page-out to virtual memory the least recently used pages in memory. As the applications on the system began to demand pages from memory, page-in activity began to occur. As the paging activity increased, the amount of free memory remained about the same. In other words, the system is swapping in pages nearly as quickly as it is paging them out while the amount of free memory remained rather small. This is a typical pattern that can be observed in Linux `vmstat` when a Linux system is experiencing swapping.

Monitoring Lock Contention on Solaris

Many Java applications that do not scale suffer from lock contention. Identifying that lock contention in Java applications can be difficult and the tools to identify lock contention are limited.

In addition, optimizations have been made in modern JVMs to improve the performance of applications that experience lock contention. For example, in Java 5, optimizations were integrated into the Java HotSpot VM (also referred to HotSpot VM hereafter) to implement much of the locking logic, the artifact resulting from Java synchronized methods and synchronized blocks, in user code rather than relying immediately on operating system lock primitives. Prior to Java 5, the HotSpot VM delegated almost all of the locking logic to operating system locking primitives. This allowed for operating system tools such as Solaris mpstat to easily monitor a Java application for lock contention by observing the "smtx" (spin on mutex) column along with observing system or kernel CPU utilization.

As a result of the Java 5 HotSpot VM optimizations to implement much of locking logic in user code, using Solaris mpstat and observing the "smtx" column and "sys" CPU utilization columns no longer work as well. Instead, an alternative approach is needed.

A high level simplistic description of the lock optimization added to Java 5 HotSpot VMs and later is given as follows; spin in a tight loop trying to acquire a lock, if not successful after a number of tight loop spins, park the thread and wait to be notified when to try acquiring the lock again. The act of parking a thread along with awaking a thread results in an operating system voluntary context switch. Hence, an application experiencing heavy lock contention exhibits a high number of voluntary context switches. The cost of a voluntary context switch at a processor clock cycle level is an expensive operation, generally upwards of about 80,000 clock cycles.

Context switching can be monitored on Solaris with mpstat by observing the "csw" column. The value reported by the "csw" column in mpstat is the total number of context switches including involuntary context switches. Involuntary context switching is also reported in mpstat in the "icsw" column. Hence, the number of voluntary context switches is the "csw" minus "icsw."

A general rule to follow is that any Java application experiencing 5% or more of its available clock cycles in voluntary context switches is likely to be suffering from lock contention. Even a 3% to 5% level is worthy of further investigation. An estimate of the number of clock cycles spent in voluntary context switching can be calculated by taking the number of thread context switches (csw) observed in an mpstat interval, minus the involuntary context switches observed in an mpstat interval, (icsw), multiplying that number by 80,000 (the general cost of a context switch in number clock cycles), and dividing it by the total number of clock cycles available in the mpstat interval.

To illustrate with an example, the following Solaris mpstat output captured at a 5 second interval from a 3.0GHz dual core Intel Xeon CPU executing a Java application shows context switches (csw) at about 8100 per 5 second interval and involuntary context switches (icsw) at about 100 per 5 second interval.

```
$ mpstat 5
CPU minf mjf xcal  intr ithr  csw icsw migr smtx srw syscl usr sys wt idl
  0    4   0    1   479  357 8201   87  658  304   0  6376   86   4  0  10
  1    3   0    1   107    3 8258   97  768  294   0  5526   85   4  0  10
CPU minf mjf xcal  intr ithr  csw icsw migr smtx srw syscl usr sys wt idl
  0    0   0    0   551  379 8179   91  717  284   0  6225   85   5  0  10
  1    2   0    0  2292    2 8247  120  715  428   0  7062   84   5  0  10
CPU minf mjf xcal  intr ithr  csw icsw migr smtx srw syscl usr sys wt idl
  0    0   0    0   562  377 8007   98  700  276   0  6493   85   5  0  10
  1    0   0    0  2550    4 8133  137  689  417   0  6627   86   4  0  11
CPU minf mjf xcal  intr ithr  csw icsw migr smtx srw syscl usr sys wt idl
  0    0   0    0   544  378 7931   90  707  258   0  6609   87   5  0   8
  1    0   0    0  2428    1 8061  125  704  409   0  6045   88   3  0   9
```

An estimate of the number of clock cycles wasted due to voluntary context switches is roughly $(8100 - 100) \times 80,000 = 640,000,000$ clock cycles. The number of clock cycles available in a 5 second interval is $3,000,000,000^1 \times 5 = 15,000,000,000$. Hence, $640,000,000 / 15,000,000,000 = 4.27\%$. About 4.27% of the available clock cycles are consumed in voluntary context switches. Based on the general rule of a Java application spending 3% to 5% or more of available clock cycles in voluntary clock cycles implies this Java application is suffering from lock contention. This lock contention is likely coming from areas where multiple threads are trying to access the same synchronized method or synchronized block of code, or a block of code that is guarded by a Java locking construct such as a `java.util.concurrent.locks.Lock`.

> **Tip**
>
> Profiling a Java application with Oracle Solaris Studio Performance Analyzer is a strategy to employ when more concrete information on lock contention and whether lock contention may be a performance concern is required. Profiling with Oracle Solaris Studio Performance Analyzer is covered in detail in Chapter 5 of this book.

Monitoring Lock Contention on Linux

It is possible to monitor lock contention by observing thread context switches in Linux with the `pidstat` command from the sysstat package. However, for `pidstat` to report context switching activity, a Linux kernel version of 2.6.23 or later is required. The use of `pidstat -w` reports voluntary context switches in a "cswch/s" column. It is important to notice that Linux `pidstat -w` reports voluntary context switches, not a sum of all context switches that Solaris `mpstat` reports. Additionally, Linux `pidstat -w` reports the number of voluntary context switches per

---

1. A 3.0 GHz processor executes 3 billion clock cycles per second.

second, not per measurement interval like Solaris `mpstat`. Therefore, the estimate of the percentage of clock cycles wasted on voluntary context switching is calculated as the number of `pidstat -w` voluntary context switches divided by the number of virtual processors. Remember that `pidstat -w` reports voluntary context switches for all virtual processors. As a result, the number of voluntary context switches times 80,000 divided by the number of clock cycles per second of the CPU provides the percentage of CPU clock cycles spent in voluntary context switches. The following is an example from `pidstat -w` monitoring a Java application having a process id of 9391 reporting results every 5 seconds.

```
$ pidstat -w -I -p 9391 5
Linux 2.6.24-server (payton)   07/10/2008

08:57:19 AM      PID   cswch/s nvcswch/s Command
08:57:26 AM     9391      3645       322      java
08:57:31 AM     9391      3512       292      java
08:57:36 AM     9391      3499       310      java
```

To estimate the percentage of clock cycles wasted on context switching, there are about 3500 context switches per second occurring on the system being monitored with `pidstat -w`, a 3.0GHz dual core Intel CPU. Hence, 3500 divided by 2, the number of virtual processors = 1750. $1750 \times 80,000 = 140,000,000$. The number of clock cycles in 1 second on a 3.0GHz processor is 3,000,000,000. Thus, the percentage of clock cycles wasted on context switches is 140,000,000/3,000,000,000 = 4.7%. Again applying the general guideline of 3% to 5% of clock cycles spent in voluntary context switches implies a Java application that may be suffering from lock contention.

Monitoring Lock Contention on Windows

On Windows, in contrast to Solaris and Linux, observing Java lock contention using built-in operating system tools is more difficult. Windows operating systems that include the Performance Monitor and `typeperf` have the capability to monitor context switches. But the capability to distinguish between voluntary and involuntary context switching is not available via a performance counter. To monitor Java lock contention on Windows, tools outside the operating system are often used, such as Intel VTune or AMD CodeAnalyst. Both of these tools have Java lock profiling capabilities along with capabilities to monitor other performance statistics and CPU performance counters.

Isolating Hot Locks

Tracing down the location in Java source code of contended locks has historically been a challenge. A common practice to find contended locks in a Java application has been to periodically take thread dumps and look for threads that tend to be blocked on the same lock across several thread dumps. An example of this procedure is presented in Chapter 4, "JVM Performance Monitoring."

Oracle Solaris Studio Performance Analyzer, which is available for Linux and Solaris, is one of the best tools the authors have used to isolate and report on Java lock contention. Using Performance Analyzer to find contended locks in a Java application is covered in detail in Chapter 5, and an example is presented in Chapter 6, "Java Application Profiling Tips and Tricks."

Other profilers can identify contended locks on Windows. Profilers that are similar in functionality to the Oracle Solaris Studio Performance Analyzer are Intel VTune and AMD CodeAnalyst.

Monitoring Involuntary Context Switches

Involuntary context switching was mentioned earlier but not explained in any detail, or how it differs from voluntary context switching. In contrast to voluntary context switching where an executing thread voluntarily takes itself off the CPU, involuntary thread context switches occur when a thread is taken off the CPU as a result of an expiring time quantum or has been preempted by a higher priority thread. Involuntary context switches can be monitored with Solaris `mpstat` by observing the "`icsw`" column.

CPU	minf	mjf	xcal	intr	ithr	csw	icsw	migr	smtx	srw	syscl	usr	sys	wt	idl
0	11	13	558	760	212	265	1	3	1	0	525	9	1	0	90
1	9	11	479	467	0	251	1	3	1	0	474	9	1	0	89
2	7	4	226	884	383	147	0	4	2	0	192	4	1	0	96
3	7	4	234	495	0	146	0	3	0	0	215	5	1	0	95

Involuntary context switching can also be observed using Solaris `prstat -m`. High involuntary context switches are an indication there are more threads ready to run than there are virtual processors available to run them. As a result it is common to observe a high run queue depth in `vmstat`, high CPU utilization, and a high number of migrations (migrations are the next topic in this section) in conjunction with a large number of involuntary context switches. Strategies to reduce involuntary context switches include using the Solaris command `psrset` to create processor sets for systems running multiple applications and assigning applications to specific processor sets, or reducing the number of application threads being run on the system. An alternative strategy, and usually less effective, is profiling the application to identify areas of the application where you can reduce CPU usage by using improved algorithms so they consume fewer CPU cycles.

Involuntary context switches can also be monitored on Linux using `pidstat -w`. But as mentioned earlier, `pidstat -w` reporting of involuntary context switching requires Linux kernel 2.6.23 or later. On Linux, creation of processor sets and assigning applications to those processor sets can be accomplished using the Linux `taskset` command. See your Linux distribution's documentation for details on how to use Linux `taskset`.

On Windows systems, applications can be assigned to a processor or set of processors by using Task Manager's Process tab. Select a target process, right-click, and select Set Affinity. Then choose the processors the selected process should execute on. On Windows Server operating systems, Windows Vista and Windows 7, an application can be launched from the command line with `start /affinity <affinity mask>`, where `<affinity mask>` is the processor affinity mask in hexadecimal. See the Windows operating system's documentation for the use of `start` command and affinity mask.

Monitoring Thread Migrations

Migration of ready-to-run threads between processors can also be a source of observed performance degradation. Most operating systems' CPU schedulers attempt to keep a ready-to-run thread on the same virtual processor it last executed. If that same virtual processor is busy, the scheduler may migrate that ready-to-run thread to some other available virtual processor. Migration of threads can impact an application's performance since data, or state information, used by a ready-to-run thread may not be readily available in a virtual processor's cache. On Solaris you can use `mpstat` and observe the "`migr`" column to monitor whether thread migrations are an issue to a Java application's performance. If you are running a Java application on a multicore system and observing a high number of migrations, a strategy to reduce thread migrations is creating processor sets and assigning Java applications to those processor sets. As a general guideline, Java applications scaling across multiple cores or virtual processors and observing migrations greater than 500 per second could benefit from binding Java applications to processor sets. In extreme cases, the Solaris kernel tunable `rechoose_interval` can be increased as a means to reduce thread migrations. The former, creating processor sets, is the preferred strategy, and the latter, tuning the kernel, should be considered only as a secondary approach.

Network I/O Utilization

Distributed Java applications may find performance and scalability limited to either network bandwidth or network I/O performance. For instance, if a system's network interface hardware is sent more traffic than it can handle, messages can be queued in operating system buffers, which may cause application delays. Additionally, other things may be occurring on the network that cause delays as well.

Identifying and monitoring a single network utilization statistic can be hard to find in bundled operating system utilities. For example, even though Linux has `netstat` with its optional sysstat package and Solaris bundles `netstat`, neither the Linux nor Solaris implementation of `netstat` reports network utilization. Both provide statistics such as packets sent and packets received per second along with errors and collisions. Collisions in a small amount are a normal occurrence of Ethernet. Large numbers of errors usually are the result of a faulty network interface card, poor wiring or auto-negotiation problems. Also, for a given number of packets received or transmitted per interval as reported by `netstat`, it is difficult to know whether the interface is being fully utilized. For example, if a `netstat -i` command reports 2500 packets per second passing through the network interface card, you do not know whether the network is at 100% utilization or 1% utilization. One conclusion you can make is network traffic is occurring. But that is about the only conclusion you can make without knowing the rated throughput of the underlying network cards and the packet sizes being trans-mitted. In short, it is difficult to tell from the output of `netstat` on Linux or Solaris to determine whether network utilization is limiting an application's performance. Regardless of the operating system running your Java application, there is a need for a tool that can show network utilization on the network interfaces your application is using. The next two subsections present tools that can be used on Solaris, Linux, and Windows to monitor network utilization.

Monitoring Network I/O Utilization on Solaris

On Solaris, a tool called `nicstat` from the freeware K9Toolkit reports network uti-lization and saturation by network interface. The K9Toolkit is also included in the Solaris Performance Tools CD 3.0 package mentioned earlier in the "Monitoring CPU Utilization on Solaris" section of this chapter. The K9Toolkit can also be downloaded from http://www.brendangregg.com/k9toolkit.html.

`nicstat` has the following command line syntax:

```
nicstat [-hnsz] [-i interface[,...]] | [interval [count]]
```

where `-h` displays a help message, `-n` shows nonlocal interfaces only, `-s` shows a summary output, `-z` skips reporting of zero values, `-i` *interface* is the network inter-face device name, *interval* is the frequency at which output is to be reported in sec-onds, and *count* is the number of samples to report.

The following is example output from `nicstat -i yukonx0 1`, which samples the network interface device `yukonx0` at a 1 second interval.

Time	Int	rKB/s	wKB/s	rPk/s	wPk/s	rAvs	wAvs	%Util	Sat
19:24:16	yukonx0	0.75	4.68	2.72	3.80	281.3	1261.9	0.00	0.00
19:24:17	yukonx0	54.14	1924.9	724.1	1377.2	76.56	1431.2	1.58	0.00
19:24:18	yukonx0	44.64	1588.4	598.0	1138.0	76.45	1429.3	1.30	0.00
19:24:19	yukonx0	98.89	3501.8	1320.0	2502.0	76.72	1433.2	2.87	0.00
19:24:20	yukonx0	0.43	0.27	2.00	3.00	222.0	91.33	0.00	0.00
19:24:21	yukonx0	44.53	1587.2	598.0	1134.0	76.26	1433.2	1.30	0.00
19:24:22	yukonx0	101.9	3610.1	1362.0	2580.0	76.64	1432.8	2.96	0.00
19:24:23	yukonx0	139.9	4958.1	1866.7	3541.4	76.73	1433.6	4.06	0.00
19:24:24	yukonx0	77.23	2736.4	1035.1	1956.2	76.40	1432.4	2.24	0.00
19:24:25	yukonx0	48.12	1704.1	642.0	1220.0	76.75	1430.3	1.40	0.00
19:24:26	yukonx0	59.80	2110.8	800.0	1517.0	76.54	1424.8	1.73	0.00

The column headings are

- `Int` is the network interface device name.
- `rKb/s` is the number of kilobytes read per second.
- `wKb/s` is the number of kilobytes written per second.
- `rPk/s` is the number of packets read per second.
- `wPk/s` is the number of packets written per second.
- `rAvs` is average bytes read per read.
- `wAvs` is the average bytes written per write.
- `%Util` is the network interface utilization.
- `Sat` is the saturation value.

As you can see a wealth of meaningful data is presented with `nicstat` to help you identify whether your distributed Java application is saturating the network. You can see there is activity occurring at the `yukonx0` network interface as shown in the number of bytes read and written yet the network utilization never reaches much above 4% utilization. As a result, you can conclude the applications running on this system are not experiencing a performance issue as a result of a saturated network.

Monitoring Network I/O Utilization on Linux

A port of the Solaris `nicstat` monitoring tool for Linux is available. The source code can be downloaded from http://blogs.sun.com/roller/resources/timc/nicstat/ nicstat-1.22.tar.gz. It requires compilation before being able to use it. It reports network utilization in the same way as described in the previous section on monitoring network utilization on Solaris.

Monitoring Network I/O Utilization on Windows

Monitoring network utilization on Windows is not as simple as adding performance counters to Performance Monitor and observing their values. It requires knowing the possible bandwidth of the network interface you are interested in monitoring and some measure of the amount of data passing through the network interface.

The number of bytes transmitted across a network interface can be obtained using the "\Network Interface(*)\Bytes Total/sec" performance counter. The "*" wildcard reports the bandwidth for all network interfaces on the system. You can use the `typeperf \Network Interface(*)\Bytes Total/sec` command to see the names of the network interfaces. Then, you can replace the wildcard "*" with the network interface you are interested in monitoring. For example, suppose the output from `typeperf \Network Interface(*)\Bytes Total/sec` shows the network interfaces as Intel[R] 82566DM-2 Gigabit Network Connection, isatap. gateway.2wire.net, Local Area Connection* 11 and you know the network interface card installed in your system is an Intel network card. You can substitute "Intel[R] 82566DM-2 Gigabit Network Connection" for the "*" wildcard when adding the performance counter to Performance Monitor or when using the `typeperf` command.

In addition to the bytes transmitted across the interface, the bandwidth of the network interface must also be obtained. It can be obtained using the "\Network Interface(*)\Current Bandwidth" performance counter. Again, the "*" wildcard should be replaced with the network interface you are interested in monitoring.

It is important to note that the Current Bandwidth performance counter reports bandwidth in bits per second. In contrast, the Bytes Total/sec reports in units of bytes per second. Therefore, the formula to calculate network utilization must compensate for the proper units, bits per second, or bytes per second. The following are two formulas that compute network utilization: the first one by adjusting the Current Bandwidth into bytes per second by dividing the Current Bandwidth by 8, and the second one by adjusting the Bytes Total/sec into bits per second by multiplying it by 8 (8 bits per byte).

```
network utilization % = Bytes Total/sec/(Current Bandwidth / 8) x 100
```

Or, alternatively as

```
network utilization % = (Bytes Total/sec * 8) / Current Bandwidth x 100
```

Network utilization can also be monitored in Windows using Task Manager and clicking on the Networking tab. An example is shown in Figure 2-9.

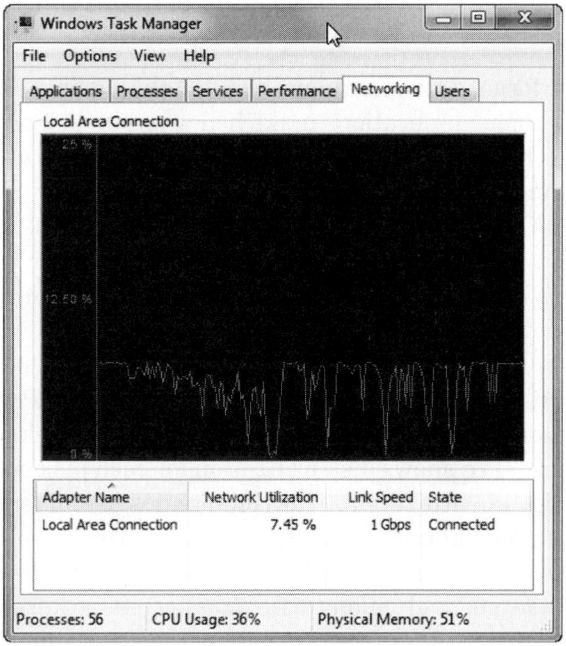

Figure 2-9 Task Manager showing network utilization

Application Performance Improvement Considerations

An application executing a large number of reads and writes to a network with small amounts of data in each individual read or write call consumes large amounts of system or kernel CPU and may also report a high number of system calls. A strategy to reduce system or kernel CPU in such an application is to reduce the number network read or write system calls. Additionally, the use of nonblocking Java NIO instead of blocking `java.net.Socket` may also improve an application's performance by reducing the number of threads required to process incoming requests or send outbound replies.

A strategy to follow when reading from a nonblocking socket is to design and implement your application to read as much data as there is available per read call. Also, when writing data to a socket, write as much data as possible per write call. There are Java NIO frameworks that incorporate such practices, such as Project Grizzly (https://grizzly.dev.java.net). Java NIO frameworks also tend to simplify the programming of client-server type applications. Java NIO, as offered in the JDK, tends to be a "bare metal" type of implementation, and there is plenty of room to make poor use of its Java APIs that can lead to disappointing application performance, and hence the suggestion of using a Java NIO framework.

Disk I/O Utilization

If an application performs disk operations, disk I/O should be monitored for possible performance issues. Some applications make heavy use of disk as a major part of its core functionality such as databases, and almost all applications utilize an application log to write important information about the state or behavior of the application as events occur. Disk I/O utilization is the most useful monitoring statistic for understanding application disk usage since it is a measure of active disk I/O time. Disk I/O utilization along with system or kernel CPU utilization can be monitored using iostat on Linux and Solaris.

To use iostat on Linux, the optional sysstat package must be installed.

To monitor disk utilization on Windows Server systems, the Performance Monitor has several performance counters available under its Logical Disk performance object.

On Solaris, iostat -xc shows disk utilization for each disk device on the system along with reporting CPU utilization. This command is useful for showing both disk utilization and system or kernel CPU utilization together. The following example shows a system that has three disks, sd0, sd2, and sd4, with disk I/O utilization of 22%, 13%, and 36%, respectively, along with 73% system or kernel CPU utilization. The other statistics from iostat are not as important for application performance monitoring since they do not report a "busy-ness" indicator.

```
$ iostat -xc 5
                       extended disk statistics          cpu
     disk r/s  w/s Kr/s Kw/s wait actv svc_t  %w  %b  us sy wt id
     sd0  3.4  1.1 17.1  9.8 0.1  0.2  16.2   1   22  3 73  8 16
     sd2  2.1  0.5 16.7  4.0 0.0  0.1  23.6   1   13
     sd4  5.2  6.0 41.4 45.2 0.2  0.4  59.2   8   36
```

To monitor disk I/O utilization and system or kernel CPU utilization on Linux you can use iostat -xm. The following is an example of iostat -xm from a Linux system showing 97% and 69% for disks hda and hdb, respectively, along with 16% system or kernel CPU utilization. Columns reporting 0 values were removed from the output for ease of reading.

```
$ iostat -xm 5

avg-cpu:  %user   %nice %system %iowait
           0.20    0.40   16.37   83.03

Device: rrqm/s  r/s    rsec/s   rMB/s  avgqu-sz await svctm %util
hda     9662.87 305.59 87798.80 42.87  1.64     5.39  3.17  97.01
hdb     7751.30 225.15 63861.08 31.18  1.18     5.24  3.11  69.94
```

Tip

The Solaris Performance Tools CD 3.0, presented in the "CPU Utilization" section earlier in this chapter contains a graphical tool called `iobar` that displays disk I/O in a `cpubar` like manner. The Solaris Performance Tools CD 3.0, also contains a command line tool called `iotop` that displays Solaris `iostat -x` information in a `prstat` or `top` manner.

One of the challenges with monitoring disk I/O utilization is identifying which files are being read or written to and which application is the source of the disk activity. Recent versions of Solaris 10 and Solaris 11 Express include several DTrace scripts in the /usr/demo/dtrace directory that can help monitor disk activity. The `iosnoop.d` DTrace script provides details such as which user id is accessing the disk, what process is accessing the disk, the size of the disk access, and the name of the file being accessed. The `iosnoop.d` script is also included in the Solaris DTraceToolKit downloadable at http://www.solarisinternals.com/wiki/index.php/ DTraceToolKit. The following is example output from executing `iosnoop.d` while launching NetBeans IDE. The entire output is not displayed since there are many files accessed during a NetBeans IDE launch. Hence, for brevity the output is trimmed.

```
$ iosnoop.d
  UID    PID D     BLOCK   SIZE    COMM PATHNAME
97734   1617 R   4140430   1024 netbeans /huntch/tmp/netbeans
97734   1617 R   4141518   1024     bash /huntch/tmp/netbeans/modules
97734   1617 R   4150956   1024     bash /huntch/tmp/netbeans/update
97734   1697 R   4143242   1024     java /huntch/tmp/netbeans/var
97734   1697 R   4141516   1024     java /huntch/tmp/netbeans/config
97734   1697 R   4143244   1024     java /huntch/tmp/netbeans/var/log
97734   1697 R   4153884   1024     java /huntch/tmp/netbeans/docs
97734   1697 R   4153884   1024     java /huntch/tmp/netbeans/docs
97734   1697 R   4153884   1024     java /huntch/tmp/netbeans/docs
97734   1697 R   4153884   1024     java /huntch/tmp/netbeans/docs
97734   1697 R   4153884   1024     java /huntch/tmp/netbeans/docs
97734   1697 R   4153884   1024     java /huntch/tmp/netbeans/docs
97734   1697 R   4153884   1024     java /huntch/tmp/netbeans/docs
97734   1697 R   4153884   1024     java /huntch/tmp/netbeans/docs
97734   1697 R  12830464   8192     java /usr/jdk1.6.0/jre/lib/rt.jar
97734   1697 R  12830480  20480     java /usr/jdk1.6.0/jre/lib/rt.jar
97734   1697 R  12830448   8192     java /usr/jdk1.6.0/jre/lib/rt.jar
97734   1697 R  12830416   8192     java /usr/jdk1.6.0/jre/lib/rt.jar
97734   1697 R  12830432   4096     java /usr/jdk1.6.0/jre/lib/rt.jar
97734   1697 R  12828264   8192     java /usr/jdk1.6.0/jre/lib/rt.jar
[... additional output removed ...]
```

The "UID" column reports the user id responsible for performing the disk access. The "PID" column is the process id of the process performing the disk access. The "D" column indicates whether the disk access is the result of a read or write, "R" = read, "W" = write. The "BLOCK" column is the disk block. The "SIZE" column is the amount of data accessed in bytes. The "COMM" column is the name of the command performing the disk access, and the "PATHNAME" column is the name of the file being accessed.

Patterns to look for in the output of iosnoop.d is repeated accesses to the same file, same disk block, by the same command, process id, and user id. For example, in the preceding output there are many disk accesses of 1024 bytes on the same disk block 4153884, which may indicate a possible optimization opportunity. It may be that the same information is being accessed multiple times. Rather than re-reading the data from disk each time, the application may be able to keep the data in memory, reuse it, and avoid re-reading and experiencing an expensive disk read. If the same data is not being accessed, it may be possible to read a larger block of data and reduce the number of disk accesses.

At a larger scale, if high disk I/O utilization is observed with an application, it may be worthwhile to further analyze the performance of your system's disk I/O subsystem by looking more closely at its expected workload, disk service times, seek times, and the time spent servicing I/O events. If improved disk utilization is required, several strategies may help. At the hardware and operating system level any of the following may improve disk I/O utilization:

- A faster storage device
- Spreading file systems across multiple disks
- Tuning the operating system to cache larger amounts of file system data structures

At the application level any strategy to minimize disk activity will help such as reducing the number of read and write operations using buffered input and output streams or integrating a caching data structure into the application to reduce or eliminate disk interaction. The use of buffered streams reduces the number of system calls to the operating system and consequently reduces system or kernel CPU utilization. It may not improve disk I/O performance, but it will make more CPU cycles available for other parts of the application or other applications running on the system. Buffered data structures are available in the JDK that can easily be utilized, such as java.io.BufferedOutputStream and java.io.BufferedInputStream.

An often overlooked item with disk performance is checking whether the disk cache is enabled. Some systems are configured and installed with the disk cache disabled. An enabled disk cache improves an application's performance that heavily relies on disk I/O. However, you should use caution if you discover the default setting of a system has the disk cache disabled. Enabling the disk cache may result in corrupted data in the event of an unexpected power failure.

> **Tip**
>
> On Solaris and Solaris 11 Express, the disk cache can be enabled when the disk is formatted using the `format -e` command. However, do not run the `format -e` command on a disk or partition where it is desirable to preserve the data. The `format -e` command destroys all data on the disk or partition where the `format` command is executed. Disk performance on Solaris can also be improved by configuring and using Oracle Solaris ZFS file systems. See the Solaris man pages for tips on how to configure and use Oracle Solaris ZFS file systems.

Additional Command Line Tools

When monitoring applications for an extended period of time such as several hours or several days, or in a production environment, many performance engineers and system administrators of Solaris or Linux systems use `sar` to collect performance statistics. With `sar`, you can select which data to collect such as user CPU utilization, system or kernel CPU utilization, number of system calls, memory paging, and disk I/O statistics. Data collected from `sar` is usually looked at after-the-fact, as opposed to while it is being collected. Observing data collected over a longer period of time can help identify trends that may provide early indications of pending performance concerns. Additional information on what performance data can be collected and reported with `sar` can be found in the Solaris and Linux `sar` man pages.

Another tool that can be useful on Solaris is `kstat`, which reports kernel statistics. Its use can be powerful for applications in need of every bit of performance they can get. There are many kernel statistics `kstat` can report on. A `kstat -l` command lists all the possible kernel statistics that can be monitored with `kstat`. The most important thing to understand about using `kstat` is that it reports the number of events since the system was last powered on. So, to monitor an application with `kstat`, running `kstat` before and after some interval of interest and then taking the difference between reported values is required. In addition, the application of monitoring interest should be the only application running when using `kstat` since `kstat` does not report on which application is correlated to the statistics, or the values reported. If more than one application is running on the system when using `kstat`, you will have no way of identifying which application is producing the values reported by `kstat`.

On Solaris, processor specific CPU performance counters can be monitored using Solaris bundled commands `cpustat` or `cputrack`. Use of these specific CPU performance counters is usually left to performance specialists looking for specific tuning optimizations but are mentioned in this section since there may be some performance specialists among the readers of this chapter.

Both `cpustat` and `cputrack` commands require a set of event counters that are specific to a processor such as AMD, Intel, or SPARC. The set of CPU performance counters may also vary within a processor family. To obtain a list of available performance counters, you can use the -h option. Additionally, CPU performance counters can also be found in the processor manufacturer's documentation. In contrast to cpustat, which gathers information from CPU performance counters for all applications on the system and tends to be more intrusive, cputrack collects CPU performance counter statistics for individual applications with little or no interference to other activities on the system. Additional details on the usage of cpustat and cputrack can be found in the Solaris man pages.

Monitoring CPU Utilization on SPARC T-Series Systems

The SPARC T-series processor from Oracle combines both chip multiprocessing and chip multithreading. Its architecture differs enough from traditional chip architectures that monitoring its CPU utilization deserves its own section. To understand CPU utilization of a SPARC T-series based system it is important to understand some of the basics of the SPARC T-series chip architecture, how it differs from traditional processor architectures, and why conventional Unix monitoring tools such as vmstat and mpstat do not truly show SPARC T-series CPU utilization.

The SPARC T-series processors have not only multiple cores, but also multiple hardware threads per core. It is easiest to explain the first generation SPARC T-series first and then extend it to its later generations. The UltraSPARC T1 is the first generation SPARC T-series processor. It has eight cores with four hardware threads per core and one pipeline per core. The UltraSPARC T2, the second generation SPARC T-series processor, consists of eight cores with eight hardware threads per core and two pipelines per core. On an UltraSPARC T1, only one hardware thread per core executes in a given clock cycle. On an UltraSPARC T2, since there are two pipelines per core, two hardware threads per core execute per clock cycle. However, what makes the SPARC T-series processors unique is the capability to switch to a different hardware thread within a core when the one that had been executing becomes stalled. Stalled is defined as a CPU state such as a CPU cache miss where the processor must wait for a memory data fetch.

Applications with a large number of concurrent software threads that tend to experience stalls tend to perform very well on a SPARC T-series processor since the amount of time spent on CPU stalls tends to be much longer than the time it takes for a SPARC T-series processor core to switch to a different runnable hardware thread. In contrast, applications with a small number of concurrent threads, especially ones that do not experience many CPU stalls, tend not to perform as well as they would on a faster clock rate traditional processor. For example, consider an application that has eight concurrent software threads that are runnable at all times with few or a very small number of CPU stalls. Such an application would utilize one hardware thread per core on an UltraSPARC T1 since there are eight cores on an UltraSPARC

T1 and only one of those four hardware threads per core can execute per clock cycle. Additionally, since only one of those four hardware threads per core can execute per clock cycle, those eight concurrent software threads will execute at a clock rate of one-fourth the clock frequency. For example, a 1.2GHz UltraSPARC T1 on such a workload would be executing each of those eight concurrent software threads at an effective clock rate of 300MHz, 1.2GHz/4 = 300MHz. In contrast, a dual CPU socket quad core Intel or AMD based system, a system with eight cores, which has a clock rate of 2.33GHz, for example, would execute each of those eight concurrent software threads at 2.33GHz since each concurrent software thread can execute on a single core and each core is a single hardware thread executing at 2.33GHz. However, in practice, few workloads operate with few memory stalls. On workloads with a much larger number of runnable threads, especially threads that experience CPU stalls, the SPARC T-series will likely perform better than an x86/x64 quad core processor since the time it takes to switch between hardware threads on a SPARC T-series is faster than the time it takes for a thread context switch on a single hardware thread per core architecture because the thread context switch may require CPU caches to be primed with data, which means the switched-to-thread will waste clock cycles waiting for data to be loaded from memory.

With a better understanding of SPARC T-series architecture and its differences from traditional single hardware thread per core processor architecture, it becomes easier to understand how to monitor a SPARC T-series based system. It is also important to realize that the Solaris operating system treats each hardware thread of a SPARC T-series as a virtual processor. This means monitoring tools such as `mpstat` report 32 virtual processors for an UltraSPARC T1 (8 cores $\times$ 4 hardware threads per core) and 64 processors for an UltraSPARC T2 (8 cores $\times$ 8 hardware threads per core). Remember that not all virtual processors in a SPARC T-series can execute on the same clock cycle. When reporting CPU utilization for a virtual processor, both `mpstat` and `vmstat` commands assume a virtual processor that is not idle, is a busy virtual processor that is making progress on processing a workload. In other words, both `mpstat` and `vmstat` will report a virtual processor as busy, or as being utilized, even when that virtual processor is stalled. Recall that on a SPARC T-series processor, a stalled software thread, which is running on a virtual processor (hardware thread), does not necessarily mean the pipeline is stalled or the entire processor core is stalled. Since the SPARC T-series processors have hardware threads reported as virtual processors, `vmstat` and `mpstat` actually report the percentage of pipeline occupancy of software threads.

Tip

More detailed information about the SPARC T-series processors can be found on the Solaris Internals wiki at http://www.solarisinternals.com/wiki/index.php/CMT_Utilization.

On systems running processors that do not have multiple hardware threads per core, idle time reported by `mpstat` or `vmstat` can be used to decide whether the system can take on additional load. On a SPARC T-series, a hardware thread being idle, which is reported as a virtual processor by `mpstat`, and a SPARC T-series processor core being idle are two different things. Remember that `mpstat` reports statistics on each hardware thread since each hardware thread is seen as a virtual processor. To understand CPU utilization of a SPARC T-series processor, both processor core utilization and core hardware thread utilization need to be observed. Processor core utilization of a SPARC T-series can be observed by monitoring the number of instructions executed by a given processor core. The Solaris `cpustat` command can monitor the number of instructions executed per hardware thread within a core. But it does not have the capability to report on the number of instructions executed per core. However, the `cpustat` data reporting the number of instructions executed per hardware thread could be aggregated to show the number of instructions executed per core. A utility called `corestat` aggregates the instruction count per hardware thread reported by `cpustat` to derive a SPARC T-series core CPU utilization. The `corestat` command is not included in Solaris distributions. But, `corestat` can be downloaded from Oracle's cool tools Web site, http://cooltools.sunsource.net/corestat/index.html. Additional information and instructions on how to use `corestat` can also be found on Oracle's cool tools Web site.

Looking at `vmstat`, `mpstat`, and `corestat` data collected on a SPARC T-series based system provides information about how the system is performing. For example, suppose `vmstat` or `mpstat` is reporting the system is 35% busy and `corestat` is reporting core utilization is 50%. Since core utilization is higher than the CPU utilization reported by `vmstat` or `mpstat`, if the system continues to take on additional similar load by adding more application threads, the system may reach core saturation before it reaches CPU saturation. As a result, this application may reach peak scalability prior to `vmstat` or `mpstat` reporting the system is 100% busy. Consider a different scenario: `vmstat` and `mpstat` are reporting the system is 100% busy and `corestat` is reporting core utilization is 40%. This indicates the system will not be able to take on additional work unless you are able to improve core utilization. Improving core utilization requires improving pipeline performance. To realize improved pipeline performance you have to focus on reducing CPU stalls. Reducing CPU stalls can be difficult and requires an in-depth understanding of the application being run on the system so that the application can better utilize the CPU caches. This usually means improving memory locality for the application. The skill necessary to reduce CPU stalls usually requires special assistance from performance engineers. These two example scenarios illustrate how important it is to monitor both CPU utilization with `vmstat` or `mpstat` and also monitor core utilization on SPARC T-series systems.

Bibliography

Linux nicstat source code download. http://blogs.sun.com/roller/resources/timc/nicstat/nicstat-1.22.tar.gz.

Microsoft Windows *typeperf* description. http://www.microsoft.com/resources/documentation/windows/xp/all/proddocs/en-us/nt_command_typeperf.mspx?mfr=true.

Oracle's cool tools Web site. http://cooltools.sunsource.net/corestat/index.html.

Project Grizzly Web site. http://grizzly.java.net.

Solaris Internals wiki. http://www.solarisinternals.com/wiki/index.php/CMT_Utilization.

Solaris K9 Toolkit and nicstat Web site and download. http://www.brendangregg.com/k9toolkit.html.

Solaris Performance Tools CD 3.0 Web site. http://www.scalingbits.com/solaris/performancetoolcd.

Tim Cook blog Web site. http://blogs.sun.com/timc/entry/nicstat_the_solaris_and_linux.

3

JVM Overview

Since its introduction in 1995, Java has evolved substantially. So too have Java Virtual Machines, (JVMs). In Java's early days, Java performance was a challenge for many applications despite its advantages of developer productivity and memory management. The integration of JIT compilers, more sophisticated garbage collectors, and improvements in the JVM runtime environment have allowed many Java applications to meet their performance requirements. Even with the many enhancements added to modern JVMs, performance and scalability remain important to application stakeholders. For example, many applications have increased their performance requirements and performance service level agreements. Additionally, new families or classes of applications are able to utilize Java technologies as a result of the performance and scalability improvements available in modern JVMs.

One of challenges introduced by modern JVMs is many users of Java technology see a JVM as a black box, which can make it a difficult task to improve the performance or scalability of a Java application. Thus, having a basic, fundamental understanding of a modern JVM is essential to the ability to improve a Java application's performance.

This chapter provides an overview of the HotSpot Java Virtual Machine, (also referred to as the HotSpot VM hereafter), architecture. Not all the information in this chapter is required to tackle the task of improving all Java application performance issues running in a HotSpot VM. Nor is this chapter an exhaustive description of the Java HotSpot VM (also referred to as the HotSpot VM hereafter). But it does present its major components and its architecture.

There are three major components of the HotSpot VM: VM Runtime, JIT compiler, and a memory manager. This chapter begins with a high level architecture view of the HotSpot VM followed by an overview of each of the three major components. In addition, information on ergonomic decisions the HotSpot VM makes automatically is included at the end of the chapter.

HotSpot VM High Level Architecture

The HotSpot VM possesses an architecture that supports a strong foundation of features and capabilities. Its architecture supports the ability to realize high performance and massive scalability. For example, the HotSpot VM JIT compilers generate dynamic optimizations; in other words, it makes optimization decisions while the Java application is running and generates high performing native machine instructions targeted for the underlying system architecture. In addition, through its maturing evolution and continuous engineering of its runtime environment and multithreaded garbage collector, the HotSpot VM yields high scalability on even the largest computer systems available.

A high level view of the HotSpot VM architecture is shown in Figure 3-1.

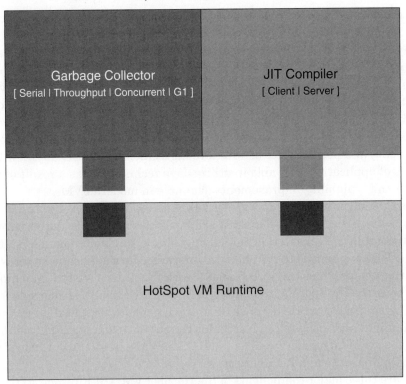

Figure 3-1 HotSpot VM high level architecture.

As shown in Figure 3-1, the JIT compiler, client or server, is pluggable as is the choice of garbage collector: Serial GC, Throughput, Concurrent, or G1. At the time of this writing, the G1 garbage collector is under development and expected to be available in Java 7 HotSpot VMs. The HotSpot VM Runtime provides services and common APIs to the HotSpot JIT compilers and HotSpot garbage collector. In addition the HotSpot VM Runtime provides basic functionality to the VM such as a launcher, thread management, Java Native Interface, and so on. Further details on VM Runtime's components and their responsibilities are described in the next section, "HotSpot VM Runtime."

Early releases of the HotSpot VM were limited to 32-bit JVMs, which have a memory address limitation of four gigabytes. It is important to note that the actual Java heap space available for a 32-bit HotSpot VM may be further limited depending on the underlying operating system. For instance, on Microsoft Windows operating systems the maximum Java heap available to a HotSpot VM is around 1.5 gigabytes. For Linux operating systems, the maximum Java heap available to the HotSpot VM is around 2.5 to 3.0 gigabytes for very recent Linux kernels and about 2 gigabytes for less recent Linux kernels. On Oracle Solaris, also referred to as Solaris hereafter, operating systems the maximum Java heap available to the HotSpot VM is around 3.3 gigabytes. The actual maximums vary due to the memory address space consumed by both a given Java application and a JVM version.

As server systems were introduced with much larger amounts of memory, a 64-bit version of the HotSpot VM was introduced. A 64-bit HotSpot VM allows these systems to utilize additional memory through the use of increased Java heaps. There are several classes of applications where using 64-bit addressing can be useful. However, with 64-bit VMs come a performance penalty due to an increase in size of the internal HotSpot VM's representation of Java objects, called *ordinary object pointers,* or *oops,* which have an increase in width from 32 bits to 64 bits. This increase in width results in fewer oops being available on a CPU cache line and as a result decreases CPU cache efficiency. The decrease in CPU cache efficiency on 64-bit JVMs often results in about a 8% to 15% performance degradation compared to a 32-bit JVM. However, beginning with more recent Java 6 HotSpot VMs, along with those found in OpenJDK, a new feature called compressed oops, which is enabled with the -XX:+UseCompressedOops VM command line option, can yield 32-bit JVM performance with the benefit of larger 64-bit Java heaps. In fact, some Java applications realize better performance with a 64-bit HotSpot VM using compressed oops than they achieve with a 32-bit VM. The performance improvement realized from compressed oops arises from being able to pack a 64-bit pointer into 32 bits by relying on alignment and possibly having an offset. In other words, the increase in performance comes from using smaller, more space efficient compressed pointers rather than full width 64-bit pointers, which improves CPU cache utilization. An application experiencing improved CPU cache utilization is one that executes faster. In addition, on some platforms such as Intel or AMD x64, 64-bit JVMs can make use of additional CPU registers, which can also improve application performance. Having additional registers available helps avoid what is known as register spilling. Register spilling occurs where there is more live state (i.e. variables) in the application than the CPU has registers. When register spilling occurs, some of the live state must be "spilled" from CPU registers to memory. Therefore, avoiding register spilling can result in a faster executing application.

Today 32-bit and 64-bit HotSpot VMs are available for the following hardware platforms and operating systems: Solaris SPARC, Solaris x86, Linux x86, and Windows x86 for both Intel Xeon and AMD along with Solaris x64, Linux x64, and Windows x64 for both Intel Xeon and AMD. Various ports of the HotSpot VM also exist for other platforms, such as Apple x64, Apple PPC, Intel Itanium, HP-UX, MIPS, and ARM.

HotSpot VM Runtime

The VM Runtime is an often overlooked part of the HotSpot VM. The VM's garbage collectors and JIT compilers tend to get more attention than the VM Runtime. However, the VM Runtime provides the core functionality of the HotSpot VM. This section provides an introduction to the HotSpot VM Runtime environment. The objective of this section is to provide a better understanding of the responsibilities and roles the Runtime plays in the VM. Having this understanding allows readers to take full performance advantage of the services provided by the VM Runtime. Not all the details presented in this section are necessary to realize a high performance Java application. However, it can be beneficial to have a basic understanding of the HotSpot VM Runtime since there may be cases where tuning a property of service provided by the VM Runtime may yield significant improvement in Java application performance.

The HotSpot VM Runtime encompasses many responsibilities, including parsing of command line arguments, VM life cycle, class loading, byte code interpreter, exception handling, synchronization, thread management, Java Native Interface, VM fatal error handling, and C++ (non-Java) heap management. In the following subsections, each of these areas of the VM Runtime is described in more detail.

Command Line Options

The HotSpot VM Runtime parses the many command line options and configures the HotSpot VM based on those options. A number of command line options and environment variables can affect the performance characteristics of the HotSpot VM. Some of these options are consumed by the HotSpot VM launcher such as the choice of JIT compiler and choice of garbage collector; some are processed by the launcher and passed to the launched HotSpot VM where they are consumed such as Java heap sizes.

There are three main categories of command line options: standard options, nonstandard options, and developer options. Standard command line options are expected to be accepted by all Java Virtual Machine implementations as required by the *Java Virtual Machine Specification.* [1] Standard command line options are stable between releases. However, it is possible for standard command line options to be deprecated in subsequent releases after the release in which it was first introduced. Nonstandard command line options begin with a -X prefix. Nonstandard command line options are not guaranteed to be supported in all JVM implementations, nor are they required to be supported in all JVM implementations. Nonstandard command line options are also subject to change without notice between subsequent releases of the Java SDK. Developer command line options in the HotSpot VM begin with a -XX prefix. Developer command line options often have specific system requirements for correct operation and may require privileged access to system configuration parameters. Like nonstandard command line options, developer command line options are also subject to change between releases without notice.

Command line options control the values of internal variables in the HotSpot VM, all of which have a type and a default value. For boolean values, the mere presence or lack of presence of an option on the HotSpot VM command line can control the value of these variables. For developer command line options (-XX options) with boolean flags, a + or - before the name of the options indicates a true or false value, respectively, to enable or disable a given HotSpot VM feature or option. For example, -XX:+AggressiveOpts sets a HotSpot internal boolean variable to true to enable additional performance optimizations. In contrast, -XX:-AggressiveOpts sets the same internal variable to false to disable additional performance optimizations. Developer command line options (the -XX options) that take an additional argument, those that are nonboolean, tend to be of the form, -XX:OptionName=<N> where <N> is some numeric value. Almost all developer command line options that take an additional argument, accept an integer value along with a suffix of k, m, or g, which are used as kilo-, mega-, or giga- multipliers for the integer value specified. There is also a small set of developer command line options that accept data passed in directly after the name of the flag without any delineation. The approach depends on the particular command line option and its parsing mechanism.

VM Life Cycle

The HotSpot VM Runtime is responsible for launching the HotSpot VM and the shutdown of the HotSpot VM. This section provides an overview of what occurs within the HotSpot VM prior to it executing a Java program and what it does when a Java program terminates or exits. A large amount of detail is presented in this section, perhaps more than necessary for purposes of performance tuning. But it is included to give you sense of the complexity involved in the starting and stopping of a Java application.

The component that starts the HotSpot VM is called the launcher. There are several HotSpot VM launchers. The most commonly used launcher is the `java` command on Unix/Linux and on Windows the `java` and `javaw` commands. It is also possible to launch an embedded JVM through the JNI interface, `JNI_CreateJavaVM`. In addition, there is also a network-based launcher called `javaws`, which is used by Web browsers to launch applets. The trailing "ws" on the `javaws` is often referred to as "web start." Hence the term "Java web start" for the `javaws` launcher.

The launcher executes a sequence of operations to start the HotSpot VM. These steps are summarized here:

1. Parse command line options.

   Some of the command line options are consumed immediately by the launcher such as `-client` or `- server`, which determines the JIT compiler to load. Other command line options are passed to the launched HotSpot VM.

2. Establish the Java heap sizes and the JIT compiler type (client or server) if these options are not explicitly specified on the command line.

   If Java heap sizes and JIT compiler are not explicitly specified as a command line option, these are ergonomically established by the launcher. Ergonomic defaults vary depending on the underlying system configuration and operating system. Ergonomic choices made by the HotSpot VM are described in more detail in the "HotSpot VM Adaptive Tuning" section later in this chapter.

3. Establish environment variables such as `LD_LIBRARY_PATH` and `CLASSPATH`.

4. If the Java `Main-Class` is not specified on the command line, the launcher fetches the `Main-Class` name from the JAR's manifest.

5. Create the HotSpot VM using the standard Java Native Interface method `JNI_CreateJavaVM` in a newly created nonprimordial thread.

   In contrast to a nonprimordial thread, a primordial thread is the first thread allocated by an operating system kernel when a new process is launched. Hence, when a HotSpot VM is launched, the primordial thread is the first thread allocated by the operating system kernel running in the newly created HotSpot VM process. Creating the HotSpot VM in a nonprimordial thread provides the ability to customize the HotSpot VM such as changing the stack size on Windows. More details of what happens in the HotSpot VM's implementation of `JNI_CreateJavaVM` are provided in the "JNI_CreateJavaVM Details" sidebar.

6. Once the HotSpot VM is created and initialized, the Java `Main-Class` is loaded and the launcher gets the Java main method's attributes from the Java `Main-Class`.

7. The Java main method is invoked in the HotSpot VM using the Java Native Interface method `CallStaticVoidMethod` passing it the marshaled arguments from the command line.

At this point the HotSpot VM is executing the Java program specified on the command line.

Once a Java program, or Java main method completes its execution, the HotSpot VM must check and clear any pending exceptions that may have occurred during the program's or method's execution. Additionally, both the method's exit status and program's exit status must be passed back to their caller's. The Java main method is detached from the HotSpot VM using the Java Native Interface method `DetachCurrentThread`. When the HotSpot VM calls `DetachCurrentThread`, it decrements the thread count so the Java Native Interface knows when to safely shut down the HotSpot VM and to ensure a thread is not performing operations in the HotSpot VM along with there being no active Java frames on its stack. Specific details of the operations performed by the HotSpot VM's Java Native Interface method implementation of `DestroyJavaVM` is described in the "DestroyJavaVM Details" sidebar.

JNI_CreateJavaVM Details

The HotSpot VM's implementation of the `JNI_CreateJavaVM` method performs the following sequence of operations when it is called during the launch of the HotSpot VM.

1. Ensure no two threads call this method at the same time and only one HotSpot VM instance is created in the process.

   Because the HotSpot VM creates static data structures that cannot be reinitialized, only one HotSpot VM can be created in a process space once a certain point in initialization is reached. To the engineers who develop the HotSpot VM this stage of launching a HotSpot VM is referred to as the "point of no return."

2. Check to make sure the Java Native Interface version is supported, and the output stream is initialized for garbage collection logging.

3. The OS modules are initialized such as the random number generator, the current process id, high-resolution timer, memory page sizes, and guard pages. Guard pages are no-access memory pages used to bound memory region accesses. For example, often operating systems put a guard page at the top of each thread stack to ensure references off the end of the stack region are trapped.

4. The command line arguments and properties passed in to the `JNI_CreateJavaVM` method are parsed and stored for later use.

5. The standard Java system properties are initialized, such as java.version, java.vendor, os.name, and so on.

6. The modules for supporting synchronization, stack, memory, and safepoint pages are initialized.

7. Libraries such as `libzip`, `libhpi`, `libjava`, and `libthread` are loaded.

8. Signal handlers are initialized and set.

9. The thread library is initialized.

10. The output stream logger is initialized.

11. Agent libraries (`hprof`, `jdi`), if any are being used, are initialized and started.

12. The thread states and the thread local storage, which holds thread specific data required for the operation of threads, are initialized.

13. A portion of the HotSpot VM global data is initialized such as the event log, OS synchronization primitives, `perfMemory` (performance statistics memory), and `chunkPool` (memory allocator).

14. At this point, the HotSpot VM can create threads. The Java version of the main thread is created and attached to the current operating system thread. However, this thread is not yet added to the known list of threads.

15. Java level synchronization is initialized and enabled.

16. bootclassloader, code cache, interpreter, JIT compiler, Java Native Interface, system dictionary, and universe are initialized.

17. The Java main thread is now added to the known list of threads. The universe, a set of required global data structures, is sanity checked. The HotSpot VMThread, which performs all the HotSpot VM's critical functions, is created. At this point the appropriate JVMTI events are posted to notify the current state of the HotSpot VM.

18. The following Java classes `java.lang.String`, `java.lang.System`, `java.lang.Thread`, `java.lang.ThreadGroup`, `java.lang.reflect.Method`, `java.lang.ref.Finalizer`, `java.lang.Class`, and the rest of the Java System classes are loaded and initialized. At this point, the HotSpot VM is initialized and operational, but not quite fully functional.

19. The HotSpot VM's signal handler thread is started, the JIT compiler is initialized, and the HotSpot's compile broker thread is started. Other HotSpot VM helper threads such as watcher threads and stat sampler are started. At this time the HotSpot VM is fully functional.

20. Finally, the `JNIEnv` is populated and returned to the caller and the HotSpot VM is ready to service new JNI requests.

DestroyJavaVM Details

The `DestroyJavaVM` method can be called from the HotSpot launcher to shut down the HotSpot VM when errors occur during the HotSpot VM launch sequence. The `DestroyJavaVM` method can also be called by the HotSpot VM during execution, after the HotSpot VM has been launched, when a very serious error occurs.

The shutdown of the HotSpot VM takes the following steps through the `DestroyJavaVM` method:

1. Wait until there is only one nondaemon thread executing noting that the HotSpot VM is still functional.

2. Call the Java method `java.lang.Shutdown.shutdown()`, which invokes the Java level shutdown hooks and runs Java object finalizers if finalization-on-exit is true.

3. Prepare for HotSpot VM exit by running HotSpot VM level shutdown hooks (those that were registered through `JVM_OnExit()`), stop the following HotSpot VM threads: profiler, stat sampler, watcher, and garbage collector threads. Post status events to JVMTI, disable JVMTI, and stop the Signal thread.

4. Call the HotSpot method `JavaThread::exit()` to release Java Native Interface handle blocks, remove guard pages, and remove the current thread from known threads list. From this point on the HotSpot VM cannot execute any Java code.

5. Stop the HotSpot VM thread. This causes the HotSpot VM to bring the remaining HotSpot VM threads to a safepoint and stop the JIT compiler threads.

6. Disable tracing at the Java Native Interface, HotSpot VM, and JVMTI barriers.

7. Set HotSpot "vm exited" flag for threads that may be running in native code.

8. Delete the current thread.

9. Delete or remove any input/output streams and release `PerfMemory` (performance statistics memory) resources.

10. Finally return to the caller.

VM Class Loading

The Hotspot VM supports class loading as defined by the *Java Language Specification*, Third Edition, [2] the *Java Virtual Machine Specification*, Second Edition, [1] and as amended by the updated *Java Virtual Machine Specification*, Chapter 5, Loading, Linking and Initializing. [3] The HotSpot VM and Java SE class loading libraries share the responsibility for class loading. The HotSpot VM is responsible for resolving constant pool symbols, that require loading, linking, and then initializing Java classes and Java interfaces. The term *class loading* is used to describe the overall process of mapping a class or interface name to a class object, and the more specific terms *loading, linking,* and *initializing* for the phases of class loading as defined by the *Java Virtual Machine Specification*. The most common reason for class loading is during bytecode resolution, when a constant pool symbol in a Java classfile requires resolution. Java APIs such as `Class.forName()`, `ClassLoader.loadClass()`, reflection APIs, and `JNI_FindClass` can initiate class loading. The HotSpot VM itself can also initiate class loading.

The HotSpot VM loads core classes such as `java.lang.Object` and `java.lang.Thread` along with many others at HotSpot VM startup time. Loading a class requires loading all Java superclasses and all Java superinterfaces. And classfile verification, which is part of the linking phase, can require loading additional classes. The loading phase is a cooperative effort between the HotSpot VM and specific class loaders such as `java.lang.ClassLoader`.

Class Loading Phases

For a given Java class or Java interface, the load class phase takes its name, finds the binary in Java classfile format, defines the Java class, and creates a `java.lang.Class` object to represent that given Java class or Java interface. The load class phase can throw a `NoClassDefFound` error if a binary representation of a Java class or Java interface cannot be found. In addition, the load class phase does format checking on the syntax of the classfile, which can throw a `ClassFormatError` or `UnsupportedClassVersionError`. Before completing the load of a Java class, the HotSpot VM must load all its superclasses and superinterfaces. If the class hierarchy has a problem such that a Java class is its own superclass or superinterface (recursively), then the HotSpot VM throws a `ClassCircularityError`. The HotSpot VM also throws an `IncompatibleClassChangeError` if the direct superinterface is not an interface, or the direct superclass is an interface.

The link phase first does verification, which checks the classfile semantics, checks the constant pool symbols, and does type checking. These checks can throw a `VerifyError`. Linking then does what is called preparation, which creates and initializes static fields to standard defaults and allocates method tables. It is worth noting at this point of execution no Java code has yet been run. The link class phase then optionally does resolution of symbolic references. Next, class initialization runs the class static initializers, and initializers for static fields. This is the first Java code that runs for this class. It is important to note that class initialization requires superclass initialization, although not superinterface initialization.

The *Java Virtual Machine Specification* specifies that class initialization occurs on the first active use of a class. However, the Java Language Specification allows flexibility in when the symbolic resolution step of linking occurs as long as the semantics of the language are held; the JVM finishes each step of loading, linking, and initializing before performing the next step; and throws errors when Java programs would expect them to be thrown. As a performance optimization, the HotSpot VM generally waits until class initialization to load and link a class. This means if class A references class B, loading class A will not necessarily cause loading of class B (unless class B is required for verification). Execution of the first instruction that references class B causes the class initialization of B, which requires loading and linking of class B.

Class Loader Delegation

When a class loader is asked to find and load a class, it can ask another class loader to do the loading. This is called *class loader delegation.* The first class loader is an initiating class loader, and the class loading that ultimately defines the class is called the defining class loader. In the case of bytecode resolution, the initiating class loader is the class loader for the class whose constant pool symbol is being resolved.

Class loaders are defined hierarchically and each class loader has a delegation parent. The delegation defines a search order for binary class representations. The Java SE class loader hierarchy searches the bootstrap class loader, the extension class loader, and the system class loader in that order. The system class loader is the default application class loader, which loads the main Java method and loads classes from the classpath. The application class loader can be a class loader from the Java SE class loader libraries, or it can be provided by an application developer. The Java SE class loader libraries implement the extension class loader, which loads classes from the lib/ext directory of the JRE (Java Runtime Environment).

Bootstrap Class Loader

The HotSpot VM implements the bootstrap class loader. The bootstrap class loader loads classes from the HotSpot VM's BOOTCLASSPATH, including for example rt.jar, which contains the Java SE class libraries. For faster startup, the Client HotSpot VM can also process preloaded classes via a feature called *class data sharing,* which is enabled by default. It can be explicitly enabled with the -Xshare:on HotSpot VM command line switch. Likewise, it can be explicitly disabled with -Xshare:off. As of this writing, the Server HotSpot VM, does not support the class data sharing feature, and class data sharing is also not supported on the Client HotSpot VM when a garbage collector other than the serial garbage collector is in use. Class data sharing is described in more detail in the "Class Data Sharing" section later in this chapter.

Type Safety

A Java class or Java interface name is defined as a fully qualified name, which includes the package name. A Java class type is uniquely determined by that fully qualified name and the class loader. In other words, a class loader defines a namespace. This means the same fully qualified class name loaded by two distinctly defined class loaders results in two distinct class types. Given the existence of custom class loaders, the HotSpot VM is responsible for ensuring that non-well-behaved class loaders cannot violate type safety. See Dynamic Class Loading in the *Java Virtual Machine,* [4] and the *Java Virtual Machine Specification* 5.3.4 [3] for additional information. The HotSpot VM ensures that when class A calls B.someMethodName(),

A's class loader and B's class loader agree on someMethodName()'s parameters and return type by tracking and checking class loader constraints.

Class Metadata in HotSpot

Class loading in the HotSpot VM creates an internal representation of a class in either an instanceKlass or an arrayKlass in the HotSpot VM's permanent generation space. The HotSpot VM's permanent generation space is described in more detailed in the "HotSpot VM Garbage Collectors" section later in this chapter. The instanceKlass refers to a Java mirror, which is the instance of java.lang.Class mirroring this class. The HotSpot VM internally accesses the instanceKlass using an internal data structure called a klassOop. An "Oop" is an ordinary object pointer. Hence, a klassOop is an internal HotSpot abstraction for a reference, an ordinary object pointer, to a Klass representing or mirroring a Java class.

Internal Class Loading Data

The HotSpot VM maintains three hash tables to track class loading. The System-Dictionary contains loaded classes, which maps a class name/class loader pair to a klassOop. The SystemDictionary contains both class name/initiating loader pairs and class name/defining loader pairs. Entries are currently only removed at a *safepoint*. Safepoints are described in more detail in the "VM Operations and Safe-points" section later in the chapter. The PlaceholderTable contains classes that are currently being loaded. It is used for ClassCircularityError checking and for parallel class loading for class loaders that support multithreaded class loading. The LoaderConstraintTable tracks constraints for type safety checking. These hash tables are all guarded by a lock; in the HotSpot VM it is called the System-Dictionary_lock. In general, the load class phase in the HotSpot VM is serialized using the Class loader object lock.

Byte Code Verification

The Java language is a type-safe language, and standard Java compilers (javac) produce valid classfiles and type-safe code; but a Java Virtual Machine cannot guarantee that the code was produced by a trustworthy javac compiler. It must reestablish type-safety through a process at link time called bytecode verification. Bytecode verification is specified in section 4.8 of the *Java Virtual Machine Specification*. The specification prescribes both static and dynamic constraints on the code that a Java Virtual Machine verifies. If any violations are found, the Java Virtual Machine throws a VerifyError and prevents the class from being linked.

Many of the constraints on bytecodes can be checked statically, such as the operand of an "ldc" bytecode must be a valid constant pool index whose type is `CONSTANT_Integer`, `CONSTANT_String`, or `CONSTANT_Float`. Other constraints that check the type and number of arguments for other instructions requires dynamic analysis of the code to determine which operands will be present on the expression stack during execution. There are currently two methods of analyzing bytecodes to determine the types and number of operands present for each instruction. The traditional method is called *type inference*. It operates by performing an abstract interpretation of each bytecode and merging type states at branch targets or exception handles. The analysis iterates over the bytecode until a steady state for the types is found. If a steady state cannot be found, or if the resulting types violate some bytecode constraint, then a `VerifyError` is thrown. The code for this verification step is present in the HotSpot VM's libverify. so external library, and uses JNI to gather whatever information is needed for classes and types.

New in the Java 6 HotSpot VMs is a second method for verification called *type verification*. In this approach the Java compiler provides the steady-state type information for each branch target or exception target, via the code attribute, `Stack-MapTable`. The `StackMapTable` consists of a number of stack map frames; each indicates the types of the items on the expression stack and in the local variables at some offset in the method. The Java Virtual Machine needs to then only perform one pass through the bytecode to verify the correctness of the types to verify the bytecode. This verification approach is faster and smaller than the traditional type inference approach for bytecode verification approach.

For all classfiles with a version number less than 50, such as those created prior to Java 6, the HotSpot VM uses the traditional type inference method to verify the classfiles. For classfiles greater than or equal to 50, the `StackMapTable` attributes are present and the new "type verification" verifier is used. Because of the possibility of older external tools that might instrument the bytecode but neglect to update the `StackMapTable` attribute, certain verification errors that occur during type-checking verification may failover to the type inference method. Should this type inference verification pass fail, only then will the HotSpot VM throw a `VerifyError`.

Class Data Sharing

Class data sharing is a feature introduced in Java 5 that was intended to reduce the startup time for Java applications, in particular small Java applications, as well as reduce their memory footprint. When the Java Runtime Environment (JRE) is installed on 32-bit platforms using the Java HotSpot JRE provided installer, the installer loads a set of classes from the system jar file into a private internal representation, and dumps that representation to a file, called a shared archive. If the

Java HotSpot JRE installer is not being used, this can be done manually. During subsequent Java Virtual Machine invocations, the shared archive is memory-mapped into the JVM, which saves the cost of loading those classes and allowing much of the JVM's metadata for these classes to be shared among multiple JVM processes.

> **Tip**
>
> As of the writing of this chapter (Java 6 Update 21), class data sharing is supported only with the HotSpot Client VM, and only with the serial garbage collector.

The primary motivation for the class data sharing feature is the decrease in startup time it provides. Class data sharing produces better results for smaller applications because it eliminates a fixed cost of loading certain Java SE core classes. The smaller the application relative to the number of Java SE core classes it uses, the larger the saved fraction of startup time.

With class data sharing, the memory footprint cost of new JVM instances is reduced in two ways. First, a portion of the shared archive, currently between five and six megabytes of space, is memory mapped read-only and therefore shared among multiple JVM processes. Previously this data was replicated in each JVM instance. Second, since the shared archive contains class data in the form in which the Hotspot VM uses it, the memory that would otherwise be required to access the original class information in the Java SE core libraries jar file, rt.jar, is not needed. These savings allow more applications to be run concurrently on the same machine. On Microsoft Windows, the footprint of a process, as measured by various tools, may appear to increase, because a larger number of pages are being mapped into the process address space. This is offset by the reduction in the amount of memory (inside Windows) that is needed to hold portions of the Java SE library jar file rt.jar. Reducing memory footprint in the HotSpot VM remains a high priority.

In the HotSpot VM, the class data sharing implementation introduces new Java subspaces into the permanent generation space that contains the shared data. The classes.jsa shared archive is memory mapped into these spaces in permanent generation at HotSpot VM startup time. Subsequently, the shared region is managed by the existing HotSpot VM memory management subsystem. Read-only shared data, which is one of the new subspaces in permanent generation includes constant method objects, symbol objects and arrays of primitives, mostly character arrays. Read-write shared data, the other new Java heap space introduced in permanent generation, consists of mutable method objects, constant pool objects, HotSpot VM internal representation of Java classes and arrays, and various `String`, `Class`, and `Exception` objects.

Interpreter

The HotSpot VM interpreter is a template based interpreter. The HotSpot VM Runtime generates the interpreter in memory at JVM startup using information stored internally in a data structure called a `TemplateTable`. The `TemplateTable` contains machine dependent code corresponding to each bytecode. A template is a description of each bytecode. The HotSpot VM's `TemplateTable` defines all the templates and provides accessor functions to get the template for a given bytecode. The template table generated in memory can be viewed using what is called a HotSpot "debug" VM and the nonproduct flag `-XX:+PrintInterpreter`.

> **Tip**
>
> A HotSpot debug VM is a version of the HotSpot VM that contains additional debugging information and additional HotSpot VM command line options that can be used together to debug, or further instrument the HotSpot VM. Its use is not recommended for production environments.

The template design of the HotSpot VM interpreter performs better than a classic switch statement loop approach. For example, a switch statement approach must perform repeated compare operations. In the worst case, the switch statement approach may be required to compare a given command with all but one bytecodes to locate the required one. Additionally, the switch statement approach must use a separate software stack to pass Java arguments. The HotSpot VM uses the native C stack to pass Java arguments. A number of HotSpot VM internal variables, such as the program counter or the stack pointer for a Java thread, are stored in C variables, that are not guaranteed to be always kept in underlying hardware registers. As a result, the management of these software interpreter data structures consumes a considerable share of total execution time. [5] Overall, the performance gap between the HotSpot VM and the real machine is significantly narrowed by the HotSpot interpreter, which makes the interpretation speed considerably higher. However, this comes at a price of large amounts of machine-specific code. For example, approximately 10,000 lines of code are dedicated to Intel x86 platforms, and about 14,000 lines of code are dedicated to SPARC platforms. The overall code size and complexity are also significantly higher, since the code supporting dynamic code generation (JIT compilation) is needed. Obviously, debugging dynamically generated machine code (JIT compiled code) is much more difficult than debugging static code. These properties certainly do not facilitate implementation of runtime evolution, but they do not make it infeasible either. [5]

There are interpreter calls out to the HotSpot VM Runtime for complex operations, which are essentially anything too complex or complicated to do in assembly language such as constant pool lookup.

The HotSpot VM interpreter is also a critical part of the overall HotSpot VM adaptive optimization story. Adaptive optimization solves the problems of JIT compilation by taking advantage of an interesting program property. Virtually all programs spend the vast majority of their time executing a minority of their code. Rather than compiling method by method, "just in time" or "ahead of time," the HotSpot VM immediately runs the program using an interpreter, and analyzes the code as it runs to detect the critical hot spots in the program. Then it focuses the attention of a global machine code optimizer on those hot spots. By avoiding compilation of infrequently executed code the HotSpot VM JIT compiler can devote more attention to the performance-critical parts of the program, without necessarily increasing the overall compilation time.

> **Tip**
>
> The term *JIT compiler* is not very descriptive for how the HotSpot VM utilizes a compiler to generate optimized machine dependent code. The HotSpot VM actually generates machine code dynamically as it observes a program's behavior rather than compiling it "just in time" or "ahead of time."

This hot spot monitoring is continued dynamically as the program runs, so that it literally adapts its performance on the fly to the program's execution and the user's needs.

Exception Handling

Java Virtual Machines use exceptions to signal that a program has violated the semantic constraints of the Java language. For example, an attempt to index outside the bounds of an array causes an exception. An exception causes a nonlocal transfer of control from the point where the exception occurred, or was thrown, to a point specified by the programmer, or where the exception is caught. [6] The HotSpot VM interpreter, its JIT compilers, and other HotSpot VM components all cooperate to implement exception handling. There are two general cases of exception handling; either the exception is thrown or caught in the same method, or it is caught by a caller. The latter case is more complicated and requires stack unwinding to find the appropriate handler. Exceptions can be initiated by the thrown bytecode, a return from a VM-internal call, a return from a JNI call, or a return from a Java call. The last case is simply just a later stage of the first three. When the VM recognizes that an exception has been thrown, the HotSpot VM Runtime system is invoked to find the nearest handler for that exception. Three pieces of information are used to find the handler: the current method, the current bytecode, and the exception object. If a handler is not found in the current method, as mentioned previously, the current activation stack frame is popped and the process is iteratively repeated for previous frames. Once the correct handler is found, the HotSpot VM execution state is updated, and the HotSpot VM jumps to the handler as Java code execution is resumed.

Synchronization

Broadly, *synchronization* is described as a mechanism that prevents, avoids, or recovers from the inopportune interleavings, commonly called *races,* of concurrent operations. In Java, concurrency is expressed through the thread construct. Mutual exclusion is a special case of synchronization where at most a single thread is permitted access to protected code or data. The HotSpot VM provides Java monitors by which threads running application code can participate in a mutual exclusion protocol. A Java monitor is either locked or unlocked, and only one thread may own the monitor at any one time. Only after acquiring ownership of a monitor may a thread enter a critical section protected by the monitor. In Java, critical sections are referred to as *synchronized blocks* and are delineated in code by the synchronized statement.

If a thread attempts to lock a monitor and the monitor is in an unlocked state, the thread immediately gains ownership of the monitor. If a subsequent second thread attempts to gain ownership of the monitor while the monitor is locked that second thread will not be permitted to proceed into the critical section until the owner releases the lock and the second thread manages to gain (or is granted) exclusive ownership of the lock. For clarification, to *enter* a monitor means to acquire exclusive ownership of the monitor and enter the associated critical section. Likewise, to *exit* a monitor means to release ownership of the monitor and exit the critical section. Additionally, a thread that has locked a monitor, *owns* that monitor. *Uncontended* refers to synchronization operations on an otherwise unowned monitor by only a single thread.

The HotSpot VM incorporates leading-edge techniques for both uncontended and contended synchronization operations, which boost synchronization performance by a large factor. Uncontended synchronization operations, which comprise the majority of synchronizations, are implemented with constant time techniques. With biased locking, a feature introduced in Java 5 HotSpot VMs with the `-XX:+UseBiasedLocking` command line option, in the best case these operations are essentially free of cost. Since most objects are locked by at most one thread during their lifetime, enabling `-XX:+UseBiasedLocking` allows that thread to bias the lock toward itself. Once biased, that thread can subsequently lock and unlock the object without resorting to expensive atomic instructions. [7]

Contended synchronization operations use advanced adaptive spinning techniques to improve throughput even for applications with significant amounts of lock contention. As a result, synchronization performance becomes so fast that it is not a significant performance issue for the vast majority of real-world programs.

In the HotSpot VM, most synchronization is handled through what is called *fast-path code*. The HotSpot VM has two JIT compilers and an interpreter, all of which will emit fast-path code. To HotSpot engineers, the JIT compilers are known as "C1" —the -client JIT compiler—and "C2"—the -server JIT compiler. C1 and C2 both emit fast-path code directly at the synchronization site. In the normal case when there is no contention, the synchronization operation will be completed entirely in fast-path code. If, however, there is a need to block or wake a thread (in monitor-enter or monitor-exit state, respectively), the fast-path code will call into the slow-path code. The slow-path implementation is C++ code, while fast-path code is machine dependent code emitted by the JIT compilers.

Java object synchronization state is encoded for every Java object internally within the HotSpot VM's object representation of that Java object in the first word, often referred to as the *mark word*. For several states, the mark word is multiplexed to point to additional synchronization metadata. The possible Java object synchronization states stored in HotSpot VM's mark word are

- **Neutral.** Unlocked.
- **Biased.** Locked/Unlocked + Unshared.
- **Stack-Locked.** Locked + Shared but uncontended. Shared means the mark points to a displaced mark word on the owner thread's stack.
- **Inflated.** Locked/Unlocked + Shared and contended. Threads are blocked in monitorenter or wait(). The mark points to a heavyweight "objectmonitor" structure.

As a side note, the mark word is also multiplexed to contain the garbage collector's object age data, and the object's identity hash code value.

Thread Management

Thread management covers all aspects of the thread life cycle, from creation through termination along with the coordination of threads within the HotSpot VM. This involves management of threads created from Java code, regardless of whether they are created from application code or library code, native threads that attach directly to the HotSpot VM, or internal HotSpot VM threads created for other purposes. While the broader aspects of thread management are platform independent, the details vary depending on the underlying operating system.

Threading Model

The threading model in the Hotspot VM is a one-to-one mapping between Java threads, an instance of java.lang.Thread, and native operating system threads. A native operating system thread is created when a Java thread is started and is reclaimed once it terminates. The operating system is responsible for scheduling all threads and dispatching them to an available CPU. The relationship between Java thread priorities and operating system thread priorities is a complex one that varies across systems.

Thread Creation and Destruction

There are two ways for a thread to be introduced in the HotSpot VM; either by executing Java code that calls the `start()` method on a `java.lang.Thread` object, or by attaching an existing native thread to the HotSpot VM using JNI. Other threads created by the HotSpot VM for internal use are discussed later. Internally to the HotSpot VM there are a number of objects, both C++ and Java, associated with a given thread in the HotSpot VM. These objects, both Java and C++, are as follows:

- A `java.lang.Thread` instance that represents a thread in Java code.
- A C++ `JavaThread` instance that represents the `java.lang.Thread` instance internally within the HotSpot VM. It contains additional information to track the state of the thread. A `JavaThread` holds a reference to its associated `java.lang.Thread` object, as an ordinary object pointer, and the `java.lang.Thread` object also stores a reference to its `JavaThread` as a raw int. A `JavaThread` also holds a reference to its associated `OSThread` instance.
- An `OSThread` instance represents an operating system thread and contains additional operating-system-level information needed to track thread state. The `OSThread` also contains a platform specific "handle" to identify the actual thread to the operating system.

When a `java.lang.Thread` is started the HotSpot VM creates the associated `JavaThread` and `OSThread` objects, and ultimately the native thread. After preparing all the HotSpot VM state, such as thread-local storage and allocation buffers, synchronization objects and so forth, the native thread is started. The native thread completes initialization and then executes a startup method that leads to the execution of the `java.lang.Thread` object's `run()` method, and then, upon its return, terminates the thread after dealing with any uncaught exceptions, and interacting with the HotSpot VM to check whether termination of this thread requires termination of the entire HotSpot VM. Thread termination releases all allocated resources, removes the `JavaThread` from the set of known threads, invokes destructors for the `OSThread` and `JavaThread`, and ultimately ceases execution when its initial startup method completes.

A native thread attaches to the HotSpot VM using the JNI call `AttachCurrent-Thread`. In response to this an associated `OSThread` and `JavaThread` instance is created, and basic initialization is performed. Next a `java.lang.Thread` object must be created for the attached thread; this is done by reflectively invoking the Java code for the `Thread` class constructor, based on the arguments supplied when the thread attached. Once attached, a thread can invoke whatever Java code it needs via other JNI methods. Finally, when the native thread no longer wishes to be involved with the HotSpot VM it can call the JNI `DetachCurrentThread` method to disassociate it from the HotSpot VM by releasing resources, dropping the reference to the `java.lang.Thread` instance, destructing the `JavaThread` and `OSThread` objects, and so on.

A special case of attaching a native thread is the initial creation of the HotSpot VM via the JNI `CreateJavaVM` call, which can be done by a native application or by the HotSpot VM launcher. This causes a range of initialization operations to take place and then acts effectively as if a call to `AttachCurrentThread` was made. The thread can then invoke Java code as needed, such as reflective invocation of the Java main method of an application. See the "Java Native Interface" section later in the chapter for further details.

Thread States

The HotSpot VM uses a number of different internal thread states to characterize what each thread is doing. This is necessary both for coordinating the interactions of threads and for providing useful debugging information if things go wrong. A thread's state transitions as different actions are performed, and these transition points are used to check that it is appropriate for a thread to proceed with the requested action at that point in time; see the discussion of safepoints for details.

From the HotSpot VM perspective the possible states of the main thread are

- **New thread.** A new thread in the process of being initialized
- **Thread in Java.** A thread that is executing Java code
- **Thread in vm.** A thread that is executing inside the HotSpot VM
- **Blocked thread.** The thread is blocked for some reason (acquiring a lock, waiting for a condition, sleeping, performing a blocking I/O operation, and so on)

For debugging purposes additional state information is also maintained for reporting by tools, in thread dumps, stack traces, and so on. This is maintained in the internal HotSpot C++ object `OSThread`. Thread states reported by tools, in thread dumps, stack traces, and so on, include

- **MONITOR_WAIT.** A thread is waiting to acquire a contended monitor lock.
- **CONDVAR_WAIT.** A thread is waiting on an internal condition variable used by the HotSpot VM (not associated with any Java object).

- **OBJECT_WAIT.** A Java thread is performing a `java.lang.Object.wait()` call.

Other HotSpot VM subsystems and libraries impose their own thread state information, such as the JVMTI system and the thread state exposed by the `java.lang.Thread` class itself. Such information is generally not accessible to, nor relevant to, the management of threads inside the HotSpot VM.

Internal VM Threads

Much to the surprise of many, the executing of a trivial "Hello World" Java program can result in the creation of a dozen or more threads in the HotSpot VM. These arise from a combination of internal HotSpot VM threads and HotSpot VM library related threads such as the reference handler and finalizer threads. The internal HotSpot VM threads are

- **VM thread.** A singleton C++ object instance that is responsible for executing VM operations. VM operations are further discussed in the next subsection.
- **Periodic task thread.** A singleton C++ object instance, also called the WatcherThread, simulates timer interrupts for executing periodic operations within the HotSpot VM.
- **Garbage collection threads.** These threads, of different types, support the serial, parallel, and concurrent garbage collection.
- **JIT compiler threads.** These threads perform runtime compilation of bytecode to machine code.
- **Signal dispatcher thread.** This thread waits for process directed signals and dispatches them to a Java level signal handling method.

All these threads are instances of the internal HotSpot C++ Thread class, and all threads that execute Java code are internal HotSpot C++ JavaThread instances. The HotSpot VM internally keeps track of all threads in a linked-list known as the `Threads_list` and is protected by the `Threads_lock`—one of the key synchronization locks used within the HotSpot VM.

VM Operations and Safepoints

The internal HotSpot VM VMThread spends its time waiting for operations to appear in a C++ object called `VMOperationQueue` and executing those operations. Typically these operations are passed on to the VMThread because they require that the HotSpot VM reach what is called a safepoint before they can be executed. In simple terms, when the HotSpot VM is at a safepoint all Java executing threads are blocked, and any threads executing in native code are prevented from returning to Java code while the safepoint is in progress. This means that a HotSpot VM operation can be executed knowing that no thread can be in the middle of modifying the Java heap, and all threads are in a state where their Java stacks are not changing and can be examined.

The most familiar HotSpot VM safepoint operation is to support garbage collection, or more specifically stop-the-world phases of garbage collection.

Tip

"Stop-the-world" in the context of garbage collection means that all Java executing threads are blocked or stopped from executing in Java code while the garbage collector frees up memory as a result of finding Java objects no longer in use by the application. If an application thread is executing in native code (i.e., JNI), it is allowed to continue, but will block if it attempts to cross the native boundary into Java code.

There many other safepoints, such as biased locking revocation, thread stack dumps, thread suspension or stopping (i.e., `java.lang.Thread.stop()` method), and numerous inspection and modification operations requested through JVMTI.

Many HotSpot VM operations are synchronous, that is, the requester blocks until the operation has completed, but some are asynchronous or concurrent, meaning that the requester can proceed in parallel with the VMThread (assuming no safepoint is initiated).

Safepoints are initiated using a cooperative, polling-based mechanism. In simplistic terms, every so often a thread asks "should I block for a safepoint?" Asking this question efficiently is not so simple. One place where the question is often asked is during a thread state transition. Not all state transitions do this, for example, a thread leaving the HotSpot VM to go to native code, but many do. Another place where a thread asks, "should I block for a safepoint?" is when JIT compiled code is returning from a method or at certain stages during loop iteration. Threads executing interpreted code do not usually ask whether they should block for a safepoint. Instead the safepoint is requested when the interpreter switches to a different dispatch table. Included as part of the switching operation is code that asks when the safepoint is over. When the safepoint is over, the dispatch table is switched back again. Once a safepoint has been requested, the VMThread must wait until all threads are known to be in a safepoint-safe state before proceeding to execute a VM operation. During a safepoint the `Threads_lock` is used to block any threads that are running. The VMThread releases the `Threads_lock` after the VM operation has been performed.

C++ Heap Management

In addition to HotSpot VM's Java heap, which is maintained by the HotSpot VM's memory manager and garbage collectors, the HotSpot VM also uses a C/C++ heap for storage of HotSpot VM internal objects and data. Within the HotSpot VM and not exposed to a user of the HotSpot VM, a set of C++ classes derived from a base class called `Arena` is used to manage the HotSpot VM C++ heap operations. The `Arena` base class and its subclasses provide a rapid C/C++ allocation layer that sits on top of the C/C++ `malloc/free` memory management routines. Each `Arena` allocates memory blocks (internally the HotSpot VM refers to them as `Chunks`) from three global `ChunkPools`. Each `ChunkPool` satisfies allocation requests for a distinct range of allocation sizes. For example, an allocation request for 1K of memory is allocated from the "small" `ChunkPool`, while a 10K allocation request is made from the "medium" `ChunkPool`. This is done to avoid wasteful memory fragmentation. The `Arena` approach for allocating memory provides better performance than directly using the C/C++ `malloc/free` memory management routines. The latter operations may require acquisition of global OS locks, which can affect scalability and impact performance.

`Arenas` are thread-local objects that cache a certain amount of memory storage. This allows for fast-path allocation where a global shared lock is not required. Likewise, `Arena` free operations do not require a lock in the common uses of releasing memory back to the `Chunks`. Arenas are also used for thread-local resource management implemented internally within the HotSpot VM as a C++ object called `ResourceArea`. `Arenas` are additionally used for handle management implemented internally within the HotSpot VM as a C++ `HandleArea` object. Both the HotSpot client and server JIT compilers use `Arenas` during JIT compilation.

Java Native Interface

The Java Native Interface, referred to as JNI hereafter, is a native programming interface. It allows Java code that runs inside a Java Virtual Machine to interoperate with applications and libraries written in other programming languages, such as C, C++, and assembly language. Although applications can be written entirely in Java, there are circumstances where Java alone does not meet the requirements of an application. Programmers can use JNI to write native methods to handle those situations when an application cannot be written entirely in Java.

JNI native methods can be used to create, inspect, and update Java objects, call Java methods, catch and throw exceptions, load classes and obtain class information, and perform runtime type checking. JNI may also be used with the Invocation API to enable an arbitrary native application to embed the Java VM. This allows programmers to easily make their existing applications Java-enabled without having to link with the VM source code. [8]

It is important to remember that once an application uses JNI, it risks losing two benefits of the Java platform. First, Java applications that depend on JNI can no longer readily run on multiple heterogeneous hardware platforms. Even though the part of an application written in the Java programming language is portable to multiple heterogeneous hardware platforms, it is necessary to recompile the part of the application written in native programming languages. In other words, using JNI loses one of the Java promises, "write once, run anywhere." Second, the Java programming language is type-safe and secure; native languages such as C or C++ are not. As a result, Java developers must use extra care when writing applications using JNI. A misbehaving native method can corrupt an entire application. For this reason, Java applications are subject to security checks before invoking JNI methods. The additional security checks and the copying of data between the Java layer and JNI layer within the HotSpot VM can infringe on an application's performance.

> **Tip**
>
> As a general rule, developers should architect their application so that native methods are defined in as few classes as possible. This entails a cleaner isolation between native code and the rest of the application. [9]

The HotSpot VM provides a command line option to aid in debugging problems with native methods using JNI called `-Xcheck:jni`. Specifying `-Xcheck:jni` causes an alternate set of debugging interfaces to be used by an application's JNI calls. The alternate interface verifies arguments to JNI calls more stringently, as well as performing additional internal consistency checks.

Internally to the HotSpot VM, the implementation of JNI functions is straightforward. It uses various HotSpot VM internal primitives to perform activities such as object creation, method invocation, and so on. In general, these are the same runtime primitives used by other HotSpot VM subsystems such as the interpreter described earlier in this chapter.

The HotSpot VM must take special care to keep track of which threads are currently executing in native methods. During some HotSpot VM activities, most notably some phases of garbage collection, one or more threads must be halted at a safepoint to guarantee that the Java memory heap is not modified to ensure garbage collection accuracy. When the HotSpot VM wants to bring a thread executing in native code to a safepoint, that thread is allowed to continue executing in native code until it attempts to either return into Java code or makes a JNI call.

VM Fatal Error Handling

The designers of the HotSpot VM believe it is important to provide sufficient information to its users and developers to diagnose and fix VM fatal errors. A common VM fatal error is an `OutOfMemoryError`. Another common fatal error on Solaris and Linux platforms is a segmentation fault. The equivalent error on Windows is called

Access Violation error. When these fatal errors occur, it is critical to understand the root cause to fix them. Sometimes the resolution to the root cause requires a change in a Java application, and sometimes the root cause is within the HotSpot VM. When the HotSpot VM crashes on a fatal error, it dumps a HotSpot error log file called hs_err_pid<pid>.log where <pid> is replaced with the process id of the crashed HotSpot VM. The hs_err_pid<pid>.log file is created in the directory where HotSpot VM was launched. Since this feature's initial introduction in HotSpot VM 1.4.2 version, many enhancements have been made to improve the diagnosability of the root cause of a fatal error. These additional enhancements include

- A memory map is included in the hs_err_pid<pid>.log error log file to make it is easy to see how memory is laid out during the VM crash.
- A -XX:ErrorFile command line option is provided so you can set the path name of the hs_err_pid<pid>.log error log file.
- An OutOfMemoryError also triggers the hs_err_pid<pid>.log file to be generated.

An additional popular feature often used to diagnose the root cause of a VM fatal error is using the HotSpot VM command line option -XX:OnError=cmd1 args...; com2 .... This HotSpot VM command line option executes the list of commands given to -XX:OnError whenever the HotSpot VM crashes. A common use of this feature is invoking a debugger such as Linux/Solaris dbx or Windows Winddbg to immediately examine the crash. For releases that do not have support for -XX:OnError, an alternative HotSpot VM command line option can be used called -XX:+Show MessageBoxOnError. This option stops the VM before it exits by displaying a dialog box saying the VM has experienced a fatal error. This provides an opportunity to attach to the HotSpot VM with a debugger prior to it exiting.

When the HotSpot VM experiences a fatal error, it internally uses a class called VMError to aggregate and dump the hs_err_pid<pid>.log file. The VMError class is invoked by operating specific code when an unrecognized signal or exception is observed.

> **Tip**
>
> The HotSpot VM uses signals internally for communication. The fatal error handler in the HotSpot VM is invoked when a signal is not recognized. This unrecognized case may originate from a fault in application JNI code, OS native libraries, JRE native libraries, or the HotSpot VM itself.

The HotSpot VM's fatal error handler had to be carefully written to avoid causing faults itself as a result of fatal errors such as StackOverflow or fatal errors when critical locks are held such as a malloc lock.

Since an `OutOfMemoryError` is possible to experience, especially on some large scale applications, it is critical to provide useful diagnostic information to users so a resolution can be quickly identified. Often it can be resolved by just simply specifying a larger Java heap size. When an `OutOfMemoryError` happens, the error message indicates which type of memory is problematic. For example, it could be a result of a Java heap space or permanent generation space being specified as too small. Beginning with Java 6, a stack trace is included in the error message produced by the HotSpot VM. Also, the `-XX:OnOutOfMemoryError=<cmd>` option was introduced so a command can be run when the first `OutOfMemoryError` is thrown. An additional useful feature worth mentioning is being able to generate a heap dump on an `Out OfMemoryError`. This can be enabled by specifying `-XX:+HeapDumpOnOutOfMemory Error` HotSpot VM command line option. There is an additional HotSpot VM command line option that allows a user to specify a path where the heap dump will be placed, `-XX:HeapDumpPath=<pathname>`.

Although applications are written with the intent to avoid thread deadlocks, developers sometimes make mistakes and deadlocks occur. When a deadlock occurs, doing a Ctrl + Break on Windows forces a Java level thread stack trace to print to standard output. On Solaris and Linux, sending a SIGQUIT signal to the Java process id does the same. With a thread stack trace, the source of the deadlock can be analyzed. Beginning with Java 6, the bundled JConsole tool added the capability to attach to a hung Java process and analyze the root cause of the deadlock. Most of the time, a deadlock is caused by acquiring locks in the wrong order.

> **Tip**
>
> The "Trouble-Shooting and Diagnostic Guide" [10] for Java 5 contains a lot of information that may be useful to diagnosing fatal errors.

HotSpot VM Garbage Collectors

> *"Heap storage for objects is reclaimed by an automatic storage management system (typically a garbage collector); objects are never explicitly de-allocated."*
> —*Java Virtual Machine Specification* [1]

The Java Virtual Machine (JVM) specification dictates that any JVM implementation must include a *garbage collector* to reclaim unused memory (i.e., unreachable objects).[1] The behavior and efficiency of the garbage collector used can heavily influence the performance and responsiveness of an application that's taking advantage of it. This section gives an introduction to the garbage collectors included in the HotSpot VM. The aim is to gain a better understanding of how garbage collection works in the HotSpot VM and, as a result, be able to take full advantage of it when designing, developing, and deploying applications.

Generational Garbage Collection

The HotSpot VM uses a *generational garbage collector,* [11] a well-known garbage collection approach that relies on the following two observations:

- Most allocated objects become unreachable quickly.
- Few references from older to younger objects exist.

These two observations are collectively known as the *weak generational hypothesis,* which generally holds true for Java applications. To take advantage of this hypothesis, the HotSpot VM splits the heap into two physical areas (also called spaces), which are referred to as generations:

- **The young generation.**   Most newly allocated objects are allocated in the young generation (see Figure 3-2), which, relatively to the Java heap, is typically small and collected frequently. Since most objects in it are expected to become unreachable quickly, the number of objects that survive a young generation collection (also referred to as a *minor* garbage collection) is expected to be low. In general, minor garbage collections are efficient because they concentrate on a space that is usually small and is likely to contain a lot of garbage objects.

- **The old generation.**   Objects that are longer-lived are eventually *promoted,* or *tenured,* to the old generation (see Figure 3-2). This generation is typically larger than the young generation, and its occupancy grows more slowly. As a result, old generation collections (also referred to as *major* garbage collections, or full garbage collections) are infrequent, but when they do occur they can be quite lengthy.

- **The permanent generation.**   This is a third area in the HotSpot VM's memory layout, and it is also shown in Figure 3-2. Even though it is also referred to as a generation, it should not be seen as part of the generation hierarchy (i.e., user-allocated objects do not eventually move from the old generation to the permanent generation). Instead, it is only used by the HotSpot VM itself to hold metadata, such as class data structures, interned strings, and so on.

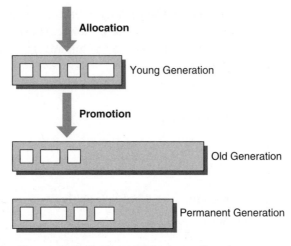

Figure 3-2 HotSpot VM generational spaces

To keep minor garbage collections short, the garbage collector must be able to identify live objects in the young generation without having to scan the entire (and potentially larger) old generation. To achieve this, the garbage collectors in the Hot-Spot VM use a data structure called a *card table*. [11] The old generation is split into 512-byte chunks called *cards*. The card table is an array with one byte entry per card in the heap. Every update to a reference field of an object must also ensure that the card containing the updated reference field is marked dirty by setting its entry in the card table to the appropriate value. During a minor garbage collection, only the areas that correspond to dirty cards are scanned to potentially discover old-to-young generation references (see Figure 3-3).

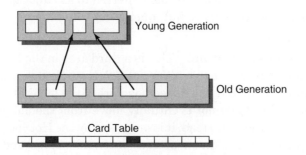

Figure 3-3 Garbage collector interaction with the card table

In cooperation with the bytecode interpreter and the JIT compiler, the HotSpot VM uses a *write barrier* [11] to maintain the card table. This barrier is a small fragment of code that sets an entry of the card table to the dirty value. The interpreter executes a write barrier every time it executes a bytecode that updates a reference field. Additionally, the JIT compiler emits the write barrier after emitting the code that updates a reference field. Although write barriers do impose a small performance overhead on the application threads, their use allows for much faster minor garbage collections, and much higher overall garbage collector efficiency, which typically improves the throughput of an application.

> **Tip**
>
> The bytecode interpreter is considered part of the HotSpot VM Runtime. Additional information on the HotSpot VM Runtime can be found in the "HotSpot VM Runtime" section earlier in this chapter. Likewise, additional information on the HotSpot JIT compiler can be found in the "HotSpot VM JIT Compilers" section later in this chapter.

A big advantage of generational garbage collection is that each generation can be managed by the garbage collection algorithm most appropriate for its characteristics. A fast garbage collector usually manages the young generation, as minor garbage collections are frequent. This garbage collector might be a little space wasteful, but since the young generation typically is a small portion of the Java heap, this is not a big problem. On the other hand, a garbage collector that is space efficient usually manages the old generation, as the old generation takes up most of the Java heap. This garbage collector might not be quite as fast, but because full garbage collections are infrequent, it doesn't have a big performance impact.

To take full advantage of generational garbage collection, applications should conform to the weak generational hypothesis, as it is what generational garbage collection exploits. For the Java applications that do not do so, a generational garbage collector might add more overhead. In practice, however, such applications are rare.

The Young Generation

Figure 3-4 illustrates the layout of the young generation of the HotSpot VM (the spaces are not drawn to proportion). It is split into three separate areas (or spaces):

- **The eden.** This is where most new objects are allocated (not all, as large objects may be allocated directly into the old generation). The eden is almost always empty after a minor garbage collection. A case where it may not be empty is described in Chapter 7, "Tuning the JVM, Step By Step."

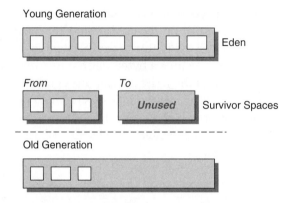

Figure 3-4 Eden and survivor spaces of young generation

- **The two survivor spaces.** These hold objects that have survived at least one minor garbage collection but have been given another chance to become unreachable before being promoted to the old generation. As illustrated in Figure 3-4, only one of them holds objects, while the other is most of the time unused.

Figure 3-5 illustrates the operation of a minor garbage collection. Objects that have been found to be garbage are marked with a gray X. As seen in Figure 3-5a, live objects in the eden that survive the collection are copied to the unused survivor space. Live objects in the survivor space that is in use, which will be given another chance to be reclaimed in the young generation, are also copied to the unused survivor space. Finally, live objects in the survivor space that is in use, that are deemed "old enough," are promoted to the old generation.

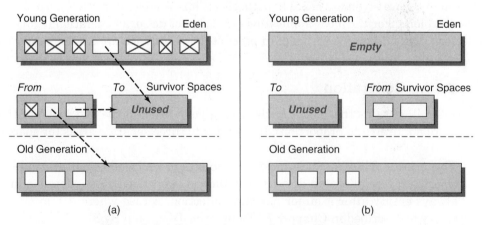

Figure 3-5 Minor garbage collection illustration

At the end of the minor garbage collection, the two survivor spaces swap roles (see Figure 3-5b). The eden is entirely empty; only one survivor space is in use; and the occupancy of the old generation has grown slightly. Because live objects are copied during its operation, this type of garbage collector is called a *copying* garbage collector. [11]

It should be pointed out that, during a minor garbage collection, there is no guarantee that the allocating survivor space will always be large enough to accommodate the surviving objects from both the eden and the other survivor space. If it overflows, the rest of the objects that need to be evacuated will be moved to the old generation. This is referred to as *premature promotion*. It causes the old generation to grow with potentially short-lived objects, and it can potentially be a serious performance issue. Further, if during a minor garbage collection the old generation becomes full and it is not possible to copy more objects into it, that minor garbage collection is typically followed by a *full garbage collection,* which collects the entire Java heap. This is referred to as *promotion failure*. Careful user-tuning, as well as some self-tuning done by the garbage collectors, typically makes the likelihood of either those two undesirable events very low. Tuning the HotSpot VM is the subject matter found in Chapter 7.

Fast Allocation

The operation of the object allocator is tightly coupled with the operation of the garbage collector. The garbage collector has to record where in the heap the free space it reclaims is located. In turn, the allocator needs to discover where the free space in the heap is before it can reuse it to satisfy allocation requests. The copying garbage collector that collects the young generation of the HotSpot VM has the advantage of always leaving the eden empty. That allows allocations into the eden to be efficient by using what's referred to as the *bump-the-pointer* technique. According to this technique, the end of the last allocated object is tracked (this is usually referred to as top), and when a new allocation request needs to be satisfied, the allocator needs only to check whether it will fit between top and the end of the eden. If it does, top is bumped to the end of the newly allocated object.

Additionally, most interesting Java applications are multithreaded, and their allocation operations need to be multithreaded safe. If they simply used global locks to ensure this, then allocation into eden would become a bottleneck and degrade performance. Instead, the HotSpot VM has adopted a technique called *Thread-Local Allocation Buffers* (TLABs), which improves multithreaded allocation throughput by giving each thread its own buffer (i.e., a small chunk of the eden) from which to allocate. Since only one thread can be allocating into each TLAB, allocation can take place quickly with the bump-the-pointer technique and without any locking. However, when a thread fills up its TLAB and needs to get a new one (an infrequent operation), it needs to do so in a multithreaded safe way. In the HotSpot VM, the `new Object()` operation is, most of the time, around ten assembly code instructions. It is the operation of the garbage collector, which empties the eden space, that enables this fast allocation.

Garbage Collectors: Spoiled for Choice

> *"The Java Virtual Machine assumes no particular type of automatic storage management system, and the storage management technique may be chosen according to the implementor's system requirements."*
>
> *—Java Virtual Machine Specification* [1]

The HotSpot VM has three different garbage collectors, as well as a fourth one that at the time of this writing is under development. Each garbage collector is targeted to a different set of applications. The next four sections describe them.

The Serial GC

The configuration of the *Serial GC* is a young generation that operates as described earlier, over an old generation managed by a *sliding compacting mark-sweep,* also known as a *mark-compact* garbage collector. [11] Both minor and full garbage collections take place in a stop-the-world fashion (i.e., the application is stopped while a collection is taking place). Only after the garbage collection has finished is the application restarted (see Figure 3-6a).

The mark-compact garbage collector first identifies which objects are still live in the old generation. It then slides them toward the beginning of the heap, leaving any free space in a single contiguous chunk at the end of the heap. This allows any future allocations into the old generation, which will most likely take place as objects are being promoted from the young generation, to use the fast bump-the-pointer technique. Figure 3-7a illustrates the operation of such a garbage collector. Objects marked with a gray X are assumed to be garbage. The shaded area at the end of the compacted space denotes reclaimed (e.g., free) space.

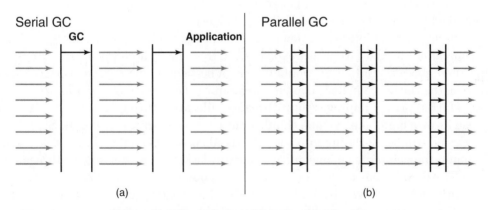

Figure 3-6 Stop-the-world garbage collection

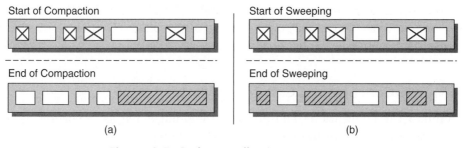

Figure 3-7 Garbage collection sequences

The Serial GC is the garbage collector of choice for most applications that do not have low pause time requirements and run on client-style machines. It takes advantage of only a single virtual processor for garbage collection work (hence, its name). Still, on today's hardware, the Serial GC can efficiently manage a lot of nontrivial applications with a few 100MBs of Java heap, with relatively short worst-case pauses (around a couple of seconds for full garbage collections). Another popular use for the Serial GC is in environments where a high number of JVMs are run on the same machine (in some cases, more JVMs than available processors!). In such environments when a JVM does a garbage collection it is better to use only one processor to minimize the interference on the remaining JVMs, even if the garbage collection might last longer. And the Serial GC fits this trade-off nicely.

The Parallel GC: Throughput Matters!

These days, a lot of important Java applications run on (sometimes dedicated) servers with a lot of physical memory and multiple processors. Ideally, the garbage collector should take advantage of all available processing resources and not leave most of them idle while it is doing garbage collection work.

To decrease garbage collection overhead and hence increase application throughput on server-style machines, the HotSpot VM includes the *Parallel GC,* also called the *Throughput GC.* Its operation is similar to that of the Serial GC (i.e., it is a stop-the-world GC with a copying young generation over a mark-compact old generation). However, both the minor and full garbage collections take place in parallel, using all available processing resources, as illustrated in Figure 3-6b. Note that earlier version of this garbage collector actually performed old collections serially. This has been rectified since the introduction of the *Parallel Old GC.*

Applications that can benefit from the Parallel GC are those that require high throughput and have pause time requirements that can be met by the worst-case stop-the-world induced full garbage collection durations along with being run on machines with more than one processor. Applications such as batch processing engines, scientific computing, and so on are well suited for Parallel GC. The Parallel GC, compared to the Serial GC, improves overall garbage collection efficiency, and as a result also improves application throughput.

The Mostly-Concurrent GC: Latency Matters!

For a number of applications, end-to-end throughput is not as important as rapid response time. In the stop-the-world garbage collection model, when a garbage collection is taking place, the application threads are not running, and external requests will not be satisfied until the application threads are restarted at the end of a garbage collection. Minor garbage collections do not typically cause long pauses. However, full garbage collections or compacting garbage collections, even though infrequent, can impose long pauses, especially when large Java heaps are involved.

To deal with this, the HotSpot VM includes the *Mostly-Concurrent GC,* also known as the *Concurrent Mark-Sweep GC (CMS)*. It manages its young generation the same way the Parallel and Serial GCs do. Its old generation, however, is managed by an algorithm that performs most of its work concurrently, imposing only two short pauses per garbage collection cycle.

Figure 3-8a illustrates how a garbage collection cycle works in CMS. It starts with a short pause, called the *initial mark,* that identifies the set of objects that are immediately reachable from outside the old generation. Then, during the *concurrent marking phase,* it marks all live objects that are transitively reachable from this set. Because the application is running and it might be updating reference fields (hence, modifying the object graph) while the marking phase is taking place, not all live objects are guaranteed to be marked at the end of the concurrent marking phase. To deal with this, the application is stopped again for a second pause, called the

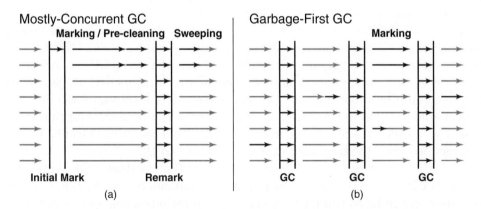

Figure 3-8 Comparison of CMS GC versus garbage first GC

remark pause, which finalizes the marking information by revisiting any objects that were modified during the concurrent marking phase. The card table data structure is reused to also keep track of modified objects. Because the remark pause is more substantial than the initial mark, it is parallelized to increase its efficiency.

To reduce further the amount of work the remark pause has to do, the concurrent *pre-cleaning* phase was introduced. As Figure 3-8a shows, it takes place after the concurrent marking phase and before the remark pause and does some of the work that would have been done during the remark pause, i.e., revisiting objects that were modified concurrently with the marking phase. Even though there is still a need for the remark pause to finalize marking (given that the application might update more objects during the pre-cleaning phase), the use of pre-cleaning can reduce, sometimes dramatically, the number of objects that need to be visited during the remark pause, and, as a result, it is very effective in reducing the duration of the remark pause.

At the end of the remark pause, all live objects in the Java heap are guaranteed to have been marked. Since revisiting objects during the pre-cleaning and remark phases increases the amount of work the garbage collector has to do (as compared to, say, the Parallel GC that only visits objects once during marking), the overall overhead of CMS also increases accordingly. This is a typical trade-off for most garbage collectors that attempt to reduce pause times.

Having identified all live objects in the old generation, the final phase of the garbage collection cycle is the *concurrent sweeping phase,* which sweeps over the Java heap, deallocating garbage objects without relocating the live ones. Figure 3-7b illustrates the operation of the sweeping phase. Again, objects marked with a gray X are assumed to be garbage, and the shaded areas in the post-sweep space denote free space. In this case, free space is not contiguous (unlike in the previous two garbage collectors, as illustrated in Figure 3-7a), and the garbage collector needs to employ a data structure (free lists, in the case of the HotSpot VM) that records which parts of the heap contain free space. As a result, allocation into the old generation is more expensive, as allocation from free lists is not as efficient as the bump-the-pointer approach. This imposes extra overhead to minor garbage collections, as most allocations in the old generation take place when objects are promoted during minor garbage collections.

Another disadvantage that CMS has, that the previous two don't, is that it typically has larger Java heap requirements. There are a few reasons for this. First, a concurrent marking cycle lasts much longer than that of a stop-the-world garbage collection. And it is only during the sweeping phase that space is actually reclaimed. Given that the application is allowed to run during the marking phase, it is also allowed to allocate memory, hence the occupancy of the old generation potentially increases during the marking phase and decreases only during the sweeping phase. Additionally, despite the garbage collector's guarantee to identify all live objects during the marking phase, it doesn't actually guarantee that it will identify all objects that are garbage. Objects that become garbage during the marking phase may or may not be reclaimed during the cycle. If they are not, then they will be reclaimed during the next cycle. Garbage objects that are not identified during a garbage collection are usually referred to as *floating garbage*.

Finally, *fragmentation* issues [11] due to the lack of compaction might also prevent the garbage collector from using all the available free space as efficiently as possible. If the old generation is full before the collection cycle in progress has actually reclaimed sufficient space, CMS reverts to an expensive stop-the-world compacting phase, similar to that of the Parallel and Serial GCs.

It should be noted that, in the latest versions of the HotSpot VM, both the concurrent phases of CMS (marking and sweeping) are parallelized, as demonstrated in Figure 3-8a. This is a useful feature when running on machines with high hardware parallelism (which are becoming more and more common). Otherwise, one concurrent CMS thread would not have been able to keep up with the work the many application threads would generate.

Compared to the Parallel GC, CMS decreases old-generation pauses—sometimes dramatically—at the expense of slightly longer young generation pauses, some reduction in throughput, and extra heap size requirements. Due to its concurrency, it also takes CPU cycles away from the application during a garbage collection cycle. Applications that can benefit from it are ones that require rapid response times (such as data-tracking servers, Web servers, and so on), and it is in fact widely used in this context.

The Garbage-First GC: CMS Replacement

The *Garbage-First GC* (aka *G1*) is a parallel, concurrent, and incrementally compacting low-pause garbage collector intended to be the long-term replacement of CMS. G1 uses a drastically different Java heap layout to the other garbage collectors in the HotSpot VM. It splits the Java heap into equal-sized chunks called regions. Even though G1 is generational, it does not have physically separate spaces for the young and old generations. Instead, each generation is a set of (maybe noncontiguous) regions. This allows G1 to resize the young generation in a flexible way.

All space reclamation in G1 takes place by evacuating the surviving objects from one set of regions to another and then reclaiming the initial (and typically larger) set of regions. Most of the time such garbage collections collect only young regions (which make up G1's young generation), and they are the equivalent of minor garbage collections. G1 also periodically performs concurrent marking cycles that identify which non-young regions are either empty or mostly empty. These are the regions that are the most efficient to collect (i.e., G1 gets back the most free space for the least amount of work), and they are scheduled for garbage collection in favor to the rest of the regions. This is where G1 gets its name from: It goes after regions with the most garbage objects in them.

Figure 3-8b shows the parallelism and concurrency in G1. Note that, apart from the concurrent marking phase, G1 also has additional short concurrent tasks. For more information on G1, please listen to the talk located at http://developers.sun.com/learning/javaoneonline/j1sessn.jsp?sessn=TS-5419&yr=2008&track=javase]. [12]

Comparisons

Table 3-1 summarizes the trade-offs between the garbage collectors that are covered in this section.

Creating Work for the Garbage Collector

This section includes a brief overview of how an application can create work for the garbage collector. Generally, there are three ways of doing so:

- **Allocation.** Garbage collections are triggered when a generation occupancy reaches a certain limit (e.g., a minor garbage collection takes place when the eden is full, a CMS cycle starts when the old generation occupancy goes over the CMS initiating limit). As a result, the higher the allocation rate of an application, the more often garbage collections are triggered.

- **Live data size.** All garbage collectors in the HotSpot VM do work proportional to the amount of live data that exists in each generation (a minor garbage collection copies all live objects as shown in Figure 3-5, a mark-compact garbage collector first needs to mark all live objects before moving them, etc.). As a result, the more live objects there are in the Java heap, the more work the garbage collector needs to do.

- **Reference updates in the old generation.** An update of a reference field in the old generation might create an old-to-young reference (which, as shown in

Table 3-1 Comparison of Garbage Collectors

	Serial GC	Parallel GC	CMS GC	G1 GC
Parallelism	No	Yes	Yes	Yes
Concurrency	No	No	Yes	Yes
Young GCs	Serial	Parallel	Parallel	Parallel
Old GCs	Serial	Parallel	Parallel & Conc	Parallel & Conc

Figure 3-3, will have to be processed during the next minor garbage collection) or might cause an object to be revisited at the pre-cleaning or the remark phase (if it takes place during a CMS marking cycle).

Typically garbage collection overhead can be reduced by reducing one or more of the preceding metrics. However, sometimes this is either impossible (e.g., it might not be possible to compress further the data that needs to be loaded into the Java heap; or it is difficult to write a useful application that does not update references at all), or even undesirable (reusing objects can reduce the allocation rate, but it is also more time-consuming to implement and maybe more error-prone too). But by avoiding some bad programming practices, it is possible to find a good balance between having low garbage collection overhead, as well as well-written, easily maintained code. Bad programming practices to avoid include object pooling (pooled objects are long-lived, hence they increase the live data size of the old generation and initializing writes to them can also increase the number of reference updates in the old generation), sloppy sizing of array-based data structures (e.g., if an `ArrayList` is initially sized too small, its backing array might subsequently need to be resized several times, causing unnecessary allocation), and so on. Expanding on this goes beyond the scope of this book, but you can find some more information in this talk. [13]

A Historical Perspective

The Serial GC was the first garbage collector included in the HotSpot VM (introduced in Java 1.3), as well as another incremental garbage collector called the *Train GC*. The latter, however, was not used very widely and was end-of-lifed in Java 6. Java 1.4.2 saw the introduction of both the Parallel GC (which only had a parallel young generation garbage collector, but a serial old generation garbage collector), as well as CMS (which also had a parallel young generation garbage collector, whereas its concurrent phases were serial). The Parallel Old GC, which parallelized the old generation of the Parallel GC, was introduced in Java 5 Update 6. The concurrent marking and sweeping phases of CMS were parallelized in Java 5 Update 6 and Java 5 Update 7, respectively. Finally, at the time of this writing, G1 GC was included in Java 6 Update 20 (and available in later Java 6 releases). Java 7 will also have G1 GC.

HotSpot VM JIT Compilers

Before diving into the details of the JITs used in the HotSpot VM it is useful to digress a bit and talk about code generation in general and the particular trade-offs of JIT compilation. This will help frame the differences between the HotSpot VM Client and Server JIT compilers when they are discussed.

Compilation is the generation of machine-dependent code from some high level language. Traditionally compilers have started from a source language like C or C++, compiling each of the individual source files into object files and then finally linking those objects into a library or executable that can then be run. Since this is a relatively infrequent task, compilation time isn't a huge constraint on static compilers, though obviously developers won't wait forever. Java on the other hand uses a compiler, `javac`, which takes the high level sources and converts them into class files. These class files are then collected into jar files for use by a Java Virtual Machine. So the Java Virtual Machine always starts with the bytecode representation of the original program and is required to convert that dynamically into machine dependent code.

All compilers have a roughly similar structure, and it is useful to describe this first. They must have a front end to take the source representation and convert it into an intermediate representation or IR. There are many different kinds of intermediate representations used in compilers, and a compiler might in fact use several since different representations can be useful for different stages of compilation. One common style of IR is called *SSA,* which stands for *static single assignment.* This is a representation that has the property that a variable is only assigned to once, and instructions directly use those values. This has the advantage that the values used by an instruction are directly visible to it. The other common style is a named form that is conceptually similar to a source language in that values are assigned to variables, or names, and instructions use the names. This gives a certain amount of flexibility and can simplify some operations such as cloning of code, but there's a less direct relationship between an instruction and the values it uses.

The IR produced by the front end is generally the focus of most optimizations in a compiler. What optimizations are supported can cover a large range and will often be driven by the time required for the optimization. The most basic classes of optimizations are simple identity transformations, constant folding, common subexpression elimination, and inlining of functions. More complicated optimizations are commonly focused around improving the execution of loops and include range check elimination, unrolling, and loop invariant code motion. Illustrating how the HotSpot VM performs each of these optimizations is outside the scope of this book and is a topic worthy to expanding upon in an entire book.

Once these high level optimizations are performed there's a back end that takes the IR and converts it into some machine representation. This stage includes instruction selection and assignment of values to machine registers. Instruction selection can be done in many ways. It can be handled in an explicit manner where the compiler writer manages all the cases directly or by using a machine description with associated rules to drive automatic instruction selection. The automated approach can be somewhat complicated to build and maintain but can often take better advantage of the details of a machine.

Once the instructions are selected registers must be assigned to all the values in the program, and code must be emitted to deal with the calling conventions of the machine. For most functions the number of values live will be greater than the number of registers on the machine. The generated code will deal with this by assigning some values to registers and moving values between the registers and the stack to free them up for other values. Moving values to the stack is referred to as spilling the value or register spilling. Again there are several approaches to this problem. For simple code generators, a round robin style local allocator will execute quickly but is only suitable for the most simple code generators.

The classic strategy for register allocation is called graph coloring and generally results in the best usage of the machine registers and the fewest spills of extra values onto the stack. A graph is built that represents which values are in use simultaneously and which registers those values can live in. If there are more values live simultaneously than there are registers available, then the least important of those values are moved to the stack so the other values can use registers. Assigning every value to a register commonly requires several rounds of graph construction and coloring. This leads to the downside of graph coloring, which is that it can be expensive both in terms of time spent and the space required for the data structures.

A simpler strategy is called linear scan register allocation. The goal in linear scan is to assign registers in a single pass over all the instructions while still producing a good register assignment. It constructs lists of ranges where a value must be in a register and then in a single pass walks over that list assigning registers to values or spilling them to the stack. This can operate quickly but isn't as good at keeping values in the same register for their whole lifetime.

Class Hierarchy Analysis

In an object-oriented language, intelligent inlining can be critical to getting good performance since code is often broken up into small methods. Java presents some interesting difficulties in this regard since by default any instance method could be overridden by a subclass, so just seeing the local type often isn't enough to know what method to inline. One way the HotSpot VM addresses this is by something called *Class Hierarchy Analysis*. This is an on-demand analysis that can be used by the compiler to determine whether any loaded subclass has overridden a particular method. The important part of this trick is that the HotSpot VM is only considering the subclasses that are loaded and does not worry about any other subclasses that it hasn't seen yet. When the compiler takes advantage of Class Hierarchy Analysis, often referred to as CHA, it records that fact in the compiled code. If later on in the execution of the program a subclass that overrides that method is requested to be loaded, then as part of the loading process the compiled code that assumed there was only one implementor is thrown out. If that compiled code is currently being executed somewhere, then a process called *deoptimization* is used to convert that compiled frame into an equivalent set of interpreter frames. This allows complete recovery from the assumptions of the CHA result. CHA is also used to identify cases where an interface or abstract class only has a single loaded implementation.

Compilation Policy

Since the JIT does not have time to compile every single method in an application, all code starts out initially running in the interpreter, and once it becomes hot enough it gets scheduled for compilation. In the HotSpot VM this is controlled through the use of counters associated with each method. Every method has two counters: the invocation counter that is incremented every time a method is entered and the backedge counter that is incremented every time control flow moves from a higher bytecode index to a lower one. The backedge counter is used to detect methods that contain loops and to cause them to get compiled earlier than they would with just an invocation counter. Whenever either counter is incremented by the interpreter it checks them against a threshold, and if they cross this threshold the interpreter requests a compile of that method. The threshold used for the invocation count is called the CompileThreshold, and the backedge counter uses a more complex formula of CompileThreshold * OnStackReplacePercentage / 100.

When a compilation is requested it is enqueued in a list that is monitored by one or more compiler threads. If a compiler thread is not busy it removes the compilation request from the queue and begins to compile it. Normally the interpreter doesn't wait for the compilation to complete. Instead it resets the invocation counter and resumes executing the method in the interpreter. Once the compile completes and the compiled code is associated with the method, then the next caller of the method begins using the compiled code. Normally this behavior of not waiting for the compile to complete is a good idea since the execution and compilation can continue in parallel. If you want the interpreter to wait for the compile to complete, then the HotSpot VM command line option -Xbatch or -XX:-BackgroundCompilation can be used to make it block waiting for the compile.

The HotSpot VM can also perform special compiles called On Stack Replacement compiles, or OSRs as they are commonly known. These are used when Java code contains a long-running loop that started executing in the interpreter. Normally the way Java code ends up in compiled code is that when invoking a method the interpreter detects that there's compiled code for it, and it dispatches to that instead of staying in the interpreter. This does not help long-running loops that started in the interpreter since they are not being invoked again.

When the backedge counter overflows, the interpreter requests a compile that starts its execution at the bytecode of backedge instead of starting at the first bytecode in the method. The resulting generated code takes an interpreter frame as its input and uses that state to begin its execution. In this way long-running loops are able to take advantage of compiled code. The act of the generated code taking an interpreter frame as its input to be its execution is called On Stack Replacement.

Deoptimization

Deoptimization is the term used in the HotSpot VM for the process of taking a compiled frame, which may be the result of several levels of inlining, and converting that compiled frame into an equivalent set of interpreter frames. This is used to recover from various kinds of optimistic optimizations that compiled code can perform. In particular it is used to recover from the assumptions of class hierarchy analysis. The server compiler also uses it for something it refers to as uncommon traps. These are special points in the generated code where the compiler has chosen to use the interpreter to deal with some execution path. Most commonly this is either because at compilation time some class was unloaded, or a path appeared to have never been executed. Some kinds of exceptions are handled in this way as well.

The HotSpot VM's JIT compilers support deoptimization by recording some metadata at every potential safepoint that describes what the state of the bytecode execution was at that point. Every safepoint already has to include the chain of methods and bytecode indexes that describe the current execution state so that things like exception stack traces and the stack walking required by security checks can be implemented. For deoptimizations the compiler additionally records the location of every value referenced by the locals and expression stack of the method, along with which lock(s) are held. This is an abstract representation of the state of the interpreter frame at that point and is sufficient to build a set of interpreter frames that resume execution in the interpreter.

At first glance it may appear as though a lot of extra values are kept alive to support this, but there are a few tricks used to reduce this. The HotSpot VM's JIT compilers use a bytecode analysis called Method Liveness that computes for every Java local field whether there's a bytecode later in the method that might use its value. These locals are considered live, and only locals that are live need to have values in the debug info state. In practice this means that the JIT compilers are not keeping many values alive solely for the purposes of deoptimization.

Once compiled code has been generated it may be invalidated for several reasons, such as class loading that invalidates a CHA optimization or because classes referenced by the code have been unloaded. In this case the space for the compiled code is returned to the code cache for use by later compiles. In the absence of explicit invalidation of compiled code it is normally never freed.

JIT compiled code has several kinds of metadata associated with it that's required to support various features of the runtime. In particular because the HotSpot VM uses precise garbage collection, compiled code has to be able to describe which locations in a compiled frame contain references to Java objects. This is accomplished using `OopMaps`, which are tables listing registers and stack locations that must be visited by the garbage collector. These are required at any location in compiled code where the system might have to stop for a safepoint. This includes all call sites and places where allocation might occur. Additionally because there are VM operations such as garbage collection, biased lock revocation, and so on that require code be able to come to a halt in a reasonable amount of time for a safepoint, every loop that does not contain calls also requires an explicit safepoint check inside it. Otherwise a long-running loop could stop the entire system from performing a garbage collection and cause it to hang. Each of these safepoints also contains all the information describing the chain of methods that were inlined and the description of the Java frame required for support of deoptimization.

Client JIT Compiler Overview

The HotSpot VM's Client JIT compiler targets applications desiring rapid startup time and quick compilation so as to not introduce jitter in responsiveness such as client GUI applications. The Client JIT compiler started life as a fast, simple code generator intended to give Java reasonable startup performance without a lot of complexity. It was conceptually similar to the interpreter in that it generated a kind of template for each kind of bytecode and maintained a stack layout that was similar to an interpreter frame. It also only inlined field accessors. In Java 1.4, the HotSpot VM's Client JIT compiler was upgraded to support full method inlining and added support for Class Hierarchy Analysis and deoptimization both of which provided a substantial improvement. The Java 5 Client JIT compiler saw few changes because a more substantial set of changes was being worked on for the Java 6 Client JIT compiler.

Java 6's Client JIT Compiler included many changes intended to improve performance across the board. The Client compiler's intermediate representation was changed to an SSA style representation, and the simple local register allocator was replaced by a linear scan register allocator. Additionally value numbering was improved by extending it across multiple blocks, and some minor improvements to memory optimizations were made. On x86 platforms, support for using SSE for floating point operations was added, which significantly improved floating point performance.

Server JIT Compiler Overview

The HotSpot VM Server JIT compiler targets peak performance and high throughput for Java applications, so its design tends to focus on using the most powerful optimizations it can. This often means that compiles can require much more space or time than an equivalent compile by the Client JIT compiler. It tends to aggressively inline as well, which often leads to large methods, and larger methods take longer to compile. It also has an extensive set of optimizations covering a large number of corner cases, which is needed to generate optimal code for any bytecodes it might see.

SSA—Program Dependence Graph

The Server JIT compiler's intermediate representation (IR) is internally called "ideal" and is an SSA style IR, but it uses a different way of representing control flow called the *program dependence graph*. The representation tries to capture the minimal set of constraints on the execution of each operation, which allows for aggressive reordering of operations and global value numbering, which reduces redundant computations. It has a rich type system that captures all the details of the Java type system and feeds that knowledge back into the optimizations.

The Server JIT compiler also takes advantage of profile information collected by execution in the interpreter. During execution of bytecodes, if a method is executed enough times, the interpreter created an object known as a `methodDataOop`, which is a container for profile information about an individual method. It has entries for recording information about the types seen at call sites along with counts of how often they are seen. All the control flow bytecodes also record how often they are taken and which direction they go. All this information is used by the Server JIT compiler to find opportunities to inline based on common types and to compute frequencies for the control flow, which drives the block layout and register allocation.

All JIT compilers of Java bytecodes have to deal with the possibility of unloaded or uninitialized classes, and the Server JIT compiler handles this by treating the path as unreached when it contains unresolved constant pool entries. In this case it emits what is called an uncommon trap for that bytecode and stops parsing that path through the method. An uncommon trap is a request to the HotSpot VM Runtime to deoptimize the current compiled method and resume execution in the interpreter where the constant pool entry that was unresolved can be processed and properly resolved. The compiled code for that method is thrown out, and executions continue in the interpreter until a new compile is triggered. Since that path has been properly resolved the new compile will compile that path normally, and future execution will use the compiled version of that path.

Uncommon traps are also used to deal with unreached paths so that the compiler does not generate code for parts of the method that are never used, resulting in smaller code and more straight-line sections of code that are generally more optimizable. The Server JIT compiler additionally uses uncommon traps to implement some kinds of optimistic optimizations. These are cases where the Server JIT compiler has decided that some behavior is likely so it proceeds as if that was the only behavior but puts in a dynamic check that it is true. If the dynamic check fails the code heads to an uncommon trap, which handles that case in the interpreter. If the uncommon trap happens often enough the HotSpot VM Runtime decides that it is really not uncommon so the code should be thrown out and regenerated without the assumption that it is uncommon. This is done for some things like predicated call sites where it appears from profile information that call site only ever sees one receiver type, so the Server JIT compiler inlines assuming that it will see this type but puts in a guard checking that the type is really the expected one. If a call site mostly sees one type but sometimes sees others, instead of emitting an uncommon trap for the other case the Server JIT compiler emits a regular call. The advantage of emitting that uncommon trap is that later code will see just the effects of the inlined version, which can result in better final generated code since a call has unknown side effects on the state of memory.

The Server JIT compiler performs a large set of optimizations on loops in the generated code, including loop unswitching, loop unrolling, and range check elimination through iteration splitting. Iteration splitting is the process of taking a loop and converting it into three loops: the preloop, the main loop, and the post loop. The idea is to compute bounds on each of the loops such that it is provable that the main loop does not need any range checks. The preloop and the post loop deal with the boundary conditions of the iteration where range checks are needed. In most cases the preloop and the post loop run a small number of times, and in many cases the post loop can be eliminated completely. This allows the main loop to run without any range checks at all.

Once a loop has had its range checks removed it is possible that it can be unrolled. Loop unrolling takes relatively simple loop bodies and creates multiple copies of the body inside the loop, while reducing the number of iterations that the loop runs. This helps amortize the cost of the loop control flow and often allows the loop body to simplify more, allowing the loop to do more work in less time. In some cases repeated unrolling can cause a loop to go away completely.

Loop unrolling enables another optimization called superword, which is a form of vectorization. Unrolling creates a parallel set of operations in the body, and if those operations are on sequential memory locations they can be collected into operations on a vector such that a single instruction performs multiple operations in the same amount of time. As of Java 6, HotSpot VMs, this is mainly focused on copying or initialization patterns, but eventually it will fully support all available SIMD (single instruction, multiple data) arithmetic operations.

Once all the high level optimizations are performed the IR (intermediate representation) is converted into a machine dependent form that is able to take advantage of all the special instructions and address modes available on the processor. The machine dependent nodes are scheduled into basic blocks based on the requirements of their inputs and the expected frequency of the blocks. The graph coloring register allocator then assigns registers to all the instructions and inserts any needed register spills. Finally the code is turned into an nmethod, which is the

HotSpot VM's internal representation of compiled bytecodes and contains all the code along with the metadata required to use the code within the HotSpot VM Runtime.

Future Enhancements

The HotSpot VM currently supports two JIT compilers, Client and Server. At the time of this writing development is underway to introduce a hybrid HotSpot JIT compiler that combines the major attributes of the Client JIT compiler and the Server JIT compiler called tiered compilation. The promise offered by tiered compilation is the rapid startup features of the Client JIT compiler and continuing to improve the performance of an application through the use of the Server JIT compiler's more advanced optimization techniques. For the adventurous or curious, tiered compilation can be enabled on recent Java 6 HotSpot VMs using the `-server-XX: +TieredCompilation` command line options. However, tiered compilation as of this writing, is not recommended as the HotSpot JIT compiler of choice for production or critical systems if using Java 6 Update 24 or earlier. If you are using Java 6 Update 25, Java 7, or later, using `-server -XX: +TieredCompilation` may be an alternative for applications typically using the Client JIT compiler. As tiered compilation improves in its optimization capabilities and matures, it is likely to be the recommended JIT compiler for both client and server families of Java applications.

HotSpot VM Adaptive Tuning

The Java 5 HotSpot VMs introduced a new feature that evaluates the underlying platform and system configuration at JVM launch time and then automatically selects the garbage collector, configures Java heap size, and chooses a runtime JIT compiler to use. In addition, this feature also introduced an adaptive means for tuning the Java heap for the throughput garbage collector. This new adaptive Java heap tuning allowed the garbage collector to dynamically tune the sizes of the Java heap to meet application behavior and object allocation rates. This combination of automatic platform dependent selection of default values and adaptive Java heap sizing to lessen the burden of manual garbage collection tuning is called *ergonomics*.

The ergonomics feature has been further enhanced in Java 6 Update 18 to improve the performance of rich client applications. In this section, the initial default values for heap sizes, garbage collector, and JIT compilers found in Java 1.4.2 HotSpot VMs are presented, followed by the default values chosen via the ergonomics feature and the Java 6 Update 18 ergonomics enhancements.

Java 1.4.2 Defaults

In the Java 1.4.2 HotSpot VM the following defaults were chosen for garbage collector, JIT compiler, and Java heap sizes:

- Serial garbage collector, i.e., `-XX:+UseSerialGC`
- Client JIT compiler, i.e., `-client`
- 4 megabyte initial and minimum Java heap size along with a 64 megabyte maximum Java heap size, i.e., `-Xms4m` and `-Xmx64m`

Java 5 Ergonomic Defaults

In the Java 5 HotSpot VMs, a category called "server-class machine" was introduced that allowed the HotSpot VM to choose a different set of default values for garbage collector, JIT compiler, and Java heap sizes. A server-class machine in the HotSpot VM is defined as a system with an underlying configuration that has two or more gigabytes of physical memory and two or more virtual processors. The number of virtual processors identified by the HotSpot VM when determining whether a system is a server-class machine is also the same value returned by the Java API `Runtime.availableProcessors()`, and generally is the same number of processors reported by operating system tools such as `mpstat` for Linux and Solaris. Also note when running a HotSpot VM in an operating system configured with a processor set, the value returned by the Java API `Runtime.availableProcessors()` is the number of virtual processors observed within the processor set, not the number of virtual processors observed system wide.

> **Tip**
>
> The definition of server-class machine does not apply to systems running a 32-bit version of the Windows operating system. These systems default to using the Serial garbage collector (`-XX:+UseSerialGC`), Client JIT compiler (`-client`), and 4 megabyte initial and minimum heap size (`-Xms4m`) along with a 64-megabyte maximum Java heap size (`-Xmx64m`).

When the HotSpot VM identifies a system as a server class machine, it selects the following defaults for garbage collector, JIT compiler, and Java heap sizes:

- Throughput garbage collector, also known as Parallel GC, i.e., `-XX:+UseParallelGC`[1]
- Server JIT compiler, i.e., `-server`

---

1. On recent Java 6 HotSpot VMs, or where the following switch is available, ergonomics may also automatically select `-XX:+UseParallelOldGC`, which also enables `-XX:+UseParallelGC`.

- 1/64 of the physical memory up to a maximum of 1GB as the initial and minimum Java heap size along with a 1/4 the total physical memory up to a maximum of 1GB as the maximum Java heap size

Table 3-2 summarizes the choices made by a Java 5 and later HotSpot VM.

Serial GC means the Serial garbage collector is chosen. Parallel GC means the Throughput garbage collector is chosen. Client means the client JIT compiler is chosen. Server means the server JIT compiler is chosen. Under (If Server Class) Default GC, JIT, and Java Heap Sizes, Client means the Client JIT compiler is chosen for a 32-bit Windows platform where other criteria for a server-class machine matched. This choice is deliberately made on 32-bit Windows platforms because historically client applications (i.e., interactive applications) are run more often on this combination of platform and operating system. Where Server is indicated, the Server JIT compiler is the only JIT compiler available in the HotSpot VM.

To print the ergonomic choices the HotSpot VM has made, the `-XX: +PrintCommandLineFlags` command line option can be used. For instance, doing a simple `java`

Table 3-2 Summary of Choices Made by a Java 5 and Later HotSpot VM

Platform	Operating System	(If Not Server Class) Default GC, JIT and Heap Sizes -Xms & -Xmx	(If Server Class) Default GC, JIT and Java Heap Sizes -Xms & -Xmx
SPARC (32-bit)	Solaris	Serial GC, Client, 4MB, 64MB	Parallel GC, Server, 1/64 RAM, max of 1/4 RAM or 1GB
i586	Solaris	Serial GC, Client, 4MB, 64MB	Parallel GC, Server, 1/64 RAM, max of 1/4 RAM or 1GB
i586	Linux	Serial GC, Client, 4MB, 64MB	Parallel GC, Server, 1/64 RAM, max of 1/4 RAM or 1GB
i586	Windows	Serial GC, Client, 4MB, 64MB	Serial GC, Client, 1/64 RAM, max of 1/4 RAM or 1GB
SPARC (64-bit)	Solaris	Parallel GC, Server, 1/64 RAM, 1/4 RAM or 1GB max	Parallel GC, Server, 1/64 RAM, max of 1/4 RAM or 1GB
x64 (64-bit)	Linux	Parallel GC, Server, 1/64 RAM, 1/4 RAM or 1GB max	Parallel GC, Server, 1/64th RAM, max of 1/4 RAM or 1GB
x64 (64-bit)	Windows	Parallel GC, Server, 1/64 RAM, 1/4t RAM or 1GB max	Parallel GC, Server, 1/64 RAM, max of 1/4 RAM or 1GB
IA-64	Linux	Parallel GC, Server, 1/64 RAM, 1/4 RAM or 1GB max	Parallel GC, Server, 1/64 RAM, max 1/4 RAM or 1GB
IA-64	Windows	Parallel GC, Server, 1/64 RAM, 1/4 RAM or 1GB max	Parallel GC, Server, 1/64 RAM, max of 1/4 RAM or 1GB

-XX:+PrintCommandLineFlags -version on any system with a Java 5 or Java 6 HotSpot VM prints the default ergonomic values. The following is an example of the output produced from a Java 5 HotSpot VM on a Sun UltraSPARC 5440 system configured with 128GB of RAM and 256 virtual processors running the Oracle 11 Express 2010.11 operating system:

```
$ java -XX: +PrintCommandLineFlags -version
-XX:MaxHeapSize=1073741824 -XX:ParallelGCThreads=85
-XX: +PrintCommandLineFlags -XX: +UseParallelGC
java version "1.6.0_14"
Java(TM) SE Runtime Environment (build 1.6.0_14-b07)
Java HotSpot(TM) Server VM (build 14.0-b15, mixed mode)
```

From the preceding output, the Java 6 HotSpot VM's launcher chose the Server JIT compiler, as shown in the last line of the output, a maximum Java heap size of 1073741824 bytes, or 1024 megabytes or 1 gigabyte along with selecting the throughput collector (-XX:+UseParallelGC) with 85 parallel gc threads (-XX:ParallelGCThreads=85). Note, -XX:MaxHeapSize is the same as the command line option -Xmx.

Java 6 Update 18 Updated Ergonomic Defaults

Java 6 Update 18 further updated the ergonomics feature to better adapt to rich client applications. The enhancements apply to when a system is identified as a non-server class machine. Remember that a server class machine is defined as a system with an underlying configuration that has 2 or more gigabytes of physical memory and two or more virtual processors. Hence these are enhancements made to systems identified as having less than 2 gigabytes of physical memory and less than two virtual processors.

For systems identified as non-server class machines, the client JIT compiler remains as the automatically selected JIT compiler. However, its Java heap sizing defaults have changed, and the settings for garbage collection are better tuned. The maximum heap size for Java 6 Update 18 is now one-half of physical memory up to a physical memory size of 192MB. Otherwise, the maximum heap size is one-fourth of physical memory up to a physical memory size of 1GB. For systems with 1GB or more of physical memory, the default maximum heap size is 256m. The initial heap size for non-server class machines is 8MB up to a physical memory size of 512MB. Otherwise, the initial and minimum heap size is 1/64 of the physical memory size between 512MB and 1GB of physical memory. At 1GB and larger physical memory, the default initial and minimum heap size is explicitly 16MB. In addition, Java 6 Update 18 sizes the young generation space at one-third of the Java heap size. However, if the concurrent collector happens to be specified explicitly with no additional Java heap sizing, initial, minimum, maximum, or young generation space sizing, Java 6 Update 18 reverts to the Java 5 ergonomic defaults.

Table 3-3 Summary of Choices Made by Java 6 Update 18 and Later

Platform	Operating System	(If Not Server Class) Default GC, JIT, and Heap Sizes -Xms & -Xmx	(If Server Class) Default GC, JIT, and Java Heap Sizes -Xms & -Xmx
SPARC (32-bit)	Solaris	Serial GC, Client, *8MB or 1/64 RAM or 16MB, 1/2 RAM or 1/4 RAM or 256MB*	Parallel GC, Server, 1/64 RAM, max of 1/4 RAM or 1GB
i586	Solaris	Serial GC, Client, *8MB or 1/64 RAM or 16MB, 1/2 RAM or 1/4 RAM or 256MB*	Parallel GC, Server, 1/64 RAM, max of 1/4 RAM or 1GB
i586	Linux	Serial GC, Client, *8MB or 1/64 RAM or 16MB, 1/2 RAM or 1/4 RAM or 256MB*	Parallel GC, Server, 1/64 RAM, max of 1/4 RAM or 1GB
i586	Windows	Serial GC, Client, *8MB or 1/64 RAM or 16MB, 1/2 RAM or 1/4 RAM or 256MB*	Serial GC, Client, 1/64 RAM, max of 1/4 RAM or 1GB
SPARC (64-bit)	Solaris	Parallel GC, Server, 1/64 RAM, 1/4 RAM or 1GB max	Parallel GC, Server, 1/64 RAM, max of 1/4 RAM or 1GB
x64 (64-bit)	Linux	Parallel GC, Server, 1/64 RAM, 1/4 RAM or 1GB max	Parallel GC, Server, 1/64 RAM, max of 1/4 RAM or 1GB
x64 (64-bit)	Windows	Parallel GC, Server, 1/64 RAM, 1/4 RAM or 1GB max	Parallel GC, Server, 1/64 RAM, max of 1/4 RAM or 1GB
IA-64	Linux	Parallel GC, Server, 1/64 RAM, 1/4 RAM or 1GB max	Parallel GC, Server, 1/4 RAM or 1GB max 4MB, 64MB
IA-64	Windows	Parallel GC, Server, 1/64 RAM, 1/4 RAM or 1GB max	Parallel GC, Server, 1/64 RAM, max of 1/4 RAM or 1GB

Table 3-3 summarizes the updated ergonomic choices made by Java 6 Update 18 when no command line options are specified. The values in the cells within Table 3-3 that have changed from the Java 5 ergonomics in Table 3-2 are in italic.

Young generation space size is also sized at 1/3 of the Java heap size for those configurations listed in the table that are in italic.

Adaptive Java Heap Sizing

An artifact of the ergonomics feature enabling the throughput collector is the enabling of an additional feature called *adaptive heap sizing*. Adaptive heap sizing attempts to optimally size the young generation and old generation spaces of the HotSpot VM by evaluating application object allocation rates and their lifetimes. The HotSpot VM monitors the

Java application's object allocation rate and their object lifetimes and then makes sizing decisions that attempt to size the young generation space such that short-lived objects are collected prior to getting promoted to old generation along with allowing longer lived objects to be promoted in a timely manner to avoid them unnecessarily being copied between survivor spaces. The HotSpot VM initially uses explicit young generation sizing such as those specified with -Xmn, -XX:NewSize, -XX:MaxNewSize, -XX:NewRatio, and -XX:SurvivorRatio as a starting point for young generation sizing. Adaptive sizing automatically adjusts young generation space sizes from those initial settings.

> **Tip**
>
> Adaptive heap sizing is available only with the throughput collectors -XX:+UseParallelGC or -XX:+UseParallelOldGC. It is not available with the concurrent collector or serial collector.

Although there exists HotSpot VM command line options that can fine-tune the policies adaptive heap sizing uses in making its dynamic heap sizing decisions, these options are rarely used outside the guidance of HotSpot VM engineers. It is much more common to disable adaptive heap sizing and explicitly size the young generation space including eden and survivor spaces. On most Java applications using the throughput collector, enabled via -XX:+UseParallelGC or -XX:+UseParallelOldGC, adaptive sizing does a good job at optimally sizing the young generation space. The family of applications that adaptive heap sizing finds the most challenging are those that have frequent fluctuations, or rapidly changing periods of object allocation rates and experience frequent phases where object lifetimes vary dramatically. Applications that fall into this category may realize better performance by disabling adaptive heap sizing using the -XX:-UseAdaptiveSizePolicy HotSpot VM command line option. Note, the "-" character after the "-XX:". The "-" character tells the HotSpot VM to disable the adaptive sizing policy. In contrast, a "+" character following the "-XX:" tells the HotSpot VM to enable the feature.

Beyond Ergonomics

Performance demanding applications often find tuning the HotSpot VM beyond its ergonomic defaults results in improved performance. The one exception to this is adaptive sizing, which is enabled automatically when using the throughput collector. Adaptive sizing tends to do well at automatically sizing the young generation space for most Java applications.

More information on tuning the HotSpot VM can be found in Chapter 7 of this book. Ergonomics is a feature that continues to evolve with each release of the

HotSpot VM with the goal of being able to meet or exceed the performance realized by specialized command line option tuning.

References

[1] Lindholm, Tim, and Frank Yellin. *Java Virtual Machine Specification, Second Edition.* Addison-Wesley, Reading, MA, 1999.

[2] Gosling, James, Bill Joy, Guy Steele, and Gilad Bracha. *Java Language Specification, Third Edition.* Chapter 12.2: Loading of Classes and Interfaces. Addison-Wesley, Boston, MA, 2005.

[3] *Amendment to Java Virtual Machine Specification, Second Edition.* Chapter 5: Linking and Initializing. http://java.sun.com/docs/books/vmspec/2nd-edition/ConstantPool.pdf.

[4] Liang, Shen, and Gilad Bracha. *Dynamic Class Loading in the Java Virtual Machine.* Proc. of the ACM Conf. on Object-Oriented Programming, Systems, Languages and Applications. 1998.

[5] Dmitriev, Mikhail. *Safe Class and Data Evolution in Large and Long-Lived Java Applications.* SML Technical Report Series, Palo Alto, CA, 2001.

[6] Gosling, James, Bill Joy, Guy Steele, and Gilad Bracha. *Java Language Specification, Third Edition.* Addison-Wesley, Reading, MA, 2005,

[7] Dice, Dave. *Biased Locking in HotSpot.* blog. http://blogs.sun.com/dave/entry/biased_locking_in_hotspot, 2006.

[8] *Java Native Interface Specification.* http://java.sun.com/javase/6/docs/technotes/guides/jni/spec.

[9] Liang, Sheng. *The Java Native Interface.* Addison-Wesley, Reading, MA, 1999.

[10] *Trouble-Shooting and Diagnostic Guide.* http://java.sun.com/j2se/1.5/pdf/jdk50_ts_guide.pdf, 2007.

[11] Jones, Richard, and Rafael Lins. *Garbage Collection.* John Wiley & Sons, Ltd., West Sussex, PO19 IUD, England, 1996.

[12] Printezis, Tony, and Paul Ciciora. *The Garbage First Garbage Collector* presentation. JavaOne Conference. San Francisco, CA, 2008. http://www.oracle.com/technetwork/java/j1sessn-jsp-155531.html

[13] Printezis, Tony, and John Coomes. *GC Friendly Programming* presentation. JavaOne Conference. San Francisco, CA, 2007. http://www.oracle.com/technetwork/java/index-jsp-156726.html

4

JVM Performance Monitoring

This chapter describes the information to monitor at the Java Virtual Machine (JVM) level of the software stack. In addition, it shows tools that can be used to monitor a JVM and what to watch for as common patterns. The details of how to make JVM tuning decisions based on the information observed can be found in Chapter 7, "Tuning the JVM, Step By Step." There is also a small section at the end of the chapter covering application monitoring.

Monitoring a JVM is an activity that should be done all the time with a production application. Since the JVM is a critical component in the software stack, it should be monitored as much as the application itself and the operating system. Analysis of JVM monitoring information indicates when JVM tuning is needed. JVM tuning should be expected anytime there is a JVM version change, operating system change (configuration or version), application version or update, or a major change in application input. A change in application input is something that can occur frequently with many Java applications that can alter the performance of a JVM. Hence, monitoring a JVM is an important activity.

There are several areas of the JVM to monitor including garbage collection, JIT compiler activity, and class loading. Many tools are available to monitor a JVM. Some monitoring tools are distributed with a JDK, some tools are free, and others are commercial. The monitoring tools covered in this chapter are either distributed with the Oracle JDK, free, or open source. Additionally, all the tools presented in this chapter are available for Windows, Linux, and Oracle Solaris (also referred to as Solaris hereafter) operating systems.

To understand the material presented in this chapter, it is helpful to understand the major components and the general operations of a modern JVM. An overview of the Java HotSpot VM and its major components is given in Chapter 3, "JVM Overview."

Definitions

Before delving into the details of what to monitor, a revisit of the definitions of performance monitoring and performance profiling presented at the beginning of Chapter 2, "Operating System Performance Monitoring," is useful. Performance monitoring is an act of nonintrusively collecting or observing performance data from an operating or running application. Performance monitoring is usually a preventative or proactive type of action and can be performed in a production environment, qualification environment, or development environment. Performance monitoring can also be a first step in a reactive situation where an application stakeholder has reported a performance issue but has not provided sufficient information or clues to a potential root cause. In this case, performance profiling likely follows the act of performance monitoring. Performance monitoring also helps identify or isolate potential issues without having a severe impact on application responsiveness or throughput.

In contrast, performance profiling is an act of collecting performance data from an operating or running application that may be intrusive on application throughput or responsiveness. Performance profiling tends to be a reactive type of activity, or an activity in response to a stakeholder reporting a performance issue. It usually has a narrower focus than performance monitoring. Profiling is rarely done in production environments. It is typically done in qualification, testing, or development environments and is often an act that follows a monitoring activity.

Performance tuning, in contrast to performance monitoring and performance profiling, is an act of changing tunables, source code, or configuration attribute(s) for the purposes of improving throughput or responsiveness. Performance tuning often follows monitoring or performance profiling activities.

Garbage Collection

Monitoring JVM garbage collection is important since it can have a profound effect on an application's throughput and latency. Modern JVMs, such as the Java HotSpot VM (also referred to as HotSpot VM hereafter), provide the ability to observe garbage collection statistics per garbage collection in either a textual form, directed to a log file, or by publishing the garbage collection statistics to a monitoring GUI.

This section begins by listing the garbage collection data of interest. Then a listing of HotSpot VM command line options to report garbage collection statistics is presented along with an explanation of the reported data. In addition, graphical tools that can be used to analyze garbage collection data is presented. And, most importantly, patterns to look for are given along with suggestions as to when JVM garbage collection tuning is advisable.

Garbage Collection Data of Interest

The data of interest in garbage collection statistics are

- The garbage collector in use
- The size of the Java heap
- The size of the young generation and old generation spaces
- The size of the permanent generation space
- The duration of minor garbage collections
- The frequency of minor garbage collections
- The amount of space reclaimed in minor garbage collections
- The duration of full garbage collections
- The frequency of full garbage collections
- The amount of space reclaimed in a concurrent garbage collection cycle
- The occupancy of the Java heap before and after garbage collections
- The occupancy of the young generation and old generation spaces before and after garbage collections
- The occupancy of the permanent generation space before and after garbage collections
- Whether it is the occupancy of the old generation space or the occupancy of the permanent generation space that triggers a full garbage collection
- Whether the application is making use of explicit calls to `System.gc()`

Garbage Collection Reporting

There is little additional overhead in the HotSpot VM to report garbage collection data. In fact, the overhead is so small it is recommended to collect garbage collection data in production environments. This section describes several different HotSpot VM command line options that produce garbage collection statistics along with an explanation of the statistics.

There are generally two different types of garbage collections: a minor garbage collection, also called a young generation garbage collection, and a full garbage collection, also called a major garbage collection. A minor garbage collection collects the young generation space. A full garbage collection generally expresses the notion of garbage collecting and compacting the old generation and permanent generation spaces. There are some exceptions to this. In the HotSpot VM, the default behavior on a full garbage collection is to garbage collect the young generation, old generation, and permanent generation spaces. In addition, the old generation and permanent generation spaces are compacted along with any live objects in young generation space being promoted to the old generation space. Hence, at the end of a full garbage collection, young generation space is empty, and old generation and permanent generation spaces are compacted and hold only live objects. The behavior of each of the HotSpot garbage collectors is described in detail in Chapter 3.

As mentioned earlier, a minor garbage collection frees memory occupied by unreachable objects in the young generation space. In contrast, the default behavior for the HotSpot VM on a full garbage collection is to free memory occupied by unreachable objects in the young generation, old generation, and permanent generation spaces. It is possible to configure the HotSpot VM to not garbage collect the young generation space on a full garbage collection prior to garbage collecting the old generation space using the command line option -XX:-ScavengeBeforeFullGC. The "–" character preceding the ScavengeBeforeFullGC disables the garbage collection of the young generation space on a full garbage collection. In contrast, a "+" character in front of ScavengeBeforeFullGC enables the garbage collection of the young generation space on a full garbage collection. As just mentioned, the default behavior for the HotSpot VM is to enable garbage collection of the young generation space on full garbage collections. It is advisable to use the default behavior and not disable garbage collection of young generation on a full garbage collection. Garbage collecting the young generation space prior to garbage collecting the old generation space usually results in less work for the garbage collector and more objects being garbage collected since objects in the old generation space may be holding object references to objects in the young generation space. If the young generation space is not garbage collected, any object in old generation space that holds a reference to an object in young generation space cannot be garbage collected.

-XX:+PrintGCDetails

Although -verbose:gc is probably the most commonly used garbage collection reporting command line option, -XX:+PrintGCDetails prints additional and more valuable garbage collection information. This subsection presents example output from -XX:+PrintGCDetails for the throughput and concurrent garbage collectors along with providing an explanation of data. Also, patterns to watch for in the output are also presented.

It is important to note the additional information produced with -XX:+PrintGCDetails can change between versions of the HotSpot VM.

An example of -XX:+PrintGCDetails output from Java 6 Update 25's throughput garbage collector, enabled via -XX:+UseParallelGC or -XX:+UseParallelOldGC, is shown in the following example. The output is spread across several lines for easier reading.

```
[GC
    [PSYoungGen: 99952K->14688K(109312K)]
    422212K->341136K(764672K), 0.0631991 secs]
    [Times: user=0.83 sys=0.00, real=0.06 secs]
```

The GC label indicates this is minor garbage collection. [PSYoungGen: 99952K->14688K(109312K)] provides information about the young generation space. PSYoungGen indicates the young generation garbage collector in use is the multithreaded young generation garbage collector used with the throughput collector, enabled with the command line option –XX:+UseParallelGC, or auto enabled with –XX:+UseParallelOldGC. Other possible young generation garbage collectors are ParNew, which is the multithreaded young generation garbage collector used with the concurrent old generation garbage collector known as CMS, and Def-New which is the single-threaded young generation garbage collector used with the serial garbage collector, enabled with the command line option –XX:+UseSerialGC. -XX:+UseSerialGC, (DefNew), can also be used in combination with the old generation concurrent garbage collector, CMS, to indicate the use of a single-threaded young generation collector. At the time of this writing the G1 garbage collector, currently under development, does not use an identifier in the same way as the other three garbage collectors to identify the output as G1 GC.

The value to the left of the ->, 99952K, is the occupancy of the young generation space prior to the garbage collection. The value to the right of the ->, 14688K, is the occupancy of the young generation space after the garbage collection. Young generation space is further divided into an eden space and two survivor spaces. Since the eden space is empty after a minor garbage collection, the value to the right of the ->, 14688K, is the survivor space occupancy. The value inside the parentheses, (109312K), is the size, not the occupancy, of the young generation space, that is, the total size of eden and the two survivor spaces.

On the next line of output, 422212K->341136K(764672K) provides the Java heap utilization (the total occupancy of both young generation and old generation spaces), before and after the garbage collection. In addition, it provides the Java heap size, which is the total size of young generation and old generation spaces. The value to the left of the ->, 422212K, is the occupancy of the Java heap before the garbage collection. The value to the right of the ->, 341136K, is the occupancy of the Java heap after the garbage collection. The value inside the parentheses, (764672K), is the total size of the Java heap.

Using the reported young generation size and the reported Java heap size, you can calculate the size of the old generation space. For example, the Java heap size is 764672K, and the young generation size is 109312K. Hence, the old generation size is 764672K − 109312K = 655360K.

0.0631991 secs indicates the elapsed time for the garbage collection.

[Times: user=0.06 sys=0.00, real=0.06 secs] provides CPU usage and elapsed time information. The value to the right of user is the CPU time used by the garbage collection executing instructions outside the operating system. In this example, the garbage collector used 0.06 seconds of user CPU time. The value to the right of sys is the CPU time used by the operating system on behalf of the garbage collector. In this example, the garbage collector did not use any CPU time executing operating system instructions on behalf of the garbage collection. The value to the right of real is the elapsed wall clock time in seconds of the garbage collection. In this example, it took 0.06 seconds to complete the garbage collection. The times reported for user, sys, and real are rounded to the nearest 100th of a second.

An example of a full garbage collection with -XX:+PrintGCDetails follows. (The output is spread across several lines for easier reading.)

```
[Full GC
    [PSYoungGen: 11456K->0K(110400K)]
    [PSOldGen: 651536K->58466K(655360K)]
    662992K->58466K(765760K)
    [PSPermGen: 10191K->10191K(22528K)],
    1.1178951 secs]
    [Times: user=1.01 sys=0.00, real=1.12 secs]
```

The Full GC label indicates it is a full garbage collection. [PSYoungGen: 11456K->0K(110400K)] has the same meaning as in a minor garbage collection (explained previously).

[PSOldGen: 651536K->58466K(655360K)] provides information about the old generation space. PSOldGen indicates the old generation garbage collector in use is the multithreaded old generation garbage collector used with the throughput collector enabled via the XX:+UseParallelOldGC command line option. In the PSOldGen row of output, the value to the left of the ->, 651536K, is the occupancy of the old generation space prior to the garbage collection. The value to the right of the ->, 58466K, is the occupancy of the old generation space after the garbage collection. The value inside the parentheses, (655360K), is the size of the old generation space.

662992K->58466K(765760K) provides the Java heap utilization. It is the cumulative occupancy of both young generation and old generation spaces before and after the garbage collection. The value to the right of the `->` can also be thought of as the amount of live data in the application at the time of the full garbage collection. Knowing the amount of live data in the application, especially while the application is in steady state is important information to have when sizing the JVM's Java heap and fine-tuning the JVM's garbage collector.

`[PSPermGen: 10191K->10191K(22528K)]` provides information about the permanent generation space. `PSPermGen` indicates the permanent generation garbage collector in use is the multithreaded permanent generation garbage collector used with the throughput collector enabled via the `-XX:+UseParallelGC` or `-XX:+UseParallelOldGC` command line options. In the `PSPermGen` row of data, the value to the left of the `->`, `10191K`, is the occupancy of the permanent generation space prior to the garbage collection. The value to the right of the `->`, `10191K`, is the occupancy of the permanent generation space after the garbage collection. The value inside the parentheses `(22528K)`, is the size of the permanent generation space.

An important observation to take notice of in a full garbage collection is the heap occupancies of the old generation and permanent generation spaces before the garbage collection. This is because a full garbage collection may be triggered by either the occupancy of the old generation or permanent generation space nearing its capacity. In the output, the occupancy of the old generation space before the garbage collection `(651536K)`, is very near the size of the old generation space `(655360K)`. In contrast, the occupancy of the permanent generation space before the garbage collection `(10191K)`, is nowhere near the size of the permanent generation space `(22528K)`. Therefore, this full garbage collection was caused by the old generation space filling up.

`1.1178951 secs` indicates the elapsed time for the garbage collection.

`[Times: user=1.01 sys=0.00, real=1.12 secs]` provides CPU and elapsed time information. Its meaning is the same as described earlier for minor garbage collections.

When using the concurrent garbage collector, CMS, the output produced by `-XX:+PrintGCDetails` is different, especially the data reporting what is happening during a mostly concurrent garbage collection of the old generation space. The concurrent garbage collector, CMS, is enabled with the `-XX:+UseConcMarkSweepGC` command line option. It also auto-enables `-XX:+UseParNewGC`, a multithreaded young generation garbage collector. An example of a minor garbage collection using the concurrent garbage collector, CMS, follows:

```
[GC
    [ParNew: 2112K->64K(2112K), 0.0837052 secs]
    16103K->15476K(773376K), 0.0838519 secs]
    [Times: user=0.02 sys=0.00, real=0.08 secs]
```

The minor garbage collection output from the concurrent garbage collector is similar to the minor garbage collection output for the throughput garbage collector. It is explained here for completeness.

The `GC` label indicates this is minor garbage collection. `[ParNew: 2112K->64K(2112K)]` provides information about the young generation space. `ParNew` indicates the young generation garbage collector in use is the multithreaded young generation garbage collector used with the CMS concurrent garbage collector. If the serial young generation garbage collector is specified to be used with CMS, the label here will be `DefNew`.

The value to the left of the `->`, `2112K`, and to the right of the `ParNew` label, is the occupancy of the young generation space prior to the garbage collection. The value to the right of the `->`, `64K`, is the occupancy of the young generation space after the garbage collection. The young generation space is further divided into an eden space and two survivor spaces. Since the eden space is empty after a minor garbage collection, the value to the right of the `->`, `64K`, is the survivor space occupancy. The value inside the parentheses `(2112K)`, is the size, not the occupancy, of the young generation space, that is, the total size of eden and the two survivor spaces. The `0.0837052 secs` output is the amount of time it took to garbage collect unreachable objects in the young generation space.

On the next line of output, `16103K->15476K(773376K)` provides the Java heap utilization (the total occupancy of both young generation and old generation spaces), before and after the garbage collection. In addition, it provides the Java heap size, which is the total size of young generation and old generation spaces. The value to the left of the `->`, `16103K`, is the occupancy of the Java heap before the garbage collection. The value to the right of the `->`, `15476K`, is the occupancy of the Java heap after the garbage collection. The value inside the parentheses `(773376K)`, is the total size of the Java heap.

Using the reported young generation size and the reported Java heap size, you can calculate the size of the old generation space. For example, the Java heap size is `773376K` and the young generation size is `2112K`. Hence, the old generation size is `773376K − 2112K = 771264K`.

`0.0838519 secs` indicates the elapsed time for the minor garbage collection including the time it took to garbage collect the young generation space and promote any objects to old generation along with any remaining final cleanup work.

`[Times: user=0.02 sys=0.00, real=0.08 secs]` provides CPU usage and elapsed time information. The value to the right of `user` is the CPU time used by the garbage collection executing instructions outside the operating system. In this example, the garbage collector used `0.02` seconds of user CPU time. The value to the right of `sys` is the CPU time used by the operating system on behalf of the garbage collector. In this example, the garbage collector did not use any CPU time executing operating system instructions on behalf of the garbage collection. The value to the right of `real` is the elapsed wall clock time in seconds of the garbage collection. In this example, it took `0.08` seconds to complete the garbage collection. The times reported for `user`, `sys`, and `real` are rounded to the nearest 100th of a second.

Recall from the description of CMS in Chapter 3 there is a mostly concurrent garbage collection cycle that can execute in the old generation space. `-XX:+PrintGCDetails` also reports garbage collection activity on each concurrent garbage collection cycle. The following example shows garbage collection output that reports an entire concurrent garbage collection cycle. The concurrent garbage collection activity is interspersed with minor garbage collections to illustrate that minor garbage collections can occur during a concurrent garbage collection cycle. The output is reformatted for easier reading, and the concurrent garbage collection data is in bold. It should also be noted that the output reported from `-XX:+PrintGCDetails` when using CMS is subject to change between releases.

```
[GC
    [1 CMS-initial-mark: 13991K(773376K)]
    14103K(773376K), 0.0023781 secs]
    [Times: user=0.00 sys=0.00, real=0.00 secs]
[CMS-concurrent-mark-start]
[GC
    [ParNew: 2077K->63K(2112K), 0.0126205 secs]
    17552K->15855K(773376K), 0.0127482 secs]
    [Times: user=0.01 sys=0.00, real=0.01 secs]
[CMS-concurrent-mark: 0.267/0.374 secs]
    [Times: user=4.72 sys=0.01, real=0.37 secs]
[GC
    [ParNew: 2111K->64K(2112K), 0.0190851 secs]
    17903K->16154K(773376K), 0.0191903 secs]
    [Times: user=0.01 sys=0.00, real=0.02 secs]
[CMS-concurrent-preclean-start]
[CMS-concurrent-preclean: 0.044/0.064 secs]
    [Times: user=0.11 sys=0.00, real=0.06 secs]
[CMS-concurrent-abortable-preclean-start]
[CMS-concurrent-abortable-clean]   0.031/0.044 secs]
    [Times: user=0.09 sys=0.00, real=0.04 secs]
[GC
    [YG occupancy: 1515 K (2112K)
    [Rescan (parallel) , 0.0108373 secs]
    [weak refs processing, 0.0000186 secs]
    [1 CMS-remark: 16090K(20288K)]
    17242K(773376K), 0.0210460 secs]
    [Times: user=0.01 sys=0.00, real=0.02 secs]
[GC
    [ParNew: 2112K->63K(2112K), 0.0716116 secs]
    18177K->17382K(773376K), 0.0718204 secs]
    [Times: user=0.02 sys=0.00, real=0.07 secs]
[CMS-concurrent-sweep-start]
```

Continued

```
[GC
    [ParNew: 2111K->63K(2112K), 0.0830392 secs]
    19363K->18757K(773376K), 0.0832943 secs]
    [Times: user=0.02 sys=0.00, real=0.08 secs]
[GC
    [ParNew: 2111K->0K(2112K), 0.0035190 secs]
    17527K->15479K(773376K), 0.0036052 secs]
    [Times: user=0.00 sys=0.00, real=0.00 secs]
[CMS-concurrent-sweep: 0.291/0.662 secs]
    [Times: user=0.28 sys=0.01, real=0.66 secs]
[GC
    [ParNew: 2048K->0K(2112K), 0.0013347 secs]
    17527K->15479K(773376K), 0.0014231 secs]
    [Times: user=0.00 sys=0.00, real=0.00 secs]
[CMS-concurrent-reset-start]
[CMS-concurrent-reset: 0.016/0.016 secs]
    [Times: user=0.01 sys=0.00, real=0.02 secs]
[GC
    [ParNew: 2048K->1K(2112K), 0.0013936 secs]
    17527K->15479K(773376K), 0.0014814 secs]
    [Times: user=0.00 sys=0.00, real=0.00 secs]
```

A CMS cycle begins with the initial mark pause and ends at the completion of the concurrent reset phase. Each of the CMS cycle phases is in bold in the preceding output beginning with the **CMS-initial-mark** and ending with the **CMS-concurrent-reset**. The **CMS-concurrent-mark** entry indicates the end of the concurrent marking phase. The **CMS-concurrent-sweep** label marks the end of the concurrent sweeping phase. The **CMS-concurrent-preclean** and **CMS-concurrent-abortable-preclean** entries identify work that can be done concurrently and is in preparation for the remark phase, denoted with the **CMS-remark** label. The sweeping phase, noted with the **CMS-concurrent-sweep** entry, is the phase that frees the space consumed by objects marked as unreachable. The final phase is indicated by the **CMS-concurrent-reset**, which prepares for the next concurrent gar bage collection cycle.

The initial mark is usually a short pause relative to the time it takes for a minor garbage collection. The time it takes to execute the concurrent phases (concurrent mark, concurrent precleaning, and concurrent sweep) may be relatively long (as in the preceding example) when compared to a minor garbage collection pause, but Java application threads are not stopped for the duration of the concurrent phases. The remark pause is affected by the specifics of the application (e.g., a higher rate of modifying objects can increase this pause time) and the time since the last minor garbage collection (i.e., a larger number of objects in the young generation space may increase the duration of this pause).

A pattern to pay particular attention to in the output is the amount in the reduction of old generation space occupancy during the CMS cycle. In particular, how much the Java heap occupancy drops between the start and end of the CMS concurrent sweep denoted in the output as **CMS-concurrent-sweep-start** and **CMS-concurrent-sweep**. The Java heap occupancy can be observed by looking at the minor garbage collections. Hence, pay attention to the minor garbage collections between the start and end of the CMS concurrent sweep phase. If there is little drop in the Java heap occupancy between the start and end of the CMS concurrent sweep phase, then either few objects are being garbage collected, meaning the CMS garbage collection cycles are finding few unreachable objects to garbage collect and as a result are wasting CPU, or objects are being promoted into the old generation space at a rate that is equal to or greater than the rate at which the CMS concurrent sweep phase is able to garbage collect them. Either of these two observations is a strong indicator the JVM is in need of tuning. See Chapter 7 for information on tuning the CMS garbage collector.

Another artifact to monitor when using the CMS garbage collector is the tenuring distribution enabled via the `-XX:+PrintTenuringDistribution` command line option. The tenuring distribution is a histogram showing the ages of objects in the young generation's survivor spaces. When an object's age exceeds the tenuring threshold it is promoted from the young generation space to the old generation space. The tenuring threshold and how to monitor the tenuring distribution along with why it is important to monitor is explained in the "Tenuring Threshold Explained" and "Monitoring the Tenuring Threshold" sections of Chapter 7.

If objects are promoted too quickly to the old generation space and the CMS garbage collector cannot keep free enough available space to meet the rate that objects are promoted from young generation to old generation, it leads to the old generation running out of available space, a situation known as a *concurrent mode failure*. A concurrent mode failure can also occur if the old generation space becomes fragmented to a point where there is no longer a hole in the old generation space large enough to handle an object promotion from the young generation space. `-XX:+PrintGCDetails` reports a concurrent mode failure in the garbage collection output with the text `(concurrent mode failure)`. When a concurrent mode failure occurs, the old generation space is garbage collected to free available space, and it is compacted to eliminate fragmentation. This operation requires all Java application threads be stopped, and it can take a noticeably lengthy duration of time to execute. Therefore, if you observe concurrent mode failures, you should tune the JVM using the guidance in Chapter 7, especially the section on fine-tuning the application for low latency.

Including Date and Time Stamps

The HotSpot VM includes command line options to include a date or time stamp on each reported garbage collection. The `-XX:+PrintGCTimeStamps` command line option prints a time stamp that is the number of elapsed seconds since the JVM started. It is printed at each garbage collection. The following is example minor garbage collection output from `-XX:+PrintGCTimeStamps` being used in combination with `-XX:+PrintGCDetails` and the throughput garbage collector. (The output is spread across several lines for easier reading.)

```
77.233: [GC
    [PSYoungGen: 99952K->14688K(109312K)]
    422212K->341136K(764672K), 0.0631991 secs]
    [Times: user=0.83 sys=0.00, real=0.06 secs]
```

Notice the `-XX:+PrintGCDetails` output is prefixed with a time stamp representing the number of seconds since the JVM started. The output for full garbage collections also prefixes the output with a time stamp. In addition, a time stamp is also printed when using the concurrent garbage collector.

Java 6 Update 4 and later include a `-XX:+PrintGCDateStamps` command line option. It produces an ISO 8601 date and time stamp. The date and time stamp have the following form; *YYYY-MM-DD*-T-*HH-MM-SS.mmm*-TZ, where:

- *YYYY* is the four-digit year.
- *MM* is the two-digit month; single-digit months are prefixed with 0.
- *DD* is the two-digit day of the month; single-digit days are prefixed with 0.
- T is a literal that denotes a date to the left of the literal and a time of day to the right.
- *HH* is the two-digit hour; single-digit hours are prefixed with 0.
- *MM* is the two-digit minute; single-digit minutes are prefixed with 0.
- *SS* is the two-digit second; single-digit seconds are prefixed with 0.
- *mmm* is the three-digit milliseconds; single- and two-digit milliseconds are prefixed with 00 and 0, respectively.
- TZ is the time zone offset from GMT.

Although the time zone offset from GMT is included in the output, the date and time of day are not printed as GMT time. The date and time of day are adjusted to local time. The following example output uses `-XX:+PrintGCDateStamps` together with `-XX:+PrintGCDetails` when using the throughput garbage collector. The output is spread across several lines for easier reading.

```
2010-11-21T09:57:10.518-0500:[GC
    [PSYoungGen: 99952K->14688K(109312K)]
    422212K->341136K(764672K), 0.0631991 secs]
    [Times: user=0.83 sys=0.00, real=0.06 secs]
```

The full garbage collections with the throughput garbage collector also prefixes a date and time stamp when using -XX:+PrintGCDateStamps. In addition, a date and time stamp are printed when using the concurrent garbage collector.

The use of date and/or time stamps allows you to measure both the duration of minor and full garbage collections along with the frequency of minor and full garbage collections. With the inclusion of date and/or time stamps, you can calculate an expected frequency that minor and full garbage collections occur. If the garbage collection durations or frequency exceed the application's requirements, consider tuning the JVM as described in Chapter 7.

-Xloggc

To facilitate offline analysis of garbage collection statistics and to direct garbage collection output to a file, the -Xloggc:<filename> HotSpot VM command line option can be used. <filename>is the name of the file where you want the garbage collection data to be stored. Offline analysis of garbage collection data can represent a wider span of time and the ability to identify patterns without having to observe the data as the application is running.

When -XX:+PrintGCDetails is used in combination with -Xloggc:<filename>, the output is automatically prefixed with a time stamp even without specifying -XX:+PrintGCTimeStamps. The time stamp is printed in the same way as -XX:+PrintGCTimeStamps is printed. Following is an example of -Xloggc:<filename> being used in combination with -XX:+PrintGCDetails with the throughput garbage collector. (The output is spread across several lines for easier reading.)

```
77.233: [GC
    [PSYoungGen: 99952K->14688K(109312K)]
    422212K->341136K(764672K), 0.0631991 secs]
    [Times: user=0.83 sys=0.00, real=0.06 secs]
```

Since -Xloggc includes a time stamp automatically in its output, it is easy to determine when minor and full garbage collections occur. In addition, you can also calculate the frequency of minor and full garbage collections. With the time stamps, you can calculate the expected frequency that minor and full garbage collections occur. If the garbage collection durations or frequency exceed the application's requirements, consider tuning the JVM as described in Chapter 7.

Application Stopped Time and Application Concurrent Time

The HotSpot VM can report the amount of time an application runs between safepoint operations and the amount of time the HotSpot VM blocks executing Java threads

using the command line options -XX:+PrintGCApplicationConcurrentTime
and -XX:+PrintGCApplicationStoppedTime. Observing safepoint operations
using these two command line options can provide useful information in understanding and quantifying the impact of JVM induced latency events. It can also be used
to identify whether a latency event of interest is the result of a JVM induced latency
from a safepoint operation, or if the latency event occurred as a result of something
in the application.

Tip

Chapter 3, "JVM Overview," describes safepoint operations in more detail.

An example using -XX:+PrintGCApplicationConcurrentTime and
-XX:+PrintGCApplicationStoppedTime in addition to -XX:+PrintGCDetails
is shown in the following:

```
Application time: 0.5291524 seconds
[GC
    [ParNew: 3968K->64K(4032K), 0.0460948 secs]
    7451K->6186K(32704K), 0.0462350 secs]
    [Times: user=0.01 sys=0.00, real=0.05 secs]
Total time for which application threads were stopped: 0.0468229 seconds
Application time: 0.5279058 seconds
[GC
    [ParNew: 4032K->64K(4032K), 0.0447854 secs]
    10154K->8648K(32704K), 0.0449156 secs]
    [Times: user=0.01 sys=0.00, real=0.04 secs]
Total time for which application threads were stopped: 0.0453124 seconds
Application time: 0.9063706 seconds
[GC
    [ParNew: 4032K->64K(4032K), 0.0464574 secs]
    12616K->11187K(32704K), 0.0465921 secs]
    [Times: user=0.01 sys=0.00, real=0.05 secs]
Total time for which application threads were stopped: 0.0470484 seconds
```

The output shows the application ran for approximately .53 to .91 seconds with
minor garbage collection pauses of approximately .045 to .047 seconds. That equates
to about 5% to 8% overhead for minor garbage collections.

Also notice there are no additional safepoints between each of the minor garbage
collections. If there happens to be additional safepoints between garbage collections,
the output will show Application time: and Total time for which application threads were stopped: messages for each safepoint that occurs between
garbage collections.

Explicit Garbage Collections

Explicit garbage collections can be identified in garbage collection output easily. The garbage collection output contains text indicating the full garbage collection is the result of an explicit call to `System.gc()`. Following is an example of a full garbage collection initiated with a call to `System.gc()` using the `-XX:+PrintGCDetails` command line option. Again, the output is spread across several lines for easier reading.

```
[Full GC (System)
    [PSYoungGen: 99608K->0K(114688K)]
    [PSOldGen: 317110K->191711K(655360K)]
    416718K->191711K(770048K)
    [PSPermGen: 15639K->15639K(22528K)],
    0.0279619 secs]
    [Times: user=0.02 sys=0.00, real=0.02 secs]
```

Notice the `(System)` label following the `Full GC` text. This indicates this is a System.gc() induced full garbage collection. If you observe an explicit full garbage collection in the garbage collection logs, investigate the reason why it is being used and then decide whether the call to System.gc() should be removed from the source code, or whether it should be disabled.

Recommended Command Line Options for Monitoring Garbage Collection

A minimum set of HotSpot VM garbage collection command line options to monitor garbage collection are `-XX:+PrintGCDetails` along with either `-XX:+PrintGCTimeStamps` or `-XX:+PrintGCDateStamps`. It may also be useful to use `-Xloggc:<filename>` to save the data to a file so the data can be further analyzed offline.

Offline Analysis of Garbage Collection Data

The purpose of doing offline analysis is to summarize garbage collection data and look for patterns of interest in the data. Offline analysis of garbage collection data can be done in a variety of different ways such as loading the data into a spreadsheet or using a charting tool to plot the data. GCHisto is a tool designed to do offline analysis. GCHisto is a free tool that can be downloaded at http://gchisto.dev.java.net. GCHisto reads garbage collection data saved in a file and presents both a tabular and graphical view of the data. Figure 4-1 shows a tabular summary from its GC Pause Stats tab.

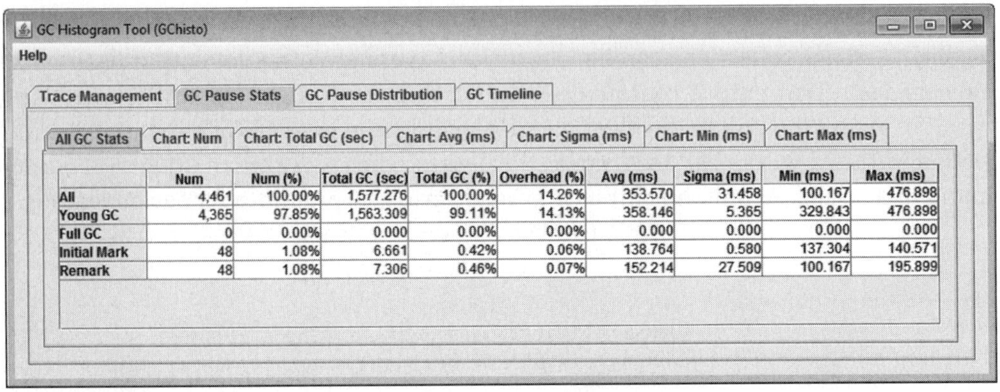

	Num	Num (%)	Total GC (sec)	Total GC (%)	Overhead (%)	Avg (ms)	Sigma (ms)	Min (ms)	Max (ms)
All	4,461	100.00%	1,577.276	100.00%	14.26%	353.570	31.458	100.167	476.898
Young GC	4,365	97.85%	1,563.309	99.11%	14.13%	358.146	5.365	329.843	476.898
Full GC	0	0.00%	0.000	0.00%	0.00%	0.000	0.000	0.000	0.000
Initial Mark	48	1.08%	6.661	0.42%	0.06%	138.764	0.580	137.304	140.571
Remark	48	1.08%	7.306	0.46%	0.07%	152.214	27.509	100.167	195.899

Figure 4-1 GC Pause Stats in GCHisto

The GC Pause Stats subtab provides information such as the number of, the overhead of, and duration of garbage collections. The additional GC Pause Stats subtabs narrow the focus to one of the aforementioned categories.

All garbage collections or phases of garbage collections that induce stop-the-world pauses have a row in the table in addition to a total on the top row. Figure 4-1 shows data from the concurrent garbage collector. Recall from Chapter 3 that the concurrent garbage collector, in addition to minor (young) and major garbage collections, also has two stop-the-world garbage collection pauses: the CMS initial mark and CMS remark. If you observe initial mark or remark pauses greater than minor garbage collection pauses, it suggests the JVM requires tuning. Initial mark and remark phases are expected to be shorter in duration than minor garbage collections.

When viewing statistics from the throughput garbage collector, since it has only two stop-the-world garbage collection pauses, only minor and full garbage collections are shown in the GC Pause Stats tab of GCHisto.

The number of minor versus full garbage collections provides a sense of the frequency of full garbage collections. This information along with the full garbage collection pause times can be evaluated against the application's requirements for frequency and duration of full garbage collections.

The garbage collection overhead (the Overhead % column) is an indicator of how well the garbage collector is tuned. As a general guideline, concurrent garbage collection overhead should be less than 10%. It may be possible to achieve 1% to 3%. For the throughput garbage collector, garbage collection overhead near 1% is considered as having a well-tuned garbage collector. 3% or higher can be an indication that tuning the garbage collector may improve the application's performance. It is important to understand there is a relationship between garbage collection overhead and the size of the Java heap. The larger the Java heap, the better the opportunity for lower

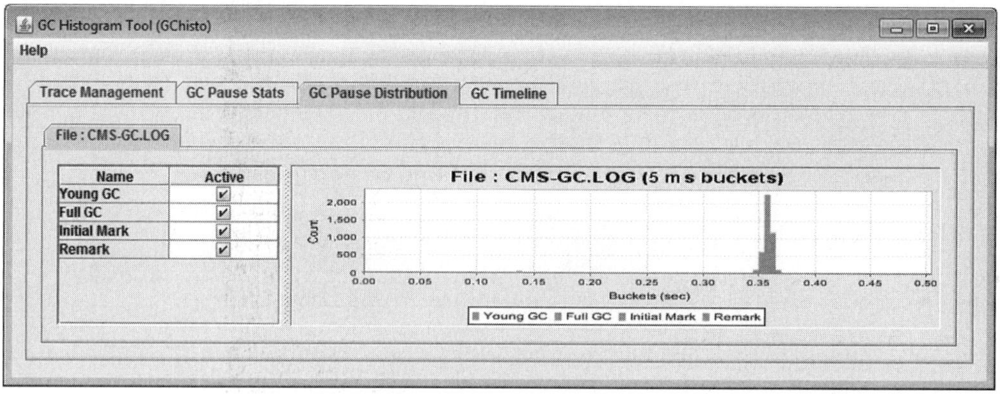

Figure 4-2 GC Pause Distribution

garbage collection overhead. Achieving the lowest overhead for a given Java heap size requires JVM tuning.

In Figure 4-1, the garbage collection overhead is a little over 14%. Applying the general guidelines just mentioned, JVM tuning will likely reduce its overhead.

The maximum pause times, the far right column, can be evaluated against the application's worst case garbage collection induced latency requirements. If any of the maximum pause times exceed the application's requirements, tuning the JVM may be a consideration. The degree and how many pause times exceed the application's requirements dictate whether JVM tuning is a necessity.

The minimum, maximum, average, and standard deviation provide information about the distribution of pause times. The distribution of pause times can be viewed by clicking on the GC Pause Distribution tab as shown in Figure 4-2.

The default view for the GC Pause Distribution shows the distribution of all garbage collection pauses. Which pause type is included in the view is controlled by selecting or deselecting the appropriate check box. The y-axis is the count of pauses and the x-axis is the pause time duration of the garbage collection event. It is generally more useful to look at full garbage collections separately since they usually have the longest duration. Looking at only minor garbage collections offers the possibility to see wide variations in pause times. A wide distribution in pause times can be an indication of wide swings in object allocation rates or promotion rates. If you observe a wide distribution of pause times, you should look at the GC Timeline tab to identify peaks in garbage collection activity. An example is shown in Figure 4-3.

The default view for the GC Timeline shows all garbage collection pauses through the entire time line. To see time stamps at the bottom of the graph (the x-axis), you must have garbage collection statistics that include either -XX:+PrintGCTimeStamps, -XX:+PrintGCDateStamps, or used -Xloggc. For

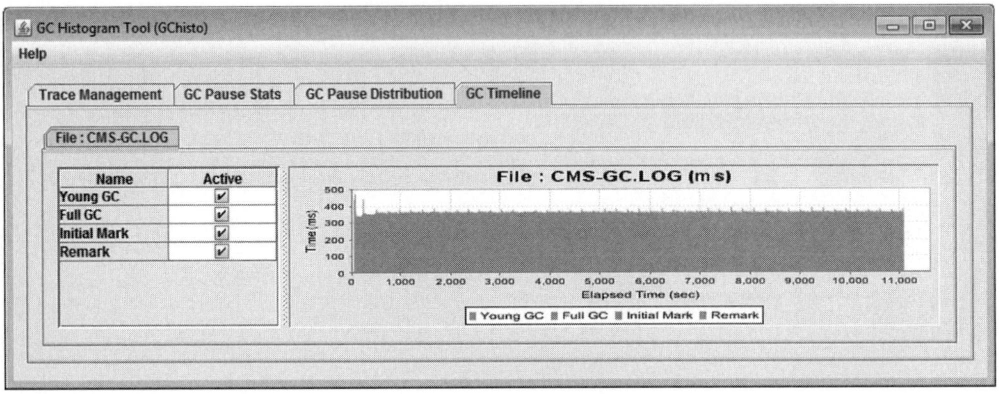

Figure 4-3 GC Timeline tab

every garbage collection pause that occurred, a tick is put on the graph illustrating the duration of the pause (y-axis) and when the pause occurred relative to the start of the JVM (the x-axis).

There are several patterns to look for in a time line. For example, you should take notice of when full garbage collections occur and how frequently. Selecting only full garbage collections as the pause type is useful for this analysis. With the time line you can observe when the full garbage collections occur relative to the start of the JVM to get a sense of when they occurred.

Selecting only minor garbage collections as the pause type to show allows you to observe peaks, or possibly repeating peaks, in garbage collection duration over time. Any observed peaks or repeating patterns can be mapped back to application logs to get a sense of what is happening in the system at that time when the peaks occur. The use cases being executed at those time periods can be candidates to further explore for object allocation and object retention reduction opportunities. Reducing object allocation and object retention during these busiest garbage collection activity time periods reduces the frequency of minor garbage collections and potentially reduces the frequency of full garbage collections.

An area of the time line can be zoomed in on by selecting an area of interest with the mouse, as illustrated in Figure 4-4.

Zooming in allows you to narrow the focus of the time line to a specific area to see each garbage collection pause. You can zoom back out by pressing the right mouse button anywhere in the graph and selecting Auto Range > Both Axes from the context sensitive menu.

GCHisto also provides the capability to load more than one garbage collection log at a time via the Trace Management tab. When multiple garbage collection logs are loaded, there is a separate tab for each garbage collection log, which allows you to

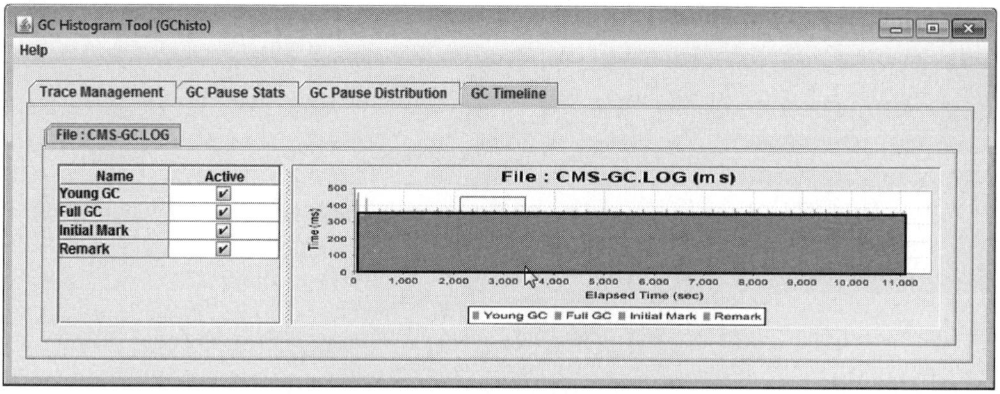

Figure 4-4 GC Timeline zooming

easily switch between logs. This can be useful when you want to compare garbage collection logs between different Java heap configurations or between different application loads.

Graphical Tools

Garbage collection can also be monitored with graphical tools, which can make the identification of trends or patterns a little easier than traversing textual output. The following graphical tools can be used to monitor the HotSpot VM: JConsole, VisualGC, and VisualVM. JConsole is distributed with Java 5 and later JDKs.

VisualGC was originally developed and packaged with jvmstat. It is available as a free download at http://java.sun.com/performance/jvmstat.

VisualVM is an open source project that brings together several existing lightweight Java application monitoring and profiling capabilities into a single tool. VisualVM is included in Java 6 Update 6 and later JDKs. It is also available as a free download from http://visualvm.dev.java.net.

JConsole

JConsole is a JMX (Java Management Extensions) compliant GUI tool that connects to a running Java 5 or later JVM. Java applications launched with a Java 5 JVM must add the `-Dcom.sun.management.jmxremote` property to allow the JConsole to connect. Java applications launched using Java 6 and later JVMs do not require this property. The following examples illustrate how to connect JConsole to an example demo application shipped with the JDK called Java2Demo. Using a Java 5 JDK, the Java2Demo application can be started using the following command line.

On Solaris or Linux:

```
$ <JDK install dir>/bin/java -Dcom.sun.management.jmxremote -jar <JDK
install dir>/demo/jfc/Java2D/Java2Demo.jar
```

`<JDK install dir>` is the path and directory where a Java 5 JDK is installed.

On Windows:

```
<JDK install dir>\bin\java -Dcom.sun.management.jmxremote -jar <JDK
install dir>\demo\jfc\Java2D\Java2Demo.jar
```

`<JDK install dir>` is the path and directory where a Java 5 JDK is installed. To start JConsole on either with a Java 6 or later JVM the `-Dcom.sun.management. jmxremote` property is not required as an argument to JConsole.

On Solaris or Linux:

```
$ <JDK install dir>/bin/jconsole
```

`<JDK install dir>` is the path and directory where Java 5 JDK is installed.

On Windows:

```
<JDK install dir>\bin\jconsole
```

`<JDK install dir>` is the path and directory where a Java 5 JDK is installed. When JConsole is launched it automatically discovers and provides the opportunity to connect to Java applications running locally or remotely. The connection dialogs differ slightly between the JConsole version shipped in Java 5 versus Java 6 as shown in Figure 4-5 and Figure 4-6, respectively.

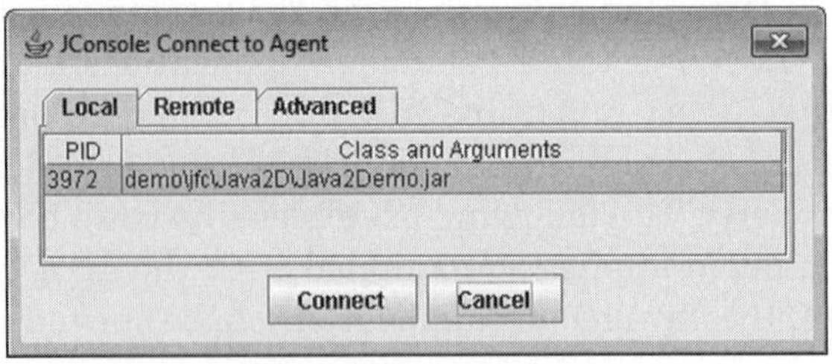

Figure 4-5 Java 5 JConsole connection dialog

Figure 4-6 Java 6 JConsole connection dialog

In Java 5 JConsoles, the applications listed in the connection dialog that can be monitored are applications that have been started with the -Dcom.sun.management. jmxremote property and applications that share the same user credentials as those of the user who has started JConsole.

With Java 6 JConsole, the applications listed in the connection dialog that can be monitored are applications that are Java 6 applications and Java 5 applications that have been started with the -Dcom.sun.management.jmxremote property, which both share the same user credentials as those of the user who has started JConsole. Java 5 applications that have not been started with the -Dcom.sun.management. jmxremote property that share the same user credentials as those of JConsole are listed but grayed out.

To monitor an application on a local system you select the Name and PID of the application from the list and click the Connect button. Remote monitoring is advantageous when you want to isolate the system resource consumption from the JConsole application from the system being monitored. To monitor an application on a remote system, the application to be monitored must be started with remote management enabled. Enabling remote management involves identifying a port number to communicate with the monitored application and establishing password authentication along with optionally using SSL for security. Information on how to enable remote management can be found in the Java SE 5 and Java SE 6 monitoring and management guides:

- Java SE 5 — http://java.sun.com/j2se/1.5.0/docs/guide/management/index.html
- Java SE 6 — http://java.sun.com/javase/6/docs/technotes/guides/management/toc. html

---

Tip

More than one Java application can be monitored with JConsole at any time by selecting the Connection > New Connection menu and selecting a different Name and PID pair.

Once a JConsole is connected to an application it will load six tabs. The default JConsole display between Java 5 and Java 6 differs. Java 6's JConsole displays a graphical representation of heap memory, thread, classes, and CPU usage. In contrast, Java 5's JConsole displays the same information but in a textual form. For the purposes of monitoring JVM garbage collection, the Memory tab is the most useful. The Memory tab in both Java 5 and Java 6 JConsole are the same. Figure 4-7 shows the JConsole Memory tab.

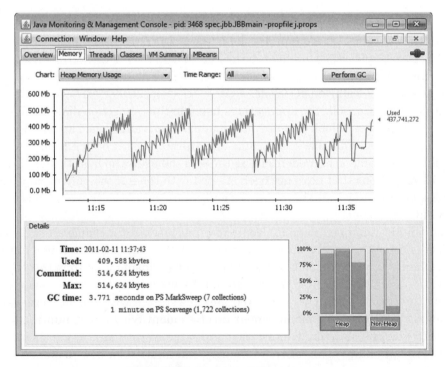

Figure 4-7 JConsole Memory tab

The Memory tab uses charts to graphically show the JVM's use of memory consumption over a period of time. Depending on the JVM being monitored and the garbage collector being used, the spaces that make up the Java heap, or memory pools as they are called in JConsole, may vary. But from their names it is straightforward to map them to following HotSpot VM space names:

- **Eden space.** The memory pool where almost all Java objects are allocated.

- **Survivor space.** The memory pool containing objects that have survived at least one garbage collection of the eden space.

- **Old or tenured space.** The memory pool containing objects that have survived some garbage collection age threshold.

- **Permanent generation space.** The memory pool containing all the reflective data of the JVM such as class and method objects. If the monitored JVM supports class data sharing, this space will be divided into read-only and read-write areas.

- **Code cache.** Applies to the HotSpot VM and contains memory that is used by the JIT compiler and for the storage of JIT compiled code.

JConsole defines heap memory as the combination of eden space, survivor space, and old or tenured space. Non-heap memory is defined as the combination of permanent generation space and code cache. You can display charts of heap memory usage or non-heap memory usage by choosing one of the options in the Chart drop-down menu. You can also view charts of specific spaces. Additionally, clicking on any of the Heap or Non-Heap bar charts in the bottom right corner switches the chart to display the selected Heap or Non-Heap space. If you hover the mouse over any of the Heap or Non-Heap bar charts in the lower right corner, a tool tip displays text indicating the memory pool or space name.

A pattern to watch for is whether the survivor space remains full for an extended period of time. This is an indication that survivor spaces are overflowing and objects are getting promoted into the old generation space before they have an opportunity to age. Tuning the young generation space can address survivor spaces overflowing.

You can also change the time range over which memory usage is displayed by selecting an option in the Time Range drop-down menu.

In the left-hand portion of the Details panel (the bottom left panel), several current JVM memory metrics are displayed including

- **Used.** The amount of memory currently used, including the memory occupied by all Java objects, both reachable and unreachable.

- **Committed.** The amount of memory guaranteed to be available for use by the JVM. The amount of committed memory may change over time. The JVM may release memory to the system, and the amount of committed memory could be less than the amount of memory initially allocated at startup. The amount of committed memory will always be greater than or equal to the amount of used memory.

- **Max.** The maximum amount of memory that can be used for memory management. Its value may change or be undefined. A memory allocation may fail if the JVM attempts to increase the used memory to be greater than committed memory, even if the amount used is less than or equal to max (for example, when the system is low on virtual memory).

- **GC time.** The cumulative time spent in stop-the-world garbage collections and the total number of garbage collection invocations including concurrent garbage collection cycles. Multiple rows may be shown, each of which represents the garbage collector used in the JVM.

Additional garbage collection monitoring capabilities are possible with JConsole. Many of these capabilities are described in the JConsole documentation found at

- Java SE 5 — http://java.sun.com/j2se/1.5.0/docs/guide/management/jconsole.html
- Java SE 6 — http://java.sun.com/javase/6/docs/technotes/guides/management/jconsole.html

VisualVM

VisualVM is an open source graphical tool that began development in 2007. VisualVM was introduced in the Java 6 Update 7 JDK and is considered the second generation of the JConsole tool. VisualVM integrates several existing JDK software tools and lightweight memory monitoring tools such as JConsole along with adding profiling capabilities found in the popular NetBeans Profiler. VisualVM is designed for both production and development environments and further enhances the capabilities of monitoring and performance analysis for the Java SE platform. It also utilizes the NetBeans plug-in architecture, which allows the ability to easily add components, add plug-ins, or extend VisualVM's existing components or plug-ins to performance monitor or profile any application.

VisualVM requires a Java 6 version to run, but it can monitor Java 1.4.2, Java 5, or Java 6 applications locally or remotely. However, there are some limitations to VisualVM's capabilities depending on the Java version used by the Java application being monitored and whether the Java application is running locally or remotely to VisualVM. Table 4-1 illustrates the VisualVM features available for a given Java application running with a given version of a JDK.

Table 4.1 VisualVM Feature Table

Feature	JDK 1.4.2 Local and Remote	JDK 5.0 Local and Remote	JDK 6.0 (Remote)	JDK 6.0 (Local)
Overview	•	•	•	•
System Properties (in Overview)				•
Monitor	•	•	•	•
Threads		•	•	•
Profiler				•
Thread Dump				•
Heap Dump				•
Enable Heap Dump on OOME				•
MBean Browser (plug-in)				•
Wrapper for JConsole plug-ins (plug-in)		•	•	•
VisualGC (plug-in)	•	•	•	•

VisualVM also includes profiling capabilities. Although profiling is covered in detail in Chapter 5, "Java Application Profiling," VisualVM's remote profiling capabilities are covered in this chapter since VisualVM's remote profiling is lightweight and fits well with monitoring activities.

VisualVM can be launched from Windows, Linux, or Solaris using the following command line. (Note the command name is `jvisualvm`, not just `visualvm`.)

```
<JDK install dir>\bin\jvisualvm

<JDK install dir> is the path and directory where JDK 6 Update 6 or later
is installed.
```

If you have downloaded the standalone VisualVM from java.net, VisualVM can be launched from Windows, Linux, or Solaris using the following command line. (Note the open source version of VisualVM available on java.net is launched using `visualvm` rather than `jvisualvm` as is done when VisualVM is launched from a JDK distribution.)

```
<VisualVM install dir>\bin\visualvm
```

<VisualVM install dir> is the path and directory where VisualVM is installed.

Alternatively, you can launch VisualVM from a directory window display such as Windows Explorer by traversing to the VisualVM installation directory and double-clicking on the VisualVM executable icon.

The initial VisualVM display shows an Applications window on the left and an empty monitoring window on the right, as shown in Figure 4-8.

The Applications panel of VisualVM has three major nodes in an expandable tree. The first major node, Local, contains a list of local Java applications VisualVM can monitor. The second node, Remote, contains a list of remote hosts and Java applications on each remote host VisualVM can monitor. The third node, Snapshots, contains a list of snapshot files. With VisualVM you can take a snapshot of a Java application's state. When a snapshot is taken, the Java application's state is saved to a file and listed under the Snapshots node. Snapshots can be useful when you want to capture some important state about the application or to compare it against a different snapshot.

Local Java applications are automatically identified by VisualVM at Java application launch time and at VisualVM launch time. For example, as shown in Figure 4-8,

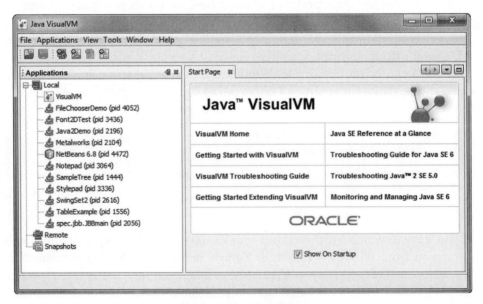

Figure 4-8 VisualVM

VisualVM automatically discovered the Java applications shown on the Local node. As additional Java applications are launched, VisualVM automatically detects them and adds them to the local node's list. As Java applications are shut down, VisualVM automatically removes them.

To monitor remote Java applications, configuration must be done on the remote system where you want to monitor the Java application. The remote system must be configured to run the jstatd daemon. The jstatd daemon is shipped in Java 5 and Java 6 JDKs. It is not included with Java 5 or Java 6 JREs. You can find the jstatd daemon in the same directory as jvisualvm and the java launcher.

The jstatd daemon launches a Java RMI server application that watches for the creation and termination of HotSpot VMs and provides an interface to allow remote monitoring tools such as VisualVM to attach and monitor Java applications remotely. The jstatd daemon must be run with the same user credentials as those of the Java applications to be monitored. Since jstatd can expose instrumentation of JVMs, it must employ a security manager and requires a security policy file. Consideration should be given to the level of access granted via the security policy so that the monitored JVM's security is not compromised. The policy file used by jstatd must conform to Java's security policy specification. The following is an example policy file that can be used with jstatd:

```
grant codebase "file:${java.home}/../lib/tools.jar" {
    permission java.security.AllPermission;
};
```

Tip

Note that the preceding example policy file allows jstatd to run without any security exceptions. This policy is less liberal than granting all permissions to all codebases but is more liberal than a policy that grants the minimal permissions to run the jstatd server. More restrictive security than this example can be specified in a policy to further limit access. However, if security concerns cannot be addressed with a policy file, the safest approach is to not run jstatd and use the monitoring tools locally rather than connecting remotely.

To use the preceding example policy and start the jstatd daemon, assuming the preceding policy is saved in a file called jstatd.policy, at the command line you would execute the following command:

```
jstatd -J-Djava.security.policy=<path to policy file>/jstatd.policy
```

Tip

Additional details on how to configure jstatd can be found at http://java.sun.com/javase/6/docs/technotes/tools/share/jstatd.html.

Once the jstatd daemon is running on the remote system, you can verify the local system can attach to the remote jstatd daemon by running the `jps` command and providing the hostname of the remote system. `jps` is a command that lists the Java applications that can be monitored. When `jps` is supplied a hostname, it attempts to connect to the remote system's jstatd daemon to discover which Java applications can be monitored remotely. When no optional hostname is supplied to `jps`, it returns a list of Java applications that can be monitored locally.

Suppose the remote system where you have configured and have the jstatd daemon running is called halas. On the local system, you would execute the following `jps` command to verify the connectivity to the remote system.

```
$ jps halas
2622  Jstatd
```

If the `jps` command returns a `Jstatd` in its output, you have successfully configured the remote system's jstatd daemon. The number preceding the `Jstatd` in the output is the process id of the jstatd daemon process. For the purposes of verifying remote connectivity, the process id is not important.

To use VisualVM to monitor a remote Java application, it needs to be configured with the remote host's name or IP address. This is done by right-clicking on the Remote node in VisualVM's Applications panel and adding the remote host information. If you want to monitor Java applications on multiple remote hosts, you must configure each remote host with a jstatd daemon, using the procedure described earlier. Then, add each remote host's information in VisualVM. VisualVM automatically discovers and provides a list of Java applications that can be monitored. Again, recall that the remote Java applications must match the user credentials of the user running VisualVM and jstatd along with those that meet the permissions specified in the jstatd policy file. Figure 4-9 shows VisualVM with a remote system configured and the Java applications it can monitor.

To monitor an application, you can either double-click on an application name or icon under the Local or Remote node. You can also right-click on the application name or icon and select Open. Any of these actions opens a window tab in the right panel of VisualVM. Local applications running with Java 6 or later have additional subtabs.

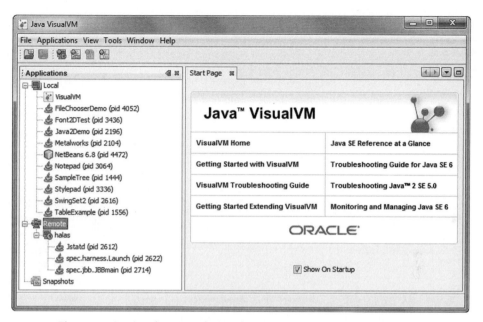

Figure 4-9 VisualVM configured to monitor remote applications

The number of subtab windows displayed in the right panel of VisualVM depends on the application's Java version, whether it is running locally or remotely, and whether any additional plug-ins have been added to VisualVM. The minimum set of window subtabs in the right panel is the Overview and Monitor subtabs. The Overview window provides a high level overview of the monitored application by showing the process id, host name where the application is running, main Java class name, any arguments passed to the application, the JVM name, the path to the JVM, any JVM flags used, whether heap dump on out of memory error is enabled or disabled, number of thread dumps or heap dumps have been taken, and, if available, the monitored application's system properties. The Monitor window displays heap usage, permanent generation space usage, classes loaded information, and number of threads. An example of the Monitor window monitoring an application running remotely under Java 6 is shown in Figure 4-10.

If a JMX connection is configured for use with the remote application, you can also request a garbage collection or heap dump from the Monitor window. To configure a JMX on the remote application, it must be started with at least the following system properties:

- `com.sun.management.jmxremote.port=<port number>`
- `com.sun.management.jmxremote.ssl=<true | false>`
- `com.sun.management.jmxremote.authenticate=<true | false>`

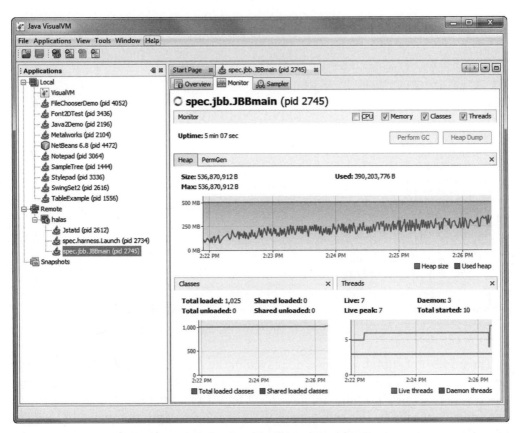

Figure 4-10 VisualVM Monitor subtab

To configure VisualVM to connect to the remote application via JMX, use the File > Add JMX Connection menu item. In the Add JMX Connection form, add the following information for each of the fields:

- `hostname:<port number>` for the Connection field. For example, if the remote application is running on a host named halas, and you configured the remote application with `com.sun.management.jmxremote.port=4433`, you enter halas:4433 in the Connection field.

- Optionally enter a display name to be displayed in VisualVM to identify the remote application via the JMX connection. By default, VisualVM uses what you entered in the Connection field as the display name.

- If you set `com.sun.management.jmxremote.authenticate=true`, enter the username and password in the Username and Password fields who are authenticated to connect remotely.

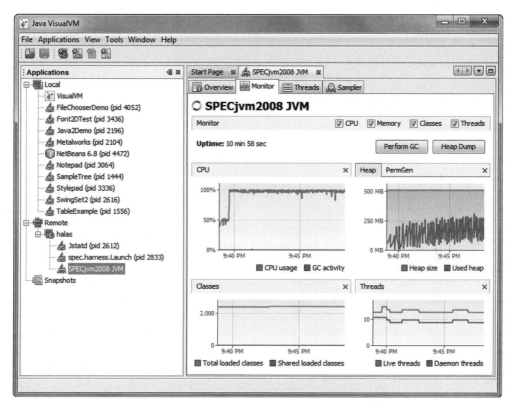

Figure 4-11 Remote monitoring via JMX

See VisualVM JMX connection documentation for additional information on configuring JMX for remote monitoring with VisualVM, http://download.oracle.com/javase/6/docs/technotes/guides/visualvm/jmx_connections.html.

After a JMX connection is configured, an additional icon is displayed in VisualVM's Application's panel representing that a remote JMX connection has been configured to the remote application. Configuring a JMX connection for remote applications in VisualVM increases the monitoring capabilities. For example, the Monitor window also shows CPU usage by the application and the ability to induce a full garbage collection or heap dump, as shown in Figure 4-11.

In addition to more capabilities in the Monitor window, an additional Threads window is also available. The Threads window shows a view of threads in the application along with a color indicating whether the thread is currently running, sleeping, blocked, waiting, or contending on a monitor lock. The Threads window is available as a view for all locally monitored applications.

The Threads window offers insight into which threads are most active, those that are involved in acquiring and releasing locks. The Threads window can be useful to observing specific thread behavior in an application, especially when operating system monitoring suggests the application may be experiencing lock contention.

An additional option available in the Threads window is the ability to create a thread dump by clicking the Thread Dump button. When a thread dump is requested, VisualVM adds a window tab displaying the thread dump and also appends a thread dump entry to the monitored application entry in the Application's window below the application being monitored. It is important to note that thread dumps are not persisted or available once VisualVM has been closed unless they are saved. Thread dumps can be saved by right-clicking on the thread dump icon or label below the application listed in the Applications panel. Thread dumps can be reloaded in VisualVM at a later time by selecting the File > Load menu item and traversing to the directory where the thread dump was saved.

VisualVM also offers profiling capabilities to both local and remote applications. Local profiling capabilities include both CPU and memory profiling for Java 6 applications. For monitoring purposes, the feature of monitoring CPU utilization or monitoring memory utilization as the application is running can be useful. However, care should be taken when invoking either of these features on a production system as they may heavily tax the running application. Being able to monitor CPU utilization while an application is running can provide information as to which methods are the busiest during times when specific events are occurring. For example, a GUI application may exhibit performance issues only in a specific view. Hence, being able to monitor the GUI application when it is in that view can be helpful in isolating the root cause.

Remote profiling requires a JMX connection to be configured and is limited to CPU profiling. It does not include memory profiling. But heap dumps can be generated from the Sampler window. They can also be generated from the Threads window. Heap dumps can be loaded into VisualVM to analyze memory usage.

To initiate remote profiling in VisualVM, first select and open a remote application from the Application panel that is configured with a JMX connection. Then select the Sampler window in the right panel. In the Sampler window click the CPU button to initiate remote profiling. Figure 4-12 shows the Sampler window after clicking the CPU button. The view of CPU utilization is presented with the method name consuming the most time at the top. The second column, Self Time %, provides a histogram view of the method time spent per method relative to the time spent in other methods. The Self Time column represents the amount of wall clock time the method has consumed. The remaining column, Self Time (CPU), reports the amount of CPU time the method has consumed. Any of the columns can be sorted in ascending or descending order by clicking on the column name. A second click on a column causes the ordering to toggle back and forth between ascending or descending.

Profiling can be stopped and resumed by clicking the Pause button. And a snapshot can be captured by clicking the Snapshot button. After a taking a snapshot,

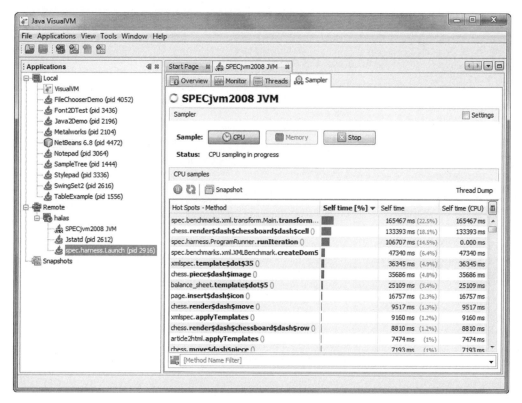

Figure 4-12 Remote CPU profiling

VisualVM displays the snapshot. The snapshot can be saved to disk. To save the snapshot to share it with another developer, to be able to load the snapshot at a later time or to compare it with another snapshot, you can export the snapshot to a file as shown in Figure 4-13. A saved snapshot can be loaded by VisualVM or the NetBeans Profiler. To load a saved snapshot with VisualVM, you select the File > Load from the main menu; filter the files by Profiler Snapshots (*.nps) to find the saved profile and have it loaded.

In the snapshot window, the call tree showing the call stacks for all threads in the captured snapshot are displayed. Each call tree can be expanded to observe the call stack and method consuming the most time and CPU. At the bottom of the snapshot window you can also view Hot Spots, which is a listing of methods with the method consuming the most Self Time at the top of the table. A combined view of the Call Tree and Hot Spots is also available. In the combined view, as you click on a call stack in the Call Tree, the table of Hot Spot methods is updated to show only the methods in the selected call stack.

Additional details on profiling Java applications can be found in Chapter 5.

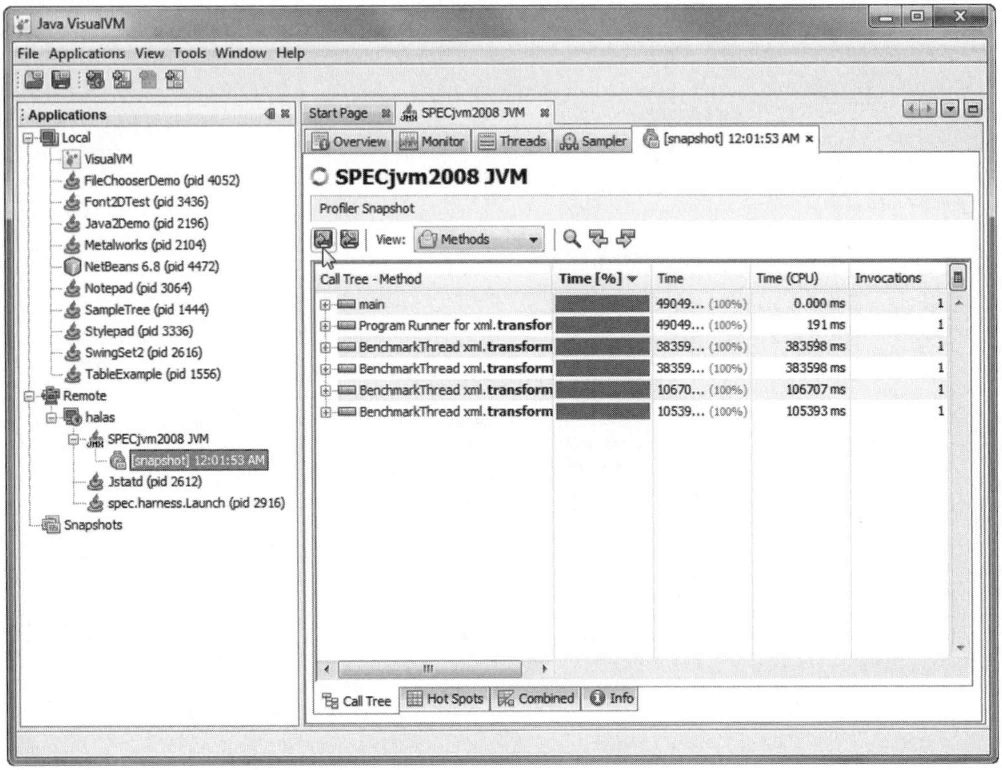

Figure 4-13 Saving a snapshot

VisualVM also has the capability to load binary heap dumps generated using jmap, JConsole, or upon reaching an OutOfMemoryError and using the -XX:+Heap DumpOnOutOfMemoryError HotSpot VM command line option. A binary heap dump is a snapshot of all the objects in the JVM heap at the time when the heap dump is taken. To generate a binary heap dump using the Java 6 jmap command, you use jmap -dump:format=b,file=<filename> <jvm pid> where <filename> is the path and filename of the binary heap dump file and <jvm pid> is the process id of the JVM running the application. For Java 5, you use jmap -heap:format=b <jvm pid> where <jvm pid> is the process id of the Java application. Java 5's jmap command places the heap dump in a file named heap.bin in the directory where the jmap command was executed. Java 6's JConsole can also generate a heap dump using its HotSpotDiagnostics MBean. Once a binary heap dump has been generated, it can be loaded in VisualVM using the File > Load menu where analysis can be performed.

VisualGC

VisualGC is a plug-in for VisualVM. VisualGC can monitor garbage collection, class loader, and JIT compilation activities. It was originally developed as a standalone GUI program. It can be used as both a standalone GUI or as a plug-in for VisualVM to monitor 1.4.2, Java 5, and Java 6 JVMs. When VisualGC was ported to a VisualVM plug-in some additional enhancements were made to make it easier to discover and connect to JVMs. The advantage of using the VisualGC plug-in over the standalone GUI is JVMs that are monitor-able are automatically discovered and displayed in VisualVM. With the standalone GUI, you have to identify the process id of the Java application you want to monitor and pass that as an argument to program launcher. The process id can be found using the jps command. An example use of the jps command is described in the previous section as part of the jstatd daemon configuration setup.

The VisualGC plug-in for VisualVM can be found in VisualVM's Plug-in Center. The Plug-in Center is accessed in VisualVM via the Tools > Plugins menu. The VisualGC plug-in can be found on the Available Plug-ins tab.

The standalone VisualGC GUI can be downloaded from http://java.sun.com/performance/jvmstat/#Download.

Regardless of whether you are using the VisualGC plug-in for VisualVM or the standalone VisualGC program, to monitor an application locally, both VisualGC and the application to be monitored must share the same user credentials. When monitoring a remote application, the jstatd daemon must be configured and running with the same user credentials as the Java application to be monitored. How to configure and run the jstatd daemon is described in the previous section.

Using the VisualGC plug-in for VisualVM is covered in this section since it is easier to use than the standalone GUI and VisualVM also offers other integrated monitoring capabilities.

After the VisualGC plug-in has been added to VisualVM, when you monitor an application listed in the Applications panel, an additional window tab is displayed in the right panel labeled VisualGC (see Figure 4-14).

VisualGC displays two or three panels depending on the garbage collector being used. When the throughput garbage collector is used, VisualGC shows two panels: the Spaces and Graphs panels. When the concurrent or serial garbage collector is

Figure 4-14 Additional VisualGC window tab

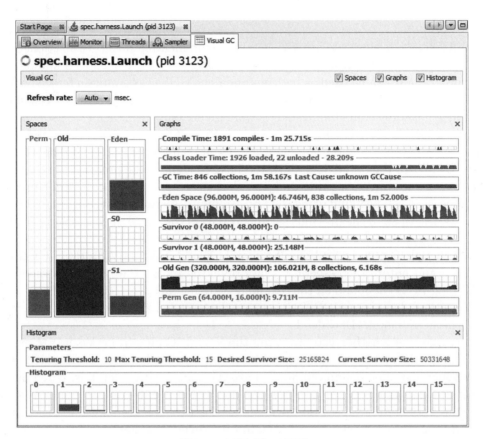

Figure 4-15 VisualGC

used a third panel is shown below the Spaces and Graphs panels called Histogram. Figure 4-15 shows VisualGC with all panel spaces.

Any of the three panels can be added or removed from the VisualGC window by selecting the appropriate check boxes in the upper-right corner.

The Spaces panel provides a graphical view of the garbage collection spaces and their space utilization. This panel is divided into three vertical sections, one for each of the garbage collection spaces: Perm (Permanent) space, Old (or Tenured) space, and the young generation space consisting of eden, and two survivor spaces, S0 and S1. The screen areas representing these garbage collection spaces are sized proportionately to the maximum capacities of the spaces as they are allocated by the JVM. Each space is filled with a unique color indicating the current utilization of the space relative to its maximum capacity. The unique color is also consistently used for each of the garbage collection spaces where they exist in both the Graphs and Histogram panels.

The memory management system within the HotSpot VM is capable of expanding and shrinking the garbage collected heap if the values set for -Xmx and -Xms differ. This is accomplished by reserving memory for the requested maximum Java heap size but committing real memory to only the amount currently needed. The relationship between committed and reserved memory is represented by the color of the background grid in each space. Uncommitted memory is represented by a lighter gray colored portion of the grid, whereas committed memory is represented by a darker gray colored portion. In many cases, the utilization of a space may be nearly identical to the committed amount of memory making it difficult to determine the exact transition point between committed and uncommitted space in the grid.

The relationship between the sizes of the eden and survivor spaces in the young generation portion of the Spaces panel is usually fixed in size. The two survivor spaces are usually identical in size and its memory space fully committed. The eden space may be only partially committed, especially earlier in an application's life cycle.

When the throughput garbage collector, enabled via -XX:+UseParallelGC or -XX:+UseParallelOldGC, is used along with the adaptive size policy feature, which is enabled by default, the relationship or ratio between the sizes of the young generation spaces can vary over time. When adaptive size policy is enabled, the sizes of the survivor spaces may not be identical and the space in young generation can be dynamically redistributed among the three spaces. In this configuration, the screen areas representing the survivor spaces and the colored region representing the utilization of the space are sized relative to the current size of the space, not the maximum size of the space. When the JVM adaptively resizes the young generation space, the screen area associated with the young generation spaces updates accordingly.

There are several things to watch for in the Spaces panel. For example, you should watch how quickly the eden space fills. Every fill and drop in the eden space represents a minor garbage collection. The rate of the fill and drop represents the minor garbage collection frequency. By watching the survivor spaces you can see how on each minor garbage collection one of the survivor spaces is occupied and the other is empty. This observation provides an understanding of how the garbage collector copies live objects from one survivor space to another at each minor garbage collection. More importantly, though, you should watch for survivor spaces overflowing. Survivor spaces overflowing can be identified by observing their occupancies at minor garbage collections. If you observe full or nearly full survivor spaces after each minor garbage collection and a growth in the space utilization in the Old generation space, survivor spaces may be overflowing. Generally, though, this observation is an indication that objects are being promoted from the young generation space to the old generation space. If they are promoted too early, or too quickly, it may result in an eventual full garbage collection. When a full garbage collection occurs, you observe the old generation space utilization drop. The frequency at which you observe a drop in the old generation space utilization is an indication of full garbage collection frequency.

The Graphs panel, shown previously in Figure 4-15, is the right panel of the VisualGC window. It plots performance statistics as a function of time for a historical view. This panel displays garbage collection statistics along with JIT compiler and class loader statistics. The latter two statistics are discussed later in this chapter. The resolution of the horizontal axis in each display is determined by the selected Refresh Rate, found just above the Spaces panel. Each sample in the Graphs panel historical view occupies 2 pixels of screen real estate. The height of each display depends on the statistic being plotted.

The Graphs panel has the following displays:

- **Compile Time.**   Discussed later in this chapter.

- **Class Loader Time.**   Discussed later in this chapter.

- **GC Time.**   Displays the amount of time spent in garbage collection activities. The height of this display is not scaled to any particular value. A nonzero value in this graph indicates that garbage collection activity occurred during the last interval. A narrow pulse indicates a relatively short duration, and a wide pulse indicates a long duration. The title bar indicates the total number of garbage collections and the accumulated garbage collection time since the start of the application. If the monitored JVM maintains the garbage collection cause and the last cause statistics, the cause of the most recent garbage collection is also displayed in the title bar.

- **Eden Space.**   Displays the utilization of the eden space over time. The height of this display is fixed, and by default the data is scaled according to the current capacity of the space. The current capacity of the space can change depending on the garbage collector being used as the space shrinks and grows over time. The title bar displays the name of the space and its maximum and current capacity in parentheses followed by the current utilization of the space. In addition, the title also contains the number and accumulated time of minor garbage collections.

- **Survivor 0 and Survivor 1.**   Displays the utilization of the two survivor spaces over time. The height of each of these two displays is fixed, and by default the data is scaled according to the current capacity of the corresponding space. The current capacity of these spaces can change over time depending on the garbage collector. The title bar displays the name of the space and its maximum and current capacity in parentheses followed by the current utilization of the space.

- **Old Gen.**   Displays the utilization of the old generation space over time. The height of the display is fixed, and by default the data is scaled according to the current capacity of the space. The current capacity of this space can change depending on the garbage collector. The title bar displays the name of the space and its maximum and current capacity in parentheses followed by the current utilization of the space. In addition, the title also contains the number and accumulated time of full garbage collections.

- **Perm Gen.** Displays the utilization of the permanent generation space over time. The height of the display is fixed, and by default the data is scaled according to the current capacity of the space. The current capacity of this space can change depending on the garbage collector. The title bar displays the name of the space and its maximum and current capacity in parentheses followed by the current utilization of the space.

The Histogram panel, shown previously in Figure 4-15, is displayed below the Spaces and Graphs panels when the concurrent or serial garbage collector is used. The throughput garbage collector does not maintain a survivor age since it uses a different mechanism for maintaining objects in the survivor spaces. As a result, the Histogram panel is not displayed when monitoring a JVM that is using the throughput collector.

The Histogram panel displays surviving object and object aging statistics. The Histogram panel contains a Parameters subpanel and a Histogram subpanel. The Parameters subpanel displays the current size of the survivor spaces and the parameters that control the promotion of objects from young to old generation space. After each minor garbage collection, if an object is still live, its age is incremented. If its age exceeds a tenuring threshold age, which is calculated by the JVM at each minor garbage collection, it is promoted to the old generation space. The tenuring threshold calculated by the JVM is displayed as the Tenuring Threshold in the Parameters panel. The maximum tenuring threshold displayed in the Parameters panel is the maximum age at which an object is held in survivor spaces. An object is promoted from young to old generation based on the tenuring threshold, not the maximum tenuring threshold.

Observing a frequent tenuring threshold less than maximum tenuring threshold is an indication objects are being promoted from young to old generation space too quickly. This is usually caused by survivor spaces overflowing. If a survivor space overflows, then objects with the highest ages are promoted to the old generation space until the utilization of the survivor space does not exceed the value displayed as the Desired Survivor Size in the Parameters panel. As mentioned earlier, survivor space overflow can cause old generation space to fill and result in a full garbage collection.

The Histogram subpanel displays a snapshot of the age distribution of objects in the active survivor space after the last minor garbage collection. If the monitored JVM is Java 5 Update 6 or later, this panel contains 16 identically sized regions, one for each possible object age. If the monitored JVM is earlier than Java 5 Update 6, there are 32 identically sized regions. Each region represents 100% of the active survivor space and is filled with a colored area that indicates the percentage of the survivor space occupied by objects of a given age.

As an application runs, you can observe long-lived objects traverse through each of the age regions. The larger the space occupied by long-lived objects, the larger the blip you will observe migrate through the age regions. When the tenuring threshold is less than the maximum tenuring threshold you see no utilization in the regions representing ages greater than the tenuring threshold since those objects have been promoted to the old generation space.

JIT Compiler

There are several ways to monitor HotSpot JIT compilation activity. Although the result of JIT compilation results in a faster running application, JIT compilation requires computing resources such as CPU cycles and memory to do its work. Hence, it is useful to observe JIT compiler behavior. Monitoring JIT compilation is also useful when you want to identify methods that are being optimized or in some cases deoptimized and reoptimized. A method can be deoptimized and reoptimized when the JIT compiler has made some initial assumptions in an optimization that later turned out to be incorrect. To address this scenario, the JIT compiler discards the previous optimization and reoptimizes the method based on the new information it has obtained.

To monitor the HotSpot JIT compiler, you can use the command line option `-XX:+PrintCompilation`. The `-XX:+PrintCompilation` command line option generates a line of output for every compilation performed. An example of this output is shown here:

```
    7          java.lang.String::indexOf (151 bytes)
    8% !       sun.awt.image.PNGImageDecoder::produceImage @ 960 (1920 bytes)
    9   !       sun.awt.image.PNGImageDecoder::produceImage (1920 bytes)
   10          java.lang.AbstractStringBuilder::append (40 bytes)
   11   n       java.lang.System::arraycopy (static)
   12 s        java.util.Hashtable::get (69 bytes)
   13   b       java.util.HashMap::indexFor (6 bytes)
   14    made zombie  java.awt.geom.Path2D$Iterator::isDone (20 bytes)
```

See Appendix A, "HotSpot VM Command Line Options of Interest," for a detailed description of the output from `-XX:+PrintCompilation`.

There are graphical tools that can monitor JIT compilation activity. However, they do not provide as much detail as the `-XX:+PrintCompilation`. At the time of this writing, JConsole, VisualVM, or the VisualGC plug-in for VisualVM do not provide information on which methods are being compiled by the JIT compiler. They only provide information that JIT compilation is taking place. Of the graphical tools,

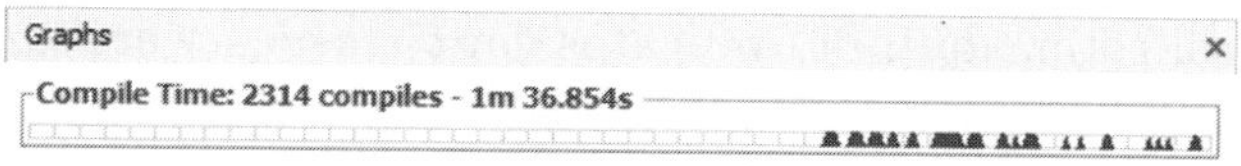

Figure 4-16 VisualGC's Graph window's compile time panel

VisualGC's Graph window's Compile Time panel, an example shown in Figure 4-16, may be the most useful since it shows pulses as JIT compilation activity occurs. It is easy to spot JIT compilation activity in VisualGC's Graphs panel.

The Compile Time display of VisualGC's Graphs panel shows the amount of time spent compiling. The height of the panel is not scaled to any particular value. A pulse in the display indicates JIT compilation activity. A narrow pulse implies a relatively short duration of activity, and a wide pulse implies a long duration of activity. Areas of the display where no pulse exists indicates no JIT compilation activity. The title bar of the display shows the total number of JIT compilation tasks and the accumulated amount of time spent performing compilation activity.

Class Loading

Many applications utilize user-defined class loaders, sometimes called custom class loaders. A JVM loads classes from class loaders and may also decide to unload classes. When classes are loaded or unloaded depends on the JVM runtime environment and the usage of class loaders. Monitoring class loading activity can be useful, especially with applications that utilize user-defined class loaders. As of this writing, the HotSpot VM loads all class metadata information in the permanent generation space. The permanent generation space is subject to garbage collection as its space becomes full. Hence, monitoring both class loading activity and permanent generation space utilization can be important to an application realizing its performance requirements. Garbage collection statistics indicate when classes are unloaded from the permanent generation space.

Unused classes are unloaded from the permanent generation space when additional space is required as a result of other classes needing to be loaded. To unload classes from permanent generation, a full garbage collection is required. Therefore, an application may suffer performance issues as a result of full garbage collections trying to make space available for additional classes to be loaded. The following output shows a full garbage collection where classes are unloaded.

```
[Full GC[Unloading class sun.reflect.GeneratedConstructorAccessor3]
[Unloading class sun.reflect.GeneratedConstructorAccessor8]
[Unloading class sun.reflect.GeneratedConstructorAccessor11]
[Unloading class sun.reflect.GeneratedConstructorAccessor6]
 8566K->5871K(193856K), 0.0989123 secs]
```

The garbage collection output indicates four classes were unloaded; `sun. reflect.GeneratedConstructorAccessor3`, `sun.reflect.Generated ConstructorAccessor8`, `sun.reflect.GeneratedConstructorAccessor11`, and `sun.reflect.GeneratedConstructorAccessor6`. The reporting of classes being unloaded during the full garbage collection provides evidence the permanent generation space may need to be sized larger, or its initial size may need to be larger. If you observe classes being unloaded during full garbage collections, you should use `-XX:PermSize` and `-XX:MaxPermSize` command line options to size the permanent generation space. To avoid full garbage collections that may expand or shrink the committed size of the permanent generation space, set `-XX:PermSize` and `-XX:MaxPermSize` to the same value. Note that if concurrent garbage collection of the permanent generation space is enabled, you may see classes being unloaded during a concurrent permanent generation garbage collection cycle. Since a concurrent permanent generation garbage collection cycle is not a stop-the-world garbage collection, the application does not realize the impact of a garbage collection induced pause. Concurrent permanent generation garbage collection can only be used with the mostly concurrent garbage collector, CMS.

> **Tip**
>
> Additional guidelines and tips for tuning the permanent generation space including how to enable concurrent garbage collection of the permanent generation space can be found in Chapter 7.

The graphical tools JConsole, VisualVM, and the VisualGC plug-in for VisualVM can monitor class loading. However, at the time of this writing, none of them display the class names of the classes being loaded or unloaded. The JConsole Classes tab, as shown in Figure 4-17, shows the number of classes currently loaded, number of classes unloaded, and total number of classes that have been loaded.

VisualVM can also monitor class loading activity in the Monitor tab via the Classes display. It shows total number of classes loaded and the number of shared classes loaded. Observing whether class data sharing is enabled on a monitored JVM can be confirmed by looking at this view. Class data sharing is a feature where classes are shared across JVMs running on the same system to reduce their memory footprint. If class sharing is being utilized by the monitored JVM, there will be a horizontal line in the graph showing the number of shared classes loaded in addition to a horizontal line showing the total number of classes loaded similar to what is shown in Figure 4-18.

You can also monitor class loading activity in the VisualGC Graph window by observing the Class Loader panel, as shown in Figure 4-19.

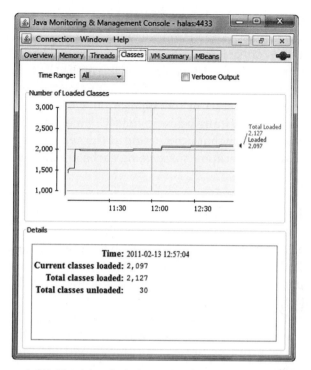

Figure 4-17 Total loaded classes and current loaded classes

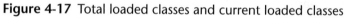

Figure 4-18 Observing class sharing in VisualVM

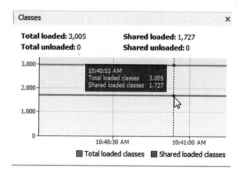

Figure 4-19 Observing class loading activity in VisualGC

In the VisualGC Graphs window, a pulse in the Class Loader panel indicates class loading or unloading activity. A narrow pulse indicates a short duration of class loading activity, and a wide pulse indicates a long duration of class loading activity. No pulse indicates no class loading activity. The title bar of the Class Loader panel shows the number of classes loaded, the number of classes unloaded, and the accumulated class loading time since the start of the application. Observing pulses in the class loader panel and directly vertically below in the GC Time panel can be an indication the garbage collection activity that is occurring at the same time could be the result of the JVM's permanent generation space being garbage collected.

Java Application Monitoring

Monitoring at the application level usually involves observing application logs that contain events of interest or instrumentation that provides some level of information about the application's performance. Some applications also build-in monitoring and management capabilities using MBeans via Java SE's monitoring and management APIs. These MBeans can be viewed and monitored using JMX compliant tools such as JConsole or using the VisualVM-MBeans plug-in within VisualVM. The VisualVM-MBeans plug-in can be found in the VisualVM plug-in center, via the Tools > Plugins menu.

The GlassFish Server Open Source Edition (also referred to as GlassFish hereafter) has a large number of attributes that can be monitored via MBeans. Using JConsole or VisualVM to monitor a GlassFish application server instance allows you to view the MBeans including their attributes and operations. Figure 4-20 shows a portion of the many GlassFish MBeans in the MBeans window in VisualVM using the VisualVM-MBeans plug-in.

You can see on the left the expanded list of GlassFish MBeans in the com.sun. appserv folder.

VisualVM can also be extended to monitor Java applications since it is built on the NetBeans Platform plug-in architecture. Plug-ins for VisualVM can be created as if they are NetBeans plug-ins. For example, a custom VisualVM plug-in to monitor a Java application can take advantage of the many rich features of NetBeans including its Visual Graph Library. Java applications that want to make available performance monitoring information can do so by developing a VisualVM plug-in. Several existing VisualVM plug-ins are available in Visual-VM's plug-in center.

Applications that have built JConsole plug-ins can use the VisualVM-JConsole plug-in to automatically integrate their custom JConsole plug-ins into VisualVM.

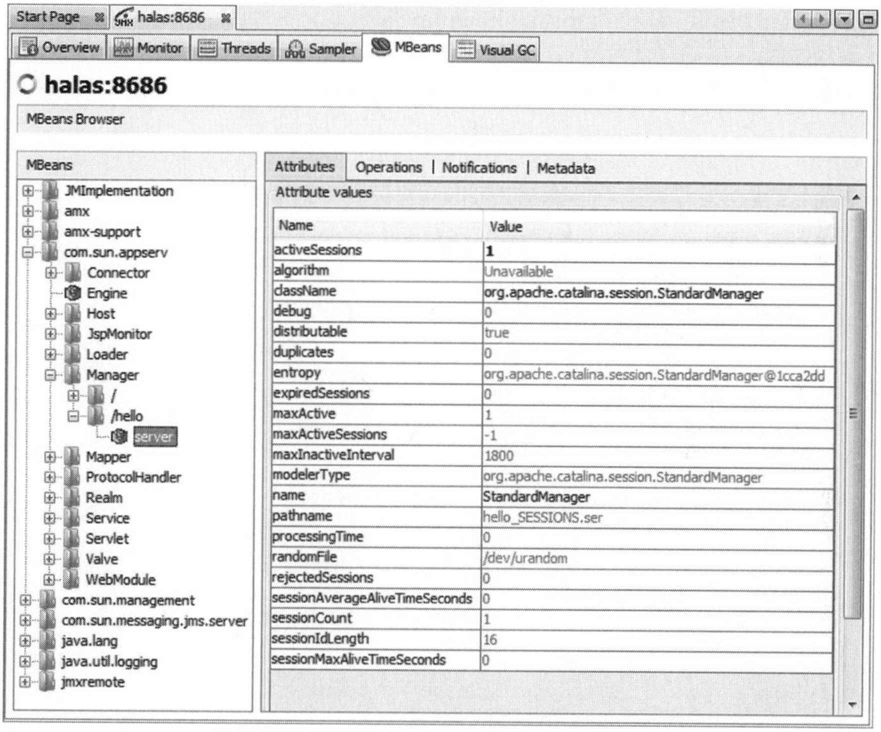

Figure 4-20 GlassFish MBeans

Quick Lock Contention Monitoring

A trick often used by the authors to get a quick sense of where lock contention is occurring in a Java application is to capture several thread dumps using the JDK's `jstack` command. This approach works well when operating in more of a monitoring role where the objective is to quickly capture some data rather than spending time to set up and configure a profiler where a more detailed analysis can be done.

The following `jstack` output is from an application that has a set of reader threads and writer threads that share a single queue. Work is placed on the queue by writer threads, and reader threads pull work from the queue.

Only the relevant stack traces are included to illustrate the usefulness of using `jstack` to rapidly find contended locks. In the `jstack` output the thread, `Read Thread-33`, has successfully acquired the shared queue lock, which is identified as a Queue object at address 0x22e88b10. This is highlighted in the output in bold as **`locked <0x22e88b10> (a Queue)`**.

All the other thread stack traces shown are waiting to lock the same lock held by the thread, Read Thread-33. This is highlighted in the other stack traces in bold as **waiting to lock <0x22e88b10> (a Queue)**.

```
"Read Thread-33" prio=6 tid=0x02b1d400 nid=0x5c0 runnable
[0x0424f000..0x0424fd94]
    java.lang.Thread.State: RUNNABLE
        at Queue.dequeue(Queue.java:69)
        - locked <0x22e88b10> (a Queue)
        at ReadThread.getWorkItemFromQueue(ReadThread.java:32)
        at ReadThread.run(ReadThread.java:23)

"Writer Thread-29" prio=6 tid=0x02b13c00 nid=0x3cc waiting for monitor
entry [0x03f7f000..0x03f7fd94]
    java.lang.Thread.State: BLOCKED (on object monitor)
        at Queue.enqueue(Queue.java:31)
        - waiting to lock <0x22e88b10> (a Queue)
        at WriteThread.putWorkItemOnQueue(WriteThread.java:54)
        at WriteThread.run(WriteThread.java:47)

"Writer Thread-26" prio=6 tid=0x02b0d400 nid=0x194 waiting for monitor
entry [0x03d9f000..0x03d9fc94]
    java.lang.Thread.State: BLOCKED (on object monitor)
        at Queue.enqueue(Queue.java:31)
        - waiting to lock <0x22e88b10> (a Queue)
        at WriteThread.putWorkItemOnQueue(WriteThread.java:54)
        at WriteThread.run(WriteThread.java:47)

"Read Thread-23" prio=6 tid=0x02b08000 nid=0xbf0 waiting for monitor entry
[0x03c0f000..0x03c0fb14]
    java.lang.Thread.State: BLOCKED (on object monitor)
        at Queue.dequeue(Queue.java:55)
        - waiting to lock <0x22e88b10> (a Queue)
        at ReadThread.getWorkItemFromQueue(ReadThread.java:32)
        at ReadThread.run(ReadThread.java:23)

"Writer Thread-24" prio=6 tid=0x02b09000 nid=0xef8 waiting for monitor
entry [0x03c5f000..0x03c5fa94]
    java.lang.Thread.State: BLOCKED (on object monitor)
        at Queue.enqueue(Queue.java:31)
        - waiting to lock <0x22e88b10> (a Queue)
        at WriteThread.putWorkItemOnQueue(WriteThread.java:54)
        at WriteThread.run(WriteThread.java:47)

"Writer Thread-20" prio=6 tid=0x02b00400 nid=0x19c waiting for monitor
entry [0x039df000..0x039dfa14]
    java.lang.Thread.State: BLOCKED (on object monitor)
        at Queue.enqueue(Queue.java:31)
        - waiting to lock <0x22e88b10> (a Queue)
        at WriteThread.putWorkItemOnQueue(WriteThread.java:54)
        at WriteThread.run(WriteThread.java:47)

"Read Thread-13" prio=6 tid=0x02af2400 nid=0x9ac waiting for monitor entry
[0x035cf000..0x035cfd14]
    java.lang.Thread.State: BLOCKED (on object monitor)
```

```
    at Queue.dequeue(Queue.java:55)
    - waiting to lock <0x22e88b10> (a Queue)
    at ReadThread.getWorkItemFromQueue(ReadThread.java:32)
    at ReadThread.run(ReadThread.java:23)

"Read Thread-96" prio=6 tid=0x047c4400 nid=0xaa4 waiting for monitor
entry [0x06baf000..0x06bafa94]
    java.lang.Thread.State: BLOCKED (on object monitor)
    at Queue.dequeue(Queue.java:55)
    - waiting to lock <0x22e88b10> (a Queue)
    at ReadThread.getWorkItemFromQueue(ReadThread.java:32)
    at ReadThread.run(ReadThread.java:23)
```

It is important to note the lock addresses, the hex number surrounded by < and >, are the same address. This is how locks are uniquely identified in jstack output. If lock addresses in the stack traces are different, they represent different locks. In other words, thread stack traces that have different lock addresses are threads that are not contending on the same lock.

The key to finding contended locks in jstack output is searching for the same lock address across multiple stack traces and finding threads that are waiting to acquire the same lock address. Observing multiple thread stack traces trying to lock the same lock address is an indication the application is experiencing lock contention. If capturing multiple jstack outputs yields similar results of observing lock contention on the same lock, it is stronger evidence of a highly contended lock in the application. Also notice that the stack trace provides the source code location of the contended lock. Being able to find the location in the source code of a highly contended lock in a Java application has historically been a difficult task. Using jstack in the manner described here can help significantly in tracking down contended locks in applications.

Bibliography

Monitoring and Management for the Java Platform. http://download.oracle.com/javase/1.5.0/docs/guide/management/.

Java SE Monitoring and Management Guide. http://download.oracle.com/javase/6/docs/technotes/guides/management/toc.html.

Connecting to JMX Agents Explicitly. http://download.oracle.com/javase/6/docs/technotes/guides/visualvm/jmx_connections.html.

VisualVM Features. https://visualvm.dev.java.net/features.html.

jvmstat 3.0 Web site. http://java.sun.com/performance/jvmstat.

Java Application Profiling

Chapter 2, "Operating System Performance Monitoring," made a clear distinction between the activities of performance monitoring, performance profiling, and performance tuning. Before jumping into the details of what is involved in performance profiling a Java application, it is worthy to revisit the performance profiling definition. Performance profiling is an activity of collecting performance data from an operating or running application that may be intrusive on application performance responsiveness or throughput. Performance profiling tends to be a reactive type of activity, or an activity in response to a stakeholder reporting a performance issue, and usually has a narrower focus than performance monitoring. Profiling is rarely done in production environments. Rather it is typically done in qualification, testing, or development environments and is often an act that follows a monitoring activity that indicates some kind of performance issue.

As suggested in Chapter 1, "Strategies, Approaches, and Methodologies," performance testing, including profiling, should be an integral part of the software development process. When performance testing is not an integral part of the software development process, profiling activities are usually performed as the result of a stakeholder complaining that performance of the application is not as he or she desires. For applications having a strong emphasis on meeting performance and scalability requirements, constructing prototypes of areas identified as being at performance risk and profiling them are ideally done early in the software development process to mitigate risk. This activity offers the opportunity to entertain alternative architectures, designs, or implementations at a stage where it is much less costly to make changes than later in the software development process.

In this chapter, the basic concepts of how to profile a Java application using a modern profiler are presented. Both method profiling and memory profiling, also known as heap profiling, are presented. Method profiling provides information about the execution time for Java methods in a Java application. The Oracle Solaris Studio Performance Analyzer (formerly known as the Sun Studio Performance Analyzer) is one of two method profilers presented in this chapter that can provide both Java and native method profile information. The Oracle Solaris Studio Performance Analyzer, often called the Performance Analyzer can also provide execution information about the internals of the Java Virtual Machine, which can help isolate potential issues observed in a Java Virtual Machine.

In contrast to method profiling, memory profiling provides information about a Java application's memory usage, that is, the number of object allocations, the size of object allocations, and which object allocations live, along with stack traces showing the method where the object allocation occurred.

Many capable profilers are available, both free and commercial, that can perform method profiling or memory profiling. This chapter shows how to use the free Oracle Solaris Studio Performance Analyzer and the free NetBeans Profiler.

Performance Analyzer offers several advanced capabilities. For example it profiles at the native level, which means it has the capability to collect accurate profiles. It also has the capability to distinguish the difference between a running thread and a paused or blocked thread. For example, it can tell the difference between when a thread is blocking on a `read()` system call versus blocking in a system call to `wait()`. As a result, Performance Analyzer reports `read()` operations as the amount of time actually spent doing a read operation and reports separately the amount time it spends blocking on a `read()`, in a call to `wait()`, waiting for more data to arrive. If it could not differentiate between those two operations and lumped both the blocked and waiting time together with the time spent in a `read()` operation it could lead to misleading information about how much time is really spent in a `read()` operation and how much time is spent blocking and waiting for more data to arrive.

The Performance Analyzer also has the capability to collect and report on Java monitor, or lock information. Monitor contention, or lock contention, is a scalability blocker for Java applications. Traditionally, tracking down and isolating hot Java monitor contention has been a difficult problem. As shown later in this chapter, the Performance Analyzer makes this task much easier. There is also an example use case shown in Chapter 6, "Java Application Profiling Tips and Tricks."

The Performance Analyzer is also easy to set up and use, as described in the next section, and can provide an enormous level of detailed information. However, one of the challenges with the Performance Analyzer is it is available on the Oracle Solaris (also referred to as Solaris hereafter) and Linux platforms only. It is not available on the Windows platform. Tools such as AMD's CodeAnalyst

Performance Analyzer and Intel's VTune could be used as alternatives on the Windows platform. They are similar tools with similar functionality as Performance Analyzer. The concepts with using a profiler such as Performance Analyzer apply to AMD's CodeAnalyst and Intel's VTune. Another good alternative to use on Windows is the NetBeans Profiler. NetBeans Profiler is also available for Solaris, Linux, and Mac OS X platforms. The NetBeans Profiler's method profiling capabilities are also covered in this chapter. In addition, memory profiling with the NetBeans Profiler is covered. Also included in this chapter is how to use the NetBeans Profiler to identify memory leaks in a Java application.

This chapter begins by presenting some profiling terminology, which should make the understanding of the tasks involved in profiling easier. The profiling terminology is followed by two major sections. The first major section describes how to use the Performance Analyzer for method profiling and isolating monitor or lock contention profiling. The second major section is followed by how to use the NetBeans Profiler for both method profiling and memory profiling along with how to use it to identify memory leaks. Chapter 6 illustrates some of the more commonly observed performance issues the book's authors have seen in Java applications.

Terminology

This section describes terms that are used throughout this chapter. Terms that are common to both the Performance Analyzer and NetBeans Profiler are described first, followed by terms specific to the Performance Analyzer and then terms specific to the NetBeans Profiler.

Common Profiling Terms

Common profiling terms include the following:

- **Profiler.** A tool that shows its users the behavior of an application as it executes. It may include both the behavior of the Java Virtual Machine and the application including both Java code and any native code.
- **Profile.** A file that contains information collected by a profiler while executing an application.
- **Overhead.** The amount of time spent by the profiler collecting the profile information instead of executing the application.
- **Call Tree.** A listing of methods in a call stack form illustrating the dynamic call stack of the program as it was run. When method profiling, looking at a call tree

can be useful when determining the hot use cases. When memory profiling, looking at a call tree can be useful to understand context of a Java object allocation.

- **Filter.**   An artifact that can be applied to either the collected profile or to the collecting of a profile that narrows the scope of information collected and/or presented.

Oracle Solaris Studio Performance Analyzer Terms

Oracle Solaris Studio Performance Analyzer terms include the following:

- **Experiment.**   An experiment or experiment file is the artifact produced by collecting a profile of an application using the Performance Analyzer. The Performance Analyzer uses the term *experiment* where many other profilers use the term *profile*.
- **collect.**   A command line tool used to collect an experiment or profile by profiling and tracing function usage. The data collected can include call stack information, microstate accounting information, Java monitor information, and hardware counter information.
- **Analyzer.**   A GUI used to view a collected experiment or experiment file.
- **er_print.**   A command line utility that can be used to view the collected experiment or experiment file. It can also be scripted to automate the processing of a collected experiment or experiment file.
- **Inclusive time.**   The amount of time taken to execute a method and all the methods it calls.
- **Exclusive time.**   The amount of time taken to execute a specific method. It does not include any time consumed by methods called by the specific method.
- **Attributed time.**   The amount of time attributed to a given method by a method that calls it or is a callee of.
- **Caller-Callee.**   A relationship of a method either being called by some method (a *caller*), or a method being called by some other method (a *callee*). The Analyzer GUI has a view that shows the *Caller-Callee* relationship of a given method.
- **System CPU.**   The amount of time, or percentage of elapsed time, a method listed in a collected experiment spends executing within the operating system kernel.
- **User CPU.**   The amount of time, or percentage of experiment elapsed time, a method listed in a collected experiment spends executing outside the operating system kernel.

NetBeans Profiler Terms

NetBeans Profiler terms include the following:

- **Instrumentation.** The insertion of counters, timers, and so on into the Java bytecode of an application to be profiled. The insertion of these counters, timers, and so on do not change the logic of an application and are removed once the profiling is terminated.
- **Heap.** The memory pool used by the Java Virtual Machine for all objects allocated in a Java application using the Java keyword *new*.
- **Garbage collection.** The operation responsible for the removal or cleaning of Java objects from the *Heap* that are no longer in use by the Java application. The Java Virtual Machine is responsible for the scheduling and executing of garbage collection.
- **Memory leak.** An object that is no longer in use by an application but cannot be *garbage collected* due to one or more Java objects holding a reference to it.
- **Self time.** The amount of time needed to execute the instructions in a method. This does not include the time spent in any other methods called by the method. Self time is analogous to the exclusive time in Oracle Solaris Studio Performance Analyzer terminology.
- **Hot spot.** A method that has a relatively large Self Time.
- **Root method.** A method selected for performance profiling.

Oracle Solaris Studio Performance Analyzer

This section covers how to use the Performance Analyzer to profile a Java application, in particular how to do method profiling and monitor profiling. The Performance Analyzer is a powerful tool. Its capabilities go well beyond profiling Java applications. It can also be used to profile C, C++, and Fortran based applications too. As mentioned earlier in this chapter, the Performance Analyzer can profile both Java code and native code. In addition, since it profiles at the native level, it can collect more accurate profiles. As a Java profiler, it is most useful as a method profiler and Java monitor/lock profiler.

> **Tip**
>
> The features of the Performance Analyzer that are most useful for method profiling Java applications are covered in this chapter. Additional features and capabilities of the Performance Analyzer can be found at the Performance Analyzer's product Web page: http://www.oracle.com/us/products/tools/050872.html.

As a method profiler, the Performance Analyzer can show the amount of time spent in user CPU, system CPU, contending for locks, and several others. However, the three categories of user CPU, system CPU, and lock contention are usually of most interest to Java applications. In addition, within each of those major categories, the collected data can be presented in either *inclusive* time or *exclusive* time. *Inclusive* time says that all the time reported includes not only the time the application spent in the selected method, but also all the methods it calls. In other words, *inclusive* time includes all the methods a selected method calls. In contrast, *exclusive* time includes only the amount of time it takes to execute the selected method. In other words, it excludes the time spent in any methods that the selected method calls.

The steps to profile a Java application with the Performance Analyzer are a little different from traditional Java profilers. When using the Performance Analyzer, there are two distinct steps to profiling. The first is collecting an experiment using the Performance Analyzer's `collect` command and executing the Java application. The second step, analysis, is viewing the collected experiment and analyzing its results with either the Performance Analyzer's Analyzer GUI tool, or using the Performance Analyzer's command line tool `er_print`.

Supported Platforms

The Performance Analyzer can profile Java applications running a Java Virtual Machine that supports the JVMTI (JVM Tool Interface). Java 5 Update 4 and later, including all Java 6 updates, support JVMTI.

> **Tip**
>
> Java 6 Update 18 and later JDKs include enhancements that provide additional information to the Performance Analyzer, which further enhances the view of the collected data.

Since the Performance Analyzer contains native code and can also profile native code, it is platform specific. The supported platforms are

- **Solaris SPARC.** Performance Analyzer 12.2 version is supported on Solaris 10 1/06 and later updates of Solaris 10 along with Solaris 11 Express. It also supports all UltraSPARC based systems and Fujitsu SPARC 64 based systems.
- **Solaris x86/x64.** Performance Analyzer 12.2 version is supported on Solaris 10 1/06 and later updates of Solaris 10 along with Solaris 11 Express.
- **Linux x86/x64.** Performance Analyzer 12.2 version is supported on SuSE Linux Enterprise Server 11, Red Hat Enterprise Linux 5, and Oracle Enterprise Linux 5.

Before using the Performance Analyzer, you should also check the Performance Analyzer documentation system requirements for the operating system versions supported and required patches. These may vary depending on the version of the Performance Analyzer. Running the Performance Analyzer's `collect` command with no arguments checks whether the platform you are running on is supported and has the required patches. Any missing required patches are reported in the output. In addition, if a valid JDK distribution is not found on the system, it too is reported.

If the Java application you want to method profile runs on a platform not listed as supported for the Performance Analyzer, you may consider running the Java application on one of the supported operating systems platforms as an alternative. Another alternative is using the NetBeans Profiler as a method profiler. One of the advantages of using the Performance Analyzer is that its intrusiveness on the Java application's performance tends be less than other Java profilers.

Downloading and Installing Oracle Solaris Studio Performance Analyzer

There are several ways to download and install the Performance Analyzer. As of this writing, the home page for the Performance Analyzer is http://www.oracle.com/technetwork/server-storage/solarisstudio/overview/index.html.

At the preceding URL, the latest version of the Performance Analyzer can be downloaded and installed for any of the supported platforms. The Performance Analyzer is a free download.

There are two different types of installation bundles for the Performance Analyzer: a package installer or tar file installer. The package installer installs the Performance Analyzer as either Solaris or Linux packages. This type of installation requires root access to the system where the Performance Analyzer is to be installed. The package installer also provides the ability for the installation to be patched. There is also a support contract option available with this type of installer. In contrast, the tar file installer does not require root access to install the Performance Analyzer. However, it is not eligible for patches or a support contract. But there is community support available through the Performance Analyzer forums, which at the time of this writing can be found at http://www.oracle.com/technetwork/server-storage/solarisstudio/community/index.html.

Tip

A large amount of detailed information is available at the Oracle Solaris Studio home page (http://www.oracle.com/technetwork/server-storage/solarisstudio/overview/index.html), including many demos, tutorials, screencasts, detailed documentation, and FAQs.

The version of the Performance Analyzer covered in this chapter is Oracle Solaris Studio Performance Analyzer 12.2 (also known as Oracle Solaris Studio 12.2). Earlier versions may have slightly different screenshots and menus than those illustrated in this chapter. Many of these differences are identified. In addition, many of the general concepts of how to use the Performance Analyzer apply to other profilers.

Capturing a Profile Experiment with Oracle Solaris Studio Performance Analyzer

As mentioned earlier, profiling with the Performance Analyzer is a two-step process. The first step is collecting the experiment, which is described in this section. The second step is viewing and analyzing the collected experiment, which is described in the following section.

One of the advantages of using the Performance Analyzer is the ease at which it can collect an experiment profile. In its simplest form, collecting an experiment profile is as easy as prefixing `collect -j` on to the java command line used to launch a Java application. The `collect` command is the Performance Analyzer command that collects the experiment profile.

Here are the general steps to collect a profile experiment.

1. Update the `PATH` environment variable to include the Performance Analyzer tools, that is, include the `bin` subdirectory of the directory where the Performance Analyzer is installed.

2. Prefix the text `collect -j` on to the Java command line used to launch the Java application you want to profile. If the Java application is launched from a script, you can update or modify the script.

3. Run the Java application and allow the Performance Analyzer `collect` command to profile the application and produce an experiment profile. By default, the experiment profile is placed in a file called test.1.er in the directory where the Java application is launched. The number in test.1.er name is incremented with each subsequent invocation of the `collect` command. Hence, if the `collect` command finds a test.1.er experiment file already exists, the `collect` command creates a new experiment file with the name test.2.er.

`Collect` Command Line Options

Many additional options may be of interest to pass to the Performance Analyzer `collect` command. Here are some that may be of particular interest when profiling Java applications:

- `-o <experiment file name>`
  When used, this option creates an experiment file name with the name specified after the `-o`.

- `-d <experiment directory path>`
  When used, this option puts the experiment file in the directory specified as experiment directory path. If `-d <experiment directory path>` is not used, the directory where the `collect` command is launched is the default directory used as the location where the experiment file is placed. Note, in a networked file system environment, it is advantageous to use a local directory/file system as the location to place the experiment to avoid unnecessary high network file system activity.

- `-p <option>`
  By default, when profiling Java applications, clock-based profiling is used with a profiling interval of approximately 10 milliseconds. This is equivalent to specifying `-p on`. In situations where it is desirable to reduce the size of the collected experiment file, using `-p lo` reduces the profiling interval to approximately 100 milliseconds. A `-p hi` can be used in situations where the profiling window of interest is small and more frequent profiling data collection is desired. Realize though, the more frequent the profiling data is collected, the larger the experiment file. This not only consumes additional file system space, it can also increase the time it takes to view the experiment file with the Analyzer GUI or command line `er_print`. A `-p <value>`, where `<value>` is a positive integer, can also be used to specify the profiling interval. The default setting for `-p`, `-p on`, tends to work well for most Java applications. There is no need to tweak the profiling interval using the `-p` option unless there is a need for a smaller experiment file, or a higher frequency of profiling data collection is needed.

- `-A <option>`
  When used, this option controls whether artifacts used by the target Java application and Java Virtual Machine should be archived or copied into the recorded experiment. The default value for `<option>` is on, which means the artifacts are archived into the experiment file. Other options include `off`, which means the artifacts are not archived into the experiment file. The other option, `copy`, means to both copy and archive the artifacts into the experiment file. If you plan to copy or read a collected experiment on a different machine than the one where the experiment was collected, you should use `-A copy`. However, keep in mind that the system where you copy or read the experiment is expected to have any source files or objects files used by the Java application to be accessible when you read and analyze the experiment.

- `-y <signal>`
  When used, this option provides the ability to control the recording of data with a `<signal>`. Whenever the signal is delivered to the collect process, the collecting of data is toggled, either from paused (no data collected) to recording, or recording to paused. When this option is used, the Java application is launched in a paused (no data collected) state and the first sending of the `<signal>` to the collect process toggles on the collecting of data. A `collect -j on -y SIGUSR2 ...` allows you the ability to send the collect process a `SIGUSR2` signal (i.e., `kill -USR2 <collect process id>`) to toggle on the collecting of experiment data and likewise toggle it off on a subsequent `SIGUSR2` signal being sent to the collect process.

- `-h <cpu counter>`
  This option is an advanced option that may not be useful for all Java application developers. But it deserves mentioning since it can be useful for computing bound Java applications whose stakeholders are looking for every bit of performance they can get. The `-h` option allows for the ability to collect CPU counters and associate them with the source code being

executed by the application. Having this ability can help isolate methods that incur costly operations, such as Java object field accesses that incur the most CPU cache misses. When a CPU cache miss occurs, there is an access to some data, possibly an access to a Java object's field, in the application that does not currently reside in the CPU cache. As a result, that data has been fetched from memory and placed in the CPU cache. It generally takes hundreds of CPU clock cycles to satisfy CPU cache misses. In addition, CPU utilization reported by modern operating systems report a CPU as being busy even when a CPU cache miss occurs. Realize that no work is actually being done in the application until the CPU cache miss is satisfied even though the operating system is reporting the CPU as being busy. Hence, for Java applications that are compute bound and are seeking additional performance, collecting CPU cache miss data with a profiler and being able to observe a Java object field or variable access that is contributing the most CPU cache misses can be crucial to improving performance of the application. There are times when alternative implementations of a Java object field access producing the most CPU cache misses can reduce CPU cache misses and improve the Java application's performance. However, it is wise to not use this command line option unless you have an application that is compute bound. In other words, it is wise to focus first on strategies such as improving application algorithms, implementations of Java application methods and reducing the amount of system CPU utilization as much as possible prior to venturing down the path of reducing CPU cache misses. This option also tends to be used by advanced Java users and a performance specialist. The -h option is also not limited to associating CPU cache misses to Java object field accesses. It can also be used with other CPU counters such as TLB (translation look-aside buffer) misses and instruction count. A full list of CPU counters that can be specified with the -h option on a platform running the application can be obtained by running the `collect` command with no arguments. Whatever the CPU counter specified with the -h option, so long as it is supported on the hardware platform where the Performance Analyzer is being used, the Performance Analyzer will associate the CPU counter events with the source code, Java or native, that generated the CPU counter event.

To use the -h `<cpu counter>` option, you specify the CPU hardware counter name after the -h. Multiple CPU counters can be profiled at the same time by comma separating the list of CPU counters. Depending on the processor, the number of CPU counters that can be specified may vary from as few as two to as many as five. As an example, to collect profile information on data loads that miss both the L1 and L2 cache on a Sun SPARC Enterprise T5120, you would specify -h `DC_miss/0,L2_dmiss_ld/1,10003` as an option to the `collect` command. As mentioned earlier, identifying the syntax of what to specify with the -h option for a CPU counter can be shown by running the collect command with no options and looking at the `Raw HW counters available for profiling` section of the output.

To illustrate how to use the Performance Analyzer to collect an experiment, suppose the task at hand is to capture a method profile of the SPECjbb2005 benchmark. For simplicity, suppose the SPECjbb2005 benchmark is launched by executing the following command line:

```
$  java -Xmx1g -cp SPECjbb2005.jar spec.jbb.Main
```

Collecting a Performance Analyzer experiment is as simple as prefixing `collect -j` on to the preceding command line (assuming you have updated your PATH environment variable to include the Performance Analyzer `bin` subdirectory):

```
$  collect -j on java -Xmx1g -cp SPECjbb2005.jar spec.jbb.Main
Creating experiment database test.1.er ...
```

The result of executing the preceding command, as the output suggests, since there is no explicit `-d` or `-o` Performance Analyzer command line option specified, an experiment file called test.1er is created in the directory where the preceding command is launched. If the `-o` and/or `-d` command line options are specified, the output from executing the command is updated to reflect the name of the experiment and the directory where the experiment is stored. Consider the following command line:

```
$  collect -j on -d /tmp -o specjbb2005.er \
    java -Xmx1g -cp SPECjbb2005.jar spec.jbb.Main
Creating experiment database /tmp/specjbb2005.er ...
```

Notice the output from the command communicates the directory where the experiment is stored and the name given to the experiment.

For some profiling tasks it is advantageous to direct the Performance Analyzer's `collect` command to not gather profiling information until a desired moment in time. This is often the case when an application has a lengthy startup or initialization phase and later has a load test run against it. In this scenario, you want to enable the collecting of profiling information at the time when the load test commences so the resulting experiment profile does not include data from the startup or initialization phase. This is accomplished using the `collect` command's `-y` option and specifying a signal for the `collect` command to listen to that toggles on and off the collecting of profile data. The `-y` option requires an operating system signal name as an argument. A commonly used operating system signal name for this purpose is `SIGUSR2`. Hence, in the scenario described here you use the `-y` option using `SIGUSR2` as the signal to toggle on and off profiling collection. For example, the `collect` command line would look like this:

```
$  collect -j on -y SIGUSR2 \
    java -Xmx1g -cp SPECjbb2005.jar spec.jbb.Main
Creating experiment database test.1.er ...
```

In this usage of the `collect` command, the Java application is launched in a paused (no data collected but application executing) state. In a separate command line window, the process id of the Java process running with `collect` must be gathered. Then the Java process running with `collect`, upon receiving a SIGUSR2 signal, toggles on the collecting of profile data. Java process id running with `collect` is accomplished using the `ps -ef | grep Xruncollector` command on Solaris or Linux, or alternatively using the `ps aux | grep Xruncollector`. The `collect` command does some initial work including adding the `-Xruncollector` command line option to the set of JVM command line options used to run the application and then the collect process exits. But the Java process continues to run with the additional `-Xruncollector` command line option. Hence, the reason for finding the Java process with a `-Xruncollector` command line option in the `ps` command output.

Sending a SIGUSR2 signal to the Java process id running with `-Xrun collector` is done on Solaris by issuing a `kill -USR2 <Java process id>` command, or on Linux by issuing a `kill -SIGUSR2 <Java process id>`. A subsequent issuing of the `kill -USR2 <Java process id>` command on Solaris or a `kill -SIGUSR2 <Java process id>` on Linux toggles off profile data collection. If this sounds too complex for your liking, you can collect the profile experiment without using the collect – y command line option and use the filtering capability in the Performance Analyzer GUI to narrow the time period of interest in the collected profile data. Filtering is also available using the command line `er_print` utility. Both the Performance Analyzer GUI and command line `er_print` utility are covered in the next several sections of this chapter.

Viewing the Collected Profile Experiment

As mentioned earlier, there are two distinct steps involved in doing method profiling using the Performance Analyzer. The first is collecting the experiment profile, which is described in the previous section, and the second is viewing the data collected in the experiment file, presented in this section.

There are two ways to view the collected data in the experiment file. One way is using the GUI, called the Analyzer, and the second way is using a command line tool called `er_print`. The Analyzer GUI approach is described first and then `er_print`. Many of the concepts presented in the Analyzer approach apply to the `er_print` approach.

Loading an experiment in the Analyzer is as simple as updating the PATH environment variable to include the Performance Analyzer `bin` directory and executing the following command:

```
$ analyzer
```

The Analyzer can also be launched with the name of the experiment to load. Assuming an experiment named test.1.er, the Analyzer loads the test.1.er experiment automatically by executing the following command:

```
$ analyzer test.1.er
```

If the Analyzer is launched without an optional experiment name, the Analyzer GUI opens a window prompting the user to select an experiment to load as shown in Figure 5-1.

The default view of the Analyzer once it has loaded a profile experiment file is shown in Figure 5-2. The Analyzer by default reports both exclusive and inclusive user CPU utilization metrics. User CPU utilization is a measure of CPU time spent executing outside system or kernel calls. The Analyzer can be configured to display many additional performance metrics. How to display additional metrics is presented later in this chapter in the "Data Presentation" section.

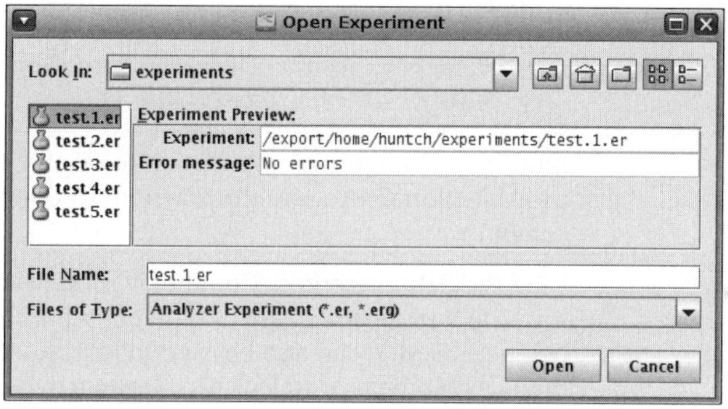

Figure 5-1 Analyzer Open Experiment

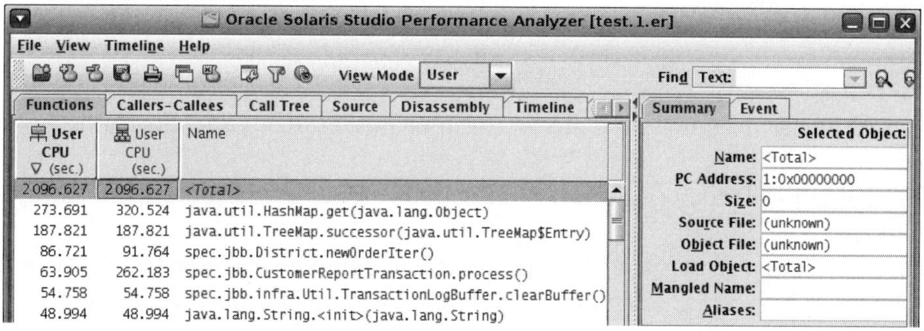

Figure 5-2 Analyzer default view

Table 5-1 Analyzer Toolbar

Icon	Description
	Open an experiment file.
	Combine an experiment's data to an existing experiment already loaded. Seldom used for Java application profiling or analysis.
	Drop an experiment's results from the experiments already loaded. Seldom used for Java application profiling or analysis.
	Collect an experiment. It tends to be easier to collect an experiment using the `collect-j` on command line than this route.
	Print the listing of data currently displayed in the Analyzer to either a file or printer. Useful when wanting a printout of the information displayed in the Analyzer.
	Create a new Analyzer window with the same experiment file loaded in both windows. If no experiment file is currently loaded, a new Analyzer window is displayed with no experiment loaded.
	Close and exit the Analyzer GUI program.
	Modify the category of information to display. Very commonly used functionality to also show System CPU and lock contention columns.
	Filter the data presented. Commonly used when wanting to focus on a particular phase or time period of the application being profiled. It can also be used to look at a subset of threads in the experiment or to look at a subtree in the call graph.
	Show and/or hide APIs or methods from logical areas. Can be useful when wanting to ignore core Java SE classes, Java HotSpot VM methods, etc.
View Mode User ▼	Switches to alternative viewing modes: User, Expert, and Machine.

The Analyzer does not save any state information about the current view prior to exit.

See Table 5-1 for an explanation of the shortcuts available on the Analyzer's toolbar.

There are two tabs on the right panel of the default Analyzer GUI view, shown previously in Figure 5-2, a Summary tab and Event tab. Information found on the Summary and Event tabs on the right panel are described in Table 5-2.

Table 5-2 Summary and Event Tab Information

Tab Name	Description
Summary	Shows all the recorded metrics for the selected object, both as values and percentages, and information on the selected object. The selected object could be a Java method, a line of source code, or a program counter. The information in the Summary tab is updated any time a new Java method, line of source code, or program counter is selected.
Event	Shows the available data for the selected Java method, source code line, or program counter, including the event type, method name, LWP Id, thread Id, and CPU Id.

| Functions | Callers-Callees | Call Tree | Source | Disassembly | Timeline | Experiments |

Figure 5-3 Analyzer left panel tabs

There are several tabs in the left panel of the default view in the Analyzer GUI. The Functions tab, as shown in Figure 5-3, is considered the "home" tab where most of your analysis work commences. The default view for the Functions tab lists inclusive and exclusive User CPU columns for Java methods in the Java application and orders the list of methods in decreasing order of exclusive User CPU time. The definitions of "exclusive" and "inclusive" terms are provided in the "Oracle Solaris Studio Performance Analyzer Terms" section earlier in the chapter. The additional tabs, shown in Figure 5-3, are described in Table 5-3.

Of the tabs in the left panel, the ones expected to be the most useful and get the most use while analyzing Java method profile experiments are Functions, Call Tree, Callers-Callees, Source, and Disassembly.

Usually the best place to start with the analysis of the experiment is using the Call Tree tab. The Call Tree tab shows the hierarchy of calls where an application spends its time. This view offers the ability to quickly recognize at a high level and in what use case(s) an application spends most of its time. Modifications made at the highest level, often a change in an algorithm, offers the biggest return in performance improvement. Although focusing on those methods that the profiles reports take the most amount of time and making implementation changes to those methods makes a certain amount of sense, stepping back at a higher level and changing the algorithm, data structures, or design will generally offer a greater performance improvement. Hence, it is useful to gain an understanding of the general operations taking the most time before focusing on the amount of time a method consumes.

The time and percent shown at each node in the Call Tree is the cumulative time spent both in the method represented by the node and everything it calls. For

Table 5-3 Tab Names

Tab Name	Description
Functions	Shows a list of methods, or functions, and their metrics, i.e., CPU utilization, lock contention, etc., that have been selected to be shown via the Metrics tab using the View > Set Data Presentation menu. The Functions tab can display inclusive metrics and exclusive metrics.
Callers-Callees	Shows the selected method, or function, from the Functions tab, in a pane in the center, with callers of that selected method or function in a pane above it, and the callees of that method or function in a pane below it.
Call Tree*	Shows the dynamic call graph of the program as a tree. Each node in the tree can be expanded or contracted.
Source	Shows the source file that contains the selected method or function, from the Functions tab, source line, or instruction. Each line in the source file for which instructions have been generated is annotated with performance metrics.
Disassembly	Shows a disassembly listing for the Java class file in either bytecode form or machine level assembly language that contains the selected method, source line, or instruction.
Timeline	Shows a chart of events as a function of time.
Experiments	The Experiments tab is divided into two panels. The top panel contains a tree that includes nodes for the artifacts in all the loaded experiments, and for each experiment loaded. The Load Objects node, a list of all load objects, is displayed with various messages about their processing. Load objects are any artifact such as Java classes, native libraries, etc., for which there is collected profile data in the experiment. The Notes area displays the contents of any notes file in the experiment. The Info area contains information about the experiments collected and the load objects accessed by the collection target, including any error messages or warning messages generated during the processing of the experiment or the load objects.

* This tab is new in Oracle Solaris Studio version 12.2.

example, in Figure 5-4, the top node, <Total>, represents the total time and percent consumed, that is, 100%. As each node underneath the <Total> node is expanded, the amount of time and percent of time reported at each node represents the cumulative time spent in that method and the methods it calls.

Expanding the nodes in the Call Tree that have the highest reported time and walking down the call traces is a good approach to identify where an application spends most of its time. For example, Figure 5-4 has nodes expanded to show 93% of the application's time is spent in a method called `spec.jbb.TransactionManager.runTxn()`. Not too surprising, it appears this application spends most of its time executing transactions.

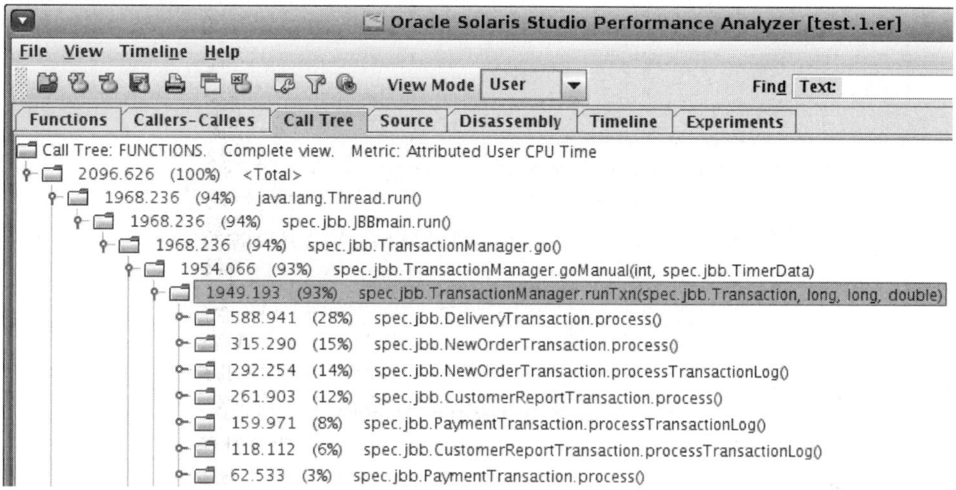

Figure 5-4 Call Tree

It also provides a good sense of the transactions or the operations of a transaction it spends the most time executing.

This call tree suggests the biggest gains in performance can be realized by improving the performance of the use case executed by `DeliveryTransaction.process()` and the use case of what appears to be a new order transaction, the logic executed by `NewOrderTransaction.process()` and `NewOrderTransaction.processTransactionLog()`. The logic in `NewOrderTransaction.process()` and `NewOrderTransaction.processTransactionLog()` account for 29% of the application time, and `DeliveryTransaction.process()` accounts for 28%. Therefore, changes to the algorithms or data structures in the use cases implemented by those three methods have the biggest impact on improving the performance of this application.

It's worth pointing out that the Call Tree view is synchronized with the Functions tab, Callers-Callees tab, Source tab, and Disassembly tab. When a node is selected in the Call Tree, a switch to any of the other tabs results in an updated view with the selected method shown. For example, if the `spec.jbb.TransactionManager.runTxn()` node is selected in the Call-Tree and the view is switched to the Callers-Callees tab, the Callers-Callee view is shown with focus on the `spec.jbb.TransactionManager.runTxn()` method. Maintaining the selected method across the different views allows you to remain focused on a particular method of interest.

Another approach, and also complementary to using the Call Tree, is to analyze the experiment using the Functions tab and identifying the hottest methods in the application. This approach focuses more on improving the implementation of a specific method. Hence, its focus tends to be more narrow than the approach of using the Call Tree.

Figure 5-5 Callers-Callee

The Functions tab shows a list of methods and their metrics (refer to Figure 5-2 for an example showing the Functions tab). As mentioned earlier, by default, the Analyzer shows the inclusive and exclusive user CPU utilization metrics. Exclusive metrics report the amount of time spent in a method and do not include any time consumed by methods it calls. In contrast, inclusive metrics report the time taken to execute a method and all the methods it calls. The displayed metrics can be changed through the View > Set Data Presentation menu. Changing the displayed metrics is described in the next section. The data displayed in the Functions tab can also be sorted by a metric column. By default, the data is sorted by exclusive user CPU utilization in descending order. When the Analyzer is configured to show multiple metrics, clicking on a different metric column changes the sort order. Methods at the top are the hottest methods for the sorted metric.

When a method is selected in the Functions list and the Callers-Callees tab is clicked on, a listing of the methods that call the selected method, "Callers," and a listing of methods that are called by the selected method, "Callees," are shown. An example view of the Callers-Callees tab is shown in Figure 5-5.

The Callers-Callees tab shows the selected method in the center panel, with callers of that method in a panel above it, and callees of that method in a panel below it. You can add callers and callees to the center panel to construct a call stack fragment as the center function. Metrics will be computed for the entire fragment. You can also set a function as the head, center, or tail of the call stack. The center panel also includes navigation buttons that let you go forward and backward in the call stack history. These are the arrow icons on the left part of the center panel.

Attributed metrics are shown in each panel. For the selected method, the attributed metric represents the exclusive metric for that method. In other words, the time spent to execute the selected method. It does not include any time spent in methods it calls. For the callees, the attributed metric represents the portion of the callee's inclusive metric that is attributable to calls from the center method. In other words, the callee's attributed metric is the amount of time the center method spent calling the callee including all the methods the callee invokes. Notice that the sum of attributed metrics for the callees and the selected method add up to the inclusive metric for the center method (not to be confused with the selected method's exclusive metric, which is shown in the center panel).

For the callers, the attributed metrics represent the portion of the selected method's inclusive metric that is attributable to calls from the callers. In other words, the attributed metric represents the time spent calling the center method including all the methods it invokes. Again, notice the sum of the attributed metrics for all callers also adds up to the inclusive metric for the selected method (again, not be confused with the selected method's exclusive metric, which is shown in the center panel).

The callers list and the callees list are sorted by a metric. If more than one column is displayed in the Callers-Callees tab, you can select the sort column by clicking on the column header. The sort column header is always displayed in bold. Also note that changing the sort metric in the Callers-Callees view changes the sort metric in the Functions tab.

The way to interpret the information shown in Figure 5-5 is as follows:

- `TransactionLogBuffer.putDollars()` and its callees contribute 45.462 User CPU seconds to the execution of the calling method `NewOrderTransaction.processTransactionLog()`.

- `TransactionLogBuffer.putDollars()` and its callees contribute 6.735 User CPU seconds to the execution of `PaymentTransaction.processTransactionLog()`.

- `TransactionLogBuffer.putDollars()` and its callees contribute 5.114 User CPU seconds to the execution of `CustomerReportTransaction.processTransactionLog()`.

- `TransactionLogBuffer.putDollars()` and its callees contribute 1.221 User CPU seconds to the execution of `OrderStatusTransaction.processTransactionLog()`.

- 10.557 User CPU seconds were spent invoking only the `TransactionLogBuffer.putDollars()` method, not including any of the methods it calls.

- `BigDecimal.toString()` and the methods it invokes contribute 29.861 User CPU seconds to `TransactionLogBuffer.putDollars()` inclusive metric.

- Similarly for `TransactionLogBuffer.putText()`, `BigDecimal.layoutChars()`, `BigDecimal.signum()`, and `String.length()`.

The Functions tab and the Callers-Callees tab can be used together by navigating through a collected experiment in the Functions tab, searching for high metric values such as User CPU, and then selecting a method of interest and clicking on the Callers-Callees tab to find out how much time is attributed to the method that has been selected.

A new feature added to the Callers-Callee tab in Performance Analyzer 12.2 allows you to build a call stack around a method of interest and see the attributed time spent in that call stack. In previous versions of Performance Analyzer, when you moved up and down the call stack, the amount of attributed time adjusted based on the method in the center of the Callers-Callees view.

To illustrate the usefulness of this new feature, consider `System.array-copy()` as being a hot method in an experiment with a value of 100 for both its inclusive and exclusive metric. Since both inclusive and exclusive metrics have the same value, it is a leaf method call, that is, no other method is called by `System.arraycopy()`. Suppose you analyze the callers of `System.arraycopy()` and observe all its use came from the `String(char[] value)` constructor. If you move `String(char[] value)` to the center to evaluate its callers, you will be analyzing `String(char[] value)`'s inclusive time. Suppose its inclusive time is 200. That 200 also includes time spent calling `System.array-copy()`, which is 100. Now, you analyze the callers of `String(char[] value)` and find there are many callers of it. As you put each of those methods that call `String(char[] value)` in the center, you find it hard to determine how much of the inclusive time from that method is actually spent in `System.array-copy()`. With Oracle Solaris Studio 12.2 you can view how much time is spent in `System.arraycopy()` for each of the call stacks that eventually call `System.arraycopy()`.

To find the amount of time a call stack spends in a given method within a call stack, you can use the Set Center button to focus on that method. Then by selecting one of the Callers and clicking the Add button, you can see in the center panel how much time is attributed to that call stack for those methods. You can similarly add Callees to the center panel too. Adding more Callers or Callees to the center panel gives you the ability to easily move up and down a call stack and easily correlate the amount of time spent in a particular method in the call stack.

To put this feature to work using the example in Figure 5-5, suppose you wanted to isolate the call stack of `PaymentTransaction.processTransactionLog()` from other callers for `TransactionLogBuffer.putDollars()`. To do this, you select and add the `PaymentTransactionLog.processTransactionLog()` to the center. The resulting view is shown in Figure 5-6.

You can see attributed metrics for `TransactionLogBuffer.putDollars()` and its callers have all been updated to reflect their attributed metrics for the call stack that isolates the `PaymentTransaction.processTransactionLog()` method from the other callers for `TransactionLogBuffer.putDollars()`. Also updated is the caller of the `PaymentTransaction.processTransactionLog()`.

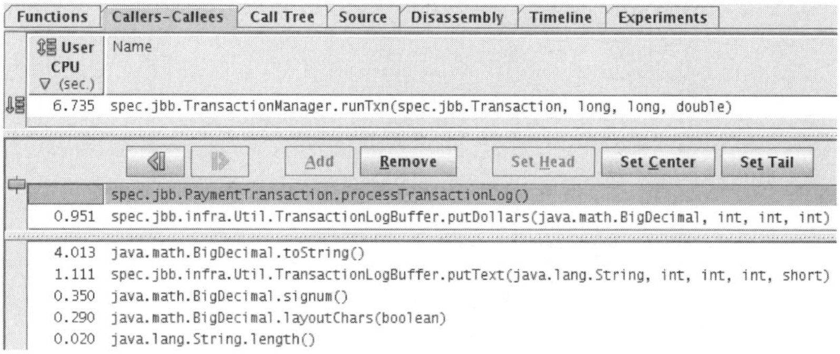

Figure 5-6 Call stack fragment

In short, this new capability allows you to build a call stack fragment and compute attributed time for its callers and callees quickly and easily. This allows you to focus on specific call stacks that call a specific hot method and isolate specific uses of that hot method.

As mentioned earlier in this section, additional metrics can be presented by the Analyzer such as System CPU and User Lock. A description of how to display additional metrics is presented in the next section.

Data Presentation

Recall from the previous section "exclusive" is defined as the amount of time taken to execute a specific method. It does not include any time consumed by methods called by the specific method. Also recall that User CPU time is the amount of time a method has spent executing outside the operating system kernel. Inclusive time, the data shown in the second column in the default Functions view, is the amount of time taken to execute a method and all the methods it calls.

Additional metrics can be added or removed from the Functions view, such as System CPU and User Lock. The way to add additional metrics is by selecting either the View > Set Data Presentation from the main menu or clicking on the Set Data Presentation shortcut in the toolbar.

See Figure 5-7 for a screenshot of the Performance Analyzer's Set Data Presentation user interface illustrating metrics that can be shown for a clock-profiling experiment. Clock-profiling is the default profiling type for Java. The metrics available in the Set Data Presentation Metric's view change depending on the type of profiling and metrics collected in the experiment.

The Metrics tab allows you to choose the metrics to display and the form in which to display them. There are three possible forms: time, value, and percentage. The list contains all metrics that are available in the loaded experiment. For each metric,

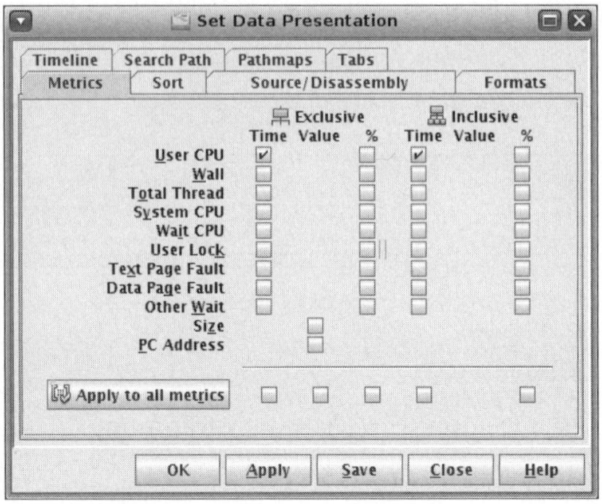

Figure 5-7 Clock-profiling's Set Data Presentation metrics

check boxes are provided for the metric forms available. Alternatively, instead of setting individual metrics, you can set all metrics at once by selecting or deselecting the check boxes in the bottom row and then clicking the Apply to all metrics" button.

You can only choose to display exclusive and inclusive metrics. Attributed metrics are always displayed in the Callers-Callees view if either the exclusive metric or the inclusive metric is displayed in the Functions view.

The metrics of most interest for Java applications are User CPU, System CPU, and User Lock. User CPU is the amount of CPU consumed executing a method outside the operating system kernel. In contrast, System CPU is the amount of CPU executed in the operating system on behalf of the method.

In addition to using the Call Tree tab for analyzing the experiment, another strategy to employ is to focus on reducing the amount of System CPU consumption since CPU time used executing system calls in the operating system is CPU time that could be used executing your program. The benefit realized from using such a strategy depends on the amount of time spent in System CPU relative to the amount of time spent in User CPU. Focusing on reducing System CPU consumption on an experiment with small amounts of System CPU consumption relative to User CPU consumption will not offer much return on investment. An example focusing on System CPU consumption is provided in Chapter 6.

The User Lock metric provides the method names that have locks and may experience lock contention in your Java application. A Java application under load with high lock contention will not scale on systems with a large number of CPUs. Hence, to improve application scaling, you need to focus on reducing lock contention. The User Lock metric tells you which locks are the most highly contended. An example is presented Chapter 6.

Functions	Callers–Callees	Call Tree	Source	Disassembly	Timeline	Experiments

User CPU (%)	Sys. CPU ▽ (%)	User Lock (%)	Name
100.00	100.00	100.00	<Total>
0.61	37.41	99.93	<JVM-System>
0.00	12.94	0.	java.io.FileInputStream.read()
1.24	9.09	0.	spec.jbb.infra.Util.TransactionLogBuffer.privText(java.1;
0.44	3.85	0.02	spec.jbb.infra.Util.TransactionLogBuffer.getLine(int)
0.55	3.15	0.00	java.lang.Integer.valueOf(int)

Figure 5-8 Functions tab with User CPU, System CPU, and User Lock

To add System CPU as a metric to display in the Functions view and Callers-Callees view, you simply select the check boxes of interest, Exclusive Time, Exclusive %, Inclusive Time, and Inclusive % corresponding to System CPU. In most cases, it is useful to display Exclusive metrics since you likely are most interested in the amount of time or percentage of time spent exclusively in a given method for some metric rather than the amount of time or percentage of time spent associated with a given method and all methods it calls.

To display monitor or lock contention information, simply select the check boxes of interest for User Lock.

Figure 5-8 shows the Functions view after selecting Exclusive % metrics for User CPU, System CPU, and User Lock.

Notice in Figure 5-8 that the list is ordered by Sys CPU %. The sorted column is identified by the bold font of the column name.

Also notice in this example, the functions list shows the vast majority of the System CPU is consumed by an entry labeled <JVM-System>. <JVM-System> is a general placeholder for time spent within the internals of the JVM performing tasks such as garbage collection, JIT compilation, class loading, and other various JVM housekeeping activities.

There are multiple format modes in which profiled experiment data can be shown in the Performance Analyzer: User mode, Expert mode, or Machine mode.

In User mode, both JIT compiled and interpreted Java methods are displayed by their method name. In addition, native method names are shown in their natural form. During execution of a Java application several instances may be available of a Java method being executed, that is, an interpreted version and possibly one or more JIT compiled versions. However, if more than one version of a Java method exists in the collected data, their information is aggregated together and reported as a single Java method. In User mode, data collected that represents internal JVM threads such as JIT compiler threads or garbage collection threads is reported under a special entry titled <JVM-System>. An example of this is found in Figure 5-8.

In User mode, the methods list in the Function's panel shows metrics against the Java methods and any native methods called. The Callers-Callees panel shows the calling relationships between Java methods and/or native methods. The Source panel shows the Java source code for Java methods with metrics on each source line. The Disassembly panel shows the bytecode generated for the Java methods with metrics on each line of bytecode. It also interleaves the Java source code if it is found by the Performance Analyzer.

Expert mode is similar to User mode except that some of the details of the JVM internals are exposed. Method and function names from JVM internal threads such as JIT compiler threads and garbage collection threads are shown in the Functions panel and Callers-Callees panel. In addition, Java methods that have spent time in the JVM Interpreter are not aggregated together with its corresponding JIT compiled information as it is in User mode. Instead, time spent in the JVM Interpreter is listed as a separate distinct item in any of the method lists. The Sources panel shows the Java source of a selected method name from the Functions panel or Callers-Callees panel. The Disassembly panel shows the bytecode generated from a selected Java method with metrics reported against each bytecode. It also may interleave Java source code if the source code is found by the Performance Analyzer.

Machine mode shows method and function names from the JVM along with any JIT compiled method names and native method names. Some of the JVM method or function names represent transition code between interpreted Java code, JIT compiled Java code, and native code. In Machine mode, multiple HotSpot JIT compilations for a given Java method may be shown as completely independent method names in the method lists even though the method names will have the same name. The Sources panel shows the Java source if the selected method in the Functions panel or Callers-Callees panel is a Java method. If the selected method is a native method, the source code will be displayed if it is available. The Disassembly panel in Machine mode shows the generated machine code, not the Java bytecode seen in User or Expert modes. Also in Machine mode, Java monitors, which delegate to operating system locking primitives are listed in the method lists as calls to operating system lock primitives such as _lwp_mutex_ on Solaris. Traversing up the call stack from an operating system locking primitive such as an _lwp_mutex_ entry in the Callers-Callees panel eventually shows the origination of the Java monitor in the form of a Java method name.

To change from User mode, choose View > Set Data Presentation from the main menu, or click on the Set Data Presentation icon in the toolbar. Then select the Formats tab where a radio button can be selected for the desired mode, User, Expert, or Machine mode. In the lower half of Figure 5-9 you can see where you can select the view mode from the Formats tab of the Set Data Presentation form.

Java developers tend to use User mode the most since they are usually not interested in viewing data that includes internal methods of the JVM. Java performance specialists tend to use all three modes, especially Expert and Machine modes, since

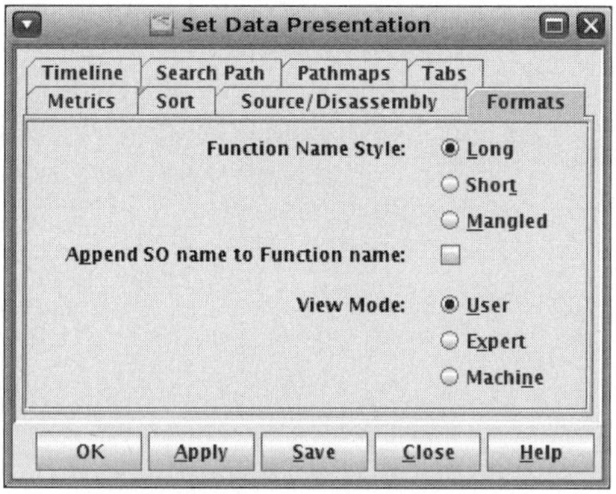

Figure 5-9 Format modes

performance specialists possess specific knowledge about the internals of the JVM and can identify if there happens to be reason for concern about the performance or scalability of the JVM.

Filtering Profile Data

Often there are time periods of an application's execution that you want to ignore when viewing a profile. For example, most of the time you are not interested in the startup or initialization phase of an application and want to ignore that information. Or there is a particular time span where performance is of concern and you want to focus on that particular time span. The Performance Analyzer has a concept called *filtering* that allows you to focus on specific time spans of interest. The Performance Analyzer allows you to select the range of profile samples collected. By default the Performance Analyzer displays all samples. Since the `collect` command of Performance Analyzer by default collects a sample once every second, it is easy to identify a time period of interest. For example, suppose an application runs for 30 minutes (1800 seconds), it takes 45 seconds to initialize, and you are not interested in viewing any performance data from the initialization phase. To exclude the first 45 seconds of profile data, you specify a filter so the first 45 samples are ignored with a range of 46–1800 as the samples to include the presentation of the profile data.

Specifying a filter in the Performance Analyzer is done through the Filter Data form, which can be accessed by selecting the View > Filter Data from the main menu or by selecting the Filter Data icon from the toolbar. Figure 5-10 illustrates a filter for limiting the data to be presented to samples 301–1720, which suggests the first 300 seconds (5 minutes) of the application profile data is to be ignored.

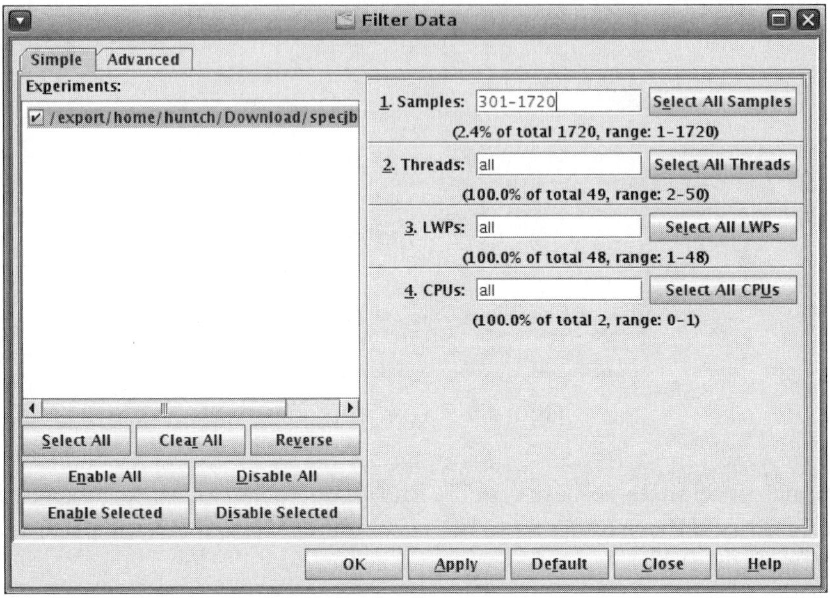

Figure 5-10 Filter Data

Command Line `er_print` Utility

In addition to the Analyzer GUI, there is also a command line utility called `er_print` that can be used to process a collected experiment profile. The `er_print` command line utility prints an ASCII text version of the various displays found in the Performance Analyzer GUI such as method lists and callers-callees of User CPU, System CPU, and User Lock consumers. The output from `er_print` is written to standard output unless it is redirected to a file. The `er_print` utility requires at least one argument, the name of one or more experiments generated with the Performance Analyzer's `collect` command.

One of the powerful capabilities of `er_print` is that it can be scripted, which makes it useful for automated performance analysis. For instance, `er_print` can be scripted to automatically process a collected experiment and output the top ten methods using the most User CPU, System CPU, and User Locks. But before talking about how to create scripts for `er_print`, it makes sense to talk about its command syntax and more generally how to use it interactively. Once these topics are covered, the task of creating scripts for `er_print` is straightforward.

The command syntax for `er_print` is

```
$ er_print [ -script <script name> | -command <er_print command> | - | -V ]
<profile experiment name>
```

The text between [and] means the arguments are optional. Text demarcated by |
means any of the options can be used between the | characters. And text between
< and > means a name of a script or file that you have created is required, or an
er_print command is required. When the -script option is not used, er_print
reads commands from the command line.

- -script <script name> says to execute the er_print script called <script
  name>, a script you have created that contains a list of er_print commands.

- -command says to execute the er_print command where command is one of
  the er_print commands, that is, -func will print a functions (methods) list.

- - says to read er_print commands entered from the keyboard. er_print
  prompts and waits for er_print commands to be entered. Using - is useful
  when used in combination with -command to execute a command and then wait
  for keyboard input for the next command. In other words, it is useful when using
  er_print for interactive command line analysis where you may not know the
  next command to execute until after viewing the previous command's output. A
  tip to keep in mind when in interactive mode: A help command will list available er_print commands.

- -V tells er_print to display version information and exit.

Multiple options can appear on the er_print command line. They are processed
in the order they appear. You can mix scripts, hyphens, and explicit commands in
any order. The default action if you do not supply any commands or scripts is to enter
interactive mode, where commands are entered from the keyboard. To exit interactive
mode type quit or press Ctrl+D.

After each command is processed, any error messages or warning messages arising
from the processing are printed.

The commands accepted by the er_print utility are listed in the following sections.

You can abbreviate any command with a shorter string as long as the command is
unambiguous. You can split a command into multiple lines by terminating a line with
a \ character. Any line that ends in \ will have the \ character removed, and the content of the next line appended before the line is parsed. There is no limit, other than
available memory, on the number of lines you can use for an er_print command.

You must enclose arguments that contain embedded blanks in double quotes. You
can split the text inside the quotes across lines.

Many of the er_print commands use a list of metric keywords. The syntax of
the list is

```
metric-keyword-1[:metric-keyword-2 ...]
```

In other words, multiple metric keywords can be specified. They need to be delimited by a : (colon) character. Metric keywords can be a combination of a metric name, metric type, donated by a metric type character, and a metric visibility character. Metric names are shown in Table 5-4. Metric type characters are shown in Table 5-5. Metric visibility characters are shown in Table 5-6.

Table 5-4 Metric Names

Metric Name	Description
user	Shows User CPU time, i.e., the amount of time spent consuming user land CPU cycles
system	Shows System CPU time, i.e., the amount of time spent consuming CPU cycles executing in operating system calls
lock	Shows User Lock time, i.e., the amount of time spent blocked, waiting to get access to a shared lock

Table 5-5 Metric Type Characters

Metric Type Character	Description
e	Shows exclusive metric value. Remember exclusive metric values represent values for only a method and not any additional value from methods it calls.
i	Shows inclusive metric value. Remember inclusive metric values represent not only the values for a method, but also includes values for methods it calls.
a	Shows attributed metric value. This is applicable only to Callers-Callees metrics.

Table 5-6 Metric Visibility Characters

Metric Visibility Character	Description
.	Shows the metric as time. This applies to timing metric metrics and hardware counters that measure cycle counts. For other metrics, it is interpreted the same as the "+" character.
%	Shows metric as a percentage of the total program metric. For attributed metrics in the Callers-Callees list, shows the metric as a percentage of the inclusive metric for the selected function.
+	Shows metric as an absolute value. For hardware counters, this value is an event count. If the hardware counter measures cycle counts, the metric is reported as time.
!	Does not show any metric value. This option cannot be used in combination with other visibility characters listed in this table.

Note, there are other metric names, but those listed in Table 5-4 are the ones most commonly used with Java applications. A full listing of all metric names available in an experiment being evaluated can be obtained using the `er_print metric_list` command.

With this information you specify which metrics you want to have selected and printed. For example, if you are interested in reporting the percentage of total time on exclusive metrics for User CPU, System CPU, and User Lock, you would enter an `er_print` command as

```
metrics e.%user:e.%system:e%lock
```

If you enter the preceding metrics command at an `er_print` command line, `er_print` will respond by saying:

```
Current metrics: e.%user:e.%system:e%lock:name
Current Sort Metric: Exclusive User CPU Time ( e.%user )
```

Notice that `er_print` is also saying that the current sort metric will be exclusive User CPU time. You can change the sort order by using the `sort` command followed by the metric name to sort by. For example, if instead of wanting to sort by exclusive User CPU time, you want to sort by exclusive User CPU time after entering the previous metrics command, you would use the following `sort` command:

```
sort e.%system
```

After entering the `sort` command, `er_print` reports the result of the command. For example, `er_print` responds with the following message after entering the preceding `sort` command:

```
Current Sort Metric: Exclusive System CPU Time ( e.%system )
```

To obtain a listing of the methods for a set of metrics, you use the `functions` command. However, the `functions` command, in the absence of a specified limit, prints all methods collected in the experiment profile. To limit the number of methods printed, you can use the `limit` command. The `limit` command tells `er_print` to limit the number of methods printed with the `functions` command to the number of methods given as an argument to the `limit` command. For example, to limit the number of methods printed with a `functions` command to 25 methods, you would use the following `limit` command:

```
limit 25
```

The `limit` command is one of the few `er_print` commands when entered that does not respond back the fact that the number of methods printed with the `functions` command now has a capped limit.

At this point you have enough information to use `er_print` to print out the top 25 methods consuming the most System CPU, User CPU, and User Lock time. However, you are probably also interested in knowing how to print out Callers-Callees information with `er_print`.

The `er_print` command `callers-callees` prints a Callers-Callees table for each of the methods printed by the `functions` command. The number of Callers-Callees table entries that are printed are constrained by the `limit` command in the same way that the `limit` command limits the number of methods printed by the `functions` command. For example, if the `limit` command limits the number of methods printed by 25, then only 25 table entries will be printed by the `callers-callees` command. For each table entry printed by the `callers-callees` command, the center method name is the name of the method from the functions list and it is marked with an asterisk. Here is example output from a `callers-callees` command:

```
Attr.     Excl.     Incl.       Name
User CPU  User CPU  User CPU
  sec.      sec.      sec.
4.440     0.        42.910      com.mydomain.MyProject.doWork()
0.        0.        4.440       *com.mydomain.MyProject.work()
4.080     0.        4.080       com.mydomain.MyProject.preProcessItem()
0.360     0.        0.360       com.mydomain.MyProject.processItem()
```

In this example, `com.mydomain.MyProject.work()` is the selected method from the methods list, the center method name, which is reportable from the `functions` command. The `com.mydomain.MyProject.work()` method is called by `com.mydomain.MyProject.doWork()`, and the `com.mydomain.MyProject.work()` method calls both `com.mydomain.MyProject.preProcessItem()` and `com.mydomain.MyProject.processItem()` methods. Also notice in this example the Attributed User CPU metric is also reported.

Another `er_print` command, `csingle`, can also print callers-callees information. In contrast to the `callers-callees` command, `csingle` prints the callers-callees of the method name passed as an argument to the `csingle` command. The `callers-callees` command prints a list of callers-callees. The length of the list of caller-callee pairs from the `callers-callees` command is constrained by the `limit` command. The `csingle` command is useful when wanting to look exclusively at callers-callees of a specific method. A common work flow when viewing profiles with `er_print` is to output the top ten methods having the highest usage of exclusive User CPU, and then print the callers-callees of the top method. This could be done interactively with `er_print` with the following sequence of `er_print` commands (`er_print` commands are shown in bold):

```
$ er_print test.er.1
(er_print) limit 10
(er_print) functions
Functions sorted by metric: Exclusive User CPU Time

Excl.      Incl.       Name

User CPU   User CPU
   sec.       sec.
3226.047   3226.047    <Total>
 372.591    521.395    com.mydomain.MyProject.work()
 314.230    314.230    com.mydomain.MyProject.doWork ()
 177.134    455.639    java.lang.Integer.valueOf(int)
 169.118    169.118    java.lang. StringBuilder.toString()
(er_print) csingle com.mydomain.myproject.work
Callers and callees sorted by metric: Attributed User CPU Time

Attr.      Name
User CPU
   sec.
 521.365     com.mydomain.MyProject.doWork()
 372.591    *com.mydomain.MyProject.work()
  66.907     java.lang.Integer.valueOf(int)
  17.342     java.lang.StringBuilder.toString()
```

Since modern JVMs include JIT compilers to compile Java bytecode into machine code for the underlying hardware platform and Performance Analyzer differentiates between interpreted methods and those that have been JIT compiled, the `csingle` command may ask for a specific version of the selected method. One of the choices will be a version of the method that had been executing in the JVM in interpreted mode, and there may be additional choices of method versions after JIT compilation. The reason there may be multiple choices after JIT compilation is the JVM's JIT compiler may have deoptimized and reoptimized the method. Having these distinct versions can be useful for JVM and JIT compiler engineers with improving

JIT compilation techniques. The following example illustrates the prompting of the csingle command asking for a version of a method.

```
(er_print) csingle java.lang.Integer.valueOf (int)
Available name list:

      0) Cancel
      1) java.lang.Integer.valueOf(int) JAVA_CLASSES:0x0 (Integer.java)
      2) java.lang.Integer.valueOf(int) JAVA_COMPILED_METHODS:0x52f70
(Integer.java)
Enter selection:
```

In the previous output, the JIT compiled version of the java.lang.Integer.valueOf(int) method is identified by the JAVA_COMPILED_METHODS text. The interpreted version is identified by the JAVA_CLASSES text. In the presence of multiple choices of a method using the csingle command, it is best to look at performance metrics for each version since you may not know how long a given version had been executing as interpreted code, or as JIT compiled code.

The metrics reported by the callers-callees and csingle commands can be controlled using the cmetrics command. Using cmetrics with no arguments tells er_print to set the callers-callees and csingle metrics to the same metrics as those specified for printing methods using the functions command. The cmetrics command can also take a list of metric keywords if you want to expand or contract the metrics reported with the callers-callees or csingle commands. For example, if you are interested in reporting only exclusive percentage System CPU time and attributed percentage System CPU time in the Callers-Callees output, you would specify the following cmetrics command:

```
cmetrics e.%system:a.%system
```

To limit the scope of information printed; in other words, in situations where you are interested in a particular time period of the collected experiment profile, you can specify a filter for er_print to use in the same way you can specify a filter in the Analyzer GUI. To limit the scope of the samples included in the printed information reported by er_print, you use the filters command. The filters command takes an argument that can be a list of one or more sample ranges with each range of samples delimited by a , (comma) character. For example, suppose you wanted to limit the scope of the information reported by er_print to be samples 61–120 and 301–360 (this suggests the data collected between 61 seconds and 120 seconds into the experiment and between 301 seconds and 360 seconds are of interest since the `collect` command samples at once per second), you would specify the following `filters` command:

```
filters 61-120,301-360
```

To direct the output produced by `er_print` to an output file you specify the `outfile` command followed by a file name you want to capture the output in. For example, to capture the output from an `er_print` sequence of commands to a file named my-output-file.txt, you would specify the following `outfile` command:

```
outfile my-output-file.txt
```

An additional `er_print` command worth mentioning is the selecting of a view mode. Recall that three view modes are available: User, Expert, and Machine. These three view modes were described earlier in the Oracle Solaris Studio Performance Analyzer Data Presentation section. As mentioned in that section, most Java developers use the User view mode. But if you want to see `er_print` output data in either Expert mode or Machine mode, the `viewmode` command can be used. The default view mode is User. To set a view mode to use with `er_print`, you append one of the view modes of User, Expert, or Machine to the `viewmode` command. For example, to set the view mode to Expert mode you specify the following `viewmode` command:

```
viewmode expert
```

At this point you have seen the basic set of `er_print` commands that allow you to make effective use of `er_print`. The next step in using `er_print` is to automate the processing of an experiment with an `er_print` script. Following are a couple of example `er_print` scripts for various tasks. Any of the following `er_print` scripts can be saved to a file and run against a collected experiment using `er_print` with the `-script` option followed by the name of the file the commands were saved as.

Example 1

Print the top 10 methods using the most percentage of exclusive System CPU time and include percentage of exclusive User CPU time and percentage of exclusive User Lock time too.

```
metrics e.%system:e.%user:e.%lock
sort e.%system
limit 10
functions
quit
```

If the preceding commands are saved in a file named, top-10-system-cpu.script, this script could be executed using `er_print` as

```
er_print -script top-10-system-cpu.script <experiment name>
```

Note that `<experiment name>` is the name of an experiment that has been collected with the Performance Analyzer `collect` command.

Example 2

Print the top 25 methods using the most exclusive User CPU time, reported as time rather than percentage. Then print the top 10 methods using the most exclusive System CPU time, reported as time rather than percentage. And then report the top 5 methods experiencing the most exclusive percentage of User Lock time. This script could be a general purpose script to report a high level view of the top consumers of CPU time, including both User CPU and System CPU along with reporting any potential lock contention issues.

```
metrics e.user
sort e.user
limit 25
functions
metrics e.system:e.%user:e.%lock
sort e.system
limit 10
functions
metrics e.%lock
sort e.%lock
limit 5
functions
quit
```

These two example scripts illustrate the power of being able to create `er_print` scripts. Many more scripts can be created and can be useful. The preceding two examples illustrate how quickly `er_print` scripts can be developed and how useful they can be as general purpose scripts that could be run against a collected experiment to give a quick overview of an application's performance. In an era of automated build and test environments, even the simple examples shown previously could be useful in an automated performance testing system to do an initial high level performance analysis. The resulting output from the preceding scripts could be further integrated into an e-mail reporting system to report the findings to interested stakeholders.

This section on `er_print` has only provided an introduction to the capabilities you can achieve utilizing `er_print`. Getting a list of `er_print` commands and their usage at any time is as simple as executing `er_print` with no arguments, that is, `er_print`.

As you use the Performance Analyzer and `er_print`, you will become more versed in its capabilities and its power.

NetBeans Profiler

Since some readers may not have the ability to do method profiling on one of the Oracle Solaris Studio Performance Analyzer's supported platforms, method profiling using the NetBeans Profiler is covered in this section. In addition, memory profiling and memory leak detection with the NetBeans Profiler are also presented. To get the most from this section, it may be useful to revisit the Common Profiling Terms and NetBeans Profiler Terms sections at the beginning of this chapter.

The NetBeans Profiler is a powerful tool that can help you identify performance problems in your application. The NetBeans Profiler is included in the NetBeans IDE and also included in a JVM monitoring tool called VisualVM. VisualVM is an open source project found at http://visualvm.dev.java.net and is also packaged with the Java HotSpot JDK beginning with Java 6 Update 7. Regardless whether you use NetBeans Profiler with NetBeans IDE or with VisualVM, it allows you to profile your Java application, determine the time used by specific methods, and examine how your application uses memory.

> **Tip**
>
> At the time of this writing, there are few differences in the functionality between the NetBeans Profiler available in NetBeans IDE and VisualVM. Both rely on the same underlying technology. One of the features absent from VisualVM is the ability to go to a specific line of source code in the NetBeans IDE editor when double-clicking on a method name while examining a profile. A feature absent in NetBeans Profiler is the profiling sampler, a lightweight profiler that's included with VisualVM 1.3.1 version (and available as a plug-in in version 1.2).

The NetBeans Profiler uses advanced technology that reduces profiling overhead, making it easier to learn about the performance of an application. The following are some of the features of the NetBeans Profiler:

- **Low overhead profiling.** You can control the profiler's performance impact on your application. Based on your selections, the performance impact ranges from extensive to none.
- **CPU performance profiling.** Time spent in every method of your application or just in selected methods can be reported.
- **Memory profiling.** You can check for excessive object allocations.
- **Memory leak detection.** The profiler's statistical reports make it easy to detect object instances that are leaking.

The act of profiling with the NetBeans Profiler presented are those followed when using the NetBeans Profiler within NetBeans IDE. However, other than some of the initial setup of selecting an application to profile, the concepts, flow of control, and so on are similar if not the same as found in VisualVM. Once you have used the NetBeans Profiler in either the NetBeans IDE or VisualVM you will find it easy to use in either tool.

Supported Platforms

The NetBeans Profiler can profile applications when they are run in a Java Virtual Machine (JVM) that supports the JVM Tool Interface (JVMTI). Java 5 Update 4 (and later) supports JVMTI. Because the NetBeans Profiler includes binary code, which is needed to communicate with the JVMTI support in the JVM, the NetBeans Profiler is platform specific. The supported platforms are as follows:

- Solaris (SPARC and x86/x64)
- Windows
- Linux
- Mac OS X

Downloading and Installing the NetBeans Profiler

The standard NetBeans IDE download includes the NetBeans Profiler and can be used directly within the NetBeans IDE. The NetBeans IDE can be downloaded from the NetBeans Web site, http://www.netbeans.org. Downloading the NetBeans IDE is as simple as selecting the download for your target platform. Once NetBeans IDE has been downloaded, you use the installation wizard to install the NetBeans IDE.

VisualVM, which also bundles the NetBeans Profiler, can be obtained by either downloading the latest version of VisualVM from http://visualvm.dev.java.net, or by downloading Oracle's Java 6 Update 7 or later JDK distribution. Java 6 Update 7 and later bundle VisualVM in its distribution.

> **Tip**
>
> The only difference between the VisualVM version available at http://visualvm.dev.java.net and what is bundled in a HotSpot JDK is the version from http://visualvm.dev.java.net may be a slightly newer version having new or additional features available in it.

The VisualVM program that is bundled with Java 6 and later releases can be found in the <install directory>/bin directory of a JDK installation. The name of the program is called *jvisualvm*. The VisualVM program in the downloaded VisualVM package from http://visualvm.dev.java.net is called *visualvm* and can be found in the <install directory>/bin directory. Note that the open source VisualVM version does not have a leading "j" character in front of the visualvm name.

The default JDK installation directory on Windows systems is C:\Program Files\ Java\<jdk release> where <jdk release> is the name of the JDK release such as jdk1.6.0_21. So, if you installed Java 6 Update 21 on a Windows system, by default the JDK installer places the *jvisualvm* program in the C:\Program Files\Java\ jdk1.6.0_21\bin directory.

The installation of NetBeans IDE on Windows systems places a launch icon on the Windows desktop for easy launching.

Starting a Method Profiling Session

The steps described here assume you are using NetBeans IDE. NetBeans IDE was chosen as the program for describing how to use NetBeans Profiler since it offers remote profiling capabilities.

> **Tip**
>
> VisualVM has a lightweight remote profiling feature different from the NetBeans IDE remote profiling feature. VisualVM's lightweight profiling feature was presented in Chapter 4.

Additionally, the steps illustrated here describe profiling remotely since usually it is most desirable to profile an application running on a target system in a qualification type of environment, and most desktop systems do not have sufficient memory resources to run both a powerful profiler and a complex application at the same time.

A remote profiling session requires the following steps:

1. Identify the remote system where the application to profile resides.
2. Start NetBeans IDE.
3. Select a profiling task, method profiling or memory profiling.
4. Specify options for the selected task.
5. Generate the remote profiling pack.
6. Configure the remote system with the remote profiling pack.
7. Start the profiling; examine the data it displays and the data it collects.

The following sequence of steps illustrates what is required to remotely profile an application using NetBeans Profiler in NetBeans IDE. In this example, the remote system's name is halas and the remote application is called SPECjvm2008's compiler. compiler workload. SPECjvm2008 can be freely downloaded at http://www.spec.org/download.html. The version of NetBeans IDE used in this example is NetBeans IDE 6.8. The JVM version used with both the NetBeans IDE and the remote application is Java 6 Update 21.

1. Identify the remote system where the application to profile resides.
   As mentioned earlier, the remote system is halas, and the application is SPECjvm2008's compiler.compiler workload.
2. Start NetBeans IDE on your desktop system.
3. Select the profiling task and method profiling.
   Select the Profile > Attach Profiler option from the main menu in NetBeans IDE. From the Attach Profiler panel, select the CPU icon on the left to select method profiling as shown in Figure 5-11. Note, if you want to perform memory profiling, select the memory icon.
4. Specify options for the selected task.
   On the right side of the Attach Profiler panel, you have several options to scope method profiling such as profiling the entire application and an option to specify a filter. A filter allows you to include or exclude specific Java classes from being included in the profiling activity. There is also a measure of intrusiveness provided by the Overhead meter. Notice in Figure 5-11, with the options to profile the entire application and a filter selected to exclude the Java core classes from the profile there is a projected profiling overhead of about 50%. If you select a filter to profile all classes, you will notice the profiling overhead jumps to 100%. Generally you will find that method profiling an entire application can be rather

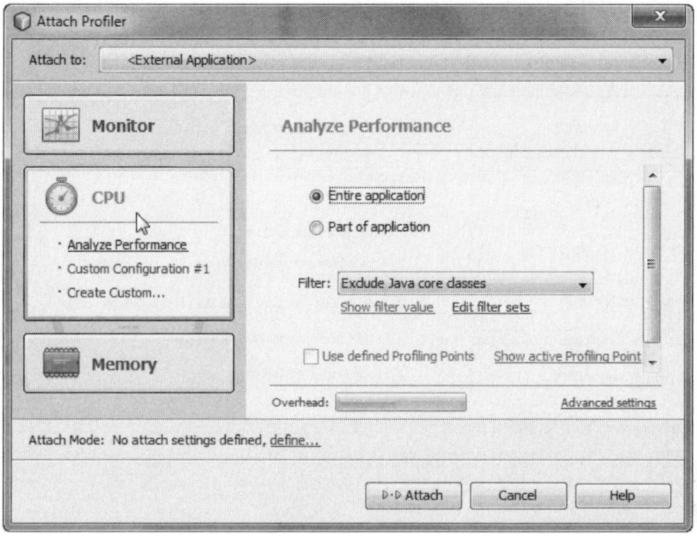

Figure 5-11 Selecting method profiling

intrusive on the application's performance. Hence, it is useful to use a filter or define a filter to use with method profiling. In other words, if you happen to have a good idea of the part or parts of the application that have performance issues, it will greatly help the intrusiveness introduced by the profiling activity if you can create and specify a filter to narrow the scope of what is profiled to that part or parts of the application.

You can also reduce the intrusiveness of the profiling by reducing the sampling rate at which profiling data is acquired from the running application. To reduce the sampling rate, you must construct a custom configuration by selecting the Create Custom option in the CPU profiling icon on the Attach Profiler panel and then clicking on the Advanced Settings option to the right of the Overhead meter; refer to Figure 5-11. Once you have clicked on the Advanced Settings option, you can specify a lower sampling interval than the 10 millisecond default as shown in Figure 5-12.

If you have not specified an Attach Mode, you must do so. Specifying an Attach Mode tells the profiler whether the JVM running the application you want to profile is running locally or remotely on a different system. You specify the Attach Mode by launching the Attach Wizard by selecting the Define Attach Mode option at the bottom of the Attach Profiler panel, shown previously in Figure 5-12.

On the Attach Wizard you specify the target type: Application, Applet, or J2EE/Web Application along with attach method, local or remote, and attach invocation, direct or dynamic. Direct attach blocks the target application from launch until

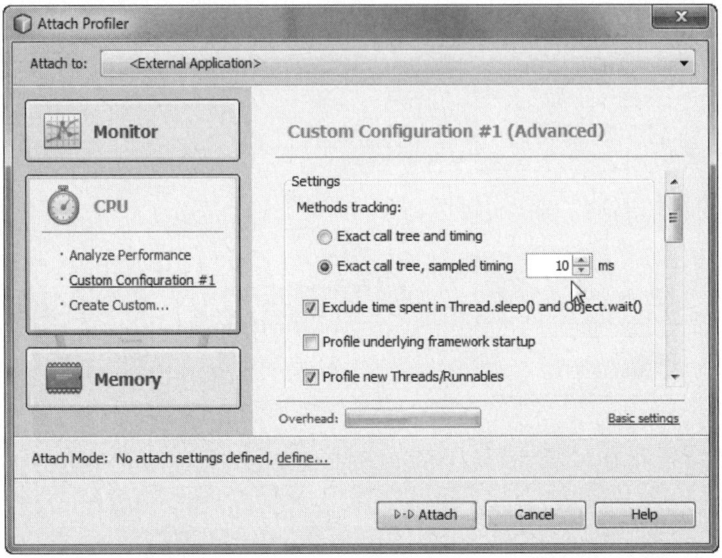

Figure 5-12 Reducing method profiling sampling interval

the profiler has attached to it. Dynamic attach allows you to attach, detach, and re-attach to the running application at any time. However, dynamic attach is not available for remote profiling or for profiling applications running on Java 5 or older JVMs.

For illustration purposes, as mentioned earlier, the example illustrated in this section assumes the target application is running remotely on a system called halas as a standalone application. Hence, on the Attach Wizard the following options are selected, also shown in Figure 5-13, Target Type is Application, Attach method is Remote, and Attach invocation is Direct.

Once the attach type is specified, you can press the Next button to proceed through the Attach Wizard.

On the next form of the Attach Wizard, you specify the hostname where the remote target application will be executed and the operating system along with specifying whether a 32-bit JVM or 64-bit JVM is being used on the target system as shown in Figure 5-14.

5. Generate the remote profiling pack.
Notice in Figure 5-13 there is a reminder that a Profiler Remote Pack is required to profile a remote application. If you have not profiled an application remotely on the target system where the application resides, you need to generate a Profiler Remote Pack. The Profiler Remote Pack makes the configuration and setup needed for the profiler to attach remotely much simpler

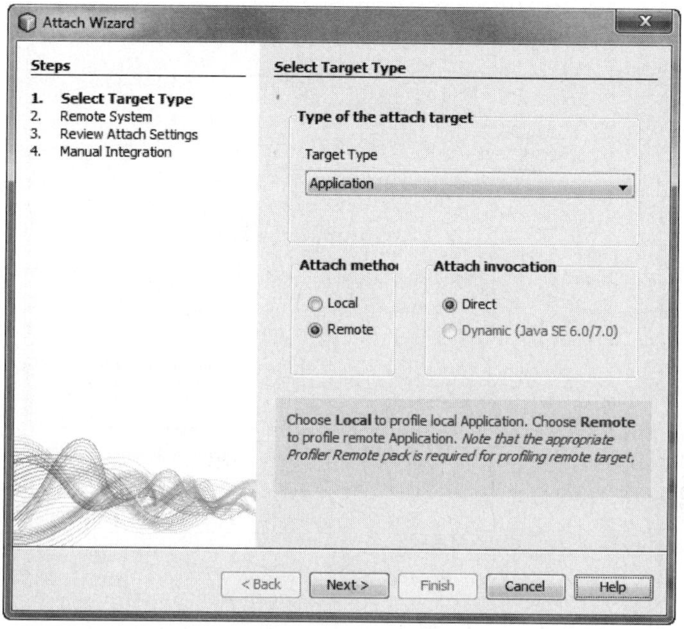

Figure 5-13 Specifying remote profiling

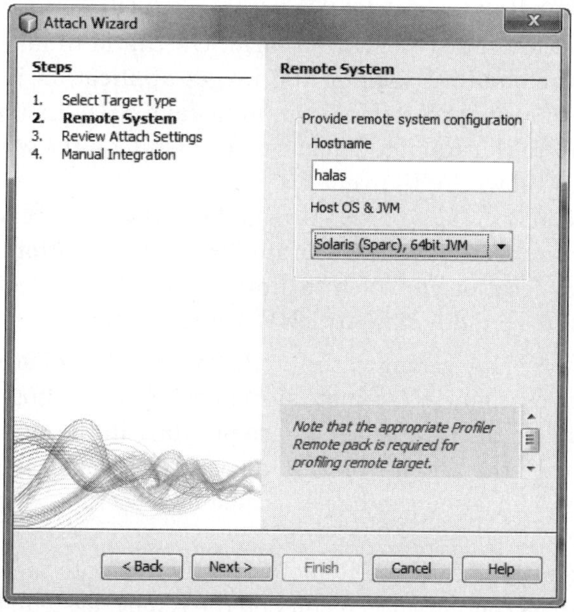

Figure 5-14 Remote host, operating system, and JVM

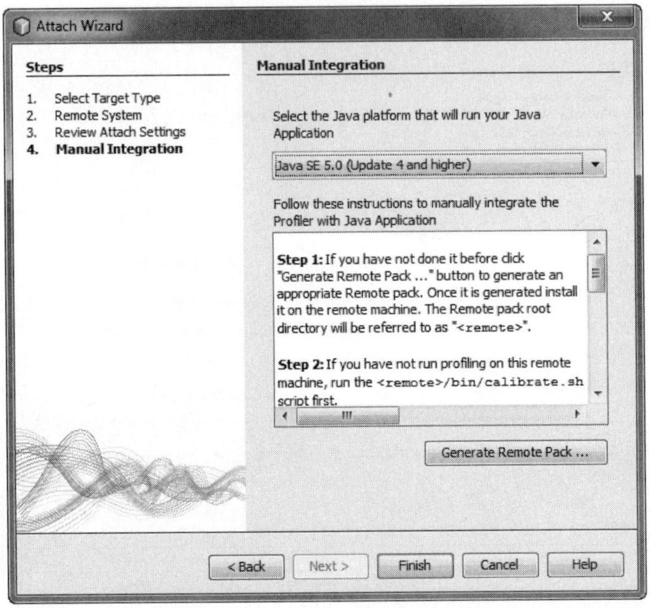

Figure 5-15 Generating Profiler Remote Pack

than doing it manually. The Profiler Remote Pack is generated by the Net-Beans Profilers on the Manual Integration form of the Attach Wizard, which is one of the next forms in the Attach Wizard. Click the Next button until you reach the Manual Integration form. On the Manual Integration form, you specify the Java SE version the target application is running. In this example, the target application is running Java SE 6. Instructions on how to generate the Profiler Remote Pack are also listed on the Manual Integration form and also shown in Figure 5-15.

Review the instructions on the form and when you are ready to generate the Profiler Remote Pack, click the Generate Remote Pack button. You are prompted for a directory location in which to store the Profiler Remote Pack. Click the Finish button to complete the Attach Wizard.

6. Configure the remote system with the Remote Profiling Pack.
Now you must configure the remote system using the Remote Profiling Pack. In addition, if this is the first time you are profiling in the remote system with a target JVM, then the target JVM will also perform some calibration of the target JVM. The calibration can be performed by a script included in the Remote Profiling Pack called `calibrate.sh`.

The first task is to copy the Remote Profiling Pack to the remote target system and unzip its contents to directory on the remote system. In the instructions given here, assume the directory that you have unzipped in the Remote Profiling Pack on the remote system is called "remote." The first task to execute on the remote system, if it has not been done previously, is to run the calibration script found in the `<remote>/bin` directory called `calibrate.sh`. Be sure to edit and update the `calibrate.sh` script with the appropriate `JAVA_HOME`, or set the `JAVA_HOME` environment variable externally to the `calibrate.sh` script prior to attempting to execute the `calibrate.sh` script. The `JAVA_HOME` environment variable must point to the base directory of the JVM you plan to use to run the remote application.

After executing the `calibrate.sh` script, you need to update the Java command line options you use to launch the target application to tell the JVM to block and wait until the Profiler has remotely connected to it. The Remote Profiler Pack has convenience scripts you can update to launch your Java application. These convenience scripts have the necessary HotSpot JVM command line option, `-agentpath`, needed for remote profiling. If you are using a Java 5 JVM you can update the `<remote>/bin/profile-15` command file or script file. If you are using a Java 6 JVM, you can update the `<remote>/bin/profile-16` command file or script file. Alternatively, you can add the appropriate `-agentpath` command line option for your platform. The command line option to specify for a Java 5 JVM or Java 6 JVM can be found in the Remote Profiling Pack's `<remote>/bin/profile-15` or `<remote>/bin/profile-16` command file or script file, respectively. When the `-agentpath` command line option is specified correctly, if you attempt to launch the target Java application, a message prints saying that the profiling agent is initializing and it is waiting for a connection from a remote profiler.

7. Start profiling; examine the data it displays and the data it collects.
Everything necessary for remote profiling is set up and configured in the previous steps. All that is left to do is launch the remote Java application and connect the Profiler to it. Launch the remote Java application with the command file or script file you updated in the `-agentpath` command line in step 6. As mentioned in step 6, when the remote Java application launches, it reports that it is waiting for the Profiler to attach. Go to your desktop system and tell the NetBeans Profiler to attach to the remote Java application. If you have forgotten how to get to the Attach Profiler panel, select the Profile > Attach Profiler option from the main menu in NetBeans IDE.

Once the NetBeans Profiler has successfully attached, the remote Java application unblocks and continues to execute. The NetBeans Profiler opens a Profiler Control Panel in NetBeans IDE with Controls, Status, Profiling

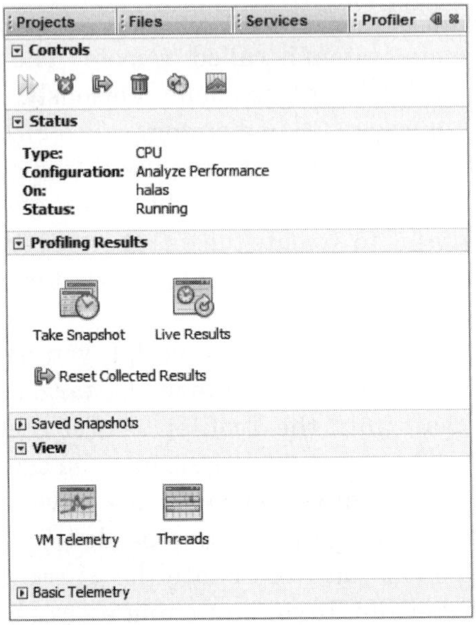

Figure 5-16 Profiler control panel

Results, Save Snapshots, View, and Basic Telemetry subpanels as shown in Figure 5-16.

Regardless of whether you are doing method profiling or memory profiling, the Profiler Control Panel looks the same. Each section of the Profiler Control Panel can be expanded or hidden by clicking the arrow icon next to the name of the section. Each of the Profiler Control Panel's subpanels is explained in more detail in the following subsections.

Controls

See Table 5-7 for an explanation of the buttons in the Profiler Control Panel Controls section.

Status

See Table 5-8 for an explanation of the entries in the Profiler Control Panel Status section.

Profiling Results

See Table 5-9 for an explanation of the entries in the Profiler Control Panel Profiling Results section.

Table 5-7 Profiler Control Panel Controls

Component	Description
▷▷	**ReRun Last Profiling** Run the last profiling command again.
🛇	**Stop** Stops the current profiling command. Also stops the target application if the application was started by the profiler.
⇨	**Reset Collected Results** Discards the already accumulated profiling results.
🗑	**Run GC** Runs garbage collection.
⏱	**Modify Profiling** Opens the Modify Profiling Task dialog box and allows you to run a new profiling command without stopping the target application.
📊	**VM Telemetry** Opens the VM Telemetry Overview in the Output window of the IDE, displaying smaller versions of the telemetry graphs.

Table 5-8 Profiler Control Panel Status

Component	Description
Type	The type of profiling: Monitor, CPU, or Memory
Configuration	Indicates whether the profiler was started with one of its preset configurations
On	An identifier indicating the name of the system where application is being profiled
Status	Running or Inactive

Table 5-9 Profiler Control Panel Profiling Results

Component	Description
📇	**Take Snapshot** Displays a static snapshot of the profiling results accumulated thus far
📇	**Live Results** Displays the current results of the profiling task
⇨	**Reset Collected Results** Discards the already accumulated profiling results

Table 5-10 Profiler Control Panel View

Component	Description
	VM Telemetry
	Opens the VM Telemetry tab. The VM Telemetry tab displays high-level data on thread activity and memory heap and garbage collection in the VM.
	Threads
	Opens the Threads tab. When Enable Threads Monitoring is selected in the Select Profiling Task dialog box, application thread activity is displayed in the Threads tab.

Table 5-11 Profiler Control Panel Basic Telemetry

Component	Description
Instrumented	When doing memory profiling, the number of classes with profiler instrumentation; when doing CPU performance profiling, the number of methods with profiler instrumentation
Filter	Type of filter (if any) that was specified
Threads	Number of active threads
Total Memory	Allocated size of the heap
Used Memory	Portion of the heap that is in use
Time Spent in GC	Percentage of time spent performing garbage collection

Saved Snapshots

Enables you to manage the profile snapshots. When you save a snapshot, the saved snapshot is displayed here. Double-clicking the name of the snapshot opens the snapshot.

View

See Table 5-10 for an explanation of the entries in the Profiler Control Panel View section.

Basic Telemetry

See Table 5-11 for an explanation of the entries in the Profiler Control Panel Basic Telemetry section. You can see the graphic presentation of some of this information by clicking the VM Telemetry and Threads buttons in the View section.

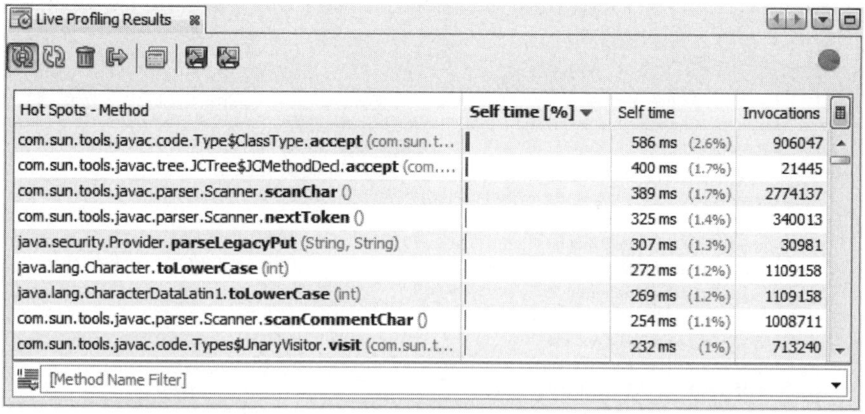

Figure 5-17 Live results while analyzing performance

Viewing Live Results

While your remote application is running you can watch the amount of time used by individual methods by clicking the Live Results icon in the Profiler Control Panel to display the Profiling Results window (shown in Figure 5-17).

This window displays all methods that have been invoked at least once. The default sort order is by descending self time, so the methods in your application that are using the most time are displayed at the top of the list. The amount of time used is displayed in two columns, one with a graph to show the percentage of time spent in each method and the other with text that displays the raw time value and the percentage. The number of invocations is also shown. The profiler updates these values as your application runs.

To change the sort order, click a column header. This sorts the table in descending order using the values from the column. Click again to sort in ascending order. Clicking the Hot Spots—Method column sorts the table by package, class, and method name. To find a specific method more quickly click on Method Name Filter at the bottom of the table and then enter the method name.

Taking a Snapshot of Results

To see more detailed information, click the Take Snapshot icon in the Profiler Control Panel. The CPU snapshot window is displayed, with the time of the snapshot as its title (shown in Figure 5-18).

The CPU snapshot window initially displays its Call Tree tab, which shows the call trees organized by thread. To switch to the Hot Spots view, just click the Hot Spots tab at the bottom of the panel. It is usually helpful to see the

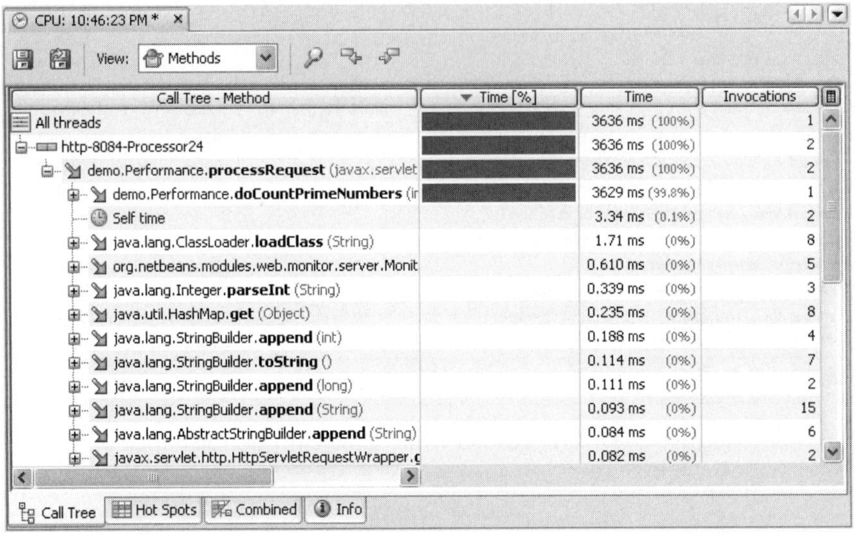

Figure 5-18 Results snapshot while analyzing performance

execution path used by your application to get from one or more of the method roots to the hot methods or hot spots in your application. To do that easily, click the Combined tab. This tab shows both the Call Tree and the Hot Spots. Clicking a method in the Hot Spot list will find that method's entry in the Call Tree, making it easy to see the relationship between a method's root and the hot spot (shown in Figure 5-19).

The Info tab displays a summary of the snapshot information: date, time, filter settings, and so on. The icons along the top of the snapshot window allow you to save the snapshot, control the granularity of the snapshot (method, classes, or packages), and search the snapshot.

The next several sections cover memory profiling.

Starting a Memory Profiling Session

The steps required to gather a memory profile with the NetBeans Profiler are similar to the steps required to gather a method profile described earlier in this chapter.

As is the case with the method profiling section, the steps presented in this section illustrate remote profiling since usually it is more desirable to profile an application running on a target system in a qualification type of environment and most desktop systems do not have sufficient memory resources to run both a powerful memory profiler and a complex application at the same time.

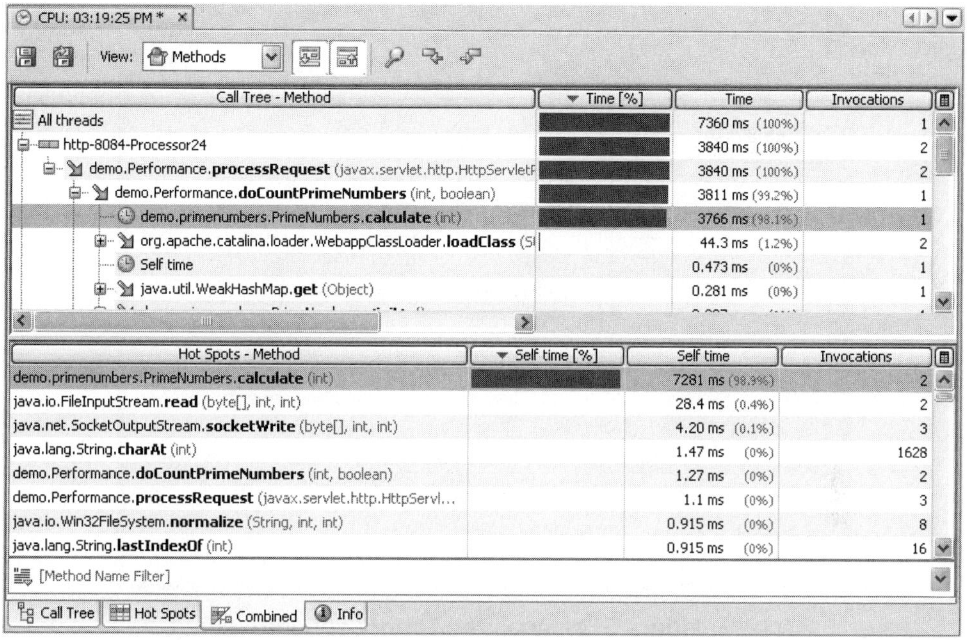

Figure 5-19 Combined view while analyzing performance

The general steps for memory profiling are as follows:

1. Identify the remote system where the application to profile resides.
2. Start NetBeans IDE on your desktop system.
3. Select the profiling task and method profiling.

   Select the Profile > Attach Profiler option from the main menu in NetBeans IDE. From the Attach Profiler panel, select the Memory icon on the left to select method profiling as shown in Figure 5-20.

4. Specify options for memory profiling.

   When you memory profile with the NetBeans Profiler you have several options. To get just a general feel for an application's object allocation footprint, select the Record object creation only since it imposes the least amount of overhead. Collected profile statistics are displayed in the live results profiling panel that suggest potential excessive object allocations in your application.

   To get a sense of the long-lived objects in your application, select the Record both object creation and garbage collection option. This option is also useful for tracking down potential memory leaks.

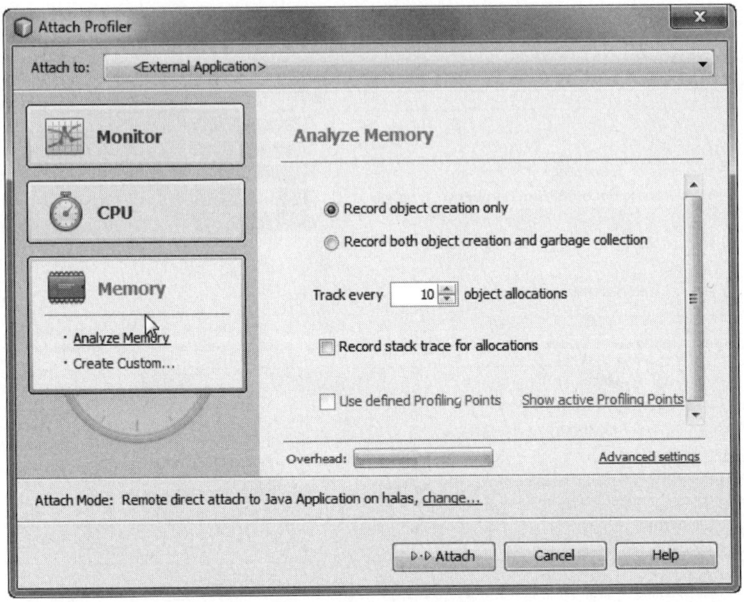

Figure 5-20 Analyze Memory options

By default, for each class used by your application, only every tenth allocation actually is tracked by the profiler. For most applications, this statistical approach dramatically lowers overhead without an impact on accuracy. You can use the spin control to change the number of allocations that are tracked, but keep in mind that lowering the value increases profiling overhead. In a complex application that you intend to profile for an extended period of time, consider increasing the value so the profiling activity is not as intrusive on the application's performance. If you find the profiling activity is too intrusive on your application, increasing Track every object allocations value reduces the profiling overhead. But increasing the Track every object allocations value, may lose some profiling accuracy if not enough samples are collected. Hence, when increasing the Track every object allocation, the application must execute longer to gain enough information from the reduce sampling frequency.

Most important though is for the profiler to report the methods that performed the object allocations, you must select the Record stack trace for Allocations option.

5. Generate the remote profiling pack.

6. Configure the remote system with the remote profiling pack; refer back to the instructions in the previous section on remote method profiling if you need assistance in how to perform these two steps.

7. Start profiling; examine the data it displays and the data it collects.

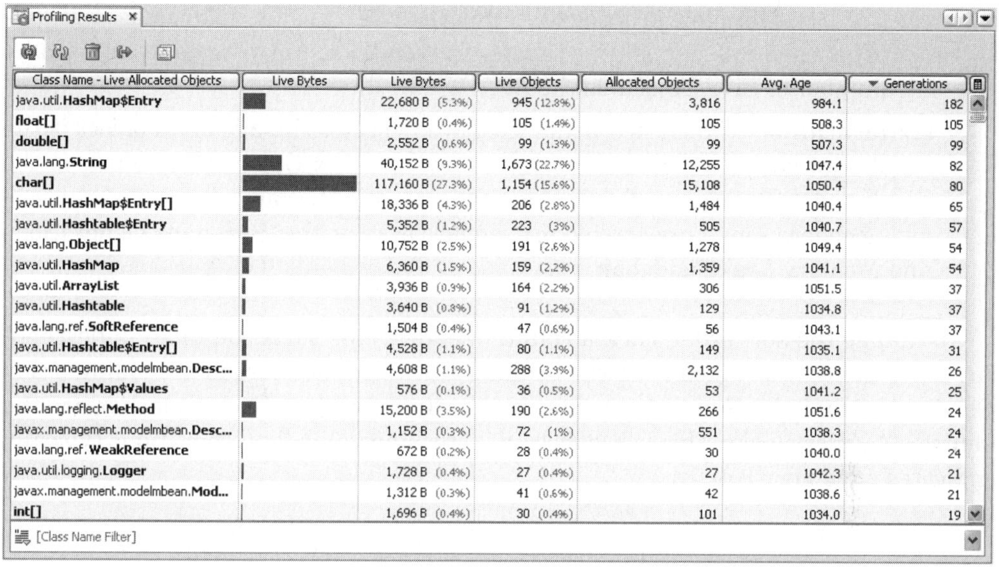

Profiling Results ✕

Class Name - Live Allocated Objects	Live Bytes	Live Bytes	Live Objects	Allocated Objects	Avg. Age	▼ Generations
java.util.**HashMap$Entry**	■	22,680 B (5.3%)	945 (12.8%)	3,816	984.1	182
float[]	┃	1,720 B (0.4%)	105 (1.4%)	105	508.3	105
double[]	┃	2,552 B (0.6%)	99 (1.3%)	99	507.3	99
java.lang.**String**	■	40,152 B (9.3%)	1,673 (22.7%)	12,255	1047.4	82
char[]	■	117,160 B (27.3%)	1,154 (15.6%)	15,108	1050.4	80
java.util.**HashMap$Entry[]**	■	18,336 B (4.3%)	206 (2.8%)	1,484	1040.4	65
java.util.**Hashtable$Entry**	┃	5,352 B (1.2%)	223 (3%)	505	1040.7	57
java.lang.**Object[]**	■	10,752 B (2.5%)	191 (2.6%)	1,278	1049.4	54
java.util.**HashMap**	■	6,360 B (1.5%)	159 (2.2%)	1,359	1041.1	54
java.util.**ArrayList**	┃	3,936 B (0.9%)	164 (2.2%)	306	1051.5	37
java.util.**Hashtable**	┃	3,640 B (0.8%)	91 (1.2%)	129	1034.8	37
java.lang.ref.**SoftReference**	┃	1,504 B (0.4%)	47 (0.6%)	56	1043.1	37
java.util.**Hashtable$Entry[]**	┃	4,528 B (1.1%)	80 (1.1%)	149	1035.1	31
javax.management.modelmbean.**Desc...**	┃	4,608 B (1.1%)	288 (3.9%)	2,132	1038.8	26
java.util.**HashMap$Values**	┃	576 B (0.1%)	36 (0.5%)	53	1041.2	25
java.lang.reflect.**Method**	■	15,200 B (3.5%)	190 (2.6%)	266	1051.6	24
javax.management.modelmbean.**Desc...**	┃	1,152 B (0.3%)	72 (1%)	551	1038.3	24
java.lang.ref.**WeakReference**	┃	672 B (0.2%)	28 (0.4%)	30	1040.0	24
java.util.logging.**Logger**	┃	1,728 B (0.4%)	27 (0.4%)	27	1042.3	21
javax.management.modelmbean.**Mod...**	┃	1,312 B (0.3%)	41 (0.6%)	42	1038.6	21
int[]	┃	1,696 B (0.4%)	30 (0.4%)	101	1034.0	19

[Class Name Filter]

Figure 5-21 Live Results while analyzing memory usage

Start the remote application. When it initializes, it blocks and waits until the Net-Beans Profiler attaches to it. Once the NetBeans Profiler has successfully attached, the remote Java application unblocks and continues to execute. The NetBeans Profiler opens a Profiler Control Panel in NetBeans IDE with Controls, Status, Profiling Results, Save Snapshots, View, and Basic Telemetry subpanels as shown previously in Figure 5-16.

Viewing Live Results

Once profiling begins, you can use the Live Results button to open a dynamic display of the heap contents (shown in Figure 5-21).

The columns displayed are

- **Allocated Objects.** The number of objects that the profiler is tracking.
- **Live Objects.** The number of the Allocated Objects that are currently on the heap and are therefore taking up memory.
- **Live Bytes.** Shows the amount of heap memory being used by the Live Objects. One column displays a graph; the other displays text.

- **Avg. Age.**   Average age of the Live Objects. The age of each object is the number of garbage collections that it has survived. The sum of the ages divided by the number of Live Objects is the Avg. Age.

- **Generations.**   Calculated using the Live Objects. The age of an object is the number of garbage collections it has survived. The Generations value is the number of different ages for the Live Objects. It is the same concept as the surviving generations, only applied to a single class; see the "Surviving Generations and Memory Leaks" sidebar.

To change the sort order, click a column header. This sorts the table in descending order using the values from the column. Click again to sort in ascending order. Sorting the table by Generations can frequently help identify classes that are the source of memory leaks. This is because an increasing value for Generations typically indicates a memory leak.

Tip

Once you have the display sorted so that the classes of interest are at the top, if you chose to track object creation and garbage collection, then you can right-click an entry and choose Stop Profiling Classes below this Line to reduce profiling overhead.

Surviving Generations and Memory Leaks

To understand the Generations column in the memory profiling results view, you have to think about the JVM's Garbage Collection process. Every time the garbage collector runs each object either survives and continues to occupy heap memory, or it is removed and its memory is freed. If an object survives, then its age has increased by a value of 1. In other words, the age of an object is simply the number of garbage collections that it has survived. The value of Generations is the number of *different* object ages.

For example, assume several objects were all allocated when your application first started. Further, another group of objects was allocated at the midpoint of your application's run. And finally, some objects have just been allocated and have only survived one garbage collection. If the garbage collector has run 80 times, then all the objects in the first group will have an age of 80, all the objects in the second group will have an age of 40, and all of the objects in the third group will have an age of 1. In this example, the value of Generations is 3, because there are three different ages among all the objects on the heap: 80, 40, and 1.

In most Java applications the value for Generations eventually stabilizes. This is because the application has reached a point where all long-lived objects have been allocated. Objects that are intended to have a shorter life span do not impact the Generations count because they will eventually be garbage collected.

If the Generations value for your application continues to increase as the application runs, it could be an indication of a memory leak. In other words, your application is continuing to allocate objects over time, each of which has a different age because it has survived a different number of garbage collections. If the objects were being properly garbage collected, the number of different object ages would not be increasing.

Taking a Snapshot of Results

To see which methods in your application are allocating objects, you must take a snapshot. Use the Take Snapshot button in the Profiler Control Panel. The resulting window has a tab labeled Memory that contains the same information as the Live Results window. Right-click a class in the list and then select the Show Allocation Stack Traces option to switch to the Allocation Stack Traces tab. Its display is similar, only the first column displays method names (shown in Figure 5-22).

> **Tip**
>
> You can right-click an entry in the Live Results window and select Take Snapshot and Show Allocation Stack Traces to quickly open a new Memory tab with the Allocation Stack Traces displayed. This is useful when spotting object allocations that are of immediate interest while observing Live Results.

The listed methods shown in the Allocation Stack Traces tab indicates which methods allocated one or more instances of the selected class. If you focus on those objects allocating the largest number of bytes and have a short average age, these become good candidates to reduce object allocations. There are many different approaches and strategies for reducing object allocations ranging from reducing underlying containers from being resized, such as StringBuilder's underlying char[ ], to object pooling, which pools a number of objects to be reused rather

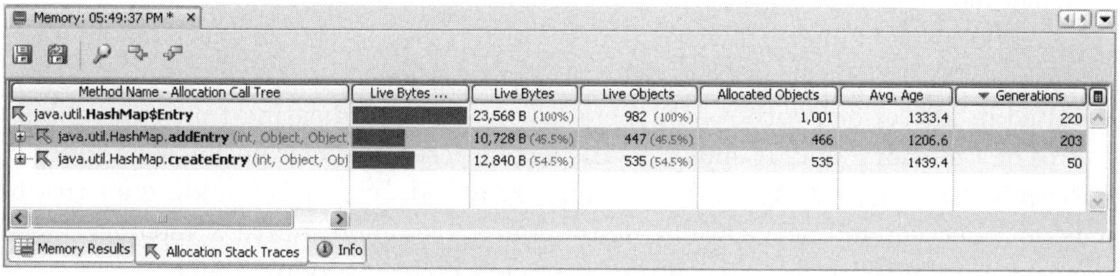

Method Name - Allocation Call Tree	Live Bytes ...	Live Bytes	Live Objects	Allocated Objects	Avg. Age	Generations	
java.util.**HashMap$Entry**		23,568 B (100%)	982 (100%)	1,001	1333.4	220	
java.util.HashMap.**addEntry** (int, Object, Object,		10,728 B (45.5%)	447 (45.5%)	466	1206.6	203	
java.util.HashMap.**createEntry** (int, Object, Obj		12,840 B (54.5%)	535 (54.5%)	535	1439.4	50	

Memory Results / Allocation Stack Traces / Info

Figure 5-22 Results snapshot while analyzing memory usage

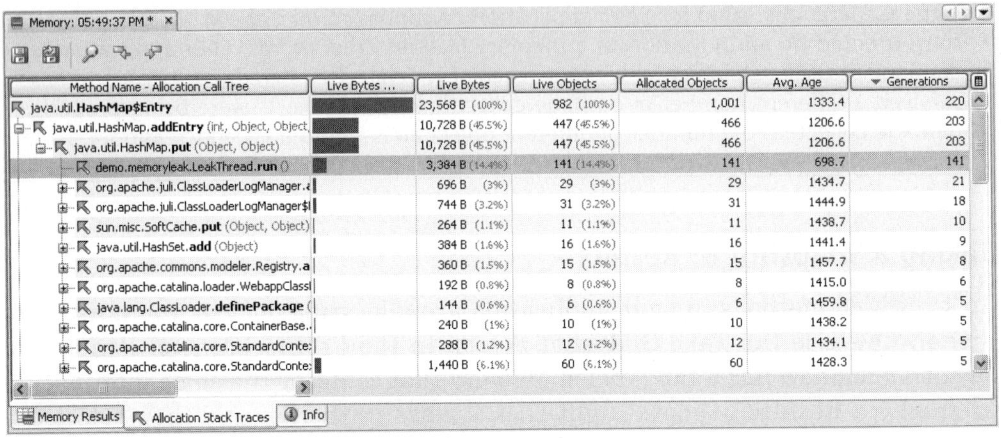

Figure 5-23 Execution paths for a method

than allocating a new one. However, it is generally not a good practice to pool objects unless there is a high cost of allocation or collecting those objects. High cost implies a lengthy duration of elapsed time to allocate or garbage collect those objects.

Isolating Memory Leaks

You can use the displayed statistics in the Allocation Stack Traces view of the Memory panel to help narrow down which of the methods is allocating class instances that are causing memory leaks. In the example shown previously in Figure 5-22, the addEntry() and createEntry() methods are both allocating instances of HashMap$Entry. Note that the Generations value for the allocations done by addEntry() is much higher than that for createEntry(). This indicates that addEntry() is where leaking instances of HashMap$Entry are being allocated. You can click the icon next to a method's name to see the different execution paths that called that method (shown in Figure 5-23).

The addEntry() method was called by put(), which in turn was called by several different methods. The calls from one of those methods, LeakThread.run(), resulted in allocations with a high Generations value, indicating that it is a likely source of a memory leak. It should be inspected to see whether perhaps it is adding entries to a HashMap that are never being removed. In general, adding entries to a Java Collection and never removing them are a common source of memory leaks. Memory profiling with NetBeans Profiler in addition to observing sources of potential unnecessary object allocations can be useful.

Analyzing Heap Dumps

In addition to memory profiling a running application, the NetBeans Profiler can also load a binary heap dump generated by the Java HotSpot VM. A binary heap dump is a snapshot of all the objects in the Java HotSpot VM at the time the heap dump is taken. One of features introduced in Java 6 HotSpot VMs is the capability to generate heap dumps on `OutOfMemoryErrors`. This is a useful feature when troubleshooting the root case that led to an `OutOfMemoryError`. Java 5 and Java 6 can both produce binary heap dumps using the `jmap` command. Binary heap dumps can also be generated using Java 6's JConsole using its HotSpotDiagnostics MBean. VisualVM can also be used to generate a binary heap of an application. How to configure the Java HotSpot VM to produce heap dumps on `OutOfMemoryErrors`, and how to use `jmap`, JConsole, or VisualVM for generating binary heap dumps are described in Chapter 4, "JVM Performance Monitoring."

Binary heap dumps can be loaded in the NetBeans Profiler by selecting Profile > Load Heap Dump from the main menu in the NetBeans IDE.

> **Tip**
>
> Since VisualVM contains a subset of the NetBeans Profiler capabilities, a common practice for VisualVM users is to generate a binary heap dump using VisualVM and then immediately analyzing it by loading the binary heap dump in VisualVM.

Once the binary heap dump has been loaded, you can analyze object allocations for opportunities to reduce or avoid unnecessary object allocations. You can think of looking at binary heap dumps as a means of doing offline memory profiling.

Bibliography

AMD CodeAnalyst Performance Analyzer. http://developer.amd.com/cpu/CodeAnalyst/Pages/default.aspx AMD Corporation.

Intel VTune Amplier XE 2011. http://software.intel.com/en-us/articles/intel-vtune-amplifier-xe/ Intel Corporation.

Itzkowitz, Marty. "Performance Tuning with the Oracle Solaris Studio Performance Tools." Oracle Develop, Oracle OpenWorld 2010 Conference. San Francisco, CA. September 2010.

Keegan, Patrick, et al. *NetBeans IDE field guide: developing desktop, web, enterprise, and mobile applications, Second Edition.* Sun Microsystems, Inc. Santa Clara, CA, 2006.

6

Java Application Profiling Tips and Tricks

Chapter 5, "Java Application Profiling," presented the basic concepts of using a modern Java profiler such as the Oracle Solaris Studio Performance Analyzer and NetBeans Profiler. It did not, however, show any specific tips and tricks in using the tools to identify performance issues and approaches of how to resolve them. This is the purpose of this chapter. Its intention is to show how to use the tools to identify performance issues and take corrective actions to resolve them. This chapter looks at several of the more common types of performance issues the authors have observed through many years of working as Java performance engineers.

Performance Opportunities

Most Java performance opportunities fall into one or more of the following categories:

- **Using a more efficient algorithm.** The largest gains in the performance of an application come from the use of a more efficient algorithm. The use of a more efficient algorithm allows an application to execute with fewer CPU instructions, also known as a shorter path length. An application that executes with a shorter path length generally executes faster. Many different changes can lead to a shorter path length. At the highest level of the application, using a different data structure or modifying its implementation can lead to a shorter path length. Many applications that suffer application performance issues often use inappropriate data structures. There is no substitute for choosing the proper data structure and algorithm. As profiles are analyzed, take notice of the data structures and the algorithms used. Optimal performance can be realized when the best data structures and algorithms are utilized.

- **Reduce lock contention.** Contending for access to a shared resource inhibits an application's capability to scale to a large number of software threads and across a large number of CPUs. Changes to an application that allow for less frequent lock contention and less duration of locking allow an application to scale better.

- **Generate more efficient code for a given algorithm.** Clocks per CPU instruction, usually referred to as CPI, for an application is a ratio of the number of CPU clock ticks used per CPU instruction. CPI is a measure of the efficiency of generated code that is produced by a compiler. A change in the application, JVM, or operating system that reduces the CPI for an application will realize an improvement in its performance since it takes advantage of better and more optimized generated code.

There is a subtle difference between path length, which is closely tied to the algorithm choice, and cycles per instruction, CPI, which is the notion of generating more efficient code. In the former, the objective is to produce the shortest sequence of CPU instructions based on the algorithm choice. The latter's objective is to reduce the number of CPU clocks consumed per CPU instruction, that is, produce the most efficient code from a compiler. To illustrate with an example, suppose a CPU instruction results in a CPU cache miss, such as a load instruction. It may take several hundred CPU clock cycles for that load instruction to complete as a result of the CPU cache miss having to fetch data from memory rather than finding it in a CPU cache. However, if a prefetch instruction was inserted upstream in the sequence of instructions generated by a compiler to prefetch from memory the data being loaded by the load instruction, it is likely the number of clock cycles required to load the data will be less with the additional prefetch instruction since the prefetch can be done in parallel with other CPU instructions ahead of the load instruction. When the load instruction occurs, it can then find the data to be loaded in a CPU cache. However, the path length, the number of CPU instructions executed is longer as a result of the additional prefetch instruction. Therefore, it is possible to increase path length, yet make better use of available CPU cycles.

The following sections present several strategies to consider when analyzing a profile and looking for optimization opportunities. Generally, optimization opportunities for most applications fall into one of the general categories just described.

System or Kernel CPU Usage

Chapter 2, "Operating System Performance Monitoring," suggests one of the statistics to monitor is system or kernel CPU utilization. If CPU clock cycles are spent executing operating system or kernel code, those are CPU clock cycles that cannot be used to execute your application. Hence, a strategy to improve the performance of an application is to reduce the amount of time it spends consuming system or kernel CPU clock cycles. However, this strategy is not applicable in applications that spend little time executing system or kernel code. Monitoring the operating system for system or kernel CPU utilization provides the data as to whether it makes sense to employ this strategy.

The Oracle Solaris Performance Analyzer collects system or kernel CPU statistics as part of an application profile. This is done by selecting the View > Set Data Presentation menu in Performance Analyzer, choosing the Metrics tab, and setting the options to present system CPU utilization statistics, both inclusive or exclusive. Recall that inclusive metrics include not only the time spent in a given method, but also the time spent in methods it calls. In contrast, exclusive metrics report only the amount of time spent in a given method.

> **Tip**
>
> It can be useful to include both inclusive and exclusive metrics when first analyzing a profile. Looking at the inclusive metrics provides a sense of the path the application executes. Looking at the general path an application takes you may identify an opportunity for an alternative algorithm or approach that may offer better performance.

Figure 6-1 shows the Performance Analyzer's Set Data Presentation form with options selected to present both inclusive and exclusive System CPU metrics. Also notice the options selected report both the raw time value and the percentage of System CPU time.

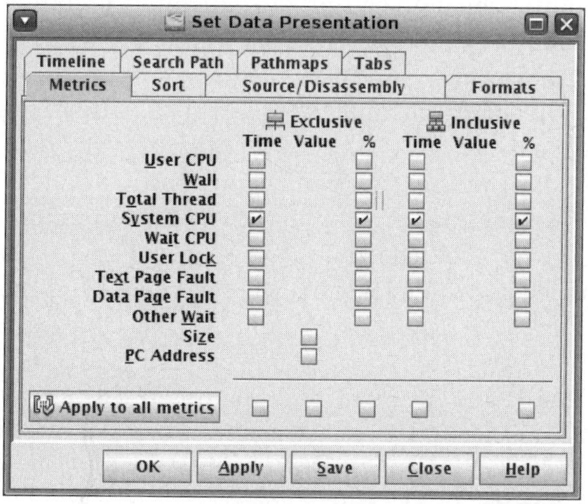

Figure 6-1 Set system CPU data presentation

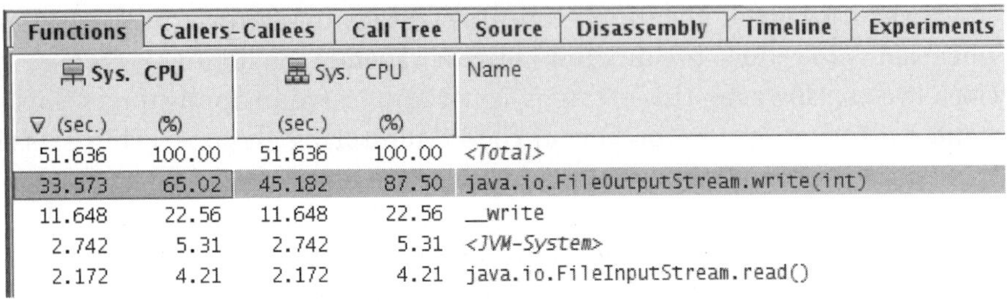

Functions	Callers–Callees	Call Tree	Source	Disassembly	Timeline	Experiments

🖥 Sys. CPU		🖧 Sys. CPU		Name
▽ (sec.)	(%)	(sec.)	(%)	
51.636	100.00	51.636	100.00	<Total>
33.573	65.02	45.182	87.50	java.io.FileOutputStream.write(int)
11.648	22.56	11.648	22.56	__write
2.742	5.31	2.742	5.31	<JVM-System>
2.172	4.21	2.172	4.21	java.io.FileInputStream.read()

Figure 6-2 Exclusive system CPU

After clicking on the OK button, the Performance Analyzer displays the profile's System CPU inclusive and exclusive metrics in descending order. The arrow in the metric column header indicates how the data is presented and sorted. In Figure 6-2, the System CPU data is ordered by the exclusive metric (notice the arrow in the exclusive metric header and the icon indicating an exclusive metric).

Figure 6-2 shows a profile from an application that exhibits high system or kernel CPU utilization. You can see this application consumed about 33.5 seconds of System CPU in the java.io.FileOutputStream.write(int) method and about 11.6 seconds in a method called __write(), or about 65% and 22.5%, respectively. You can also get a sense of how significant the improvement can be realized by reducing the System CPU utilization of this application. The ideal situation for an application is to have 0% System CPU utilization. But for some applications that goal is difficult to achieve, especially if there is I/O involved, since I/O operations require a system call. In applications that require I/O, the goal is to reduce the frequency of making a system call. One approach to reduce the call frequency of an I/O system call is buffer the data so that larger chunks of data are read or written during I/O operations.

In the example shown in Figure 6-2, you can see the file write (output) operations are consuming a large amount of time as illustrated by the java.io.FileOutputStream.write(int) and __write() entries. To identify whether the write operations are buffered, you can use the Callers-Callees tab to walk up the call stack to see what methods are calling the FileOutputStream.write(int) method and the __write method. You walk up the call stack by selecting one of the callees from the upper panel and clicking the Set Center button. Figure 6-3 shows the Callers-Callees of the FileOutputStream.write(int) method.

The callers of FileOutputStream.write(int) are ExtOutputStream.write(int) and OutImpl.outc(int). 85.18% of the System CPU attributed to FileOutputStream.write(int) comes from its use in ExtOutputStream.write(int) and 14.82% of it from OutImpl.outc(int). A look at the implementation of ExtOutputStream.write(int) shows:

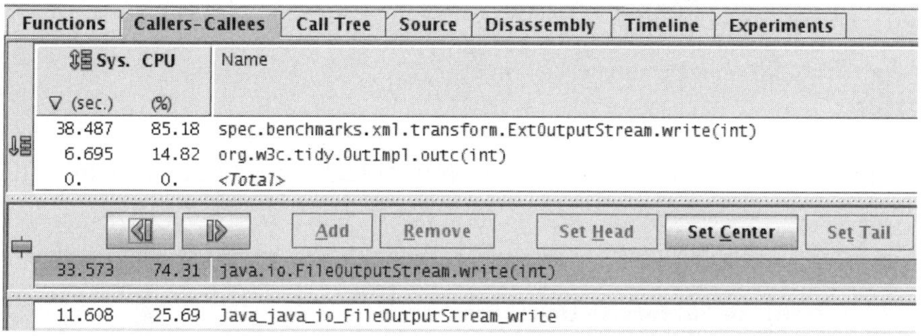

Sys. CPU (sec.)	(%)	Name
38.487	85.18	spec.benchmarks.xml.transform.ExtOutputStream.write(int)
6.695	14.82	org.w3c.tidy.OutImpl.outc(int)
0.	0.	*Total*
33.573	74.31	java.io.FileOutputStream.write(int)
11.608	25.69	Java_java_io_FileOutputStream_write

Figure 6-3 FileOutputStream.write(int) callers and callees

```
public void write(int b) throws IOException {
    super.write(b);
    writer.write((byte)b);
}
```

A look at the implementation of `super.write(b)` shows it is not a call to `FileOutputStream.write(int)`:

```
public void write(int b) throws IOException {
    crc = crc * 33 + b;
}
```

But the writer field in `ExtOutputStream` is declared as a `FileOutputStream`:

```
private FileOutputStream writer;
```

And it is initialized without any type of buffering:

```
writer = new FileOutputStream(currentFileName);
```

`currentFileName` is a field declared as a `String`:

```
private String currentFileName;
```

Hence, an optimization to be applied here is to buffer the data being written to `FileOutputStream` in `ExtOutputStream` using a `BufferedOutputStream`. This is done rather quickly and easily by chaining or wrapping the `FileOutputStream` in a `BufferedOutputStream` in an `ExtOutputStream`. Here is a quick listing of the changes required:

```
// Change FileOutputStream writer to a BufferedOutputStream
// private FileOutputStream writer;
private BufferedOutputStream writer;
```

Then chain a `BufferedOutputStream` and `FileOutputStream` at initialization time:

```
// Initialize BufferedOutputStream
// writer = new FileOutputStream(currentFileName);
writer = new BufferedOutputStream(
            new FileOutputStream(currentFileName));
```

Writing to the `BufferedOutputStream`, instead of the `FileOutputStream`, in `ExtOutputStream.write(int b)` does not require any update since `BufferOutputStream` has a `write()` method that buffers bytes written to it. This `ExtOutputStream.write(int b)` method is shown here:

```
public void write(int b) throws IOException {
    super.write(b);
    // No update required here,
    // automatically uses BufferedOutputStream.write()
    writer.write((byte)b);
}
```

The other uses of the `writer` field must be inspected to ensure the use of `BufferedOutputStream` operates as expected. In `ExtStreamOutput`, there are two additional uses of the `writer` field, one in a method called `reset()` and another in `checkResult()`. These two methods are as follows:

```
public void reset() {
    super.reset();
    try {
        if (diffOutputStream != null) {
            diffOutputStream.flush();
            diffOutputStream.close();
            diffOutputStream = null;
        }
        if (writer != null) {
            writer.close();
        }
    } catch (IOException e) {
        e.printStackTrace();
```

```
        }
    }
    public void checkResult(int loopNumber) {
        try {
            writer.flush();
            writer.close();
        } catch (IOException e) {
            e.printStackTrace();
        }
        check(validiationProperties.getProperty(propertyName));
        outProperties.put(propertyName, "" + getCRC());
        reset();
    }
```

The uses of `writer` as a `BufferedOutputStream` works as expected. It should be noted that the API specification for `BufferedOutputStream.close()` indicates it calls the `BufferedOutputStream.flush()` method and then calls the `close()` method of its underlying output stream, in this case the `FileOutputStream.close()` method. As a result, the `FileOutputStream` is not required to be explicitly closed, nor is the `flush()` method in `ExtOutputStream.checkResult(int)` required. A couple of additional enhancements worth consideration are

1. A `BufferedOutputStream` can also be allocated with an optional buffered size. The default buffer size, as of Java 6, is 8192. If the application you are profiling is writing a large number of bytes, you might consider specifying an explicit size larger than 8192. If you specify an explicit size, consider a size that is a multiple of the operating systems page size since operating systems efficiently fetch memory that are multiples of the operating system page size. On Oracle Solaris, the `pagesize` command with no arguments reports the default page size. On Linux, the default page size can be obtained using the `getconf PAGESIZE` command. Windows on x86 and x64 platforms default to a 4K (4096) page size.

2. Change the `ExtOutputStream.writer` field from an explicit `BufferedOutputStream` type to an `OutputStream` type, that is, `OutputStream writer = new BufferedOutputStream()`, instead of `BufferedOutputStream writer = new BufferedOutputStream()`. This allows for additional flexibility in type of `OutputStream`, for example, `ByteArrayOutputStream`, `DataOutputStream`, `FilterOutputStream`, `FileOutputStream`, or `BufferedOutputStream`.

Looking back at Figure 6-3, a second method calls `FileOutputStream.write(int)` called `org.w3c.tidy.OutImpl.outc(int)`, which is a method from a third-party library used in the profiled application. To reduce the amount of system CPU utilization used in a third-party supplied method, the best approach is to file a bug or enhancement request with the third-party library provider and include the information from the profile. If the source is accessible via an open source license and has acceptable license terms, you may consider further investigating and including additional information in the bug or enhancement request report.

After applying the changes identified in `ExtOutputStream`, using the `BufferedOutputStream` and its default constructor (not including the two additional enhancements just mentioned), and collecting a profile, the amount of system CPU utilization drops substantially. Comparing the profiles in Figure 6-4 to those in Figure 6-2, you can see the amount of inclusive system CPU time spent in `java.io.FileOutputStream` has dropped from 45.182 seconds to 6.655 seconds (exclusive system CPU time is the second column).

Executing this application workload outside the profiler in a performance testing environment prior to making the modifications reports it took this application 427 seconds to run to completion. In constrast, the modified version of the application workload that uses the `BufferOutputStream` in the same performance testing environment reports it runs to completion in 383 seconds. In other words, this application realized about a 10% improvement in its run to completion execution.

In addition, looking at the Callers-Callees tab for `java.io.FileOutputStream.write(int)`, only the call to `org.w3c.tidy.OutImpl.outc(int)` remains as a significant consumer of the `FileOutputStream.write(int)` method. The Callers-Callees of `FileOutputStream.write(int)` are shown in Figure 6-5.

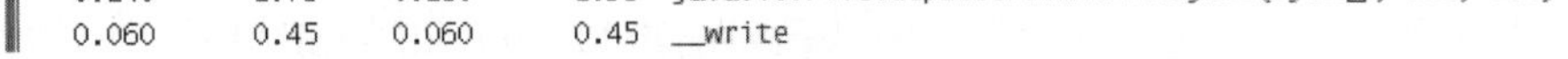

Functions	Callers–Callees	Call Tree	Source	Disassembly	Timeline	Experiments

🖥 Sys. CPU		🖧 Sys. CPU		Name
▽ (sec.)	(%)	(sec.)	(%)	
13.479	100.00	13.479	100.00	<Total>
6.655	49.37	6.655	49.37	java.io.FileOutputStream.write(int)
3.052	22.64	3.052	22.64	<JVM-System>
2.412	17.89	2.412	17.89	java.io.FileInputStream.read()
0.240	1.78	0.260	1.93	java.io.FileOutputStream.writeBytes(byte[], int, int)
0.060	0.45	0.060	0.45	__write

Figure 6-4 Reduced system CPU utilization

Functions	Callers–Callees	Call Tree	Source	Disassembly	Timeline	Experiments

🔢 Sys. CPU ▽ (sec.)	Name
6.655	org.w3c.tidy.OutImpl.outc(int)

◁	▷	Add	Remove	Set Head	Set Center	Set Tail

6.655	java.io.FileOutputStream.write(int)

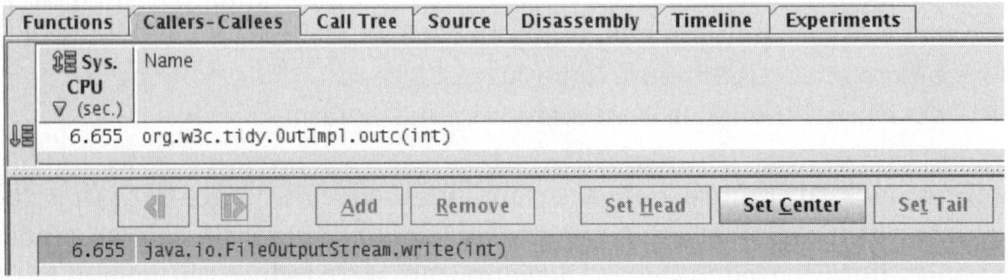

Figure 6-5 Callers-Callees after changes

Comparing the Callers-Callees in Figure 6-5, after the changes to `ExtStream Output`, with the Callers-Callees in Figure 6-3, prior to the changes, you can see the amount of attributable time spent in `org.w3c.tidy.OutImpl.outc(int)` stays close to the same. This should not be a surprise since the changes made to `ExtStreamOutput` now use `BufferedOutputStream`. But recall that the `BufferedOutputStream` invokes a `FileOutputStream` method when any of the underlying buffer in the `BufferedOutputStream` becomes full, the `BufferedOutputStream.flush()` method is called, or when the `Buffered-OutputSteam.close()` method is called. If you look back at Figure 6-4 you see a `FileOutputStream.writeBytes(byte[],int,int)` method. This is the method that the `BufferedOutputStream` calls from `ExtStreamOut-put`. Figure 6-6 shows the Callers-Callees tab for the `FileOutputStream. writeBytes(byte[],int,int)`.

Selecting `java.io.FileOutputStream.write(byte[],int,int)` method from the upper Callee panel and clicking the Set Center button illustrates that `Buff-eredOutputStream.flushBuffer()` is its callee; see Figure 6-7.

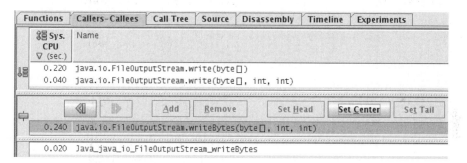

Figure 6-6 Callers-Callees of FileOutputStream.writeBytes(byte[],int,int)

Figure 6-7 Callers-Callees of FileOutputStream.writeBytes(byte[], int, int)

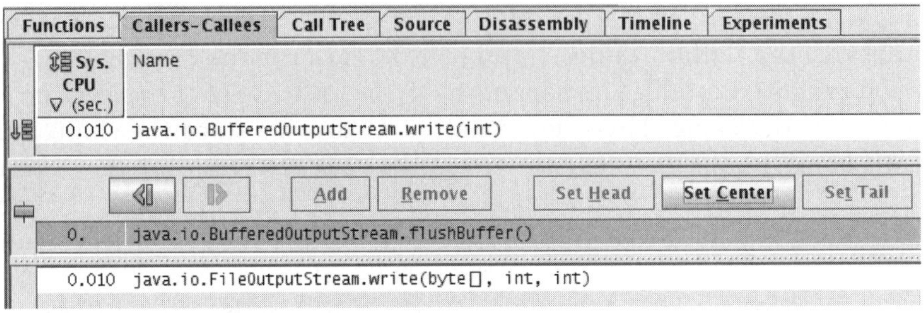

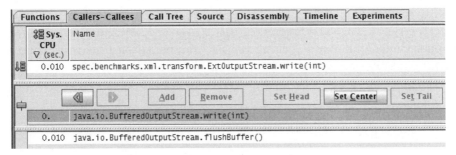

Figure 6-8 Callers-Callees of BufferedOutputStream.flushBuffer()

Figure 6-9 Callers-Callees of BufferedOutputStream.write(int)

Selecting the `BufferedOutputStream.flushBuffer()` method in the upper Callee panel and clicking the Set Center button shows the callee of `java.io.BufferedOutputStream.flushBuffer()` is `BufferedOutputStream.write(int)`. The Callers-Callees of `BufferedOutputStream.flushBuffer()` are shown in Figure 6-8.

Selecting the `BufferedOutputStream.write(int)` method in the upper Callee panel and clicking the Set Center button shows the callee of `java.io.BufferedOutputStream.write(int)` is `ExtOutputStream.write(int)`, the method that has been modified. The Callers-Callees of `BufferedOutputStream.write(int)` are shown in Figure 6-9.

As mentioned earlier, the next step in reducing System CPU utilization for this application requires a modification to a third-party library, a library that holds the implementation of `org.w3c.tidy.OutImpl.outc(int)`. It may be possible for the maintainers of the third-party library to implement a similar modification to `OutImpl.outc(int)` as just described and implemented for `ExtOutputStream.write(int)`. However, the performance improvement realized will likely not be as significant since the profile suggests there is more System CPU utilization attributed to the call path of `ExtOutputStream.write(int)` than to `OutImpl.outc(int)`; refer to Figure 6-3 for attributable System CPU utilization on callers of `FileInput-Stream.write(int)`. In addition, looking at the amount of System CPU utilization consumed in `OutImpl.outc(int)`, about 6.6 seconds, compared to the total application runtime of 383 seconds is rather small, about 1.5%. Hence, a modification to reduce the amount of System CPU utilization spent in `OutImpl.outc(int)` would likely not yield more than 1% to 2% improvement.

> **Tip**
>
> Applications that perform network I/O can employ a similar, general approach to reduce system CPU utilization as that just described in this section. That is, buffer both the data in the input and output stream used to write and read the data.

An additional strategy to reduce system CPU utilization for applications performing large amounts of network I/O is utilizing Java NIO nonblocking data structures. Java NIO was introduced in Java 1.4.2 with many runtime performance improvements added in Java 5 and Java 6. Java NIO nonblocking data structures allow for the ability to read or write as much data as possible in a single call to a network I/O (read or write) operation. Remember that every network I/O call eventually results in the invocation of an operating system's system call, which consumes system CPU utilization. The challenge with using Java NIO nonblocking data structures is it is more difficult to program than using blocking Java NIO or the older, more traditional Java SE blocking data structures such as `java.net.Socket`. In a Java NIO nonblocking output operation, you can write as many bytes as the operating system allows to be written. But you have to check the return value of the output operation to determine whether all the bytes you asked to be written have indeed been written. In a Java NIO nonblocking input operation, where you read as many bytes as are available, you have to check how many bytes have been read. You also have to implement some complex programming logic to deal with partially read protocol data units, or multiple protocol data units. That is, you may not be able to read enough bytes in a single read operation to construct a meaningful protocol data unit or message. In the case of blocking I/O, you simply wait until you generally read the specified number of bytes that constitute a full protocol data unit or message. Whether to migrate an application to utilize nonblocking network I/O operations should be decided upon by the application's performance needs. If you want to take advantage of the additional performance promised by using nonblocking Java NIO, you should consider using a general Java NIO framework to make the migration easier. Several popular Java NIO frameworks are available such as Project Grizzly (https://grizzly.dev.java.net) and Apache MINA (http://mina.apache.org).

Another area where high System CPU utilization may show up is in applications experiencing heavy lock contention. Identifying lock contention in a profile and approaches to reduce lock contention are discussed in the next section.

Lock Contention

In early JVM releases, it was common to delegate Java monitor operations directly to operating system monitors, or mutex primitives. As a result, a Java application experiencing lock contention would exhibit high values of system CPU utilization since operating system mutex primitives involve system calls. In modern JVMs Java monitors are mostly implemented within the JVM in user code rather than immediately delegating them to operating system locking primitives. This means Java applications can exhibit lock contention yet not consume system CPU. Rather, these applications first consume user CPU utilization when attempting to acquire a lock. Only applications that experience severe lock contention may show high system CPU utilization since modern JVMs tend to delegate to operating system locking primitives as a last resort. A Java application running in a modern JVM that experiences lock contention tends to show symptoms of not scaling to a large number of application threads, CPU cores, or a large number of concurrent users. The challenge is finding the source of the lock contention, that is, where are those Java monitors in the source code and what can be done to reduce the lock contention.

Finding and isolating the location of highly contented Java monitors is one of the strengths of the Oracle Solaris Performance Analyzer. Once a profile has been collected with the Performance Analyzer, finding the highly contented locks is easy.

The Performance Analyzer collects Java monitor and lock statistics as part of an application profile. Hence, you can ask the Performance Analyzer to present the Java methods in your application using Java monitors or locks.

> **Tip**
>
> You can also view locks used within the JVM with the Performance Analyzer, but that requires setting the presentation view mode to Machine Mode.

By selecting the View > Set Data Presentation menu in Performance Analyzer and choosing the Metrics tab, you can ask the Performance Analyzer to present lock statistics, both inclusive or exclusive. Remember that inclusive lock metrics include not only the lock time spent in a given method but also the lock time spent in methods it calls. In contrast, exclusive metrics report only the amount of lock time spent in a given method.

Figure 6-10 shows the Performance Analyzer's Set Data Presentation form with options selected to present both inclusive and exclusive lock information. Also notice the options selected report both the time value and the percentage spent locking.

After clicking OK, the Performance Analyzer displays the profile's lock inclusive and exclusive metrics in descending order. The arrow in the metric column header indicates how the data is presented. In Figure 6-11, the lock data is ordered by the exclusive metric (notice the arrow in the exclusive metric header and note the icon indicating an exclusive metric).

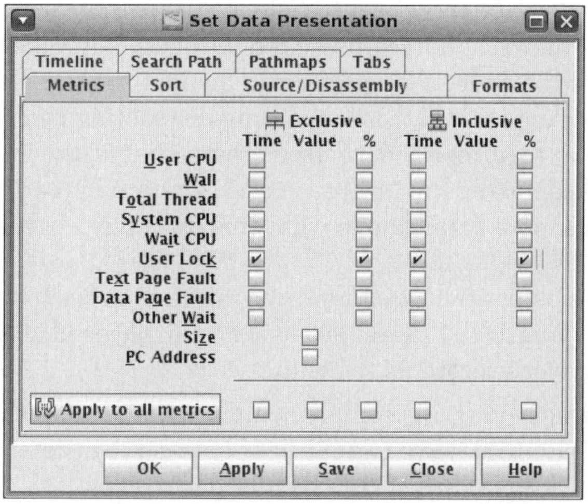

Figure 6-10 Set user lock data presentation

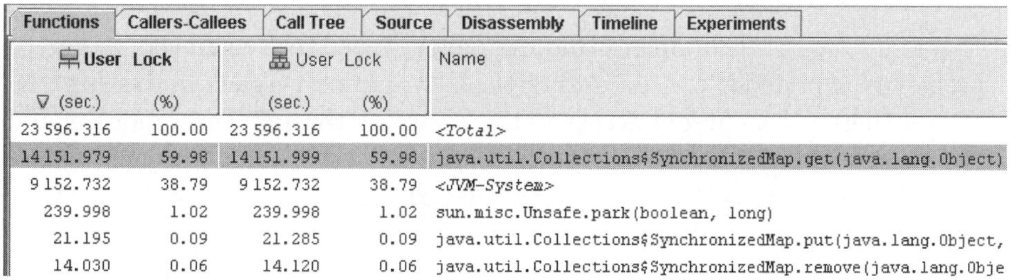

User Lock (sec.)	User Lock (%)	User Lock (sec.)	User Lock (%)	Name
23 596.316	100.00	23 596.316	100.00	<Total>
14 151.979	59.98	14 151.999	59.98	java.util.Collections$SynchronizedMap.get(java.lang.Object)
9 152.732	38.79	9 152.732	38.79	<JVM-System>
239.998	1.02	239.998	1.02	sun.misc.Unsafe.park(boolean, long)
21.195	0.09	21.285	0.09	java.util.Collections$SynchronizedMap.put(java.lang.Object,
14.030	0.06	14.120	0.06	java.util.Collections$SynchronizedMap.remove(java.lang.Obje

Figure 6-11 Java monitors/locks ordered by exclusive metric

> **Tip**
>
> Before blindly looking only at lock metrics in Performance Analyzer, an application should be exhibiting scalability symptoms. The classic scaling symptoms occur when executing an application on a system with a large number of CPUs, CPU cores, or hardware threads does not show an expected scaling in performance throughput relative to a system with a smaller number of CPUs, CPU cores, or hardware threads, or leaves CPU utilization unused. In other words, if an application is not showing scaling issues, then there is no need to investigate an application's locking activity.

The screenshot taken in Figure 6-11 is from a simple example program (complete source code for the remaining examples used in this chapter can be found in Appendix B, "Profiling Tips and Tricks Example Source Code") that uses a `java.util.HashMap` as a data structure to hold 2 million fictitious tax payer records and performs updates to those records stored in the `HashMap`. Since this example is multithreaded and the operations performed against the `HashMap` include adding a new record, removing a new record, updating an existing record, and retrieving a record, the `HashMap` requires synchronized access, that is, the `HashMap` is allocated as a synchronized `Map` using the `Collections.synchronizedMap()` API. The following list provides more details as to what this example program does:

- Creates 2 million fictitious tax payer records and places them in an in-memory data store, a `java.util.HashMap` using a tax payer id as the `HashMap` key and the tax payer's record as the value.

- Queries the underlying system for the number of available processors using the Java API `Runtime.availableProcessors()` to determine the number of simultaneous Java threads to execute concurrently.

- Uses the number returned from `Runtime.availableProcessors()` and creates that many `java.util.concurrent.Callable` objects to execute concurrently in an allocated `java.util.concurrent.ExecutorService` pool of `Executors`.

- All `Executors` are launched and tax payer records are retrieved, updated, removed, and added concurrently by the `Executor` threads in the `HashMap`. Since there is concurrent access to the `HashMap` through the actions of adding, removing, and updating records, `HashMap` access must be synchronized. The `HashMap` is synchronized using the `Collections.synchronizedMap()` wrapper API at `HashMap` creation time.

From the preceding description, it should be of little surprise this example program experiences lock contention when a large number of threads are trying to concurrently access the same synchronized `HashMap`. For example, when this program is run on a Sun SPARC Enterprise T5120 Server configured with an UltraSPARC T2 processor, which has 64 virtual processors (the same value as that returned by the Java API `Runtime.availableProcessors()`), the performance throughput reported by the program is about 615,000 operations per second. But only 8% CPU utilization is reported due to heavy lock contention. Oracle Solaris mpstat also reports a large number of voluntary thread context switches. In Chapter 2, the "Memory Utilization" section talks about high values of voluntary thread context switches being a potential indicator of high lock contention. In that section, it is said that the act of parking a thread and awaking a thread after being notified both result in an operating system voluntary context switch. Hence, an application experiencing heavy lock contention also exhibits a high number of voluntary context switches. In short, this application is exhibiting symptoms of lock contention.

Capturing a profile of this example program with the Performance Analyzer and viewing its lock statistics, as Figure 6-11 shows, confirms this program is experiencing heavy lock contention. The application is spending about 59% of the total lock time, about 14,000 seconds, performing a synchronized `HashMap.get()` operation. You can also see about 38% of the total lock time is spent in an entry labeled *<JVM-System>*. You can read more about this in the "Understanding JVM-System Locking" sidebar. You can also see the calls to the `put()` and `remove()` records in the synchronized `HashMap` as well.

Figure 6-12 shows the Callers-Callees of the `SynchronizedMap.get()` entry. It is indeed called by the `TaxPayerBailoutDBImpl.get()` method, and the `SynchronizedMap.get()` method calls a `HashMap.get()` method.

Understanding JVM-System Locking

A JVM-System entry in Performance Analyzer indicates time spent within the JVM internals. In the context of looking at lock contention statistics in Performance Analyzer, this is the amount or percentage of time spent in locks within the internals of the JVM. This may sound alarming when looking at the amount of time spent in the JVM-System in Figure 6-11.

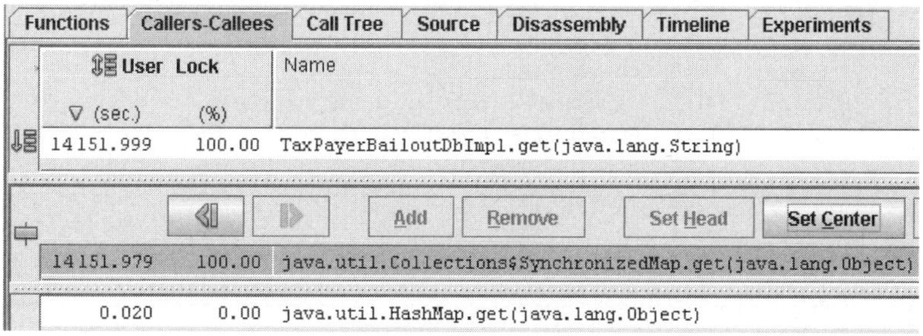

Figure 6-12 Callers-Callees of synchronized HashMap.get()

Hence, this requires a little further explanation and clarification. Recall from Chapter 5 that switching from a Data Presentation Format of User mode to either Expert mode or Machine mode shows the internal operations of the JVM and puts them in the JVM-System entry seen in User mode. Also remember that switching to Expert mode or Machine mode also shows highly contended Java monitors as a form of a _lwp_mutex, __lwp_cond_wait, or __lwp_park type of entry and isolates the locking within Java APIs with those found within the JVM. Figure 6-13 shows the same profile but is switched from User mode to Expert mode in the Performance Analyzer.

Comparing Figure 6-11 to Figure 6-13 suggests the JVM-System entry has resolved into __lwp_condition_wait and __lwp_park operations. The sum of the __lwp_condition_wait and __lwp_park are close to what is reported for JVM-System in Figure 6-11. Your initial reaction may be the JVM is also experiencing lock contention. However, selecting the __lwp_cond_wait entry and selecting the Callers-Callees tab and walking up the call stack, the source of the locking activity associated with __lwp_cond_wait, in other words the locking activity associated with the JVM-System entry, is shown in Figure 6-14.

All five of the methods shown in Figure 6-14 are internal JVM methods. Notice that over 95% of the attributable lock time is spent in GCTaskManager::get_task(unsigned).

Functions	Callers-Callees	Call Tree	Source	Disassembly	Timeline	Experiments

🖳 User Lock		🖧 User Lock		Name
▽ (sec.)	(%)	(sec.)	(%)	
23 596.316	100.00	23 596.316	100.00	*<Total>*
14 151.979	59.98	14 151.999	59.98	java.util.Collections$SynchronizedMap.get(java.lang.Object)
8 874.037	37.61	8 874.037	37.61	___lwp_cond_wait
279.726	1.19	279.726	1.19	__lwp_park

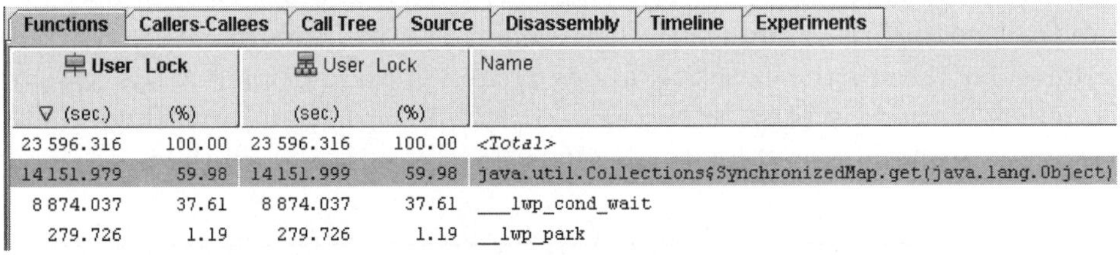

Figure 6-13 Switching from User mode to Expert mode

Functions	Callers-Callees	Call Tree	Source	Disassembly	Timeline	Experiments

⬍ User Lock		Name
▽ (sec.)	(%)	
8 401.507	95.54	GCTaskManager::get_task(unsigned)
278.455	3.17	VMThread::loop()
112.078	1.27	CompileBroker::compiler_thread_loop()
1.411	0.02	WaitForBarrierGCTask::wait_for()
0.010	0.00	SafepointSynchronize::begin()

◁|	|▷	Add	Remove	Set Head	Set Center

0.	0.	Monitor::wait(bool,long,bool)
8 793.461	100.00	Monitor::IWait(Thread*,long)

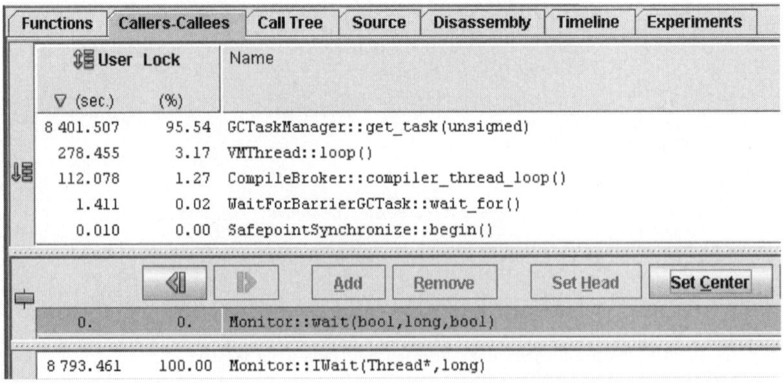

Figure 6-14 Traversing up the call stack of callers of __lwp_cond_wait

This method is part of the garbage collection subsystem of the Java HotSpot VM. This garbage collection method blocks and waits on a queue for work to do on behalf of the garbage collector subsystem. Each of the method names listed in Figure 6-14 represent areas of the Java HotSpot VM that may block and wait for some work to be placed on their respective work queue. For example, the VMThread::loop() method blocks on a queue for work to do on behalf of the Java HotSpot VM. You can think of the VMThread as the "kernel thread" of the Java HotSpot VM. The CompilerBroker::compile_thread_loop() method blocks and waits for work to do on behalf of the JIT compilation subsystem and so on. As a result, the entries reported as the JVM-System entry in User Mode can be ignored as being hot locks in this profile.

Continuing with the example program, the reaction from many Java developers when he or she observes the use of a synchronized HashMap or the use of a java.util.Hashtable, the predecessor to the synchronized HashMap, is to migrate to using a java.util.concurrent.ConcurrentHashMap.[1] Following this practice and executing this program using a ConcurrentHashMap instead of a synchronized HashMap showed an increase of CPU utilization of 92%. In other words, the previous implementation that used a synchronized HashMap had a total CPU utilization of 8% while the ConcurrentHashMap implementation had 100% CPU utilization. In addition, the number of voluntary context switches dropped substantially from several thousand to less than 100. The reported number of operations per second performed with the ConcurrentHashMap implementation increased by a little over 2x to 1,315,000, up from 615,000 with the synchronized HashMap. However, seeing only a 2x performance improvement while utilizing 100% CPU utilization compared to just 8% CPU utilization is not quite what was expected.

Tip

When performance testing, observing an unexpected result or observing a result that looks suspicious is a strong indication to investigate performance results and revisit testing methodology.

Capturing a profile and viewing the results with the Performance Analyzer is in order to investigate what happened. Figure 6-15 shows the hot methods as java.util.Random.next(int) and java.util.concurrent.atomic.AtomicLong.compareAndSet(long, long).

Using the Callers-Callees tab to observe the callers of the java.util.concurrent.atomic.AtomicLong.compareAndSet(long,log) method shows java.util.Random.next(int) as the most frequent callee. Hence, the two hottest methods in the profile are in the same call stack; see Figure 6-16.

---

1. java.util.concurrent.ConcurrentHashMap was introduced in the Java 5 SE class libraries and is available in Java 5 and later Java JDKs/JREs.

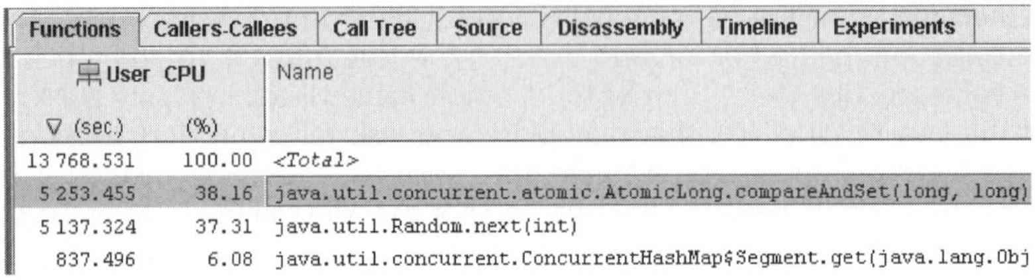

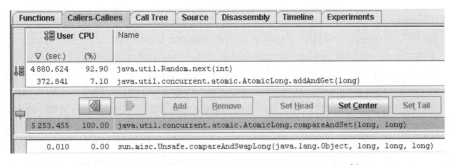

| Functions | Callers-Callees | Call Tree | Source | Disassembly | Timeline | Experiments |

User CPU		Name
▽ (sec.)	(%)	
13 768.531	100.00	*<Total>*
5 253.455	38.16	`java.util.concurrent.atomic.AtomicLong.compareAndSet(long, long)`
5 137.324	37.31	`java.util.Random.next(int)`
837.496	6.08	`java.util.concurrent.ConcurrentHashMap$Segment.get(java.lang.Obj`

Figure 6-15 Hot methods in the ConcurrentHashMap implementation of the program

| Functions | Callers-Callees | Call Tree | Source | Disassembly | Timeline | Experiments |

User CPU		Name
▽ (sec.)	(%)	
4 880.624	92.90	`java.util.Random.next(int)`
372.841	7.10	`java.util.concurrent.atomic.AtomicLong.addAndGet(long)`

| ◁ | ▷ | Add | Remove | Set Head | Set Center | Set Tail |

| 5 253.455 | 100.00 | `java.util.concurrent.atomic.AtomicLong.compareAndSet(long, long)` |
| 0.010 | 0.00 | `sun.misc.Unsafe.compareAndSwapLong(java.lang.Object, long, long, long)` |

Figure 6-16 Callers of AtomicLong.compareAndSet

| Functions | Callers-Callees | Call Tree | Source | Disassembly | Timeline | Experiments |

User CPU		Name
▽ (sec.)	(%)	
9 304.999	92.20	`TaxCallable.updateTaxPayer(long, TaxPayerRecord)`
218.853	2.17	`BailoutMain.getRandomAddress()`
182.518	1.81	`BailoutMain.getRandomTaxPayerId()`
180.056	1.78	`BailoutMain.getRandomName()`
104.963	1.04	`BailoutMain.getRandomSSN()`
90.563	0.90	`BailoutMain.getRandomCity()`
10.707	0.11	`BailoutMain.getRandomState()`

| ◁ | ▷ | Add | Remove | Set Head | Set Center | Set Tail |

| 74.712 | 0.74 | `java.util.Random.nextInt(int)` |
| 10 017.948 | 99.26 | `java.util.Random.next(int)` |

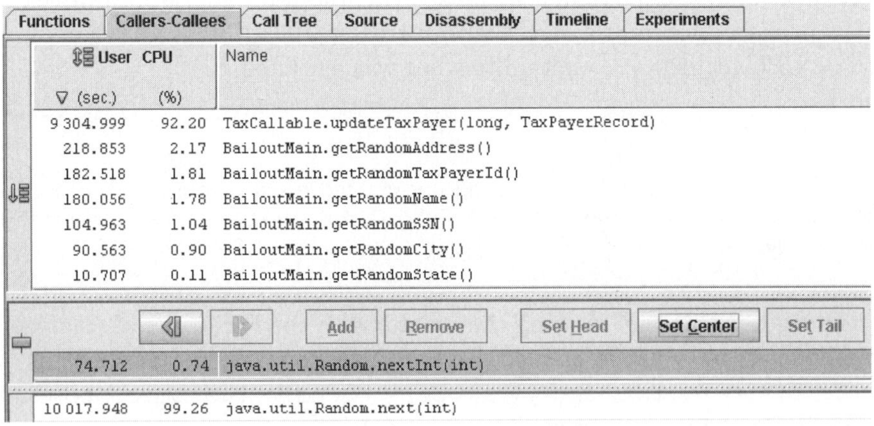

Figure 6-17 Callers and callees of Random.nextInt(int)

Figure 6-17 shows the result of traversing further up the call stack of the callers of `Random.next(int)`. Traversing upwards shows `Random.next(int)` is called by `Random.nextInt(int)`, which is called by a `TaxCallable.updateTaxPayer(long, TaxPayerRecord)` method and six methods from the `BailoutMain` class with the bulk of the attributable time spent in the `TaxCallable.updateTaxPayer(long, TaxPayerRecord)` method.

The implementation of `TaxCallable.updateTaxPayer(long, TaxPayerRecord)` is shown here:

```
final private static Random generator = BailoutMain.random;
// these class fields initialized in TaxCallable constructor
final private TaxPayerBailoutDB db;
private String taxPayerId;
private long nullCounter;
private TaxPayerRecord updateTaxPayer(long iterations,
                                      TaxPayerRecord tpr) {
    if (iterations % 1001 == 0) {
        tpr = db.get(taxPayerId);
    } else {
        // update a TaxPayer's DB record
        tpr = db.get(taxPayerId);
        if (tpr != null) {
            long tax = generator.nextInt(10) + 15;
            tpr.taxPaid(tax);
        }
    }
    if (tpr == null) {
        nullCounter++;
    }
    return tpr;
}
```

The purpose of `TaxCallable.updateTaxPayer(long, TaxPayerRecord)` is to update a tax payer's record in a tax payer's database with a tax paid. The amount of tax paid is randomly generated between 15 and 25. This randomly generated tax is implemented with the line of code, `long tax = generator.nextInt(10) + 15`. `generator` is a class instance `static Random` that is assigned the value of `BailoutMain.random` which is declared in the `BailoutMain` class as `final public static Random random = new Random(Thread.currentThread().getId())`. In other words, the `BailoutMain.random` class instance field is shared across all instances and uses of `BailoutMain` and `TaxCallable`. The `BailoutMain.random` serves several purposes in this application. It generates random fictitious tax payer ids, names, addresses, social security numbers, city names and states which are populated in a tax payer database, a `TaxPayerBailoutDB` which uses a `ConcurrentHashMap` in this implementation variant as its storage container. `BailoutMain.random` is also used, as described earlier, to generate a random tax for a given tax payer.

Since there are multiple instances of `TaxCallable` executing simultaneously in this application, the static `TaxCallable.generator` field is shared across all `TaxCallable` instances. Each of the `TaxCallable` instances execute in different threads, each sharing the same `TaxCallable.generator` field and updating the same tax payer database.

This means all threads executing `TaxCallable.updateTaxPayer(long, TaxPayerRecord)` trying to update the tax payer database must access the same Random object instance concurrently. Since the Java HotSpot JDK distributes the Java SE class library source code in a file called `src.zip`, it is possible to view the implementation of `java.util.Random`. A `src.zip` file is found in the JDK root installation directory. Within the `src.zip` file, you can find the `java.util.Random.java` source code. The implementation of the `Random.next(int)` method follows (remember from the Figure 6-17 that `Random.next(int)` is the method that calls the hot method `java.util.concurrent.atomic.AtomicLong.compareAndSet(int,int)`).

```
private final AtomicLong seed;
private final static long multiplier = 0x5DEECE66DL;
private final static long addend = 0xBL;
private final static long mask = (1L << 48) - 1;
protected int next(int bits) {
    long oldseed, nextseed;
    AtomicLong seed = this.seed;
    do {
      oldseed = seed.get();
      nextseed = (oldseed * multiplier + addend) & mask;
    } while (!seed.compareAndSet(oldseed, nextseed));
    return (int)(nextseed >>> (48 - bits));
}
```

In `Random.next(int)`, there is a do/while loop that performs an `AtomicLong.compareAndSet(int,int)` on the old seed and the new seed (this statement is highlighted in the preceding code example in bold). `AtomicLong` is an atomic concurrent data structure. Atomic and concurrent data structures were two of the features added to Java 5. Atomic and concurrent data structures typically rely on some form of a "compare and set" or "compare and swap" type of operation, also commonly referred to as a CAS, pronounced "kazz".

CAS operations are typically supported through one or more specialized CPU instructions. A CAS operation uses three operands: a memory location, an old value, and a new value. Here is a brief description of how a typical CAS operation works. A CPU atomically updates a memory location (an atomic variable) if the value at that location matches an expected old value. If that property fails to hold, no changes are made. To be more explicit, if the value at that memory location prior to the

CAS operation matches a supplied expected old value, then the memory location is updated with the new value. Some CAS operations return a boolean value indicating whether the memory location was updated with the new value, which means the old value matched the contents of what was found in the memory location. If the old value does not match the contents of the memory location, the memory location is not updated and false is returned.

It is this latter boolean form the `AtomicLong.compareAndSet(int, int)` method uses. Looking at the preceding implementation of the `Random.next(int)` method, the condition in the do/while loop does not exit until the `AtomicLong` CAS operation atomically and successfully sets the `AtomicLong` value to the `nextseed` value. This only occurs if the current value at the `AtomicLong`'s memory location has a value of the `oldseed`. If a large number of threads happen to be executing on the same `Random` object instance and calling `Random.next(int)`, there is a high probability the `AtomicLong.compareAndSet(int, int)` CAS operation will return false since many threads will observe a different `oldseed` value at the `AtomicLong`'s value memory location. As a result, many CPU cycles may be spent spinning in the do/while loop found in `Random.next(int)`. This is what the Performance Analyzer profile suggests is the case.

A solution to this problem is to have each thread have its own `Random` object instance so that each thread is no longer trying to update the same `AtomicLong`'s memory location at the same time. For this program, its functionality does not change with each thread having its own thread local `Random` object instance. This change can be accomplished rather easily by using a `java.lang.ThreadLocal`. For example, in `BailoutMain`, instead of using a static `Random` object, a static `ThreadLocal<Random>` could be used as follows:

```
// Old implementation using a static Random
//final public static Random random =
//                   new Random(Thread.currentThread.getid());

// Replaced with a new ThreadLocal<Random>
final public static ThreadLocal<Random> threadLocalRandom =
      new ThreadLocal<Random>() {
         @Override
         protected Random initialValue() {
            return new Random(Thread.currentThread().getId());
         }
      };
```

Then any reference to or use of `BailoutMain.random` should be replaced with `threadLocalRandom.get()`. A `threadLocalRandom.get()` retrieves a unique `Random` object instance for each thread executing code that used to use `BailoutMain.random`. Making this change allows the `AtomicLong`'s CAS operation in `Random.next(int)` to succeed quickly since no other thread is sharing the same `Random` object instance. In short, the do/while in `Random.next(int)` completes on its first loop iteration execution.

After replacing the `java.util.Random` in `BailoutMain` with a `ThreadLocal<Random>` and re-running the program, there is a remarkable improvement performance. When using the static `Random`, the program reported about 1,315,000 operations per second being executed. With the static `ThreadLocal<Random>` the program reports a little over 32,000,000 operations per second being executed. 32,000,000 operations per second is almost 25x more operations per second higher than the version using the static `Random` object instance. And it is more than 50x faster than the synchronized `HashMap` implementation, which reported 615,000 operations per second.

A question that may be worthy of asking is whether the program that used the synchronized `HashMap`, the initial implementation, could realize a performance improvement by applying the `ThreadLocal<Random>` change. After applying this change, the version of the program that used a synchronized `HashMap` showed little performance improvement, nor did its CPU utilization improve. Its performance improved slightly from 615,000 operations per second to about 620,000 operations per second. This should not be too much of a surprise. Looking back at the profile, the method having the hot lock in the initial version, the one that used a synchronized `HashMap`, and shown in Figure 6-11 and Figure 6-12, reveals the hot lock is on the synchronized `HashMap.get()` method. In other words, the synchronized `HashMap.get()` lock is masking the `Random.next(int)` CAS issue uncovered in the first implementation that used `ConcurrentHashMap`.

One of the lessons to be learned here is that atomic and concurrent data structures may not be the holy grail. Atomic and concurrent data structures rely on a CAS operation, which in general employs a form of synchronization. Situations of high contention around an atomic variable can lead to poor performance or scalability even though a concurrent or lock-free data structure is being used.

Many atomic and concurrent data structures are available in Java SE. They are good choices to use when the need for them exists. But when such a data structure is not available, an alternative is to identify a way to design the application such that the frequency at which multiple threads access the same data and the scope of the data that is accessed is minimized. In other words, try to design the application to minimize the span, size, or amount of data to be synchronized. To illustrate with an example, suppose there was no known implementation of a `ConcurrentHash-Map` available in Java, that is, only the synchronized `HashMap` data structure was available. The alternative approach just described suggests the idea to divide the tax payer database into multiple `HashMaps` to lessen the amount or scope of data that needs to be locked. One approach might be to consider a `HashMap` for tax payers in each state. In such an approach, there would be two levels of `Maps`. The first level `Map` would find one of the 50 state `Maps`. Since the first level `Map` will always contain a mapping of the 50 states, no elements need to be added to it or removed from it. Hence, the first level `Map` requires no synchronization. However, the second level state maps require synchronized access per state `Map` since tax payer records can be added, removed, and updated. In other words, the tax payer database would look something like the following:

```
public class TaxPayerBailoutDbImpl implements TaxPayerBailoutDB {
    private final Map<String, Map<String,TaxPayerRecord>> db;
    public TaxPayerBailoutDbImpl(int dbSize, int states) {
        db = new HashMap<String,Map<String,TaxPayerRecord>>(states);
        for (int i = 0; i < states; i++) {
            Map<String,TaxPayerRecord> map =
                Collections.synchronizedMap(
                    new HashMap<String,TaxPayerRecord>(dbSize/states));
            db.put(BailoutMain.states[i], map);
        }
    }
...
```

In the preceding source code listing you can see the first level `Map` is allocated as a `HashMap` in the line `db = new HashMap<String, Map<String, TaxPayerRecord>>(dbSize)` and the second level `Map`, one for each of the 50 states is allocated as a synchronized `HashMap` in the for loop:

```
for (int i = 0; i < states; i++) {
    Map<String,TaxPayerRecord> map =
        Collections.synchronizedMap(
            new HashMap<String,TaxPayerRecord>(dbSize/states));
    db.put(BailoutMain.states[i], map);
}
```

Modifying this example program with the partitioning approach described here shows about 12,000,000 operations per second being performed and a CPU utilization of about 50%. The number of operations per second is not nearly as good as the 32,000,000 observed with a `ConcurrentHashMap`. But it is a rather large improvement over the single large synchronized `HashMap`, which yielded about 620,000 operations per second. Given there is unused CPU utilization, it is likely further partitioning could improve the operations per second in this partitioning approach. In general, with the partitioning approach, you trade-off additional CPU cycles for additional path length, that is, more CPU instructions, to reduce the scope of the data that is being locked where CPU cycles are lost blocking and waiting to acquire a lock.

Volatile Usage

JSR-133, which was introduced in Java 5, addressed many issues in the Java Memory Model. This is well documented at http://jcp.org/jsr/detail?id=133 by the JSR-133 Expert Group with further material at http://www.cs.umd.edu/~pugh/java/memoryModel/ maintained by Dr. Bill Pugh. One of the issues addressed with JSR-133 is the use of the Java keyword `volatile`. Fields in Java objects that are declared as volatile are usually used to communicate state information among threads. The inclusion of JSR-133 into Java 5 and later Java revisions, ensures that a thread that reads a volatile field in an object is guaranteed to have the value that was last written to that volatile field, regardless of the thread that is doing read or write, or the location of where those two threads are executing, that is, different CPU sockets, or CPU cores. The use of a volatile field does limit optimizations a modern JVM's JIT compiler can perform on such a field. For example, a volatile field must adhere to certain instruction ordering. In short, a volatile field's value must be kept in sync across all application threads and CPU caches. For instance, when a volatile field's value is changed by one thread, whose field might be sitting in a CPU cache, any other thread that might have a copy of that volatile field in its CPU cache, a different CPU cache than the other thread that performed the change, must have its CPU cache updated before its thread reads that volatile field found in its local CPU cache, or it must be instructed to retrieve the updated volatile field's value from memory. To ensure CPU caches are updated, that is, kept in sync, in the presence of volatile fields, a CPU instruction, a memory barrier, often called a *membar* or *fence,* is emitted to update CPU caches with a change in a volatile field's value.

In a highly performance sensitive application having multiple CPU caches, frequent updates to volatile fields can be a performance issue. However, in practice, few Java applications rely on frequent updates to volatile fields. But there are always exceptions to the rule. If you keep in mind that frequent updates, changes, or writes to a volatile field have the potential to be a performance issue (i.e., reads of a volatile field are okay, not a cause for performance concern), you will likely not experience performance issues when using volatile fields.

A profiler, such as the Performance Analyzer, that has the capability to gather CPU cache misses and associate them to Java object field access can help isolate whether the use of a volatile field is a performance issue. If you observe a high number of CPU cache misses on a volatile field and the source code suggests frequent writes to that volatile field, you have an application that is experiencing performance issues as a result of its usage of volatile. The solution to such a situation is to identify ways in which less frequent writes are performed to the volatile field, or refactor the application in a way to avoid the use of the volatile field. Never remove the use of a volatile field if it breaks program correctness or introduces a potential race condition. It is much better to have an underperforming application than it is to have an incorrect implementation, or one that has the potential for a race condition.

Data Structure Resizing

Java applications tend to make high use of Java SE's `StringBuilder` or `String-Buffer` for assembling `Strings` and also make high use of Java objects that act as containers of data such as the Java SE Collections classes. Both `StringBuilder` and `StringBuffer` use an underlying `char[]` for their data storage. As elements are added to a `StringBuilder` or `StringBuffer`, the underlying `char[]` data storage, may be subject to resizing. As a result of resizing, a new larger `char[]` array is allocated, the char elements in the old `char[]` are copied into the new larger `char[]` array, and the old `char[]` discarded, that is, available for garbage collection. Similar resizing can also occur in Java SE Collections classes that use an array for their underlying data store.

This section explores ways to identify data structure resizing, in particular `StringBuilder`, `StringBuffer`, and Java SE Collections classes resizing.

StringBuilder/StringBuffer Resizing

When a `StringBuilder` or `StringBuffer` becomes large enough to exceed the underlying data storage capacity, a new char array of a larger size, 2x larger in the OpenJDK `StringBuilder` and `StringBuffer` implementation (used by Java Hot-Spot Java 6 JDK/JRE), is allocated, the old char array elements are copied into the new char array, and the old char array is discarded. A version of the implementation used by `StringBuilder` and `StringBuffer` follows:

```java
char[] value;
int count;

public AbstractStringBuilder append(String str) {
    if (str == null) str = "null";
      int len = str.length();
    if (len == 0) return this;
    int newCount = count + len;
    if (newCount > value.length)
        expandCapacity(newCount);
    str.getChars(0, len, value, count);
    count = newCount;
    return this;
}

void expandCapacity(int minimumCapacity) {
    int newCapacity = (value.length + 1) * 2;
    if (newCapacity < 0) {
        newCapacity = Integer.MAX_VALUE;
    } else if (minimumCapacity > newCapacity) {
      newCapacity = minimumCapacity;
    }
    value = Arrays.copyOf(value, newCapacity);
}
```

Continuing with the fictitious tax payer program example from the previous section (full listing of the source code used in this section can be found in Appendix B in the section "First Resizing Variant"), `StringBuilder` objects are used to assemble random `Strings` representing tax payer names, addresses, cities, states, social security numbers, and a tax payer id. It also uses the no argument `StringBuilder` constructor. Hence, the program is likely to be subject to `StringBuilder`'s underlying `char[]` being resized. A capture of a memory or heap profile with a profiler such as NetBeans Profiler confirms that is the case. Figure 6-18 shows a heap profile from NetBeans Profiler.

In Figure 6-18, you can see that `char[]`, `StringBuilder`, and `String` are the most highly allocated objects and also have the largest amount of live objects. In the NetBeans Profiler, selecting and right-clicking on the `char[]` class name in the far left column as shown in Figure 6-19 shows the allocation stack traces for all `char[]` objects.

In the `char[]` stack allocation traces, shown in Figure 6-20, you can see an entry for `java.lang.AbstractStringBuilder.expandCapacity(int)`, which is

Class Name – Live Allocated Objects	Live Bytes ▼	Live Bytes	Live Objects	Allocated Objects
char[]		118,792,912 B (63.6%)	2,460,612 (44.9%)	2,926,057
java.lang.**String**		30,427,464 B (16.3%)	1,267,811 (23.1%)	1,267,815
java.lang.**StringBuilder**		14,524,080 B (7.8%)	907,755 (16.6%)	1,266,550
TaxPayerRecord		8,453,440 B (4.5%)	211,336 (3.9%)	211,336
java.util.**HashMap$Entry**		5,067,552 B (2.7%)	211,148 (3.9%)	211,148
java.util.concurrent.atomic.**AtomicLong**		3,380,416 B (1.8%)	211,276 (3.9%)	211,276
StateAndId		3,378,960 B (1.8%)	211,185 (3.9%)	211,185
java.util.**HashMap$Entry[]**		2,868,112 B (1.5%)	37 (0%)	67
byte[]		11,416 B (0%)	6 (0%)	8

Figure 6-18 Heap profile

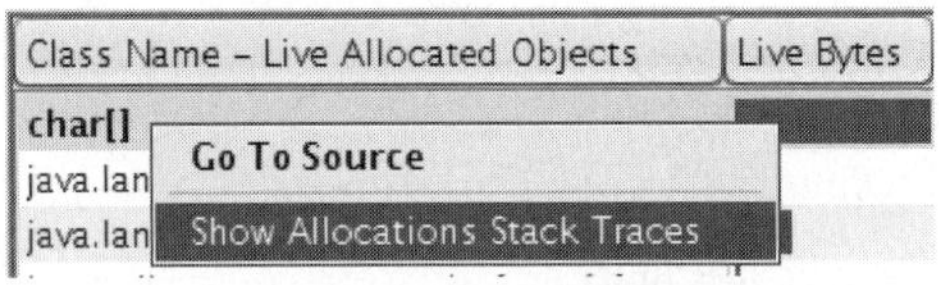

Class Name – Live Allocated Objects	Live Bytes
char[]	
java.lan **Go To Source**	
java.lan Show Allocations Stack Traces	

Figure 6-19 Showing allocation stack traces

Method Name – Allocation Call Tree	Live Bytes...	Live Objects ▼	Allocated Objects
▽ ▮ char[]		2,460,612 (100%)	2,926,048
▷ ▮ java.util.Arrays.**copyOfRange** (char[], int, int)		1,268,072 (51.5%)	1,268,073
▷ ▮ java.lang.AbstractStringBuilder.**<init>** (int)		911,056 (37%)	1,266,982
▽ ▮ java.util.Arrays.**copyOf** (char[], int)		281,480 (11.4%)	390,988
▽ ▮ java.lang.AbstractStringBuilder.**expandCapacity** (int)		281,480 (11.4%)	390,988
▷ ▮ java.lang.AbstractStringBuilder.**append** (char)		281,476 (11.4%)	390,984
▷ ▮ java.lang.AbstractStringBuilder.**append** (String)		4 (0%)	4

Figure 6-20 char[] allocations from expanding StringBuilders

called from `AbstractStringBuilder.append(char)` and `AbstractString-Builder.append(String)` methods. The `expandCapacity(int)` method calls `java.util.Arrays.copyOf(char[], int)`. Looking back at the previous source code listing, you can see where `AbstractStringBuilder.append(String str)` calls `expandCapacity(int)` and calls `Arrays.copyOf(char[] int)`.

You can also see from Figure 6-20, over 11% of the current live `char[]` objects are from resized `StringBuilder char[]`. In addition, there are a total of 2,926,048 `char[]` objects that have been allocated, and of those, 390,988 `char[]` allocations occurred as a result of `StringBuilder char[]` resizing. In other words, about 13% (390,988/2,926,048) of all `char[]` allocations are coming from resized `StringBuilder char[]`s. Eliminating these `char[]` allocations from resizing improves the performance of this program by saving the CPU instructions needed to perform the new `char[]` allocation, copying the characters from the old `char[]` into the new `char[]`, and the CPU instructions required to garbage collect the old discarded `char[]`.

In the Java HotSpot JDK/JRE distributions, both the `StringBuilder` and `StringBuffer` offer no argument constructors that use a default size of 16 for their underlying char array data storage. These no argument constructors are being used in this program. This can be seen in the profile by expanding the `java.lang.AbstractStringBuilder.<init>(int)` entry seen in Figure 6-20. The expansion of the `java.lang.AbstractStringBuilder.<init>(int)` entry, shown in Figure 6-21, shows it is called by a no argument `StringBuilder` constructor.

In practice, few `StringBuilder` or `StringBuffer` object instances result in having consumed 16 or fewer char array elements; 16 is the default size used with the no argument `StringBuilder` or `StringBuffer` constructor. To avoid `StringBuilder` and `StringBuffer` resizing, use the explicit size `StringBuilder` or `StringBuffer` constructor.

A modification to the example program follows, which now uses explicit sizes for constructing `StringBuilder` objects. A full listing of the modified version can be found in Appendix B in the section "Second Resizing Variant."

Recent optimizations in Java 6 update releases of the Java HotSpot VM analyze the usage of `StringBuilder` and `StringBuffer` and attempt to determine the

Method Name – Allocation Call Tree	Live Bytes...	Live Objects ▼	Allocated Objects
▽ ▨ char[]	■■	2,460,612 (100%)	2,926,048
▷ ▨ java.util.Arrays.**copyOfRange** (char[], int, int)	■	1,268,072 (51.5%)	1,268,073
▽ ▨ java.lang.AbstractStringBuilder.**<init>** (int)	■	911,056 (37%)	1,266,982
▷ ▨ java.lang.StringBuilder.**<init>** ()	■	911,055 (37%)	1,266,981
▷ ▨ java.lang.StringBuffer.**<init>** (int)		1 (0%)	1
▽ ▨ java.util.Arrays.**copyOf** (char[], int)	■	281,480 (11.4%)	390,988
▽ ▨ java.lang.AbstractStringBuilder.**expandCapacity** (int)	■	281,480 (11.4%)	390,988
▷ ▨ java.lang.AbstractStringBuilder.**append** (char)	■	281,476 (11.4%)	390,984
▷ ▨ java.lang.AbstractStringBuilder.**append** (String)		4 (0%)	4

Figure 6-21 Uses of StringBuilder default constructor

```
public static String getRandomTaxPayerId() {
    StringBuilder sb = new StringBuilder(20);
    for (int i = 0; i < 20; i++) {
        int index =
            threadLocalRandom.get().nextInt(alphabet.length);
        sb.append(alphabet[index]);
    }
    return sb.toString();
}

public static String getRandomAddress() {
    StringBuilder sb = new StringBuilder(24);
    int size = threadLocalRandom.get().nextInt(14) + 10;
    for (int i = 0; i < size; i++) {
        if (i < 5) {
            int x = threadLocalRandom.get().nextInt(8);
            sb.append(x + 1);
        }
        int index =
            threadLocalRandom.get().nextInt(alphabet.length);
        char c = alphabet[index];
        if (i == 5) {
            c = Character.toUpperCase(c);
        }
        sb.append(c);
    }
    return sb.toString();
}
```

optimal char array size to use for a given `StringBuilder` or `StringBuffer` object allocation as means to reduce unnecessary `char[]` object allocations resulting from `StringBuilder` or `StringBuffer` expansion.

Measuring the performance impact after addressing `StringBuilder` and `StringBuffer` resizing will be done in combination with addressing any Java Collection classes resizing, the topic of the next section.

Java Collections Resizing

The addition of the Java Collections to Java SE offered an enormous boost to developer productivity by providing containers with interfaces allowing the ability to easily switch between alternative concrete implementations. For example, the `List` interface offers an `ArrayList` and `LinkedList` concrete implementation.

Java Collections Definition

As of Java 6, there were 14 interfaces in the Java SE Collections:

Collection, Set, List, SortedSet, NavigableSet, Queue, Deque, BlockingQueue, BlockingDeque, Map, SortedMap, NavigableMap, ConcurrentMap, and ConcurrentNavigableMap

The following is a listing of the most common concrete implementations of the Java SE Collections:

HashMap, HashSet, TreeSet, LinkedHashSet, ArrayList, ArrayDeque, LinkedList, PriorityQueue, TreeMap, LinkedHashMap, Vector, Hashtable, ConcurrentLinkedQueue, LinkedBlockingQueue, ArrayBlockingQueue, PriorityBlockingQueue, DelayQueue, SynchronousQueue, LinkedBlocking-Deque, ConcurrentHashMap, ConcurrentSkipListSet, ConcurrentSkipListMap, WeakHashMap, IdentityHashMap, CopyOnWriteArrayList, CopyOnWriteArraySet, EnumSet, and EnumMap

Some of the Collections' concrete implementations are subject to potential expensive resizing as the number of elements added to the Collection grows such as `ArrayList`, `Vector`, `HashMap`, and `ConcurrentHashMap` since their underlying data store is an array. Other Collections such as `LinkedList` or `TreeMap` often use one or more object references between the elements stored to chain together the elements managed by the Collection. The former of these, those that use an array for the Collection's underlying data store, can be subject to performance issues when the underlying data store is resized due to the Collection growing in the number of elements it holds. Although these Collections classes have constructors that take an optional size argument, these constructors are often not used, or the size provided in an application program is not optimal for the Collection's use.

Tip

It is possible that there exists concrete implementations of Java Collections classes, such as LinkedList and TreeMap, that use arrays as underlying data storage. Those concrete implementations may also be subject to resizing. Collecting a heap profile and looking at collection resizing will show which Java Collections classes are resizing.

As is the case with `StringBuilder` or `StringBuffer`, resizing of a Java Collections class that uses an array as its data storage requires additional CPU cycles to allocate a new array, copy the old elements from the old array, and at some point in the future garbage collect the old array. In addition, the resizing can also impact Collection's field access time, the time it takes to dereference a field, because a new underlying data store, again typically an array, for the Collection's underlying data store may be allocated in a location in the JVM heap away from the object references stored within the data store and the other fields of the Collection. After a Collection resize occurs, it is possible an access to its resized field can result in CPU cache misses due to the way a modern JVM allocates objects in memory, in particular how those objects are laid out in memory. The way objects and their fields are laid out in memory can vary between JVM implementations. Generally, however, since an object and its fields tend to be referenced frequently together, an object and its fields laid out in memory within close proximity generally reduce CPU cache misses. Hence, the impact of Collections resizing (this also applies to `StringBuffer` and `StringBuilder` resizing) may extend beyond the additional CPU instructions spent to do the resizing and the additional overhead put on the JVM's memory manager to having a lingering higher field access time due to a change in the layout of the Collection's fields in memory relative the Collection object instance.

The approach to identifying Java Collections resizing is similar to what was described earlier for identifying `StringBuilder` and `StringBuffer` resizing, collecting heap or memory profile with a profiler such as NetBeans Profiler. Looking at the source code for the Java Collection classes helps identify the method names that perform the resizing.

Continuing with the fictitious tax payer program, the program variant in which tax payer records were populated into multiple `HashMaps` using a tax payer's state of residence as a key into a second `HashMap` where a tax payer's id is used as an index is a good example of where Collections resizing can occur. A full source code listing from this variant can be found in Appendix B in the section "First Resizing Variant." The source code, found in `TaxPayerBailoutDbImpl.java`, that allocates the `HashMaps` follows:

```java
private final Map<String, Map<String,TaxPayerRecord>> db;

public TaxPayerBailoutDbImpl(int numberOfStates) {
    db = new HashMap<String,Map<String,TaxPayerRecord>>();
    for (int i = 0; i < numberOfStates; i++) {
        Map<String,TaxPayerRecord> map =
                Collections.synchronizedMap(
                    new HashMap<String,TaxPayerRecord>());
        db.put(BailoutMain.states[i], map);
    }
}
```

Here you can see the `HashMaps` are using a `HashMap` constructor that takes no arguments. As a result, the `HashMap` relies on a default size for its underlying mapping array. The following is a portion of OpenJDK's `HashMap.java` source code that shows the default size chosen for a `HashMap`'s underlying data storage.

```java
static final int DEFAULT_INITIAL_CAPACITY = 16;
static final float DEFAULT_LOAD_FACTOR = 0.75f;

public HashMap() {
    this.loadFactor = DEFAULT_LOAD_FACTOR;
    threshold =
            (int)(DEFAULT_INITIAL_CAPACITY * DEFAULT_LOAD_FACTOR);
    table = new Entry[DEFAULT_INITIAL_CAPACITY];
    init();
}
void init() {
}
```

Two factors decide when the data storage for a `HashMap` is resized: the capacity of the data storage and the load factor. The capacity is the size of the underlying data storage. That's the `HashMap.Entry[]`'s size. And the load factor is a measure of how full the `HashMap` is allowed to reach before the `HashMap`'s data storage, the `Entry[]`, is resized. A `HashMap` resize results in a new `Entry[]` being allocated, twice as large as the previous `Entry[]`, the entries in the `Entry[]` are rehashed and put in the `Entry[]`. The CPU instructions required to resize a `HashMap` are greater than what is required by `String-Builder` or `StringBuffer` resizing due to the rehashing of the `Entry[]` elements.

In Figure 6-18, you can see a row for `java.util.HashMap$Entry[]`. For this entry you can see there are 67 allocated objects, and 37 of them are live at the time of the profile snapshot. This suggests that 37/67, about 55%, are still live. That also suggests 45% of those `Entry[]` objects that had been allocated have been garbage collected. In other words, the `HashMaps` are experiencing resizing. Notice that the total bytes consumed by `HashMap.Entry[]` objects is much less than those consumed by `char[]` objects. This suggests the impact of eliding the `HashMap` resizing is likely to be less than the impact realized from eliding the `StringBuilder` resizing.

Figure 6-22 shows the allocation stack traces for `HashMap.Entry[]`. Here you can see some of those `HashMap.Entry[]` allocations result from a `HashMap.resize(int)` method call. In addition, you can see the no argument `HashMap` constructor is being used, which also allocates a `HashMap.Entry[]`.

Since this example program populates 50 different `HashMaps` with a total of 2,000,000 fictitious records, each of those 50 `HashMaps` hold about 2,000,000 / 50 = 40,000 records. Obviously, 40,000 is much greater than the default size of 16 used by the no argument `HashMap` constructor. Using the default load factor of .75, and the fact that each of the 50 HashMap holds 40,000 records, you can determine a size for the HashMaps so they will not resize (40,000 / .75 = ~ 53,334). Or simply passing the total number of records to store divided by the number of states, divided by the default load factor, i.e., (2,000,000 / 50) / .75, to the `HashMap` constructor that holds the records. Following is the modified source code for `TaxPayerBailoutDbImpl.java` that elides `HashMap` resizing:

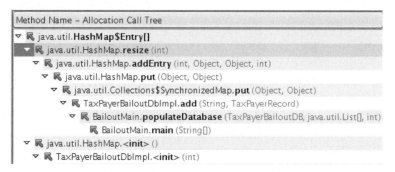

Figure 6-22 HashMap.Entry[] allocation stack traces

```
    private final Map<String, Map<String,TaxPayerRecord>> db;
    private final int dbSize = 2000000;

    public TaxPayerBailoutDbImpl(int dbSize, int numberOfStates) {
        final int outerMapSize = (int) Math.ceil(numberOfStates / .75);
        final int innerMapSize =
                (int) (Math.ceil((dbSize / numberOfStates) / .75));
        db =
            new HashMap<String,Map<String,TaxPayerRecord>>(outerMapSize);
        for (int i = 0; i < numberOfStates; i++) {
            Map<String,TaxPayerRecord> map =
                Collections.synchronizedMap(
                    new HashMap<String,TaxPayerRecord>(innerMapSize));
            db.put(BailoutMain.states[i], map);
        }
    }
```

In this example program, both `StringBuilder` and `HashMap` resizing occur during the initialization phase of the program, the phase of the program that populates a `Map` of `Maps` with fictitious, randomly generated tax payer records. Hence, to measure the performance impact of eliding the `StringBuilder` and `HashMap` resizing, the initialization phase of this program has been instrumented with a time stamp at the beginning of the program and after the `Map` of `Maps` has been populated. A modified version of this example program, one that uses the no argument `HashMap` constructor, calculates and reports the time it takes to populate the `HashMaps` with 2,000,000 records, can be found in Appendix B in the section "First Resizing Variant."

When this variant of the program is run on a Sun SPARC Enterprise T5120 Server configured with 64 virtual processors (the same value as that returned by the Java API `Runtime.availableProcessors()`), the amount of time it takes to complete the initialization phase is 48.286 seconds.

Tip

Since the populating of records is single threaded and the Sun SPARC Enterprise T5120 Server has a 1.2GHz clock rate, a processor with a smaller number of cores with a higher clock rate will likely report a shorter duration time needed to populate the 2,000,000 records in the HashMaps.

Updating this program variant with the changes described in this section to address both `StringBuilder` and `HashMap` resizing and running on the same Ultra-SPARC T5120 system with the same JVM command line options reports it takes 46.019 seconds to complete its initialization phase. That's about a 5% improvement in elapsed time. The source code for this variant can be found in Appendix B in the section "Second Resizing Variant."

Applying the data resizing strategy reduces the application's path length, the total number of CPU instructions required to execute the program, and potentially more efficient use of CPU cycles due to fewer possibilities of CPU cache misses as a result of frequently accessed data structure fields being laid out in memory next to each other.

You may have noticed that the initialization phase in this program is single threaded. But the system it is being executed on has a CPU that is multicore and multithreaded per core. The Sun SPARC Enterprise T5120 Server this program is executing on has 8 cores, and 8 hardware threads per core. It is a chip multi-threading type of CPU chip, CMT for short. In other words, 8 cores and 8 hardware threads per core means it has 64 virtual processors. That also means the Java API, `System.availableProcessors()`, returns a value of 64. A next step to improve the performance of the initialization phase of this program is to refactor it to utilize all of those 64 virtual processors. This is the topic of the next section.

Increasing Parallelism

Modern CPU architectures have brought multiple cores and multiple hardware execution threads to developer desktops. This means there are more CPU resources available to do additional work. However, to take advantage of those additional CPU resources, programs executed on them must be able to do work in parallel. In other words, those programs need to be constructed or designed in a multithreaded manner to take advantage of the additional hardware threads.

Java applications that are single threaded cannot take advantage of additional hardware threads on modern CPU architectures. Those applications must be refactored to be multithreaded to do their work in parallel. In addition, many Java applications have single-threaded phases, or operations, especially initialization or startup phases. Therefore, many Java applications can improve initialization or startup performance by doing tasks in parallel, that is, making use of multiple threads at the same time.

The example program used in the previous sections "Lock Contention" and "Data Structure Resizing" has a single-threaded initialization phase where random fictitious tax payer records are created and added to a Java `Map`. This single-threaded initialization phase could be refactored to being multithreaded. The single-threaded form, as it was run in the "Lock Contention" and "Data Structure Resizing" sections, when run on the same Sun SPARC Enterprise T5120 Server, reports it takes about 45 to 48 seconds for the initialization phase to complete. Since there are 64 virtual processors on an a Sun SPARC Enterprise T5120 Server, 63 of those 64 virtual processors are idle doing little or no work during the initialization phase. Therefore, if the initialization phase could be refactored to utilize those additional 63 virtual processors, the elapsed time it takes to execute the initialization phase should be significantly less.

The key to being able to refactor single-threaded phases of a program to be multi-threaded is constrained by the program's logic. If there is a loop of execution involved, and much of the work performed within that loop is independent of what happens within each loop iteration, it may be a good candidate to be refactored into a multithreaded version. In the case of the fictitious tax payer program, Map records are added to a ConcurrentMap. Since a ConcurrentMap can handle multiple threads adding records to it and the records can be created independently of each other, the work performed in the single-threaded loop can be broken up and spread among multiple threads. With a Sun SPARC Enterprise T5120 Server that has 64 virtual processors, the work that is being done in the single-threaded loop could be spread across those 64 virtual processors.

Here is the core part of the single-threaded loop logic (full implementation can be found in Appendix B in the section "Increasing Parallelism Single-Threaded Implementation"):

```
// allocate the database
TaxPayerBailoutDB db = new TaxPayerBailoutDbImpl(dbSize);
// allocate list to hold tax payer names
List<String>[] taxPayerList = new ArrayList[numberOfThreads];
for (int i = 0; i < numberOfThreads; i++) {
    taxPayerList[i] = new ArrayList<String>(taxPayerListSize);
}
// populate the database and tax payer list with random records
populateDatabase(db, taxPayerList, dbSize);

...

private static void populateDatabase(TaxPayerBailoutDB db,
                                     List<String>[] taxPayerIdList,
                                     int dbSize) {
    for (int i = 0; i < dbSize; i++) {
        // make random tax payer id and record
        String key = getRandomTaxPayerId();
        TaxPayerRecord tpr = makeTaxPayerRecord();
        // add tax payer id & record to database
        db.add(key, tpr);
        // add tax payer id to to tax payer list
        int index = i % taxPayerIdList.length;
        taxPayerIdList[index].add(key);
    }
}
```

The core part of refactoring the for/loop to be multithreaded results in creating a Runnable, or Callable, along with an ExecutorService to execute the Runnables or Callables in addition to ensuring the implementation of a TaxPayerBailoutDB and taxPayerIdList are thread safe. That is, the data they hold will not be corrupted as a result of having multiple threads writing data to them simultaneously. Following are segments of source code that contain the most relevant parts to the multithreaded refactoring (full implementation can be found in Appendix B in the section "Increasing Parallelism Multithreaded Implementation"):

```
    // allocate the database
    TaxPayerBailoutDB db = new TaxPayerBailoutDbImpl(dbSize);
    List<String>[] taxPayerList = new List[numberOfThreads];
    for (int i = 0; i < numberOfThreads; i++) {
        taxPayerList[i] =
                Collections.synchronizedList(
                    new ArrayList<String>(taxPayerListSize));
    }

    // create a pool of executors to execute some Callables
    int numberOfThreads = System.availableProcessors();
    ExecutorService pool =
        Executors.newFixedThreadPool(numberOfThreads);
    Callable<DbInitializerFuture>[] dbCallables =
        new DbInitializer[numberOfThreads];
    for (int i = 0; i < dbCallables.length; i++) {
        dbCallables[i] =
            new DbInitializer(db, taxPayerList, dbSize/numberOfThreads);
    }

    // start all db initializer threads running
    Set<Future<DbInitializerFuture>> dbSet =
        new HashSet<Future<DbInitializerFuture>>();
    for (int i = 0; i < dbCallables.length; i++) {
        Callable<DbInitializerFuture> callable = dbCallables[i];
        Future<DbInitializerFuture> future = pool.submit(callable);
        dbSet.add(future);
    }

    // A Callable that will execute multi-threaded db initialization
    public class DbInitializer implements Callable<DbInitializerFuture> {
        private TaxPayerBailoutDB db;
        private List<String>[] taxPayerList;
        private int recordsToCreate;

        public DbInitializer(TaxPayerBailoutDB db,
                             List<String>[] taxPayerList,
                             int recordsToCreate) {
            this.db = db;
            this.taxPayerList = taxPayerList;
            this.recordsToCreate = recordsToCreate;
        }

        @Override
        public DbInitializerFuture call() throws Exception {
            return BailoutMain.populateDatabase(db, taxPayerList,
                                                recordsToCreate);
        }
    }

    static DbInitializerFuture populateDatabase(TaxPayerBailoutDB db,
                                     List<String>[] taxPayerIdList,
                                     int dbSize) {
        for (int i = 0; i < dbSize; i++) {
            String key = getRandomTaxPayerId();
            TaxPayerRecord tpr = makeTaxPayerRecord();
            db.add(key, tpr);
```

```
            int index = i % taxPayerIdList.length;
            taxPayerIdList[index].add(key);
        }
        DbInitializerFuture future = new DbInitializerFuture();
        future.addToRecordsCreated(dbSize);
        return future;
    }
```

After applying the refactoring to make the initialization phase multithreaded by dividing up the number of records to be added to the Map to run in 64 threads rather than 1 thread, the time it takes to perform the initialization phase drops from about 45 seconds to about 3 seconds on the Sun SPARC Enterprise T5120 Server. A higher clock rate dual or quad core desktop system may not observe as much of an improvement. For example, the author's dual core desktop system realized about a 4 second improvement, 16 seconds down to about 12. The larger the number of virtual processors that additional parallel work can be spread among, the greater the potential performance improvement.

This simple example illustrates the potential benefit of being able to take advantage of additional virtual processors on a system that may be idle for some phase of an application by making that phase multithreaded.

High CPU Utilization

Sometimes an application simply cannot meet service level performance or scalability agreements even though performance efforts have reduced system CPU utilization, have addressed lock contention, and other optimization opportunities have been addressed. In such cases, doing an analysis of the program logic and the algorithms used is the direction to take. Method profilers such as the Performance Analyzer or NetBeans Profilers do a good job at collecting information about where in general an application spends most of its time.

The Performance Analyzer's Call Tree tab is good at providing an application's hottest use case by showing the call stack trees. This information can be leveraged to answer questions in a more abstract way, such as how long does it take the application to perform a unit of work, or perform a transaction, use case, and so on so long as the person looking at the profile has sufficient understanding of the implementation to be able to map a method entry point as the beginning of a unit of work, beginning of a transaction, use case, and so on. Being able to analyze the profile in this way provides the opportunity to step back, look at a higher level, and ask questions such as whether the algorithms and data structures being used are the most optimal or are there any alternative algorithms or data structures that might yield better performance or scalability. Often the tendency when analyzing profiles is to focus primarily on the methods that consume the most time in an exclusive metric kind of way, that is, focusing only on the contents of a method rather than at a higher level unit of work, transaction, use case, and so on.

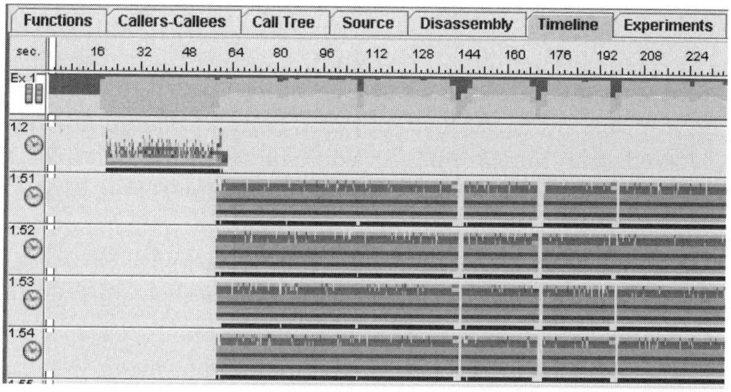

| Functions | Callers-Callees | Call Tree | Source | Disassembly | Timeline | Experiments |

Figure 6-23 Performance analyzer timeline view

Other Useful Analyzer Tips

Another useful strategy to employ when using the Performance Analyzer is to look at the Timeline view in the Performance Analyzer GUI (see Figure 6-23).

The Timeline view provides a listing of all threads, one in each row of the listing, that executed during the time when the profile was collected. At the top of the Timeline view is a timeline of seconds that have passed since the initiation of the collection of the profile. If the recording of the profiling data is enabled at Java application launch time, then the timeline contains data since the launching of the Java application. For each horizontal row, a thread within the application, a unique color is used to distinguish the method the application was executing in at the time of the sample. Selecting a thread, one of the rows within a colored area shows the call stack, their method names in the Call Stack for Selected Event panel, executing at the time the sample was taken. Figure 6-24 is a screenshot of the Call Stack for Selected Event panel for the selected thread, thread 1.2 in Figure 6-23.

Hence, by looking at the timeline, you can determine which threads are executing in the program at any particular point in time. This can be useful when looking for opportunities to multithread single-threaded phases or operations in an application. Figure 6-23, shows the single-threaded program variant presented in the "Increasing Parallelism" section earlier in the chapter. In Figure 6-23, you can see from the timeline, from about 16 seconds to a little past 64 seconds, the thread labeled as Thread 1.2, is the only thread that appears to be executing. The timeline

Figure 6-24 Performance analyzer's call stack for selected event panel

in Figure 6-23, suggests the program may be executing its initialization or beginning phase as a single threaded. Figure 6-24 shows a Call Stack for the Selected Event after clicking in the region of Thread 1.2 between the timeline of 16 seconds and 64 seconds. Figure 6-24 shows the call stack that's being executed during the selected thread and selected timeline sample. As you can see in Figure 6-24, a method by the name `BailoutMain.populateDatabase()` is being called. This is the method identified in the "Increasing Parallelism" section earlier in the chapter as one that could be multithreaded. Hence, this illustrates how you can use the Performance Analyzer to identify areas or phases of an application that could benefit from parallelism.

Another useful tip when using the Timeline view is make note of the range of seconds for some time period of interest that has caught your attention in the timeline. Then use the filtering capability to narrow the profile data loaded by the Analyzer GUI. After applying the filter, the Functions and Callers-Callees views show data only for the filtered range. In other words, filtering allows you to focus exclusively on the profile data collected within the period of interest. To illustrate with an example, in Figure 6-23, Thread 1.2 between 16 and 64 seconds is the only thread executing. To narrow the focus of the collected profile data to that particular time range, the Analyzer can be configured to load only the profile data between 16 and 64 seconds using the View > Filter Data menu and specifying 16-64 samples in the Filter Data form's Samples field as shown in Figure 6-25.

Filtering allows for the ability to eliminate data collected outside an area of interest, which leads to more accurate analysis since only the data of interest is being presented.

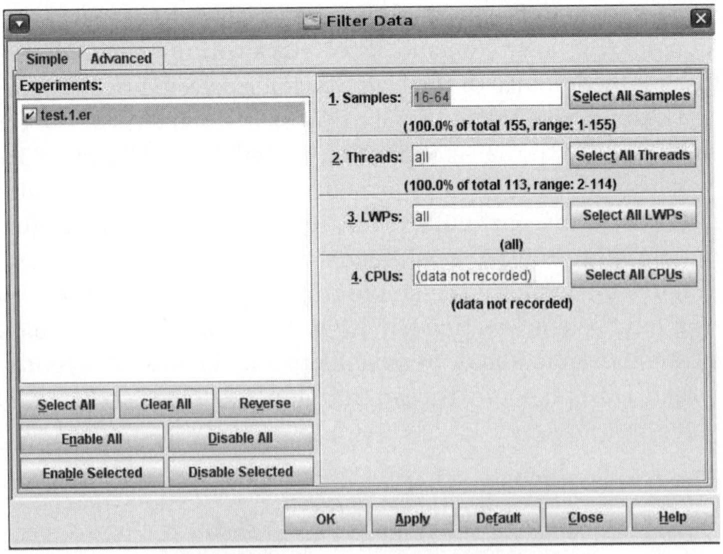

Figure 6-25 Filtering the range of samples to view in performance analyzer

There are many additional features of the Performance Analyzer, but this chapter presents those likely to be the most useful when profiling and analyzing Java applications. Additional details on using Performance Analyzer for profiling Java applications, including the Java EE application, can be found at the Performance Analyzer product Web site: http://www.oracle.com/technetwork/server-storage/solarisstudio/overview/index.html.

Bibliography

Keegan, Patrick, et al., *NetBeans IDE field guide: developing desktop, web, enterprise, and mobile applications,* 2nd Edition. Sun Microsystems, Inc., Santa Clara, CA, 2006.

Oracle Solaris Studio 12.2: Performance Analyzer. Oracle Corporation. http://dlc.sun.com/pdf/821-1379/821-1379.pdf.

JSR-133: Java Memory Model and Thread Specification. JSR-133 Expert Group. http://jcp.org/en/jsr/summary?id=133.

The Java Memory Model. Dr. Bill Pugh. http://www.cs.umd.edu/~pugh/java/memoryModel/.

7

Tuning the JVM, Step by Step

A modern JVM (Java Virtual Machine) is a complex piece of software with the capability and flexibility to adapt to many different application families and domains. Though many applications perform well with the default settings of a JVM, some applications require additional JVM tuning to meet their performance requirements. Due to the wide variety of applications that can be run on a modern JVM, a large number of JVM attributes can be tuned for running an application. Unfortunately, a well-tuned JVM configuration used for one application may not be well suited for another application. As a result, understanding how to tune a JVM is a necessity.

Tuning a modern JVM is largely an art, but some fundamentals, when well understood and followed, can make the task much simpler. This chapter presents those fundamentals and a general step-by-step process to tune the Java HotSpot VM (also referred to as HotSpot VM hereafter). To gain the most from this chapter, you should be familiar with the information presented in Chapter 3, "JVM Overview," in particular the "HotSpot VM Garbage Collectors" and "HotSpot VM JIT Compilers" sections.

This chapter begins by examining the methodology employed in the step-by-step tuning process, including any assumptions. Following these assumptions, there is an examination of the application requirements you need to know before embarking on tuning the HotSpot VM, requirements for a suggested testing infrastructure, and the garbage collection command line options to use to collect data. This is followed by several sections describing the step-by-step process of tuning the HotSpot VM behaviors such as startup time, memory footprint, throughput, and latency. This chapter also includes some edge case configurations where a final JVM configuration may deviate from the general guidelines and process presented in this chapter. These edge cases, as the term implies, are unusual but are included to show that exceptional configurations exist along with an explanation as to why they work well. The chapter concludes by examining some additional HotSpot VM command line options that may offer an application additional performance.

> **Tip**
>
> It is important to note that any change in the application, the data it operates on, or the hardware platform it runs on requires performance testing and qualification that may include JVM tuning.

This chapter is structured so that tuning for a particular aspect such as latency or throughput can be accomplished by turning to those sections. However, familiarity with the overall tuning process is helpful.

Methodology

The methodology presented in this chapter follows the work flow illustrated in Figure 7-1. It begins with a clear understanding of an application's performance requirements, which should be ranked in priority order by application stakeholders. This category of requirements is known as systemic requirements. In contrast to functional requirements, which dictate functionally what an application computes or produces for output, systemic requirements dictate a particular aspect of an application's operation such as its throughput, response time, the amount of memory it consumes, startup time, availability, manageability, and so on.

The next section takes a closer look at each systemic requirement important to the tuning process.

Performance tuning a JVM involves many trade-offs. When you emphasize one systemic requirement, you usually sacrifice something in another. For example, minimizing memory footprint usually comes at the expense of throughput and/or latency. Or, as you improve manageability, say by reducing the number of JVMs you use to deploy an application, you sacrifice some level of availability of the application since running fewer JVMs puts a larger portion of an application at risk should there be an unexpected failure. Such a situation results in a larger portion of the application being unavailable to its users. Since there are trade-offs when emphasizing systemic requirements, it is crucial to the tuning process to understand which are most important to the application's stakeholders.

Once you know which systemic requirements are most important, the next step is to choose a JVM deployment model. Choosing one involves making a decision about whether to deploy an application in multiple JVMs or in a single JVM. The

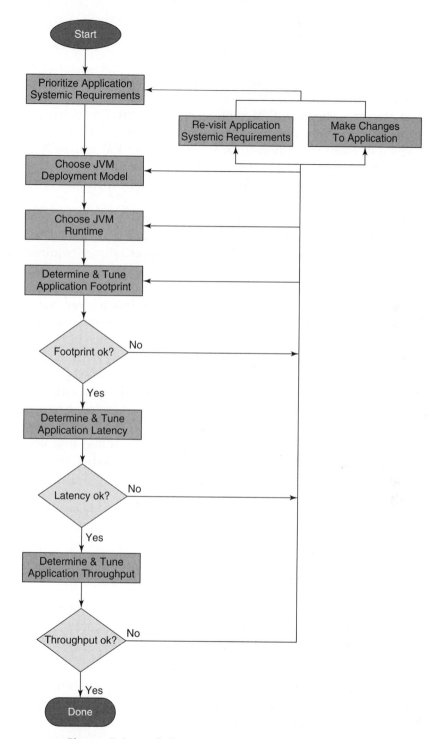

Figure 7-1 Work flow of tuning the JVM, step by step

availability, manageability, and memory footprint systemic requirements play a role in choosing an appropriate JVM deployment model.

The next step is to choose a JVM runtime environment. The HotSpot VM offers several runtime choices including a 32-bit client VM primarily focused on rapid startup time and small memory footprint, and a server VM primarily focused on high throughput available in both 32-bit and 64-bit VMs. Systemic requirements for high throughput, responsiveness, and startup and initialization time determine the best choice for a JVM runtime.

Next, the process moves to tuning the garbage collector to meet your application's memory footprint, pause time/latency, and throughput requirements. It begins by tuning to meet footprint requirements and then to meet latency requirements and finally to meet throughput requirements.

The tuning process presented iterates repeatedly through measurement and configuration refinement. It may take several iterations within a given step before you are able to meet applicable systemic requirements. In addition, it is possible that tuning done in one area may require revisiting previous steps in the process. For example, suppose you are not satisfied with latency after several iterations of trying to tune the garbage collector. In such an event, a change in the JVM deployment model may be necessary. Another possible outcome may be that either application changes must be made or that revisiting the application's systemic requirements is needed.

For some applications and their systemic requirements, it may take several iterations of this process until the application's stakeholders are satisfied with the application's performance.

Assumptions

The step-by-step tuning process assumes application execution has the following phases:

- An initialization phase where the application initializes important data structures and other necessary artifacts to begin its intended use
- A steady state phase where the application spends most of its time and where the application's core functionality is executed
- An optional summary phase where an artifact such as a report may be generated, such as that produced by executing a benchmark program just prior to the application ending its execution

The steady state phase—where an application spends most of its time—is the phase of most interest.

Testing Infrastructure Requirements

To make informed decisions about an application's memory footprint, latency, throughput, and startup time, along with confirming that the initial JVM runtime environment decision is appropriate for the application, the data collected from executing experiments must reflect what is expected to be observed when the application is in production. Hence, it is important to have a performance testing environment that replicates a production system and the expected production load. The testing environment must be capable of testing realistic production conditions under realistic production loads. Included in the performance testing environment should be all of the hardware and software components required to run the application in production.

In short, the performance testing environment should be close to, if not a replica of, the production environment and include the capability to capture metrics of interest, namely memory footprint, latency, throughput, and startup time. The better the testing environment replicates the production environment running with a realistic production load, the more accurate and better informed tuning decisions will be.

Application Systemic Requirements

Recall from the "Methodology" section earlier in the chapter that systemic requirements dictate a particular aspect of an application's operation such as its throughput, response time, the amount of memory it consumes, its availability, its manageability, and so on. In contrast, functional requirements dictate what an application computes or the output it produces.

The next several sections define application systemic requirements that can be optimized by the step-by-step tuning process.

Availability

Availability is a measure of the application being in an operational and usable state. An availability requirement expresses to what extent an application, or portions of an application, are available for use when some component breaks or experiences a failure.

In the context of a Java application, higher availability can be accomplished by running portions of an application across multiple JVMs or by multiple instances of the application in multiple JVMs. One of the trade-offs when emphasizing availability is increased manageability costs. Introducing additional JVMs means additional JVMs must be managed, which comes at a higher cost and usually more complexity.

A trivial example of an availability requirement is "the application shall be deployed in a manner in which an unexpected software component failure does not render the entire application unusable."

Manageability

Manageability is a measure of the operational costs associated with running and monitoring the application along with how easy it is to configure the application. A manageability requirement expresses the ease with which the system can be managed. In general, the fewer the number of JVMs used to run an application, the lower the operational costs associated with running and monitoring the application. Configuration tends to be easier with fewer JVMs, but the application's availability may be sacrificed.

A simple example of a manageability requirement is "the application shall be deployed in the fewest possible number of JVMs due to limited staffing resources."

Throughput

Throughput is a measure of the amount of work that can be performed per unit time. A throughput requirement ignores latency or responsiveness. Usually, increased throughput comes at the expense of either an increase in latency and/or an increase in memory footprint.

An example of a performance throughput requirement is "the application shall execute 2500 transactions per second."

Latency and Responsiveness

Latency, or responsiveness, is a measure of the elapsed time between when an application receives a stimulus to do some work and that work is completed. A latency or responsiveness requirement ignores throughput. Usually, increased responsiveness or lower latency, comes at the expense of lower throughput and/or an increase in memory footprint.

An example of a latency or responsiveness requirement is "the application shall execute trade requests to completion within 60 milliseconds."

Memory Footprint

Memory footprint is a measure of the amount of memory required to run an application at a some level of throughput, some level of latency, and/or some level of availability and manageability. Memory footprint is usually expressed as either the amount of Java heap required to run the application and/or the total amount of memory required to run the application. Usually, an increase in memory footprint via an increase in Java heap size can improve throughput or reduce latency, or both. As the memory made available for an application is decreased, throughput or latency is generally sacrificed. The footprint of an application may limit the number of application instances you can run on a machine with a given memory size.

An example of a memory footprint requirement is "the application shall execute on a system having at least 8 gigabytes of memory as a single application or on a system with 24 gigabytes of memory with three additional application instances."

Startup Time

Startup time is a measure of the amount of time it takes for an application to initialize. With Java applications, there may also be interest in the amount of time it takes to reach a point where a modern JVM has optimized the hot portions of the application. The time it takes to initialize a Java application is dependent on many factors including but not limited to the number of classes loaded, the number of objects that require initialization, how those objects are initialized, and the choice of a HotSpot VM runtime, that is, client or server.

Leaving aside the number of classes loaded, the number of objects that require initialization, and how those objects are initialized, a faster startup time using the HotSpot client runtime comes at the expense of more highly optimized generated code, that is, potentially higher throughput and lower latency. In contrast, the HotSpot server runtime has a longer startup time as a result of the time it takes to gain more knowledge of the application's use of Java, along with the time it takes to produce highly optimized generated machine code.

An example of a startup time requirement is "the application shall complete its initialization phase within 15 seconds."

Rank Systemic Requirements

The first step in the tuning process is prioritizing the application's systemic requirements. Doing so involves getting the major application stakeholders together and agreeing upon the prioritization. This exercise should be done as part of the application architecture and design phase since it provides clarity as to which requirements are most important.

Ranking the systemic requirements in order of importance to the application stakeholders is critical to the tuning process. The most important systemic requirements drive some of the initial decisions. For example, if availability is more important than manageability, then the JVM deployment model decision will be one that uses multiple JVMs. In contrast, if manageability is more important than availability, then a single JVM deployment model will be the initial choice.

Making decisions about JVM deployment and JVM runtime is discussed in more detail in the next two sections.

Choose JVM Deployment Model

The JVM deployment model choice amounts to whether to deploy your application in a single JVM instance or across multiple JVM instances. Which is best suited for your application is a function of the systemic requirements ranking along with some potential constraints. For example, suppose you want to deploy your application in a 64-bit JVM to leverage the ability to configure a larger Java heap. If the application is dependent upon third-party native code components for which 64-bit versions are either not available or not supported by the third-party vendor, you may be forced to use a 32-bit JVM and tune around a smaller than optimal Java heap.

Single JVM Deployment Model

Deploying a Java application in a single JVM has the advantage of reducing manageability cost since there are fewer JVMs to manage. The total memory used by the application will also be smaller since there is memory overhead associated with each deployed JVM.

The challenge associated with deploying a Java application in a single JVM is that the availability of the application is at higher risk in the event of a catastrophic application or JVM failure. In effect, the application has a single point of failure.

Multiple JVM Deployment Model

Deploying a Java application in multiple JVMs has the advantages of improved availability and potential for lower latency. With the application deployed across multiple JVMs an application or JVM failure may take only a portion of the application down rather than all of it as would occur with a single JVM deployment. A multiple JVM deployment may also allow for lower latency. In a multiple JVM deployment, Java heap sizes tend to be smaller, and smaller Java heaps may allow for shorter garbage collection pauses. Garbage collection pauses are usually the most significant inhibitor of an application's ability to meet latency requirements. In addition, a multiple JVM deployment may also help with throughput if there are application level scalability bottlenecks. Distributing the load across multiple JVMs may allow the application to scale to higher load.

With multiple JVMs, JVMs can be bound to processor sets. Binding JVMs to processor sets prevents application and JVM threads from migrating across hardware threads bound to different CPU caches. Thread migrations outside CPU cache boundaries can negatively impact performance due to increased CPU cache misses or thrashing.

The challenge with deploying a Java application in multiple JVMs is that monitoring, managing, and maintaining multiple JVMs requires more effort than a single JVM.

General Advice

There is not necessarily a "best" JVM deployment model. The most appropriate choice depends on which systemic requirements (manageability, availability, etc.) are most important.

A constraint to be aware of is that deploying in a single JVM may necessitate the use of a 64-bit JVM if running the Java application has a large enough memory footprint to warrant the need for a Java heap size larger than what a 32-bit JVM can handle. If you use a 64-bit JVM, make sure any third-party software components used in the application are supported by the third-party software vendor(s). In addition, if there any native components such as those that use JNI (Java Native Interface), regardless of whether they are third-party software components or ones developed along with the application, make sure they are compiled with a 64-bit compiler.

Generally, the authors' experience with JVM deployment models has been the fewer the JVMs the better. With fewer JVMs, there are fewer JVMs to monitor and manage along with less total memory footprint.

Choose JVM Runtime

Choosing a JVM runtime for a Java application is about making a choice between a runtime environment that tends to be better suited for one or another of client and server type applications.

> **Tip**
> More specific detailed information on the implementation of the HotSpot VM Runtime can be found in the "HotSpot VM Runtime" section of Chapter 3.

Client or Server Runtime

There are two types of JVM runtimes to choose from when using the HotSpot VM: client or server. The client runtime is specialized for rapid startup, small memory footprint, and a JIT compiler with rapid code generation. The server runtime offers more sophisticated code generation optimizations, which are more desirable in server applications. Many of the optimizations found in the server runtime's JIT compiler require additional time to gather more information about the behavior of the program and to produce better performing generated code.

There is a third HotSpot VM runtime under development called *tiered,* which combines the best of the client and server runtimes, that is, rapid startup time and high performing generated code. If you are using Java 6 Update 25, Java 7, or later, you may consider using tiered server runtime as a replacement for the client runtime. The tiered server runtime is enabled with the `-server -XX:+TieredCompilation` command line options. At the time of this writing, it is not mature enough to recommend as a replacement for either a client or server runtime. If you are using Java 6 Update 24 or earlier, the tiered server runtime is also not mature enough to recommend as a replacement for either client or server runtimes.

> **Tip**
>
> If you do not know which runtime to initially choose, start with the server runtime. If startup time or memory footprint requirements cannot be met and you are using Java 6 Update 25 or later, try the tiered server runtime. If you are not running Java 6 Update 25 or later, or the tiered server runtime is unable to meet your startup time or memory footprint requirement, switch to the client runtime.

32-Bit or 64-Bit JVM

In addition to a client and server runtime, there is also a choice between 32-bit and 64-bit JVMs. The 32-bit JVM is the default for the HotSpot VM. The choice of using a 32-bit or 64-bit JVM is dictated by the memory footprint required by the application along with whether any third-party software used in the application supports 64-bit JVMs and if there are any native components in the Java application. All native components using the Java Native Interface (JNI) in a 64-bit JVM must be compiled in 64-bit mode. Determining the memory footprint necessary to run your Java application is discussed in the next section of this chapter.

Table 7-1 provides some guidelines for making an initial decision on whether to start with a 32-bit or 64-bit JVM. Note that client runtimes are not available in 64-bit HotSpot VMs.

Table 7-1 Guidelines for Deciding on a 32-Bit or 64-Bit JVM

Operating System	Java Heap Size	32-Bit or 64-Bit JVM
Windows	Less than 1300 megabytes	32-bit
Windows	Between 1500 megabytes and 32 gigabytes*	64-bit with -d64 -XX:+UseCompressedOops command line options
Windows	More than 32 gigabytes	64-bit with -d64 command line option
Linux	Less than 2 gigabytes	32-bit
Linux	Between 2 and 32 gigabytes*	64-bit with -d64 -XX:+UseCompressedOops command line options
Linux	More than 32 gigabytes	64-bit with -d64 command line option
Oracle Solaris	Less than 3 gigabytes	32-bit
Oracle Solaris	Between 3 and 32 gigabytes*	64-bit with -d64 -XX:+UseCompressedOops command line options
Oracle Solaris	More than 32 gigabytes	64 bit with -d64 command line option

* Best performance in the 64-bit HotSpot VM with -XX:+UseCompressedOops is realized around 26 gigabytes or less of maximum Java heap size. HotSpot VM versions later than Java 6 Update 18 automatically enable -XX:+UseCompressedOops by default based on maximum Java heap size.

Garbage Collectors

Before moving to the next step of the tuning process, an initial garbage collector must be chosen. Several garbage collectors are available in the HotSpot VM: serial, throughput, mostly concurrent, and garbage first.

Tip

More specifics about the HotSpot VM garbage collectors are presented in the "HotSpot VM Garbage Collectors" section of Chapter 3.

Since it is possible for applications to meet their pause time requirements with the throughput garbage collector, start with the throughput garbage collector and migrate to the concurrent garbage collector if necessary. If migration to the concurrent garbage collector is required, it will happen later in the tuning process as part of the Determine and Tune Application Latency step; see Figure 7-1 for an illustration of the JVM tuning process.

The throughput garbage collector is specified by the HotSpot VM command line option -XX:+UseParallelOldGC or -XX:+UseParallelGC. If

-XX:+UseParallelOldGC is not available in the version of the HotSpot VM you are using, use -XX:+UseParallelGC. The difference between the two is that -XX:+UseParallelOldGC enables both a multithreaded young generation garbage collector and a multithreaded old generation garbage collector, that is, both minor garbage collections and full garbage collections are multithreaded. -XX:+UseParallelGC enables only a multithreaded young generation garbage collector. The old generation garbage collector used with -XX:+UseParallelGC is single threaded. Using -XX:+UseParallelOldGC also automatically enables -XX:+UseParallelGC. Hence, if you want to use both a multithreaded young generation garbage collector and a multithreaded old generation garbage collector, you need only specify -XX:+UseParallelOldGC.

GC Tuning Fundamentals

This section describes three major attributes of garbage collection performance, three fundamental garbage collection tuning principles, and the garbage collection information to collect when tuning a HotSpot VM garbage collector. Understanding the important trade-offs among the attributes, the tuning principles, and what information to collect is crucial to JVM tuning.

The Performance Attributes

- **Throughput.**   A measure of the garbage collector's ability to allow an application to run at peak performance without regard to the duration of garbage collection pause times or the amount of memory it requires
- **Latency.**   A measure of the garbage collector's ability to allow an application to experience a minimal amount of, or completely eliminate, pause time or application jitter induced by the garbage collector
- **Footprint.**   A measure of the amount of memory a garbage collector requires to operate efficiently

A performance improvement for one of these attributes almost always is at the expense of one or both of the other attributes. Put another way, the performance of one the attributes is usually compromised in favor of performance improvements in one or both of the other attributes. However, for most applications, rarely are all three performance attributes equally important. Usually, one or two of them are more important than the other(s).

As is the case with knowing which systemic requirements are most important to an application, it is also necessary to know which of the three performance attributes are the most important. Identifying which of these attributes are most important will map to similar application systemic requirements that are most important to the application.

The Principles

There are also three fundamental principles to understand when it comes to tuning a JVM's garbage collector.

- At each minor garbage collection, maximize the number of objects reclaimed. The authors call this the Minor GC Reclamation Principle. Adhering to this principle helps reduce the number and frequency of full garbage collections experienced by the application. Full garbage collections typically have the longest duration and as a result are the number one reason for applications not meeting their latency or throughput requirements.

- The more memory made available to the garbage collector, that is, the larger the Java heap space, the better the garbage collector and application perform when it comes to throughput and latency. The authors call this the GC Maximize Memory Principle.

- Tune the JVM's garbage collector for two of the three performance attributes: throughput, latency, and footprint. The authors call this the 2 of 3 GC Tuning Principle.

The exercise of tuning a JVM's garbage collector while keeping these three principles in mind makes the task of meeting your application's performance requirements much easier.

Command Line Options and GC Logging

The JVM tuning decisions made in the remainder of the tuning process utilize metrics observed from monitoring garbage collections. Collecting this information in garbage collection logs is the best approach. This means garbage collection statistics gathering must be enabled via HotSpot VM command line options. Enabling garbage collection logging, even in production systems, is a good idea. It has minimal overhead and provides a wealth of information that can be used to correlate application level events with garbage collection or JVM level events. For example, an application may exhibit a lengthy pause at some point during its operation. Having garbage collection logging enabled allows you to recognize whether the lengthy pause event was the result of a garbage collection or the artifact of some other kind of event, perhaps generated by the application.

If you are unfamiliar with the terms young generation space, old generation space, permanent generation space, eden space, survivor space, tenuring, or promotion, read the "HotSpot VM Garbage Collectors" section of Chapter 3. Understanding these terms is essential to tuning the JVM.

Several HotSpot VM command line options are of interest for garbage collection logging. The following is the minimal set of recommended command line options to use:

```
-XX:+PrintGCTimeStamps -XX:+PrintGCDetails -Xloggc:<filename>
```

`-XX:+PrintGCTimeStamps` prints a time stamp representing the number of seconds since the HotSpot VM was launched until the garbage collection occurred. `-XX:+PrintGCDetails` provides garbage collector-specific statistics and thus varies depending on the garbage collector in use. `-Xloggc:<filename>` directs the garbage collection information to the file named `<filename>`.

Here is example output using the preceding three garbage collection logging command line options in conjunction with the parallel throughput garbage collector enabled via `-XX:+UseParallelOldGC` or `-XX:+UseParallelGC` from Java 6 Update 21 (output is split across several lines for easier reading):

```
45.152: [GC
    [PSYoungGen: 295648K->32968K(306432K)]
    296198K->33518K(1006848K), 0.1083183 secs]
    [Times: user=1.83 sys=0.01, real=0.11 secs]
```

`45.152` is the number of seconds since the JVM launched and so tells when this garbage collection occurred. The `GC` label indicates this is a minor garbage collection, or young generation garbage collection.

`[PSYoungGen: 295648K->32968K(306432K)]` provides information on the young generation space. `PSYoungGen` indicates the young generation garbage collector in use is the multithreaded young generation garbage collector used with the throughput collector. Other possible young generation garbage collectors are `ParNew`, which is the multithreaded young generation garbage collector used with the concurrent old generation garbage collector known as CMS, and `DefNew`, which is the single-threaded young generation garbage collector used with the serial garbage collector. At the time of this writing the G1 garbage collector, which is currently under development, does not use an identifier in the same way as the other three garbage collectors to identify the output as G1 GC.

The value to the left of the ->, 295648K, is the occupancy of the young generation space prior to the garbage collection. The value to the right of the ->, 32968K, is the occupancy of the young generation space after the garbage collection. Young generation space is further divided into an eden space and two survivor spaces. Since the eden space is empty after a minor garbage collection, the value to the right of the ->, 32968K, is the amount of space consumed in survivor space. It can also be interpreted as the survivor space occupancy. The value inside the parentheses (306432K), is the size of the young generation space, that is, the total size of eden and the two survivor spaces.

296198K->33518K(1006848K) provides the Java heap utilization (cumulative occupancy of both young generation and old generation spaces) before and after the garbage collection. In addition, it provides the Java heap size, which is the total size of young generation and old generation. The value to the left of the ->, 296198K, is the occupancy of the Java heap before the garbage collection. The value to the right of the ->, 33518K, is the occupancy of the Java heap after the garbage collection. The value inside the parentheses (1006848K), is the total size of the Java heap.

From the young generation occupancy and Java heap occupancy, you can quickly calculate the occupancy of the old generation space. For example, the Java heap size is 1006848K, and the young generation heap size is 306432K. Hence, the old generation heap size is 1006848K − 306432K = 700416K. Before the garbage collection, 296198K − 295648K = 550K is the occupancy of the old generation space. After the garbage collection, 33518K − 32968K = 550K is the occupancy of the old generation space. In this example, since there is no change in occupancy of the old generation space before and after the garbage collection, no objects were promoted from the young to old generation. This is an important observation to make when looking at garbage collections since this data confirms the Minor GC Reclamation Principle. If an object is promoted to the old generation and later becomes unreachable, then the maximum number of objects was not reclaimed in the minor garbage collection and thus would violate the Minor GC Reclamation Principle. More on what to look for in garbage collection logs can be found in later sections of this chapter.

0.1083183 secs indicates the elapsed time for the garbage collection.

[Times: user=1.83 sys=0.01, real=0.11 secs] provides CPU and elapsed time information. The value to the right of user is the CPU time used by the garbage collection in user mode, that is, while executing in the JVM. In this example, the garbage collector used 1.83 seconds of CPU time in user mode. The value to the right of sys is the CPU time used by the operating system on behalf of the garbage collector. In this example, the garbage collection used 0.01 seconds of operating system CPU time. The value to the right of real is the elapsed wall clock time in seconds of the garbage collection. In this example, it took 0.11 seconds to complete the garbage collection. The times reported for user, sys, and real are rounded to the nearest 100th of a second.

If you are interested in a time stamp that reflects a calendar date and time, you can specify the -XX:PrintGCDateStamps command line option. The output of -XX:+PrintGCDateStamps shows the year, month, day, and time of day the garbage collection occurred and was introduced in Java 6 Update 4. The following is example output using -XX:+PrintGCDateStamps together with -XX:+PrintGCDetails.

```
2010-11-21T09:57:10.518-0500: [GC
    [PSYoungGen: 295648K->32968K(306432K)]
    296198K->33518K(1006848K), 0.1083183 secs]
    [Times: user=1.83 sys=0.01, real=0.11 secs]
```

The date stamp field, 2010-11-21T09:57:10.518-0500, uses the ISO 8601 date and time stamp. The output has the following form: *YYYY-MM-DDTHH-MM-SS.mmm*-TZ where:

- *YYYY* is the four-digit year.
- *MM* is the two-digit month; single-digit months are prefixed with 0.
- *DD* is the two-digit day of the month; single-digit days are prefixed with 0.
- *T* is a literal that denotes a date to the left of the literal and a time of day to the right.
- *HH* is the two-digit hour; single-digit hours are prefixed with 0.
- *MM* is the two-digit minute; single-digit minutes are prefixed with 0.
- *SS* is the two-digit second; single-digit seconds are prefixed with 0.
- *mmm* is the three-digit milliseconds; single- and two-digit milliseconds are prefixed with 00 and 0, respectively.
- *TZ* is the time zone offset from GMT.

Although the time zone offset from GMT is included in the output, the date and time of day are not printed as GMT time. The date and time of day are adjusted to local time.

When tuning the HotSpot VM for low latency the following two command line options are useful since they report the amount of time the application has been blocked due to a VM safepoint operation and how long the application has executed between safepoint operations.

```
• -XX:+PrintGCApplicationStoppedTime
• -XX:+PrintGCApplicationConcurrentTime
```

A safepoint operation puts the JVM into a state where all Java application threads are blocked and any thread executing in native code is prevented from returning to the VM to execute Java code. Safepoint operations are required when the VM must perform an internal operation with all Java threads in a known blocked state and unable to change the Java heap.

> **Tip**
>
> The "VM Operations and Safepoints" section of Chapter 3 describes safepoint operations in more detail.

Since safepoint operations block Java code execution, it is useful to know if an observed response time in an application is strongly correlated with a safepoint operation. Hence, being able to observe when application threads are blocked from executing as a result of a safepoint operation (the amount of time reported by -XX:+PrintGCApplicationStoppedTime) along with application log information can help identify whether an observed response time that exceeds application requirements is the result of a VM safepoint operation, or whether it is an artifact of some other event in the application or system. The use of the command line option -XX:+PrintSafepointStatistics can help distinguish garbage collection safepoints from other safepoints.

The -XX:+PrintGCApplicationConcurrentTime command line option can be used to determine whether the application was executing, and for how long, during some time period of interest where an observed response time exceeds application requirements.

Table 7-2 summarizes the garbage collection command line options presented in this section and offers suggestions for when their use is most applicable:

Table 7-2 Recommended GC Logging Command Line Options

GC Command Line Option	Most Applicable
-XX:+PrintGCTimeStamps -XX:+PrintGCDetails -Xloggc:<filename>	Minimal set of command line options to enable for all applications.
-XX:PrintGCDateStamps	Use when wanting to see a calendar date and time of day rather than a time stamp indicating the number of seconds since the JVM was launched. Requires Java 6 Update 4 or later.
-XX:+PrintGCApplicationStoppedTime -XX:+PrintGCApplicationConcurrentTime -XX:+PrintSafepointStatistics	Useful when tuning an application for low response time/latency to help distinguish between pause events arising from VM safepoint operations and other sources.

Determine Memory Footprint

Up to this point in the tuning process, no measurements have been taken. Only some initial choices have been made such as a JVM deployment model, a JVM runtime environment, what garbage collection statistics to collect, and the garbage collection principles to follow. This step of the tuning process provides a good estimate of the amount of memory or Java heap size required to run the application. The outcome of this step identifies the live data size for the application. The live data size provides input into a good starting point for a Java heap size configuration to run the application. It also determines whether the application's footprint requirements should be revisited or whether some application changes must be made to meet footprint requirements.

> **Tip**
>
> Live data size is the amount of memory in the Java heap consumed by the set of long-lived objects required to run the application in its steady state. In other words, it is the Java heap occupancy after a full garbage collection while the application is in steady state (see Figure 7-3).

Constraints

The input in this step is how much physical memory can be made available to the JVM. The choice of a single JVM deployment model or multiple JVM deployment model plays a significant role. The following list helps determine how much physical memory can be made available to the JVM(s):

- Will the Java application be deployed in a single JVM on a machine where it is the only application running? If that is the case, then all the physical memory on the machine can be made available to JVM.

- Will the Java application be deployed in multiple JVMs on the same machine? Or will the machine be shared by other processes or other Java applications? If either case applies, then you must decide how much physical memory will be made available to each process and JVM.

In either of the preceding scenarios, some memory must be reserved for the operating system.

HotSpot VM Heap Layout

Before taking some footprint measurements, it is important to have an understanding of the HotSpot VM Java heap layout. This understanding helps in determining

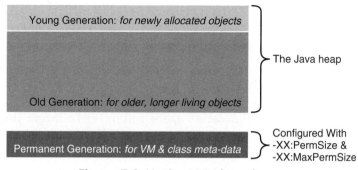

Figure 7-2 HotSpot VM heap layout

the Java heap size to use with the application and in fine-tuning the space sizes that impact the performance of the garbage collector.

The HotSpot VM has three major spaces: young generation, old generation, and permanent generation. These three spaces are shown in Figure 7-2.

When a Java application allocates Java objects, those objects are allocated in the young generation space. Objects that survive, that is, those that remain live, after some number of minor garbage collections are promoted into the old generation space. The permanent generation space holds VM and Java class metadata as well as interned Strings and class static variables.

The -Xmx and -Xms command line options specify the initial and maximum total size of the young generation and old generation spaces. This initial and maximum size is also referred to as the Java heap size. The value specified for -Xms is the initial and minimum size and -Xmx is the maximum size. When the value for -Xms is smaller than the value for -Xmx, the amount of space consumed by young and old generation spaces is allowed to grow or contract depending on the needs of the application. The growth of the Java heap will never be larger than -Xmx, and the Java heap will never contract smaller than -Xms. Java applications emphasizing throughput or latency tend to set both -Xms and -Xmx to the same value. Growing or contracting the size of either the young generation space or old generation space requires a full garbage collection. Full garbage collections can reduce throughput and induce larger than desired latencies.

The young generation space is specified using any one of the following command line options:

- -XX:NewSize=<n>[g|m|k]
  The initial and minimum size of the young generation space. <n> is the size. [g|m|k] indicates whether the size should be interpreted as gigabytes,

megabytes, or kilobytes. The young generation space will never be smaller than the value specified.[1] `-XX:MaxNewSize=<n>[g|m|k]` should also be specified when using `-XX:NewSize=<n>[g|m|k]`.

- `-XX:MaxNewSize=<n>[g|m|k]`
  The maximum size of the young generation space. `<n>` is the size. `[g|m|k]` indicates whether the size should be interpreted as gigabytes, megabytes, or kilobytes. The young generation space will never be larger than the value specified. `-XX:NewSize=<n>[g|m|k]` should also be specified when using `-XX:MaxNewSize=<n>[g|m|k]`.

- `-Xmn<n>[g|m|k]`
  Sets the initial, minimum, and maximum size of the young generation space. `<n>` is the size. `[g|m|k]` indicates whether the size should be interpreted as gigabytes, megabytes, or kilobytes. The young generation space size will be set to the value specified.

`-Xmn` is convenient to size both the initial and maximum size of the young generation space. It is important to note that if `-Xms` and `-Xmx` are not set to the same value and `-Xmn` is used, a growth or contraction in the Java heap size will not adjust the size of the young generation space. The size of the young generation space will remain constant with any growth or contraction of the Java heap size. Therefore, `-Xmn` should be used only when `-Xms` and `-Xmx` are set to the same value.

The size of the old generation space is implicitly set based on the size of the young generation space. The initial old generation space size is the value of `-Xms` minus `-XX:NewSize`. The maximum old generation space size is the value of `-Xmx` minus `-XX:MaxNewSize`. If `-Xms` and `-Xmx` are set to the same value and `-Xmn` is used, or `-XX:NewSize` is the same value as `-XX:MaxNewSize`, then the old generation size is `-Xmx` (or `-Xms`) minus `-Xmn`.

The permanent generation space is sized with the following command line options:

- `-XX:PermSize=<n>[g|m|k]`
- The initial and minimum size of the permanent generation space. `<n>` is the size. `[g|m|k]` indicates whether the size should be interpreted as gigabytes, megabytes, or kilobytes. The permanent generation space will never be smaller than the value specified.
- `-XX:MaxPermSize=<n>[g|m|k]`
- The maximum size of the permanent generation space. `<n>` is the size. `[g|m|k]` indicates whether the size should be interpreted as gigabytes, megabytes, or

---

1. The actual size allocated by the HotSpot VM may be slightly adjusted depending on the memory system of the hardware platform and the operating system. This is true of all the command lines listed on this page.

kilobytes. The permanent generation space will never be larger than the value specified.

Java applications with an emphasis on performance should size both the initial and maximum permanent generation sizes (`-XX:PermSize` and `-XX:MaxPermSize`) to the same value since growing or contracting the permanent generation space requires a full garbage collection.

If any Java heap size, initial or maximum size, young generation size, or permanent generation size is not specified, the HotSpot VM automatically chooses values based on the system configuration it discovers through an adaptive tuning feature called ergonomics.

Tip

Additional information on HotSpot adaptive tuning, including the default values chosen for Java heap sizes, can be found in the "HotSpot VM Adaptive Tuning" section of Chapter 3.

It is important to understand that a garbage collection occurs when any one of the three spaces, young generation, old generation, or permanent generation, is in a state where it can no longer satisfy an allocation event. In other words, a garbage collection occurs when any one of those three spaces is considered full and there is some request for additional space that is not available. When the young generation space does not have enough room available to satisfy a Java object allocation, the HotSpot VM performs a minor garbage collection to free up space. Minor garbage collections tend to be short in duration relative to full garbage collections.

Objects that remain live for some number of minor garbage collections eventually get promoted (copied) to the old generation space. When the old generation space no longer has available space for promoted objects, the HotSpot VM performs a full garbage collection. It actually performs a full garbage collection when it determines there is not enough available space for object promotions from the next minor garbage collection. This is a less costly approach rather than being in the middle of a minor garbage collection and discovering that the promotion of an object will fail. Recovering from an object promotion failure is an expensive operation. A full garbage collection also occurs when the permanent generation space does not have enough available space to store additional VM or class metadata.

If a full garbage collection is triggered by old generation space being full, both old generation space and permanent generation space are garbage collected, even if the permanent generation space is not full. Likewise, if a full garbage collection event is triggered by permanent generation space being full, both old generation and permanent generation spaces are garbage collected even if the old generation space is not full. In addition, the young generation space is also garbage collected before the old generation space on a full garbage collection unless the `-XX:-ScavengeBeforeFullGC` command line option is specified. `-XX:-ScavengeBeforeFullGC` will disable young generation space garbage collection on full garbage collections.

Heap Size Starting Point

To begin the heap size tuning process, a starting point is needed. The approach described in this section may start with a larger Java heap size than is necessary to run the Java application. The purpose of this step is to gather some initial data and further refine the heap size to more reasonable values later in the tuning process.

As mentioned earlier in the "Choose JVM Runtime" section, start with the throughput garbage collector. Remember that the throughput garbage collector is specified with the `-XX:+UseParallelOldGC` command line option. If the HotSpot VM you are using does not accept `-XX:+UseParallelOldGC` as a valid command line option, use `-XX:+UseParallelGC` instead.

If you have a good sense of the amount of the Java heap space the Java application will require, you can use that Java heap size as a starting point for setting `-Xmx` and `-Xms`. If you do not know what Java heap size the Java application will require, you can start with the Java heap size the HotSpot VM automatically chooses. Starting the Java application without specifying a `-Xmx` or `-Xms` value provides some initial data for a Java heap size. In other words, it's a starting point. The Java heap size will be refined a bit later in this tuning step.

The suggested command line options to use for capturing data in garbage collection logs are described earlier in this chapter in the "Command Line Options and GC Logging" section. The garbage collection logs show the Java heap size in use. The initial and maximum heap sizes in use can also be viewed using the HotSpot command line option `-XX:+PrintCommandLineFlags`. `-XX:+PrintCommandLineFlags` prints the selected initial and maximum heap sizes at HotSpot VM initialization time as `-XX:InitialHeapSize=<n>  -XX:MaxHeapSize=<m>`, where `<n>` is the initial Java heap size in bytes and `<m>` is the maximum Java heap size in bytes.

Regardless of whether you specify an explicit Java heap size using a command line option, or use the default size, attempt to put the application in the phase where you expect it to spend most of its operating time, that is, its steady state phase. You must have sufficient load generation capabilities and the ability to drive the application with a load representative of what is expected in production.

If you observe OutOfMemoryErrors in the garbage collection logs while attempting to put the application into its steady state, take notice of whether the old generation space or the permanent generation space is running out of memory. The following example illustrates an OutOfMemoryError occurring as a result of a too small old generation space:

```
2010-11-25T18:51:03.895-0600: [Full GC
    [PSYoungGen: 279700K->267300K(358400K)]
    [ParOldGen: 685165K->685165K(685170K)]
    964865K->964865K(1043570K)
    [PSPermGen: 32390K->32390K(65536K)],
    0.2499342 secs]
    [Times: user=0.08 sys=0.00, real=0.05 secs]
Exception in thread "main" java.lang.OutOfMemoryError: Java heap space
```

The important parts of the garbage collection output are highlighted in bold. Since the throughput garbage collector is in use, the old generation statistics are identified by ParOldGen. The fields that follow ParOldGen, 685165K->685165K(685170K), indicate the old generation space's occupancy before the full garbage collection, after the full garbage collection, and the size of the old generation space, respectively. From this output, you can conclude that the old generation space is too small, since the old generation space occupancy after the full garbage collection, the value to the right of the bold -> is very near the same value as the configured old generation size, the value between the (and). Hence, the JVM reports an OutOfMemoryError and suggests that Java heap space has run out of memory. In contrast, the permanent generation space occupancy (32390K), identified with the row beginning with the PSPermGen label, is nowhere near its capacity of (65536K).

The following example shows an OutOfMemoryError occurring as a result of a too small permanent generation space:

```
2010-11-25T18:26:37.755-0600: [Full GC
    [PSYoungGen: 0K->0K(141632K)]
    [ParOldGen: 132538K->132538K(350208K)]
    32538K->32538K(491840K)
    [PSPermGen: 65536K->65536K(65536K)],
    0.2430136 secs]
    [Times: user=0.37 sys=0.00, real=0.24 secs]
java.lang.OutOfMemoryError: PermGen space
```

Again, the important parts of the garbage collection output are highlighted bold. Since the throughput garbage collector is in use, the permanent generation statistics are identified by PSPermGen. The fields that follow PSPermGen, 65536K->65536K(65536K), indicate the permanent generation space's occupancy before the full garbage collection, after the full garbage collection, and the size of the permanent generation space, respectively. It is easy to conclude that the permanent generation space is not large enough since the permanent generation space occupancy after the full garbage collection, the value to the right of the ->, is the same as the configured permanent generation size, the value between (and). Hence, the

OutOfMemoryError suggests that PermGen space has run out of memory. In contrast, the old generation space occupancy is much less than its capacity, `132538K` versus `350208K`.

If you observe an OutOfMemoryError in the garbage collection logs, try increasing the Java heap size to 80% to 90% of the physical memory you have available for the JVM. Pay particular attention to the heap space that incurred the OutOfMemoryError and be sure to increase its size. For example, increase `-Xms` and `-Xmx` for old generation space OutOfMemoryErrors, and increase `-XX:PermSize` and `-XX:MaxPermSize` for permanent generation OutOfMemoryErrors. Keep in mind the limitations of the Java heap sizes based on the hardware platform and whether you are using a 32-bit or 64-bit JVM. After increasing the Java heap size check the garbage collection logs for OutOfMemoryErrors. Repeat these steps, increasing the Java heap size at each iteration, until you observe no OutOfMemoryErrors in the garbage collection logs.

Once the application is running in its steady state without experiencing Out-OfMemoryErrors, the next step is to calculate the application's live data size.

Calculate Live Data Size

As mentioned earlier, the live data size is the Java heap size consumed by the set of long-lived objects required to run the application in its steady state. In other words, the live data size is the Java heap occupancy of the old generation space and permanent generation space after a full garbage collection while the application is running in its steady state.

The live data size for a Java application can be collected from the garbage collection logs. The live data size provides the following tuning information for

- An approximation of the amount of old generation Java heap occupancy consumed while running the application in steady state
- An approximation of the amount of permanent generation heap occupancy consumed while running the application in steady state

In addition to the live data size, the full garbage collections at steady state also provide the worst case latency to expect due to full garbage collections.

To get a good measure of an application's live data size, it is best to look at the Java heap occupancy after several full garbage collections. Make sure these full garbage collections are occurring while the application is running in its steady state.

If the application is not experiencing full garbage collections, or they are not occurring very frequently, you can induce full garbage collections using the JVM monitoring tools VisualVM or JConsole. Both are bundled with HotSpot JDK distributions and can instruct a monitored JVM to induce a full garbage collection. VisualVM can be launched with the `jvisualvm` command and JConsole with the `jconsole` command. VisualVM is available in Java 6 Update 7 or later.

To force full garbage collections, monitor the application with VisualVM or JConsole and click the Perform GC button in the VisualVM or JConsole window. A command line alternative to force a full garbage collection is to use the HotSpot JDK distribution `jmap` command. `jmap` requires the `-histo:live` command line option and the JVM process id for this purpose. The JVM process id can be acquired using the JDK's `jps` command. For example, if the Java application's JVM process id is 348, the `jmap` command line to induce a full garbage collection would look like

```
$ jmap -histo:live 348
```

The `jmap` command induces a full garbage collection and also produces a heap profile that contains object allocation information. For the purposes of this step, you can ignore the generated heap profile.

Initial Heap Space Size Configuration

This section describes how to use live data size calculations to determine an initial Java heap size. Figure 7-3 shows the fields that identify an application's live data size. It is wise to compute an average of the Java heap occupancy and garbage collection duration of several full garbage collections for your live data size calculation. The more data you collect, the better the estimate for a Java heap size starting point.

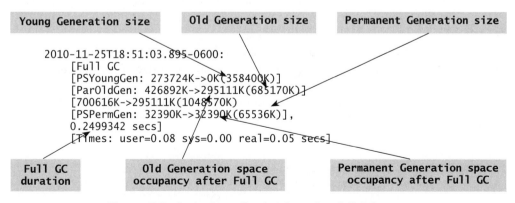

Figure 7-3 Garbage collection log after full GC event

Using the live data size information, an informed decision can be made on an initial Java heap size to use along with an estimate of the worst case latency due to full garbage collections.

As a general rule, the initial and maximum Java heap size command line options, -Xms and -Xmx, should be set to a value between three and four times larger than the live data size of the old generation space. In the full garbage collection data shown in Figure 7-3, the old generation space occupancy after the full garbage collection is 295111K, or about 295 megabytes. Hence, the live data size is about 295 megabytes. Therefore, the suggested initial and maximum Java heap size to specify for this application should be a value between 885 and 1180 megabytes, that is, -Xms1180m -Xmx1180m for four times the live data size. In Figure 7-3, the Java heap size in use is 1048570K, about 1048 megabytes. This Java heap size is at the upper end of the recommendation.

Also as a general rule, the initial and maximum permanent generation size, -XX:PermSize and -XX:MaxPermSize, should be 1.2x to 1.5x larger than the live data size of the permanent generation space. In the example full garbage collection shown in Figure 7-3, the permanent generation space occupancy after the full garbage collection is 32390K, or about 32 megabytes. Hence, the suggested initial and maximum permanent generation space size to specify for this application should be between 38 megabytes and 48 megabytes, that is, -XX:PermSize=48m -XX:MaxPermSize=48m, for 1.5 times the permanent generation live data size. In Figure 7-3, the permanent generation space size in use is 65536K, about 65 megabytes. Although this is above the recommended size of 38 to 48 megabytes, 17 additional megabytes in the context of a 1 gigabyte Java heap space is not worth worrying about.

As an additional general rule, the young generation space should be 1 to 1.5 times the old generation space live data size. In the example full garbage collection shown in Figure 7-3, the live data size is about 295 megabytes. As a result, the suggested young generation size should be between 295 and 442 megabytes. In Figure 7-3, the young generation space size is 358400K, about 358 megabytes. 358 megabytes is within the recommended size.

If the initial and maximum Java heap size is 3x to 4x the live data size and the young generation space is 1x to 1.5x the live data size, the size of the old generation space should be between 2x to 3x the live data size.

The combined Java command line applying these general sizing rules based on the garbage collection data in Figure 7-3 is

```
$  java -Xms1180m -Xmx1180m -Xmn295m
       -XX:PermSize=48m -XX:MaxPermSize=48m
```

Table 7-3 Guidelines for Calculating Java Heap Sizing

Space	Command Line Option	Occupancy Factor
Java heap	`-Xms and -Xmx`	3x to 4x old generation space occupancy after full garbage collection
Permanent Generation	`-XX:PermSize` `-XX:MaxPermSize`	1.2x to 1.5x permanent generation space occupancy after full garbage collection
Young Generation	`-Xmn`	1x to 1.5x old generation space occupancy after full garbage collection
Old Generation	Implied from overall Java heap size minus the young generation size	2x to 3x old generation space occupancy after full garbage collection

Guidelines to follow when calculating Java heap sizing are summarized in Table 7-3.

Additional Considerations

This section presents additional items to keep in mind when determining the application's memory footprint. It is important to know that the Java heap size calculated in the previous section does not represent the full memory footprint of a Java application. A better way to determine a Java application's total memory use is by monitoring the application with an operating system tool such as `prstat` on Oracle Solaris, `top` on Linux, and Task Manager on Windows. The Java heap size may not be the largest contributor to an application's memory footprint. For example, applications may require additional memory for thread stacks. The larger the number of threads, the more memory consumed in threads stacks. The deeper the method calls executed by the application, the larger the thread stacks. There may also be native libraries that allocate memory as well as I/O buffers used by the application that require additional memory. The memory footprint estimate for an application must include any additional memory use.

Keep in mind that a possible outcome of this step in the tuning process may be that the application's memory requirements cannot be met. If that is the case, either the application memory footprint requirements must be revisited and revised, or application changes must be made. A possible activity may include Java heap profiling and making changes to the application to reduce object allocations or object retention. A reduction in object allocations, more importantly, object retention helps reduce the live data size.

The Java heap sizes calculated in this step are a starting point. These sizes may be further modified in the remaining steps of the tuning process, depending on the application's requirements.

Tune Latency/Responsiveness

The objective of this step in the tuning process is to meet the application's latency requirements. The activities performed in this step involve several iterations of refining the Java heap size configuration, evaluating garbage collection duration and frequency, possibly switching to a different garbage collector, and further fine-tuning of space sizes in the event of a change to a different garbage collector.

There are two possible outcomes of this step:

- **Application latency requirements are met.** If the tuning activities performed in this step result in being able to meet the application's latency requirements, you can continue to the next step in the tuning process, Determine and Tune Application Throughput described in the next major section "Tune Application Throughput."

- **Application latency requirements are not met.** If you are not able to meet the application's latency requirements after performing the tuning activities described in this section, you must either revisit the application's latency requirements or implement changes in the application that improve latency. Possible activities that may drive changes to improve the application's latency might include

    a. Heap profiling and making changes to the application to reduce object allocation or object retention

    b. Changing the JVM deployment model to lessen the amount of work or load taken on by a JVM

    Either of these two choices reduces the JVM's object allocation rate and therefore garbage collection frequency.

This step begins by looking at the latency impact of the garbage collector starting with the initial Java heap size established in the previous section "Determine Memory Footprint."

The following activities are involved in evaluating the garbage collector's impact on latency:

- Measuring minor garbage collection duration

- Measuring minor garbage collection frequency

- Measuring worst case full garbage collection duration

- Measuring worst case full garbage collection frequency

Measuring garbage collection duration and frequency is crucial to refining the Java heap size configuration. Minor garbage collection duration and frequency measurements drive the refinement of the young generation size. Measuring the worst case full garbage collection duration and frequency drive old generation sizing decisions and the decision of whether to switch from using the throughput garbage collector, enabled via `-XX:+UseParallelOldGC` or `-XX:+UseParallelGC`, to using the concurrent garbage collector, enabled via `-XX:+UseConcMarkSweepGC`. The decision to switch to the concurrent garbage collector is made if the throughput collector's worst case full garbage collection duration or frequency is too high compared to the application's latency requirements. If a switch is made, additional tuning of the concurrent garbage collector may be required, as discussed later in this section.

Each of the previously mentioned activities is elaborated on in the next several subsections. Before exploring each of these in more detail, several inputs to this step are worth mentioning. They are described in the next subsection.

Inputs

There are several inputs to this step of the tuning process. They are derived from the systemic requirements for the application.

- **The acceptable average pause time target for the application.** The average pause time requirement(s) are compared against what is measured or observed for minor garbage collection duration.

- **The frequency of minor garbage collection induced latencies that are considered acceptable.** The frequency of minor garbage collections is compared against what is considered tolerable. The frequency of these latency events is generally not as important to application stakeholders as their duration.

- **The maximum pause time incurred by the application that can be tolerated by the application's stakeholders.** The maximum latency requirement(s) are compared against what is measured as the worst case full garbage collection duration.

- **The frequency of the maximum pause time that is considered acceptable by the application's stakeholders.** The frequency of maximum pause times is essentially the frequency of full garbage collections. Again, most application stakeholders are more interested in the average and maximum pause times than the frequency at which they occur.

Once the inputs are known, garbage collection duration and frequency statistics can be collected beginning with the Java heap size determined in the previous section "Determine Memory Footprint" along with specifying the throughput garbage collector enabled via the HotSpot command line option `-XX:+UseParallelOldGC` or `-XX:+UseParallelGC`. By examining the statistics, young generation space and old generation space sizes can be tuned to meet the above inputs. Refining the young generation space and old generation space sizes through the evaluation of observed minor garbage collection duration and frequency along with evaluating worst case full garbage collection duration and frequency are the topics of the next two subsections.

Refine Young Generation Size

Sizing decisions for the young generation space are made by evaluating garbage collection statistics and observing minor garbage collection durations and frequency. An example of how to size a young generation space using garbage collection statistics follows.

Although the time it takes to perform a minor garbage collection is directly related to the number of reachable objects in the young generation space, generally the smaller the young generation space, the shorter the minor garbage collection duration. Regardless of the impact on the minor garbage collection duration, decreasing the size of the young generation space increases the frequency of minor garbage collections. This is because a smaller young generation space fills up in less time at the same object allocation rate. Likewise, an increase in the young generation space size decreases the frequency of minor garbage collections.

When examining garbage collection data and observing minor garbage collections that are too lengthy, the corrective action is to reduce the size of the young generation space. If minor garbage collections are too frequent, then the corrective action is to increase the size of the young generation space.

To illustrate with an example, the minor garbage collections shown in Figure 7-4 were produced with the following HotSpot VM command line options: `-Xms6144m -Xmx6144m -Xmn2048m -XX:PermSize=96m -XX:MaxPermSize=96m -XX:+UseParallelOldGC`.

Figure 7-4 shows the average duration of the minor garbage collections as .054 seconds. The average frequency of those minor garbage collections is one every 2.147 seconds. When calculating the average duration and frequency, the larger the number of minor garbage collections in the calculation, the better the estimate of the average duration and average frequency. It is also important to use minor garbage collections known to have occurred while the application is running in its steady state.

The next step is to compare the observed average minor garbage collection duration to the application's average latency requirement. If the observed average minor garbage collection duration is greater than the application's latency requirement, decrease the size of young generation space and run another experiment. Collect garbage collection statistics and reevaluate the data.

If the observed frequency of minor garbage collections is greater than the application's latency requirement (they occur too frequently), increase the size of the young generation space and run another experiment. Collect garbage collection statistics and reevaluate the data.

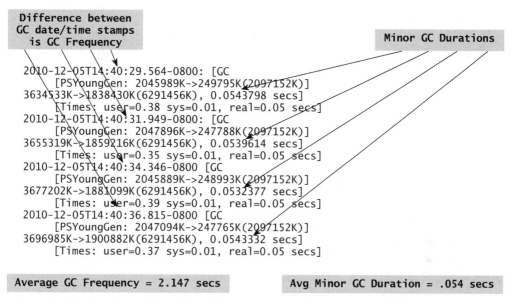

Figure 7-4 Example minor GC average duration and average frequency

It may require several iterations before you are able to meet the application's average latency requirement. As you change the size of the young generation space, try to keep the size of old generation space the same. An example is described in the next paragraph.

Using the garbage collection data in Figure 7-4, if the application's latency requirement is 40 milliseconds, the observed average minor garbage collection duration from the preceding example of 54 milliseconds (.054 seconds) is greater than the application's latency requirement. The Java heap space configuration used to produce the data in Figure 7-4 was -Xms6144m -Xmx6144m -Xmn2048m -XX:PermSize=96m -XX:MaxPermSize=96. This means the old generation size is 4096 megabytes (old generation size is -Xmx minus -Xmn). A decrease in the young generation size by about 10% and keeping old generation size the same results in the following adjusted HotSpot VM command line options:

```
-Xms5940m -Xmx5940m -Xmn1844m
-XX:PermSize=96m -XX:MaxPermSize=96 -XX:+UseParallelOldGC
```

Notice the decrease in value for -Xmn from 2048m to 1844m and the Java heap size (-Xmx and -Xms) reduction from 6144m to 5940m. Both young generation space (-Xmn) and Java heap size (-Xmx and -Xms) are reduced by 204 megabytes, about 10% of the 2048 megabytes configured for the previous young generation size.

If the application requirements suggest it can tolerate longer pause times than what are observed and measured in the garbage collection data, the young generation size can be increased. Again, try to keep the size of the old generation space constant.

Regardless of whether the young generation heap size is increased or decreased, collecting garbage collection statistics and recalculating the average minor garbage collection duration must be done and evaluated against the application's latency requirements. It may require several iterations of changing young generation size.

To illustrate the exercise of increasing the young generation size as a result of an application's requirement for minor garbage collection frequency being greater than the calculated average minor garbage collection frequency, suppose the application's requirement for minor garbage collection frequency is one every 5 seconds. In the example in Figure 7-4, the average minor garbage collection frequency is one every 2.147 seconds. Since the application's requirement for minor garbage collection frequency is greater than the calculated frequency, the young generation size should be increased. A rough estimate of how much to increase the young generation size is to look at the current size of the young generation space and look at the average minor garbage collection frequency. In this example, it takes on average 2.147 seconds to fill a 2048 megabyte young generation space. Assuming a steady object allocation rate, an increase of about 2.3 (5 / 2.17) seconds is needed. In other words, if it takes 2.17 seconds to fill a space of 2048 megabytes, it will take about 5 seconds to fill a space of 4700 megabytes. Hence, the size of a young generation space needed to meet a 5 second minor garbage collection frequency target is about 4700 megabytes. The following is an updated set of HotSpot VM command line options based on this analysis:

```
-Xms8796m -Xmx8796m -Xmn4700m
-XX:PermSize=96m -XX:MaxPermSize=96 -XX:+UseParallelOldGC
```

Notice the increase in both young generation size, -Xmn, and the Java heap size, -Xmx and -Xms, from their original values of 2048m and 6144m.

Additional general guidelines to keep in mind as the young generation size is changed are

- **The old generation space size should be not be much smaller than 1.5x the live data size.** See the previous section "Determine Memory Footprint" for live data size definition and additional old generation sizing guidelines.

- **Young generation space size should be at least 10% of the Java heap size, the value specified as -Xmx and -Xms.** A very small young generation size can be counterproductive. It leads to frequent minor garbage collections.

- **When increasing the Java heap size, be careful not to exceed the amount of physical memory available to the JVM.** A Java heap size that consumes enough memory to cause the underlying system to swap to virtual memory results in poor garbage collector and application performance.

If at this stage, taking into account only minor garbage collection induced latencies, you are not able to meet the application's average pause time or latency requirements through sizing the young generation space, you must either make changes to the application, change the JVM deployment model to deploy the application across additional JVMs, or revisit the application's average pause time latency requirements.

If you can meet the application's latency requirements focusing only on the minor garbage collections, then you can proceed to sizing the old generation space in an effort to meet the application's worst case pause time and worst case pause time frequency. This is the topic of the next subsection.

Refine Old Generation Size

The objective of this task is to evaluate the worst case pause time induced by a full garbage collection and the frequency of full garbage collections.

As in the previous section, "Refine Young Generation Size," garbage collection statistics are required. The data of interest are full garbage collection duration and frequency. The duration of full garbage collections that occur in steady state indicate the worst case full garbage collection induced pause time for the application. If multiple full garbage collections occur in steady state, then calculate an average worst case pause time. More data implies a better estimate.

Calculating the elapsed time between full garbage collections by taking the difference between full garbage collection date or time stamps provides the worst case full garbage collection frequency. Figure 7-5 shows an example of two full garbage collections with durations identified and frequency computed.

```
                        Full GC duration
2010-12-05T15:10:11.231-0800: [Full GC
    [PSYoungGen: 455832K->0K(2097152K)]
    [ParOldGen: 4194289K->1401197K(4194304K)]
4650121K->1401197K(6291456K)
    [PSPermGen: 66329K->59470K(98304K)],
1.3370216 secs]
    [Times: user=7.03 sys=0.11, real=1.34 secs]
... minor GC events omitted ...
2010-12-05T15:35:41.853-0800: [Full GC
    [PSYoungGen: 1555832K->0K(2097152K)]
    [ParOldGen: 4194196K->1402217K(4194304K)]
5750028->1402217K(6291456K)
    [PSPermGen: 61351K->59667K(98304K)],
1.4299125 secs]
    [Times: user=7.56 sys=0.09, real=1.43 secs]

    Average Full GC Frequency = 25 min, 30.622 secs
    *Elapsed time between Full GCs

    Average Full GC Duration = 1.383 secs
```

Figure 7-5 Example full GC average duration and frequency

If no full garbage collections are found in the garbage collection data, they should be induced as described earlier in the "Calculate Live Data Size" subsection. In addition, an estimate of the full garbage collection frequency should be calculated by looking at the object promotion rate, the rate that objects get copied from the young generation space to the old generation space. How to calculate the promotion rate is described in the next several paragraphs.

> **Tip**
>
> Minor garbage collections immediately and shortly following a full garbage collection should not be used in this calculation since it may take up to 15 minor garbage collections before object promotions are observed. The 15 minor garbage collections may be the result of object aging. Object aging is described in further detail later in this chapter.

Following are several example minor garbage collections. These are used to illustrate how to calculate the frequency of full garbage collections.

```
2010-12-05T14:40:29.564-0800: [GC
    [PSYoungGen: 2045989K->249795K(2097152K)]
    3634533K->1838430K(6291456K), 0.0543798 secs]
    [Times: user=0.38 sys=0.01, real=0.05 secs]
2010-12-05T14:40:31.949-0800: [GC
    [PSYoungGen: 2047896K->247788K(2097152K)]
    3655319K->1859216K(6291456K), 0.0539614 secs]
    [Times: user=0.35 sys=0.01, real=0.05 secs]
```

```
2010-12-05T14:40:34.346-0800 [GC
    [PSYoungGen: 2045889K->248993K(2097152K)]
    3677202K->1881099K(6291456K), 0.0532377 secs]
    [Times: user=0.39 sys=0.01, real=0.05 secs]
2010-12-05T14:40:36.815-0800 [GC
    [PSYoungGen: 2047094K->247765K(2097152K)]
    3696985K->1900882K(6291456K), 0.0543332 secs]
    [Times: user=0.37 sys=0.01, real=0.05 secs]
```

From the preceding garbage collections, the following is known:

- The Java heap size is 6291456K or 6144 megabytes (6191456 / 1024).
- The young generation size is 2097152K or 2048 megabytes (2097152 / 1024).
- The old generation size is 6144 − 2048 = 4096 megabytes.

Subtracting the live data size, calculated earlier as part of the analysis done in the "Determine MemoryFootprint" section, from the old generation size produces the amount of available old generation space. For this example, assume the live data size is 1370 megabytes. An old generation size of 4096 megabytes and a live data size of 1370 megabytes means there are 2726 megabytes of free space in the old generation (4096 − 1370 = 2726).

How long it takes to fill 2726 megabytes of free space in the old generation is determined by the young to old generation promotion rate. The promotion rate is calculated by looking at the increase in the occupancy of the old generation space along with the date or time stamp at each minor garbage collection. The occupancy of the old generation space is the difference between the occupancy of the Java heap after a minor garbage collection minus the occupancy of the young generation space after that same minor garbage collection. Using the preceding example minor garbage collections, the occupancy of the old generation space after each minor garbage collection is

1588635K, for the first minor garbage collection

1611428K, for the second minor garbage collection

1632106K, for the third minor garbage collection

1653117K, for the fourth minor garbage collection

The increase in the old generation space size at each garbage collection is

22793K, between the first and second minor garbage collection

20678K, between the second and third minor garbage collection

21011K, between the third and fourth minor garbage collection

The average promoted at each minor garbage collection is about 21494K, or about 21 megabytes.

The remaining data needed to calculate the promotion rate is the minor garbage collection frequency. In the preceding example garbage collections, the average minor garbage collection frequency is one every 2.147 seconds. Therefore, the promotion rate is 21,494K bytes / 2.147 seconds, or about 10,011K bytes (10 megabytes) per second. The time it takes to fill 2726 megabytes of available old generation space is 272.6 seconds, 2726/10 = 272.6, about 4.5 minutes.

Therefore, based on an analysis of the example garbage collections given earlier, this application has an estimated worst case full garbage collection frequency of about one every 4.5 minutes. This estimate can easily be checked by running the application in steady state for more than 4.5 minutes and observing a full garbage collection.

If the estimated or observed full garbage collection frequency is more than the application's requirement for worst case latency frequency, you should increase the size of the old generation space. This reduces the full garbage collection frequency. As you increase the size of the old generation space, keep the size of the young generation space constant.

If You Are Observing Only Full Garbage Collections

When modifying the size of the old generation space, it is possible the old generation size may become out of balance with the young generation size and result in the application experiencing only full garbage collections. Usually this occurs when the old generation space is not large enough to hold all the objects being promoted from the young generation space, even after a full garbage collection. This situation can be identified in garbage collection statistics as illustrated here:

```
2010-12-06T15:10:11.231-0800: [Full GC
    [PSYoungGen: 196608K->146541K(229376K)]
    [ParOldGen: 262142K->262143K(262144K)]
    458750K->408684K(491520K)
    [PSPermGen: 26329K->26329K(32768K)],
    17.0440216 secs]
    [Times: user=11.03 sys=0.11, real=17.04 secs]
2010-12-05T15:10:11.853-0800: [Full GC
    [PSYoungGen: 196608K->148959K(229376K)]
    [ParOldGen: 262143K->262143K(262144K)]
    458751K->411102K(6291456K)
    [PSPermGen: 26329K->26329K(32768K)],
    18.1471123 secs]
    [Times: user=12.13 sys=0.12, real=18.15 secs]
2010-12-05T15:10:12.099-0800: [Full GC
    [PSYoungGen: 196608K->150377K(229376K)]
    [ParOldGen: 262143K->262143K(262144K)]
    458751K->412520K(6291456K)
    [PSPermGen: 26329K->26329K(32768K)],
    17.8130416 secs]
    [Times: user=11.97 sys=0.12, real=17.81 secs]
```

The key indicator that the old generation space is not large enough is that little space has been reclaimed in the old generation space (the values to the right of the ParOldGen label), and a large portion of the young generation space remains occupied after each full garbage collection. When not enough space is available in the old generation to handle promoted objects from the young generation, objects "back up" into the young generation space as observed in the preceding output.

If you are able to meet your application's worst case latency requirements after several iterations of sizing the old generation space, you are finished with this JVM tuning step. You can proceed to the next step in the tuning process presented in the next major section "Tune Application Throughput."

If you are not able to meet your application's worst case latency requirements due to full garbage collection duration being too long, then you should switch to using the concurrent garbage collector. Increasing the size of the old generation space generally does not result in a heroic reduction in full garbage collection time with the throughput garbage collector. The concurrent garbage collector has the capability to garbage collect the old generation space mostly concurrently while the application is running. The concurrent garbage collector is enabled with the HotSpot command line option:

```
-XX:+UseConcMarkSweepGC
```

Fine-tuning the concurrent garbage collector is described in the next subsection.

Fine-Tune Latency with the Concurrent Garbage Collector

With the concurrent garbage collector, also known as CMS, the old generation garbage collector executes mostly concurrently with application threads. This presents an opportunity to reduce both the garbage collection induced worst case latency frequency and the worst case latency duration to the lengthiest minor garbage collection. CMS does not perform compaction, so this is accomplished by avoiding a stop-the-world compacting garbage collection of the old generation space. An old generation overflow initiates a stop-the-world compacting garbage collection.

> **Tip**
>
> There is a subtle difference between a stop-the-world compacting garbage collection and a full garbage collection. In CMS, when there is not enough available space in old generation space to handle object promotions from the young generation space, a stop-the-world compacting garbage collection occurs only in the old generation space. When a full garbage collection occurs, both the young generation and old generation space are garbage collected except when `-XX:-ScavengeBeforeFullGC` is in use.

The goal with tuning the concurrent garbage collector is to avoid a stop-the-world compacting garbage collection. However, that is much easier said than done. In some application deployments they are unavoidable, especially when memory footprint constraints exist.

The CMS garbage collector requires more fine-tuning compared to other HotSpot VM garbage collectors—in particular, further fine-tuning young generation space size and potentially tuning when to initiate the old generation's concurrent garbage collection cycle.

When migrating to the concurrent garbage collector from the parallel garbage collector, you can expect slightly longer minor garbage collection durations in situations where objects are promoted from the young generation space to the old generation space due to slower object promotion into old generation. CMS allocates memory in old generation space from free lists. In contrast, the throughput garbage collector must only bump a pointer in a thread-local allocation promotion buffer. In addition, since the old generation garbage collector thread executes mostly concurrently with application threads, you can expect lower application throughput. However, the worst case latency frequency should be much less, since unreachable objects in the old generation space can be garbage collected while the application is running and thus prevent the old generation space from filling.

With CMS, if the space available in the old generation space is exhausted, a single-threaded stop-the-world compacting garbage collection occurs. This type of garbage collection in CMS usually has a longer duration than a full garbage collection with the throughput garbage collector. As a result, the absolute worse case latency duration with CMS may be greater than the worst case latency with the throughput garbage collector. Running out of old generation space and experiencing a stop-the-world compacting garbage collection will catch the attention of your application stakeholders due to the lengthy disruption in application responsiveness. Therefore, it is important to avoid running out of old generation space. A general guideline to follow when migrating to the concurrent garbage collector from the throughput garbage collector is to increase the size of the old generation space by an additional 20% to 30% to allow the concurrent garbage collector to execute efficiently.

Several forces at work make tuning the concurrent garbage collector challenging. One is the rate at which objects get promoted from the young generation space to the old generation space. Another is the rate at which the concurrent old generation garbage collector thread reclaims space. The third is the fragmenting of the old generation space as a result of the concurrent garbage collector reclaiming objects that reside between reachable objects. This creates holes between reachable objects in the old generation space and thus fragments the available space.

Fragmentation can be addressed by several different means. One is through compaction of the old generation space. Compacting the old generation space is accomplished with a stop-the-world compacting garbage collection. As mentioned earlier, a stop-the-world compacting garbage collection can take a long time and is an event to avoid since it is likely the largest and most significant contributor to an application's worst case latency duration. A second means to address fragmentation is to increase the size of the old generation space. This may not completely address the fragmentation issue, but it helps delay the amount of time it takes for the old generation space to become fragmented to a point where a compaction is required. Generally, the more memory made available to the old generation space, the longer until a compaction is necessary due to fragmentation. A goal to strive for is making the old generation space large enough to avoid a heap fragmentation induced stop-the-world compacting garbage collection during the application's life cycle. In other words, apply the GC

Maximize Memory Principle. An additional way to help deal with fragmentation is to reduce the rate at which objects get promoted into the old generation space from the young generation, that is, apply the Minor GC Reclamation Principle.

The tenuring threshold controls when objects are promoted from the young generation into the old generation. The tenuring threshold, further described later, is computed internally by the HotSpot VM based on the occupancy of the young generation space, more specifically the occupancy of the survivor space. The role of survivor spaces is described next followed by a discussion of the tenuring threshold.

Survivor Spaces Explained

Survivor spaces are part of the young generation space (see Figure 7-6). Additional details on the eden and survivor spaces can be found in "The Young Generation" section of Chapter 3.

The young generation space in all HotSpot garbage collectors is subdivided into an eden space and two survivor spaces.

> **Tip**
>
> In contrast to the concurrent garbage collector, the throughput garbage collector by default enables a feature called adaptive sizing, which automatically sizes eden and survivor spaces. But the general operation of how objects are allocated in eden and copied to and between survivor spaces is the same.

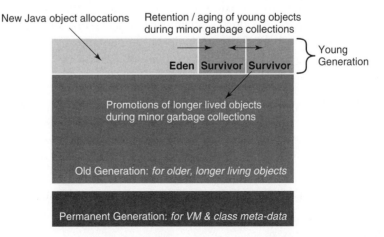

Figure 7-6 Eden and survivor spaces

One of the survivor spaces is labeled the "from" survivor space, and the other survivor space is labeled the "to" survivor space. The role of the survivor spaces and their labeling will make more sense shortly.

Eden space is where new Java objects are allocated. For instance, in a Java program, a statement such as

```
Map<String, Long> map = new HashMap<String, Long>();
```

allocates a new `HashMap` object and any objects the `HashMap` constructor allocates in the eden space. When the eden space becomes full, a minor garbage collection occurs. Any live objects are copied from the eden space into the "to" survivor space along with any surviving objects in the "from" survivor space. Upon completion of the minor garbage collection, the eden space is empty, the "from" survivor space is empty, and the "to" survivor space contains the live objects. Then the survivor spaces swap their labels in preparation for the next minor garbage collection. The now empty "from" survivor space takes on the "to" label, and the "to" survivor space takes on the "from" label. Therefore, at the end of a minor garbage collection both the eden space and one of the survivor spaces are empty. The other survivor space holds the live objects that survived the minor garbage collection.

If during a minor garbage collection, the "to" survivor space is not large enough to hold all of the live objects being copied from the eden space and the "from" survivor space, the overflow will be promoted to the old generation space. Overflowing into the old generation space may cause the old generation space to grow more quickly than desired and result in an eventual stop-the-world compacting full garbage collection. Again, a stop-the-world compacting full garbage collection is something to avoid as much as possible when tuning a Java application with low latency requirements. In other words, try to adhere to the Minor GC Reclamation Principle.

Avoiding survivor space overflow is accomplished by sizing the survivor spaces so they are large enough to hold surviving objects long enough to age for some period of time. Effective aging results in only long-lived objects being promoted to the old generation space.

Tip

Aging is the means by which objects are retained in the young generation until they are no longer reachable, so as to preserve old generation space for longer-lived objects.

The survivor spaces are sized using the HotSpot command line option:

```
-XX:SurvivorRatio=<ratio>
```

The <ratio> must be a value greater than 0. -XX:SurvivorRatio=<ratio> expresses the ratio of space between each survivor space and the eden space. The following equation can be used to determine the survivor space size:

```
survivor space size = -Xmn<value>/(-XX:SurvivorRatio=<ratio> + 2)
```

The reason for the + 2 in the equation is there are two survivor spaces. The larger the value specified as the ratio, the smaller the survivor space size.

To illustrate, suppose the young generation size is specified as -Xmn512m and -XX:SurvivorRatio=6. With these two settings, the young generation space will have two survivor spaces sized at 64 megabytes each and 384 megabytes of eden space. 512/(6 + 2) = 64 megabytes for each of the two survivor spaces leaves 384 megabytes for the eden space.

Using the same young generation size, -Xmn512m, but changing to -XX:SurvivorRatio=2 results in survivor space sizes of 128 megabytes each and an eden space of 256 megabytes. 512/(2 + 2) = 128 megabytes for each survivor space leaving 256 megabytes for eden space.

For a given young generation size, decreasing the survivor ratio increases the size of survivor spaces and decreases the size of the eden space. Likewise, increasing the survivor ratio decreases the size of the survivor spaces and increases the size of the eden space. It is important to recognize that decreasing the size of the eden space results in more frequent minor garbage collections. In contrast, increasing the size of the eden space results in less frequent minor garbage collections. It is also important to recognize that the more frequently garbage collections occur, the more quickly objects age.

To fine-tune the survivor space sizes and refine the young generation heap size, monitor the tenuring threshold. The tenuring threshold determines how long objects are retained in the young generation's survivor spaces. The tenuring threshold, how to monitor to it, and how to tune survivor spaces are described next.

Tenuring Threshold Explained

The term "tenuring" is synonymous with promoting. In other words, tenuring means object promotion into the old generation space. The HotSpot VM calculates a tenuring threshold at each minor garbage collection to determine when an object will be promoted. The tenuring threshold is an object age. An object's age is the number of minor garbage collections it has survived. When an object is first allocated, its age is 0. After the next minor garbage collection, if an object survives in the young generation, its age is 1. If it survives a second minor garbage collection, its age is 2, and so on. Objects in the young generation space whose age exceeds the HotSpot

VM calculated tenuring threshold are promoted to the old generation space. In other words, the tenuring threshold determines how long objects are retained, or aged, in the young generation space.

> **Tip**
>
> Effective object aging in the young generation to prevent them from being prematurely promoted to the old generation space reduces the rate that the old generation occupancy increases. This reduces the frequency at which the CMS garbage collection cycle must execute and also reduces the likelihood of fragmentation.

The tenuring threshold calculation is based on the amount of space required to hold reachable objects in the young generation space and the target survivor space occupancy after a minor garbage collection. The young generation garbage collector used with CMS, called "ParNew" GC,[2] calculates the tenuring threshold. There is also a HotSpot VM command line option, -XX:MaxTenuringThreshold=<n>, that can be used to ask the HotSpot VM to promote objects to the old generation space only after an object's age exceeds the value of <n>. The internally calculated tenuring threshold never exceeds the value of the max tenuring threshold. The max tenuring threshold can be set to a value ranging from 0–15 for Java 5 Update 6 and later, 0–31 for Java 5 Update 5 and earlier.

> **Tip**
>
> It is not recommended to set the max tenuring threshold value to 0. This causes objects to be immediately promoted from young generation to old generation on the next minor garbage collection after an object has been allocated. This will grow the old generation space very rapidly and result in frequent full garbage collections.
>
> It is also not recommended to set the max tenuring threshold to a value larger than the possible maximum. That will result in objects being retained in survivor spaces until survivor spaces overflow. If they overflow, objects are promoted to the old generation nondiscriminantly, that is, they are not promoted based on their age. As a result, short-lived objects may be promoted before longer-lived objects, which prevents effective object aging.

The HotSpot VM uses the max tenuring threshold as its calculated tenuring threshold when the target survivor space occupancy is at or below what the HotSpot VM attempts to maintain. See the "Tuning Target Survivor Space Occupancy" sidebar for more information. If the HotSpot VM believes it cannot maintain the target

---

2. "ParNew GC" is explicitly enabled using -XX:+UseParNewGC. It is automatically enabled when using CMS, -XX:+UseConcMarkSweepGC.

survivor space occupancy, it uses a tenuring threshold lower than the maximum to preserve the target survivor space occupancy. Any objects older than the tenuring threshold are promoted to the old generation space. In other words, when the amount of space consumed by surviving objects exceeds the target survivor space occupancy, an overflow situation occurs. An overflow may cause objects to be promoted to the old generation too soon and result in the old generation space filling more quickly than desired, which in turn results in the concurrent garbage collector running more frequently, reducing application throughput, and increasing the probability of fragmentation. All of which may lead to more frequent stop-the-world compacting garbage collections. Remember, a stop-the-world compacting garbage collection of the old generation space is a high latency garbage collection induced event.

Which objects are promoted in an overflow situation are determined by evaluating their ages against the tenuring threshold. Objects older than the tenuring threshold are promoted to the old generation space. Therefore, it is important to monitor the tenuring threshold to avoid survivor space overflow. This is the topic of the next subsection.

Monitoring the Tenuring Threshold

As mentioned earlier, the max tenuring threshold, not to be confused with the internally calculated tenuring threshold, can be set using the HotSpot VM command line option `-XX:MaxTenuringThreshold=<n>`. Determining the optimal value requires monitoring the tenuring distribution, or object age distribution, using the HotSpot VM command line option:

```
-XX:+PrintTenuringDistribution
```

The output from `-XX:+PrintTenuringDistribution` shows how effectively objects age in the survivor spaces. The pattern to watch for in the output produced by `-XX:+PrintTenuringDistribution` is that the number of bytes surviving at each object age decreases as the object age increases and whether the tenuring threshold calculated by the HotSpot VM is equal to or stays close to the value set for the max tenuring threshold.

`-XX:+PrintTenuringDistribution` produces tenuring distribution information at each minor garbage collection. It can also be used in combination with other garbage collection command line options such as `-XX:+PrintGCDateStamps`, `-XX:+PrintGCTimeStamps`, and `-XX:+PrintGCDetails`. When fine-tuning survivor space sizes for effective object aging, you should include `-XX:+PrintTenuring Distribution` statistics in your garbage collection data. It is also useful to capture tenuring distribution data in production environments to obtain a log to help identify application events should a stop-the-world compacting garbage collection occur.

Here is an example of the output produced from `-XX:+PrintTenuring`
`Distribution`:

```
Desired survivor size 8388608 bytes, new threshold 1 (max 15)
 - age   1:   16690480 bytes,   16690480 total
```

In this example the max tenuring threshold is set to 15, indicated by `(max 15)`.
The internally calculated tenuring threshold is 1, indicated by `new threshold 1`.
`Desired survivor size 8388608 bytes` is the size of one of the survivor spaces
times the target survivor ratio. The target survivor ratio is a value the HotSpot VM
uses as the target occupancy percentage of the survivor space. You can read more
on how to use the desired survivor size information later in the chapter. Below the
header information is a listing of object ages. There is a row printed for each object
age with the number of bytes at that age, `16690480 bytes` for age 1 in this example.
There is also a total number of bytes reported in each row. When there is more than
one age row, the value for the total is the cumulative number of bytes for that age row
and the preceding rows. Example output showing more than one age row is shown
a little later.

In the preceding example output, since the desired survivor size (8388608) is
less than the number of total surviving bytes (16690480), a survivor space overflow
occurred, that is, some objects were promoted to old generation as a result of this
minor garbage collection. A survivor space overflow suggests survivor spaces may be
too small. In addition, since the max tenuring threshold is 15 and the HotSpot VM
internally calculated a tenuring threshold of 1, it further suggests survivor spaces
are too small.

Tip

In general, observing a new tenuring threshold value that is consistently less than the max
tenuring threshold or observing a desired survivor size that is smaller than the number of
total surviving bytes (the value for the last row of object ages and the far right column) are
indications that the survivor spaces are too small.

If you observe that survivor spaces are too small, increase their size. A procedure
to determine how to size survivor spaces is described next.

Sizing Survivor Spaces

There is an important concept to keep in mind when changing the size of survivor spaces.
If the size of the young generation space is not changed when changing the survivor space

size, an increase in survivor space size decreases the size of the eden space. Decreasing the size of the eden space increases the frequency of minor garbage collections. Therefore, if the current young generation size is pushing up against the application's minor garbage collection frequency requirements, the size of the eden space should be kept the same when increasing the size of survivor space. In other words, the young generation size should be increased whenever the size of the survivor spaces is increased.

If there is room for increased minor garbage collection frequency, then there is a choice to be made between using some of the eden space to increase the survivor space, or making the young generation space larger. It is generally a better choice, if there is memory available, to increase the size of young generation rather than reduce the size of the eden space. By keeping the eden size constant, the minor garbage collection frequency is subject to less change as a result of increasing the size of the survivor spaces.

Using the output from `-XX:+PrintTenuringDistribution`, the total number of bytes for all object ages along with the target survivor space occupancy can be used to calculate a survivor space size to use with your application. Repeating the previous example:

```
Desired survivor size 8388608 bytes, new threshold 1 (max 15)
- age   1:   16690480 bytes,   16690480 total
```

The total number of surviving bytes is 16690480. The concurrent garbage collector by default uses a target survivor space occupancy of 50%. Using this information, the survivor spaces should be sized to a value of at least 33,380,960 bytes, that is, 16690480/50% = 33,380,960. 33,380,960 is about 32 megabytes. This calculation provides the estimated survivor space size needed to age objects more effectively and prevent overflow. To obtain a better estimate of the survivor space size to use, you should monitor the tenuring distribution over a period of time while the application is running in steady state and use the additional total surviving bytes data as a better estimate of the survivor space size to use.

To age objects effectively for the application in this example, the survivor space size should be increased to at least 32 megabytes. If the following set of HotSpot command line options produced the example print tenuring threshold output data given previously,

```
-Xmx1536m -Xms1536m -Xmn512m -XX:SurvivorRatio=30
```

and there is a desire to maintain the minor garbage collection frequency close to what had been observed, then increasing the survivor space sizes to 32 megabytes requires an updated set of HotSpot command line options such as

```
-Xmx1568m -Xms1568m -Xmn544m -XX:SurvivorRatio=15
```

where the size of the young generation space is increased, the size of the eden space is kept about the same, and the survivor space size is increased. Notice that both the size of the Java heap, -Xmx and -Xms, and young generation space, -Xmn, are increased by 32 megabytes. In addition, -XX:SurvivorRatio=15 sizes both survivor spaces at 32 megabytes each ($544/(15 + 2) = 32$). That leaves the eden space the same size as the previous configuration at 480 megabytes ($512 - 16 - 16 = 480$ for the first configuration and $544 - 32 - 32 = 480$ for the second configuration).

If there are constraints that do not allow for an increase in the young generation size, then an increase in survivor space size comes at the expense of reducing the eden size. Here is an example that keeps the young generation size the same but increases the size of survivor spaces from 16 megabytes to 32 megabytes each and decreases the size of the eden space from 480 megabytes to 448 megabytes ($512/(14 + 2) = 32$ and $512 - 32 - 32 = 448$).

```
-Xmx1536m -Xms1536m -Xmn512m -XX:SurvivorRatio=14
```

Again, remember that reducing the eden space size results in more frequent minor garbage collections. But objects will be retained in the young generation for a longer period of time relative to the original heap sizing due to the increase in survivor space size.

Suppose running the same application again with the revised heap size where the eden size is kept constant, that is, using the following set of HotSpot command line options,

```
-Xmx1568m -Xms1568m -Xmn544m -XX:SurvivorRatio=15
```

produced the following tenuring distribution:

```
Desired survivor size 16777216 bytes, new threshold 15 (max 15)
- age   1:    6115072 bytes,    6115072 total
- age   2:     286672 bytes,    6401744 total
- age   3:     115704 bytes,    6517448 total
- age   4:      95932 bytes,    6613380 total
- age   5:      89465 bytes,    6702845 total
- age   6:      88322 bytes,    6791167 total
- age   7:      88201 bytes,    6879368 total
- age   8:      88176 bytes,    6967544 total
- age   9:      88176 bytes,    7055720 total
- age  10:      88176 bytes,    7143896 total
- age  11:      88176 bytes,    7232072 total
- age  12:      88176 bytes,    7320248 total
```

In this tenuring distribution output, the survivor space is not overflowing since the total surviving bytes, 7320248, the last column, last row, is less than the desired survivor size of 16777216 and the tenuring threshold is equal to the max tenuring threshold. This suggests that objects are aging effectively and there is no survivor space overflow.

In this example, since there are few objects reclaimed beyond age 3, you might consider testing a configuration where the max tenuring threshold is set to 3, that is, -XX:MaxTenuringThreshold=3. Such a set of command line options looks like

```
-Xmx1568m -Xms1568m -Xmn544m -XX:SurvivorRatio=15
-XX:MaxTenuringThreshold=3
```

The trade-off between this configuration and the previous one is that the latter may avoid some unnecessary copying of objects between the "from" and "to" survivor spaces at each minor garbage collection. Looking at the tenuring distribution across many minor garbage collections during steady state suggests whether objects eventually get promoted to the old generation, or whether they eventually are garbage collected. If you observe tenuring distributions in your garbage collections with a similar pattern to the one shown previously, which rarely show object ages as high as 15 with no survivor space overflow, you should leave the max tenuring threshold at its default maximum value of 15. In this situation, the objects at ages where it appears little is being reclaimed are not long-lived objects since they are eventually garbage collected because they never reach the max tenuring threshold of age 15. They are garbage collected in a minor garbage collection since they remain in the young generation space rather than being promoted to the old generation space. With the concurrent collector, any objects promoted to the old generation space that are eventually garbage collected increase the probability of fragmentation and/or the probability of a stop-the-world compacting garbage collection. Neither of these is desirable. It is generally better to err on the side of copying objects too many times between the survivor spaces than it is to promote objects to the old generation too quickly.

You may have to repeat the steps of monitoring tenuring distribution, updating survivor spaces, or in general reconfiguring young generation space size several times until you are satisfied with the application's latency due to minor garbage collections. If you find minor garbage collection durations are too long, you should start decreasing the size of the young generation space until you are able to meet the application's minor garbage collection duration latency requirements. Although reducing the size of the young generation space may promote objects to the old generation space more quickly and contribute to a higher probability of fragmentation, if the concurrent garbage collector can keep up with the rate at which objects are promoted, this situation may be better than the consequences of not meeting the application's latency requirements. If you are not able to meet the application's minor garbage collection duration latency or frequency requirements, you must either revisit the application's requirements, make some application changes, or possibly change JVM deployment models to lessen the load on the JVM instance.

If you are able to meet application latency requirements for minor garbage collection duration and frequency, you can continue with the next step of tuning the initiation of the CMS garbage collection cycle. Tuning the initiation of the CMS garbage collection cycle is presented in the subsection "Initiating the CMS Collection Cycle" later in the chapter.

Tuning Target Survivor Space Occupancy

The target survivor space occupancy is the survivor space occupancy the HotSpot VM attempts to enforce after a minor garbage collection. It can be tuned with the HotSpot VM command line option -XX:TargetSurvivorRatio=<percent>. The value to specify with this command line option is actually a percentage of survivor space occupancy, rather than a ratio. Its default value is 50.

Through extensive testing of a wide variety of different types of application workloads by the HotSpot VM engineering team, a 50% target survivor space occupancy tends to work best for most applications since it helps absorb spikes in surviving objects seen at minor garbage collections.

Tuning the target survivor occupancy is rarely required. However, if your application has a relatively consistent object allocation rate, you may consider raising the target survivor space occupancy to something as high as 80 or 90. This can help reduce the amount of survivor space needed to age objects. The challenge with setting -XX:TargetSurvivorRatio=<percent> higher than the default is that the HotSpot VM may not be able to better adapt object aging in the presence of spikes in object allocation rates, which can lead to promoting objects earlier than desired. Using CMS, promoting objects too soon can contribute to increasing old generation occupancy, which may lead to a higher probability of fragmentation since some promoted objects may not be long-lived objects and must be garbage collected in a future concurrent garbage collection cycle. Remember, fragmentation is a situation to avoid since it contributes to the eventual likelihood of a stop-the-world compacting garbage collection.

Initiating the CMS Collection Cycle

Once the young generation space size, including eden and survivor spaces, has been refined to meet application minor garbage collection induced latency requirements, attention can shift to tuning the CMS garbage collector in an attempt to avoid worst case latency duration and minimize worst case latency frequency. The goal is to maintain available old generation space and consequently avoid stop-the-world compacting garbage collections.

Stop-the-world compacting garbage collections are the worst case garbage collection induced latency. In some applications it may not be possible to entirely avoid them, but the tuning advice offered in this section at least reduces their frequency.

Successful tuning of the CMS garbage collector requires being able to garbage collect objects in the old generation space at a rate that is at least as fast as the rate that objects get promoted from the young generation space. Not being able to meet this criteria is what is termed "losing the race." The consequence of losing the race is experiencing a stop-the-world compacting garbage collection. The key to not losing the race is a combination of having a large enough old generation space and initiating the start of the CMS garbage collection cycle soon enough to allow it to reclaim space at a rate faster than the promotion rate.

The initiation of a CMS cycle is based on the occupancy of old generation space. If the CMS cycle starts too late, it will lose the race. It does not reclaim objects rapidly enough to avoid running out of old generation space. If the CMS cycle starts too early, it introduces unnecessary overhead and impacts application throughput. It is generally better to initiate the CMS cycle too early rather than too late since the consequences of starting it too late are worse than starting it too early.

The HotSpot VM tries to adaptively figure out at what occupancy it should initiate the start of a CMS garbage collection cycle. There are some cases where it does not do a good enough job to avoid stop-the-world compacting garbage collections. If you observe stop-the-world compacting garbage collections, you can tune when the CMS cycle should start. Stop-the-world compacting garbage collections in CMS are identified in garbage collection output by concurrent mode failure. The following is an example:

```
174.445: [GC 174.446: [ParNew: 66408K->66408K(66416K), 0.0000618
secs]174.446: [CMS (concurrent mode failure): 161928K->162118K(175104K),
4.0975124 secs] 228336K->162118K(241520K)
```

The meaning of all the output fields is not as important as the concurrent mode failure. If you are observing concurrent mode failures in your garbage collection output, you can instruct the HotSpot VM to initiate the start of the CMS cycle earlier using the command line option:

```
-XX:CMSInitiatingOccupancyFraction=<percent>
```

The value specified is the percentage of old generation occupancy at which the CMS garbage collection cycle should start. For instance, if you would like the CMS cycle to start at an old generation space occupancy of 65%, you set -XX:CMSInitiating OccupancyFraction=65. A second HotSpot command line option should be used in conjunction with -XX:CMSInitiatingOccupancyFraction=<percent> called

```
-XX:+UseCMSInitiatingOccupancyOnly
```

`-XX:+UseCMSInitiatingOccupancyOnly` instructs the HotSpot VM to always use the `-XX:CMSInitiatingOccupancyFraction` as the occupancy of the old generation space to initiate a CMS cycle. If `-XX:+UseCMSInitiatingOccupancyOnly` is not used, the HotSpot VM uses the `-XX:CMSInitiatingOccupancyFraction` as the occupancy percentage to start only the first CMS cycle. It then attempts to adaptively adjust when to start the CMS cycle for subsequent CMS cycles, that is, it no longer uses the specified `-XX:CMSInitiatingOccupancyFraction` after the first CMS cycle.

> **Tip**
>
> When specifying when to initiate the CMS cycle, it is important to use both `-XX:CMSInitiating OccupancyFraction=<percent>` and `-XX:+UseCMSInitiatingOccupancyOnly` together.

The occupancy specified with `-XX:CMSInitiatingOccupancyFraction` should be larger than the occupancy percentage of the old generation corresponding to the live data size. Remember from the "Determine Memory Footprint" section earlier in the chapter that the live data size for an application is the heap occupancy after a full garbage collection. If `-XX:CMSInitiatingOccupancyFraction` is not larger than the occupancy percentage at the live data size, the CMS collector will run constantly. As a general guideline, `-XX:CMSInitiatingOccupancyFraction` should be a percentage of old generation occupancy corresponding to at least 1.5x the live data size. For instance, if the following Java heap configuration is in use

```
-Xmx1536m -Xms1536m -Xmn512m
```

then the old generation size is 1024 megabytes ($1536 - 512 = 1024$). If the live data size for the application is 350 megabytes, then the threshold of old generation space occupancy that the CMS cycle should be started should be around 525 megabytes, or about 51% occupancy ($525/1024 = 51\%$). This is a starting point, and it will be further refined through monitoring garbage collection statistics. The updated command line options for initiating the CMS cycle at 51% old generation occupancy are

```
-Xmx1536m -Xms1536m -Xmn512m
-XX:CMSInitiatingOccupancyFraction=51
-XX:+UseCMSInitiatingOccupancyOnly
```

How early or late the CMS cycle should start depends on the rate that objects are promoted from the young generation space to the old generation space, that is, the growth rate of the old generation space. If the old generation space fills up slowly, you can start the CMS cycle later. If the old generation space fills up quickly, you should start the CMS cycle earlier, but not lower than the occupancy percentage of the live data size. Rather than starting the CMS cycle lower than the live data size, you should increase the size of the old generation space.

Knowing whether the CMS cycle starts too early or too late can be identified by evaluating the garbage collection data. Here is an example where the CMS cycle starts too late. For ease of reading, the output has been trimmed to show garbage collection type, heap occupancy, and duration.

```
[ParNew 742993K->648506K(773376K), 0.1688876 secs]
[ParNew 753466K->659042K(773376K), 0.1695921 secs]
[CMS-initial-mark 661142K(773376K), 0.0861029 secs]
[Full GC 645986K->234335K(655360K), 8.9112629 secs]
[ParNew 339295K->247490K(773376K), 0.0230993 secs]
[ParNew 352450K->259959K(773376K), 0.1933945 secs]
```

Notice the Full GC shortly after the `CMS-initial-mark`. The `CMS-initial-mark` is one of several phases reported during a CMS cycle. All the phases of a CMS cycle are described in "The Mostly-Concurrent GC: Latency Matters" section of Chapter 3.

Here is an example where the CMS cycle is started too early. For ease of reading, the output has been trimmed to show garbage collection type, heap occupancy, and duration.

```
[ParNew 390868K->296358K(773376K), 0.1882258 secs]
[CMS-initial-mark 298458K(773376K), 0.0847541 secs]
[ParNew 401318K->306863K(773376K), 0.1933159 secs]
[CMS-concurrent-mark: 0.787/0.981 secs]
[CMS-concurrent-preclean: 0.149/0.152 secs]
[CMS-concurrent-abortable-preclean: 0.105/0.183 secs]
[CMS-remark 374049K(773376K), 0.0353394 secs]
[ParNew 407285K->312829K(773376K), 0.1969370 secs]
[ParNew 405554K->311100K(773376K), 0.1922082 secs]
[ParNew 404913K->310361K(773376K), 0.1909849 secs]
[ParNew 406005K->311878K(773376K), 0.2012884 secs]
[CMS-concurrent-sweep: 2.179/2.963 secs]
[CMS-concurrent-reset: 0.010/0.010 secs]
[ParNew 387767K->292925K(773376K), 0.1843175 secs]
[CMS-initial-mark 295026K(773376K), 0.0865858 secs]
[ParNew 397885K->303822K(773376K), 0.1995878 secs]
```

The beginning of a CMS cycle is indicated by a `CMS-initial-mark` and the end by `CMS-concurrent-sweep` and `CMS-concurrent-reset`. Notice that the heap occupancy reported in the first CMS-initial-mark is 298458K. Then notice that the ParNew minor garbage collections report little change in heap occupancy between CMS-initial-mark and CMS-concurrent-reset. The heap occupancy at the completion of a ParNew minor garbage collection is the value to the right of the ->. In this example, very little garbage is being collected during a CMS cycle as indicated by the small drop in heap occupancy between CMS-initial-mark and CMS-concurrent-reset. The corrective action here is to start the CMS cycle at a higher old generation occupancy percentage using -XX:CMSInitiating OccupancyFraction and -XX:+UseCMSInitiatingOccupancyOnly. Based on the initial occupancy at the CMS-initial-mark of 298458K, and a Java heap size of 773376K, it appears the CMS cycle is starting at about 35% to 40% occupancy, (298458K/773376K = 38.5%). Using a setting of -XX:CMSInitiatingOccupancy Fraction=50 and -XX:+UseCMSInitiatingOccupancyOnly would force the CMS cycle to start at a higher heap occupancy.

Here is an example where a CMS cycle is reclaiming a large amount of old generation space, yet not experiencing a stop-the-world compacting garbage collection, that is, no concurrent mode failures. Again, for ease of reading, the output has been trimmed to show garbage collection type, heap occupancy, and duration.

```
[ParNew 640710K->546360K(773376K), 0.1839508 secs]
[CMS-initial-mark 548460K(773376K), 0.0883685 secs]
[ParNew 651320K->556690K(773376K), 0.2052309 secs]
[CMS-concurrent-mark: 0.832/1.038 secs]
[CMS-concurrent-preclean: 0.146/0.151 secs]
[CMS-concurrent-abortable-preclean: 0.181/0.181 secs]
[CMS-remark 623877K(773376K), 0.0328863 secs]
[ParNew 655656K->561336K(773376K), 0.2088224 secs]
[ParNew 648882K->554390K(773376K), 0.2053158 secs]
[ParNew 489586K->395012K(773376K), 0.2050494 secs]
[ParNew 463096K->368901K(773376K), 0.2137257 secs]
[CMS-concurrent-sweep: 4.873/6.745 secs]
[CMS-concurrent-reset: 0.010/0.010 secs]
[ParNew 445124K->350518K(773376K), 0.1800791 secs]
[ParNew 455478K->361141K(773376K), 0.1849950 secs]
```

In this example, the occupancy at the beginning of the CMS cycle indicated by CMS-initial-mark is 548460K. Between the start and end of the CMS cycle, indicated by the CMS-concurrent-reset, there is a rather dramatic drop in the occupancy reported in the ParNew minor garbage collections. In particular, there is a drop from 561336K to 368910K just prior to the end of the CMS-concurrent-sweep. This suggests that about 190 megabytes were garbage collected during the CMS cycle (561336K − 368910K = 192426K = 187.91 megabytes). Also notice the occupancy reported at the first ParNew minor garbage collection after CMS-concurrent-sweep is 350518K. This suggests that more than 190 megabytes have been collected during the CMS cycle (561336K − 350518K = 210818K = 205.88 megabytes).

If you decide to fine-tune the start of the CMS cycle, be sure to try several different old generation occupancy percentages. Monitoring the garbage collection data and analyzing them leads you to what is the most appropriate for your application.

Explicit Garbage Collections

If you observe full garbage collections, which are initiated by an explicit call to `System.gc()`, there are two ways to deal with them when using the concurrent garbage collector:

1. You can request the HotSpot VM to execute them as a concurrent garbage collection cycle using the HotSpot VM command line option:

```
-XX:+ExplicitGCInvokesConcurrent
```

or

```
-XX:+ExplicitGCInvokesConcurrentAndUnloadsClasses
```

The first requires Java 6 or later. The second requires Java 6 Update 4 or later. It is generally better to use `-XX:+ExplicitGCInvokesConcurrentAnd UnloadsClasses` if the JDK version you are using supports it.

2. You can ask the HotSpot VM to ignore explicit calls to `System.gc()` by using the Hotspot command line option:

```
-XX:+DisableExplicitGC
```

This command line option also ignores explicit calls to `System.gc()` in the other HotSpot VM garbage collectors.

Be careful when disabling explicit garbage collection. Doing so may have a non-trivial performance impact on the Java application. There may also be situations where timely object reference processing is required and garbage collections are not happening frequently enough for that to occur. Applications using Java RMI may be subject to this. It is advisable when explicitly disabling explicit garbage collection to have a reason for doing so. Likewise, it is advisable to have a reason for using `System.gc()` in an application.

Explicit garbage collections can be identified in the garbage collection output rather easily. The garbage collection output contains text indicating that the full garbage collection is the result of an explicit call to `System.gc()`. The following is an example of such a full garbage collection:

```
2010-12-16T23:04:39.452-0600: [Full GC (System)
    [CMS: 418061K->428608K(16384K), 0.2539726 secs]
    418749K->4288608K(31168K),
    [CMS Perm : 32428K->32428K(65536K)],
    0.2540393 secs]
    [Times: user=0.12 sys=0.01, real=0.25 secs]
```

Notice the `(System)` label following the `Full GC` text. This indicates that `System.gc()` induced the full garbage collection. If you observe an explicit full garbage collection in the garbage collection logs, determine why it is happening and then decide whether it should be disabled, whether the call should be removed from the source code, or whether it makes sense to specify an invocation of a CMS concurrent garbage collection cycle.

Concurrent Permanent Generation Garbage Collection

Full garbage collections may also occur as a result of a full permanent generation space. Monitoring the garbage collection data looking for full garbage collections and then observing the occupancy of the permanent generation space identifies whether they occur as a result of permanent generation space filling up. Here is an example full garbage collection initiated by permanent generation space filling up:

```
2010-12-16T17:14:32.533-0600: [Full GC
    [CMS: 95401K->287072K(1048576K), 0.5317934 secs]
    482111K->287072K(5190464K),
    [CMS Perm : 65534K->58281K(65536K)], 0.5319635 secs]
    [Times: user=0.53 sys=0.00, real=0.53 secs]
```

Notice the occupancy of the permanent generation space, identified by the `CMS Perm` label. The permanent generation size is the value between the parentheses, `65536K`. The permanent generation occupancy before the full garbage collection is the value to the left of the `->`, `65533K`. The permanent generation occupancy after the full garbage collection is the value to the right of the `->`, `58281K`. Seeing that the permanent generation occupancy before the full garbage collection, `65534K`, is near the permanent generation size, `65536K`, suggests that this full garbage collection was triggered by the permanent generation running out of space. Also notice that the old generation space is not close to running out of space and that there is no evidence of a CMS cycle being active, which later would indicate that it has lost the race.

The HotSpot VM by default does not garbage collect the permanent generation space with CMS despite the CMS Perm label reported in the garbage collection output. To enable CMS permanent generation garbage collection, you must specify the following HotSpot VM command line option:

```
-XX:+CMSClassUnloadingEnabled
```

If you are using Java 6 Update 3 or earlier, you must also specify the following command line option in addition to -XX:+CMSClassUnloadingEnabled:

```
-XX:+CMSPermGenSweepingEnabled
```

You can control the occupancy percentage of the permanent generation space to initiate CMS permanent generation garbage collection using

```
-XX:CMSInitiatingPermOccupancyFraction=<percent>
```

This option takes a percentage as an argument in the same fashion as -XX:CMS InitiatingOccupancyFraction. It is the percentage of permanent generation occupancy at which the CMS cycle should start. It also requires the use of -XX:+CMSClassUnloadingEnabled. If you want -XX:CMSInitiatingPerm OccupancyFraction to always be used as the percentage of permanent generation occupancy to initiate a CMS cycle, you must also specify:

```
-XX:+UseCMSInitiatingOccupancyOnly
```

CMS Pause Time Tuning

Two phases of a CMS cycle are stop-the-world phases where application threads are blocked. These two phases are the initial mark phase and the remark phase. Although the initial mark phase is single threaded, it rarely takes long to execute, usually much less than any other garbage collection pause. The remark phase is multithreaded. The number of threads used in the remark phase can be controlled by the following HotSpot VM command line option:

```
-XX:ParallelGCThreads=<n>
```

As of Java 6 Update 23, it defaults to the number returned by the Java API Runtime.availableProcessors() if the number returned is less than or equal to 8; otherwise, it defaults to 5/8 the number returned by `Runtime.available` `Processors()`. In cases where multiple applications are running on the same system, it is advisable to set the number of parallel garbage collection threads to a number lower than the default. Otherwise, garbage collections may intrude on the performance of other applications as a result of a large number of garbage collection threads executing at the same time.

The duration of the remark phase can in some cases be reduced by specifying

```
-XX:+CMSScavengeBeforeRemark
```

This command line option forces the HotSpot VM to perform a minor garbage collection prior to a CMS remark. Doing a minor garbage collection just prior to a remark can minimize the amount of work for the remark phase by reducing the number of objects in the young generation space that may be reachable from the old generation space.

If the application has a large number of Reference or finalizable objects to be processed, specifying the following HotSpot VM command line option can help reduce garbage collection duration:

```
-XX:+ParallelRefProcEnabled
```

This option can be used in combination with other HotSpot VM garbage collectors. It uses multiple rather than a single reference processing thread. This option does not enable many threads to run method finalizers. It uses many threads to discover finalizable objects that need to be enqueued for notification.

Next Steps

On completion of this step of the tuning process you have either determined that you are not able to meet application latency requirements or have been able to meet application latency requirements using the throughput or concurrent garbage collector. If you are not able to meet application latency requirements, you can consider using some of the additional performance command line options described in the "Additional Performance Command Line Options" section later in this chapter. Otherwise, you must either revisit application latency requirements, make changes to the application, possibly doing some profiling to identify problematic areas, or consider alternative JVM deployment models to spread the load across more JVM instances. If you are able to meet application latency requirements, you can continue to the next step in the tuning process, presented in the next section, "Tune Application Throughput."

Tune Application Throughput

If you have made it this far through the tuning process, it is good to know that this is the final step. In this step you measure application throughput and fine-tune the JVM for high throughput.

The main input into this step is the application's throughput performance requirements. An application's throughput is something measured at the application level, not at the JVM level. Thus, the application must report some kind of throughput metric, or some kind of throughput metric must be derived from the operations it is performing. The observed application throughput can then be compared to the application's throughput requirements. When the observed application throughput meets or exceeds the throughput requirements, you are finished with the tuning process. If you need additional application throughput to meet the throughput requirements, then you have some additional JVM tuning work to do.

Another important input into this step is the amount of memory that can be made available to the deployed Java application. As the GC Maximize Memory Principle says, the more memory that can be made available for the Java heap, the better the performance. This is true not only for throughput performance, but also for latency performance.

It is possible that the application's throughput requirements cannot be met. In that case, the application's throughput requirements must be revisited, application changes must be made, or a change in the JVM deployment model is required. Once one or more of those alternatives have been explored, you can iterate through the tuning process again.

In arriving at this step, you either settled on using the throughput garbage collector enabled via `-XX+UseParallelOldGC` or `-XX:+UseParallelGC`, or you switched to the concurrent garbage collector, CMS, as part of the previous step, Determine and Tune Application Latency, described in the "Tune Latency/Responsiveness" section earlier in the chapter. If you switched to using CMS, the options for increasing application throughput are presented next. If you are using the throughput garbage collector, the means to achieve additional throughput are described after those for using CMS.

CMS Throughput Tuning

The options for obtaining additional application throughput when using CMS are pretty much limited to the following alternatives or combination of alternatives:

- Explore using some of the additional command line options presented in the "Additional Performance Command Line Options" section.

- Increase the size of the young generation space. Increasing the size of the young generation space reduces the minor garbage collection frequency, which reduces the total number of minor garbage collections required over the same period of time.

- Increase the size of the old generation space. Increasing the size of the old generation space decreases the CMS cycle frequency and reduces the probability of fragmentation, which reduces the likelihood and frequency of concurrent mode failures along with stop-the-world compacting garbage collections.

- Further refine the young generation heap sizes as described in the previous section "Tune Latency/Responsiveness." Refining the young generation's eden and survivor spaces for optimal object aging to reduce the amount of objects being promoted from young generation to old generation reduces the total number of CMS cycles. But there are trade-offs to consider when refining eden and survivor space sizes as described in the "Tune Latency/Responsiveness" section.

- Further refine the initiating of the CMS cycle by starting it later as described in the previous section, "Tune Latency/Responsiveness." Starting the CMS cycle later may result in less frequent CMS cycles. But a consequence of starting the CMS cycle later is it introduces a higher probability of experiencing a concurrent mode failure and stop-the-world compacting garbage collection.

Any of these choices, or any combination of choices, causes the garbage collector to use fewer CPU cycles, leaving more CPU cycles to execute the application. The first two alternatives offer the likelihood of realizing more throughput improvement with lower risk of a high latency induced stop-the-world compacting garbage collection.

As a guideline, overhead with CMS, including minor garbage collection times should be less than 10%. You may be able to drive the overhead down to as little as 1% to 3%. Generally, if you are currently observing garbage collection overhead with CMS at 3% or less, there probably is little additional throughput performance improvement to be realized without a lot of effort.

Throughput Garbage Collector Tuning

The goal to accomplish in fine-tuning the throughput garbage collector for performance throughput is to avoid full garbage collections as much as possible or ideally avoid them indefinitely during steady state. This requires optimal object aging, which is accomplished through explicit fine-tuning of survivor spaces. You can make the eden space larger, which reduces minor garbage collection frequency and ensures there is sufficient old generation space to hold the application's live data size. Add a little additional old generation space to deal with situations where objects may not be optimally aged and some non-long-lived objects get promoted into the old generation space. Since object aging is done by counting the number of minor garbage collections an object has survived and object aging is limited to a count of 15 for Java 5 Update 16 and later 31 for previous JDKs, making the eden space larger decreases the frequency of minor garbage collections, which increases the length of time an object can age, assuming survivor spaces are not overflowing.

The HotSpot VM's throughput garbage collector, enabled via `-XX:+UseParallelOldGC` and `-XX:+UseParallelGC`, offers the best throughput of all the HotSpot VM garbage collectors. The throughput garbage collector by default utilizes a feature called adaptive sizing. Adaptive sizing automatically attempts to size the young generation's eden and survivor spaces for optimal object aging based on object allocation and survival rates. See Figure 7-6 for a depiction of eden and survivor spaces. The intention of adaptive sizing is to provide ease of use, that is, easy JVM tuning, yet offer reasonable throughput performance. Adaptive sizing works well for most applications. However, disabling adaptive sizing and fine-tuning eden space, survivor spaces, and old generation space sizes is an option for applications in search of that last bit of throughput. Disabling adaptive sizing does cost some flexibility with changing application behavior, either within a run of the application, or as its data changes over time.

To disable adaptive sizing, use

```
-XX:-UseAdaptiveSizePolicy
```

Note the - symbol after the `-XX:`. This indicates that the feature described by `UseAdaptiveSizePolicy` is to be disabled. Only the throughput garbage collector supports adaptive sizing. Attempting to enable or disable adaptive sizing on garbage collectors other than the throughput garbage collector (`-XX:+UseParallelOldGC` or `-XX:UseParallelGC`) results in no effect, that is, it is a "no-op."

An additional HotSpot VM command line option to produce more details on survivor space occupancy, whether survivor spaces overflowed and object promotions from the young to old generation in the garbage collection logs, is `-XX:+PrintAdaptiveSizePolicy`. It is best used in conjunction with `-XX:+PrintGCDetails` and either `-XX:+PrintGCDateStamps` or `-XX:+PrintGCTimeStamps`. Here is an example of the garbage collection output produced with `-XX:+PrintGCDateStamps`, `-XX:PrintGCDetails`, `-XX:-UseAdaptiveSizePolicy` (disable adaptive sizing), and `-XX:+PrintAdaptiveSizePolicy`:

```
2010-12-16T21:44:11.444-0600:
    [GCAdaptiveSizePolicy::compute_survivor_space_size_and_thresh:
        survived: 224408984
        promoted: 10904856
        overflow: false
        [PSYoungGen: 6515579K->219149K(9437184K)]
    8946490K->2660709K(13631488K), 0.0725945 secs]
    [Times: user=0.56 sys=0.00, real=0.07 secs]
```

The additional information begins with the text, `GCAdaptiveSizePolicy`. The value to the right of the `survived` label is the amount of surviving bytes in the "to" survivor space. In other words, it is the occupancy of the "to" survivor space after the minor garbage collection. In this example, the survivor space occupancy is 224,408,984 bytes. The value to the right of the `promoted` label is the number of bytes promoted from the young generation space to the old generation space, 10,904,856 bytes. The text to the right of the `overflow` label indicates whether surviving objects overflowed into the old generation space; in other words, whether enough survivor space is available to hold the surviving objects from garbage collecting the eden space and "from" survivor space. For reaching optimal performance throughput, it is desirable for survivor spaces to not overflow while the application is running in steady state.

To begin fine-tuning, you should begin by disabling adaptive sizing and capture additional survivor space statistics in the garbage collection logs using both `-XX:-UseAdaptiveSizePolicy` and `-XX:+PrintAdaptiveSizePolicy`. This provides some initial data to drive the tuning decisions. Suppose, for example, the previous set of command line options used are

```
-Xmx13g -Xms13g -Xmn4g -XX:SurvivorRatio=6
-XX:+UseParallelOldGC -XX:PrintGCDateStamps -XX:+PrintGCDetails
```

The set of command line options should be updated to include disabling adaptive sizing and the capture of additional survivor space statistics:

```
-Xmx13g -Xms13g -Xmn4g -XX:SurvivorRatio=6
-XX:+UseParallelOldGC -XX:PrintGCDateStamps -XX:+PrintGCDetails
-XX:-UseAdaptiveSizePolicy -XX:+PrintAdaptiveSizePolicy
```

First look for full garbage collections during application steady state. Including date or time stamps can be helpful in identifying when the application transitions from an initialization phase to a steady state phase. For example, if you know the application takes 30 seconds to complete its initialization phase and begin its steady state phase, you can look for the garbage collections that occur after those 30 seconds have elapsed.

Observing full garbage collections in steady state may suggest that short-lived objects may be getting promoted to the old generation space. If there are full garbage collections occurring in steady state, first confirm that the old generation space is sized at about 1.5x the live data size, the occupancy of the old generation space after a full garbage collection. If need be, increase the size of the old generation space to preserve the 1.5x general guideline. This ensures you have a reasonable amount of head room to work with should the application experience unexpected spikes in object allocation rates that result in short-lived objects getting promoted to old generation or there is some other unexpected event that results in objects getting promoted too quickly. Having this additional head room will delay, or possibly prevent, a full garbage collection from occurring during steady state application execution.

After confirming sufficient old generation space is available, start looking at each minor garbage collection occurring in steady state. First look to see whether survivor spaces are overflowing. If survivor spaces are overflowing on a minor garbage collection, the output shows the overflow field as true; otherwise, the overflow field will be false. An example where a survivor space is overflowing is

```
2010-12-18T10:12:33.322-0600:
    [GCAdaptiveSizePolicy::compute_survivor_space_size_and_thresh:
        survived: 446113911
        promoted: 10904856
        overflow: true
        [PSYoungGen: 6493788K->233888K(9437184K)]
    7959281K->2662511K(13631488K), 0.0797732 secs]
    [Times: user=0.59 sys=0.00, real=0.08 secs]
```

If survivor spaces are overflowing in steady state, objects are promoted to the old generation space before they have an opportunity to fully age and die. In other words, it is likely objects are getting promoted into the old generation space too quickly. Frequent survivor space overflows tend to lead to frequent full garbage collections. Increasing survivor space size prevents overflow and therefore reduces the frequency of full garbage collections. How to tune survivor space size is the next topic.

Tuning Survivor Spaces

The objective of tuning survivor space size is to retain or age short-lived objects in the young generation as long as possible before they are promoted to the old generation space. Begin by looking at each minor garbage collection occurring in steady state, in particular the number of survived bytes. Consider ignoring data from several minor garbage collections as the application transitions from an initialization state to steady state since there may be some long-lived objects allocated in the initialization phase requiring some additional aging before being promoted to old generation. For most applications, ignoring 5 to 10 minor garbage collections as the application enters steady state usually covers this case.

The number of survived bytes at each minor garbage collection is identified in each minor garbage collection as part of the additional data printed with -XX:+PrintAdaptiveSizePolicy. In the following example output, the number of survived bytes is 224,408,984.

```
2010-12-16T21:44:11.444-0600:
   [GCAdaptiveSizePolicy::compute_survivor_space_size_and_thresh:
      survived: 224408984
      promoted: 10904856
      overflow: false
      [PSYoungGen: 6515579K->219149K(9437184K)]
   8946490K->2660709K(13631488K), 0.0725945 secs]
   [Times: user=0.56 sys=0.00, real=0.07 secs]
```

Using the maximum number of survived bytes along with knowing the target survivor space occupancy, you can determine the worst case survivor space size to age objects most effectively during steady state. If a target survivor space occupancy is not specified by -XX:TargetSurvivorRatio=<percent>, the target survivor space occupancy defaults to 50%.

Tune survivor spaces for the worst case scenario first. This is done by finding the maximum survived bytes in minor garbage collections between full garbage collections occurring in steady state, ignoring the first 5 to 10 minor garbage collections after entering application steady state. Finding the maximum survived bytes can be simplified by writing an awk or perl script to process the data or by pulling the data into a spreadsheet.

Sizing survivor spaces for effective object aging is unfortunately not as simple as merely setting the survivor space size to a value at or slightly higher than the maximum survived bytes obtained from the garbage collection logs. There are other things to keep in mind. Increasing survivor space size without increasing the size of the young generation space results in a smaller eden space. A decrease in the eden space size increases the frequency of minor garbage collections. An increase in minor garbage collection frequency decreases the length of time an object has to age in survivor spaces. As a result, objects are subject to promotion to old generation sooner, causing the old generation to fill up faster and eventually provoking a full garbage collection. Therefore, you should try to keep the size of the eden space constant when increasing the size of survivor spaces. You should increase the size of the young generation by the amount of the survivor space increase yet maintain the old generation size. Increasing young generation space at the expense of old generation space has its consequences. If the live data size is greater than the size of the old generation, the application will likely experience nonstop full garbage collections and may also throw OutOfMemoryErrors. Therefore, be careful when reconfiguring spaces so you do not take too much from the old generation space. If the application footprint requirements allow it, and there is sufficient available memory, the best option is increasing the size of the Java heap (-Xms and -Xmx) rather than taking from the old generation space.

Also, remember the HotSpot VM by default targets survivor space occupancy after a minor garbage collection at 50%. If the -XX:TargetSurvivorRatio=<percent> command line option is in use, then it uses <percent> as the target survivor space occupancy. If the survivor space occupancy trends above this target, objects are promoted to the old generation before they have reached their maximum age. To calculate the minimum survivor space required to effectively age the maximum survived bytes, the maximum survived bytes must be divided by the target survivor space occupancy, 50%, or the percent specified with -XX:TargetSurvivorRatio=<percent>.

To illustrate with an example, consider the following command line options:

```
-Xmx13g -Xms13g -Xmn4g -XX:SurvivorRatio=6
-XX:+UseParallelOldGC -XX:-UseAdaptiveSizePolicy
-XX:PrintGCDateStamps -XX:+PrintGCDetails -XX:+PrintAdaptiveSizePolicy
```

The overall JVM heap size is 13 gigabytes. The young generation space size is 4 gigabytes. The old generation space size is 9 gigabytes ($13 - 4 = 9$). The survivor spaces each have a size of 512 megabytes (4 gigabytes/(6 + 2) = .5 gigabytes = 512 megabytes). Suppose an analysis of the garbage collection logs finds the maximum bytes survived during application steady state as 495,880,312 bytes, about 473 megabytes (495,880,312/(1024 * 1024) = 473). Since there is no explicit use of -XX:Target SurvivorRatio=<percent> in the set of command line options, the target survivor space occupancy is the default 50%. A minimum survivor space size to set, or one that is slightly higher, based on the worst case survived bytes in this example is 495,880,312/50% = 991,760,624 bytes, about 946 megabytes.

From the initial command line options above, a 4 gigabyte young generation space is divided into two survivor spaces at 512 megabytes each and an eden space at 3 gigabytes ($4 - (.5 \times 2) = 3$). The analysis of the worst case survived bytes suggests survivor spaces should be at least 946 megabytes each. A 1024 megabyte survivor space, in other words 1 gigabyte, is pretty close to the 946 megabytes needed for each survivor space. To preserve the rate at which object ages are incremented, that is, the frequency of minor garbage collections, the eden size must remain at or near the same size of 3 gigabytes. Hence, the young generation space must be sized with or near 1024 megabytes for each survivor space along with 3 gigabytes of eden space for a total young generation space of 5 gigabytes. In other words, the young generation size should be 1024 megabytes, or 1 gigabyte, larger than was specified in the initial configuration. Changing only -Xmn4g to -Xmn5g results in a 1 gigabyte reduction in the old generation space. The ideal configuration is increasing the Java heap size (-Xmx and -Xms) by 1 gigabyte. But if memory footprint requirements or the amount of memory available on the system do not allow for it, then ensure the resulting old generation space is comfortably larger than the live data size. A general guideline to follow is the old generation size should be 1.5x larger than the live data size.

Assuming the application's footprint requirements allow it and there is enough memory available, an updated command line for increasing the size of the survivor spaces to accommodate the worst case bytes survived during steady state while maintaining eden space and old generation space size is

```
-Xmx14g -Xms14g -Xmn5g -XX:SurvivorRatio=3
-XX:+UseParallelOldGC -XX:-UseAdaptiveSizePolicy
-XX:PrintGCDateStamps -XX:+PrintGCDetails -XX:+PrintAdaptiveSizePolicy
```

This sizes old generation space at 9 gigabytes ($14 - 5 = 9$), same size as before; young generation space at 5 gigabytes, 1 gigabyte (1024 megabytes) larger than before; survivor spaces at 1 gigabyte (1024 bytes) each, ($5/(3 + 2) = 1$); and eden space at 3 gigabytes ($5 - (1 \times 2) = 3$).

You may have to do several resizing iterations until you achieve application peak throughput that fits within the application's memory footprint requirements. The peak throughput is expected to be found in a configuration that is most effective at aging objects in the survivor spaces.

As a general guideline, garbage collection overhead with the throughput garbage collector should be less than 5%. If you are able to drive the overhead down to as little as 1% or less, you may not be able to do much better without doing some very extensive or specialized JVM tuning in addition to what is presented in this chapter.

If you are not able to increase the size of the young generation space while maintaining the size of the eden space and are either unable to maintain the size of the old generation space or are concerned with falling too close to the live data size for the old generation space size or are bounded by the amount of memory you can make available for the Java heap, there is an additional alternative to explore. When looking at the maximum survived bytes at each minor garbage collection in steady state, calculate the minimum, maximum, average, standard deviation, and median survived bytes. These calculations offer information about the application's object allocation rate, that is, is it fairly steady without wide swings, or does it experience wide swings? If it does not have wide swings, that is, there is not a large gap between minimum and maximum or the standard deviation is small, try several configurations raising the target survivor occupancy percentage (-XX:TargetSurvivorRatio=<n>) from its default of 50, to 60, 70, 80, or possibly 90. This is an option to consider in the presence of memory constraints, that is, application memory footprint requirements or other limitations. Setting the target survivor occupancy higher than the default of 50 for applications having wide swings in object allocations can, however, result in survivor space overflow.

Tuning Parallel GC Threads

The number of throughput garbage collector threads should also be tuned based on the number of applications running on the same system and the underlying hardware platform. As mentioned in the "CMS Pause Time Tuning" subsection earlier in the chapter, in cases where multiple applications are running on the same system, it is advisable to set the number of parallel garbage collection threads to a number lower than the default using the command line option -XX:ParallelGCThreads=<n>.

Otherwise, garbage collections may intrude heavily on the performance of the other applications due to a large number of garbage collection threads executing at the same time. As of Java 6 Update 23, the number of parallel garbage collection threads defaults to the number returned by the Java API Runtime.availableProcessors() if the number returned is less than or equal to 8; otherwise, it defaults to 5/8 the number returned by Runtime.availableProcessors(). A general guideline for the number of parallel garbage collection threads to set in the presence of multiple applications on the same system is taking the total number of virtual processors (the value returned by Runtime.availableProcessors()) and dividing it by the number of applications running on the system, assuming that load and Java heap sizes are similar among the applications. If the load or Java heap sizes differ substantially, then some weighting of the number of parallel garbage collection threads for each Java application is a better approach.

Deploying on NUMA Systems

If the application is deployed on a NUMA (Non-Uniform Memory Architecture) system, an additional HotSpot VM command line option that can be used with the throughput garbage collector is

```
-XX:+UseNUMA
```

This command line option leverages the relationship of CPU to memory location to allocate objects in memory local to where the allocating thread is executing. The premise at work here is that the thread that allocates the object is the one that is most likely to access it in the near future. By allocating objects in local memory, it takes less time to fetch the object from memory by the same thread than if the object had been allocated in remote memory.

The -XX:+UseNUMA command line option should only be used when a JVM spans a topology of CPU to memory where access times from CPU to memory differ. For example, if a JVM is deployed in a processor set on a NUMA system, but the processor set does not contain a CPU to memory topology such that access times differ, then -XX:+UseNUMA should not be used.

Next Steps

If you have reached this point of the JVM tuning process and you are not able to meet the application's throughput requirements, you can explore using the command line options presented in the section "Additional Performance Command Line Options" later in the chapter. If none of the additional command line options in that section allow you to meet your application's throughput performance requirements, then you must either revisit application performance requirements, change the application, or change the JVM deployment model. Once one or more of those alternatives are chosen, you can again iterate through the tuning process.

Edge cases where some of the general JVM tuning guidelines may not apply are described in the next section.

Edge Cases

In some situations the general guidelines presented in the step-by-step JVM tuning process do not apply. This section explores those possibilities.

Some applications have very large object allocation rates with a small number of long-lived objects. Such applications may require a much larger young generation space than old generation space. An example of such an application is the SPEC benchmark SPECjbb2005.

Some applications experience a small number of object promotions. These applications may not require an old generation space much larger than the live data size since the growth of old generation space occupancy is very slow.

Some applications with low latency requirements using the CMS collector run well with a small young generation space to keep minor garbage collection induced latencies short and a large old generation space. In such a configuration, it is likely objects will be promoted to the old generation quickly rather than aging effectively in survivor spaces. Instead, CMS garbage collects these objects after they are promoted. The likelihood of fragmentation of the old generation space is mitigated by a large old generation space.

Additional HotSpot command line options that may offer application improved performance are described in the next section.

Additional Performance Command Line Options

Several additional HotSpot VM command line options not mentioned previously in this chapter may offer a Java application improved latency or throughput performance through JIT compiler code generation optimizations and other HotSpot VM performance capabilities. These optimizations and features along with the HotSpot VM command line options that enable them are presented in this section.

Latest and Greatest Optimizations

When new performance optimizations are integrated into the HotSpot VM they are usually introduced under the command line option -XX:+AggressiveOpts.

New optimizations are introduced under this command line option as a way to isolate the latest and greatest optimizations from those that have proved stable over time. Applications that are more interested in stability over performance can choose to not use this command line option because the introduction of new optimizations may result in unexpected JVM behavior. It also allows for applications in search of every bit of performance they can get to take on a little more risk using a JVM configuration that enables the new optimizations.

As new optimizations demonstrate stability, they are made the default. It may be several update releases before they become the default.

Using the -XX:+AggressiveOpts command line option should be considered if the application stakeholders are looking for additional performance and are willing to accept the additional small risk associated with enabling the most recent optimizations.

Escape Analysis

Escape analysis is a technique that evaluates the scope of a Java object. In particular, if a Java object allocated by some executing thread can ever be seen by a different thread, the object "escapes." If a Java object does not escape, additional optimization techniques can be applied. Hence, the optimization technique is called *escape analysis*.

Escape analysis optimizations in the HotSpot VM are enabled with the following command line option:

```
-XX:+DoEscapeAnalysis
```

It was introduced in Java 6 Update 14 and is automatically enabled with -XX:+AggressiveOpts. It is enabled by default beginning with Java 6 Update 23, but otherwise disabled in previous Java 6 Updates.

The HotSpot VM JIT compiler can apply any of the following optimization techniques through escape analysis:

- **Object explosion.** Object explosion is a technique where an object's fields are allocated in places other than the Java heap and can potentially be eliminated. For example, an object's fields can be placed directly in CPU registers or object allocation can be done on the stack rather than the Java heap.

- **Scalar replacement.** Scalar replacement is an optimization technique to reduce memory accesses. Consider the following Java class that acts as a holder for the related values of a length and width of a rectangle:

```java
public class Rectangle {
    int length;
    int width;
}
```

  The HotSpot VM can optimize the allocation and use of a nonescaping Rectangle class instance by allocating both the length and width fields directly in CPU registers without allocating a Rectangle object. As a result there is no need to dereference a Rectangle object pointer to load its length and width fields into CPU registers each time those fields are accessed. The net effect is a reduction in memory accesses.

- **Thread stack allocation.** Thread stack allocation, as the name implies, is an optimization technique that allocates an object in a thread's stack frame rather than the Java heap. An object that never escapes can be allocated in a thread's stack frame since no other thread will ever see the object. Thread stack allocation reduces the number of objects allocated to the Java heap, which reduces the frequency of garbage collection.

- **Eliminate synchronization.** If an object allocated by a thread never escapes and the thread locks the allocated object, the lock can be eliminated by the JIT compiler since no other thread ever sees the allocated object.

- **Eliminate garbage collection read/write barriers.** If an object allocated by a thread never escapes, it is reachable only from thread-local roots, so stores of its address into other objects do not need a read or write barrier. A read or write barrier is only needed if the object can be seen by a different thread, which usually occurs if the allocated object is assigned to a field of some other object that can be seen by another thread, and thus escapes.

Biased Locking

Biased locking is an optimization technique that biases an object to the thread that last acquired the lock. In uncontended lock situations where only one thread ever locks the object, near lock-free overhead can be realized.

Biased locking was introduced in Java 5 Update 6. It is enabled with the HotSpot VM command line option -XX:+UseBiasedLocking.

Java 5 HotSpot JDKs require the explicit enabling of biased locking to use the feature. Biased locking is automatically enabled with -XX:+AggressiveOpts in Java 5 HotSpot VMs. In Java 6 HotSpot JDKs, biased locking is enabled by default.

Experience has shown this feature is useful for most Java applications. However, some applications do not perform well using it—for example, applications where the thread that acquires a lock is usually not the same as the thread that acquired it last. An example is an application where locking activity is dominated by locking around a worker thread pool and worker threads. In this family of Java applications, since a stop-the-world safepoint operation is required to revoke a bias, it may be beneficial to explicitly disable biased locking by specifying -XX:-UseBiasedLocking. If you suspect your application may fit this family of Java applications you should conduct a performance experiment to compare the performance of biased locking enabled (-XX:+UseBiasedLocking) versus disabled (-XX:-UseBiasedLocking).

Large Pages

Memory in a computer system is divided into fixed sized blocks called pages. Memory accesses by a program translate a virtual memory address to a physical memory address. Virtual to physical memory address mappings are held in a page table. To reduce the cost of accessing a page table on every memory access, a fast cache of virtual to physical address translations is often used. This cache is called a translation lookaside buffer, or TLB for short.

Accessing a TLB to satisfy a virtual to physical address mapping request is much faster than walking the page tables to find the mapping. A TLB usually has a fixed number of entries it can hold. An entry in a TLB is a mapping of a memory address range based on the page size. Therefore, a larger page size allows for a larger range of memory addresses per entry and per TLB. With a wider range of addresses represented in a TLB, fewer address translation requests miss the address range found in the TLB. When a request for an address translation is not found in the TLB, it is called a TLB miss. When a TLB miss occurs, walking the page table in memory is usually required. Walking the page table is an expensive operation compared to finding the address translation in the TLB. Hence, the benefit of using large pages is reduced TLB misses.

The HotSpot VM has support for using large pages on Oracle Solaris (also referred to as Solaris hereafter), Linux, and Windows. Usually processors support several different page sizes. Page sizes can also be different based on a processor or processor family. In addition, operating system configuration may be required to utilize large pages.

The procedure required to use large pages in the HotSpot VM for Solaris, Linux, and Windows is described in the next subsections.

Large Pages on Solaris

```
Using large pages on Solaris is enabled by default. It can also be
specified with the command line option -XX:+UseLargePages.
```

On Solaris, large pages work with no additional specialized operation system configuration.

On Solaris SPARC processors, several different page sizes are available depending on the processor. The default page size on all SPARC processors is 8 kilobytes. UltraSPARC-III and UltraSPARC-IV processors also support 4 megabyte pages. UltraSPARC-IV+ supports up to 32 megabyte pages. At the time of this writing, SPARC T-series supports up to 256 megabyte pages.

On Intel and AMD systems, page sizes range from 4 kilobytes, to 2 megabytes for x64, to 4 megabytes through page size extension, to 1 gigabyte on recent AMD64 and Intel Xeon and Core systems.

A list of page sizes supported on a platform can be obtained using the Solaris `pagesize -a` command. Here is an example output from the Solaris `pagesize -a` command on a system running an UltraSPARC T2 processor:

```
$ pagesize -a
8192
65536
4194304
268435456
```

The values reported by the `pagesize` command are in bytes. The output shows 8 kilobyte, 64 kilobyte, 4 megabyte, and 256 megabyte pages are possible page sizes.

> The HotSpot VM can also be configured to use a specific page size with the command line option -XX:LargePageSizeInBytes=<n>[g|m|k]

The value of `<n>` is the size and the trailing g, m, or k represents gigabytes, megabytes, and kilobytes. Therefore, to use 256 megabyte pages, you specify `-XX:LargePageSizeInBytes=256m`. This command line option is useful when you want to explicitly specify the page size to use. If the underlying platform does not support the page size specified, the HotSpot VM falls back to using the default page size for the given platform.

Large Pages on Linux

As of this writing, using large pages on Linux requires operating system configuration modifications in addition to using the command line option `-XX:+UseLargePages`. The Linux modifications required can vary depending on the Linux distribution and Linux kernel. To enable large pages on Linux it is advisable to consult a Linux administrator or your Linux distribution documentation for the appropriate changes. Once the Linux operating system configuration changes have been made, the command line option `-XX:+UseLargePages` must be used. For example:

```
$ java -server -Xmx1024m -Xms1024m -Xmn256m -XX:+UseLargePages ...
```

If large pages are not set up properly, the HotSpot VM will still accept `-XX:+UseLargePages` as a valid command line option, but it will report it was not able to acquire large pages and will fall back to using the default page size for the underlying platform.

Large Pages on Windows

Use of large pages on Windows requires changing Windows security settings to lock pages into memory for the user running the Java application. This is done through the Group Policy Editor. To launch the Group Policy Editor and make this configuration change, follow these steps:

1. From the Start menu, select Run and type gedit.msc. This opens the Group Policy editor.

2. In the Group Policy editor, expand the Computer Configuration. Then expand Windows Settings, expand Security Settings, expand Local Policies, and select the User Rights Assignment folder.

3. Double-click on the Lock page in memory entry in the right panel.

4. In the Local Security Policy Setting dialog, click the Add button.

5. In the Select Users or Groups dialog, add the account name of the user who will run the Java application.

6. Click the Apply and OK buttons to apply the changes. Then quit the Group Policy editor.

After changing the configuration to lock pages in memory, remember to reboot to activate the policy change.

Then add `-XX:+UseLargePages` to the set of command line options used to run the application. For example:

```
$ java -server -Xmx1024m -Xms1024m -Xmn256m -XX:+UseLargePages ...
```

Bibliography

Printezis, Tony, and Charlie Hunt. "Garbage Collection Tuning in the Java HotSpot Virtual Machine." http://developers.sun.com/learning/javaoneonline/sessions/2009/pdf/TS-4887.pdf.

Printezis, Tony, and Charlie Hunt. "Step-by-Step: Garbage Collection Tuning in the HotSpot Virtual Machine." JavaOne 2010 Conference, San Francisco, California.

Goetz, Brian, Tony Printezis, and John Coomes. "Inside Out: A Modern Virtual Machine Revealed." http://developers.sun.com/learning/javaoneonline/sessions/2009/pdf/TS-5427.pdf.

"How to: Enable the Lock Pages in Memory Option" (Windows). http://msdn.microsoft.com/en-us/library/ms190730.aspx.

Hohensee, Paul, and David Dagastine Keenan. "High Performance Java Technology in a Multi-core World. JavaOne 2007 Conference, San Francisco, California.

"Dot-Com & Beyond." Sun Professional Services, Built to Last: Designing for Systemic Qualities. Sun Professional Services.com Consulting, 2001.

ISO 8601:2004. International Organization for Standardization. http://www.iso.org/iso/catalogue_detail?csnumber=40874.

Masamitsu, Jon. "What the Heck's a Concurrent Mode?" http://blogs.sun.com/jonthecollector/entry/what_the_heck_s_a.

8

Benchmarking Java Applications

It is a common practice to evaluate the performance of an application or make inferences about the performance of an application through the use of benchmarks. Benchmarks are programs specifically developed to measure the performance of one or more elements of a computing system. In the context of Java software, benchmarks are Java programs intended to measure the performance of one or more elements of a system where the Java program is being executed. These elements can include the entire hardware and software stack or be limited to a small segment of functionality in a Java program. The latter is often described as a *micro-benchmark* since it has a much narrower focus. Benchmarks used to make the broader evaluation of a system's performance, that is, the entire hardware and software stack, are often industry standard benchmarks such as those developed under the collaboration of industry competitors such as those developed at SPEC (Standard Performance Evaluation Corporation). In contrast, micro-benchmarks tend to be created by developers since micro-benchmarks have a narrow or specific performance question to be analyzed.

Developing benchmarks, especially micro-benchmarks, to execute in a modern Java Virtual Machine (JVM) introduces numerous challenges that can often lead an observer and a developer of a benchmark to improper or incorrect conclusions due to one or more of the many runtime optimizations that can be made by modern JVMs such as the Java HotSpot VM (also referred to as HotSpot VM hereafter). The development of Java benchmarks, including micro-benchmarks, is largely an art. This chapter describes several potential issues to be aware of when writing Java benchmarks, including micro-benchmarks, and how to identify potential issues with a micro-benchmark along with tips to effectively write Java benchmarks. Additionally, how to identify performance improvements or regressions with benchmarks through the use of the design of experiments and statistical methods to improve confidence in arriving at conclusions are also presented. To gain the most from this chapter, it may be helpful to read or review the "HotSpot VM JIT Compilers" section of Chapter 3, "JVM Overview." Doing so will help you learn about some of the complex optimizations a modern JVM's JIT compiler can perform on a Java application.

Challenges with Benchmarks

This section presents several unintentional mistakes developers experience when developing Java benchmarks or Java micro-benchmarks. Remember that benchmarks measure a much broader area of a system than micro-benchmarks, which measure specific portions, or small segments of functionality.

Benchmark Warm-up

One of the most common unintentional errors made by developers of Java benchmarks and Java micro-benchmarks is not including a warm-up period, or not having a sufficiently long warm-up period where a JVM's JIT compiler can identify and produce optimizations. A warm-up period provides the HotSpot VM's JIT compiler the opportunity to collect information about a running program and make intelligent dynamic optimization decisions based on the "hot" code paths taken by the executing program. By default, the HotSpot Server VM executes a block of Java byte code 10,000 times before the HotSpot Server JIT compiler produces native machine code for that block of Java bytecode. The HotSpot Client VM begins producing native machine code at 1,500 iterations. Since HotSpot Client and HotSpot Server JIT compilers produce native machine code after an application has been running for a period of time, the JIT compiler may be actively produce native machine code during a measurement interval of an executing benchmark. Additionally, HotSpot's JIT compilers consume some CPU cycles to make optimization decisions to generate native machine code. As a result, an experiment that involves executing a benchmark that does not include a warm-up period or a long enough warm-up period has a high probability of reporting inaccurate findings.

A strategy to ensure the JIT compiler has ample opportunity to determine the best optimizations and produce native machine code is to incorporate into the benchmark or micro-benchmark a sufficient warm-up period. This warm-up period should be long enough that the benchmark or micro-benchmark has reached benchmark steady state and JIT compiler steady state.

Tip

During warm-up, it is important to execute the code paths that will be measured during the measurement interval. One of the advantages of a JIT compiler is that runtime feedback can be used to optimize for the common case. If parts of a micro-benchmark are not executed during warm-up, the JIT compiler may presume that the code is infrequently executed and concentrate on optimization opportunities elsewhere.

A good way to ensure a HotSpot JIT compiler has reached steady state, finished its optimizations, and generated optimized code for a benchmark is to execute a run of the benchmark with the HotSpot VM command line option `-XX:+PrintCompilation` along with instrumenting the benchmark to indicate when it has completed the warm-up period. `-XX:+PrintCompilation` causes the JVM to print a line for each method as it optimizes or deoptimizes. Following is a small portion of output produced by `-XX:+PrintCompilation` on a micro-benchmark.

```
11         java.util.Random::nextInt (60 bytes)
12         java.util.Random::next (47 bytes)
13         java.util.concurrent.atomic.AtomicLong::get (5 bytes)
14         java.util.HashSet::contains (9 bytes)
15         java.util.HashMap::transfer (83 bytes)
16         java.util.Arrays$ArrayList::set (16 bytes)
17         java.util.Arrays$ArrayList::set (16 bytes)
18         java.util.Collections::swap (25 bytes)
19         java.util.Arrays$ArrayList::get (7 bytes)
20         java.lang.Long::<init> (10 bytes)
21         java.lang.Integer::longValue (6 bytes)
22         java.lang.Long::valueOf (36 bytes)
23         java.lang.Integer::stringSize (21 bytes)
24         java.lang.Integer::getChars (131 bytes)
```

For a detailed explanation of the output produced by `-XX:+PrintCompilation`, see Appendix A, "HotSpot VM Command Line Options of Interest." Being able to understand the meaning of the output generated from `-XX:+PrintCompilation` is not as important as when the information is emitted. The goal in the context of developing a benchmark is to not see any output from `-XX:+PrintCompilation` while the benchmark is executing in a measurement interval.

Tip

`-XX:+PrintCompilation` used in conjunction with instrumentation reporting when the warm-up cycle is completed helps identify whether the benchmark you are executing is indeed executing with JIT compiled native machine code. In addition, specifying different warm-up period lengths can provide additional evidence that the JIT compiler has reached steady state.

An example that illustrates the use of a warm-up period and instrumentation for a micro-benchmark follows. Specifics of what is being benchmarked are deliberately not included. The example's intent is to illustrate the usefulness of adding instrumentation to be able to identify when the benchmark has completed the warm-up period and when the JIT compiler has reached steady state, that is, when it has completed its optimizations.

```java
public static void main(String[] args) {
    int warmUpCycles = 1000000;
    int testCycles = 50000000;
    SimpleExample se = new SimpleExample();
    System.err.println("Warming up benchmark ...");
    long nanosPerIteration = se.runTest(warmupCycles);
    System.err.println("Done warming up benchmark.");
    System.err.println("Entering measurement interval ...");
    nanosPerIteration = se.runTest(testCycles);
    System.err.println("Measurement interval done.");
    System.err.println("Nanoseconds per iteration : +
                        nanosPerIteration);
}

private long runTest(int iterations) {
    long startTime = System.nanoTime();
    // Execute the test 'iterations' number of times.

    // Deliberately leaving out specifics of what is
    // being performance tested in this benchmark.

    long elapsedTime = System.nanoTime();
    return (elapsedTime - startTime)/iterations;
}
```

In the preceding example there may be an issue in the length of time to execute the method runTest(). It may not be sufficiently long enough, which can result in a small or misleading nanoseconds per iteration value. This topic is further discussed in a later section of this chapter, "Use of Time Java APIs." In addition, if you are observing -XX:+PrintCompilation output during the measurement interval, JIT compiler activity is taking place and the benchmark has not reached JIT compiler steady state. This can usually be corrected by increasing the length of the warm-up period and possibly adding multiple warm-up periods.

Tip

A good idiom for effective micro-benchmark implementations is to use and execute the same method(s) during warm-up periods(s) as those executed during the measurement interval.

After observing no output from -XX:+PrintCompilation indicating the JIT compiler has completed its optimizations prior to executing in the measurement interval(s) on several executions of the benchmark, the benchmark should be executed several times without `-XX:+PrintCompilation` to observe if the reported performance results are consistent. If they are not consistent, the benchmark may be suffering from another challenge of creating benchmarks or micro-benchmarks.

Garbage Collection

The impact of garbage collection pauses is often overlooked in the execution of benchmarks, especially micro-benchmarks. Since garbage collections can pause application threads, or consume CPU cycles concurrently, results from executing a benchmark experiencing garbage collections can lead to incorrect conclusions (unless it is the performance of garbage collectors, which is the purpose of the benchmark). Therefore it is important to tune the garbage collector and size the Java heap appropriately for the benchmark being executed. The ideal situation is to avoid garbage collections during the measurement interval of a benchmark. For some benchmarks it may not be possible to avoid garbage collections. In either case, it is important to tune the JVM's garbage collector for that benchmark's workload to minimize its impact on the reported performance results. For micro-benchmarks it is important to avoid a garbage collection during the measurement interval since micro-benchmarks usually are short in execution time and usually do not require a large Java heap. If garbage collections cannot be avoided in a micro-benchmark, the serial garbage collector, `-XX:+UseSerialGC`, should be used along with explicitly setting the initial heap size, `-Xms`, the maximum heap size, `-Xmx`, to the same value and explicitly setting the young generation heap size using `-Xmn`.

> **Tip**
>
> A common practice used in micro-benchmarks, which are subject to garbage collections during a measurement interval is to call `System.gc()` several times prior to entering the measurement interval. `System.gc()` is called several times since Java objects with finalizers may require multiple garbage collections to be freed. In addition, the `System.runFinalization()` API can be called explicitly to help in asking the JVM to complete the execution of `finalize()` methods on unreachable objects whose finalizers are waiting to be executed or partially executed.

To tune the JVM's garbage collector for a benchmark, other than a micro-benchmark, which may incur garbage collections during its measurement interval, tune the JVM as described in Chapter 7, "Tuning the JVM, Step by Step."

To observe the behavior of the garbage collector when executing a benchmark use the `-verbose:gc` JVM command line flag to get an indication of the impact of garbage collection on the benchmark's performance. As mentioned earlier, the ideal situation is for the benchmark to complete its performance measurement interval without experiencing a garbage collection. Adding `-verbose:gc` to the command line along with adding instrumentation that indicates the phase of the benchmark shows whether garbage collections are occurring during the measurement interval. This is a similar approach as described in the previous section "Benchmark Warm-up."

Use of Time Java APIs

Until the introduction of the `System.nanoTime()` Java API, most Java benchmarks or micro-benchmarks used the `System.currentTimeMillis()` Java API to take a time stamp at the beginning and end of a measurement interval and then calculated the difference between the end time and start time to report an elapsed time it took to execute the code of interest.

There is a degree of accuracy issue with using the Java API `System.currentTimeMillis()` and `System.nanoTime()`. Although the value returned by `System.currentTimeMillis()` is the current time in milliseconds, the accuracy of the value at a millisecond level depends on the operating system. The Java API specification for `System.currentTimeMillis()` explicitly states that although the value returned is a millisecond, the granularity of the returned value depends on the underlying operating system. This specification provides the opportunity to use operating system APIs that may report milliseconds, but updates to the millisecond counter may occur at lesser intervals such as every 30 millisecond intervals. The specification is intentionally loose so that the Java API could be satisfied across a wide range of operating systems, some of which may not be able to report millisecond accuracy. The issue with using the Java API `System.nanoTime()` is similar. Although the method provides nanosecond precision, it does not provide nanosecond accuracy. The Java API specification for `System.nanoTime()` states there is no guarantee about how frequently the values returned by `System.nanoTime()` are updated.

Hence, when using `System.currentTimeMillis()` to measure elapsed time, the measurement interval needs to be sufficiently large enough such that the degree of accuracy of `System.currentTimeMillis()` does not matter. In other words, the measurement interval needs to be large relative to a millisecond (i.e., many seconds or possibly as much as minutes). The same applies to using `System.nanoTime()`. For example, depending on the underlying operating system, `System.nanoTime()`, as described in the Java API specification, returns the current value of the most precise available system timer. The most precise available system timer may not have nanosecond accuracy. It is advisable to know the granularity and accuracy of these two Java APIs for the platform or operating system where the benchmark will be executed. If you do not know, if the source code is available, looking at the underlying implementation of these two Java APIs to gain an understanding of the granularity and accuracy should be considered, especially if the measurement intervals are narrow or very small relative to a millisecond, if you are using `System.currentTimeMillis()`, or nanosecond, if you are using `System.nanoTime()`.

> **Tip**
>
> It is a good practice to use `System.nanoTime()` to obtain start and end time stamps for measurement intervals in micro-benchmarks. Then report the elapsed time difference between the end and start time stamps or report the elapsed nanoseconds per iteration of the operation of interest, or alternatively report the number of iterations per second. The most important criterion is to ensure the micro-benchmark has run long enough to reach steady state and the measurement interval is long enough.

Optimizing Away Dead Code

Modern JVMs have the capability to identify code that is never called through the form of static analysis, through runtime observation, and through a form of light-weight profiling. Since micro-benchmarks rarely produce significant output, it is often the case some portions of micro-benchmark code can be identified as dead code by a JVM's JIT compiler. In extreme cases the code of interest being measured could be completely optimized away without the creator or executor of the micro-benchmark knowing. The following micro-benchmark, which attempts to measure the time it takes to calculate the twenty-fifth Fibonacci[1] number is an example where a modern JVM's JIT compiler can find dead code and eliminate it.

```java
public class DeadCode1 {

    final private static long NANOS_PER_MS = 1000000L;
    final private static int NUMBER = 25;

    // Non-recursive Fibonacci calculator
    private static int calcFibonacci(int n) {
        int result = 1;
        int prev = -1;
        int sum = 0;
        for (int i = 0; i <= n; i++) {
            sum = prev + result;
            prev = result;
            result = sum;
        }
```

---

1. Fibonacci, also known as Leonardo di Pisa, in his thirteenth century book *Liber abaci* posed the following question: Two young rabbits, one of each sex, are placed on an island. A pair of rabbits do not reproduce until they are two months old. After they are two months old, each pair of rabbits produces another pair each month. What is an equation that models the number of pairs of rabbits on the island after n months, assuming no rabbits die? The Fibonacci sequence. [1]

```
        return result;
    }

    private static void doTest(long iterations) {
        long startTime = System.nanoTime();
        for (long i = 0; i < iterations; i++)
            calcFibonacci(NUMBER);
        long elapsedTime = System.nanoTime() - startTime;
        System.out.println("    Elapsed nanoseconds -> " +
                           elapsedTime);
        float millis = elapsedTime / NANOS_PER_MS;
        float itrsPerMs = 0;
        if (millis != 0)
            itrsPerMs = iterations/millis;
        System.out.println("    Iterations per ms ---> " +
                           itrsPerMs);
    }

    public static void main(String[] args) {
        System.out.println("Warming up ...");
        doTest(1000000L);
        System.out.println("Warmup done.");
        System.out.println("Starting measurement interval ...");
        doTest(900000000L);
        System.out.println("Measurement interval done.");
        System.out.println("Test completed.");
    }
}
```

Notice in this example there is a warm-up period of one million iterations and a measurement interval of 900 million iterations. However, in doTest(), the call to method calcFibonacci(int n) can be identified as dead code and subsequently optimized into a no-op and eliminated. A no-op is defined as an operation or sequence of operations that has no effect on the state or output of a program. A JIT compiler could potentially see that no data computed in calcFibonacci() escapes that method and may eliminate it. In other words, the JIT compiler can determine that calcFibonacci() is a no-op and can eliminate the call to it as a performance optimization. The preceding micro-benchmark executed with a Java 6 HotSpot Server VM on a 2GHz AMD Turion running Oracle Solaris 10 produced the following output:

```
Warming up ...
    Elapsed nanoseconds -> 282928153
    Iterations per ms -> 3546.0
Warmup done.
Starting measurement interval ...
    Elapsed nanoseconds -> 287452697
    Iterations per ms -> 313588.0
Measurement interval done.

Test completed.
```

Comparing the iterations per millisecond during the warm-up period and measurement interval suggests the HotSpot Server JIT compiler has managed to increase the performance of calculating the twenty-fifth Fibonacci number by almost 9,000%. A speed up of 9,000% does not make sense. This is pretty strong evidence something is wrong with the implementation of this micro-benchmark.

If this benchmark is updated with the following modifications the reported iterations per millisecond change drastically:

1. Modify the `doTest()` method to store the returned result of the called method, `calcFibonacci(int n)`.

2. Print the stored result returned from the called `calcFibonacci(int n)` method after the elapsed time has been calculated in the `doTest()` method.

An updated implementation follows:

```java
public class DeadCode2 {

    final private static long NANOS_PER_MS = 1000000L;
    final private static int NUMBER = 25;

    private static int calcFibonacci(int n) {
        int result = 1;
        int prev = -1;
        int sum = 0;
        for (int i = 0; i <= n; i++) {
            sum = prev + result;
            prev = result;
            result = sum;
        }
        return result;
    }

    private static void doTest(long iterations) {
        int answer = 0;
        long startTime = System.nanoTime();
        for (long i = 0; i < iterations; i++)
            answer = calcFibonacci(NUMBER);
        long elapsedTime = System.nanoTime() - startTime;
        System.out.println("    Answer -> " + answer);
        System.out.println("    Elapsed nanoseconds -> " +
                    elapsedTime);
        float millis = elapsedTime / NANOS_PER_MS;
        float itrsPerMs = 0;
        if (millis != 0)
            itrsPerMs = iterations/millis;
        System.out.println("    Iterations per ms ---> " +
                    itrsPerMs);
    }
```

Continued

```
    public static void main(String[] args) {
        System.out.println("Warming up ...");
        doTest(1000000L);
        System.out.println("Warmup done.");
        System.out.println("Starting measurement interval ...");
        doTest(900000000L);
        System.out.println("Measurement interval done.");
        System.out.println("Test completed.");
    }
}
```

Executing this modified version produces the following output:

```
Warming up ...
    Answer -> 75025
    Elapsed nanoseconds -> 28212633
    Iterations per ms -> 35714.0
Warmup done.
Starting measurement interval ...
    Answer -> 75025
    Elapsed nanoseconds -> 1655116813
    Iterations per ms -> 54380.0
Measurement interval done.

Test completed.
```

Now, the difference between the reported iterations per millisecond between warm-up and measurement interval is about 150%. Observing a speed up of 150% is more believable than the 9,000% observed in the earlier version of the micro-benchmark. But if this version of the micro-benchmark is executed with -XX:+PrintCompilation, there appears to be some compilation activity occurring during the measurement interval.

Executing the preceding modified micro-benchmark version with the addition of -XX:+PrintCompilation shows the following output:

```
Warming up ...
    1       DeadCode2::calcFibonacci (31 bytes)
    1%      DeadCode2::doTest @ 9 (125 bytes)
    1%  made not entrant DeadCode2::doTest @ 9 (125 bytes)
    Answer -> 75025
    Elapsed nanoseconds -> 38829269
    Iterations per ms -> 26315.0
Warmup done.
Starting measurement interval ...
    2       DeadCode2::doTest (125 bytes)
    2%      DeadCode2::doTest @ 9 (125 bytes)
    Answer -> 75025
    Elapsed nanoseconds -> 1650085855
    Iterations per ms -> 54545.0
Measurement interval done.

Test completed.
```

The way to eliminate the compilation activity reported during a measurement interval is to add a second warm-up period. A second warm-up period can also help show whether the benchmark is indeed fully warmed by comparing the second warm-up period's iterations per millisecond to that which is reported by the measurement interval. Although compilation activity occurs during the second warm-up interval, if the second warm-up period is very long relative to the compilation activity time, then the iterations per millisecond should be close to the measurement interval iterations per millisecond.

The following is a modified version of the micro-benchmark that includes a second warm-up period of the same length as the measurement interval.

```java
public class DeadCode3 {

    final private static long NANOS_PER_MS = 1000000L;
    final private static int NUMBER = 25;

    private static int calcFibonacci(int n) {
        int result = 1;
        int prev = -1;
        int sum = 0;
        for (int i = 0; i <= n; i++) {
            sum = prev + result;
            prev = result;
            result = sum;
        }
        return result;
    }

    private static void doTest(long iterations) {
        int answer = 0;
        long startTime = System.nanoTime();
        for (long i = 0; i < iterations; i++)
            answer = calcFibonacci(NUMBER);
        long elapsedTime = System.nanoTime() - startTime;
        System.out.println("    Answer -> " + answer);
        System.out.println("    Elapsed nanoseconds -> " +
                            elapsedTime);
        float millis = elapsedTime / NANOS_PER_MS;
        float itrsPerMs = 0;
        if (millis != 0)
            itrsPerMs = iterations/millis;
        System.out.println("    Iterations per ms ---> " +
                            itrsPerMs);
    }

    public static void main(String[] args) {
        System.out.println("Warming up ...");
        doTest(1000000L);
        System.out.println("1st warmup done.");
        System.out.println("Starting 2nd warmup ...");
        doTest(900000000L);
```

Continued

```
          System.out.println("2nd warmup done.");
          System.out.println("Starting measurement interval ...");
          doTest(900000000L);
          System.out.println("Measurement interval done.");
          System.out.println("Test completed.");
      }
}
```

The output from executing the modified version with `-XX:+PrintCompilation`
follows:

```
Warming up ...
  1       DeadCode3::calcFibonacci (31 bytes)
  1%      DeadCode3::doTest @ 9 (124 bytes)
  1%  made not entrant  DeadCode3::doTest @ 9 (124 bytes)
      Answer -> 75025
      Elapsed nanoseconds -> 40455272
      Iterations per ms -> 25000.0
1st warmup done.
Starting 2nd warmup ...
  2       DeadCode3::doTest (124 bytes)
  2%      DeadCode3::doTest @ 9 (124 bytes)
      Answer -> 75025
      Elapsed nanoseconds -> 1926823821
      Iterations per ms -> 46728.0
2nd warmup done.
Starting measurement interval ...
      Answer -> 75025
      Elapsed nanoseconds -> 1898913343
      Iterations per ms -> 47418.0
Measurement interval done.
Test completed.
```

By adding the second warm-up period, compilation activity no longer occurs in the
measurement interval. In addition, comparing the iterations per millisecond in the
second warm-up period to that of the measurement interval, the cost of the compilation activity during the second warm-up period is very small, less than 700 iterations
per millisecond, or about a 1.5% difference.

To reduce the chances of code in micro-benchmarks from being identified as being
dead code or drastically simplified, the following programming practices should be
integrated:

- Make the computation nontrivial.
- Print computation results immediately outside the measurement interval or
  store the computed results for printing outside the measurement interval.

To make the computation nontrivial pass in arguments to the methods being measured and return a computation result from methods being measured. Additionally,

vary the number of iterations used in the measurement interval within the benchmark or alternatively in different runs of the benchmark. Then compare the iterations per second values to see whether they remain consistent as the number of iterations is varied while also tracking the behavior of the JIT compiler with `-XX:+PrintCompilation`.

Inlining

The HotSpot VM Client and Server JIT compilers both have the ability to inline methods. This means that the target method at a call site is expanded into the calling method. This is done by the JIT compiler to reduce the call overhead in calling methods and results in faster execution. In addition, the inlined code may provide further optimization opportunities in that the combined code may be simplified or eliminated in ways not possible without inlining. Inlining can also produce surprising observations in micro-benchmarks. This section presents an example that illustrates what can happen to a micro-benchmark as a result of inlining optimization decisions made by the HotSpot Client JIT compiler.

Consider the following micro-benchmark, which attempts to measure the performance of `String.equals(String s)` when both `String` objects are the same `String` object.

```java
public class SimpleExample {

    final private static long ITERATIONS = 5000000000L;
    final private static long WARMUP = 10000000L;
    final private static long NANOS_PER_MS = 1000L * 1000L;

    private static boolean equalsTest(String s) {
        boolean b = s.equals(s);
        return b;

    }

    private static long doTest(long n) {
        long start = System.nanoTime();
        for (long i = 0; i < n; i++) {
            equalsTest("ABC");
        }
        long end = System.nanoTime();
        return end - start;
    }

    private static void printStats(long n, long nanos) {
        float itrsPerMs = 0;
        float millis = nanos/NANOS_PER_MS;
        if (millis != 0) {
            itrsPerMs = n/(nanos/NANOS_PER_MS);
        }
```

Continued

```
            System.out.println("    Elapsed time in ms -> " + millis);
            System.out.println("    Iterations / ms ----> " + itrsPerMs);
        }

    public static void main(String[] args) {
        System.out.println("Warming up ...");

        long nanos = doTest(WARMUP);
        System.out.println("1st warm up done.");
        printStats(WARMUP, nanos);

        System.out.println("Starting 2nd warmup ...");
        nanos = doTest(WARMUP);
        System.out.println("2nd warm up done.");
        printStats(WARMUP, nanos);

        System.out.println("Starting measurement interval ...");
        nanos = doTest(ITERATIONS);
        System.out.println("Measurement interval done.");
        System.out.println("Test complete.");
        printStats(ITERATIONS, nanos);
    }
}
```

Based on the information presented in the "Optimizing Away Dead Code" section earlier in this chapter, the SimpleExample.equalsTest("ABC") method call from within the for/loop in method doTest() could be optimized away into dead code since the result of the call to method SimpleExample.equalsTest(String s) never escapes the SimpleExample.doTest(long n) method. However, executing the preceding micro-benchmark with a Java 6 HotSpot Client VM suggests this is not the case. The following output is from a Java 6 HotSpot Client VM executing the preceding micro-benchmark using -XX:+PrintCompilation.

```
Warming up ...
  1       java.lang.String::hashCode (60 bytes)
  2       java.lang.String::charAt (33 bytes)
  3       java.lang.String::equals (88 bytes)
  4       SimpleExample::equalsTest (8 bytes)
 1%       SimpleExample::doTest @ 7 (39 bytes)
1st warm up done.
Elapsed time in ms -> 96
Iterations / ms ----> 104166
  5       java.lang.String::indexOf (151 bytes)
Starting 2nd warmup ...
  6       SimpleExample::doTest (39 bytes)
2nd warm up done.
    Elapsed time in ms -> 95
    Iterations / ms ----> 105263
Starting measurement interval ...
Measurement interval done.
```

```
Test complete.
    Elapsed time in ms -> 42870
    Iterations / ms ----> 116631
```

The preceding output shows there is small improvement in the iterations per millisecond between the first warm-up period and the second warm-up period or measurement interval. It is less than 20%. The output also shows JIT compiler optimizations were performed for `String.equals()`, `SimpleExample.equalsTest()`, and `SimpleExample.doTest()`. Although the JIT compiler has performed optimizations for those methods, it may not have optimized any part of the micro-benchmark into dead code. To gain a further understanding of what is happening with a micro-benchmark and the JIT compiler, a HotSpot debug VM can be used. A HotSpot debug VM has additional instrumentation enabled within it so more can be learned about what the JVM is doing as it is executing a program.

Tip

HotSpot debug VMs with support for Java 6 and later can be downloaded from the OpenJDK open source project on java.net at https://openjdk.dev.java.net.

With a HotSpot debug VM, additional information about the optimizations and decisions made by the JIT compiler can be observed. For example, with a HotSpot debug VM a micro-benchmark executed with the `-XX:+PrintInlining` command line option reports which methods have been inlined. Executing this micro-benchmark with a HotSpot debug VM using `-XX:+PrintInlining`, as shown in the following example, indicates `String.equals(String s)` is not inlined since the `String.equals(String s)` method is too large.

```
- @ 2    java.lang.String::equals (88 bytes)  callee is too large
  @ 16   SimpleExample::equalsTest (8 bytes)
- @ 2    java.lang.String::equals (88 bytes)  callee is too large
```

The output suggests that increasing the inlining size could result in the `String.equals(Object o)` being inlined since the output says 88 bytes of byte code from `String.equals(Object o)` is too large to be inlined. The following output shows the effect of increasing the inlining size to 100 bytes of bytecode using the HotSpot command line option `-XX:MaxInlineSize=100` to inline the `String.equals(Object o)` method. The micro-benchmark reported results change rather dramatically as illustrated in the following example.

```
Warming up ...
   1        java.lang.String::hashCode (60 bytes)
   2        java.lang.String::charAt (33 bytes)
   3        java.lang.String::equals (88 bytes)
   4        SimpleExample::equalsTest (8 bytes)
   1%       SimpleExample::doTest @ 7 (39 bytes)
1st warm up done.
Elapsed time in ms -> 21
Iterations / ms ----> 476190
   5        SimpleExample::doTest (39 bytes)
2nd warm up done.
   6        java.lang.String::indexOf (151 bytes)
Elapsed time in ms -> 18
Iterations / ms ----> 555555
Test complete.
Elapsed time in ms -> 8768
Iterations / ms ----> 570255
```

The output again reports the same methods are JIT compiled. But comparing the elapsed time reported to execute the warm-up periods and measurement
interval to the time reported to execute the warm-up periods and measurement
interval when -XX:MaxInlineSize=100 is not specified is quite different. For
example, previously 96, 95, and 42,870 milliseconds were reported, respectively.
But after specifying -XX:MaxInlineSize=100, reported elapsed times dropped
to 21, 18, and 8,768 milliseconds, respectively. What happened? Can inlining possibly increase the performance of a method that much? The HotSpot debug VM
can be used to confirm the String.equals(Object o) method is inlined when
-XX:MaxInlineSize=100 is added by using -XX:+PrintInlining and executing
the micro-benchmark. The following output confirms the String.equals(Object o)
method is indeed inlined, which was not inlined in a previous run when not explicitly
setting -XX:MaxInlineSize=100.

```
@ 2    java.lang.String::equals (88 bytes)
@ 16   SimpleExample::equalsTest (8 bytes)
 @ 2    java.lang.String::equals (88 bytes)
```

Based on the reported elapsed time and iterations per millisecond, the micro-
benchmark is now starting to look like a candidate for a modern VM JIT compiler identifying dead code and eliminating it as an optimization, similar to
what was discussed in the "Optimizing Away Dead Code" section earlier in
this chapter. Setting the inlined size so that String.equals(Object o)
was inlined resulted in the JIT compiler identifying dead code in the micro-
benchmark and optimizing it away. Capturing a profile of both configurations,
one using -XX:MaxInlineSize=100 and one without, using a profiler such

as Oracle Solaris Studio Performance Analyzer where the generated assembly code can be viewed, can show that the HotSpot Client JIT compiler will indeed identify dead code and optimize away the call to `String.equals(Object o)`. For tips on how to capture a profile and view assembly language instructions generated by the HotSpot JIT compilers with Oracle Solaris Studio Performance Analyzer, see Chapter 5, "Java Application Profiling," and Chapter 6, "Java Application Profiling Tips and Tricks." The generated assembly code can also be viewed using a HotSpot debug VM and adding the HotSpot `-XX:+PrintOptoAssembly` command line option. The generated assembly code is printed as standard output by default and can be saved to a file by redirecting standard output to a file.

If the same micro-benchmark is executed in a HotSpot Server VM, the reported performance will be similar to that seen by the HotSpot Client VM when explicitly setting `-XX:MaxInlineSize=100`. The HotSpot Server VM's JIT compiler in its default configuration will inline and identify dead code in this micro-benchmark since its uses more aggressive inlining policies. This does not imply you should always use the HotSpot Server VM or go through an exercise of collecting inlining data from a debug HotSpot VM and then trying to set `-XX:MaxInlineSize` to an optimal size for your application. Both the HotSpot Server VM and HotSpot Client VM have undergone rigorous performance testing of a large number of benchmarks and workloads. It is only after careful analysis of the performance data has the default inlining size been chosen.

Obviously the micro-benchmark presented in this section would require some modifications to more accurately measure the performance of a `String.equals(Object o)` operation where the object being compared is the same `String` as those modifications described earlier in the "Optimizing Away Dead Code" section. But that is not the intent of this section. Rather, the purpose of this section is to illustrate the potential effect inlining can have on the observed results of a micro-benchmark. Using a HotSpot debug VM to observe inlining decisions made by HotSpot can help avoid some of the pitfalls that may occur as a result of inlining decisions made by the HotSpot JIT compiler. Additionally, capturing profiles with Oracle Solaris Studio Performance Analyzer and viewing the generated assembly code can help identify whether the JIT compiler is identifying dead code and optimizing away that dead code.

When developing a micro-benchmark to model the behavior of a larger benchmark or application, be aware of the potential impact inlining can have on the results of a micro-benchmark implementation. If a micro-benchmark does not sufficiently model a target operation of interest, where methods in the micro-benchmark may or may not get inlined in a similar way as they would in a target application can lead to some misleading conclusions.

Deoptimization

JIT compilers are widely known for their capability to perform optimizations. But there are situations when JIT compilers perform deoptimizations. For example, once a Java application starts running, methods become hot; the JIT compiler makes optimization decisions based on what it has learned from the executing program. Sometimes the optimization decisions may turn out to be incorrect. When the JIT compiler notices it has made an incorrect decision in a previous optimization, the JIT compiler performs a deoptimization. Often, a JIT compiler deoptimization will, a short time later, be followed by a reoptimization once a number of execution times threshold has been reached. The mere fact that deoptimizations occur suggests that such an event could happen while executing a benchmark or micro-benchmark. Not recognizing that a deoptimization event has occurred may result in an incorrect performance conclusion. In this section an example is provided in which initial optimizations made by a HotSpot Server JIT compiler are followed by deoptimizations and reoptimizations.

The following is a declaration for a Shape interface, which has one method called area(). Below the Shape interface are class declarations for Square, Rectangle, and RightTriangle, which implement the Shape interface.

```java
// Shape interface
public interface Shape {
    public double area();
}

// Square class
public class Square implements Shape {

    final private double side;

    public Square(double side) {
        this.side = side;
    }

    private Square(){side = 0;}

    public double area() {
        return side * side;
    }
}

// Rectangle class
public class Rectangle implements Shape {

    final private double length, width;

    public Rectangle(double length, double width) {
        this.length = length;
        this.width = width;
    }
```

```
        private Rectangle(){length = width = 0;}

        public double area() {
            return length * width;
        }
    }

// RightTriangle class
public class RightTriangle implements Shape {

    final private double base, height;

    public RightTriangle(double base, double height) {
        this.base = base;
        this.height = height;
    }

    private RightTriangle(){base = height = 0;}

    public double area() {
        return .5 * base * height;
    }
}
```

Consider the following micro-benchmark implementation, which has the objective to compare the time it takes to calculate the area for each of the Shapes: Square, Rectangle, and RightTriangle.

```
public class Area {
    final static long ITERATIONS = 5000000000L;
    final static long NANOS_PER_MS = (1000L * 1000L);
    final static StringBuilder sb = new StringBuilder();

    private static void printStats(String s, long n,
                                   long elapsedTime){
        float millis = elapsedTime / NANOS_PER_MS;
        float rate = 0;
        if (millis != 0) {
            rate = n / millis;
        }
        System.out.println(s + ": Elapsed time in ms -> " + millis);
        System.out.println(s + ": Iterations per ms --> " + rate);
    }

    private static long doTest(String str, Shape s, long n) {
        double area = 0;
        long start = System.nanoTime();
        for (long i = 0; i < n; i++) {
            area = s.area();
        }
        long elapsedTime = System.nanoTime() - start;
        sb.append(str).append(area);
```

Continued

```
            System.out.println(sb.toString());
            sb.setLength(0);
            return elapsedTime;
    }

    public static void main(String[] args) {
        String areaStr = "     Area: ";
        Shape s = new Square(25.33);
        Shape r = new Rectangle(20.75, 30.25);
        Shape rt = new RightTriangle(20.50, 30.25);

        System.out.println("Warming up ...");
        long elapsedTime = doTest(areaStr, s, ITERATIONS);
        printStats("     Square", ITERATIONS, elapsedTime);
        elapsedTime = doTest(areaStr, r, ITERATIONS);
        printStats("     Rectangle", ITERATIONS, elapsedTime);
        elapsedTime = doTest(areaStr, rt, ITERATIONS);
        printStats("     Right Triangle", ITERATIONS, elapsedTime);
        System.out.println("1st warmup done.");

        System.out.println("Starting 2nd warmup ...");
        elapsedTime = doTest(areaStr, s, ITERATIONS);
        printStats("     Square", ITERATIONS, elapsedTime);
        elapsedTime = doTest(areaStr, r, ITERATIONS);
        printStats("     Rectangle", ITERATIONS, elapsedTime);
        elapsedTime = doTest(areaStr, rt, ITERATIONS);
        printStats("     Right Triangle", ITERATIONS, elapsedTime);
        System.out.println("2nd warmup done.");

        System.out.println("Starting measurement intervals ...");
        elapsedTime = doTest(areaStr, s, ITERATIONS);
        printStats("     Square", ITERATIONS, elapsedTime);
        elapsedTime = doTest(areaStr, r, ITERATIONS);
        printStats("     Rectangle", ITERATIONS, elapsedTime);
        elapsedTime = doTest(areaStr, rt, ITERATIONS);
        printStats("     Right Triangle", ITERATIONS, elapsedTime);
        System.out.println("Measurement intervals done.");
    }
}
```

This implementation uses two warm-up periods along with a measurement interval for calculating the area of a Square, Rectangle, and RightTriangle. Both elapsed time in milliseconds and the number of iterations per millisecond are reported in each interval. As shown in the following output, executing this micro-benchmark with Java 6 HotSpot Server VM produces some surprising results. When comparing the elapsed time and iterations per millisecond between the first warm-up period and the second warm-up period, the performance of calculating a Square's area has decreased by about 29%. Additionally, comparing the elapsed time and iterations per millisecond between the first warm-up period and the measurement interval also shows a decrease of about 29%.

```
Warming up ...
    Area: 641.6089
    Square: Elapsed time in ms -> 11196
    Square: Iterations per ms --> 446588
    Area: 627.6875
    Rectangle: Elapsed time in ms -> 17602
    Rectangle: Iterations per ms --> 284058
    Area: 310.0625
    Right Triangle: Elapsed time in ms -> 33894
    Right Triangle: Iterations per ms --> 147518
1st warmup done.
Starting 2nd warmup ...
    Area: 641.6089
    Square: Elapsed time in ms -> 15766
    Square: Iterations per ms --> 317138
    Area: 627.6875
    Rectangle: Elapsed time in ms -> 17679
    Rectangle: Iterations per ms --> 282821
    Area: 310.0625
    Right Triangle: Elapsed time in ms -> 33339
    Right Triangle: Iterations per ms --> 149974
2nd warmup done.
Starting measurement intervals ...
    Area: 641.6089
    Square: Elapsed time in ms -> 15750
    Square: Iterations per ms --> 317460
    Area: 627.6875
    Rectangle: Elapsed time in ms -> 17595
    Rectangle: Iterations per ms --> 284171
    Area: 310.0625
    Right Triangle: Elapsed time in ms -> 33477
    Right Triangle: Iterations per ms --> 149356
Measurement intervals done.
```

The observed decrease in performance is the result of the JIT compiler making some initial optimization decisions that later turned out to be incorrect. For example, there are optimizations a modern JIT compiler can make when it observes only one class implementing an interface. When executing this micro-benchmark, the JIT compiler first performed an aggressive optimization thinking only `Square` implemented the `Shape` interface. As the micro-benchmark began calculating the area for the `Rectangle`, the JIT compiler had to undo the aggressive optimization it performed previously when calculating the `Square`'s area. As a result, a deoptimization occurred and a subsequent reoptimization was performed. Being able to identify whether deoptimizations are occurring can be identified using `-XX:+PrintCompilation`. When `-XX:+PrintCompilation` output contains the text "made not entrant," it is an indication a previous compilation optimization is being discarded and the method executes in the interpreter until it is executed enough times to trigger a recompilation.

The following output is from executing the `Area` micro-benchmark with a Java 6 HotSpot Server VM with `-XX:+PrintCompilation`.

```
Warming up ...
   1         com.sun.example.Square::area (10 bytes)
   1%        Area::doTest @ 11 (78 bytes)
     Area: 641.6089
     Square: Elapsed time in ms -> 11196
     Square: Iterations per ms --> 446588
   2         Area::doTest (78 bytes)
   1%  made not entrant  Area::doTest @ 11 (78 bytes)
   2%        Area::doTest @ 11 (78 bytes)
   3         com.sun.example.Rectangle::area (10 bytes)
     Area: 627.6875
     Rectangle: Elapsed time in ms -> 17602
     Rectangle: Iterations per ms --> 284058
   2   made not entrant  Area::doTest (78 bytes)
   4         com.sun.example.RightTriangle::area (14 bytes)
     Area: 310.0625
     Right Triangle: Elapsed time in ms -> 33894
     Right Triangle: Iterations per ms --> 147518
1st warmup done.
Starting 2nd warmup ...
     Area: 641.6089
     Square: Elapsed time in ms -> 15766
     Square: Iterations per ms --> 317138
     Area: 627.6875
     Rectangle: Elapsed time in ms -> 17679
     Rectangle: Iterations per ms --> 282821
     Area: 310.0625
     Right Triangle: Elapsed time in ms -> 33339
     Right Triangle: Iterations per ms --> 149974
2nd warmup done.
Starting measurement intervals ...
     Area: 641.6089
     Square: Elapsed time in ms -> 15750
     Square: Iterations per ms --> 317460
     Area: 627.6875
     Rectangle: Elapsed time in ms -> 17595
     Rectangle: Iterations per ms --> 284171
     Area: 310.0625
     Right Triangle: Elapsed time in ms -> 33477
     Right Triangle: Iterations per ms --> 149356
Measurement intervals done.
```

Several deoptimizations occurred during the execution of the Area micro-benchmark. The preceding output indicates the deoptimizations are an artifact of the three virtual call sites for Shape.area() of which Square, Rectangle, and RightTriangle implement coupled with the way this micro-benchmark is written. Although deoptimizations are possible with virtual call sites, what is shown in this example is not intended to suggest to software developers to avoid writing software that utilizes interfaces and multiple classes implementing that interface. The intent is to illustrate a pitfall that can occur with the creation of micro-benchmarks and show it is difficult to know what the JIT compiler is doing as it attempts to improve the performance of an application.

> **Tip**
>
> Software developers should concentrate their efforts on good software architecture, design, and implementation and not worry about trying to outsmart a modern JIT compiler. If a change to a software architecture, design, or implementation is needed to overcome some artifact of a JIT compiler, it should be considered a bug or deficiency of the JIT compiler.

An improvement to the implementation of this micro-benchmark would be to call each `area()` method of `Square`, `Rectangle`, and `RightTriangle` one right after the other in the warm-up intervals rather than attempting to warm up each `Shape`'s `area()` individually. This allows the JIT compiler to see all three implementations of the `Shape.area()` interface prior to making aggressive optimization decisions.

Micro-benchmark Creation Tips

Creating Java micro-benchmarks can be difficult to create or model what you intend to performance measure as a result of the optimizations performed by JIT compilers. Many optimizations are performed by the JIT compiler, many more than the several presented in this chapter. In fact, an entire book could be dedicated to the subject. Additionally, not only the type of optimization but also when the optimization is made transparent to most stakeholders of a Java application. While this is a nice attribute, or feature of a JIT compiler, it can greatly complicate the creation of effective micro-benchmarks to truly measure what they intend to measure. However, some general guidelines and principles can help avoid some of the common pitfalls in writing micro-benchmarks. Following is a list of guidelines.

1. Identify exactly what you want to know and design an experiment to answer what you want to know. Do not get distracted with artifacts that are not important to what you really want to know.

2. Make sure the work being done in the measurement interval is always the same constant amount of work.

3. Compute and report multiple metrics such as elapsed time, iterations per unit of time, or unit of time per iteration. Report these metrics after warm-up period(s) and after the measurement interval.

   Be aware of the accuracy and granularity of how time is measured, especially when using `System.currentTimeMillis()` and `System.nanoTime()`.

   Execute multiple runs varying the amount of cycles or duration of the measurement interval. Then compare the elapsed time metrics and pay close attention to the iterations per unit of time or unit of time per iteration metric.

The latter metric should be nearly the same as the duration of measurement interval is changed so long as the benchmark has reached steady state and has been sufficiently warmed up.

4. Make sure the micro-benchmark has reached steady state prior to the measurement interval. A general guideline to follow is to ensure the micro-benchmark has been running for at least 10 seconds. Use of HotSpot's `-XX:+PrintCompilation` can help confirm the benchmark has reached steady state along with inserting instrumentation that indicates the execution phase of the micro-benchmark. The goal is to have the micro-benchmark fully warmed prior to the measurement interval and that further optimizations or deoptimizations are not occurring during the measurement interval.

5. Run multiple iterations of the benchmark to ensure the observed results are repeatable. Running multiple iterations can provide additional confidence to your findings.

6. As you execute the experiments and observe results, question whether the results make sense. If the results are unexpected or suspicious, investigate or revisit the design of the experiment to validate the observed results.

7. Avoid creating dead code in the micro-benchmark by making computations nontrivial, passing arguments that change on occasion to methods of interest, returning results from a method of interest, and printing computation results outside the measurement interval.

8. Be aware of the effect inlining may have on the micro-benchmark. If suspicious of the observed results, use a HotSpot debug VM to observe the inlining decisions made by a HotSpot JIT compiler and use the `-XX:+PrintInlining` and `-XX:+PrintCompilation` command line options.

9. Make sure other applications are not intruding on the system when executing the micro-benchmark. Small or simple applications added to a desktop window manager such as a weather applet or stock ticker can intrude on the system while executing a micro-benchmark.

10. When wanting to know exactly what the JIT compiler is generating for optimized code, use Oracle Solaris Studio Performance Analyzer or a HotSpot debug VM along with `-XX:+PrintOptoAssembly` to view the generated assembly code.

11. Micro-benchmarks with small data sets or data structures can become cache sensitive. The micro-benchmark may report results that vary from run to run or vary from machine to machine.

12. For micro-benchmarks that utilize multiple threads, realize that thread scheduling may not be deterministic, especially under heavy load.

Design of Experiments

Designing an experiment to observe, quantify, or evaluate performance is a critical step in performance testing and developing benchmarks. It is also a step often overlooked or a step in which insufficient time is spent. The design of an experiment determines what claims or inferences about performance will be able to be made. An incorrect or incomplete design may fail to provide answers to the question or questions initially set forth.

The design of an experiment must clearly state the question to be answered. For example, a potential question might initially begin as being able to identify whether a given benchmark could realize a performance improvement from increasing the size of the HotSpot VM young generation heap space by 100 megabytes. But that question is incomplete. For example, what constitutes a performance improvement? Is any observable increase regardless of magnitude the question to be answered? Is it important to know, or be able to estimate, the magnitude of the improvement? How much of an improvement is important to the stakeholders? Is an improvement of 1% or greater considered to be important? Is 5% or greater considered to be important? Is there any concern about measuring a potential regression? Or, is it sufficient to know there is an improvement and not a regression? Being able to identify an improvement is a different question from being able to identify a regression or alternatively being able to identify both an improvement or a regression.

Hence, it is important when stating the question to be answered by an experiment, to quantify in some manner what is considered important. Continuing to use the example of increasing the size of the young generation space on a HotSpot VM by 100 megabytes, the question to be answered might be rephrased as, Does increasing the young generation heap space on a HotSpot VM version 1.6.0-b105 by 100 megabytes improve the score of the SPECjbb2005 benchmark by at least 1% or more on an Oracle X4450 system configured with two dual-core Intel Xeon 7200 processors and 16G of PC205300 667 MHz ECC fully buffered DDR2 DIMMs running Oracle Solaris 10 x64 update 4.

> **Tip**
>
> The more explicit the problem statement, the easier it is to construct a hypothesis, build an experiment to test the hypothesis, and be able to draw good conclusions toward answering the questions in the problem statement.

Once the problem statement is clearly stated, the next step of formulating a hypothesis that provides an answer to the problem statement can begin. Formulating a good hypothesis is important to the ability to make inferences about findings. For example, using the example problem statement, a possible hypothesis would be, Is the improvement from making this change at least 1%. The first step might be to execute a version of the SPECjbb2005 benchmark using a baseline young generation heap space configuration. Then execute a version of the SPECjbb2005 benchmark only changing the baseline young generation space configuration by increasing that value by 100 megabytes. Then compute the difference between the observed scores for the baseline configuration versus a specimen that increased the young generation heap space by 100 megabytes. If the observed difference happens to be greater than or equal to 1% of the baseline score, then the hypothesis would be considered true. Otherwise, the hypothesis would be considered false. Contrast this example hypothesis with a problem statement and hypothesis that wants to know if there is an improvement regardless of the magnitude in the SPECjbb2005 score by increasing the size of the young generation space by 100 megabytes. The hypothesis for this latter problem statement could be taking the difference between observed scores. Then if the difference is greater than 0, the hypothesis would be considered true; otherwise, it would be considered false. Consider the likelihood for each of these two hypotheses of incorrectly accepting a given hypothesis as true when indeed it is false. Additionally, consider the likelihood of rejecting a given hypothesis as false when it indeed is true. Considering the number of outcomes that may render a difference in scores being greater than 0, and the number of outcomes with differences in scores greater than or equal to 1%, it should be obvious the population of differences in scores being greater than or equal to 1% is much smaller than the population of differences in scores being greater than 0. Hence, the probability of drawing the right conclusion greatly depends on the problem statement and the hypothesis. This illustrates the importance of quantifying the performance improvement that is considered to be important in the problem statement.

To improve confidence in the inferences or conclusions being drawn from an experiment, statistical methods can be used.

Use of Statistical Methods

Statistical methods incorporate the mathematical science of statistics as a means (no pun intended) to help design an experiment around the question(s) to be answered and arrive at conclusions or make inferences about the data collected. In the context of benchmarking, applying or using statistical methods is a way to strengthen the design of an experiment and subsequently add a level of confidence to the inferences or conclusions drawn from an experiment.

It is important to keep in mind that in some experiments statistical methods are not required to convince stakeholders of a conclusion or an outcome of an experiment. In other situations statistical methods may help in gaining confidence in drawing conclusions from an experiment. Note, however, that using statistical methods will not provide the ability to prove a hypothesis is absolutely true. Rather statistical methods help in quantifying to a certain level of confidence, a probability, that a given hypothesis is true.

This section provides general advice the authors believe is beneficial when using statistical methods in performance testing Java applications. The intent is not to present an in-depth discussion of statistical methods or cover all the details of statistical analysis. Statistics textbooks may use as many as three, four, or more chapters to cover the statistics material found in this section.

Compute an Average

One of the challenges with performance testing and performance tuning is being able to identify if a change of some kind somewhere in an application—whether at the application level, JVM level, operating system level, or hardware level—results in a performance improvement or regression. To help identify performance improvements or regressions, performance engineers often execute benchmarks multiple times and compute an average of the metric of interest for both a baseline (prior to any change) and a specimen (after a change). The average, also called a *mean* and denoted as $\bar{x}$ can be calculated using the following formula:

$$\overline{X} = \frac{1}{n} \cdot \sum_{i=1}^{n} X_i$$

Hence, the average for the baseline is the sum of all observations from executing the baseline divided by the number of baseline executions. Likewise, the average for the specimen is the sum of all observations from executing the specimen divided by the number of specimen executions. Once the average has been calculated for a baseline and specimen, a difference between the baseline average and specimen average can be computed to estimate the difference between baseline and specimen. The resulting value from a difference between two averages is also known as the difference in means.

Compute a Standard Deviation

In addition to computing an average for a baseline and specimen, a measure of a baseline or specimen's variability can be evaluated by computing a sample standard deviation. The sample standard deviation can be calculated using the following formula where s is the sample standard deviation, n is the number of observations in the sample, x is the ith observation, and $\bar{x}$ is the average.

$$s = \sqrt{\frac{1}{n-1} \sum_{i=1}^{n} (X_i - \overline{X})^2}$$

The magnitude of the sample standard deviation provides a quantifiable measure of the variability between scores reported for a baseline or specimen in the same units of measure as the observations and average.

Calculate a Confidence Interval

With a sample standard deviation and an average, an estimate can be made as to a baseline's or specimen's true average within a range to a certain probability or level of confidence, called a confidence interval. The higher the confidence level for a given sample standard deviation and average, the wider the confidence interval, or range of values for estimating the true average. Likewise, the lower the confidence level the narrower the confidence interval. This should be intuitive since an increase in the level of confidence necessitates a wider range of values to deal with the increased probability the true average lies within a given range. Another strategy that can narrow a confidence interval or increase the level of confidence in estimating a range of values for the true average is to increase the number of observations or runs of the experiment. It stands to reason that by increasing the number of observations in an experiment, more information is gathered about what is being measured, and as a result additional confidence in the estimate of the true average for a baseline or specimen is realized. Looking at the equation for computing an average, sample standard deviation and confidence interval also provide evidence that increasing the number of observations can narrow the width of a confidence interval.

> **Tip**
>
> Regardless of the statistical method chosen, the larger the sample size or number of observations, more information will be provided to the experiment and analysis.

The level of confidence chosen is a decision left to the stakeholders or designer of an experiment. Most statisticians choose confidence levels at 90%, 95%, or 99%. It should be noted that no one confidence level is necessarily right or wrong.

A confidence interval estimating the true average is calculated using the following formula where: $\bar{x}$ is the average, s is the sample standard deviation, n is the sample size, $t_{\alpha/2}$ is the t-value for $n - 1$ degrees of freedom for a given α, which is $1 - $ confidence level chosen (i.e., 95%).

$$\overline{X} \pm t_{\frac{\alpha}{2}} \cdot \left(\frac{s}{\sqrt{n}} \right)$$

> **Tip**
>
> Tables containing t-values for samples sizes at different α levels can be found in statistics textbooks and on the Internet.

Another possible approach using statistical methods to add confidence in identifying performance improvements or regressions is to compare the confidence intervals that estimate the true average for a baseline and specimen. If there is no overlap between the confidence intervals, then an appropriate conclusion would be to claim there is indeed a difference in performance between the baseline and specimen at the specified level of confidence. Being able to estimate the magnitude of the difference between a baseline and specimen average requires calculating a confidence interval on the difference of means between the baseline and specimen.

A confidence interval for estimating the true difference in means of a baseline and specimen can be calculated using the following formula where $\overline{X}_1$ is the average for sample 1, $\overline{X}_2$ is the average for sample 2, s is the pooled sample standard deviation of sample 1 and sample 2, n_1 is the sample size of sample 1, n_2 is the sample size of sample 2, $t_{\frac{\alpha}{2}}$ is the t-value for $n_1 + n_2 - 2$ degrees of freedom for a given α, which is $1 -$ confidence level chosen (i.e., 95%).

$$(\overline{X}_1 - \overline{X}_2) \pm t_{\frac{\alpha}{2}} \cdot s \cdot \sqrt{\frac{1}{n_1} + \frac{1}{n_2}}$$

As mentioned earlier, s in the preceding formula is a pooled standard deviation of sample 1 and sample 2's standard deviations. The pooled standard deviation is defined:

$$s = \sqrt{\frac{(n_1 - 1) \cdot s_1^2 + (n_2 - 1) \cdot s_2^2}{(n_1 + n_2 - 2)}}$$

s_1 and s_2 are the sample standard deviations for sample 1 and sample 2. n_1 and n_2 are the sample sizes for sample 1 and sample 2.

A confidence interval on the true difference of means communicates to a given level of confidence that the true difference between baseline and specimen is within a range of values calculated by the confidence interval. Keep in mind that it may not be important to the stakeholders to have an estimate for the true difference in performance. The stakeholders may only be interested in knowing whether there is sufficient evidence to infer there is a difference in mean performance equal to or greater than some number or value, not an estimate of the true mean difference. The criteria of whether estimating the magnitude of the true difference, or whether a difference of some value or greater exists is important, should be specified earlier in the design of the experiment.

Use of Hypothesis Tests

Another statistical methods approach is to use hypothesis testing such as a t-test to compare results between a baseline to specimen. In this approach, a hypothesis, more formally known as a null hypothesis, is formulated based on a problem statement, that is, what you want to know. Then data is collected and a t-statistic is calculated based on the collected observations. The t-statistic is compared to a value obtained from a Student's t-distribution for an α (alpha) and degrees of freedom. α is the risk level at which you are willing to incorrectly accept the null hypothesis as true when it is really false, also known in statistical terms as a Type I Error. One of the most common α levels chosen by statisticians is 0.05. Other common α levels chosen are

0.10 and 0.01. The degrees of freedom when comparing a baseline to specimen is the total number of observations in both samples − 2 since the t-statistic calculation uses observations from both the baseline and specimen. To illustrate this approach with an example, suppose you want to know if increasing the JVM maximum heap size from 1500 megabytes to 1800 megabytes increases the number of messages per second an application is processing by at least 1%. A possible hypothesis in this example could be whether the difference in means between a baseline (a configuration that uses a JVM maximum heap size of 1500 megabytes) and a specimen (a configuration that uses a JVM maximum heap size of 1800 megabytes) is greater than 1% of the baseline messages per second throughput.

> **Tip**
>
> When forming a null hypothesis it is generally a poor decision to test for no difference in means or that a baseline and specimen are equal. Most statistical methods are designed to test that the difference between means is significantly different than what is observed by chance. Claiming there is no difference between a baseline and specimen is different from claiming there is insufficient information to conclude or infer a difference exists. In short, statistically it is difficult to show there is no difference in means.

Once a null hypothesis is specified, a number of samples should be collected running the same workload as a baseline and specimen. Then the baseline and specimen averages, standard deviations, and difference of means should be calculated along with calculating t using the following formula.

$$t = \frac{\overline{X}_1 - \overline{X}_2}{S_{\overline{X}_1 - \overline{X}_2}} \; where \; S_{\overline{X}_1 - \overline{X}_2} = \sqrt{\frac{(n_1 - 1) \cdot s_1^2 + (n_2 - 1) \cdot s_2^2}{(n_1 + n_2 - 2)} \cdot \left(\frac{1}{n_1} + \frac{1}{n_2}\right)}$$

In the preceding formula, $\overline{X}_1$ and $\overline{X}_2$ are the averages for sample 1 and sample 2, s_1 and s_2 are the sample standard deviations for sample 1 and sample 2, and n_1 and n_2 are the sample sizes for sample 1 and sample 2.

Using a t-table, found in many statistics textbooks or on the Internet, locate the t-value in the t-table for the degrees of freedom (total number of observations in the two samples − 2) for an α of 0.05. You can alternatively choose a different α or risk level that you and your experiment's stakeholders are willing to accept such as 0.01. If the calculated t using the preceding formula is greater than the t-value found in the t-table, then you can conclude to $1 - \alpha$ confidence there is a difference of at least 1% or more improvement in the messages per second throughput by increasing the JVM maximum heap size from 1500 megabytes to 1800 megabytes.

Continuing with the previous example, suppose you have selected an α of 0.05 for this experiment and have collected a total of 20 observations, 10 baseline observations, and 10 specimen observations, along with calculating a t at 3.44 using the preceding formula. The t-value in a t-table for an α of 0.05 and 18 degrees of freedom (20 observations − 2) is 1.734. Since the calculated t-statistic of 3.44 is greater than the t-value found in the t-table for an α of 0.05, you can conclude there is at least a 1% improvement in the message throughput by increasing the JVM maximum heap size from 1500 megabytes to 1800 megabytes. In a situation where you find that the calculated t is less than or equal to the t-value found in the t-table, there are two possible explanations. Either there is indeed not a 1% improvement in the message throughput, or you do not have enough information to claim an improvement of 1% or more. The latter possibility is also known in statistical terms as a Type II Error. The contributing factors to experiencing a Type II Error are high variability in the observations and a small number of observations. An experiment having a large number of observations and small variability is less likely to experience a Type II Error. Another important note, if the hypothesis of this example was slightly different such that you wanted to know if there was an improvement or a regression of 1% or more, not just an improvement of 1% or more, the t-table lookup would use 0.025, one-half the 0.05 α level in the table lookup rather than 0.05 since the hypothesis reflects either an improvement or a regression. In other words, the hypothesis requires what is called a two-tailed test. A one-tailed test is what you use when you want to know only about either an improvement or regression exclusively.

Software packages and software libraries, such as Apache Commons, can perform statistical calculations including the ability to report a p-value based on a set of observations. A p-value is the probability of rejecting a null hypothesis when the null hypothesis is in fact true. As mentioned earlier, a null hypothesis is formulated based on what you want to learn from your experiment or problem statement. In statistical terms, the p-value represents the probability of making what is called a Type I Error. A Type I Error is an outcome where the null hypothesis is accepted as true when it is indeed false. The quantity 1 − p-value is the probability of accepting the null hypothesis as true if the null hypothesis is in fact true. To illustrate the concepts with an example, suppose the calculated p-value is .03. The probability of making a Type I Error is .03. In other words, there is a 3% chance that the null hypothesis is accepted as true when it is indeed false. In addition, there is a 97% (1 − the p-value) chance, or you are 97% confident that there exists at least a 1% or greater improvement in the messages per second throughput performance of the application as a result of increasing the maximum Java heap size from 1500 megabytes to 1800 megabytes.

Tip

It is important to realize that you cannot claim or make the inference that you are 97% confident that the magnitude of the performance improvement is the calculated difference in means. This is not the hypothesis tested. Rather, the hypothesis tested is whether there was an improvement of at least 1% or more in the message throughput. In other words, a magnitude of 1% or more is what was tested, not the magnitude of the difference in means. An estimate of the true mean difference, if desired, could be calculated using a confidence interval as described earlier in this section.

When using statistical software packages and software libraries it is a good practice to double-check the reported values with calculations done by hand. Often software packages and software libraries have multiple or similar statistics routines that can lead to confusion in deciding which routine is appropriate for your analysis. Additionally, some software packages or libraries provide routines for one-tailed tests only. You may have to adjust the α given to these routines based on what the software is assuming, one- or two-tailed tests.

Tips for Using Statistical Methods

It is important to recognize the presence of any of the following: small sample sizes, high variability within samples, the desire to observe a small magnitude of an improvement or regression, and using a small α, impacts the ability to show there is indeed statistical significant evidence to claim an improvement or regression exists, or that no improvement or regression exists. In other words, the smaller sample size, the higher the variability, the smaller the magnitude of an improvement or regression you deem as important, or the higher the desired confidence level in the experiment's outcome, the more likely it is you will arrive at a conclusion that there is not sufficient information to claim there is a statistically significant conclusion. Likewise, the larger the sample size, the smaller the variability within the samples, the larger the magnitude of the improvement or regression you deem as important, or the lower the confidence level that a performance improvement or regression exists, the more likely it is you will be able to claim a statistically significant conclusion.

The following list offers additional advice when using statistical methods:

1. Realize that using statistical methods gives you the ability to quantify your findings to some level of confidence. Statistical methods will not provide 100% proof that a hypothesis is true or a hypothesis is false.

2. Make sure you clearly define what you want to learn. This helps in choosing an appropriate statistical method and analysis.

3. There is not one specific statistical method or analysis that will always be the best for every experiment. Often multiple analyses or methods can render the same conclusion. Do not get too hung up on the details of the method or analysis. Choose a method that best answers what you want to know.

4. Keep the statistical analysis simple. The more complex the methods and analysis techniques, the more difficult it will be to explain the findings to others who have interest in the results.

5. The larger the sample size or the number of observations, the less likely it is that an incorrect conclusion will be drawn.

6. Ask yourself if the results and conclusions you are arriving at as a result of doing the analysis make sense. If they do not make sense, double-check the

data, confirm what you are seeing is indeed correct, confirm the methods you are using make sense, and validate any assumptions that you may have made. Some adverse or unexpected event may have occurred while executing the experiment and as a result may be leading you to an inaccurate conclusion.

7. Realize some experiments do not require statistical methods to arrive at a proper conclusion. For example, if the purpose of the experiment is to determine whether there is at least a 1% improvement as a result of some change and the observed difference from a single observation of a baseline and specimen is 10%, then statistical methods are probably not necessary to conclude there is at least 1% improvement realized with the change. Keep in mind that if the 10% improvement is suspicious, you should double-check the data, the system configuration, and so on to confirm some adverse event has not occurred. Hence, a second or third execution of both the baseline and specimen may be needed to add sufficient confidence without relying on statistical methods.

Reference

[1] Rosen, Kenneth H. *Discrete Mathematics and Its Applications,* First Edition. Copyright AT&T Information Systems, Inc., publisher McGraw-Hill, Inc., 1988.

Bibliography

Apache Commons. http://commons.apache.org/. The Apache Software Foundation. Forest Hill, MD.

Snedecor, George W., and William G. Cochran. *Statistical Methods, Eighth Edition.* Iowa State University Press, Ames, IA, 1989.

Benchmarking Multitiered Applications

The Java Enterprise Edition (referred to as Java EE hereafter), is a widely used platform for the deployment of distributed multitiered enterprise applications. These applications are often the public face of the business on the Internet and a well-designed, user-friendly online presence is critical to the success of the business. The ability to serve large numbers of concurrent users on a 24×7 basis is a necessity, and any disruption or poor quality of service can lead to permanent loss of customers. Performance, scalability, and reliability considerations should be incorporated into the design and development of enterprise applications so that they can provide a rich user experience.

The performance capability of applications is studied through the use of benchmarks. In this chapter, some of the general principles behind developing benchmarks for multitiered applications are discussed. The first part looks at some of the characteristics of these applications and how benchmarks can be designed to meet the requirements of simulating complex user interactions. The second part deals with performance analysis of applications as well as monitoring and tuning of the Java EE container in which these applications are deployed.

Benchmarking Challenges

Chapter 8, "Benchmarking Java Application," discussed some of the challenges faced while developing Java SE benchmarks. Benchmarking enterprise applications brings a set of additional challenges due to the distributed and complex nature of these applications. Some of the application characteristics that need to be addressed while developing enterprise benchmarks are as follows:

- **Multitiered nature of enterprise applications.** Enterprise applications are often multitiered systems with the presentation tier, application tier, and persistence tier deployed on physically or logically separated systems. The distributed nature of the application makes the benchmark more complex to develop and deploy as well as makes it more difficult to isolate performance bottlenecks. Issues relating to network connectivity between the different components is another factor that needs to be taken into consideration while benchmarking distributed systems.

- **User scaling.** Applications are required to support large numbers of concurrent requests reliably while maintaining the overall quality of service. User demand increases as the business grows, and applications servicing these customers should be capable of meeting the increased user load. The term "user scalability" is used to define the capability of a system to scale up to meet increased user load. It is important to have a clear understanding of how the application behaves to increasing load and also to identify the limits of the application beyond which the performance may degrade substantially. For example, an application that performs well on a database with a small data set may perform poorly as the size of the database increases. Large user scalability studies are difficult to carry out due to the high resource requirements (may require a large number of machines connected on a high speed network) and the time and effort involved.

- **Vertical and horizontal scaling.** Enterprise applications are usually distributed across multiple JVMs and/or hardware nodes. Highly scalable systems are designed in such a way that each tier can scale independently to meet the growing customer demand. The load is balanced to the various systems through the use of hardware or software load balancers. The two main modes of scaling, horizontal and vertical, are characterized by how the application responds to the addition of hardware resources. In vertical scaling, a single instance of the application meets the increased demand by fully utilizing the additional CPU and memory resources provided to it. A horizontally scaled application on the other hand, meets growing customer demand by increasing the number of application instances on an existing system or on additional hardware nodes. Understanding the scalability characteristics of an application is essential and must be an integral part of the performance analysis. As in the case of user scalability studies, large scale horizontal and vertical scalability studies can be expensive due to the high resource requirements. However, in most cases, it is possible to understand the scalability characteristics from a study with a limited number of nodes and extrapolating it to larger clusters of machines.

- **Access by different types of clients.** The applications maybe accessed by a wide variety of clients including cell phones, PDAs, browsers, standalone clients, and Web service clients just to name a few, using a wide variety of communication protocols. Simulating different clients is an important consideration while developing benchmarks, especially if these invocations traverse different code paths. The presence of various types of caches (browser cache, proxy cache, etc.) between the client device and the server makes modeling the access pattern by clients more complex.

- **Secure interactions.** Applications often need to support both secure and nonsecure access. It is important to understand the impact of enabling security to the overall performance of the application. Defining benchmarks with the appropriate mix of secure and nonsecure transactions requires good insight into the application usage pattern, which may not be available in all cases.

- **Session maintenance.** User states maintained as part of the application are sometimes required to be saved into a persistent store to account for loss of data in case of a system failure. Maintaining the shopping cart in a persistent HTTP session is a well-known example of this. Session persistence is an expensive operation and is an important performance characteristic to be studied. Several factors affect the performance of these highly available applications, which increases the complexity of the benchmark.

- **Service availability.** Availability of an application is defined as the percentage of time it is operational and is typically defined in *nines notation*. For example, 2-nines availability corresponds to 99% up time (or a downtime of 8.76 hours/year), and 5-nines availability translates to 99.999% up time (or 5 minutes/year). The service and data availability requirements vary over a wide range depending on how critical the application is. Benchmarking the applications under various scenarios, including the injection of failure conditions, allows estimation of the availability rating of the application. Due to the large number of components often distributed over multiple tiers, obtaining an accurate estimate of the availability of an enterprise application is a complex and difficult task.

- **Difference in payload sizes.** Size of the payload that is processed/transmitted is one of the most important factors that affect the performance of enterprise applications. For similar requests, the response payload size may vary depending on different parameters. For example, a request to get an invoice may result in a small invoice consisting of one line item or one with thousands of line times. It is important that benchmarks are designed in such a way that changes in application behavior can be easily studied for varying payload sizes.

- **Load due to asynchronous requests.** Business applications are often required to handle asynchronous requests (e.g., user requests posted to message queues, asynchronous Web service invocations, etc.) while servicing existing users. Processing these asynchronous requests requires additional system resources, which may affect the response time characteristics of the other user requests. It is important to add simulated asynchronous requests into the benchmark so that the effect of these interactions can be studied.

- **Presence of firewalls.** For security purposes, firewalls are often present between the different tiers and can affect the overall performance. In the initial phase of the performance analysis where the focus may be on identifying performance bottlenecks in the software, performance tests can often be done without the firewalls. It is a good practice to do an evaluation of the performance impact of these systems in a deployed configuration before the system goes live.

- **Dependence on external entities.** Some enterprise applications have to communicate with external entities as part of their request processing. A Web 2.0 mashup that obtains part of its data from an external Web service is an example of this. One challenge faced in the benchmarking of such applications is the lack of predictability of the results due to the dependence of the benchmark on entities outside the benchmark setup. Replacing the external entity with an emulator that is deployed within benchmark setup is often required to address this issue.

It should be noted that for most applications, only a subset of the previously mentioned features is applicable. Since the purpose of the benchmark is to study the application behavior as closely as possible, it is important that the benchmark addresses all relevant aspects of the application.

Enterprise Benchmark Considerations

This section looks at some of the important considerations in the design of an enterprise benchmark. The discussion uses the example of benchmarking a Web application. However, these principles can be applied to the benchmarking of other enterprise applications as well. Performance considerations for designing enterprise applications are not considered here but are discussed in later chapters.

Defining the System Under Test (SUT)

One important aspect to consider is defining the boundaries of the system under test (SUT, commonly pronounced as "sut"). This may seem obvious but is often overlooked. The importance of defining a SUT is to ensure that we are actually measuring what is deemed important. This is especially critical for the benchmarking of one or more components of a multitier application.

> **Tip**
>
> The SUT should include components whose performance is to be measured and exclude external systems that the application depends on but are not part of the performance evaluation. The overall performance of the system as measured by the benchmark should be limited by the performance of one of the components within the SUT and not by any of the external systems.

Take the example of a Web application that accesses data from a database. Depending on the scope of the benchmark, the database may or may not be part of the SUT. If the benchmark is designed to analyze the performance of the Web application including the database interaction, then the database should be considered to be part of the SUT. Under these circumstances, the overall performance of the system may be limited by either the application server or the database.

Alternatively, consider a scenario in which a benchmark is used to compare the performance of an application deployed on application servers from different vendors. Since the purpose of this study is to evaluate the performance of the application server tier, the SUT would consist of only the application server, and the database would be considered external to the SUT. In this case, a valid benchmark result would require the overall performance to be limited by the application server and not by the database. If the database turns out to be the bottleneck, the benchmark should be rerun after tuning the database so that it is not the limiting factor.

Developing Micro-benchmarks

A combination of micro- and macro-benchmarks is often required to study the performance of complex enterprise applications distributed over multiple tiers. The purpose of the micro-benchmark is to evaluate the performance characteristics of a small section of the application while the macro-benchmark is used to analyze the performance of the entire system.

There are several advantages in developing micro-benchmarks that focus on specific user scenarios. They are easy to develop, and their limited scope allows easy identification of performance bottlenecks. It is most effective to develop micro-benchmarks for the most common use cases. However, keep in mind that micro-benchmarks may at times identify false positive bottlenecks. These bottlenecks may be an artifact of the benchmarking process itself (e.g., several concurrent users simultaneously accessing the same Web page leading to lock contention; in the real world scenario, the concurrent access may be limited due to users carrying out different activities), or the overall impact of this issue may be trivial when the whole application is taken into consideration. In other words, the micro-benchmark use case may be a small percentage of all the interactions and may not be significant in the global scope.

> **Tip**
>
> Develop micro-benchmarks for the most common use cases to identify performance bottlenecks. It is a good practice to carry out a thorough evaluation of the impact of the performance problem identified by the micro-benchmark before investing significant resources in analyzing and fixing it.

Micro-benchmarks are the first step in the performance evaluation process. Since these benchmarks typically address only a single interaction at a time, they are not useful in evaluating the overall performance of an application where multiple components interact with each other. A more complex macro-benchmark that evaluates the performance of the entire application in a realistic fashion is required for this. The steps involved in the development of such a macro-benchmark are discussed next.

Defining the User Interaction Model

A macro-benchmark simulates a real world user load, which allows us to understand the performance characteristics of an application. The first step in benchmark development is defining the user interaction model, which describes the paths traversed by the user as he or she uses the application. A Markov chain is often used to simulate user interactions in a realistic fashion.

An easy-to-understand description of Markov chain is provided in Wikipedia as follows:

> Markov chain is a discrete-time stochastic process with the Markov property. Having the Markov property means that, *given the present state,* future states are independent of the past states. In other words, the present state description fully captures all the information that can influence the future evolution of the process. Thus, given the present, the future is conditionally independent of the past. At each time instant the system may change its state from the current state to another state, or remain in the same state, according to a certain probability distribution. The changes of state are called transitions, and the probabilities associated with various state-changes are termed transition probabilities.

It is easier to explain the Markov chain with an example. Figure 9-1 shows the interaction model for a simple online store that supports the browsing of a catalog and purchasing an item. A shopper, who acts as the client in this interaction model, starts by accessing the home page (interaction: home). The shopper then browses

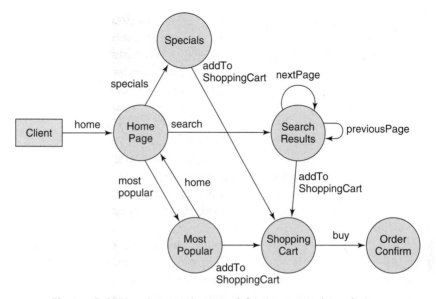

Figure 9-1 User interaction model using a Markov chain

through the specials, visits the most popular items, or searches for an item and browses through the results using the page navigational aids (interactions: next-Page, previousPage). A small set of shoppers continue to shop by adding items into the shopping cart. From the shopping cart page, the shopper may decide to go back to the search results, buy the items, or go back to the home page. Typically, only a small percentage of shoppers add items to the shopping cart and a smaller percentage ultimately buys the product. To fully capture the application usage pattern, an accurate model needs to be constructed. Developing such a model is often a difficult task that requires access pattern analysis, input from business experts, and so on.

A variety of tools are available in the market that can capture the interaction paths. Most of them have the capability to capture the key clicks as a user navigates the Web site, and this can later be replayed to simulate the interaction. JMeter (http://jakarta.apache.org/jmeter/), the Open Source load testing tool from the Apache Software Foundation, is one of the most popular tools in this area. Other options include the use of Live HTTP Headers or Firebug plug-in for Firefox or Developer Tools for Chrome. The main challenge in developing the model is getting an accurate estimate of the state transition probabilities. The task of estimating transition probabilities may be simpler for preexisting applications since it may be possible to glean the user interaction data using Web analytics tools. It is a good practice to define the various transition probabilities as configurable parameters since it will enable easy simulation of different user interaction scenarios.

> **Tip**
>
> The first step in benchmark development is to define the user interaction model. A Markov chain can be used to simulate user interactions in a realistic fashion.

If an application supports different types of clients, Web browsers, RMI and Web service clients, mobile devices, and so on, and the application behavior is different for the different client requests, the model should incorporate the different interactions. As in the case of transition probabilities, it is a good practice to include the proportion of the various client types as configurable parameters. This allows the performance of each client type to be studied in isolation by setting its proportion to 100% and others to 0%.

Browsers/proxies cache scripts, style sheets, and images and different client types need to be taken into account while developing Web benchmarks. Clients that represent visitors who do not have the resources cached need to make subsequent requests to fetch the necessary artifacts, whereas clients that represent visitors with cached content need to fetch only the dynamic content. The load impact of noncached users may be heavier than that of the cached users and hence these two types of users have to be treated differently in the benchmark. Performance results from Yahoo! have shown that roughly half of Yahoo!'s users have an empty cache. To get an accurate proportion for your Web application, some experimentation may be required.

> **Tip**
>
> It is important to incorporate different client access patterns into the benchmark including the presence of browser/proxy caches.

Navigation of any Web site by real users includes delays between subsequent requests, often described as the think time. The think time may vary depending on the resource that is accessed; a user likely spends more time filling out a form than reading a simple page. In an enterprise benchmark, the think time is defined as the elapsed time between the completion of one request and the start of the next request. This delay can either be a fixed value throughout the benchmark or a value calculated based on a probability density function that allows a certain amount of randomness to be injected into the benchmark. For example, the think time could be a randomly selected value from a set of uniformly distributed values between min and max with a mean of $(min + max)/2$. Use of a negative exponential distribution is recommended since it most closely models Web user interaction.

As mentioned, think time is an important parameter for Web users. However, for asynchronous interactions, say, a Web service or JMS client, the rate at which messages are injected into the system, *injection rate,* may be the more important criteria. The performance of asynchronous applications is often defined in terms of the highest injection rate it can support without failures. Injection rate is often described in terms of cycle time as follows:

```
injection rate = 1 / cycle time
```

Cycle time defines the elapsed time between the start of one request and the start of the next one. Cycle time includes the invocation time for a request (amount of time elapsed between the start of the request and the end of the response) plus the delay time (amount of time elapsed between the completion of a response and the start of the next request). Thus the delay time is calculated as the difference between the cycle time and the invocation time and varies depending on the invocation cost. If the invocation time is greater than the cycle time, the client makes the next request without any delay. If the invocation time is consistently higher than the defined cycle time, it is clear that the application is unable to meet the current injection rate and would signify a failure condition for the benchmark. Cycle time thus enables clients to inject requests to the system as close to the desired rate as possible. As in the case of think time, randomness is often injected into the system by varying the delay time according to a predefined probability distribution.

Additional complexities are added to the benchmark if the application has high availability requirements. If service and data availability requirements are specified, the benchmarks should incorporate the injection of one or more failure conditions into the system during the benchmark run. Calculating the availability metric is a complex task and is beyond the scope of this book.

Applications often use HTTP sessions or stateful session beans to maintain user data for an active session. In a typical case, this session information is stored in memory and would be lost if the JVM is terminated. However, most applications and Web servers, including GlassFish Server Open Source Edition (also referred to as GlassFish hereafter) provide a high availability feature in which these sessions are saved in persistent storage to ensure that the user data stored in sessions is not lost in case of a server crash. Several factors affect the performance of session persistence (described in Chapter 10, "Web Application Performance"), and they should be taken into account while developing benchmarks for high availability applications.

> **Tip**
>
> Benchmarks that measure session persistence performance should take into account the different factors that affect session replication.

For example, performance of highly available systems is greatly affected by the size of data stored in the sessions. Hence the benchmark may want to introduce session size as a parameter while studying the performance of these systems.

Defining the Performance Metrics

The next step in the design of the benchmark is to identify the important performance metrics. First, let's review a few definitions:

- **Request.**   Invocation of a single resource from the server.
- **Round-trip time.**   The elapsed time between the instant at which a request is started and the instant at which the response is completed.
- **Think time.**   The elapsed time between the instance at which a response is completed and the instance at which a new request is started.
- **Page view.**   A collection of one or more requests associated with rendering a single Web page. The requests include the specified page as well as other related artifacts (style sheets, script files and images, etc.).
- **User transaction.**   A collection of one or more page requests.

Unlike the terms request, round-trip time, and think time, which are simple to understand, the other metrics are more complex and need further discussion. The following two sections provide a more detailed description of the last two terms.

Page View

A page view defines the work involved in rendering a page and may span multiple requests. In the simplest case it consists of a single request.

> **Tip**
>
> Typically, a single page request consists of multiple requests to fetch other referenced artifacts including style sheets, JavaScript files, images, and so on.

For example, accessing http://java.sun.com/ using my browser resulted in a total of 65 requests. It should be noted that the presence of caches and content delivery networks (CDN) can reduce the number of requests served by the application server associated with a page request.

How do you check whether a request has been successful? One simple way is to check the status code of the response with any value of 400 or higher considered to be a failure. Other options include verifying the size of the response or parsing the response to verify its validity. Irrespective of the method used for verification, it is important that any failures encountered during the course of a benchmark be reported in the results.

User Transaction

A user transaction is defined as a set of associated page requests. The purpose of defining user transactions is to divide the application into a set of manageable pieces with each piece being a collection of associated user interactions. In the simplest case, a transaction may involve only a single page request (e.g., accessing the home page), but in other cases a user transaction may be a collection of several page requests. The following transactions can be defined for the online store described in Figure 9-1. Even though home is the access point for all transactions, it is not included in other transactions for simplicity.

- **home.**   Access the home page only (10%).
- **specials.**   Access the specials page (20%).
- **search.**   Search for an item in the catalog. Navigate the search results; 2 forward, 1 backward (40%).
- **mostPopular.**   Access the list of most popular items including browsing through the results (30%).
- **addToCart.**   Add an average of n items to the cart from the search result. Delete 1 item from the cart. (30% of search, 20% of specials, and 10% of most popular).
- **buy.**   Buy items in the shopping cart; confirm items in the list (10%).

The next step is to define transactional probabilities (shown in parentheses in the preceding list), which are often collected using Web analytics tools, request logs, or based on business projections. For our example, the model defines that of all the users, 10% access the home page and return without any further interaction, while 40% access the search page (includes navigation of search results), 30% pick most-Popular, and 20% select specials. Some of the search page users (30%) then go on to add an average of n items into the shopping cart. A further 10% proceed with the buy transaction. Once the user interaction model has been defined, the benchmark driver can be implemented to traverse the various paths through the application to simulate real world user load. It is recommended that the transitional probabilities be set as configurable parameters to make it easy to study different user interaction scenarios, including the ability to study the performance of a single transaction in isolation.

Response Time

From an end user point of view, this is the overall time taken for a page to render fully and to be interactive. Even though it is important to measure the end user page load time, if the focus of the benchmark is on measuring server-side performance, the metric of interest is only a portion of the overall render time, the time taken to generate the HTML page and deliver it to the client. Since the focus of this book is on server-side performance, the discussion is limited to the development of benchmarks that measure server performance.

During the course of the benchmark run, a page may be requested multiple times. And, the response time measured for each request/response iteration needs to be stored. At the end of the run it is useful to analyze the response time data for each page request and calculate the following:

- Maximum
- Average
- 90th or 99th percentile
- Standard deviation

The two most commonly used measures are the average and the 99th percentile response times. The average response time is calculated as the arithmetic mean of the response time of all the successful requests, and the 99th percentile response time describes the time at which 99% of all successful requests have completed. In Web benchmarks, it is not uncommon for the distribution of response times to have a long tail, with a small number of requests with high response time values even though the vast majority of the requests have small response times. These outliers may be caused due to full garbage collections, database check pointing, network glitches, and so on. For applications that have strict response time requirements, the maximum value may be used as the primary metric of interest.

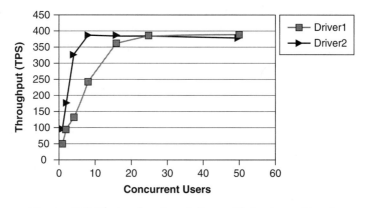

Figure 9-2 Throughput variation with increased load

A successful transaction typically requires each of its individual component requests be completed while meeting specified success criteria. The common success criteria are a combination of 99th percentile response time and data integrity requirements. For the *search* transaction mentioned previously, the success criteria may be defined as the 99th percentile response time for each of the individual page requests be less than or equal to 1 second. An additional data integrity constraint can be specified that at least ten items be returned as part of the search result.

Throughput

The performance of a system is usually described in terms of throughput, the capacity of a system in servicing user requests. Throughput may be defined in a variety of ways, number of successful transactions completed per second, number of operations per second, amount of data processed (bytes/second), and so on. Figure 9-2 shows the variation in throughput for increasing user load. For a well-behaved system, the throughput initially increases as the number of concurrent users increases while the response times of the requests stay relatively flat (see Figure 9-3). The system resources are underutilized during the initial period, allowing the system to accommodate the increased user load. However, once the system has reached peak capacity (as indicated by 100% CPU usage in Figure 9-4), the system throughput remains steady and the response time increases linearly with increasing load.

Throughput can be used as the primary metric to measure the performance of an application deployed on a particular hardware configuration. This works effectively if all the user transactions are equally heavy. However, this often is not the case. For example, in our online store example, a *buy* transaction that uses secure communication may be more expensive than a simple *search* transaction, which would translate to a higher average response time for *buy* than for *search*. This necessitates the need to specify different response time requirements for different transactions. Under

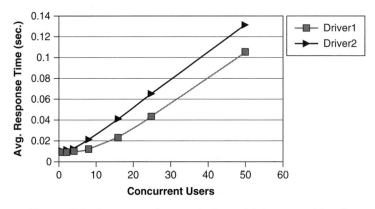

Figure 9-3 Response time variation with increased load

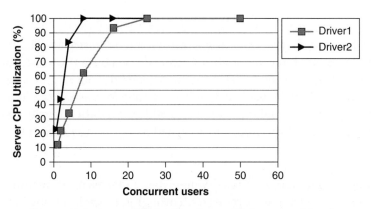

Figure 9-4 Server CPU utilization with increased load

such conditions, the benchmark would be defined as a set of transactions with each transaction having a passing response time requirement (often 99th percentile). Any transaction that does not meet the response time metric would be deemed as failed. The overall benchmark metric would then be defined as the maximum load that the benchmark can handle without any transaction failure.

Scaling the Benchmark

Scaling a benchmark typically means increasing the user load (the number of concurrent requests) to the application. A driver framework is used to generate the concurrent requests as well as measure the response time for each individual request. A variety of open source driver frameworks is available in the marketplace—Apache JMeter, Faban, just to name two—as well as commercially available products. Most of the driver frameworks fall under one of these two categories.

- **Single client process with multiple concurrent threads.** Each thread simulates a real world user and works in parallel to the other threads. Since all the threads occur within a single JVM, it is easy to control and synchronize the execution of the various simulated users. Collating the data and generating a report is also easy with this method. This type of client is easy to develop and to set up. However, it has some disadvantages. It may be difficult to scale beyond a certain number of users due to the JVM memory size limitations. The performance measurement may be skewed by bottlenecks within the client; for example, full garbage collection within the client may cause large pause times that may be incorrectly attributed to poor server performance. User load limitation due to lack of availability of client resources is another drawback of this approach. During benchmarking, the enterprise applications are typically deployed on server class machines with multiple cores and often multiple network interfaces. To saturate the server in a single client JVM approach, an equally powerful load generation machine may be required.

- **Centrally controlled distributed multithreaded clients.** In this case, the user load is generated by a set of client processes where each process is similar to the one explained previously. These clients may be co-located on the same machine or may span across multiple machines. A central controller is required to control the life cycle of each of these clients. This approach has several advantages. No upper limit on the user load that can be generated; the concurrent users can be increased easily by adding more client processes. The distributed nature of this framework allows the use of a large number of low end client machines to generate enough load to saturate the server without being limited by the client resources. The primary disadvantage of this approach is the complexity of setting up and configuring a potentially large number of client systems. The distributed benchmark framework that we use for our tests is Faban, an open source offering from Oracle (http://faban.sunsource.net/).

It is often the case that the size of the database an application uses is proportional to the total number of users it supports. In some cases, the number of users in the database is the same as the number of active users accessing the application, whereas in other cases, only a small proportion of the overall users is active at any given time. A social network application is a classic example of the latter case, where the application may have a large number of registered individuals but only a small proportion of them are active at any given time. Increasing the size of the benchmark database is an important consideration in the scaling of the benchmark. As the number of concurrent users of a benchmark is increased, it is a good practice to increase the database size to reflect the increase in the user population.

Depending on the benchmark, other aspects of the benchmark may need to be scaled as well. For example, to understand the performance impact of session size for a high availability application, the benchmark needs to be run with a range of session sizes thus scaling the benchmark with respect to session size. To have a complete understanding of the performance of the application, it is good practice to carry out all the relevant scalability experiments.

Little's Law Verification

The driver framework in a benchmark is responsible for generating the appropriate load as well as measure the various performance metrics including throughput and response times. It is important to pick a driver framework that provides accurate results for the benchmark. In many cases, due diligence is not applied to check the validity of the testing harness, and the inaccurate results produced by the driver are taken at face value.

To illustrate this point, consider the following example of a benchmark used to measure the performance of a Web service. The test was designed to identify the maximum number of concurrent clients that the application can support with an average response time of 300ms. Two different benchmark drivers were used:

- **Driver1.** A heavy client that submits the request, reads in the response, and processes the receiving data before proceeding to submit the next request.
- **Driver2.** A light client that submits the request and reads the response without any processing of the received data before submitting the next request.

Figure 9-2, Figure 9-3, and Figure 9-4 show the throughput, response time, and server CPU utilization for increasing the number of concurrent users for both the clients. The maximum throughputs measured by both the drivers are about the same. Both drivers were able to fully saturate the server, but note that Driver1 (heavy client) requires more concurrent users than Driver2 (thin client) to saturate the server.

Even though both the drivers reported similar maximum throughput numbers, the response time data is different. Figure 9-3 shows that the response times measured for a specified number of concurrent users using Driver1 is lower than that measured using Driver2. Table 9-1 shows the maximum number of users supported with an average response time of 300 milliseconds for the two drivers.

Table 9-1 Maximum Number of Users That Can Be Supported by the Application

Driver	Maximum Users
Driver1	133
Driver2	115

It is pretty clear that there is something wrong with this data set—the maximum capacity of a server cannot change based on the testing harness. But which one is wrong? We can use Little's Law to verify the validity of both data sets.

Little's Law states the following: The long-term average number of customers in a stable system L, is equal to the long-term average arrival rate, multiplied by the long-term average time a customer spends in the system, W, or:

Applying this to our benchmark, L is the number of concurrent users, is the throughput, and W is the average response time. Thus Little's Law can be used to calculate the number of active concurrent users given the throughput and the response time. To verify the validity of the results, we calculate the number of concurrent users for both drivers using the measured throughout and response time values. Table 9-2 shows the calculated values of concurrent users for both drivers. For Driver2, the values reported by the driver match the calculated values. However, this is not the case for Driver1 where the calculated value is roughly 20% lower than the one specified by the framework.

This explains the anomaly seen in the response time data shown in Figure 9-3. The reason for the lower response time for Driver1 is the smaller number of concurrent users loading the application. To verify this, the response times were plotted against the calculated users as opposed to the number of users specified by the driver harness as shown in Figure 9-5. The data confirms that overestimating the number of users by Driver1 was the reason for the discrepancy in our performance metric. Once the data has been calibrated, the maximum capacity of the server is the same irrespective of the driver framework used.

The preceding example highlights the importance of the verification of results produced by any testing framework, especially for ones that involve user scalability analysis.

Table 9-2 Specified Versus Calculated Concurrent Users

Specified Users	Calculated Users–Driver1	Calculated Users–Driver2
1	.44	.95
2	.84	1.95
4	1.32	3.92
8	2.92	8.07
16	8.32	15.81
25	16.66	24.94
50	40.71	49.97

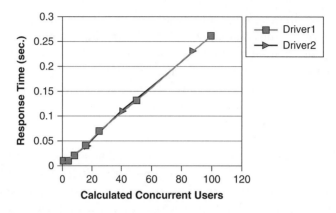

Figure 9-5 Response time for calculated concurrent users

Tip

Use Little's law ($L = \lambda * W$; L = number of users, λ = throughput, W = avg. response time) to verify that the actual number of concurrent users generating load is indeed equal to the number of users reported by the driver framework.

Think Time

Think time is used to denote the time a user takes to process the information that has been received (e.g., to read a page, complete a form, etc.). In benchmark design, the think time is represented as a delay introduced between subsequent requests. The type and amount of delay depends on the application and may vary from request to request (e.g., reading a page may take less time than filling out a form). There are a variety of ways to incorporate think times into a benchmark. They include introducing a fixed time between requests, recording the think time while a real user navigates the site and replaying it, and selecting the value from a probability distribution. Some of the distributions that can be used include a randomly distributed value between a minimum and maximum or a negative exponential probability distribution (with a maximum of five times the mean value). For Web applications, the negative exponential distribution, the time between events in a Poisson process, is considered to be the best option. It should be noted that delays are meant to be present between successive page requests but not when requesting content (CSS, JavaScript, images) considered part of a page request.

Figure 9-6 shows the variation in throughput with increasing active users for a simple Web application for various fixed user think times in milliseconds. In the legend for Figure 9-6, tt is an abbreviation for think time. Figure 9-7 shows the

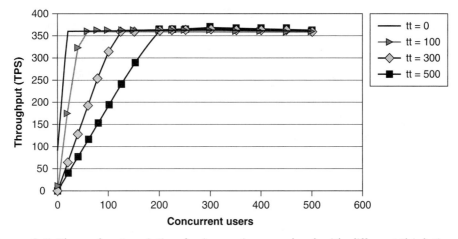

Figure 9-6 Throughput variation for increasing user load with different think times

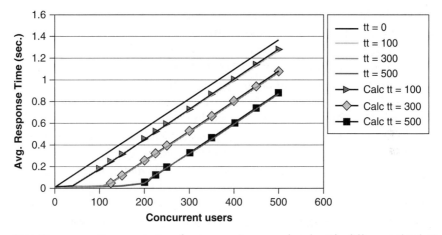

Figure 9-7 Response time variation for increasing user load with different think times

variation of the average response times for the same tests. The throughput measured as the number of successful operations per second increases initially as the number of users increases up to a maximum value and then remains steady. With a think time of 300 milliseconds, the peak throughput of the system is achieved at around 150 concurrent users.

As seen in Figure 9-8, the overall load on the system is determined by the number of active requests being processed at the server, which is a function of the number of concurrent users and think time. For the same user load, increasing the think time reduces the number of active requests at the server, which allows it to support more users.

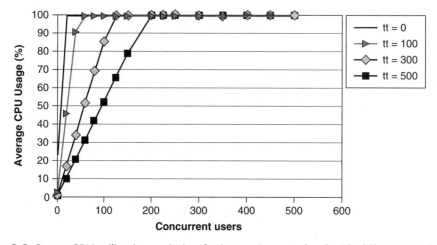

Figure 9-8 Server CPU utilization variation for increasing user load with different think times

How does think time affect the server's performance? The performance of a server is dictated mainly by the number of concurrent requests being processed and to a limited extent by the total number of open connections (this may not be the case if the connections become very large, say, >10,000). The introduction of think time means that some of the active users will be in a passive state where they are not requesting any resources from the server. In other words, the number of active users processed by the server is less than the number of total users.

As seen in the earlier section, one commonly used performance metric is the maximum number of users an application can support with the average response time equal to, or smaller than a specified value. One way to ascertain this metric for varying think times is to run multiple tests with different think times and for increasing user loads as shown previously in Figure 9-7. If we define the response time limit for our experimental application to be 500ms, then without think time the application can support about 180 users, while that number increases to about 290 once a think time of 300ms is introduced.

Is there a way to use the performance data generated by the tests run without think time and use it to extrapolate how the application performance would change for different think times? The answer is yes. Little's Law comes in handy here as well. With the introduction of think time, the relationship between the number of concurrent users, N, the arrival rate, λ, the average response time, W, and the average think time, T, is as follows:

$$\lambda = N/(W + T)$$

The arrival rate is the rate at which requests arrive at the server. An estimate of the peak arrival rate can be obtained from running experiments without think time and measuring the peak throughput. So given the peak throughput, we can calculate the number of concurrent users for a given think time and response time or conversely, we can calculate the average response time for a specified number of users running with an average think time of T seconds. Figure 9-7, shown previously, shows the calculated response time along with the measured times for three different think times. As can be seen from the graph, the calculated value is very close to the measured value. In our experiments, the peak arrival rate turns out to be around 362. Using the equation listed earlier, our experiments show that we can support a maximum of 290 users with a think time of 300ms and an average response time of 500ms (N = 362*[0.5 + 0.3] = 290).

Tip

The arrival rate equation, $\lambda = N/(W + T)$, provides a means by which we can compute the capacity of a system under different think times and response time requirements based on the results of a small set of no think time experiments.

Scalability Analysis

As the user load on an enterprise application increases, the need for compute resources at the server go up as well. The increased user demand can be met by either vertical, horizontal, or hybrid scaling. In vertical scaling, more resources are provided to a single instance of the application to meet the increased throughput requirement. This is often achieved by deploying the application on a larger SMP (symmetric multiprocessing) or a CMT (chip multithreading) system. This is suitable for applications that can fully utilize all the available resources without being inhibited by limitations in application design, JVM's garbage collection, lock contention, network, disk I/O limitations, and so on.

In horizontal scaling, the increased demand is met by the addition of more application instances deployed on additional (usually smaller) systems. The multiple systems are typically fronted by a load balancer that distributes the user load among the various available instances. This is a flexible way to scale the application to meet extremely large user load. The main disadvantage of this model is the difficulty of managing and maintaining the large numbers of deployed applications, Java EE containers, and hardware systems.

The hybrid scaling model is a mixture of both the vertical and horizontal models. In this case, within a single SMP system, applications are deployed on multiple application server instances, and further scalability is achieved by the addition of more systems. As in the case of horizontal scaling, this requires a load balancer to route the requests to the appropriate instance.

Scalability analysis is often necessary to identify the best deployment configuration for the application, especially for deploying applications on large SMP or CMT systems.

The application may be unable to fully utilize all the available resources due to various reasons. Vertical scaling studies (plotting maximum throughput versus number of hardware threads) allows the identification of scalability bottlenecks that can then be rectified. It also allows us to identify the configuration that maximizes the resource utilization. For example, excessive lock contention may inhibit an application to scale beyond a certain number of cores. In such cases, it may be better to select a hybrid deployment model in which multiple application server instances are run on a single system for optimal resource utilization.

Some of the conditions that cause poor scalability of enterprise applications are lock contention, disk or network I/O bottleneck, JVM garbage collection, inappropriate application server tuning (mainly incorrect pool sizes), and dependence on slow external systems (databases, Web services, etc.). The "Monitoring Subsystems" section, later in the chapter, describes how these different parameters can be monitored.

Running the Benchmark

This section looks at some of the best practices for setting up and running multitiered benchmarks as well as identifies a set of monitoring tools useful to identify potential problems.

Isolate the SUT

Isolate the SUT if possible. The "Defining the System Under Test" section earlier in the chapter described the need for identifying the SUT to ensure that the benchmark generates accurate results.

> **Tip**
>
> For multitiered benchmarks, whenever possible, it is a good practice to isolate the SUT into an environment that can be easily monitored.

For example, it is ideal if the driver, SUT, database, and external systems can be deployed on separate machines allowing each of these systems to be monitored separately. However, lack of machine availability and other limitations may not make this deployment possible. One combination often employed is to isolate the SUT on one system and aggregate all the other components (driver, database, etc.) onto a second machine.

> **Tip**
>
> It is a good performance practice to carry out network throughput and latency tests during the benchmark setup phase to understand the capacity of the various communication channels and to identify and eliminate high latency communication links.

It is also a good practice in the setup and configuration of a benchmark to consider leveraging operating system capabilities such as processor sets, or partitioning off portions of a system so they are viewed as distinct systems, such as virtualization or Oracle Solaris zones. Creating processor sets allows for the ability to tie a process, a Java application running in a JVM, to a set of processors. Doing so can improve CPU cache utilization. Whether CPU cache utilization is improved depends on which virtual processors are assigned to a processor and the underlying CPU chip architecture, in particular its cache size and cache boundaries, that is, how many virtual processors a CPU cache spans, or how many virtual processors share the same CPU cache. Virtualization, or use of Oracle Solaris zones, can further isolate applications into domains since virtualization or zones provide the appearance of a distinct system.

There are often situations in which an application depends on one or more external third-party components that may be connected over a network, say, a Web 2.0 mashup application that obtains data from an external source through a Web service call. In this case, even though the response time of a request processed by the application includes the time required to access the data from the external source, while benchmarking, it is better to consider this resource to be external to the SUT.

Since repeatability is important in benchmarking, it is advisable not to have dependencies on systems outside the confines of the benchmark setup. One commonly used approach in these types of scenarios is to include a simulator within the benchmark setup that mimics the external service.

Resource Monitoring

For CPU bound applications, a benchmark designed to study the peak capacity of an application should be able to fully utilize the CPU resources within the SUT. In most cases, underutilization of CPU resources during benchmark runs is undesirable and is often an indicator of software or hardware bottlenecks (unless the benchmark is run at a reduced load).

> **Tip**
>
> Because of the multitiered nature of enterprise applications, it is important to monitor the resource utilization of all the systems involved in the benchmark and to ensure that the benchmark is not throttled due to lack of resources on systems external to the SUT.

The following should be monitored:

- CPU utilization
- Kernel and user memory utilization
- Network I/O utilization

- Disk I/O utilization
- JVM

Chapter 2, "Operating System Performance Monitoring," and Chapter 4, "JVM Performance Monitoring," as well as the "Monitoring Subsystems" section later in this chapter describe how the various components just mentioned can be monitored.

Ramp Up and Steady State Intervals

Chapter 8 described the warm-up requirements for Java benchmarks. These requirements hold true for enterprise benchmarks as well. Additionally, a few other requirements are worth considering:

- **Ramp up time.** This is the elapsed time for ramping up the load to the required limit. It is preferable to increase the load gradually rather than starting all the clients simultaneously. During the ramp up phase, the number of concurrent clients is increased based on a predefined function such that all clients are started by the end of the ramp up period. This time also serves as the warm-up period for the JVM(s) within the SUT.
- **Steady state time.** This is the elapsed time during which benchmark measurements are made. This should be long enough to collect meaningful results as well as provide enough data points that allow clients to meet the proportionality requirements. The steady state should also be long enough to include important episodes that occur during the lifetime of an application, for example, full garbage collection, database checkpoint, and so on.
- **Ramp down time.** The load is reduced gradually during this phase.

Managing Repeatability

An important requirement for any benchmark is to ensure it can generate repeatable and consistent results. The presence of several components distributed over multiple tiers can make repeatability a challenge for enterprise benchmarks. Benchmarks with performance metrics that have wide variability between runs make it difficult to assess whether the improvements or regressions are real, even with the use of statistical methods as described in Chapter 8. The repeatability problem, which can introduce wide swings in variability, can be mitigated by incorporating a series of pretest steps that reset all the components to a known state. Some of the steps to consider are given in the following list. All these steps may not be required for all benchmarks.

- Reboot all systems.
- Restart all the JVMs.

- Restore database to original state (may require data reload).
- Restore file systems to original state.
- Restore message queues to original state.
- Clock synchronization across all systems.

Running Asynchronous Benchmarks

So far in the chapter, synchronous benchmarks have been discussed in which the response time for a transaction can be measured at the client as the round-trip time taken to complete the request/response cycle. However, the situation is different for benchmarking applications involving asynchronous requests (JMS or one-way Web service requests). In this case, the client will not be able to measure the time taken to process the request due to the one-way nature of the request and hence a different approach is needed to measure the performance of the application. One way to achieve this is to have the time stamp of when the request was sent packaged as part of the payload or within the message header if appropriate. The message consumer can record the message arrival time and use the packaged time information to calculate the transmission time of the message. The transmission start and end times will be synchronized if the producer and consumer are deployed on the same machine. However, if they are deployed on multiple machines, the time calculation will be incorrect if the clocks on the two systems are not synchronized.

> **Tip**
>
> For multitiered asynchronous benchmarks, it is a good practice to synchronize the clocks on all the systems before the start of the benchmark run. Clock synchronization can be achieved through the use of Network Time Protocol (NTP) or using the rdate utility available on Oracle Solaris and Linux systems.

To account for cases in which the clocks within different systems that are part of the benchmark drift apart by large amounts during the benchmark run, it is recommended that a comparison of the system clocks be done as part of a post benchmark audit process and any run with large difference in system times be discarded.

Use Statistical Methods

Readers are encouraged to refer to the "Use of Statistical Methods" section in Chapter 8 for a detailed discussion on the use of statistical methods in benchmarking. Since several components are involved in an enterprise benchmark, the amount of variability of the benchmark scores for repeated runs tends to be high. Hence one tip worth repeating here from the Use of Statistical Methods section is Regardless of the statistical method chosen, the larger the sample size or number of observations, more information will be provided to the experiment and analysis.

Application Server Monitoring

In a typical multitiered enterprise application deployment, the clients, application server instances, database, and external systems that the application depends on may be deployed on disparate systems. Since each of these systems contributes to the overall performance of the application, it is important to monitor and tune the performance of each of these components. Even though in a live deployment, the clients are typically outside the monitoring realm, in a benchmark scenario performance monitoring of the client is also essential. Undetected client-side bottlenecks may raise undue concerns about the performance of the application.

The typical attributes monitored at the operating system level are CPU, kernel, and user memory, and network and disk I/O utilization. At the JVM level, garbage collection, lock contention, and class loading need to be monitored. Chapter 2 and Chapter 4 describe how to monitor these attributes for the various operating systems as well as provide a set of general guidelines for identifying potential issues.

For applications with heavy database interaction, it is important to tune the database for optimal performance. A rich set of tools from database and other third-party vendors is available for monitoring and analyzing the performance of databases. The details of database monitoring are beyond the scope of this book and are not covered here.

This section discusses how the system, JVM, and application server monitoring can help identify some of the common problems encountered in distributed applications. The different parameters that can be monitored to analyze the performance of JSP/servlets and EJBs are described in Chapter 10 and Chapter 12, "Java Persistence and Enterprise Java Beans Performance." But first, let's take a brief look at the monitoring framework within GlassFish; the Open Source Java EE server from Oracle is provided. Readers not using GlassFish can skip ahead to the "Monitoring Subsystems" section.

GlassFish Monitoring

The monitoring framework built into GlassFish allows users to monitor the different containers as well as the applications deployed within the application server. Clients can connect to the application server in several ways to monitor the server instance.

- Administration console
- Administration command line interface (admin CLI)
- JConsole, VisualVM, or other JMX clients

Administration Console

The GlassFish application server provides a browser-based administration user interface that allows users to administer as well as monitor server instances that are part of a domain. The administration GUI can be accessed via http://<host name>:<admin port>/(Default admin port: 4848). The examples provided in this section are based on GlassFish V3.

Monitoring data can be accessed by clicking on the Monitoring button on the Common Tasks pane on the left side, which brings up the default monitoring page. Monitoring is disabled by default. It can be enabled dynamically for the various components or services by clicking on the Configure Monitoring link. Figure 9-9 shows a screenshot of the monitoring configuration panel. The monitoring level of each individual component can be modified independently of each other. Monitoring of a component is enabled by setting its value to either low or high. The difference between these two levels is component dependent. For example, in the case of HTTP service, both the low and high level provide the same set of data, whereas in the case of EJB container, application specific monitoring data is available only when the level is set too high.

The cost associated with enabling monitoring can vary depending on the number of modules enabled. A performance drop of about 5% to 8% can be expected if monitoring is enabled for one or two modules. Due to its intrusive nature, monitoring should only be enabled on production systems during periods of data collection.

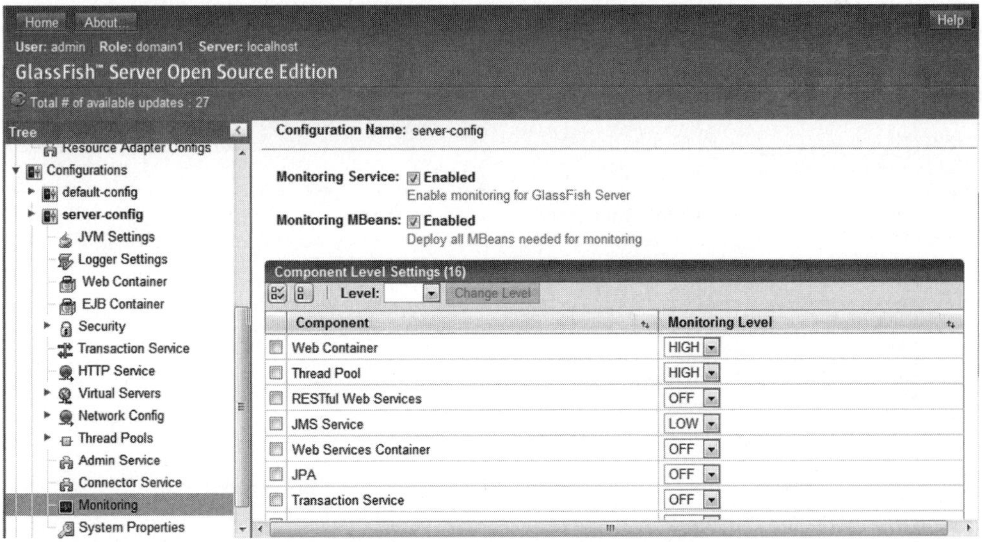

Figure 9-9 Configuration panel of GlassFish administration console to enable monitoring of different components

The data on the monitoring page is separated into different categories. The Runtime tab can be used to monitor a variety of subsystems including the JVM, server, HTTP service, thread pool, and so on. The pertinent data can be viewed by selecting the appropriate item from the drop-down box. The Applications tab can be used to get statistics about the performance of individual applications, and the Resources tab provides data about the deployed resources.

JConsole/VisualVM

The application server behavior can be studied by introspecting the various built-in MBeans using JConsole. JConsole is a JMX (Java Management eXtensions) compliant GUI tool that can connect to a running 5.0 version of later JDK. Refer to Chapter 4 for more details about how to start JConsole and use it for JVM monitoring. This section describes how JConsole can be used to monitor application server statistics.

JConsole can connect to a local or remote instance of the application server. When connecting to a local system, select the appropriate server instance represented by the name *ASMain*. Note that there may be more than one listing if multiple instances of the application server are running. JConsole is a rather heavyweight process, and running it locally may affect the performance of the application server due to the sharing of the CPU resources. The JMX service URL to connect to a remote server instance can be obtained from the administration console. On the bar on the left-hand side, select Configurations > server-config > Admin Service. JMX connector settings including the JMX port are displayed as shown in Figure 9-10. To connect via JConsole, use the <host>:<JMXPort> in the remote connection dialog box.

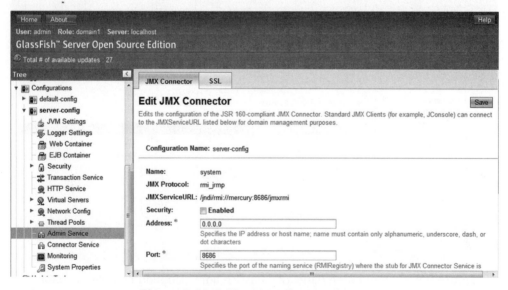

Figure 9-10 JMX connections settings

Once connection has been established, JConsole can be used to monitor the performance of the JVM as well as some of the other properties of the application server that are exposed as MBeans. The performance monitoring and analysis of the JVM are described in detail in Chapter 4 and are not covered here.

To view the application server specific MBeans, click on the MBeans tab and then the amx node. amx contains both configuration parameters as well as monitored values. The monitored performance metrics are classified as *<module>*-mon nodes. For example, *request-mon* node provides request statistics as shown in Figure 9-11. To view the monitored value, click the attribute of interest on the navigation tree and double-click on the value field on the right-hand pane. It is possible to add custom MBeans to expose application specific data; see Chapter 10.

VisualVM, the graphical JVM visualization tool, can also be used to monitor the JVM used within the GlassFish application server (requires JDK 6 Update 7 or later). VisualVM can connect to both local and remote instances of the application server. To monitor GlassFish-specific attributes, the GlassFish VisualVM plug-in needs to be installed. The latest version of the plug-in can be downloaded from https://visualvm. dev.java.net/plugins.html. Once monitoring is enabled on the server instance, the

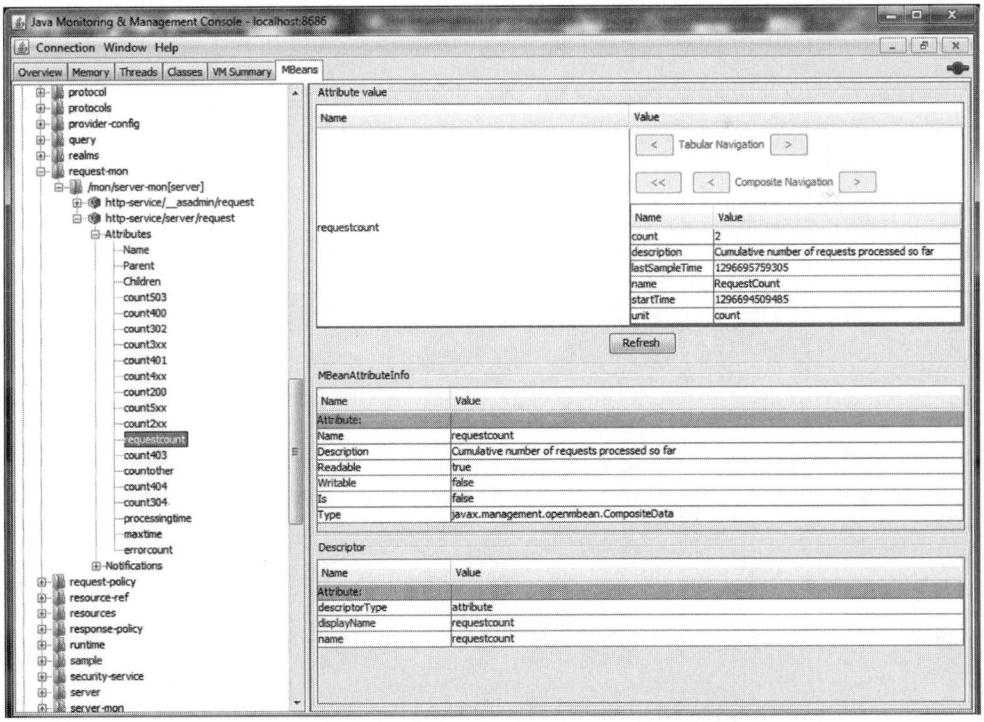

Figure 9-11 Using JConsole to view application server statistics

GlassFish plug-in for VisualVM can be used to monitor the various attributes. Refer to Chapter 4 for more details on how to use VisualVM.

asadmin CLI

GlassFish provides a Command Line Interface (CLI) that allows users to monitor the performance of the various components of the server. The CLI can be used to list all the monitorable components, set the monitoring levels for items of interest, and get the performance data from a running system on either a local or a remote system. This is achieved through the use of the administrative command, `asadmin` (or asadmin.bat in the case of Windows), which is available under the bin directory of the GlassFish installation. A detailed description of `asadmin` usage can be obtained by using the `asadmin --help` command.

Since monitoring is turned off by default, the first step is to enable monitoring of components. The list of all available monitorable services can be obtained using the following command:

```
asadmin --host <host> --port <port> get "<server-name>.monitoring-service.
module-monitoring-levels.*"
<host> and <port> are the host name and port of the DAS, resptively.
<server-name> is the name of the server to be monitored (default: server).
```

A sample listing follows:

```
asadmin --host host1 --port 4848 get server.monitoring-service.
module-monitoring-levels.*
server.monitoring-service.module-monitoring-levels.
connector-connection-pool=OFF
server.monitoring-service.module-monitoring-levels.connector-service=OFF
server.monitoring-service.module-monitoring-levels.ejb-container=OFF
server.monitoring-service.module-monitoring-levels.http-service=HIGH
server.monitoring-service.module-monitoring-levels.
jdbc-connection-pool=OFF
server.monitoring-service.module-monitoring-levels.jersey=OFF
server.monitoring-service.module-monitoring-levels.jms-service=OFF
server.monitoring-service.module-monitoring-levels.jpa=OFF
server.monitoring-service.module-monitoring-levels.jvm=OFF
server.monitoring-service.module-monitoring-levels.orb=OFF
server.monitoring-service.module-monitoring-levels.security=OFF
server.monitoring-service.module-monitoring-levels.thread-pool=OFF
server.monitoring-service.module-monitoring-levels.transaction-service=OFF
server.monitoring-service.module-monitoring-levels.web-container=HIGH
server.monitoring-service.module-monitoring-levels.
web-services-container=OFF
Command get executed successfully.
```

The monitoring level for each individual component can be changed using the `asadmin set` command as follows:

```
asadmin set <server-name>.monitoring-service.
module-monitoring-levels.<service>=<level>
<server-name> is the name of the server to be monitored (default: server).
<service> is service module of interest.
<level> can be OFF, LOW or HIGH.
```

For example, to enable monitoring of the http-service, run the following command:

```
asadmin set server.monitoring-service.module-monitoring-levels.
http-service=HIGH
```

Once monitoring has been enabled for a module, the special flag `--monitor` (or `-m`) can be used in conjunction with `asadmin` to list and retrieve the required performance data. To list all the available monitoring nodes within a service use the following command:

```
asadmin --host <host> --port <port> list -m "<server-name>.<module>*"

<module> is the service of interest (eg: network).
```

To get the values of all the attributes within a monitoring node, use the `get` command as follows:

```
asadmin --host <host> --port <port> get -m
"<server-name>.<module>.<service>.*"

<service> is the specific service within the module that is of interest
(eg: server.network.http-listener-1)
```

The preceding command prints all the attributes and can be overwhelming. By specifying the full dotted name of an attribute, only the data specific to that attribute can be obtained. For example, to monitor how busy the HTTP request processing threads are, use the attribute `server.network.http-listener-1.thread-pool.currentthreadsbusy-count`.

The `get` command supports data collection at periodic intervals using the parameters `--interval` and `--iterations`.

The `asadmin monitor` command is another alternative to display a variety of statistics for the various components. The usage is as follows:

```
asadmin monitor --type monitor_type
```

where `type` is one of the following values: `httplistener`, `jvm`, or `webmodule`. The `-help` command can be used to get a detailed description of the monitor command.

Monitoring Subsystems

Performance monitoring helps identify some of the potential issues that may impact the performance of an application. This section describes some of the important parameters that should be monitored.

Java Virtual Machine

Performance of the JVM associated with the Java EE container is the most important factor that determines the overall performance of an enterprise application. JVM monitoring is thus an essential part of the performance analysis. Chapter 4 provides a detailed description of the various performance monitoring tools that can be used for this purpose. In this section specific details about how these tools can be used to monitor a running application server instance are discussed.

As in the case of any Java application, enterprise applications are affected by garbage collection performance. The Java EE container creates objects as part of the Web, EJB, Web service, or JMS request processing in addition to the object allocations that are part of the application's business method processing. The performance impact of garbage collection of application sever-generated objects has been shown to be low. However, setting up large resource pools as well as large processing thread pools can have adverse performance impacts due to increased garbage collection overhead. Maintaining session information (via HTTP session objects or stateful session beans) is another source of increased memory usage, so it is important to appropriately tune the various containers within the application server instance. Advice on tuning the Java HotSpot VM can be found in Chapter 7, "Tuning the JVM, Step by Step."

> **Tip**
>
> Monitoring and tuning of the JVM associated with the JavaEE container are essential, and users should apply the performance tips and best practices provided in other parts of this book to improve the performance of the JVM embedded within the application server.

JVM command line options can be added to the GlassFish server instance using the Administration Console or through the `asadmin` CLI. The following example shows how to enable GC monitoring in GlassFish.

- Use JVM command line options, `-verbose:gc`, `-XX:+PrintGCDetails`, or `-XX:+PrintGCTimeStamps`.
  Use the Administration Console. After logging in, select the application server instance of interest. Select the JVM Setting tab and then the JVM Options tab. Click the Add JVM Option button and type in the required option in the new text field. Save the page and restart the server instance.
- Use `asadmin` CLI:

```
asadmin create-jvm-options \\-verbose\\:gc
asadmin create-jvm-options \\-XX\\:+PrintGCDetails
asadmin create-jvm-options \\-XX\\:+PrintGCTimeStamps
```

  The output is written to the file <path to server instance>/logs/server.log.
- Use the `jstat` command line tool to monitor local or remote instances (remote monitoring requires the installation and configuration of jstatd). The vmid associated with the server instance can be identified by the class name ASMain as shown in the output of the `jps` command. Use of jstat, jps and configuring jstatd are covered in Chapter 4.

```
#jps
19151 ASMain
20190 Jps
```

- Use JConsole or VisualVM (refer to the earlier section on connection information).

Thread Dumps

Threads dumps are an easy way to capture a snapshot of what the threads are executing at a point in time, and this can be used to get a quick synopsis of the application execution. They provide a variety of useful information including lock contentions, usages of the various pools, I/O activity, as well as a quick feel about the load on the system. There are multiple ways to generate thread dumps for a running server instance as shown here:

- The `jstack` utility bundled in JDK 6 (available in the Oracle Solaris and Linux versions of JDK 5) can be used to collect the threads dump for any Java application including the application server, either local or remote. To connect `jstack` to a local GlassFish server instance, first use `jps` to identify the server process identified by the class name ASMain. Refer to http://java.sun.com/javase/6/docs/technotes/tools/share/jstack.html to learn more about the available options as well as how to connect to remote instances.

- The Threads tab in JConsole.

- Use the Threads Inspector plug-in to VisualVM. Refer to https://visualvm.dev.java.net/plugins.html for more information on how to use this plug-in.

- Use the `asadmin` command, `asadmin generate-jvm-report --type thread`.

Even though thread dumps provide only a snapshot of the execution state, it is an easy-to-use, minimally intrusive method than can often provide useful data. Chapter 4 discusses how this information can be used to identify lock contention in an application that inhibits scalability. The analysis can also provide a variety of additional information including unanticipated file system interaction as well as network interactions with slow external systems including databases (details are provided later in the section).

Network I/O

Since network performance is critical to distributed systems, it is important to ensure that the network is designed to meet the demands of the application. The two measures of interest are throughput and latency. Throughput describes how much data flows over a channel in a given period of time. Two terms closely related to throughput, but not identical, are network speed and bandwidth. Speed refers to the rated speed of the networking technology (e.g., Gigabit Ethernet is rated at 1 gigabit per second), and bandwidth refers to the theoretical data capacity. Network throughput is the practically measured data transfer capacity over a communication channel. Network bandwidth can be measured using the Java version of Test TCP (TTCP), available at http://www.netcordia.com/files/java-ttcp.zip, or uperf, a network performance tool that supports modeling and replay of various networking patterns, available at http://www.uperf.org/.

The other important aspect is the network latency, which describes how long it takes for the data to arrive after it has been requested. Network latency is an important contributor to the overall response time for requests and should be taken into account while setting up a benchmark. The ping utility available in Oracle Solaris (also referred to as Solaris hereafter), Linux, and Windows can be used to measure the network latency between two systems. The `ping` command usage and the associated output for the various platforms are given in the following sections.

Solaris

This is `ping` usage and output for Solaris:

```
# ping -s webcache.east.sun.com 32 5
PING webcache.east.sun.com: 32 data bytes
40 bytes from cache3bur.East.Sun.COM (129.148.13.2): icmp_seq=0.
time=78.0 ms
40 bytes from cache3bur.East.Sun.COM (129.148.13.2): icmp_seq=1.
time=77.6 ms
...
----webcache.east.sun.com PING Statistics----
5 packets transmitted, 5 packets received, 0% packet loss
round-trip (ms)  min/avg/max/stddev = 77.5/77.7/78.0/0.18
```

Linux

This is `ping` usage and output for Linux:

```
# ping -c 5 -s 32 webcache.east.sun.com
PING webcache.east.sun.com (129.148.9.2) 32(60) bytes of data.
40 bytes from cache1bur.East.Sun.COM (129.148.9.2): icmp_seq=0 ttl=239
time=79.1 ms
40 bytes from cache1bur.East.Sun.COM (129.148.9.2): icmp_seq=1 ttl=239
time=78.4 ms
...
--- webcache.east.sun.com ping statistics ---
5 packets transmitted, 5 received, 0% packet loss, time 4039ms
rtt min/avg/max/mdev = 78.261/78.628/79.103/0.456 ms, pipe 2
```

Windows

This is `ping` usage and output for Windows:

```
D:\>ping webcache.east.sun.com

Pinging webcache.east.sun.com [129.148.13.2] with 32 bytes of data:

Reply from 129.148.13.2: bytes=32 time=78ms TTL=240
Reply from 129.148.13.2: bytes=32 time=78ms TTL=240
...

Ping statistics for 129.148.13.2:
    Packets: Sent = 4, Received = 4, Lost = 0 (0% ]
Approximate round trip times in milli-seconds:
    Minimum = 77ms, Maximum = 78ms, Average = 77ms
```

Tip

It is a good performance practice to carry out network throughput and latency tests during the benchmark setup phase to understand the capacity of the various communication channels and to identify and eliminate high latency communication links.

The "Network I/O Utilization" section of Chapter 2 describes tools to monitor the network utilization of a system at the operating system level as well as a set of best practices that improve the performance of the application's network interactions. The amount of system time as a proportion of the overall CPU usage time will be high for Web applications servicing large numbers of users because of the high network I/O involved.

It is common to find enterprise applications that interact with external applications over the network as part of a request processing cycle. The application may create a new socket connection for each request or may reuse an already existing connection. The creation and closing of sockets are expensive operations, and this overhead may even be a significant part of the overall network communication cost, especially if the amount of data transferred is small. How can runtime monitoring be used to figure out if too many new connections are being created? This can be done using the netstat utility available on Solaris, Windows, and Linux. netstat -a provides the state of active connections (sample output for Solaris follows; the output is slightly different for other platforms, but all of them indicate the state of a connection). Connections in TIME_WAIT state indicate sockets that are closed, and a large number of these are usually a good indicator of new connection creation/closure. The other piece of information to watch for is the client port number; a constantly changing port number is a telltale sign of new connection creation.

```
#netstat -a
<edited>
Local Address          Remote Address          <edited>    State
-------------          --------------------    --------    ------
jes-x4600-1.10000      jes-x4600-1.42850       ...         TIME_WAIT
jes-x4600-1.10000      jes-x4600-1.42851       ...         TIME_WAIT
jes-x4600-1.42860      jes-x4600-1.10000       ...         TIME_WAIT
jes-x4600-1.42883      jes-x4600-1.10000       ...         ESTABLISHED
jes-x4600-1.10000      jes-x4600-1.42883       ...         ESTABLISHED
```

Tip

It is a good performance practice to create a pool of socket connections and reuse them as appropriate rather than creating a new connection for each request. Setting up appropriate timeout values would allow these resources to be released if they are not used frequently.

Performance of External Systems

As mentioned earlier, multitier enterprise applications interact with other external systems including databases over the network. A slow external system can affect the response time for a request if the network interaction is in the request processing path as is often the case with database interactions. There are several ways to identify slow database performance including the use of sophisticated database analysis tools. In some cases, a simple thread dump analysis helps you identify the problem quickly, and the authors often use this approach as a simple first level method to identify slow network or database performance. It should be noted that this is just a coarse-grained approach and should not be the final determining factor and preclude you from carrying out more sophisticated techniques even if this test does not identify any problems.

The way to identify slow external systems is to look for threads that are waiting for a response as shown in the following stack snippet. A combination of a large number of threads in the network I/O state and the availability of spare CPU cycles on the application tier clearly indicate that the performance of the application is hampered by slowness of either the network or the external system.

```
"httpSSLWorkerThread-8081-62" daemon prio=3 tid=0x00c84c00 nid=0xcf
runnable
 [0x3bc7e000..0x3bc7faf0]
    java.lang.Thread.State: RUNNABLE
        at java.net.SocketInputStream.socketRead0(Native Method)
        at java.net.SocketInputStream.read(SocketInputStream.java:129)
        at com.mysql.jdbc.util.ReadAheadInputStream.
        fill(ReadAheadInputStream.java:113)
        ..
        at com.mysql.jdbc.Connection.execSQL(Connection.java:3283)
        ..
        at javax.servlet.http.HttpServlet.service(HttpServlet.java:831)
 ..
"httpSSLWorkerThread-8081-61" daemon prio=3 tid=0x01102000 nid=0xce
runnable
 [0x3bd7fe000..0x3bd7fa70]
    java.lang.Thread.State: RUNNABLE
        at java.net.SocketInputStream.socketRead0(Native Method)
    java.lang.Thread.State: RUNNABLE
        at java.net.SocketInputStream.socketRead0(Native Method)
        at java.net.SocketInputStream.read(SocketInputStream.java:129)
        at com.mysql.jdbc.util.ReadAheadInputStream.
        fill(ReadAheadInputStream.java:113)
 ..
"httpSSLWorkerThread-8081-60" daemon prio=3 tid=0x01101000 nid=0xcd
runnable
 [0x3be7e000..0x3be7fbf0]
    java.lang.Thread.State: RUNNABLE
        at java.net.SocketInputStream.socketRead0(Native Method)
        at java.net.SocketInputStream.read(SocketInputStream.java:129)
```

BTrace, the dynamic Java tracing utility (available at http://kenai.com/projects/btrace/pages/Home) can also be used to identify slow database interactions. A sample that measures the JDBC statement execution time for all queries follows. A more

sophisticated JDBC query tracking script (JdbcQueries.java) that displays the execution time of each SQL statement is available as part of the BTrace samples found at
the BTrace Project Web site.

```java
package com.sun.btrace.samples;

import static com.sun.btrace.BTraceUtils.*;
import java.sql.Statement;
import java.util.Map;
import com.sun.btrace.AnyType;
import com.sun.btrace.BTraceUtils;
import com.sun.btrace.aggregation.*;
import com.sun.btrace.annotations.*;

/**
 * BTrace script to print timings for all executed JDBC statements on an
 * event. Use --full parameter to display the histogram.
 */
@BTrace
public class JdbcAnyQuery {
    private static Map<Statement, String> preparedStatementDescriptions
        = newWeakMap();
    private static Aggregation histogram =
        newAggregation(AggregationFunction.QUANTIZE);
    private static Aggregation average =
        newAggregation(AggregationFunction.AVERAGE);
    private static Aggregation max =
        newAggregation(AggregationFunction.MAXIMUM);
    private static Aggregation min =
        newAggregation(AggregationFunction.MINIMUM);
    private static Aggregation count =
        newAggregation(AggregationFunction.COUNT);
    private static boolean full = $(2) != null &&
        strcmp("--full", $(2)) == 0;
    @TLS
    private static long timeStampNanos;

    @OnMethod(clazz = "+java.sql.Statement", method = "/execute.*/")
    public static void onExecute(AnyType[] args) {
        timeStampNanos = timeNanos();
    }
    @OnMethod(clazz = "+java.sql.Statement", method = "/execute.*/",
location = @Location(Kind.RETURN))
    public static void onExecuteReturn() {
      AggregationKey key = newAggregationKey("Generic Query");
        int duration = (int) (timeNanos() - timeStampNanos) / 1000;
        addToAggregation(count, key, duration);
        addToAggregation(average, key, duration);
        addToAggregation(histogram, key, duration);
        addToAggregation(max, key, duration);
        addToAggregation(min, key, duration);
    }

    @OnEvent(value="reset")
    public static void onReset() {
        println ("Data reset");
```

```
            clearAggregation(count);
            clearAggregation(min);
            clearAggregation(max);
            clearAggregation(average);
            clearAggregation(histogram);
        }

        @OnEvent()
        public static void onEvent() {
            println("Results. All times are in microseconds");
            println("-----------------------------------------------");
            printAggregation("Count", count);
            printAggregation("Min", min);
            printAggregation("Max", max);
            printAggregation("Average", average);
            if (full) {
                printAggregation("Histogram", histogram);
            }
            println("-----------------------------------------------");
        }
    }
```

Running the script provides the following output:

```
# /home/binu/Utils/btrace/bin/btrace `jps |grep ASMain  | awk '{print
$1}'` /home/binu/Utils/btrace/samples/JdbcAnyQuery.java

^CPlease enter your option:
        1. exit
        2. send an event
        3. send a named event
2
Results. All times are in microseconds
---------------------------------------------
Count
   Generic Query                                              32
Min
   Generic Query                                             922
Max
   Generic Query                                          146336
Average
   Generic Query                                           13341
---------------------------------------------
```

Based on the query execution times, a determination can be made of whether the application performance is impaired by a slow database.

Disk I/O

The "Disk I/O Utilization" section of Chapter 2 describes how to collect disk usage statistics for the various operating systems. Several parts of the Java EE container code involve disk interaction in addition to the application level disk usage. The various disk activities carried out by the application server instance are presented in the following list, and they vary depending on the type of request that is processed and the application server configuration.

- Accessing static files (HTML, CSS, image, Javascript files) as part of the Web request
- Writing to access and server logs
- Writing to transaction logs as part of distributed transactions
- Writing of persistent JMS messages as well as JMS transaction logging

A typical Web request for a static content involves the Web container reading the required resource from the file system before streaming it over the network. In the classic Web usage pattern, the user requests are predominantly HTTP GETs, which translate to large amounts of read system calls involving disk I/O if the data is not cached in memory. However, with the advent of Web 2.0, users interacting with the system often upload a variety of content including images, audio, and video. These types of transactions involve storing content in a local or distributed file system and are very write intensive. So the disk/file system interaction is a critical component of Web application performance.

It is common practice to enable access logging (default is no access logging on GlassFish) to collect data regarding the user requests. See Chapter 10 for more information about tuning the access log files.

GlassFish supports several levels of logging that can be customized individually for the different subsystems. As the logging level is made more and more fine-grained from the default level of INFO, the increased write activity can cause disk bottlenecks. Excessive logging adversely affects the performance of the application as well as causes scalability issues. Some of the logging best practices include

- Set the server log level to the minimum required level.
- When required for debugging, be specific about the component that needs the increased log level.
- Specify appropriate logging level within the application code. Printing to the standard output and standard error causes the output to be written to the log file if the log level of the component is set to INFO or higher. In cases where the application cannot be modified, this logging can be eliminated by reducing the log level to WARNING.

The Transaction Manager writes information to the transaction log file as part of transaction processing, which may cause disk bottlenecks. The large service times due to busy disks may result in poor system performance, degrade scalability, and in the worst case cause transactions to be aborted. In cases where disk performance is an issue, it is recommended that the application server instance be configured to have the transaction log file on a fast disk (best choice would be a solid state disk, also know as an SSD) or a disk array with write cache. The location of the transaction log directory can be configured using the administration console (on the left navigation bar, select Configuration > Transaction Service and specify the new location in the Transaction Log Location field) or the `asadmin` CLI as follows:

```
asadmin set server.transaction-service.tx-log-dir=<PATH LOCATION>
```

Processing of persistent or transactional JMS messages is disk intensive. Persistent JMS messages need to be saved, which results in writes to the file system since the default message store is file based. (DB store is also supported, but file store has shown to have better performance.) JMS transactions (single or two-phase) involve transaction logging, which cause disk activity. As in the case of distributed transaction logging, it is recommended to configure the JMS file/transaction store to be on a fast disk or write cache enabled disk array for optimal performance.

Tip

It is a good performance practice to use SSDs or disk arrays with write caches for transaction logging and for storing JMS messages.

Thread dump analysis is useful for identifying unanticipated file system interactions as well. One example of this is the loading of XML factory classes, which may involve searches through the various jar files to identify the appropriate instance to load. Repeated loading of these factory classes is expensive (more details about this are provided in Chapter 11, "Web Services Performance") and should be avoided. Thread dump analysis is often an effective way to identify this problem as shown in the following stack trace snippet of loading a javax.xml.transform.TransformerFactory.newInstance.

```
"p: thread-pool-1; w: 9" daemon prio=3 tid=0x09f1ac00 nid=0xe2 runnable
[0x2dc43000..0x2dc44bf0]
    java.lang.Thread.State: RUNNABLE
        at java.util.zip.ZipFile.getEntry(Native Method)
        at java.util.zip.ZipFile.getEntry(ZipFile.java:149)
        - locked <0x3f8a30b0> (a java.util.jar.JarFile)
        at java.util.jar.JarFile.getEntry(JarFile.java:206)
        at java.util.jar.JarFile.getJarEntry(JarFile.java:189)
```

Continued

```
at sun.misc.URLClassPath$JarLoader.getResource(URLClassPath.
java:754)
.... <deleted> ...
at javax.xml.transform.FactoryFinder.newInstance(FactoryFinder.
java:147)
at javax.xml.transform.FactoryFinder.find(FactoryFinder.java:233)
at javax.xml.transform.TransformerFactory.
newInstance(TransformerFactory.java:102)
```

It is important to note that thread dump analysis is a coarse-grained approach and may not identify all potential problems.

Another tool available in Solaris for I/O monitoring is the iosnoop DTrace script, the use of which is described in detail in Chapter 2.

Monitoring and Tuning Resource Pools

One important step in tuning an enterprise application is the proper configuration of the various resource pools. Tuning JDBC connection pools for applications that interact with databases is an example of this. The external interaction typically involves network I/O, which can cause the thread to be in a blocked state while waiting for the external resource to complete the interaction. The blocked thread uses up one of the connections from the pool, thereby reducing the number of available connections that can be used by other processing threads. If the pool size is too small, other threads wait for a connection to be available resulting in underutilization of CPU resources. Setting the pool size too high causes waste of resources both within the application server as well as the database. Most application servers provide three tuning parameters: minimum, steady state, and maximum connections.

Tip

One general tuning guideline is to set the steady state pool size to the number of hardware threads and maximum size to be equal to the maximum size of the HTTP worker thread pool (plus ORB thread pool size if remote EJBs or MDBs are invoked).

Further tuning of the connection pool can be attained by monitoring the server under load and taking corrective actions based on the observed values.

The GlassFish monitoring framework allows the inspection of the different resources including JMSConnectionFactories, resource adapters, and JDBC connections pools. Monitoring of these systems can be enabled by setting the level too high. To obtain a list of all the available resources, use the following command:

```
asadmin list -m "*resources*"
server.resources
server.resources.SpecJPool
server.resources.__TimerPool
server.resources.jms/QueueConnectionFactory
```

Data within the individual resources can be obtained using the `asadmin get -m` command as shown in the following example:

```
asadmin get -m "server.resources.SpecJPool.*"
```

Inspection of the various JDBC connection pool statistics allows us to understand whether the pool is appropriately sized. The two most important attributes to check are `numconnfree-current` and `waitqueuelength-count`. If the value of `numconnfree-current` is consistently zero and `waitqueuelength-count` is greater than zero, this indicates that the pool is configured to a smaller size than that required by the application. Typically this causes underutilization of the server's CPU resources, and the corrective action would be to increase the maximum pool size if the external resource (e.g., database) can handle the increased number of connections.

The connection pool monitoring statistics are useful for identifying potential connection leaks. The attributes `numconnacquired-count` and `numconnreleased-count` indicate the number of connections acquired and released, respectively. Under steady state, the number of connections acquired and released should be the same. Any mismatch indicates a potential connection leak. A nonzero value for the attribute `numpotentialconnleak-count` is another indicator of a potential leak.

Profiling Enterprise Applications

Enterprise applications deployed within the GlassFish application server behave like any other Java application, and profiling techniques used for Java applications work here as well. Chapter 5, "Java Application Profiling," and Chapter 6, "Java Application Profiling Tips and Tricks," provide both an introduction into using modern Java profilers and tips and tricks to employ to identify performance issues in Java applications. Readers are encouraged to read both chapters to understand how to improve the performance of their enterprise applications. In this section, how to attach and collect the profile data to introspect enterprise applications deployed on the GlassFish application server is presented. Once the data is collected the techniques described in Chapters 5 and 6 can be used to analyze the performance of the application.

As described in Chapter 5 the Oracle Solaris Studio Performance Analyzer collects profile information in an experiment file with a command line utility called `collect`, or often referred to as the *Collector*. Also remember that the Oracle Solaris Studio Performance Analyzer runs on Solaris (both SPARC and x86/x64) and Linux x86/x64 platforms. Profiling on the Windows platform can be done using the NetBeans Profiler. Both approaches are covered in this section beginning with the Performance Analyzer approach. Before reading this section it may be useful to read Chapter 5 to obtain an understanding of how to use the Performance Analyzer and NetBeans Profiler.

There is no `asadmin` command that allows the user to collect the necessary profiling data using the Performance Analyzer for the GlassFish application server. Generating profiling data using the Performance Analyzer requires the user to start the Java application using the Performance Analyzer's `collect` command. Since GlassFish uses a command launcher to start the application server process, some shell script creation is necessary to start the application server with the Performance Analyzer `collect` command.

Viewing the results of the collected experiment file is done using the Performance Analyzer's GUI program called Analyzer, or through a command line utility called `er_print`. How to use the Performance Analyzer GUI or command line `er_print` to view the results of a collected experiment is described in Chapter 5.

For other application servers implemented in the Java language, they too can be profiled on Solaris and Linux using the Performance Analyzer. To collect profiling data, the Java command line that launches the application needs to be updated to use the Performance Analyzer `collect` command as described in Chapter 5. Then the collected profile can be viewed and analyzed with either the Analyzer GUI or command line `er_print`.

The NetBeans Profiler can also be used to profile the GlassFish application server. NetBeans Profiler supports profiling of many popular application servers and Web servers right out of the box such as GlassFish, Tomcat, Weblogic, and JBoss. It also uses wizards to make the task of attaching the profiler simple and straightforward. A review of Chapter 5's coverage of how to use the NetBeans Profiler provides sufficient information to capture a profile of an application running in an application server along with providing information on how to view the profile data.

Bibliography

Dellamaggiore, Nick, and Eishay Smith. "LinkedIn: A Professional Social Network Built with Java Technologies and Agile Practices." http://www.slideshare.net/linkedin/linkedins-communication-architecture.

Tharakan, Royans. "What is scalability?" http://www.royans.net/arch/what-is-scalability/.

Beltran, Vicenç, Jordi Guitart, David Carrera, Jordi Torres, Eduard Ayguadé, and Jesus Labarta. "Performance Impact of Using SSL on Dynamic Web Applications." http://www.bsc.es/media/389.pdf.

Hines, Bill, Tom Alcott, Roland Barcia, and Keys Botzum. "IBM WebSphere Session Management." http://www.informit.com/articles/article.aspx?p=332851.

McDougall, Richard. "Availability—What It Means, Why It's Important, and How to Improve It." http://www.sun.com/blueprints/1099/availability.pdf.

Harris, James, Americo J. Melara, Hugh Smith, and Phillip Nico. "Performance analysis of the Linux firewall in a host." http://courseware.ee.calpoly.edu/3comproject/Published%20Papers/security.pdf.

"Markov Chain." Wikipedia. http://en.wikipedia.org/wiki/Markov_chain.

Halili, Emily H. "Functional Testing with Jmeter." http://www.packtpub.com/article/functional-testing-with-jmeter.

Theurer, Tenni. "Performance Research, Part 1: What the 80/20 Rule Tells Us about Reducing HTTP Requests." http://yuiblog.com/blog/2006/11/28/performance-research-part-1/.

Theurer, Tenni. "Performance Research, Part 2: Browser Cache Usage–Exposed!" http://www.yuiblog.com/blog/2007/01/04/performance-research-part-2/.

King, Andy, and Konstantin Balashov. *Speed Up Your Site: Web Site Optimization,* New Riders Publishing, Indianapolis, IN, 2003.

Standard Performance Evaluation Corporation (unknown author). SPECjms2007 Design Document. http://www.spec.org/jms2007/docs/DesignDocument.html.

Little, John D. C., and Stephen C. Graves. "Little's Law." http://web.mit.edu/sgraves/www/papers/Little%27s%20Law-Published.pdf.

bmwiz. "Estimating Max. Concurrent Users Supported." http://testnscale.com/blog/performance/estimating-max-users/.

Gunther, Niel. "Using Think Times to Determine Arrival Rates." http://perfdynamics. blogspot.com/2010/05/using-think-times-to-determine-arrival.html.

Oracle. "Oracle GlassFish Server 3.0.1 Administration Guide." http://download.oracle. com/docs/cd/E19798-01/821-1751/821-1751.pdf.

Infoblox. "Java TTCP." http://www.netcordia.com/community/files/folders/tools/ entry103.aspx.

Sun Microsystems, Inc. Performance Applications Engineering Group. "uperf–A Network Performance Tool." http://www.uperf.org/.

Sun Microsystems, Inc. "BTrace–Dynamic Tracing Utility for Java." http://kenai.com/ projects/btrace.

10

Web Application Performance

Over the last decade, the complexities of Web applications have increased tremendously. Not only are they expected to support increasingly complex features, they also are expected to handle hundreds of thousands, if not millions, of requests per day. It has become common to deploy these applications on a Java EE based Web container. To achieve optimal performance, it is important to architect the application appropriately as well as tune the container that it runs on. This chapter discusses how to monitor and tune a Web container for optimal performance as well as some of the best practices that should be used in applications.

Before diving in, a discussion about the scope of this chapter is provided. The area of high performance Web site development has been discussed at length in the literature; dozens of books have been written, thousands of blogs and articles can be found on the Web, and several Web sites are dedicated to this area. This is a vast topic that warrants that type of a comprehensive coverage. Before discussing what is covered here, to set expectations right, it is appropriate to enumerate a few topics not covered in this chapter.

The architecture of a large scale Web site is complex, involving many hardware and software components. The Web container that originates the content is one of the most important pieces in this puzzle, but it is just one piece nonetheless. This chapter does not cover how to architect a high performance site in terms of components to use or network layout. The scope is limited to discussing how to tune a Java EE based Web container for optimal performance. Users who are not familiar with Web architecture design may want to turn to one of the dozen books available on this subject.

Several factors contribute to the performance of a Web site: page delivery time of the server, network latency, and browser page display time. It has been well documented that a poorly designed page can result in large page display times and end user dissatisfaction. Hence generating a Web page that the browser can display efficiently is one of the most important steps in the design of a Web application. Steve Souders discusses several Web page optimization techniques in his two books *High Performance Web Sites* and *Even Faster Web Sites*. It is recommended that users incorporate these optimization techniques in the page generation process. The performance of the server in delivering the required pages is also an important factor in overall performance. This chapter identifies a set of best practices specifically for Java EE-based Web applications that provide low latency and high scalability.

Java EE consists of several individual specifications, and a variety of technologies are bundled into the Web container. Not all of them are discussed here—JSF and Jersey, just to name two. The goal here is to provide an overview of how to monitor performance of a Web application and to provide a set of best practice guidelines for some of the most commonly used techniques.

The chapter is organized as follows. The benchmarking section highlights some important factors to consider when developing Web benchmarks. This is followed by a brief description of the different components within the Web container. The next section deals with how to monitor and tune the Web container for optimal performance. The chapter concludes with a look at some of the best practices for Web applications.

Benchmarking Web Applications

Chapter 9, "Benchmarking Multitiered Applications," described the general principles behind developing enterprise benchmarks. In this section, we highlight a few items specific to Web applications.

- Development of benchmarks based on a Markov chain is useful for applications that have complex access patterns. However, in cases where page accesses are independent of each other, the complexity of the benchmark can be reduced by using a benchmark that accesses pages based on the proportion of the anticipated traffic.

- Replay of access logs is a great mechanism for simulating production load. Web servers in production environments are typically set up to capture requests that are served by the server. Refer to the "Access Logging" section later in the chapter for more information on setting up the access log on the Glass-Fish server. Designing a benchmark that can replay the log lines allows you to mimic production load as closely as possible. Requests that modify data (POST, PUT, DELETE) often need special attention. A replicated data store that can be repopulated easily may be required so that the integrity of the production data is not compromised when data modification requests are replayed. Additionally, the logger mechanism may have to be augmented to collect post and put data.

- Even though the focus in this book is on measuring the time taken for the server to deliver a page, it is important to study the user-perceived page load time since studies show that more than 90% of the time may be taken at the client side.

- If a page has multiple Ajax requests, it is important to measure the overall performance of the page by combining all associated requests.

- Applications that behave differently for different users pose additional benchmark development challenges. A social networking application that delivers content based on the requesting user is an example of this type of application. For such applications, it is important to understand how the application behavior is affected by who is requesting the page. Requests from non-signed-in users are typically delivered from a cache, and these types of requests are a load test on the caching infrastructure. Even within signed-in users, there may be a wide disparity in application logic based on user profile. For example, a user with a few friends may have different performance characteristics than one with many friends. Developing an accurate benchmark model for such applications may be tricky and difficult. In addition to request distribution based on page URLs, a secondary distribution based on the requesting user profile is also required.

Web Container Components

This section provides a brief description of the various components within a Web container instance. The discussion is based on the GlassFish Server Open Source Edition (also referred to as GlassFish hereafter), which is the reference implementation for Java EE 6. Even though this discussion uses GlassFish as the example, the Web container architecture discussed here is similar to that used by many other containers available on the market.

A GlassFish deployment is based on the concept of one or more domains controlled by a domain administration server. A domain may contain one or more clusters, which in turn is a collection of server instances, along with one or more standalone server instances. For the purpose of this discussion, we focus only on the components within the container that are relevant to performance.

The container is built on a set of nested components as shown in Figure 10-1. The server consists of one or more connectors that share a single engine component. The engine in turn contains one or more virtual hosts each with one or more applications (Context). Within each application are Java Servlets and JSPs. A few concepts are

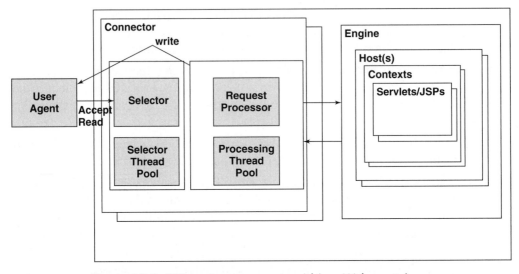

Figure 10-1 Different components within a Web container

shared in some of the components. Both the connector and the engine use the concept of pipeline and valves. A pipeline is a series of steps that the incoming request goes through during its processing cycle. The pipeline consists of a set of default valves or tasks but is configurable, and new valves can be added to provide additional functionalities.

HTTP Connector

As of V2, the GlassFish Web container uses the Grizzly NIO framework (http://grizzly.java.net/), which allows the server to scale to many concurrent clients. The entry point into Grizzly is the Selector module where the NIO selectors are created. The selector thread pool allows multiple selectors to be run in parallel to provide better scalability. The Selector is task based and creates the following tasks:

- Accept task to handle new connections (NIO OP_ACCEPT event)
- Read task for reading the request (NIO OP_READ event)
- Processor task for processing the request

The read task is responsible for preprocessing the request; to read data from the stream to ensure that there is enough information to start processing the request. Once a request is ready for processing, a processor task is created and scheduled for execution on the request processing thread pool (request processor in Figure 10-1).

The threads in the request processing thread pool are responsible for processing incoming requests and committing the response back to the client. In all cases, other than the asynchronous processing defined in Servlet 3.0 specification, all the instructions involved in a request process are executed in a single thread including any I/O operations (database interaction, external Web service calls, etc.). The processor consists of a series of pipelined operations, including stream processing and protocol parsing. Additionally, the pipeline also includes special handlers like HTTP file cache, which if enabled allows static files to be delivered from the Grizzly file cache for improved static file delivery performance.

In addition to the NIO based Grizzly connector, GlassFish also supports a blocking connector called the Coyote connector. The blocking connector is based on Java I/O and follows a thread per request model. In this mode, when a new connection is created, a thread is assigned to handle all requests on that connection. After a request has been processed, if the connection is not closed by the client, the processing thread blocks waiting for additional requests until the connection times out. The blocking connector works well for handling multiple requests from a single client but suffers from scalability problems since a thread has to be dedicated to each open connection. The connector is thus typically limited to handling a couple of thousands of connections at best. The problem is especially acute for cases where the user makes requests at a low rate. In this case, the server has to reject new connections due to lack of available processing threads even though the server has plenty of computational capacity left.

Since the NIO based connector uses a limited set of worker threads for handling all connections, it can scale to several thousand connections. Performance tests have shown that GlassFish can handle upwards of 10,000 connections.

Servlet Engine

The connector hands off the request to the servlet engine for processing. A single engine shared by multiple connectors is composed of multiple nested components starting with one or more virtual hosts. Virtual hosting allows multiple domains to be serviced by a single server. GlassFish allows multiple virtual hosts to be configured using the Administration Console. Virtual hosting is a convenience feature and does not impact the performance of applications deployed in it. A host can support multiple applications with each application identified by a unique context root. The engine pipeline consists of a series of valves with each valve responsible for a specific operation. The valve hierarchy is configurable, and users can add their own valves to implement custom features.

Applications are isolated from each other through the use of separate class loaders for every application. Each application can contain one or more Java Servlets and JSPs. The container handles the application life cycle during deployment and undeployment. Applications can attach listeners to be invoked during context initialization and destruction as well as have custom code invoked during the creation and destruction of a Servlet (init() and destroy() methods). In addition to user-defined Servlets, the container has two built-in Servlets, the DefaultServlet and the JspServlet. The DefaultServlet is responsible for handling static files (html, css, JavaScript, images, etc.) deployed as part of the application.

By default, GlassFish supports dynamic modification of JSPs allowing changes to be reflected immediately without application redeployment. Requests mapped to a JSP page are handled by the JspServlet, which first checks whether the JSP file has been modified since it was last compiled. If it is, the JSP page is compiled and service method invoked. The support for dynamic changes does have a performance impact and is discussed in more detail in the "Best Practices" section later in the chapter.

Web Container Monitoring and Performance Tunings

Chapter 9 discussed how the various containers within an application server can be monitored to identify potential performance bottlenecks and use the observed values to tune the container for optimal performance. By tuning the containers appropriately, we hope to maximize the use of the system resources. For most Web applications, the goal would be to eliminate performance bottlenecks and be able to scale the application either vertically or horizontally as the user load increases.

Before talking about the various parameters that can be monitored, some of the container level configuration settings that have performance implications are discussed. It is important to note that the items discussed here are applicable to most application servers; GlassFish is used as an example to show how the various parameters can be tweaked.

Development and Production Container Modes

There may be configuration settings applicable to the container that affect its performance. It is important to select appropriate container settings for optimal performance. For example, the GlassFish Web container supports two different modes —development mode and production mode. The difference between the two modes is the way in which the container handles changes made to a deployed JSP. In the development mode, auto-reloading of the JSP is enabled, in which each page is checked to see whether any changes have been made to it. This mode allows developers to see the effect of the changes without the need to redeploy the application. There is a performance penalty for achieving the flexibility offered by the development mode. The container saves the last compiled time of the JSP file, and for each request this value is checked against the last modified time of the file in the file system. If the file is newer than the compiled version in memory, the file is reloaded thus allowing the modifications to be visible right away. In addition to the expense involved in the file timestamp check (due to a system call), the synchronized nature of this check reduces the container's capability to process the same JSP file by multiple threads in parallel thus reducing the scalability of the application. In the production mode, auto-reloading is disabled, which means that the application needs to be redeployed for any changes to be visible.

By default, GlassFish in a developer profile sets the container to be in developer mode. To achieve best performance in a production environment, the container should be configured to be in production mode. To configure GlassFish in production mode, add the following lines to the <DOMAIN_DIR>/config/default-web.xml> file under the JspServlet definition:

```
<init-param>
    <param-name>development</param-name>
    <param-value>false</param-value>
</init-param>
<init-param>
    <param-name>genStrAsCharArray</param-name>
    <param-value>true</param-value>
</init-param>
```

The default-web.xml is only read during application deployment. So the application has to be redeployed for this change to take effect.

Even in production mode, it is possible to check the freshness of the page periodically through the use of the checkInterval property. By default, the check Interval value is set to zero, which results in background compilation being turned off. By setting a value higher than zero, the container can be configured to check for changes even in production mode. However, for best performance the checkInterval value should be set to zero.

Presence of Security Manager

The Java security manager manages the security policy that determines whether access to a protected resource is permitted to code. Based on a security policy file, the security manager provides access of protected resources to code loaded from specific locations, signed by particular entities, and executed for a set of users. The security manager is required only if your application runs untrusted code and can be turned off if the application runs trusted code.

In GlassFish, the Java security manager is disabled by default but can be easily enabled by adding the System property `java.security.manager` as a JVM argument through the Administration Console or using the `asadmin` CLI. Once the security manager is enabled, it will be in effect for all the applications deployed on that instance of the application server.

A performance cost is associated with enabling the security manager. The Java runtime keeps track of the sequence of method calls made as a program executes. When access to a protected resource is requested, the entire call stack, by default, is evaluated to determine whether the request access is permitted. This security check is expensive, thereby increasing the overall execution time of any operation that involves access of protected resources (for example, file and network I/O). In performance tests conducted in our lab using a simple online trading application, enabling the security manager (using the default security.policy file) resulted in a 33% reduction in throughput.

It is important to note that disabling the security manager does not affect the application server's capability to provide authentication and authorization.

JVM Tunings

One of the most important performance tunings that need to be applied to a Web container is tuning the JVM that the container runs on. These include the selection of the JVM compiler as well as the garbage collection settings appropriate for the application.

Chapter 3, "JVM Overview," provides details of the client and the server JIT compilers. Most Web containers in production environments are expected to run continuously over a long period of time between restarts. The server JIT compiler that provides the best performance is ideally suited for such cases. Unless the client JIT compiler is specified (which is the default behavior for the GlassFish application server), the JVM ergonomics automatically selects the appropriate JIT compiler for server class machines.

> **Tip**
>
> Java EE containers that are used in production mode should select the server JIT compiler. For server class machines, the JVM typically selects this option automatically unless the `-client` option is provided (which is the default for the GlassFish server in development mode). Server compiler can be enabled by specifying the `-server` JVM option.

As discussed earlier, the GlassFish application server sets the client compiler as the default by specifying the `-client` option. This is due to the fact that the default server is configured in development mode for application developer use. The servers used in this mode are expected to be restarted often and lower server startup time is more important than achieving the best performance. The client compiler is thus a better fit for this type of use.

The other important JVM subsystem to be tuned for production deployments is the garbage collection. The selection of the garbage collector and the various tuning parameters play an important role in the overall performance of the container. Users are encouraged to review Chapter 7, "Tuning the JVM, Step by Step," for more information on the selection of the appropriate garbage collector as well as for tuning the GC for optimal performance.

The garbage collection characteristics of a Web container depend both on the container as well as the deployed application. Even though Web applications vary widely, in the vast majority of cases, the object retention is limited to the duration of the processing of the request. In a typical scenario, many `String` and `char` arrays are created by the container when a request is being processed, and these objects are eligible for garbage collection once the response is committed. These short-lived objects can often be reclaimed from the young generation space. If the young generation space is small, this can lead to some of the objects being promoted unnecessarily to the old generation space. Since JDK 1.4, the size of the young generation space is based on the value set as the Java HotSpot VM's NewRatio, the default value of which varies with the hardware (Server VM: SPARC=2, x86=8). Java HotSpot's NewRatio sets the ratio of young generation space to old generation space. GlassFish sets the NewRatio value to 2, but in general, for Web containers running on x86 based systems, the performance can be improved by increasing the size of the young generation space by setting the following `-XX:NewSize=<size>` and `-XX:MaxNewSize=<size>` where size is one-third of the maximum Java heap size, which is set by the command line option `-Xmx`.

The choice of the garbage collector depends on the application requirements. Since Web containers are deployed on server class machines with multiple CPUs, and are designed to service large number of requests in parallel, the throughput collector would be able to provide the highest overall system throughput. The downside of using this collector is the large pause times encountered during the full garbage collection cycles, which may lead to poor user experience. The CMS collector is a better choice for Web applications that require low pause times.

GlassFish and other Web containers embed an RMI server to service client requests. It is important to tune the garbage collection for RMI to control periodic full garbage collections. By default RMI invokes distributed garbage collection every 60 seconds. Distributed garbage collection is done via a call to `System.gc()`. Distributed garbage collection frequency can be tuned using the following two properties, `-Dsun.rmi.dgc.client.gcInterval` and `-Dsun.rmi.dgc.server.gcInterval`. Both properties accept a numeric value. The default value is 3,600,000 milliseconds, in other words 1 hour. Setting these two properties to a value of `Long.MAX_VALUE`, effectively sets the interval between distributed garbage collections to infinity. In addition, the `-XX:+DisableExplicitGC` Java HotSpot VM command line option disables distributed garbage collection. The important thing to know with tuning distributed garbage collection is that if the application requires timely reference processing, then setting the interval to `Long.MAX_VALUE` or disabling distributed garbage collection is not a recommended practice. Otherwise, disabling or setting the interval to `Long.MAX_VALUE` is acceptable. You may need to do some analysis of your application to determine whether it relies on frequent reference processing.

HTTP Service and Web Container

This section discusses the important parameters within the Web container that can be monitored. The examples are based on the GlassFish V3 application server, but the general principles should apply to other application servers as well. It should be noted that identification of issues often requires several of the parameters to be monitored in combination. Refer to Chapter 9 for a more detailed description of GlassFish monitoring, including how to enable monitoring for the different containers.

The monitoring data of interest in the Web container fall under two categories: HTTP Service and Web Container. The monitoring levels for these components need to be changed to low (setting a value of high has the same effect) to turn on the data collection. The examples in this section are based on GlassFish V3.

HTTP Listener

The HTTP listener provides data regarding the connection queues, thread pools, file caches, and keep-alives. The different nodes that can be monitored under the http-listener-x are shown in the following example. To view this in the Administration Console, click on the Monitor tab of the server instance, select the Server tab, and choose the http-listener-x element from the drop-down menu. A sample listing of the elements that can be monitored under http-listener-1 follows:

```
asadmin list -m "server.*http-listener-1.*"
server.network.http-listener-1.keep-alive
server.network.http-listener-1.file-cache
server.network.http-listener-1.thread-pool
server.network.http-listener-1.connection-queue
```

Thread Pool

The most important parameter that affects performance is the size of the request processing thread pool. A request processing thread pool is configured with each listener to process the incoming request as described in the Web container architecture section. By default, GlassFish sets the maximum size of the thread pool to be 5. This is usually sufficient for developer class machines consisting of one or two CPUs. However, this value should be modified for production deployments on large servers.

The best practice in tuning the thread pool configuration is to first change it to a set of initial values based on some general guidelines, monitor the thread pool under load conditions, and then modify the values if required based on the findings. A reasonable set of starting values for the thread pool is given in Table 10-1.

The request processing thread pool (http-thread-pool) values can be changed using the `asadmin` command or through the Administration Console (Select the Configuration node and then the Server-config node, followed by Thread Pools. In the panel, select the http-thread-pool and click to edit the values). The following example shows how to use `asadmin` to set the values for a four-core server.

```
asadmin set "configs.config.server-config.thread-pools.thread-pool.http-
thread-pool.min-thread-pool-size=4"
asadmin set "configs.config.server-config.thread-pools.thread-pool.http-
thread-pool.min-thread-pool-size=8"
```

Once a thread starts processing a request, that thread is used to execute all the application logic until the response is committed. Any I/O interaction that is part of the application (examples: invocation of remote EJBs, database interactions, communicating with slow clients, file system interactions) can cause the thread to be in I/O wait state, thereby making the CPU resources available for other threads to run. For such applications, configuring the thread pool with too few threads can cause requests to be queued for processing while CPU resources are available. By monitoring the request processing thread pool as well as CPU utilization, a determination can be made if the pool size needs to be increased. Before proceeding with this tuning, lock contention and/or resource contention in other parts of the system (e.g., all threads waiting on a slow disk I/O) that can cause poor CPU utilization should be identified and eliminated. Refer to Chapter 2, "Operating System Performance Monitoring," and Chapter 4, "JVM Performance Monitoring," for more details on how to identify performance bottlenecks.

The HTTP thread pool utilization can be understood by monitoring the `current threadsbusy-count` attribute, which shows the status of the server at the time

Table 10-1 Thread Count Settings for the Thread Pool

Attribute	Initial Value
Initial Thread Count	Number of hardware threads
Thread Count	2 X Number of hardware threads

Table 10-2 Thread Pool Tuning Hints

Attribute	Description	Tuning Hints
`maxthreads-count`	Maximum number of threads allowed in the thread pool	Size this value based on the CPU utilization and currentthreadsbusy-count. Increase the value if all the threads are being used on a consistent basis and CPU resources are still available. Setting the pool size to an excessive high value can have detrimental performance effects due to increased context switches, cache misses, etc.
`currentthreadsbusy-count`	Number of request processing threads currently in use in the listener thread pool serving requests	If this value is consistently equal to the maxthreads-count, it signifies that there is enough load on the system to keep the request processing pool fully utilized.

of statistics collection. The other attribute of interest, `maxthreads-count`, is a static value based on the configuration setting. Table 10-2 provides further information.

Tip

Tuning the HTTP request processing pool appropriately is essential for obtaining maximum performance. A good starting value for `http-service.request-processing.thread-count` is twice the number of cores for non-CMT type CPUs and the number of virtual processors for a CMT type CPU. Monitor the `currentthreadsbusy-count` value to verify the efficacy of the setting and make further changes as required.

Acceptor Thread, Connection Queue, and Keep Alive

Unlike GlassFish V2 where the connection queue statistics are maintained in the HTTP listener, in V3, the transport layer, TCP, maintains the data. The connection queue is where connections waiting to be serviced are kept. The requests are taken out of the queue and serviced by one of the available processing threads. As expected, as the number of requests waiting to be serviced increases, the response times for those requests also increase. Additionally, the server rejects new requests if the number of items in the queue reaches a maximum configured value (default is 4096). Some of the parameters that can be configured for the transport layer and the connection queue and their default values are as follows:

```
asadmin get "configs.config.server-config.*tcp.*"
configs.config.server-config.network-config.transports.transport.tcp.
acceptor-threads=1
configs.config.server-config.network-config.transports.transport.tcp.
buffer-size-bytes=8192
configs.config.server-config.network-config.transports.transport.tcp.
max-connections-count=4096
```

The `acceptor-thread` property defines the number of selector threads. Since the selector thread handles the request read task for servers that handle a large number of connections, the default value of a single thread would not be optimal. For best performance, set this value equal to the number of the processors in the system. Table 10-3 summarizes this information.

The `max-connections-count` property is used to specify the maximum number of entries in the connection queue. Once the queue length reaches maximum capacity, the server rejects any new requests. The `buffer-size-bytes` property specifies the size of the send and receive buffers. For most applications, there is no need to change the send and receive buffer sizes since the default values provide the optimum performance. This value may be increased for applications that deal with large incoming or outgoing payloads. Any modifications to this value should be accompanied by appropriate changes to the operating system level TCP buffer sizes.

Monitoring the connection queue allows the server load to be evaluated and to take appropriate actions when the load increases beyond a certain level. The GlassFish monitoring framework can be used to inspect the various connection queue statistics using the admin CLI or through the Administration Console.

```
asadmin get -m "server.network.http-listener-1*connection-queue.*"
```

Some important parameters, their descriptions, and how to interpret the values are given in Table 10-4.

HTTP/1.1 by default uses persistent connections in which a single connection is used by the client to make multiple requests. The server maintains the connection in the keep-alive state enabling the user agent to make subsequent requests on the same connection rather than create a new connection for every request (HTTP/1.0). The server closes a connection if one of the following conditions are met.

Table 10-3 Acceptor Threads Tuning Hint

Attribute	Description	Tuning Hints
acceptor-threads	Number of selector threads	For multiprocessor systems, set this value to the number of available processors.

Table 10-4 Connection Queue Tuning Hints

Attribute	Description	Comments
`countqueued-count`	Number of connections currently in the queue	A request in the queue will be processed when a processing thread becomes available. Consistently high values suggest high load on the system, incorrect thread pool tuning, or lock contention within the application.
`countqueued*minuteaverage-count`	Average number of connections queued in the last 1, 5, or 15 minutes	Useful for filtering out short load spikes.
`countoverflows-count`	Number of times the queue has been too full to accommodate a connection	Rejection of client connections results in poor user experience. If clients can tolerate higher response times, increasing the queue size can reduce the connection rejections. Potential solution for a highly loaded system is to scale the application server tier vertically or horizontally.

- The time elapsed between now and the last request exceeds the value specified for the `timeout-in-seconds` parameter.

- The number of requests using a connection exceeds the value specified by the `max-connections` parameter.

The `max-connections` parameter is used to prevent malicious clients from tying up a thread indefinitely when the Coyote blocking connector is used. This restriction can be eliminated by setting the value to –1 (minus one) if the instance uses the Grizzly NIO connector or if the instance is accessed only by trusted clients.

The default keep-alive values are as follows:

```
asadmin get -m server.network.http-listener-1.keep-alive.*
server.http-service.keep-alive.maxrequests-count = 250
server.http-service.keep-alive.secondstimeouts-count = 30
```

The GlassFish monitoring framework can be used to inspect the various keep-alive statistics using the admin CLI or through the Administration Console.

```
asadmin get -m server.network.http-listener-1.keep-alive.*
server.network.http-listener-1.keep-alive.countconnections-count = 1869
server.network.http-listener-1.keep-alive.countflushes-count = 0
server.network.http-listener-1.keep-alive.counthits-count = 359873
server.network.http-listener-1.keep-alive.countrefusals-count = 1428
server.network.http-listener-1.keep-alive.counttimeouts-count = 0
server.network.http-listener-1.keep-alive.maxrequests-count = 250
server.network.http-listener-1.keep-alive.secondstimeouts-count = 30
```

Some important parameters, their descriptions, and how to interpret the values are given in Table 10-5. All values are totals since the start of monitoring and hence will increase monotonically. To collect relevant values, the statistics for the period of interest can be obtained by collecting the values at the start of the measurement interval and then subtracting those numbers from the subsequent values. The information presented in Table 10-5 pertains to statistics collected during the measurement interval.

Table 10-5 Keep-Alive Tuning Hints

Attribute	Description	Comments
countconnections-count	Number of connections in keep-alive mode	If this value is consistently high (several hundreds/core), consider decreasing the maximum requests or reducing the timeout value.
counthits-count	Number of cache lookup hits	A high hit rate (keep-alive. counthits-count/request. countrequests-count) means that the current settings are working well.
countrefusals-count	Number of keep-alive connections that were rejected for exceeding the maximum number of requests allowed per connection	The configuration attribute keep-alive. max-requests limits the number of requests allowed for a connection. The client has to open a new connection for subsequent requests. It is advisable to keep this at the default value if the HTTP connector is run in blocking mode. A value of –1 (signifies unlimited requests) can be set for HTTP connectors running in nonblocking mode (default connector) or if servicing trusted clients.
counttimeouts-count	Number of keep-alive connections that timed out	The default keep alive timeout is 30 seconds. Increase this value if most of your returning clients take longer than this interval for making subsequent requests. A very high value can cause the number of connections to be kept alive unnecessarily thereby degrading the performance.

Request Processing

Inspecting the various request processing counts can provide some insight into the type of requests being processed by the server, and the data can be used to improve the performance of the application. The various request processing metrics can be obtained using the `asadmin` CLI command as shown here (output is edited for better readability).

```
asadmin get -m "server.http-service.server.request.*" | grep 'count.*\-count'
server.http-service.server.request.count200-count = 1
server.http-service.server.request.count302-count = 0
server.http-service.server.request.count304-count = 0
server.http-service.server.request.count404-count = 0
server.http-service.server.request.count5xx-count = 0
server.http-service.server.request.countrequests-count = 1
```

Some parameters of interest, their descriptions, and comments about what the values mean are given in Table 10-6.

The value of the `count302-count` parameter needs to be analyzed in detail to see whether performance improvements can be achieved by modifying the application. A Servlet can either forward or redirect a request to a new URL at the end of processing as shown in the following code snippets.

```
public void processRequest (HttpServletRequest request,
        HttpServletResponse response)
        throws ServletException, IOException {
    ...
    request.getRequestDispatcher(url).forward (request, respsonse);
}
public void processRequest (HttpServletRequest request,
        HttpServletResponse response)
        throws ServletException, IOException {
    ...
    response.sendRedirect(url);
}
```

In the case of forward, the servlet container forwards the request internally, and the browser is unaware of the change in URL. Any reload of the page at the browser results in the request being sent to the original URL. Redirect on the other hand is a two-step process. In the first step, the servlet container sends a response with the status 302 Moved Temporarily along with the new URL specified in the Location header field. The browser then makes a request to the specified URL. Since the browser is aware of the new URL, a page reload results in fetching contents from the new location. Due to the additional round-trip communication involved in redirect, it

Table 10-6 Explanation of Response Code Values

Attribute	Description	Comments
`countrequests-count`	Total number of requests serviced by the server since startup	
`count200-count`	Number of responses with a status code of 200 OK	`count200-count/countrequests-count` indicates the percentage of requests serviced normally.
`count302-count`	Number of requests that were redirected	A redirect results in two browser requests instead of one. See following discussion for more details.
`count304-count`	Number of requests in which the resource has not been changed since last accessed	A high percentage of these responses indicates possibility of resource caching. It may be possible to reduce these types of requests by setting appropriate HTTP caching headers. Refer to http://www.w3.org/Protocols/rfc2616/rfc2616-sec13.html for more information about HTTP caching.
`count404-count`	Number of times in which the server could not find anything matching the request URI	High values typically suggest incorrect resource references within applications that need to be corrected. See following discussion for more details.
`count5xx-count`	Number of reported server errors	For a healthy application, this value should be zero. It is important to evaluate the cause of the server errors and fix them since they result in poor user experience.

may be slightly slower than forward. However, depending on the application state, in some situations redirect may be a better choice. An example is the redirection at the end of a POST request processing that may change the state of the application. This would avoid data being submitted multiple times due to users accidentally reloading the page. (There are ways to detect multiple submissions and take corrective actions, but they are beyond the scope of this discussion.)

Tip

Forwarding a request to a new location performs slightly better than redirection. In addition to performance, other application-specific factors should also be taken into consideration to determine whether forward or redirect should be used.

Status code 404 represents the number of times a requested resource was not found. High values for `count404-count` parameter often point to the presence of incorrect resource references within the application. Searching for nonexistent resources is expensive and should be avoided. The monitoring framework does not provide any information regarding the resource that generated this error, though this information can be gleaned from the access logs. (Note: GlassFish in developer profile does not turn on access logging by default.)

One of the common sources of 404 errors is the absence of a favicon.ico icon for the site. Most modern browsers request the icon file (favicon.ico), if the location of the icon is not defined within a page. One option to reduce these errors is to create a 1x1 pixel blank image as the favicon.ico. Applying proper caching headers allows this image to be cached thereby eliminating subsequent requests.

Applications

Performance statistics for individual applications can be obtained by enabling the monitoring level of the Web container to be LOW or HIGH.

```
asadmin set server.monitoring-service.module-monitoring-levels.
web-container=LOW
```

Unlike the EJB container, there is no difference in the displayed output between the LOW and HIGH values. The monitoring framework provides a variety of application level statistics including the response times of individual servlets as well as details regarding HTTP sessions. The `asadmin list -m` command can be used to obtain a list of all available servlets as shown in the following example.

```
asadmin list -m "server.applications.TestWebapp*"
server.applications.TestWebapp.server.ControlServlet
server.applications.TestWebapp.server.default
server.applications.TestWebapp.server.jsp
```

By default, the time statistics for all the JSPs are listed under the `JspServlet` (identified as `jsp`) and the delivery of static content under the `default` servlet. Combining the service times for all the JSPs under a single node may not be useful for a variety of applications. Unfortunately, this is a limitation of the current implementation, and the only available workaround is to redeploy the application with a modified web.xml file that maps the JSP to a servlet and then specifying the appropriate URL pattern as shown in the following example web.xml snippet.

```
<servlet>
   <servlet-name>ElTesterJsp</servlet-name>
   <jsp-file>/elTester.jsp</jsp-file>
</servlet>
<servlet-mapping>
   <servlet-name>ElTesterJsp</servlet-name>
   <url-pattern>/elTester.jsp</url-pattern>
</servlet-mapping>
```

Once the application is redeployed, the JSP of interest (/elTester.jsp) can be monitored as a servlet (server.applications.TestWebapp.server.ElTesterJsp). The following command shows how to get a few interesting request processing statistics for a servlet in the Web application named TestWebapp.

```
asadmin get -m
server.applications.TestWebapp.server.ControlServlet.maxtime-count server.
applications.TestWebapp.server.ControlServlet.processingtime-count server.
applications.TestWebapp.server.ControlServlet.requestcount-count
server.applications.TestWebapp.server.ControlServlet.maxtime-count = 112
server.applications.TestWebapp.server.ControlServlet.processingtime-count =
1173395
server.applications.TestWebapp.server.ControlServlet.requestcount-count =
3746651
```

The data of interest include the number of serviced requests, the maximum time taken for a request, and the cumulative processing time. The average response time for the servicing of a request can be obtained by dividing the cumulative processing time by the number of serviced requests. Since all values are cumulative since monitoring was enabled, some number crunching (storing the baseline values for both number of requests and service times and subtracting it from the observed values) is required to evaluate the response time characteristics for a specific period.

As seen in the preceding example, the Web application monitoring framework has several limitations and is only useful as a coarse-grained monitoring tool. However, most Web applications need more sophisticated monitoring. The way to achieve this is by adding performance statistics within the application and exposing them through JMX. The advantage of this method is that the developer can add different types of performance statistics including request counts, elapsed times of various calls (e.g., query execution times at the database), cache hit/miss rates if applicable, and so on. The JMX based monitoring approach does not have to be limited to performance statistics but can be used to display any useful application-specific information.

Since the applications are long running, it is advisable to use a count-based or time-based sampling window to calculate the performance statistics. In this approach, a moving sampling window with a fixed set of sample data are maintained; old values are dropped as new ones are added. In a count-based window, the number of samples is fixed, whereas in a time-based window all the samples within a time interval are saved. The Statistics package under the Apache Commons Math project provides a framework for descriptive statistics that can be used for this purpose. More information about the package can be found at http://commons.apache.org/math/userguide/stat.html#a1.2_Descriptive_statistics. The following section describes how application level monitoring can be added to a Web application. In this example, a sample MBean is developed to capture the request count and response time statistics for a single servlet. For simplicity, data for all types of requests irrespective of paths or request method are aggregated. In real production deployments, users may want to add logic to subdivide data for different request types appropriately (e.g., GET versus POST).

First, define the MBean that will be exposed. A sample is shown here:

```java
/**
 * Describes the data that will be exposed through JMX.
 */
public interface StatsMBean {
    /**
     * @return The request count
     */
    public int getCount();

    /**
     * @return Name of the stat object
     */
    public String getName();

    /**
     * @return Description of the stat object
     */
    public String getDescription();

    /**
     * @return The mean response time in milliseconds
     */
    public double getMean();

    /**
     * @return The response time std. dev. in milliseconds
     */
    public double getStandardDeviation();

    /**
     * @return The Minimum response time in milliseconds
     */
    public double getMin();

    /**
     * @return The maximum response time in milliseconds
```

```
   */
   public double getMax();
   /**
    * @return The median response time in milliseconds
    */
   public double getTP50();
   /**
    * @return The 90th percentile response time in milliseconds
    */
   public double getTP90();
   /**
    * @return The 99th percentile response time in milliseconds
    */
   public double getTP99();

   /**
    * Clear the sample data
    */
   public void reset();
}
```

The next step is to implement the MBean. The following code sample uses a count-based sample window. The Javadocs have been removed for brevity.

```
import org.apache.commons.math.stat.descriptive.DescriptiveStatistics;
import org.apache.commons.math.stat.descriptive.
SynchronizedDescriptiveStatistics;
import java.util.concurrent.atomic.AtomicInteger;

public class Stats implements StatsMBean {
      private static final int DEFAULT_ITEM_COUNT = 1000;
      private String description;
      private String name;
      private AtomicInteger count;

      private DescriptiveStatistics stats;

      public Stats(String name, String description) {
            this (name, description, DEFAULT_ITEM_COUNT);
      }

      public Stats(String name, String description, int sampleCount) {
            this.name = name;
            this.description = description;
            stats = new SynchronizedDescriptiveStatistics(sampleCount);
            count = new AtomicInteger();
      }

      public void addValue (double v) {
            stats.addValue(v);
            count.incrementAndGet();
      }
}
```

```
    public int getCount() {
        return count.get();
    }

    public double getMin() {
        return stats.getMin();
    }

    public double getMax() {
        return stats.getMax();
    }

    public double getTP50() {
        return stats.getPercentile(50.0);
    }

    public double getTP90() {
        return stats.getPercentile(90.0);
    }

    public double getTP99() {
        return stats.getPercentile(99.0);
    }

    public double getStandardDeviation() {
        return stats.getStandardDeviation();
    }

    public String getName() {
        return name;
    }

    public String getDescription() {
        return description;
    }

    public double getMean() {
        return stats.getMean();
    }

    // Reset the stats
    public void reset() {
        stats.clear();
        count.set(0);
    }
}
```

The MBean needs to be registered so that it is visible to the user. One approach is to add the register and unregister logic in a servlet context listener that gets invoked as part of the servlet initialization and destruction life cycle. A sample context listener and the web.xml configuration snippet follow. The StatsExporter is a utility class used to export and unexport the various MBeans that are part of this application. It should be noted that for simplicity no special error handling code is included.

```java
import javax.servlet.ServletContextListener;
import javax.servlet.ServletContextEvent;
import javax.servlet.ServletContext;

public class ControlServletContextListener
    implements ServletContextListener {
    public void contextInitialized(
        ServletContextEvent servletContextEvent) {
        // Register the MBean for this Servlet
        ServletContext context =
            servletContextEvent.getServletContext();
        String path = context.getContextPath();
        StatsMBean statsMBean = new Stats(path, "ServletRequest stats");
        String statName =
            "javaperfbook.web.sample:name=ServletRequest ("+path+" )";
        StatsExporter.getInstance().export(statName, statsMBean);
        context.setAttribute("statsMBean", statsMBean);
    }

    public void contextDestroyed(
        ServletContextEvent servletContextEvent) {
        StatsExporter.getInstance().unExportAll();
    }
}

import javax.management.*;
import java.lang.management.ManagementFactory;
import java.util.Set;
import java.util.HashSet;
import java.util.Iterator;
import java.util.logging.Logger;

public class StatsExporter {
    private static StatsExporter instance = new StatsExporter();
    private Set<ObjectName> exportBeans = new HashSet<ObjectName>();
    private static Logger logger =
        Logger.getLogger(StatsExporter.class.getName());

    public static StatsExporter getInstance() {
        return instance;
    }

    public void export (String name, StatsMBean bean) {
        try {
            ObjectName oName = new ObjectName(name);
ManagementFactory.getPlatformMBeanServer()
                            .registerMBean(bean, oName);
            exportBeans.add(oName);
        } catch (MalformedObjectNameException e) {
            handleException(e);
        } catch (NotCompliantMBeanException e) {
            handleException(e);
        } catch (MBeanRegistrationException e) {
            handleException(e);
        } catch (InstanceAlreadyExistsException e) {
            handleException(e);
        }
```

```
    }

    private void unexport (ObjectName oName) {
        try {
            ManagementFactory.getPlatformMBeanServer()
                            .unregisterMBean(oName);
        } catch (MBeanRegistrationException e) {
            handleException(e);
        } catch (InstanceNotFoundException e) {
            handleException(e);
        }
    }

    public void unExportAll() {
        Iterator<ObjectName> iter = exportBeans.iterator();
        while (iter.hasNext()) {
            unexport(iter.next());
        }
        exportBeans.clear();
    }

    private void handleException (Exception e) {
        logger.warning(e.getMessage());
        e.printStackTrace();
    }
}
```

```xml
<web-app xmlns="http://java.sun.com/xml/ns/javaee"...
    ...
    <listener>
        <display-name>ContextListener</display-name>
        <listener-class>
            javaperfbook.web.sample.ControlServletContextListener
        </listener-class>
    </listener>
</web-app>
```

The last step is to measure the elapsed time and add the data to the Stats object. Typically, this is achieved through the use of a servlet filter as shown in the following code sample. In this example, only the response time and the request count are measured. If the response length is required, the filter can provide a response wrapper that calculates the size of the response and exposes that through an MBean.

```java
import javax.servlet.*;
import java.io.IOException;

public class StatsFilter implements Filter {
    private FilterConfig config;
```

```
    public void doFilter(ServletRequest req,
                        ServletResponse resp,
                        FilterChain chain)
       throws ServletException, IOException {
       long start = System.nanoTime();
       chain.doFilter(req, resp);
       double elapsed = (System.nanoTime()-start)/1e6;
       Stats stat = (Stats) config.getServletContext().
                                getAttribute("statsMBean");
       if (stat ! = null) {
           stat.addValue(elapsed);
       }
    }

    public void init(FilterConfig config) throws ServletException {
       this.config = config;
    }

    public void destroy() {
    }
}
```

Figure 10-2 shows the custom MBeans viewed using JConsole. The application-specific data can be viewed by selecting the MBeans tab and then clicking on the javaperfbook.web.sample node on the left navigation tree.

Best Practices

This section covers the various performance best practices that should be considered during the development and deployment of the Web application. The "Servlet and JSP Best Practices" section includes performance tips that can enhance the performance of servlets and JSPs. This is followed by a set of performance techniques that address issues common across many Web applications: data compression, content caching, session persistence, and static file delivery. The "Access Logging" section later in the chapter describes a way for users to capture performance metrics that can be used to improve the performance of deployed applications.

Servlet and JSP Best Practices

This section describes a set of best practices that should be considered while developing servlets and/or JSPs.

Use of Init Method and ContextListener

The *init* method of the servlet and JSP can be used to cache static data and resource references. The Web container initializes a servlet before it is ready to service any requests. This operation is carried out only once as part of a servlet's life cycle.

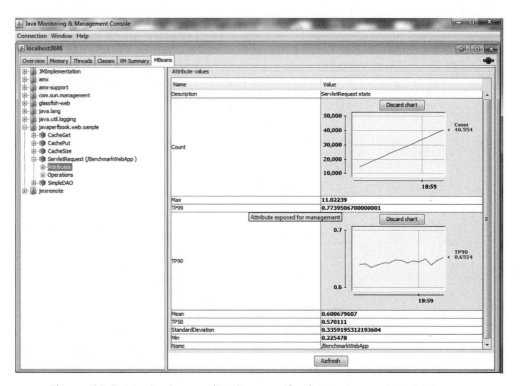

Figure 10-2 Monitoring application-specific data using custom MBeans

```
public class SampleServlet extends HttpServlet {
    public void init() {
        ....
    }
    ...
}
```

The `init()` method can thus be used to carry out expensive one-time operations. Some of these operations include creation and caching of static content, and in the case of J2EE 1.4 based applications, reading configuration information and initialization and caching of resource references including JNDI lookup of `DataSources`. In Java EE 5, resource injection allows easy access to resources and hence the use of the `init()` method for this purpose is no longer required.

Similar to the Servlet's `init()` method, the `jspInit()` method is called once during the initialization of a JSP page. By providing a user-defined `jspInit()` method within the JSP, it is possible to carry out one-time operations. The most common use of this is to create and cache static data. The use of `jspInit()` is not a common practice.

Context listeners invoked as part of the servlet life cycle are useful for initializing and clearing application-specific data. The listener is specified in the web.xml as follows:

```
<webapp ..>
    ..
    <listener>
        <display-name>ContextListener</display-name>
        <listener-class>
            javaperfbook.web.sample.ControlServletContextListener
        </listener-class>
    </listener>
</webapp>
```

The listener is called when the servlet context is initialized and destroyed. Refer back to the "Applications" section earlier in the chapter for information on how to use a context listener for initializing the application-specific JMX MBeans.

Use Appropriate JSP Include Mechanism

JSP supports two ways to include the contents of a resource in a page:

- **Include directive.** `<%@ include file="relativeURL" %>` adds the text of the included file to the page. This include process is static, which means that the text is incorporated into the JSP page at compilation time. If the included file is a JSP page, its JSP elements are translated and included in this page. The side effect of this is that any changes made to the included file are not reflected in the page that includes it even when dynamic reloading of JSPs is enabled. The changes are only visible when changes are made to the top level page that causes regeneration of the included content.

- **Include action.** `<jsp:include page="relativeURL" />` allows the addition of static or dynamic resources to the page. If the resource is static, its content (obtained through the invocation of the default servlet) is included in the calling page. If the included resource is dynamic, the results from its invocation are included in the calling page. The attribute `flush="true"|"false"` can be used to specify whether the content of the calling page needs to be flushed before including the resource. The default value for this attribute is false. The `<jsp:param>` clause can be used to pass one or more name/value pairs as parameters to the included resource. The dynamic nature of the include action allows modifications made to included pages to be visible without the need for any changes to be made to the top level page.

Since the page directive includes the contents of the referenced resource at compile time, this mechanism provides improved performance for including HTML and other static content. The page action on the other hand should be used for situations in which the required content to be included is the dynamically generated response from the referenced resource.

> **Tip**
>
> Use the include directive if the referenced resource is static and use the include action to incorporate a dynamically generated response from a resource.

Trim Whitespaces

Whitespaces within the text of a JSP page, even though not significant, are preserved. This means that some extraneous characters are processed and transmitted by the Web container that is not required by the browser for displaying the content.

Preserving the whitespaces within the template text of a JSP can result in blocks of whitespaces in the rendered output making the HTML source difficult to read. There is also a performance cost of encoding and transmitting the extraneous characters. The JSP 2.1 specification provides the following example. The following code snippet (where α represents the end-of-line character(s))

```
<%@ taglib prefix="c" uri="http://java.sun.com/jsp/jstl/core" %>α
<%@ taglib prefix="x" uri="http://java.sun.com/jsp/jstl/xml" %>α
Hello World!
```

would generate the following output:

```
α
α
Hello World!
```

The trim directive, `<%@ page trimDirectiveWhitespaces="true" %>` can be used to eliminate the superfluous characters. The preceding directive needs to be added to all pages that require the trimming of whitespaces. Additionally, the behavior of a group of JSPs can be configured via the web.xml. The following example configuration trims whitespaces for all the JSPs in the application.

```
<web-app ...>
<jsp-config>
 <jsp_property-group>
  <url-pattern>
   *.jsp
  </url-pattern>
```

```
                   <trim-directive-whitespaces>
                     true
                   </trim-directive-whitespaces>
                  </jsp_property-group>
                 </jsp-config>
                 <web-app>
```

This behavior can be achieved systemwide by adding the following lines to the domain's default-web.xml file under the jsp servlet element (`<servlet-name>jsp</servlet-name>`):

```
<init-param>
      <param-name>trimSpaces</param-name>
      <param-value>true</param-value>
</init-param>
```

It should be noted that the preceding directive only eliminates whitespaces in template text and does not remove other types of whitespaces, for example, indentations added by the user for better readability.

In certain cases where you do not want to incur the cost of transmitting extraneous characters, say, when delivering content over low bandwidth networks, the server should generate the content in the most compact form, stripping away all the unnecessary whitespaces. One option to achieve this is to include a servlet filter that removes the extra whitespaces from the output (example: http://coldjava.hypermart. net/servlets/trimflt.htm). It is important to note that addition of the filter adds extra processing cost during the service of the request. The second option is to compact the JSP using an external process prior to deployment. Users must write a custom compactor since GlassFish does not bundle such a utility.

If your application includes CSS and JavaScript files, it is important to minify and optionally compress these to reduce overall size of the file that needs to be transmitted across the network. Several CSS/JavaScript minifiers are available on the market, including YUICompressor (http://developer.yahoo.com/yui/compressor/), a Java-based compressor from Yahoo. Additionally, if the Web container can be configured to send compressed versions of the CSS and JavaScript files, enabling compression can reduce the payload size further for user agents that support compression.

Tip

Trimming whitespaces can reduce the size of the file that needs to be transmitted across the wire, thereby improving performance, especially for clients connected via slow networks. Minifying CSS and JavaScript files along with the use of compression can further reduce the file transfer cost.

Use of jsp:useBean Action

The jsp:useBean action is used to locate or instantiate a bean with a specific name and scope. This action supports two instantiation options, beanName versus class, as well as multiple values for the scope attribute. It is important to select the appropriate values for these attributes that provide the required functionality as well as the best performance.

The JSP 2.0 syntax reference page (http://java.sun.com/products/jsp/syntax/2.0/syntaxref20.html) describes the steps taken by <jsp:useBean> to locate or instantiate the bean.

1. Attempts to locate a bean with the scope and name you specify.

2. Defines an object reference variable with the name you specify.

3. If it finds the bean, stores a reference to it in the variable. If you specified type, gives the bean that type.

4. If it does not find the bean, instantiates it from the class you specify, storing a reference to it in the new variable. If the class name represents a serialized template, the bean is instantiated by java.beans.Beans.instantiate.

5. If jsp:useBean has instantiated (rather than located) the bean, and if it has body tags or elements (between <jsp:useBean> and </jsp:useBean>), executes the body tags.

The bean instantiation depends on whether the class or the beanName attribute is specified. If class="package.class" is specified, the bean is instantiated using the new keyword. If beanName="{package.class | <%= expression %>}" is specified, the bean is instantiated from a class, a serialized template, or an expression that evaluates to a class or serialized template. The use of beanName provides flexibility (can evaluate which class to load at runtime) in instantiating the required bean. In this case, the bean is instantiated by the java.beans.Beans.instantiate method. If the value specified by the beanName attribute represents a class or a serialized template, the bean's instantiation involves loading of the resource by the Classloader. Figure 10-3 shows a snippet of a profile during the invocation of the following simple JSP page.

```
<jsp:useBean beanName="perfbook.SimpleBean" type="perfbook.SimpleBean"
id="sbean" scope="page"/>
<html>
    <body>
bean value = ${sbean.value}
    </body>
</html>
```

Call Tree - Method	Time [%] ▼	Time	Invocations	
⊟ ▨ httpSSLWorkerThread-8080-17		311 ms (100%)	1	
⊟ ▨ javax.servlet.http.HttpServlet.**service** (javax.servlet.ServletRequest, javax.servlet.ServletResponse)		311 ms (100%)	195	
⊟ ▨ org.apache.jasper.servlet.JspServlet.**service** (javax.servlet.http.HttpServletRequest, javax.servlet.http.HttpServlet		311 ms (99.8%)	195	
⊟ ▨ org.apache.jasper.servlet.JspServlet.**serviceJspFile** (javax.servlet.http.HttpServletRequest, javax.servlet.http		305 ms (97.8%)	195	
⊟ ▨ org.apache.jasper.servlet.JspServletWrapper.**service** (javax.servlet.http.HttpServletRequest, javax.servlet.		303 ms (97.3%)	195	
⊟ ▨ javax.servlet.http.HttpServlet.**service** (javax.servlet.ServletRequest, javax.servlet.ServletResponse)		302 ms (96.9%)	195	
⊟ ▨ org.apache.jasper.runtime.HttpJspBase.**service** (javax.servlet.http.HttpServletRequest, javax.servle		301 ms (96.8%)	195	
⊟ ▨ org.apache.jsp.usebeanName_jsp._**jspService** (javax.servlet.http.HttpServletRequest, javax.se		301 ms (96.8%)	195	
⊟ ▨ java.beans.Beans.**instantiate** (ClassLoader, String)		206 ms (66.3%)	195	
⊟ ▨ java.beans.Beans.**instantiate** (ClassLoader, String, java.beans.beancontext.BeanContex		206 ms (66.2%)	195	
⊞ ▨ java.beans.Beans$1.**run** ()		196 ms (62.9%)	195	
⊞ ▨ org.apache.jasper.servlet.JasperLoader.**loadClass** (String)		3.84 ms (1.2%)	195	
⏱ Self time		3.1 ms (1%)	195	
⊞ ▨ java.lang.Class.**newInstance** ()		1.92 ms (0.6%)	195	
⊞ ▨ java.lang.String.**concat** (String)		0.957 ms (0.3%)	195	
⊞ ▨ java.lang.String.**replace** (char, char)		0.267 ms (0.1%)	195	
⏱ java.beans.Beans$1.**<init>** (ClassLoader, String)		0.094 ms (0%)	195	
⏱ Self time		0.163 ms (0.1%)	195	
⊞ ▨ org.apache.jasper.runtime.PageContextImpl.**evaluateExpression** (String, Class, javax.servl		50.7 ms (16.3%)	584	
⊞ ▨ org.apache.jasper.runtime.JspFactoryImpl.**releasePageContext** (javax.servlet.jsp.PageCor		11.1 ms (3.6%)	194	
⊞ ▨ org.apache.jasper.runtime.JspFactoryImpl.**getPageContext** (javax.servlet.Servlet, javax.se		8.40 ms (2.7%)	195	
⊞ ▨ org.apache.coyote.tomcat5.CoyoteResponseFacade.**setContentType** (String)		6.70 ms (2.1%)	195	
⊞ ▨ org.apache.jasper.runtime.PageContextImpl.**getAttribute** (String, int)		6.38 ms (2%)	195	
⏱ Self time		3.13 ms (1%)	195	
⊞ ▨ org.apache.coyote.tomcat5.CoyoteResponseFacade.**setHeader** (String, String)		1.93 ms (0.6%)	195	
⊞ ▨ org.apache.jasper.runtime.JspWriterImpl.**write** (char [])		1.77 ms (0.6%)	973	

Figure 10-3 Bean instantiation cost when using beanName attribute

As Figure 10-3 shows, instantiation of the bean accounts for two-thirds of the invocation cost. (Note: The effect of bean instantiation is exaggerated because of the trivial nature of the JSP.) The use of the `beanName` attribute, though it provides a lot of flexibility, is significantly more expensive than using the `className` attribute.

> **Tip**
>
> Use the `beanName` attribute only in cases where it is absolutely required; use the `className` attribute in all other cases.

The `scope` attribute defines the scope in which the bean exists. The possible values include `page`, `request`, `session`, and `application`, with `page` being the default. The meanings of the different values are as follows:

- **page.**   The bean can be used within the enclosing JSP page or any of the page's static include files until the page sends a response back to the client or forwards a request to another resource.

- **request.**   The bean can be used from any JSP page processing the same request until a JSP page sends a response to the client or forwards the request to another resource.

- **session.**   The bean can be used from any JSP page in the same session as the JSP page that created the bean. The bean exists across the entire session, and any page that participates in the session can use it.

- **application.** The bean can be used from any JSP page in the same application as the JSP page that created the bean.

There are performance implications for the value that you select for the `scope` attribute. In `application` scope, the bean is created only once, and hence the initialization expense is amortized over the entire life of the application. However, the long life span of the bean increases the memory footprint of the application.

When `session` scope is used, the bean is maintained in memory as long as the session is active, which also increases the memory footprint. In cases where the user does not invalidate the session, the server maintains the session in memory until the session timeout expires. More details about the performance impact of session maintenance are provided in the "Session Persistence" subsection later in this chapter.

If the `scope` is `request` or `page`, a new object is created when the page is invoked. In these modes, the objects are relatively short-lived and garbage collected quickly. However, as discussed in the earlier section, the cost of bean instantiation can be high and as a result reduce the overall performance of the application.

Expression Language

JSP 2.0 supports an expression language (EL) that makes it easy to access data stored in JavaBeans components. A bean can be accessed using the `${name}` syntax and can be used in static text or any custom or standard tag attribute that can accept an expression. EL can be used in lieu of JSP scriptlets (code fragments specified within `<% %>`) or JSP expressions (used to generate a value based on the evaluation of an expression, specified using the `<%= expression %>` syntax). JSP EL along with JSP Standard Tag Library (JSTL) and/or custom tag libraries make development of complex JSPs easier than using scriptlets.

From a developer standpoint, using EL is a better choice than using scriptlets. However, from a performance perspective, the use of EL adds extra overhead in resolving the variable names to objects and in evaluating expressions. In the case of a scriptlet, the necessary code is injected directly into the generated servlet during the compilation phase that eliminates the need for variable lookups and the complexities of expression evaluations. Due to the additional overhead incurred by EL, it is typical to have the rendering times for EL-based JSPs to be slightly higher than that of an equivalent scriptlet based page.

The difference in performance depends on the amount of expression evaluations as well as the amount of other work involved in generating the output. For example, the performance impact of rendering a list of objects may be low if most of the time is spent generating the list, say, looking up from a database. If on the other hand, the list generation is inexpensive, the variable evaluation cost dominates, causing EL to perform poorer than a scriptlet. To show the performance difference, a simple JSP that lists a set of shapes along with its properties was profiled. The HTML snippet for the scriptlet-based JSP is shown here:

```
<tbody>
    <% List<Shape> list = sc.getRandomShapes();
    for (Shape shape: list) {
    %>
        <tr style="background-color: <% = shape.getColor() %>">
            <td><%= shape.getType() %></td>
                <td><%= shape.getAreaStr() %></td>
                <td><%= shape.getPerimeterStr() %></td>
        </tr>
    <% } %>
</tbody>
```

The HTML snippet for the EL-based JSP follows. In this case, to highlight the expense of the expression evaluation, the scriptlet-based code to get the list of shapes was maintained.

```
<tbody>
    <% List<Shape> list = sc.getRandomShapes();
    for (Shape shape: list) {
    pageContext.setAttribute("shape", shape);
    %>
    <tr style="background-color: ${shape.color}">
      <td>${shape.type}</td>
            <td>${shape.areaStr}</td>
            <td>${shape.perimeterStr}</td>
            </tr>
    <% } %>
</tbody>
```

Figure 10-4 shows the execution times for the two pages for 100 shapes during the profiling session.

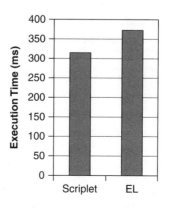

Figure 10-4 Sample performance comparison of scriptlet and EL

Figure 10-5 and Figure 10-6 show the profiles generated during the execution of the two pages. By comparing the time taken within the `jspService` method between the two profiles, it is clear that the slower performance of the EL-based JSP is due to the added cost of expression evaluation. In both cases, the `String.format` method takes around 105ms. However, in the case of EL, there is additional overhead in evaluating the expression and resolving the value. Since there is a small performance degradation for each expression evaluation, the difference in performance between the two implementations would increase as the number of expressions increases.

> **Tip**
>
> Even though the use of Expression Language makes JSP development easier, evaluation of many expressions within a JSP can reduce its performance. Use scriptlets for pages that require the best possible performance.

HTTP Compression

HTTP compression helps reduce the size of the textual data transferred from the server to the client. If the browser supports compression (as specified by the Accept-Encoding header), the server can be configured to transmit compressed data that is

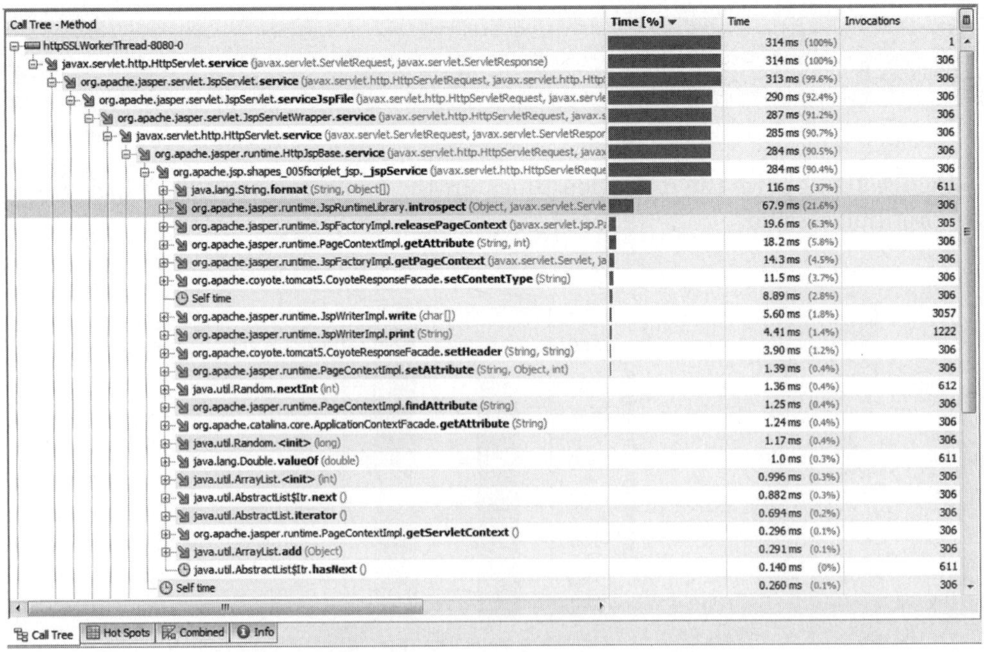

Figure 10-5 Profile for a scriptlet-based JSP

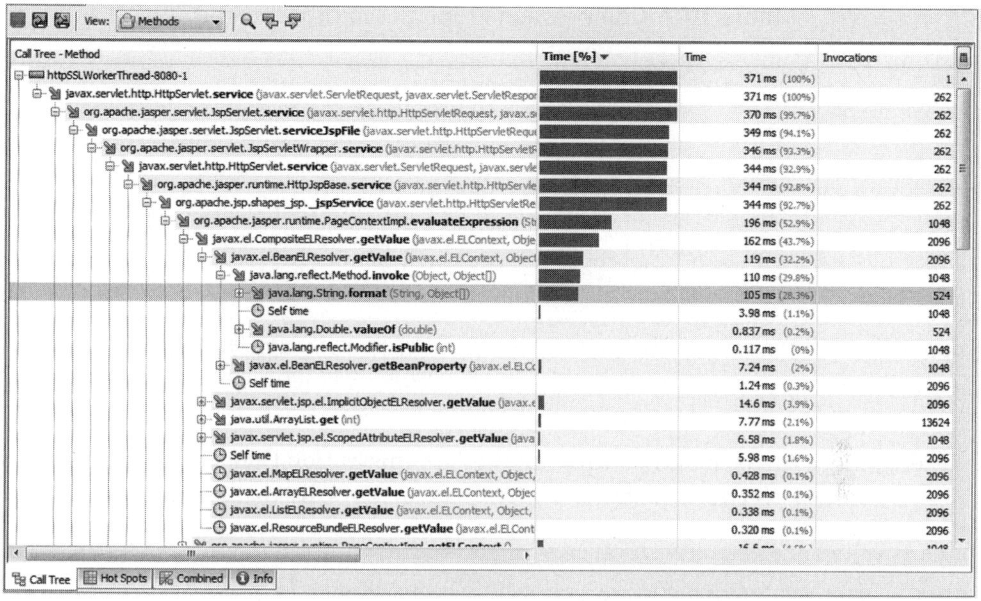

Figure 10-6 Profile for an EL-based JSP

then decoded at the browser. The amount of compression that can be achieved varies. Andy King and Konstantin Balashov have noted that HTML and CSS files can typically be compressed by about 80% and JavaScript files by an average of 70%.

Currently GlassFish supports on-the-fly compression in which the content is compressed as part of the response delivery for each request. Another approach is to deploy both compressed and uncompressed versions of the static files (e.g., index.html and index.html.gz) in the application, and a compression filter delivers the appropriate file based on the encoding accepted by the client. However, there is no built-in support for this mode in GlassFish.

The use of on-the-fly compression is a trade-off between lower bandwidth and higher CPU and memory usage, both at the client and the server. The smaller payload size can result in lower transmission cost thereby improving the user response time. The transmission latency is a higher percentage of the overall response time for clients connected over slow networks, and hence compression may improve the performance for such clients. However, the increased CPU resources required for compressing the data can reduce the overall throughput of the Web container. The additional cost incurred at the client for decoding the compressed content should also be taken into consideration while compression is enabled.

The GlassFish application server supports gzip compression and can be configured to use it by adding the properties listed in Table 10-7 to the http-listener.

Table 10-7 Compression Properties in http-listener

Property	Value	Comment
`Compression`	`on|off|force`	Use `on` or `off` to enable or disable compression. `force` compresses all types of files including images.
`compressableMimeType`	`text/ html, text/ css/, text/ javascript, ...`	A comma-separated list of mime types that should be compressed.
`compressionMinSize`	`<min value>`	Compression is applied only if the data size is larger than this value.

These values can be modified through the Administration Console (configs > config > server-config > Network Listener > http-listener-X) or by using `asadmin`.

```
asadmin get "configs.config.server-config.network-config.protocols.protocol.
http-listener-1.http.*" | grep compress
configs.config.server-config.network-config.protocols.protocol.http-
listener-1.http.compressable-mime-type=text/html,text/xml,text/plain
configs.config.server-config.network-config.protocols.protocol.http-
listener-1.http.compression=off
configs.config.server-config.network-config.protocols.protocol.http-
listener-1.http.compression-min-size-bytes=2048
```

A simple performance test was run to understand the performance impact of using compression. The test consisted of delivering a copy of the java.sun.com page (about 40 kilobytes in size in uncompressed form) to two different types of clients, one connected via a fast network and the other one over a slow DSL connection. For a single request, the page delivery time was essentially the same when the client was connected via a fast network. However, when the client had a slow network connection (from a laptop over a VPN), the latency for the compressed version was substantially lower, 280ms for compressed versus 510ms for the uncompressed version. Even though the server was able to handle low request rates without issues, it started throwing `OutOfMemoryErrors` when the load was increased, which makes this configuration useless in production settings. This issue may be solved in future releases of the product. It is important to note that compression is a CPU-intensive task, and enabling compression can result in increased resource consumption, thereby reducing the overall throughput of the system.

Another compression technique that works across all application servers is to include a compression servlet filter. The filter intercepts all outgoing requests and compresses the response as appropriate.

> **Tip**
>
> Enabling HTTP compression may reduce page delivery times for clients connected via slow networks.

Content Caching

In the current generation of Web applications, the generated content falls into two major categories: a set of generic pages for browsing users and another set of customized pages if the user is known. As the site grows in popularity and needs to support hundreds of thousands of users, different caching strategies are required to support these many users. One performance optimization used routinely is the caching of frequently used content. In this section, we discuss some of the factors that affect the performance of Web applications that interact with distributed caches like Memcached.

Before starting the discussion, it is import to emphasize a few points. This section highlights the effects of different components involved in the interaction and is not meant to be a performance comparison of the different implementations. The data is generated based on a synthetic workload, and the performance of individual applications may differ from what is shown here. Users are strongly encouraged to run their own performance tests to identify implementations that provide the best performance for their application.

Distributed caches are shared by multiple application instances and are used to store a variety of application content including full HTML pages (e.g., pages delivered to non-signed-in users), snippets of pages (e.g., HTML snippet of top ten items), or results from an expensive database query (e.g., list of photos for a user), just to name a few. We look at an example of a Web application using Memcached (http://memcached.org/), the most popular distributed caching solution, to store a top 100 list of items. What is of interest are the factors that affect the performance of storing a set of Java-based data objects.

Figure 10-7 shows the various components involved in the storing and retrieval of these objects to and from the cache. To store an object in cache, a binary representation of the object needs to be created first. This functionality is represented by the serialize component in Figure 10-7. The choice of the serializer depends on several factors including ease of use, extensibility, and, of course, performance. A variety of serialization technologies are available on the market with each considered by its supporters to be superior over others. It is worth reiterating a point made earlier. The intent of this section is not to compare the performance of all available serialization technologies but to select a couple of options that show how the choice of these components affects the overall performance of your application. Each developer is encouraged to experiment with different serialization (and compression) technologies available on the market and select the one that best suits his or her overall need.

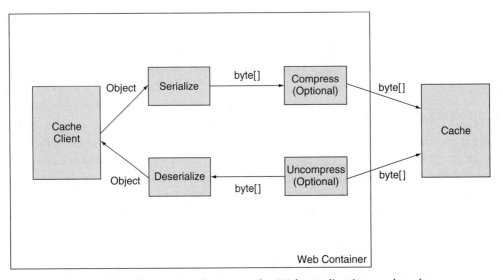

Figure 10-7 Interaction between the Web application and cache

For the purpose of discussion, the Jackson serializer for JSON and JAXB for XML were selected. Both the packages generate a textual representation of the Object from which the binary data can be extracted. Once the binary payload representing the Object is obtained, it can optionally be compressed to reduce its size. There are pros and cons for including compression, which are discussed a little later. Since any data compressed during storage needs to be uncompressed during retrieval, it is important to save the information regarding the type of compression used, if any, as part of the data that is stored. The binary payload is then transferred over the network to the distributed cache. During data retrieval, the order of the components is reversed with the uncompress step, if required, followed by deserialization to obtain the Object that was stored. The two compression libraries used for our testing were GZIP that is part of the JDK and the open source LZF library (https://github.com/ning/compress).

Several factors relating to performance affect the choice of the serialization and compression components, including the size of the generated payload in compressed and uncompressed form, latency of operation, and CPU and network resource requirements during storage and retrieval. Higher payload size results in higher network transfer cost as well as reduced cache efficiency since for a given cache size, fewer items can be stored in the cache. The other important factors are the overall efficiency of each component in terms of latency of individual operation as well as the capability to handle multiple concurrent requests.

To show how the choice of serialization and compression technologies affect performance, a sample benchmark application was developed. The following code snippet shows the sample cached class, the Jackson based JSON serializer, and the LZF based compressor. The XML serializer and GZIP compressor are not shown for brevity.

```java
public class SimpleDataContainer implements Serializable {
    private String name;
    private long lastUpdatedTime;
    private List<SimpleData> dataList;
    private Date createdDate;
...
```

```java
public class SimpleData implements Serializable {
    private long id;
    private long createdTime;
    private long lastUpdatedTime;
    private String author;
    private String description;
...
```

```java
import org.codehaus.jackson.map.ObjectMapper;
import org.codehaus.jackson.map.type.TypeFactory;
import org.codehaus.jackson.type.JavaType;

import java.io.IOException;
import java.io.ByteArrayOutputStream;
import java.io.ByteArrayInputStream;

public class JsonDataSerializer<T> implements DataSerializer<T> {
    private static ObjectMapper mapper = new ObjectMapper();
    JavaType type;

    public JsonDataSerializer(Class<T> type) {
        this.type = TypeFactory.type(type);
    }

    public byte[] serialize(T object) throws IOException {
        ByteArrayOutputStream bos = new ByteArrayOutputStream();
        mapper.writeValue(bos, object);

        return bos.toByteArray();
    }

    public T deSerialize(byte[] buf) throws IOException {
        ByteArrayInputStream bis = new ByteArrayInputStream(buf);
        T obj = (T) mapper.readValue(bis, type);
        return obj;
    }

    public SerializationMode getSerializationMode() {
        return SerializationMode.JSON_SERIALIZATION;
    }
}
```

```java
import com.ning.compress.lzf.LZFOutputStream;
import com.ning.compress.lzf.LZFInputStream;

import java.io.IOException;
import java.io.ByteArrayOutputStream;
import java.io.ByteArrayInputStream;

public class LZFCompressor extends Compressor {
    public byte[] compress(byte[] buf) throws IOException {
        ByteArrayOutputStream bos = new ByteArrayOutputStream();
        LZFOutputStream os = new LZFOutputStream(bos);
        os.write(buf);
        os.close();
        return bos.toByteArray();
    }

    public byte[] uncompress(byte[] buf) throws IOException {
        LZFInputStream is = new LZFInputStream(new
ByteArrayInputStream(buf));
        byte[] data = new byte[8192];
        int count;
        ByteArrayOutputStream bos = new ByteArrayOutputStream();
        while ((count=is.read(data)) != -1) {
            bos.write(data, 0, count);
        }
        is.close();
        return bos.toByteArray();
    }

    public CompressionMode getCompressionMode() {
        return CompressionMode.LZF;
    }
}
```

A benchmark operation consisted of a put and get of a cache object. Typically, the number of get operations is significantly more than the put operations. However, in this benchmark, to study the performance impact of both operations, a single request consisted of a put followed by a get. The overall performance of the system was measured in terms of number of operations that could be completed for a given set of concurrent requests. Figure 10-8 shows the throughput for varying payload sizes with eight concurrent requests. As expected, the overall throughput reduces as the size increases. Across all size ranges, the Jackson based JSON serializer provides slightly better performance than the JAXB based XML serializer.

At small payload sizes, adding compression may have a detrimental impact on performance. So it is a good performance practice to set up a size threshold above which compression should be applied. Additionally, the performance benefit of compression depends on the type of compressor used. The gzip compressor that is part of the JDK performs poorly at high concurrencies. The primary reason for this is the lack of scalability of the implementation due to lock contention at memory allocation in the native code. The scalability can be improved by using alternate malloc libraries such as libumem for Oracle Solaris. The LZF compressor on the other hand

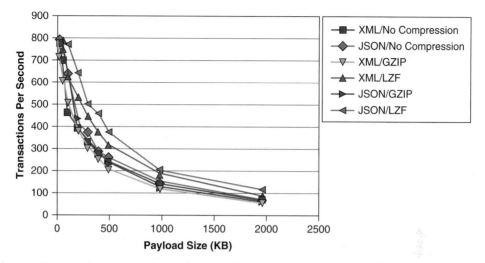

Figure 10-8 Performance of serializers and compressors as part of the cache interaction

provides great benefit at large payload sizes. Reducing the amount of data that needs to be transferred across the network decreases the latency, reduces the bandwidth requirement, and provides increased cache capacity.

The compression efficiency is defined as the ratio of the compressed size to the uncompressed size. Several factors affect the compression ratio. Since the benchmark data is highly synthetic with large amounts of repeating elements, measuring the compression ratio for this test case is misleading. Overall, gzip offers better compression than LZF in terms of compression size, whereas LZF provides significantly faster compression but with a lower compression ratio.

In addition to several types of serializers being available, there are multiple implementations within each type. The large number of choices can make the identification of the optimum solution difficult. The best way to identify the best option for your application is through experimentation.

> **Tip**
>
> Serialization and compression technologies play a significant role in the overall performance of the caching solution. It is recommended that the user do experiments to identify the best performing solution/implementation to each of these components.

Session Persistence

An HTTP session object is often used to store application information for a specific user. The Web container is responsible for maintaining the session, and the application can access the session object through the HttpServletRequest or from within a JSP. By default, most containers including GlassFish maintain only an in-memory copy of the sessions, which means that the session information is lost in case of server failure. However, for some applications, this data loss is unacceptable, and they require a persistent session solution where the data is available even in case of a server crash.

There are several ways the high availability feature can be implemented. One option is to write the session information to a shared data store that is accessible from two or more servers. The HA-DB based solution available in GlassFish V2 Enterprise Edition is an example of this. An alternate solution that is available in GlassFish V3.1 is the in-memory replication scheme in which a copy of the session stored in one server is replicated and maintained in memory of a backup server. In case of primary server failure, the backup server can service the requests without any data loss. The implementation details of both these schemes are beyond the scope of this book. In this section we cover the factors that affect performance when session persistence is enabled.

As in the case of distributed caching, some form of serialization mechanism is required to transform the Java objects saved in the session into a byte stream that can be transported across containers or stored in a common data store. GlassFish uses the Java object serialization through the use of ObjectOutputStream and ObjectInputStream. Additionally, the payload size is further reduced through compression. The overall cost of session persistence consists of certain fixed costs (replica identification, transport initialization, and so on) and some variable costs that depend on what is stored in the session. The two main factors that affect the latter are the size of the payload that needs to be transported and the complexity of items stored in the session.

The correlation between object size and cost is straightforward since larger objects take longer to serialize/unserialize as well as transport across the network. For example, a larger String object takes longer to serialize and transport.

Object complexity impacts the overall performance substantially. Objects with multiple levels of inheritance are expensive to serialize as well as generate larger size payload. So for optimum performance, keep the items in the session as simple as possible. Before adding any item into a session, verify that the data is absolutely required to be maintained in the session.

There are instances in which a complex data object, say, a user preference object created from a database, is required to be kept in the session. In this case, the object in question can be recreated in case it is not found in the session. In such cases, it is optimal to identify such attributes as nonpersistent using the transient keyword. Transient attributes are maintained in the in-memory session but are not serialized as part of the session persistence, thereby improving the performance. In case of a failover, the transient attributes are recreated in the new session.

HTTP Server File Cache

Java EE containers are designed to deliver dynamic content and are not especially well suited for handling static content. However, the majority of Web applications require at least a few static files to be delivered to the clients. Application servers typically provide optimized static file handling mechanisms. In this section, we discuss HTTP Server File Cache, a caching feature provided by the GlassFish server that improves the static content delivery performance. Even though the details provided here are vendor specific, similar optimization options are available in other application servers as well.

File Cache within the HTTP Server caches frequently used static files in memory, which eliminates the need to read the resource from the file system for every request.

The following conditions need to be met for a file to be added to the cache:

- The request has to be for a static resource serviced by the default servlet. Files with URI mappings to custom servlets will not be cached.
- The total number of cached files should be less than the value specified by max file count.
- A file will be added to the cache only if space is available in the cache.

The amount of time a file is retained in the cache is decided by the `max-age-in-seconds` parameter. The age of a file in the cache is calculated as the difference between the current time and the time when the file was added to the cache. The file entry is removed from the cache when its age is greater than `max-age-in-seconds`. The files are either read into the JVM heap or memory mapped based on the size of the file.

File caching can improve performance by eliminating the disk I/O associated with the reading of a file for every request in the absence of the cache. However, file cache increases the memory footprint of the server instance. Small files are cached in the JVM heap, which increases the garbage collection cost, and large files that are memory mapped increase the resident memory of the process.

The file cache statistics can be monitored if the `http-service` monitoring level is set too high. Use the `asadmin get -m` command to view the various file cache statistics as shown in the following example:

```
asadmin get -m "server*http-listener-1.file-cache*" | grep '\-count'
server.network.http-listener-1.file-cache.contenthits-count = 0
server.network.http-listener-1.file-cache.contentmisses-count = 0
server.network.http-listener-1.file-cache.heapsize-count = 0
server.network.http-listener-1.file-cache.hits-count = 0
server.network.http-listener-1.file-cache.infohits-count =0
server.network.http-listener-1.file-cache.infomisses-count = 0
server.network.http-listener-1.file-cache.mappedmemorysize-count = 0
server.network.http-listener-1.file-cache.maxheapsize-count = 0
server.network.http-listener-1.file-cache.maxmappedmemorysize-count = 0
server.network.http-listener-1.file-cache.misses-count = 0
```

The cache can be tuned based on the cache hit rate, `hits-count` / (`hits-count` + `misses-count`). A very high value of the hit rate suggests that the cache is working well, and no further tuning is required. A low hit rate may indicate the need for further tuning—by either increasing the `max-age` or the size of the cache.

The following factors should be taken into consideration while tuning the file cache: the number and size of the files, the frequency of the file request, the heap space configured for the instance, and the amount of available memory.

- Set the number of files to be cached based on the number of files that are commonly accessed. For most cases, the default value of 1024 will suffice.

- Set the maximum age of a cache entry based on how often clients access a given resource. It is recommended that this value be set large enough so as to incur several hits before the file is removed from the cache. Since a cached entry is served even if the underlying resource changes, it is not recommended that a high value be set for files that change frequently. Setting a very high value for this can also cause caching of infrequently used files, which can impact the performance negatively.

- Set the cache size based on the amount of heap and the overall memory available. It is recommended that this parameter be set to a value large enough to accommodate the commonly accessed files. Setting this value to be a large proportion of the heap can cause frequent garbage collection thereby reducing the overall performance. Since files beyond a certain size are memory mapped, the memory associated with this cache is external to the JVM heap. Caching these files increase the process memory, and it is important to ensure that the overall memory does not go beyond the available process memory (4GB for 32-bit JVM). If the amount of physical memory in the system is limited, it is recommended that the space allocated be reduced so that the overall process memory is lower than the available physical memory.

Access Logging

Web containers are designed to log details about the requests served by them. Processing these logs can provide a wealth of information that can be used to identify poorly performing request paths, understand application usage patterns, as well as provide baseline data for developing benchmarks. A log replay benchmark driver that can replay access logs is one of the best benchmarking tools to mimic production load in a test environment. Some of the attributes of interest include, but are not limited to, the request rate, user agent, client IP address, request type, path, response status, response length, response time, referrer, and/or specific request or response headers.

The GlassFish server in the developer profile by default does not enable access logging. Access logging can be turned on as well as configured at the http-service level either through `asadmin` or the Administration Console. To configure access logging via the Administration Console, first click on the Configurations link on the navigation tree on the left side bar. Select the appropriate configuration for the server, and then select http-service. Check the Access Logging check box to enable logging. The following `asadmin` commands can be used to get/set the access logging properties via the command line.

To turn on access logging, use the following command:

```
asadmin set configs.config.server-config.http-service.access-log.
rotation-enabled=true
```

Enabling access logging increases the write operations to the disk. In GlassFish, the request information is buffered in memory and subsequently written to the disk when the buffer is full (this can be configured to be time based, where the logs are written at periodic intervals). The performance impact of access logging is negligible under most conditions. However, for systems under very heavy load, the periodic disk write operations may interfere with the processing of other requests if the same set of disks is used for storing content, transaction logging, or as the persistent message store. Under these conditions, it is preferable to dedicate a set of disks, SSD, or a disk array with write cache for access logging so that it does not interfere with other operations.

For GlassFish V3, the access logs are written to the install_dir/domains/domain_name/logs/access directory. Based on the log rotation interval (default: 1 day), a new log file of the form server_access_log_<suffix>.txt is written to the access log directory. The default suffix date is of the form yyyy-MM-dd, which can be changed if required. The number of log files retained is based on the `max-history-files` attribute. The default value of −1 results in all files being retained indefinitely. This may result in a large number of files for long-running servers, so it is recommended to limit the number of saved logs to a few days. This can be achieved by setting the `max-history-files` attribute to the number of days the logs are to be retained. The log lines are stored in memory and are written to disk when either the buffer becomes full or the write interval has expired. Based on user needs, these values can be configured using the `asadmin set` command.

The `format` attribute defines what values will be logged in each log line and can be set using the `asadmin set` command as follows:

```
asadmin set 'configs.config.server-config.http-service.access-log.
format=%datetime% %user.agent% %referer% %session.userId% %response.header.
TRACE% %http-uri% %query-str% %http-method% %status% %response.length%
%time-taken%'
```

The format described in the preceding example produces the following log line.

```
"02/Jan/2011:10:47:24 -0800" "Mozilla/5.0 (Macintosh; U; Intel Mac OS X
10.5; en-US; rv:1.9.2.13) Gecko/20101203 Firefox/3.6.13" "NULL-REFERER"
"1293993380" "1bc8bedf-d87d-4309-9dce-37787cddf9e4" "/BenchmarkWebApp/main/
session" "listSize=10&stringSize=10000" "GET" 200 137 "2"
```

Most of the attribute names are self-explanatory, for example, `response.length` specifies the size of the response in bytes, and `time-taken` describes the response time. Any request header of interest can be defined using `%header.<headerName>%`. Similarly, `%session.sessionAttribute%` and `%response.header.header Name%` can be used to get session attributes and response headers, respectively.

Two attributes, `session.userId` and `response.header.TRACE` need further explanation. The first one is for applications that require users to sign in to interact with certain parts of the site. Maintaining the user id in a session is one way to track signed-in users. Having this information in the access log is useful in a variety of ways including tracking the number of requests per session, identifying the request paths and the response times associated with each of these requests. If the application performance varies based on the user, these logs are valuable in identifying users who are subject to poor performance and in identifying performance bottlenecks.

The `response.header.TRACE` information is useful for applications that use one or more Restful services to service a user request. In such cases, a single user request would result in HTTP requests to multiple back-end services each of which will log the request that it receives. To trace a single request through these multitude of distributed systems and to identify performance issues, some form of request tracing is required. One way to achieve this is to allocate a unique identifier to each request at the request entry point and to propagate the unique identifier to each service in the pipeline. The access logs can then be grouped based on the trace identifier to identify all the request paths and response times associated with each front-end request. There are a variety of ways in which this tracing can be achieved. A simple filter-based approach is described here.

A servlet filter inspects each request and adds a trace identifier in case the trace is not found in the request header. The filter further sets the trace as a local thread variable within the processing thread so that it can be passed along to any subsequent HTTP request involved in this request processing cycle. The use of a thread local variable limits the use of this solution to a synchronous request processing model. The sample code for the TraceFilter and the TraceManager follows:

```
import javax.servlet.*;
import javax.servlet.http.HttpServletRequest;
import javax.servlet.http.HttpServletResponse;
import java.io.IOException;

public class TraceFilter implements Filter {
    public void doFilter(ServletRequest req,
                         ServletResponse resp,
                         FilterChain chain)
        throws ServletException, IOException {
        // Set up the trace if not already present.
        TraceManager traceManager = null;
        if (req instanceof HttpServletRequest &&
            resp instanceof HttpServletResponse) {
            HttpServletRequest hreq = (HttpServletRequest) req;
            HttpServletResponse hres = (HttpServletResponse) resp;
            traceManager = new TraceManager();
            traceManager.setTrace(hreq, hres);
        }

        chain.doFilter(req, resp);

        if (traceManager ! = null)
            traceManager.removeTrace();
    }
    ...
}
import javax.servlet.http.HttpServletRequest;
import javax.servlet.http.HttpServletResponse;
import java.util.UUID;

public class TraceManager {
    private static ThreadLocal<String> traceTLS = new ThreadLocal<String>();
    public static final String TRACE_HEADER = "TRACE";

    public String getTrace() {
        String trace = traceTLS.get();
        if (trace = = null)
            trace = UUID.randomUUID().toString();
        return trace;
    }

    public void setTrace (HttpServletRequest req,
                          HttpServletResponse res) {
        String trace = req.getHeader(TRACE_HEADER);
        if (trace = = null) {
            trace = UUID.randomUUID().toString();
            req.setAttribute(TRACE_HEADER, trace);
        }
        res.setHeader(TRACE_HEADER, trace);
```

```
        traceTLS.set(trace);
        logger.fine("Trace set to " + trace);
    }

    public void removeTrace() {
        traceTLS.remove();
    }
}
```

We end this section with a short discussion regarding access log file aggregation. As the Web site grows in popularity with hundreds of thousands of page views a day, hundreds of servers may be required to handle the requests. Aggregating the log files distributed across these many disparate machines turns out to be a challenge. One possible solution is to use open source log aggregators such as Scribe (https://github .com/facebook/scribe) in combination with collector, an open source Java based scribe client (https://github.com/pierre/collector) to aggregate the logs and store them in the Hadoop Distributed File System (http://hadoop.apache.org/hdfs/) where they can be easily searched and collated. A special log appender valve may have to be written for GlassFish to seamlessly integrate with these solutions, the implementation details of which are beyond the scope of this book.

Bibliography

Theurer, Tenni. "Performance Research, Part 1: What the 80/20 Rule Tells Us about Reducing HTTP Requests." http://yuiblog.com/blog/2006/11/28/performance-research-part-1/.

Exceptional Performance team, various authors. "Best Practices for Speeding Up Your Web Site." http://developer.yahoo.com/performance/rules.html.

"Web Performance Best Practices." http://code.google.com/speed/page-speed/docs/rules_intro.html

Souders, Steve. *High Performance Web Sites*. O'Reilly Media. September 2007. ISBN 978-0-596-52930-7.

Souders, Steve. *Even Faster Web Sites*. O'Reilly Media. June 2009. ISBN 978-0-596-52230-8.

JSR 316: JavaTM Platform, Enterprise Edition 6 (Java EE 6) Specification. http://jcp.org/en/jsr/detail?id=316.

Arcand, Jeanfrancois. "Grizzly 1.5 Architecture Overview." http://weblogs.java.net/blog/jfarcand/archive/20070712_Grizzly_Architecture.pdf.

Chetty, Damodar. "An Overview of Tomcat 6 Servlet Container: Part 1." http://www.packtpub.com/article/an-overview-of-tomcat-6-servlet-container-1.

Chetty, Damodar. "An Overview of Tomcat 6 Servlet Container: Part 2." http://www.packtpub.com/article/an-overview-of-tomcat-6-servlet-container-2.

Oracle GlassFish Server 3.0.1 Administration Guide. http://download.oracle.com/docs/cd/E19798-01/821-1751/821-1751.pdf.

"Apache Commons Math, Statistics." http://commons.apache.org/math/userguide/stat.html.

"Trim Filter." http://www.servletsuite.com/servlets/trimflt.htm.

"YUI Compressor." http://developer.yahoo.com/yui/compressor/.

"Jackson Java JSON-processor." http://jackson.codehaus.org/.

## 11

Web Services Performance

Service Oriented Architecture (SOA) is an architectural style that enables complex business applications to be built from smaller individual services distributed over the network. It has become the industry's de facto standard for building and deploying business solutions that are agile enough to meet the demands of business partners and customers. Web services have emerged as the most widely used technology for implementing SOA. A Web service is a software system accessible over a network that supports machine-to-machine interaction. It is a platform and programming language neutral system that exposes standardized interfaces accessible over a set of standard Internet communication protocols; typically described using Web Services Description Language (WSDL). Web services communicate using the Simple Object Access Protocol (SOAP) and use eXtensible Markup Language (XML) for describing the exchanged messages.

With increasing SOA adoption by enterprises, both new and existing enterprise applications are being exposed as Web services. The loose coupling enables enterprises to harness the power of existing services more efficiently. However, this also brings new challenges, especially in terms of performance and scalability, as the same services are invoked by a large number of clients. Performance and scalability should be important considerations in the design, implementation, and deployment of Web services. In this chapter we look at different aspects relating to Web service performance: how to measure Web service performance, the important factors that affect performance, and best practices for commonly encountered use cases.

This chapter is divided as follows. Since Web services rely on XML as the underlying data exchange format, the first part covers XML performance. The various stages involved in the XML document processing life cycle are discussed along with performance tips and recommendations. The second part of this chapter focuses on Web services performance, which starts with a brief look at the implementation of the Java API for XML Web Services (JAX-WS) Reference Implementation. This is followed by a discussion on Web services benchmarking and a description of the various factors that affect Web service performance. A look at a set of best practices for the common uses cases concludes the chapter.

XML Performance

Since Web services rely on XML as the underlying data exchange format, XML processing is one of the core elements within the Web services stack. The Java platform supports XML processing through the Java API for XML Processing (JAXP) as well as the Java API for XML Binding (JAXB).

JAXP provides a set of XML processing APIs that enable applications to parse, transform, and query XML documents. JAXP is a standard component in the Java platform with a reference implementation of JAXP 1.4 bundled in Java SE 6. JAXP supports a number of different industrywide standards to process XML documents: Simple API for XML (SAX), Document Object Model (DOM), and the Streaming API for XML (StAX).

JAXB allows developers to access and process XML documents as Java objects. The first step in the use of JAXB is to compile the XML schema representing the document to generate a set of Java classes. JAXB also provides a runtime that enables the easy conversion of XML documents to Java objects (unmarshalling) and Java objects to XML (marshalling). Since the use of the JAXB compiler is a one-time operation, the performance of the compiler is not addressed here. Instead, the focus is on the marshalling and unmarshalling performance.

In this section the performance aspects related to the use of various parsers and serializers are discussed starting with a brief look at the steps involved in a typical XML processing cycle. This is followed by discussions about the factors that affect XML performance and a description of best practices. The section concludes with a recommendation of which parser is the most appropriate for certain purposes.

XML Processing Life Cycle

Processing of an XML document typically involves the following steps: Parse or unmarshall, access, modify, and serialize or marshall, as shown in Figure 11-1. These are logically defined processing units and may be accomplished within a single step (e.g., SAX) or may be distinct steps (e.g., DOM). Additionally, depending on the use case and the type of parser you use, all four steps may not be exercised.

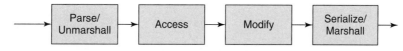

Figure 11-1 Typical XML document processing

- **Parse/Unmarshall.** Scan through the XML document processing elements and attributes and possibly build an in-memory tree in the case of a DOM parser or a Java object in JAXB. Parsing is a prerequisite for any processing of an XML document.

- **Access.** Extract the data from the elements and attributes of parts of the document into the application. For example, given an XML document for an invoice, the application might want to retrieve the prices for each item in the invoice.

- **Modify.** Change the textual content of elements or attributes and possibly also the structure of the document by inserting or deleting elements. This does not apply to SAX. As an example, an application might need to update the prices of some of the items in an invoice or insert or delete some items.

- **Serialize/Marshall.** Convert the in-memory representation to a textual form that is written to a disk file or forwarded to a network stream. SAX parser does not support this functionality.

Parse/Unmarshall

If using JAXP, the first step in parsing a document is the creation of the parser, `SAXParser`, `XMLStreamReader`, or `DocumentBuilder` depending on the API selected (SAX, StAX, and DOM, respectively). This is carried out through the use of appropriate factory objects as shown in the following code snippet below.

```java
// SAX Parser
import javax.xml.parsers.SAXParserFactory;
import javax.xml.parsers.SAXParser;
SAXParserFactory spf = SAXParserFactory.newInstance();
SAXParser sp = spf.newSAXParser();

// StAX XMLStreamReader
import javax.xml.stream.XMLInputFactory;
import javax.xml.stream.XMLStreamReader;
XMLInputFactory xif = XMLInputFactory.newInstance();
```

```
XMLStreamReader reader = xif.createXMLStreamReader (inputStream);

// DOM Parser
import javax.xml.parsers.DocumentBuilderFactory;
import javax.xml.parsers.DocumentBuilder;
DocumentBuilderFactory dbf=DocumentBuilderFactory.newInstance();
DocumentBuilder db = dbf.newDocumentBuilder();
```

The use of the abstract factory pattern allows the developer to select the parser implementation to be used at runtime. However, initialization of the `Factory` object is an expensive operation since it involves file system search to identify the appropriate factory implementation to load. The Java documentation for `DocumentBuilder-Factory.newInstance()` uses the following ordered lookup procedure to determine the `DocumentBuilderFactory` implementation class to load:

- Use the `javax.xml.parsers.DocumentBuilderFactory` system property.

- Use the properties file lib/jaxp.properties in the JRE directory. This configuration file is in standard `java.util.Properties` format and contains the fully qualified name of the implementation class with the key being the system property defined previously.

- Use the Services API (as detailed in the JAR specification), if available, to determine the classname. The Services API looks for a classname in the file META-INF/services/javax.xml.parsers.DocumentBuilderFactory in jars available to the runtime.

- Platform default `DocumentBuilderFactory` instance.

The factory lookup procedures for `SAXParserFactory` and `XMLInputFactory` are similar to that of `DocumentBuilderFactory`. The factory loading time can be reduced by specifying the default implementation class as a System property or in the lib/jaxp.properties file. Table 11-1 shows the various default factory implementation classes for the implementation of Oracle's Java 6.

Table 11-1 Default Parser Factory Implementation Classes

Factory	Property	Default Implementation Class
SAXParserFactory	javax.xml.parsers. SAXParserFactory	com.sun.org.apache. xerces.internal.jaxp. SAXParserFactoryImpl
DocumentBuilderFactory	javax.xml.parsers. DocumentBuilder Factory	com.sun.org.apache. xerces.internal.jaxp. DocumentBuilderFactoryImpl
XMLInputFactory	javax.xml.stream. XMLInputFactory	com.sun.xml.internal. stream.XMLInputFactoryImpl

JAXP does not mandate that the factory instances be thread-safe. Even though some of the default factory implementations in the JDK are thread-safe for parser creations, it is a good practice to avoid the concurrent use of JAXP factories from multiple threads. Sharing of a single `Factory` object should only be used if the implementation provides a thread-safe guarantee (e.g., Woodstox StAX parser, JDK's default `DocumentBuilderFactory`).

> **Tip**
>
> Since creation of a `Factory` instance is expensive, it is advisable to reuse existing `Factory` objects. Share a singleton `Factory` instance for thread-safe implementations. Otherwise, reuse a pool of instances among multiple threads or store it as a `ThreadLocal` variable.

JAXP provides a pluggable architecture that allows users to plug-in different implementations. There are instances in which implementations from other vendors outperform the default implementation within JAXP. In such cases, it is a good practice to use the better performing implementation rather than the default one (see performance data at the end of this section). One example of this is the use of Woodstox, the open source StAX parser (http://woodstox.codehaus.org/) that outperforms Oracle Java Streaming XML Parser (SJSXP), the default StAX parser within JAXP. There are a variety of ways to configure JAXP to use the new implementation.

- Add the jar file containing the parser to the classpath (the jar file should specify the implementation class in META-INF/services/<ParserProperty> where `ParserProperty` is the property defined in Table 11-1). For example, to use Woodstox, all that is required is to add the jar file to the classpath.

- Specify the factory class using the appropriate system property. For example, to use Woodstax parser, set the following system property:

```
javax.xml.stream.XMLInputFactory=com.ctc.wstx.stax.WstxInputFactory
```

- Specify the factory class in the properties file lib/jaxp.properties in the JRE directory.

The parser instances created from the factory instance, `SAXParser`, `XMLStream Reader`, and `DocumentBuilder`, are not thread-safe and cannot be shared among multiple threads. Parser creation is a heavyweight operation and may take a significant portion of the XML processing cost, especially for small documents. Both SAX and DOM parsers provide a reset method that allows the parser to be reset for later reuse. So in cases where a lot of small documents are to be processed, it is a good practice to create a pool of parser instances that can be reused. Each thread would get a parser from the pool, use it to parse the document, reset the parser, and return it to the pool after completing the parsing operation. Unfortunately, the current version of the StAX specification does not provide a standard mechanism for resetting the XMLStreamReader.

Tip

For parsing small documents using SAX and DOM, it is a good performance practice to create a pool of Parser instances that can be reused.

While using JAXB for document processing, the Unmarshaller needs to be first created as shown in the following code snippet.

```
// JAXB Unmarshaller
import javax.xml.bind.JAXBContext;
import javax.xml.bind.Unmarshaller;
JAXBContext jc = JAXBContext.newInstance("mypackage");
Unmarshaller u = jc.createUnmarshaller();
```

JAXBContext creation is an expensive operation, and creation of multiple instances should be avoided if possible. JAXBContext is thread-safe and can be shared among multiple threads. For best performance, create a single instance for the whole application. However, Unmarshaller is not thread-safe and should not be used concurrently by multiple threads. But Unmarshaller objects can be pooled and reused. It is a good practice to use a pool of Unmarshaller objects for processing small documents.

Tip

While using JAXB, it is a good practice to reuse a single instance of JAXBContext. For unmarshalling small documents, create a pool of Unmarshaller instances that can be reused.

Access

Referring to Figure 11-1, the next step in the document processing is the access of elements and attributes within the document. In the case of streaming parsers, this step is closely linked to the parsing process, whereas in the case of DOM and JAXB this is a secondary step of navigating the in-memory DOM tree or the Java objects created during the parsing phase. Streaming parsers provide content to the application as they become available, discarding the previous contents. The parser does not cache any content in memory, and it is the responsibility of the application to store the contents that may be necessary for further processing. DOM and JAXB, on the other hand, store the document in memory allowing random access of any element in the document. Since streaming parsers do not store the entire document contents in memory, the objects created by them are short-lived.

> **Tip**
>
> The memory usage for JAXB and DOM is higher than that of streaming parsers (SAX and StAX), especially for large documents.

Modify

In-memory parsers allow modifications to be made to the document. Since the JAXB unmarshaller creates a set of related Java objects to represent the document in memory, no special JAXB related APIs are required to access and modify the document. Access and modification of the DOM objects on the other hand are done using the DOM APIs. To obtain optimal performance, the following points are worth noting while using the DOM APIs:

- Before you retrieve a list of attributes, first check to see whether that `Node` has attributes using the `hasAttributes` method. Invocation of `getAttributes` for an `Element` node causes the unnecessary creation of an `AttributeMap` object even if the element has no attributes.

- The methods `getElementsByTagName` and `getElementsByTagNameNS` are expensive operations since they traverse the DOM tree searching for nodes that match the name and the namespace URI. Applications should consider implementing custom traversal methods that search in parts of the tree.

- In DOM Level 2, renaming and moving nodes from one document to the other can be expensive, since these operations involve creating new nodes, copying the contents of the old node to the new ones, and inserting the nodes at the appropriate places in the tree. Consider using the `renameNode` and `adoptNode` APIs defined in DOM Level 3 specification for renaming a node and moving a node from one document to the other. In most cases, `renameNode` simply changes the name of the given node. However, under certain circumstances, this API can be forced to create a new node, copy all the contents, and insert the node at the appropriate place. This rare case happens most often when the application attempts to mix namespace-aware and non-namespace-aware nodes in a single document. `adoptNode` attempts to adopt a node from another document to this document. This allows the applications to move a subtree from one document to another without making a copy of the subtree.

- Avoid unnecessary error checking if all operations performed by the application on the DOM are legal. DOM Level 3 adds the `setStrictErrorChecking` attribute to specify whether error checking is enforced. When set to false, the implementation is free to not test every possible error case normally defined on DOM operations.

- DOM by default, enables the defer-node-expansion mode in which the document components are initially represented with a compact format that is expanded to a full DOM representation as the tree is traversed. Even though this mode offers better performance for large documents, it leads to poor performance and larger memory size for small documents (0K-10K). So for small documents, higher performance can be achieved by disabling the defer-node-expansion feature identified by the URI http://apache.org/xml/features/dom/defer-node-expansion.

Serialize/Marshall

The last step in the XML document processing is the serialization or marshalling to write the document to an output stream. StAX, DOM, and JAXB provide APIs to achieve this task. The serializer classes, `XMLStreamWriter` (StAX), `Transformer` (DOM), and `Marshaller` (JAXB), are created through the use of factory as in the case of parsers or `JAXBContext` objects in the case of JAXB. Reusing an instance of the factory object provides significant performance benefits since factory object creation is expensive. When working with small documents, creating a pool of writers or marshallers improves the performance.

Validation

Validation of the XML document is sometimes required as part of the business process to guarantee reliability of the application. *Validation* is the process of verifying that an XML document is an instance of a specified XML *schema*. An XML schema defines the content model (also called a *grammar* or *vocabulary*) that its instance documents represent. Some of the popular XML schema include Document Type Declaration (DTD), W3C XML Schema, and RELAX NG. By default, the parsers are set to be nonvalidating but can be easily configured to be validating. Even though Web services are based on XML schema and do not support DTDs, processing of DTD-based XML documents are widely used and hence discussed here for completeness.

Validation is an expensive process, since the parser needs not only to parse an XML document but also to parse the schema document, build an in-memory representation of this schema, and then use this internal schema representation to validate the XML document.

> **Tip**
>
> Turning on validation significantly reduces parser performance.

In cases where validation is required, the following items are worth considering.

- Processing and validating against a DTD is normally cheaper than processing and validating against a W3C Schema.
- Avoid the use of a lot of external entities (external DTDs or imported schemas) as this requires the opening and reading of those files, which reduces the performance.
- Avoid the use of many default attributes as this increases the validation cost.

If the application has a limited set of schemas against which you want to validate XML documents, consider compiling (parsing the schema and building in-memory representation) and caching schemas, since it can significantly improve the performance of applications. In particular, if most of the XML documents your application processes are relatively small, then schema compilation can consume a significant portion of the overall processing time of your XML documents. JAXP provides APIs that allow applications to reuse schemas and hence improve the performance of validating parsers.

> **Tip**
>
> If your application has a limited set of schemas against which you want to validate XML documents, consider caching schemas.

To use schema caching, the first step is to compile the schema using the `Schema Factory` object as shown in the following code snippet. Unlike the `ParserFactory` objects discussed earlier, `SchemaFactory` object is not thread-safe and should not be shared by multiple threads. `SchemaFactory` implementation in Java SE 6 supports W3C XML Schema 1.0 and RELAX NG 1.0. Because the XML DTD is strongly tied to the parsing process and has a significant effect on the parsing process, it is impossible to define the DTD validation as a process independent from parsing. For this reason, JAXP does not define the semantics for the XML DTD caching.

The `SchemaFactory` object is used to compile the schema and create the `Schema` class, which is the in-memory representation of the schema. The `Schema` class can then be used either to create parsers that are optimized for validating documents based on that schema or to create validators that can validate different XML input sources (SAX, DOM, or Stream). The following code snippet shows how to use a validator to validate a document using SAX.

```
// SchemaFactory instantiation
import javax.xml.validation.SchemaFactory;
import javax.xml.validation.Schema;
import javax.xml.transform.stream.StreamSource;
import javax.xml.validation.Validator;
import javax.xml.transform.sax.SAXResult;
SchemaFactory sf =
  SchemaFactory.newInstance(XMLConstants.W3C_XML_SCHEMA_NS_URI);

StreamSource ss1 = new StreamSource("schema1.xsd");
StreamSource ss2 = new StreamSource("schema2.xsd");

// Compile the schemas
Schema schemas = sf.newSchema (new Source[] {ss1, ss2});

// Create the validator
Validator validator = schemas.newValidator();

// Configure the validator
validator.setErrorHandler (errorHandler);

// Create the SAXSource
SAXSource saxSource = new SAXSource (inputSource);

//Validate the specified input and send the augmented validation
//result to the handler.
validator.validate (saxSource, new SAXResult(contentHandler));
```

Resolving External Entities

Another factor that affects the parsing performance is the presence of external entities or DTD references within the XML document. External entities, including external DTD subsets, need to be loaded from either the file system or over the network and subsequently parsed. Loading and parsing of these external entities can seriously impact the performance of your application especially if these entities have to be accessed over a slow network.

One way to improve the performance is to load the entities into memory using an entity resolver. Write a custom entity resolver that caches the contents of the entity the first time it is read. The cached in-memory content will be delivered for the subsequent calls to resolve the entity. The cache may even be preloaded at application startup time to reduce the XML processing cost of the first request.

In some cases, applications may want to bundle the DTDs or schemas along with the application so that they can be read from the local file system rather than accessing them over the network. XML Catalogs provide a way for your application to use local copies of these artifacts without modifying the XML instance document by mapping external references to local resources. The application then uses a resolver that consults the catalog to resolve the external references. You can use the Apache XML Commons Resolver package that is part of the Apache xml-commons project. You can find more information regarding the resolver at http://xml.apache.org/commons/components/resolver/ and the package can be downloaded from http://www.axint.net/apache/xml/commons/xml-commons-resolver-1.2.zip. The following code sample shows how to set up a custom entity resolver that uses both caching as well as a catalog resolver.

```java
public class Processor {
    public void parse() {
        // Set up the parser to use this entity resolver
        SAXParser parser =
            SAXParserFactory.newInstace().newSAXParser();
        XMLReader reader = parser.getXMLReader();

        // set up the reader correctly
        reader.setContentHandler (myHandler);
        reader.setEntityResolver (new CustomEntityResolver());
        reader.parse (...);
    }
}

// Set up a custom Entity resolver
import org.xml.sax.EntityResolver;
import javax.xml.parsers.SAXParser;
import org.xml.sax.InputSource;
import org.xml.sax.XMLReader;
import org.apache.xml.resolver.tools.CatalogResolver;

public class CustomEntityResolver implements EntityResolver {
    // cache to hold the Entity
    private ConcurrentHashMap<String, InputSource> entityCache =
        new ConcurrentHashMap<String, InputSource>();
    CatalogResolver cResolver = new CatalogResolver();
    public InputSource resolveEntity (String publicId,

    String systemId) throws SAXException, IOException {
    // Check of publicId is ignored for simplicity
    if (systemId != null) {
        InputSource is = entityCache.get(systemId);
        if ( is != null) {
            // return cached version
            return is;
        }
        else {
            // Use catalog to resolve it
            is = cResolver.resolveEntity (publicId, systemId);
            entityCache.put (systemId, is);
            return is;
        }
    }

    // Let the default entity resolver resolve it.
    return null;
    }
}
```

The catalog resolver uses one or more catalog entry files to resolve the references that it encounters. A catalog entry file is made up of a number of catalog entries. A simple catalog file follows. For more information on catalog files, refer to http://www.oasis-open.org/committees/entity/specs/cs-entity-xml-catalogs-1.0.html.

```
<?xml version="1.0" encoding="UTF-8"?>
<catalog xmlns="urn:oasis:names:tc:entity:xmlns:xml:catalog">
        <public publicId="-//Sun Microsystems, Inc.//DTD Enterprise
JavaBeans 2.0//EN" uri="dtds/ejb-jar_2_0.dtd"/>
        <system systemId="http://java.sun.com/dtd/ejb-jar_2_0.dtd"
uri="dtds/ejb-jar_2_0.dtd/>
    </catalog>
```

Two methods can be used to specify how the `CatalogResolver` can find the catalog files to be used. Set the system property `xml.catalog.files` to a semicolon-separated list of catalog entry files (e.g., `-Dxml.catalog.files=catalogs/cat1.xml;catalogs/cat2.xml`) or add the `CatalogManager.properties` file to the classpath. The `CatalogResolver` uses a `CatalogManager` that searches the classpath for the previously mentioned file. An example of the properties file follows:

```
# Catalogs are relative to this properties file
relative-catalogs=false
# Catalog list
catalogs=catalogs/cat1.xml;catalogs/cat2.xml
```

The `relative-catalogs` attribute may seem a little counterintuitive; a value of true means that the paths are left unchanged and any relative path will be relative to where the JVM was started. A value of false on the other hand means that the files are relative to the location of the `CatalogManager.properties` file.

Tip

If your document refers to external DTDs and/or contains references to external entities, consider setting up a custom entity resolver that caches the contents of the external entities to avoid the performance penalty of repeatedly loading the entities from external sources. Use XML Catalogs to map external references to locally stored files.

SAX provides two features that allow you to avoid processing of external entities: http://xml.org/sax/features/external-general-entities and http://xml.org/sax/features/external-parameter-entities. If these features are disabled, the SAX parser will not report the entity content when it encounters an external entity reference but instead reports the name of the entity to the `skippedEntity` callback of the content handler.

Partial Processing of XML Documents

There are instances in which only a small portion of a large document needs to be processed. Streaming parsers allow processing to be terminated by the application at any given time, and in the case of SAX parser, this is done by the content handler throwing a `SAXException`. It should be noted that all parsers have to parse the XML content in a sequential manner before the content can be accessed. For streaming parsers, the cost of retrieving content information at the beginning of the document is less expensive than accessing similar information situated further down the stream. In the case of in-memory parsers, the entire document stream has to be parsed irrespective of the location of the element before the content can be accessed.

> **Tip**
>
> In cases where a small portion of the document situated toward the beginning of the document is to be accessed, streaming parsers have a performance advantage over in-memory parsers.

Both DOM and JAXB also support partial processing of the documents: DOM through the use of DOM Level 3 load and save APIs, and JAXB by accepting the XML infoset in different forms (DOM, SAX, StreamSource). If random access of information in a small portion of a large document is required, partial processing using in-memory parsers is an efficient solution. The following section describes how to do this in DOM and JAXB.

DOM Level 3 Load and Save specification provides a set of APIs that allow applications to load, save, and filter documents. The document can be examined and its structure modified during parsing by asking the parser to accept, skip, or reject a node and its children from the resulting tree. The application can also interrupt parsing using the filter API to load only a part of the document. These APIs thus allow you to store a smaller document in memory that reduces the memory footprint of the in-memory DOM tree. The following code snippet shows how the Load and Save APIs can be used to load a selected node into the DOM tree. In this example, an invoice document containing several nodes, including a `Summary` node is parsed. The filter is set up to skip all nodes except the `Summary` node.

```
// Use load and save APIs
import org.w3c.dom.DOMConfiguration;
import org.w3c.dom.DOMImplementation;
import org.w3c.dom.Document;
import org.w3c.dom.Element;
import org.w3c.dom.Node;
```

```java
import org.w3c.dom.bootstrap.DOMImplementationRegistry;
import org.w3c.dom.ls.DOMImplementationLS;
import org.w3c.dom.ls.LSParser;
import org.w3c.dom.ls.LSParserFilter;
import org.w3c.dom.traversal.NodeFilter;

public class PartialDOM {
    public void processPartial (String docLocation) {
        System.setProperty (DOMImplementationRegistry.PROPERTY,
  "com.sun.org.apache.xerces.internal.dom.DOMImplementationSourceImpl");
        try {
            DOMImplementationRegistry registry =
                DOMImplementationRegistry.newInstance();
            DOMImplementation domImpl =
                registry.getDOMImplementation("LS 3.0");
            DOMImplementationLS implLS =
                (DOMImplementationLS)domImpl;
            LSParser parser =
            implLS.createLSParser(
                DOMImplementationLS.MODE_SYNCHRONOUS,
                "http://www.w3.org/2001/XMLSchema");

            // Configure the parser if required
            DOMConfiguration config=parser.getDomConfig();
            // Set up the filter
            parser.setFilter(new InputFilter());
            Document document = parser.parseURI("invoice.xml");
        }
        catch (ClassCastException ex) {
            ex.printStackTrace();
        }
        catch (InstantiationException ex) {
            ex.printStackTrace();
        }
        catch (IllegalAccessException ex) {
            ex.printStackTrace();
        }
        catch (ClassNotFoundException ex) {
            ex.printStackTrace();
        }
    }
    private static class InputFilter implements LSParserFilter {
        private boolean skip = true;
        public InputFilter () {}

        public short acceptNode(Node node) {
            return NodeFilter.FILTER_ACCEPT;
        }

        public int getWhatToShow() {
            return NodeFilter.SHOW_ELEMENT;
        }

        public short startElement(Element element) {
            if (element.getTagName().equals("Summary") || !skip) {
                System.out.println ("accepted element - " +
                                        element.getTagName());
                skip = false;
```

```
                                return NodeFilter.FILTER_ACCEPT;
                    }
                    else
                                return NodeFilter.FILTER_SKIP;
            }

            public short EndElement (Element element) {
                    if (element.getTagName().equals("Summary")) {
                            skip = true;
                            return NodeFilter.FILTER_ACCEPT;
                    }
                    else
                            return NodeFilter.FILTER_SKIP;
                    }
            }
    }
}
```

Similar to DOM, JAXB also provides APIs that allow applications to unmarshall a part of the document into JAXB objects. The JAXB unmarshaller accepts the XML infoset as SAX, DOM, or Stream sources. The following code snippet shows how JAXB can be used along with a SAX parser to bind only a small portion of the document. In this example, we parse an invoice document and bind only the Summary element.

```
import java.io.File;
import javax.xml.bind.JAXBContext;
import javax.xml.bind.JAXBException;
import javax.xml.bind.Unmarshaller;
import javax.xml.parsers.SAXParserFactory;
import org.xml.sax.XMLReader;
import com.sun.xmltest.genjaxb20.ubl07.InvoiceSummaryType;

public class JAXBPartialUnmarshaller {

    public static void main(String[] args) throws Exception {
        JAXBContext jc =
            JAXBContext.newInstance("com.sun.xmltest.genjaxb20.ubl");
        Unmarshaller unmarshaller = jc.createUnmarshaller();
        // install the callback on Summary instance
        unmarshaller.setListener(new Unmarshaller.Listener() {
            public void beforeUnmarshall(Object target,
                                         Object parent) {}
            public void afterUnmarshall(Object target,
                                         Object parent) {
                if(target instanceof InvoiceSummaryType) {
                    InvoiceSummaryType ist =
                        (InvoiceSummaryType) target;
                    // We have the object - access a field
                    System.out.println ("value = " +
                        ist.getSubtotalAmount().
                            getValue().floatValue());
                    // Can stop the parsing if required by
                    // throwing an exception.
```

```
                        }
                }
        });
        // create a new XML parser
        SAXParserFactory factory = SAXParserFactory.newInstance();
        factory.setNamespaceAware(true);
        XMLReader reader = factory.newSAXParser().getXMLReader();
        reader.setContentHandler
            (unmarshaller.getUnmarshallerHandler());
        for (String arg : args) {
        // parse all the documents specified via the command line.
        reader.parse(new File(arg).toURI().toString());
    }
}
```

Selecting the Right API

As discussed in earlier sections, a variety of APIs is available for XML processing. Ease of use is often the most important factor in selecting the API. This is a strong argument for using JAXB, which hides the complexities of XML to Java mapping from the developer allowing them to work directly with Java objects. One of the important advantages that DOM provides is the flexibility that allows applications to support documents whose schemas may often change. Performance should also be an important consideration in the selection process.

The three charts shown in Figure 11-2, Figure 11-3, and Figure 11-4 show the comparative performance of parsing and accessing the elements for a 900 kilobyte invoice document. The data was collected using a modified version of XMLTest (http://java.net/projects/xmltest/), an XML micro-benchmark developed by Sun Microsystems. The benchmark runs a number of concurrent threads each of which creates a SAXParser or XMLStreamReader or DocumentBuilder or Unmarshaller based on the type of test, parses the preloaded in-memory document stream, accesses a set of elements (the proportion of elements to be accessed is configurable), and optionally writes the output to an in-memory buffer. The benchmark measures the total number of transactions that can be completed by all the threads within a specified period of time. In all cases, the factory objects are created only once per thread, but the parsers/unmarshallers are created for each iteration. Pooling of parsers/unmarshallers was not carried out so that the parser/unmarshaller creation times could be studied. The tests were run against the SAX, DOM, StAX, and JAXB implementations bundled with JDK 6 Update 4 as well as the Woodstox parser (version 3.2.5). It should be noted that the data is based on running the tests against a single document type and may vary slightly for other types of XML documents. It is a good practice to carry out performance experiments with the specific documents of interest to identify the API that best suits your performance needs.

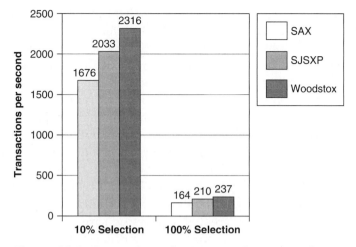

Figure 11-2 Comparison of parsing performance of SAX,
Oracle's SJSXP, and Woodstox streaming parsers

Figure 11-2 compares the performance of SAX, Oracle's (SJSXP), and Woodstox StAX parsers that access different proportions of the document. In the case of 10% selection, the parser exits after accessing 10% of the content, whereas the entire document is scanned in the 100% selection case. The StAX parsers perform better than SAX in both cases, with Woodstox providing the best performance in all cases. As expected, accessing a smaller portion of the document provides higher throughput than traversing the entire document.

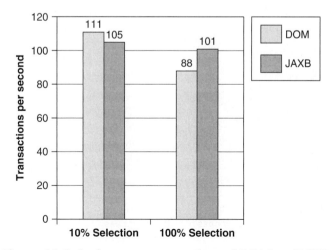

Figure 11-3 Performance comparison of DOM and JAXB

Figure 11-3 shows the performance data for DOM and JAXB for the operations described in Figure 11-2. The DOM and JAXB performance is significantly lower than that of SAX and StAX even when the entire document is scanned. The difference is even more pronounced when only a portion of the document is required to be traversed. The effectiveness of in-memory parsers can also be clearly seen here. Since streaming parsers do not support bidirectional traversal, multiple parse cycles are required for accessing elements in a nonsequential manner. For in-memory parsers, the cost of traversal is low compared to the cost of building the in-memory tree. In-memory parsers may be a better fit if a large portion of the document is to be traversed and in cases where random access of elements is required.

Between the two in-memory parsers, JAXB has a larger cost of building the in-memory tree because of the higher binding overhead incurred by JAXB. However, once the JAXB object has been created, traversing through its various elements is cheaper than that for DOM. In our case, JAXB is a better choice if the entire document is required to be accessed. It is important to note that the comparative performance between DOM and JAXB is dependent on the size and schema of the document.

Figure 11-4 shows the performance impact of serializing the in-memory document to an output stream. The set of bars on the left represents the cost of building the in-memory representation as well as traversing the entire document. The bars on the right include the additional expense of serialization of the document into an in-memory output stream. The JAXB serialization performs better than DOM serialization. In cases where the in-memory object is required to be converted back to XML, JAXB is a better choice.

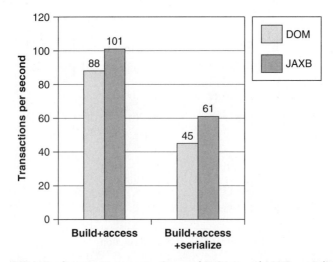

Figure 11-4 Performance comparison of DOM and JAXB serialization

> **Tip**
>
> Use streaming parsers for processing large documents or if only a small portion of the document is accessed. The default StAX parser typically outperforms the default SAX parser.
>
> Use in-memory parsers, DOM or JAXB, if random access of elements is required. Creation of JAXB objects tends to be more expensive than creating the equivalent DOM tree, but it is cheaper to navigate the JAXB object once it has been built. Use JAXB if random access of multiple elements is involved.
>
> JAXB marshalling performance is superior to DOM serialization.

JAX-WS Reference Implementation Stack

The Java platform supports Web services through the Java API for XML-based Web services (JAX-WS), which has been defined as JSR 224 within the Java Community Process. JAX-WS 2.x is part of Java SE 5, Java SE 6 as well as Java EE 5. The JAX-WS specification defines the following: mappings between WSDL 1.1 and Java, the client and service APIs, a set of annotations as well as the specifics related to the SOAP binding. Even though JAX-WS based Web services can be deployed using Java SE 5 or Java SE 6, Web services often need enterprise features provided by Web or application servers (such as scalable HTTP connection handling, transaction support, etc.). All examples in this chapter are based on the JAX-WS Reference Implementation (JAX-WS RI) that is part of the GlassFish Server Open Source Edition (also referred to as GlassFish hereafter). Users can download GlassFish from https://glassfish.java.net/.

JAX-WS Reference Implementation (JAX-WS RI) provides a set of tools that make it easy for developers to develop Web services as well as a runtime for deploying those services. Developers have the choice of exposing a Java class as a Web service or generating the necessary artifacts from a predefined WSDL. The Web service can then be deployed into an environment that supports the JAX-WS runtime, which is often a Java EE container. In this chapter, we look at the performance characteristics of the deployed Web services without delving into performance issues related to the Web service development tools.

JAX-WS RI is built on top of several standard components including Java API for XML Processing (JAXP), Streaming API for XML (StAX), Java API for XML Binding (JAXB), and SOAP with Attachments API for Java (SAAJ). Figure 11-5 shows the different layers within the JAX-WS runtime at the client and the server. In a typical SOAP request-response message exchange, the client invokes the service endpoint of the Web service deployed at the server and receives a response back from the server. At the client side, the application delegates the responsibility of the Web service invocation to the JAX-WS implementation. JAX-WS runtime creates the SOAP envelope,

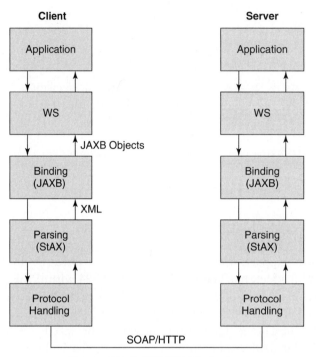

Figure 11-5 JAX-WS RI stack

uses JAXB to marshall the Java objects to XML, and the appropriate payload is written to the network buffer to be sent to the server.

At the server side, the data goes through a similar series of steps but in the reverse order in which the SOAP payload is read from the network and the appropriate operation of the endpoint is invoked. The server first reads the payload from the network stream, selects the right decoder—SOAP decoder in the case of SOAP messages—parses the payload, processes the headers as required, and passes the SOAP body to JAXB to unmarshall the XML to the appropriate Java objects, and the right method in the endpoint implemented by the application is invoked. The response from the server to the client traces a similar path through the stack but in the other direction.

A Web service call from the client to the server thus involves several components, all of which contribute to the processing cost of that invocation. Web services that use HTTP are greatly affected by the HTTP request processing performance within the Web container as well as network performance. The remaining invocation cost is a combination of the data processing expense incurred by the JAX-WS stack at the outbound and inbound sides and the time spent in the application code involved in processing the message at the service endpoint. In cases where the application code is minimal, the Web services performance is dictated by how good the JAX-WS implementation is. Several factors including the type and size of the message affect the performance of this layer. This is covered in more detail in the "Factors That Affect Web Service Performance" section.

In some cases, the data processing in the service endpoint implementation is complex and time consuming, in which case the overall performance of the Web service is influenced by the application performance more so than by any other factor. To distinguish Web services performance as opposed to application performance, the rest of this chapter assumes a small amount of application code. To understand the performance characteristics of a Web service, a benchmark is required. The next section describes how to develop a Web service micro-benchmark that can be used to accurately measure Web service performance.

Web Services Benchmarking

Development of a micro- or macro-benchmark is sometimes required to understand the performance characteristics of your Web service. The benchmark is useful in identifying potential performance bottlenecks, comparing different application designs, and evaluating JAX-WS implementations from different vendors. The general principles behind developing benchmarking multi-tiered applications discussed in Chapter 9, "Benchmarking Multi-tiered Applications," should be considered while developing a Web services benchmark. In this section, issues relating specifically to Web service benchmarking are discussed.

As described in the previous section, a typical request-response message exchange involves the execution of the application code at the service endpoint, which contributes to the overall response time of the method invocation.

> **Tip**
>
> If the Web service benchmark is used to compare the performance of implementations from different vendors, keep the application code to a minimum to accurately compare the performance of the Web service infrastructure.

In this section, we look at three parameters important for a Web service benchmark:

- Payload messages
- Types of operations
- Client driver

While describing the benchmark Web service, use schema types and message definitions similar to that used in the application. However, in some cases, the messages are complex, and developing a micro-benchmark using these messages is not practical due to the difficulties involved in developing simple clients capable of generating the required messages (e.g., the client having to generate invoices or purchase orders that typically come from external vendors). In such cases, the benchmark may have to resort to using simpler messages. It should be noted that use of nonrepresentative overly simple messages may not provide an accurate characterization of your application.

Another factor to consider while defining the service is the size of the payload to be tested since the payload size greatly affects Web service performance.

> **Tip**
>
> It is a good practice to design messages whose size can be changed easily. One common practice is to define the message as a list of `MessageTypes`. The size of the payload can be increased by increasing the number of items in the list.

Web services often define different types of operations; for example, receiving simple requests and sending large payloads in response, or receiving large payloads and sending a simple acknowledgment in return. The third category of operations receives large payloads and responds with similar sized payloads. Different layers in the Web service stack are responsible for the processing of incoming request and outgoing response messages.

> **Tip**
>
> It is a good practice to test the different operational signatures used by the application. An echo operation often serves as a good test case: The application processes the incoming message and returns the same message.

The easiest way to develop a Web service client is to use the JAX-WS client APIs, from here on referred to as the *thick client*. Figure 11-6 shows the use of thick client for benchmark measurement. A Web service invocation from a thick client to a server traverses the JAX-WS stack on both the client and the server, and the overall response time for the invocation includes the processing time at the client and the server. In this case, both the client and the server should be considered to be part of the system under test (SUT).

The thick client test scenario has several advantages:

- Easy to implement
- Measures the performance of the JAX-WS implementation at both the client and server

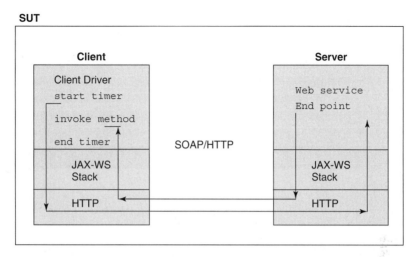

Figure 11-6 Web service benchmark using a JAX-WS client

- Can handle fault conditions
- Represents a real life use case in which both the client and server are part of the single application deployment

However, it also has a significant disadvantage. In a client-server test, to generate sufficient load on the server, an equally powerful client system is required. This challenge is especially daunting when you need to study the performance and scalability characteristics of a Web service deployed on a large multicore system. For such cases, the *thin client* approach described next is more suitable.

In the thin client mode, a simple HTTP driver is used to deliver the SOAP message to the Web service endpoint as shown in Figure 11-7. The HTTP driver is a simple client that posts the message to the server and receives the response. In its simplest form, the driver assumes that the Web service is fully functional, checking only the HTTP response code and discarding the return messages, thus making it incapable of handling any Web service specific fault conditions. More complex forms of the HTTP driver may parse the output for diagnostic purposes.

Since the processing time within the HTTP driver is small, the Web services processing time at the server is the primary contributor to the response time of an interaction, making this a pure server benchmark. Unlike the thick client mode, the processing power required for the client system is only a fraction of that of the server, making this mode ideally suited for scalability analysis of Web services on large multicore systems.

One of the challenges in the thin client test scenario is the ability to load the correct SOAP message to be used by the HTTP driver. One simple solution is to

SUT

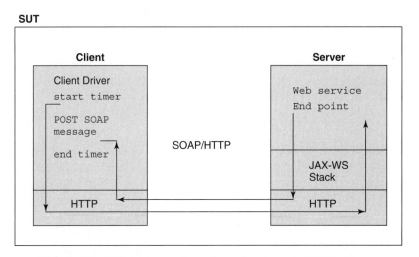

Figure 11-7 Web service benchmark using an HTTP driver

capture the request using an intermediary like Apache TCPMon and saving it to a file. The HTTP driver during its initialization, reads the contents from the file into memory and reuses it for subsequent requests. The primary drawback of this method is the requirement to capture the required messages for each test case. A second more complex scenario involves the use of a JAX-WS handler to capture the request dynamically during the driver initialization. A JAX-WS handler, `LoggingHandler`, that implements `SOAPHandler<SOAPMessageContext>` is first added to the handler list of the client binding. During the initialization of the driver, a thick client is first created and a single invocation of the required operation is carried out by this client. This causes the `handleMessage()` method of the `LoggingHandler` to be called allowing the `LoggingHandler` to save the request payload into memory. The in-memory payload is used by the HTTP driver for subsequent requests.

The two primary benchmark metrics that need to be measured are throughput and response time. Throughput defines the number of operations completed within a specified period of time, and the response time defines the time taken for the successful invocation of an operation. Refer to the "Use of Time Java APIs" section in Chapter 8, "Benchmarking Java Applications," to understand how to make accurate benchmark time measurements.

Measuring the response time of a single request is valuable, but it is often not the most important metric in Web services performance analysis. Web services typically need to be highly scalable and capable of handling large numbers of concurrent requests. The performance of the entire system measured in terms of throughput or maximum number of sustainable concurrent clients is a more relevant performance metric, especially for large multicore throughput systems.

Factors That Affect Web Service Performance

Several factors influence the performance of Web services including

- Message size
- Complexity of schema elements
- Implementation of endpoint
- Presence of handlers

Web service applications may also include other technologies defined by the different WS-* specifications. The JAX-WS reference implementation supports a variety of these specifications including WS-Security, WS-Policy, WS-Addressing, WS-ReliableMessaging, WS-Transactions, and so on. The overall performance of the Web service application is affected by the presence of these additional features. The performance impact of adding each one varies by a wide margin, from minimal impact due to WS-Addressing to extremely large impact when WS-Security is enabled. Analysis of the performance impact of the different specifications is beyond the scope of this book.

The performance data shown in this chapter was generated using WS-Test, a Web services benchmark developed by Sun Microsystems. WS-Test is a thick client benchmark that is useful for understanding the performance of the Web services stack. It includes test cases for measuring the performance of sending and receiving simple payloads to complex documents.

Effect of Message Size

The size of the message can dramatically affect Web service performance. As the message size increases, the amount of time taken to process the message increases. Figure 11-8 shows the variation in throughput for different message sizes measured using the echoDoc test case of WSTest benchmark in which an Invoice document (based on the UBL invoice schema) with multiple line items was transferred between the client and the server. The size of the payload was increased by increasing the number of line items included in the invoice. Throughput is measured in terms of number of transactions completed within a second where a transaction is defined as a complete request-response cycle.

As seen in Figure 11-8 the throughput decreases as the message size increases. This behavior is explained by the larger processing cost at each layer of the Web service stack when the payload size increases. Referring to Figure 11-5 at the client, as the message size is increased, the binding layer needs to process more elements and

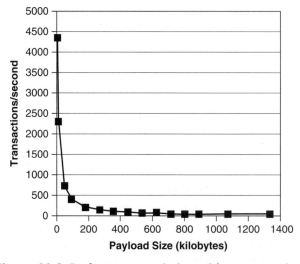

Figure 11-8 Performance variation with message size

write more data to the underlying network stream. The cost at the transport layer is higher due to the increased cost of copying and processing larger buffers and the additional cost of transferring larger amounts of data over the network. At the server, the cost at the parsing and binding layers is increased due to the larger amount of characters that need to be scanned and unmarshalled, respectively.

The JVM memory usage is another factor that needs to be taken into account with increased memory allocation and garbage collection costs. In some extreme cases with very large payloads, memory shortage may reduce the performance drastically making the Web service unusable. The "Working with XML Documents" section later in the chapter provides some best practices on working with very large payloads.

Tip

Using smaller sized messages can improve the performance of your Web service.

An important question often asked is about the granularity of the service; single invocation exchanging a large message versus multiple invocations of smaller messages. Figure 11-9 shows the variation in throughput normalized with respect to message size. Initially the performance improves as the payload size increases until it reaches a maximum. Further increase in payload size causes a drop in performance. In this particular test, the best performance was achieved for a payload size of 450 kilobytes. So to transfer a fixed amount of data, it is more efficient to send a few large

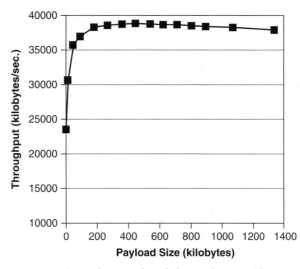

Figure 11-9 Variation of normalized throughput with message size

messages rather than sending a large number of smaller messages. A setup overhead is incurred for each service invocation (connection handling, header processing, etc.), and for small messages, this overhead would be a significant portion of the overall processing cost, whereas for large messages, data processing cost would dominate, dwarfing the invocation overhead. Garbage collection overhead also rises for increasing message size thereby reducing the throughput.

Tip

Payload size should be an important Web service design consideration. It is important to identify the optimum message size for your application.

Web service invocation granularity should be designed around the use of the optimum message size. If possible, small messages should be combined to create a larger message of the optimum message size allowing a single invocation to replace multiple requests with smaller payloads. Similarly, a single invocation with a large message may be split into multiple invocations.

Performance Characteristics of Various Schema Types

Web Service Descriptor Language (WSDL) is used to describe what a Web service does. It defines an XML grammar to describe the services as collections of communication endpoints capable of exchanging messages. Within WSDL, the `types` element encloses data type definitions relevant for the exchanged messages. XML schema definition is used as the default type system. The mapping of XML schema types is delegated to JAXB within the JAX-WS stack. Table 11-2 shows a partial list of XML schema to Java type mapping in JAX-WS 2.0.

Web service performance is greatly influenced by the choice of message schema. Figure 11-10 shows the comparative performance of echoing an array of 100 elements comprised of a single schema type, and observing the effect of changing the schema type of this array.

The schema types `boolean`, `short`, and `int` share similar performance and are the best among all types. Significantly lower to these three types are the `float` and `double` where the difference between the two is small. Note that a marked distinction in performance exists between the use of schema types `xsd:int` and `xsd:integer`. The cost of marshalling and unmarshalling is the primary reason for the performance difference between each data type. Of all the numerical types, `decimal` is the least efficient.

Table 11-2 XML Schema to Java Type Mapping

XML Schema Type	Java Data Type
xsd:string	java.lang.String
xsd:integer	java.math.BigInteger
xsd:int	int
Xsd:long	long
xsd:short	short
xsd:float	float
xsd:double	double
xsd:decimal	java.math.BigDecimal
xsd:boolean	boolean
xsd:byte	byte
xsd:base64Binary	byte[]
xsd:hexBinary	byte[]
xsd:unsignedInt	long
xsd:unsignedShort	int
xsd:unsignedByte	short
xsd:time	javax.xml.datatype.XMLGregorianCalendar
xsd:date	javax.xml.datatype.XMLGregorianCalendar
xsd:dateTime	javax.xml.datatype.XMLGregorianCalendar

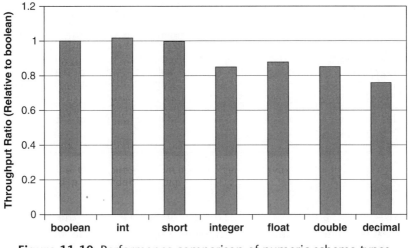

Figure 11-10 Performance comparison of numeric schema types

Tip

Use the higher performing data types if these types can meet the application requirements. For example, use `xsd:int` or `xsd:long` instead of `xsd:integer` if the data values are within a range that can be represented by the corresponding Java primitive types.

All date and time related XML schema types are mapped to a single Java type, `javax.xml.datatype.XMLGregorianCalendar`. Even though different schema types are mapped to the same Java type, the performance of these different types is not the same. Figure 11-11 shows the performance of three different schema

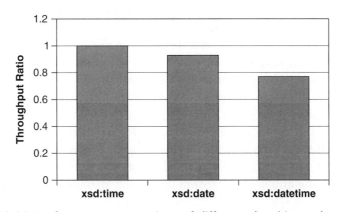

Figure 11-11 Performance comparison of different date/time schema types

Table 11.3 Schema and Java Type Mapping of any Type

```
<xsd:element name="person">           import org.w3c.dom.Element;
  <xsd:complexType>                   @XmlRootElement
    <xsd:sequence>                    class Person {
      <xsd:element name="name"          public String getName();
type="xsd:string"/>                     public void setName(String);
      <xsd:any processContents="skip"
maxOccurs="unbounded" minOccurs="0" />  @XmlAnyElement
    </xsd:sequence>                     public List<Element> getAny();
  </xsd:complexType>                  }
</xsd:element>
```

types—time, date, and dateTime. The use of dateTime is the most expensive, followed by date. The marshalling/unmarshalling cost and the varying size of the serialized XML message are the reasons why the performance differs among these three types. As in the case of numeric types, use the highest performing schema type that meets the application requirement whenever possible. Use the dateTime only in cases where both the date and time are required.

The binary data types, base64Binary and hexBinary are covered in more detail in the section "Processing Binary Payload" later in the chapter. The last schema type that is discussed in this section is the any type. The mapping of any is dependent on the processContents attribute. An any element with processContents="skip" allows the user to bind any well-formed XML to a DOM Element interface. Table 11-3 shows an example of a schema and the associated mapping.

An any element with processContents="strict" (this is the default in the absence of the processContents attribute) means any XML elements placed here must have corresponding schema definitions. JAXB binds any such element to an Object, and during unmarshalling, all elements encountered are converted into corresponding JAXB objects (including JAXBElements if necessary) and placed in this field. If the unmarshaller encounters elements that cannot be unmarshalled, DOM elements are produced instead. The option processContents="lax" means any XML elements can be placed here, but if their element names match those defined in the schema, they have to be valid.

As described previously, any can be used for XML elements whose schema has not been defined. The JAXB binds such elements to the DOM Element interface that allows applications to process the XML fragments or documents. However, a penalty has to be paid for the use of any. Figure 11-12 compares the performance of sending and receiving a 100 kilobyte UBL invoice document as either a JAXB object mapped using a schema or a DOM Element mapped using any. In this example, the throughput for the test using any is about 35% of that using an object defined in the schema.

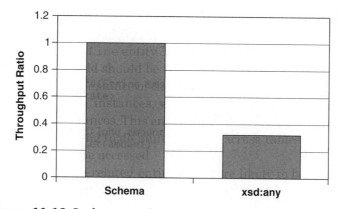

Figure 11-12 Performance impact of using *any* schema type

> **Tip**
>
> Use schema bound elements whenever possible limiting the use of *any* type to meet specific requirements.

The complexity of the message schema also plays an important role. Marshalling and unmarshalling documents consisting of arrays contained within arrays or deeply nested elements incurs significant processing cost. In summary, to achieve best performance, keep the messages small and simple.

Endpoint Implementation

A JAX-WS based Web service can be implemented as an EJB or a Servlet endpoint. Since a service invocation to either endpoint goes through the same parsing and binding layers of the JAX-WS stack, you would expect the performance to be fairly equivalent. However, this is not the case in the implementation of JAX-WS RI included within GlassFish V2. Invocation of an EJB endpoint entails some additional costs, which reduces its performance significantly compared to a Servlet endpoint. Figure 11-13 compares the performance between two similar Web services, one implemented with an EJB endpoint and the other with a Servlet endpoint. The performance of the EJB endpoint is roughly two-thirds that of the Servlet endpoint.

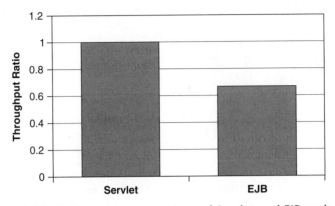

Figure 11-13 Performance comparison of Servlet and EJB endpoints

The performance difference is due to the additional processing involved in the security handlers within the EJB container. This issue is being worked on by the JAX-WS RI team and may be fixed in a later release.

Tip

A Web service implemented as a Servlet endpoint performs better than that implemented as an EJB endpoint in the version of JAX-WS RI bundled in GlassFish V2. The difference in performance may be eliminated in later releases of JAX-WS.

Handler Performance

Handlers are message interceptors that can be easily plugged into the JAX-WS runtime to do additional processing of the inbound and outbound messages. JAX-WS defines two types of handlers, logical handlers and protocol handlers. Protocol handlers are specific to a protocol and may access or change the protocol-specific aspects of a message. Logical handlers are protocol-agnostic and cannot change any protocol-specific parts (like headers) of a message. Logical handlers act only on the payload of the message. Figure 11-14 shows how the logical and message handlers are invoked during a request and response.

Handlers provide an easy mechanism to access and modify inbound and outbound messages. They are easy to develop since a basic handler needs to implement just three methods: handleMessage(), which is called for both inbound and outbound messages; handleFault(), to handle fault conditions; and close(), which is called at the end of the message invocation. The handlers can access the message via the MessageContext interface.

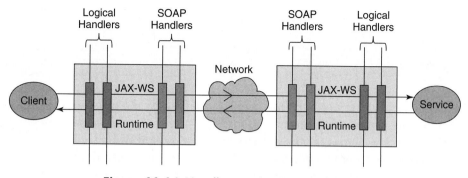

Figure 11-14 Handler mechanism in JAX-WS

The JAX-WS specification defines a specific protocol handler for the SOAP binding, `javax.xml.ws.handler.soap.SOAPHandler`, which receives a `SOAPMessage` object. The `SOAPMessage` is based on DOM, which means that the entire message is loaded in memory as a DOM tree. In contrast, the JAX-WS RI without handlers works in a streaming fashion, which provides much better performance.

Logical handlers extend `javax.xml.ws.handler.LogicalHandler` and access the message payload through the `LogicalMessage` interface as either a `Source` or a JAXB object. In JAX-WS RI, the payload data is accessed as a `DOMSource`, which requires the creation of a DOM representation of the payload. This causes significant performance degradation as shown in Figure 11-15. Reading the payload as a JAXB object causes further degradation in performance due to the added expense of unmarshalling and marshalling of the object from a `DOMSource`.

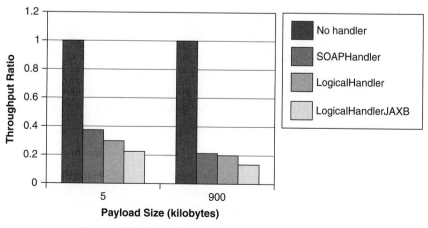

Figure 11-15 Performance impact of handlers

> **Tip**
>
> The handler mechanism provides an easy way for applications to access inbound and outbound messages. Addition of `Handlers` degrades the overall performance significantly.

In summary, Web service performance is influenced by the size and complexity of the message as well as the presence of any `Handlers`. The response time of a Web service increases as the payload size increases. However, if Web service performance is measured in terms of transactions per byte of data transferred, the performance increases as the payload size is increased up to an optimum payload size beyond which the performance decreases. Different schema types show different performance characteristics, and this should be taken into account while designing Web services. Use the higher performing data types if these types can meet the application requirements. Addition of SOAP `Handlers` degrades the overall performance significantly, especially for large documents.

Performance Best Practices

Web services participating in complex business processes are expected to service a variety of operations. In addition to the supporting request-response of simple messages, they may have to process large XML documents of the order of several megabytes or process binary data such as images or audio files.

Consider a simple order processing service for example. The client first submits a purchase order consisting of several line items. The service processes the order, which could be potentially very large, by iterating over each line item and then sending an acknowledgment back to the client. At a later time, the client may inquire about the status of the order (simple request/response messages) to check whether the work has been completed or invoke a request to get the invoice (potentially very large). The process is completed with the client submitting a scanned copy of the signed invoice as an image back to the service. A complete work flow consists of several steps, each involving a different message exchange model. Certain best practices can be applied in the design and implementation of the sample purchase order service that would make it perform significantly better than the simple out-of-the-box implementation. This section describes some of these best practices.

Processing Binary Payload

XML, being a textual format, requires all elements including binary data to be represented as characters when embedded in an XML document. Binary data specified using XML schema type `base64Binary` and `hexBinary` is converted to text using Base64 encoding, which traverses the binary data stream and creates a textual representation of the data using 64 characters ([a-z]-[A-Z]-[0-9] +/). The encoded text is roughly about one-third larger in size than the original binary data. Transmission of a SOAP document containing binary data thus entails binary to text encoding at the sender and text to binary decoding at the receiver. The encoding/decoding costs along with the bloated message size make transmission of binary data, especially large binary data such as images and audio files expensive.

The SOAP Message Transmission Optimization Mechanism (MTOM) together with XML-binary Optimized Packaging (XOP) were proposed to address the inefficiencies encountered in the transmission of binary data in SOAP documents. The W3C XOP specification describes XOP as follows:

> A means of more efficiently serializing XML infosets that have certain types of content. An XOP package is created by placing a serialization of the XML infoset inside of an extensible packaging format (such as MIME Multipart/Related). Then selected portions of its content that are base64-encoded binary data are extracted and re-encoded (i.e., the data is decoded from base64) and placed into the package. The locations of those selected portions are marked in the XML with a special element that links to the packaged data using URIs. In a number of important XOP applications, binary data need never be encoded in base64 form. If the data to be included is already available as binary octet stream, then either an application or other software acting on its behalf can directly copy that data into a XOP package, at the same time preparing suitable linking elements for use in the root part; when parsing a XOP package, the binary data can be made available directly to applications, or, if appropriate, the base64 binary character representation can be computed from the binary data.

MTOM provides an optimization for exchanging messages between SOAP nodes using an XOP-based selective encoding. This allows the binary blobs of type `base64Binary` or `hexBinary` to be transmitted as MIME attachments in a way that is transparent to the application. Since the binary data is an attachment and not part of the XML payload, base64 encoding of the binary data is not required.

JAX-WS 2.0 supports MTOM for the optimal transmission of binary data as follows:

- The binary attachment is packaged in a MIME multipart message.
- An `<xop:include>` element is used to mark where the binary data is.
- The actual binary data is kept in a different MIME part.

The Base64 encoded as well as the MTOM on-the-wire message corresponding to the following schema appear in the following two examples.

```
<xsd:complexType name="Synthetic">
    <xsd:sequence>
        <xsd:element name="barray" type="xsd:base64Binary" />
    </xsd:sequence>
</xsd:complexType>
```

Base64 Encoded In-line Message

```
Content-Type: text/xml;charset="utf-8"
...
<?xml version="1.0" ?>
 <S:Envelope xmlns:S="http://schemas.xmlsoap.org/soap/envelope/">
  <S:Body>
   <echoSynthetic
xmlns="http://www.sun.com/wstest/testcases/test/wsdltypes">
    <synthetic>
       <barray>AAAAAAAAAAAAAAA==</barray>
    </synthetic>
   </echoSynthetic>
  </S:Body>
 </S:Envelope>
```

MTOM Message

```
--uuid:e18b7da7-8169-44a0-9465-cd9d2694850d
Content-Id: <rootpart*e18b7da7-8169-44a0-9465-cd9d2694850d@example.jaxws.sun.
com
>
Content-Type: application/xop+xml;charset=utf-8;type="text/xml"
Content-Transfer-Encoding: binary
<?xml version="1.0" ?>
 <S:Envelope xmlns:S="http://schemas.xmlsoap.org/soap/envelope/">
  <S:Body>
   <echoSynthetic xmlns="http://www.sun.com/wstest/testcases/test/wsdltypes">
    <synthetic>
     <barray>
       <Include xmlns="http://www.w3.org/2004/08/xop/include"
href="cid:3falce96-
3f3e-4db9-bee8-c04e85b852a4@example.jaxws.sun.com"/>
     </barray>
    </synthetic>
   </echoSynthetic>
  </S:Body>
 </S:Envelope>
--uuid:e18b7da7-8169-44a0-9465-cd9d2694850d
Content-Id: <3falce96-3f3e-4db9-bee8-c04e85b852a4@example.jaxws.sun.com>
Content-Type: application/octet-stream
Content-Transfer-Encoding: binary
```

If your message contains binary data, you should use MTOM for the optimized transmission of the payload.

> **Tip**
>
> Use MTOM for the transmission of large binary payloads.

The process for enabling MTOM at the server and client for JAX-WS RI is described in the following paragraphs. There are multiple ways of enabling MTOM at the server. Two of them are given in the following list.

- Annotating the Service Endpoint Interface (SEI) with @MTOM as shown in the following code snippet:

```
@javax.xml.ws.SOAP.MTOM
@javax.xml.ws.WebService
public class TestServiceImpl implements TestService {
    ...
}
```

- Setting the `enable-mtom` element within the `port-component` element of the Web services deployment descriptor (webservices.xml).

```
<webservices ..>
   <port-component>
      ...
      <enable-mtom>true</enable-mtom>
   </port-component>
</webservice>
```

- At the client side, the MTOM support is automatically enabled if the server WSDL advertises that it supports MTOM.
- IT can also be enabled programmatically as follows:

```
import javax.xml.ws.soap.MTOMFeature;

TestServicePortType test =
     new TestService().getTestServicePort ( new MTOMFeature());
```

A performance cost is associated with enabling MTOM: the cost of packaging the message as a MIME package. Does this cost offset the benefits, making it more expensive to use MTOM over base64 encoding? There is no straightforward answer since it depends on the size of the payload and the MTOM implementation. The cost of base64 encoding/decoding is proportional to the data size and the larger size of the encoded payload adds to the message transmission cost. Since MTOM does not do any data processing, the MTOM setup cost is fixed and does not depend on the size of the binary data. So for small messages, the setup cost associated with MTOM may be more than transmitting the data as encoded inline text. Experiments have shown that this limit is around 5–6 kilobytes. This value may vary depending on the server type, container type, and the MTOM implementation that you use. If you work with small binary data, for optimum performance, it is a good practice to carry out experiments in your environment to identify whether MTOM should be enabled. JAX-WS provides APIs that allow users to set a threshold value above which MTOM should be enabled. At the server side, this can be achieved through the use of @MTOM (threshold = <value in bytes>) annotation.

At the client side, the threshold can be specified as an argument to the MTOM Feature constructor (e.g., getTestServicePort (new MTOMFeature (6000))). Alternatively, this can also be achieved by setting the MTOM_THRESHOLD_VALUE property in the RequestContext object as shown in the following code snippet:

```
TestServicePortType proxy = new TestService().getTestServicePort();
java.util.Map<String, Object> requestContext = ((BindingProvider)proxy).
getRequestContext();
requestContext.put (
com.sun.xml.ws.developer.JAXWSProperties.MTOM_THRESHOLD_VALUE, 6000);
```

As the size of the attachment becomes sufficiently large, JVM memory limitations and high GC costs become a factor since the entire data needs to be read into memory. The Metro 1.2 implementation of JAX-WS RI provides memory optimizations to the attachment handling mechanism that allows the application to process large payloads (several megabytes in size). If the size of the MIME part is larger than a predefined value (1 megabyte), during processing, the attachment is written to a temporary file with only a portion of the data loaded into memory, thus enabling JAX-WS to reduce the memory usage. However, it should be noted that the lower memory usage comes with the added overhead of file I/O operations.

The performance of the attachment handing mechanism has been further enhanced with the introduction of a JAX-WS RI specific data handler, StreamingDataHandler. The StreamingDataHandler is a specialized data handler that applications can use, through the use of readOnce() method, to eliminate the file I/O operations mentioned previously if the attachments are consumed sequentially. This is usually the case with a single attachment or when the application consumes the MIME parts in the same order as they are attached. The StreamingDataHandler thus allows even large attachments to be processed efficiently as small payloads with reduced memory usage. Another convenience method within this handler is the moveTo method that allows the application to move the downloaded attachment to a new location. The following code snippet shows the use of `StreamingDataHandler` at the client and server sides.

At the client, the `StreamingAttachmentFeature` allows the user to specify a threshold value below which the attachment is kept in memory without writing to the file system. It is important to enable HTTP chunking so that the data is sent in chunks rather than the connection buffering the entire attachment before sending the request.

```java
import javax.xml.ws.soap.MTOMFeature;
import com.sun.xml.ws.developer.StreamingAttachmentFeature;
import com.sun.xml.ws.developer.JAXWSProperties;

public EchoDocPortType initProxy() {
    MTOMFeature feature = new MTOMFeature();
    // Configure such that whole MIME message is parsed eagerly,
    // Attachments under 4MB are kept in memory
    StreamingAttachmentFeature stf =
        new StreamingAttachmentFeature(null, true, 4000000L);
    EchoDocPortType proxy =
        new EchoDocService().getEchoDocPort(feature, stf);
    java.util.Map<String, Object> ctxt =
        ((BindingProvider)proxy).getRequestContext();

    // Enable HTTP chunking mode, otherwise HttpURLConnection buffers
    ctxt.put(JAXWSProperties.HTTP_CLIENT_STREAMING_CHUNK_SIZE, 8192);
    return proxy;
}
```

The `StreamingDataHandler` can be used at the server side to specify that the attachment below a specified threshold be read as chunks into memory rather than written to the file system.

```java
import com.sun.xml.ws.developer.StreamingDataHandler;

public void echoDoc (EchoOctetDocAttachIn ecd) {
    DataHandler dh = ecd.getDoc();
    try {
            java.io.InputStream is;
            if (dh instanceof StreamingDataHandler) {
                    is = ((StreamingDataHandler)dh).readOnce();
            }
            else {
                    is = dh.getInputStream();
            }

            // Process the data using the InputStream
            // Close the stream as well as the data handler.
            is.close();
            dh.close();
    }
    catch (Exception e) {
            e.printStackTrace();
    }
}
```

> **Tip**
>
> To reduce memory requirements for transferring large attachments, use the JAX-RI specific `StreamingDataHandler`.

Working with XML Documents

JAX-WS provides an abstraction layer that allows developers to work with Java objects without having to deal with the hassle of generating Java objects from XML representations. Even though the implementation hides the complexities from the developer, the application has to pay the processing cost of the various layers that make the binding possible. For most cases, this is the best approach to take, but may not be the best option if you work with large documents (more than 500 kilobytes). In such cases, under load, the memory requirements may be so high that the server is unable to perform efficiently due to the prohibitively high cost of garbage collection. This section details some of the alternative approaches that can be used when working with large documents.

Sending XML Document as Attachment Using MTOM

The previous section described the use of MTOM to transmit binary BLOBs. MTOM can also be used to transmit XML documents. JAX-WS provides a facility that allows certain MIME types to be mapped to specific Java types, which makes it easier for applications to send and receive different data types. A schema element of type `base64 Binary` can be optionally annotated with the attribute `xmime:expectedContentTypes` to indicate the Java mapping of the element. The `xmime:expectedContentTypes` to Java type mapping supported by JAXB 2.0 is shown in Table 11-4.

Table 11.4 Java Type Mapping for Different MIME Types

MIME Type	Java Type
`image/gif`	`java.awt.Image`
`image/jpeg`	`java.awt.Image`
`text/plain`	`Java.lang.String`
`text/xml or application/xml`	`Java.xml.transform.Source`
`*/*`	`Javax.activation.DataHandler`

To send XML payloads as attachments, you would specify the element type as base64Binary with the attribute xmime:expectedContentTypes set to text/xml, application/xml, or application/octet-stream. Depending on the MIME type, wsimport maps the data to either a java.xml.transform.Source or javax.activation.DataHandler. Table 11-5 shows the schema definition and the associated code necessary to parse the document using a StAX parser. Note that creation of XMLInputFactory is expensive and should be cached if possible. Also keep in mind that the default XMLInputFactory implementation within the JDK is not thread-safe, which necessitates the factory to be either pooled or stored as a thread local variable to be used in a multithreaded environment.

The use of a StAX parser reduces the memory requirements as well as eliminates the JAXB unmarshalling cost. The downside of this approach is that the

Table 11.5 Schema Definition and Code Snippet for Attaching an XML Document

```
<xsd:element name="echoDocAttachIn">
  <xsd:complexType>
    <xsd:sequence> <xsd:element
        name="doc"
        type="xsd:base64Binary"
        xmime:expectedContentTypes="t
ext/xml"/>
    </xsd:sequence>
  </xsd:complexType>
</xsd:element>
```

```
public String echoDocAttach
(EchoDocAttachIn ecd) {
    Source source = ecd.getDoc();
    try {
        XMLInputFactory sFactory =
XMLInputFactory.newInstance();
        XMLStreamReader reader =
sFactory.createXMLStreamReader
(source);
    }
      catch (Exception e) {
        . . .
    }
}
```

```
//<xsd:element name="echoDocAttachIn">
  <xsd:complexType>
    <xsd:sequence> <xsd:element
        name="doc"
        type="xsd:base64Binary"
        xmime:expectedContentTypes="a
pplication/octet-stream"/>
    </xsd:sequence>
  </xsd:complexType>
</xsd:element>
```

```
public String echoDocAttach
(EchoDocAttachIn ecd) {
    DataHandler dh = ecd.getDoc();
    try {
        XMLInputFactory sFactory =
XMLInputFactory.newInstance();
        XMLStreamReader reader =
sFactory.createXMLStreamReader (dh.
getInputStream());
    }
      catch (Exception e) {
        . . .
    }
}
```

user will not be able to leverage the binding facilities provided by JAX-WS and will have to rely on custom XML message processing. One case in which this approach is effective is when only a small portion of the document is required to be parsed.

Consider the scenario of a discount calculation Web service that receives an invoice, extracts the buyer id, looks up the discount percentage for that buyer, and returns the discount value back to the sender. The application should be able to deal with very large payloads (invoices may contain a large number of line items), and only partial processing of the document is required to extract the data of interest. In the common Java-centric approach, JAX-WS creates an Invoice object in memory and then invokes the application method, which extracts the buyer id from the object. In addition to the parsing and binding cost, the memory footprint of the application is also increased as the entire message has to be read and the object created in memory. Working directly on the XML message may be a better choice in this case. By transmitting the payload as an attachment, the server can access the XML document directly. Figure 11-16 shows the data from a test case in which the server extracts just one element (located toward the beginning of the document) from an invoice. As expected, using the attachment mode for partial processing provides better performance compared to JAX-WS. The performance difference increases as the payload size increases, since JAX-WS has to parse and bind larger amounts of data to create the required JAXB object for the bigger payload.

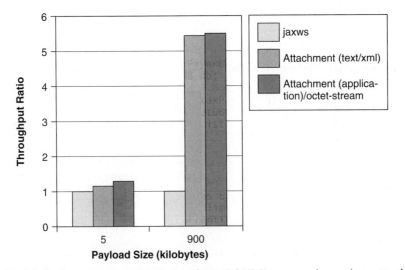

Figure 11-16 Performance comparison of partial XML processing using attachments

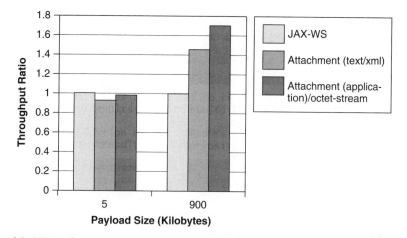

Figure 11-17 Performance comparison of full XML processing using attachments

The practice of sending XML documents as attachments does not have to be restricted to the use case described previously. It can also be used if using a custom streaming parser is deemed to be more efficient than using the binding framework within JAX-WS. Figure 11-17 shows the comparative performance of a client making a direct Web service invocation versus sending the document as an attachment where the entire document is traversed using a StAX parser. The tests were conducted for invoice documents of two different sizes, 5 kilobytes and 900 kilobytes. For small sized payloads, the performance between all three is comparable, whereas for large payloads, using attachments is a better performance option.

> **Tip**
>
> In cases where it is more efficient to work directly with XML payload, sending XML documents as attachments is a good alternative. To send XML documents as attachments, set the element type to `base64Binary` with the attribute `xmime:expectedContentTypes` specified as `application/octet-stream`.

Using the Provider Interface

JAX-WS provides another way to work at the XML message level through the use of `javax.xml.ws.Provider` interface. The Provider is a low level generic API that allows services to work with messages or payloads. The service instance's `invoke()` method is called for each message received for the service. The `Provider` instance can be configured to either receive the entire protocol message or just the message payload. The configuration is achieved through the use of `ServiceMode`

annotation of the `Provider` instance. `@ServiceMode(value=MESSAGE)` can be used
to indicate that the instance wants to receive and send the entire protocol message.
`@ServiceMode(value=PAYLOAD)` indicates that the provider instance is interested
in the message payload only. For the SOAP binding, `MESSAGE` mode allows the provider to get access to the entire SOAP message, whereas the `PAYLOAD` mode provides
access to the contents of the SOAP Body. The following code sample shows a sample
Web service that processes the message payload as a source.

```
import javax.xml.ws.Provider;
import javax.xml.transform.Source;
import javax.xml.ws.Service;
import javax.xml.ws.ServiceMode;
import javax.xml.ws.WebServiceProvider;

@WebServiceProvider
@ServiceMode(value=Service.Mode.PAYLOAD)
public class InvoiceProcessService implements Provider<Source> {
    //Cache factory when appropriate
    private XMLInputFactory sFactory = XMLInputFactory.newInstance();
    public InvoiceProcessService() {}
    public Source invoke (Source request) {
        // Obtain a StAX Reader from the source
        try {
            XMLStreamReader reader =
                staxFactory.createXMLStreamReader(request);
        }
        catch (XMLStreamException ex) {
            return processError();
        }
        return processPayload (reader);
    }
}
```

On arrival of a message, the `invoke()` method of the `InvoiceProcessorService`
is called. Since we have specified the `ServiceMode` to be `PAYLOAD`, the SOAP Body
is passed to the method (the entire SOAP message is delivered in the case of MES-
SAGE). Once the payload is available as a `Source`, it can then be parsed using any
XML parser as described in the previous section.

In addition to the `Source` based provider, JAX-WS also defines a `SOAPMessage` based
provider where the message is delivered to the application as a `SOAPMessage` (which is
based on DOM). This provider only supports the `MESSAGE` `ServiceMode`, and the SOAP
body can be retrieved using the `getSOAPBody()` method.

Additionally, the JAX-WS RI provides an implementation specific `Message` based
provider. The `Message` object is an optimized structure that allows efficient access
to the message stream. As in the case of the `SOAPMessage` provider, this one works
only with the `MESSAGE` `ServiceMode`. Applications can access the envelope or
the payload through a variety of methods including `readEnvelopeAsSource()`,

readAsSOAPMessage(), readPayload(), readPayloadAsJAXB(), and readPay-
loadAsSource(). It is important to note that the `Message` object allows reading
of the data only once. So if multiple passes of the stream are required, a copy of the
message has to be created (using `message.copy()`). The `Message` based provider
is implemented as follows.

```
import import com.sun.xml.ws.api.message.Message;

public class CustomMessageProvider implements Provider<Message> {
    ..
        public Message invoke(Message message) {..}
}
```

By default, providers support the `SOAPBinding` but can be configured to support
HTTP binding instead, using the `@BindingTypeAnnotation` as follows:

```
@WebServiceProvider()
@ServiceMode(value=Service.Mode.PAYLOAD)
@BindingType (value=HTTPBinding.HTTP_BINDING)
public class SourceProviderDocService implements Provider<Source> { .. }
```

The combination of the `ServiceMode=PAYLOAD` and `BindingType=HTTP_Bind-
ing` allows the provider to receive XML messages sent over HTTP as opposed to the
SOAP messages expected by providers in the default mode.

Since providers allow applications to access the XML payload directly, the following questions are worth asking: Is it possible to achieve better performance by
writing custom providers rather than using JAX-WS? Is it more efficient to use
XML/HTTP rather than using SOAP? The answer depends on how the application
processes the incoming message. If only a small portion of the document is parsed
as described in the previous section, using custom providers may give better performance than using JAX-WS. However, in the majority of the cases, use of a custom
provider results in the application performing poorer than using JAX-WS.

Figure 11-18 compares JAX-WS performance to different types of providers:
`SourceSOAP` is a `Source` based provider with SOAP binding and `ServiceMode`
set to `PAYLOAD`, `SourceHTTP` is a `Source` based provider with `ServiceMode` set
to `PAYLOAD` and `BindingType` set to `HTTPBinding`, `SOAPMessage` is a `SOAP`
`Message` based provider, and `Message` is a `Message` based provider. The performance results were based on an `echoMessage` test in which the service receives
an invoice document that is bound to a JAXB object and the same object is echoed
back to client. In the case of `SOAPMessage` provider, the application uses the
`SOAPMessage` directly without creating a JAXB object. The poor performance of
the `SOAPMessage` provider is to be expected since the provider needs to convert

the payload to the DOM based `SOAPMessage`. However, the extremely poor performance of `Source` based provider is surprising. The main reasons for this are the inefficiencies involved in the interaction between the codec, the parser, and the binding layers. The JAX-WS stack, built on top of a `Message` based provider has several optimizations including the use of proprietary internal APIs for its interaction between the different layers, the sharing of symbol table information between StAX and JAXB, and the efficient marshalling of the JAXB objects directly into the output stream. The providers on the other hand have to use a standards based layered approach that substantially increases the overall message processing cost. The results shown here are based on a fairly complex schema. The performance degradation for simpler and smaller documents may be smaller than what is shown here.

Figure 11-18 also compares the performance of providers that handle SOAP versus Plain Old XML (POX), `SourceSOAP` versus `SourceHTTP`. The data shows that there is no difference in performance between the two message types (for SOAP messages without any additional headers). Additional performance cost may be incurred for SOAP messages that incorporate header information that requires extra processing (e.g., WS-Security headers for message encryption and/or digital signature). As mentioned earlier, the cost of processing the SOAP envelope is significantly less than that of other components and hence using POX does not provide any tangible performance benefits.

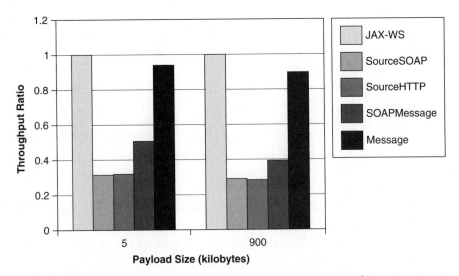

Figure 11-18 Performance impact of using providers

Fast Infoset

The SOAP 1.2 specification defines a SOAP message as an XML Information Set (XML Infoset). While XML 1.0 is the most commonly used serialization, a variety of other binary encodings can be used for improved performance. MTOM and XOP can be used for optimized binary encodings of XML content within SOAP 1.2 payloads as described in the sections "Processing Binary Payloads" and "Sending XML Document as Attachment Using MTOM" earlier in the chapter. These specifications enable encoding of XML content as MIME body parts and encapsulation of those parts within SOAP 1.2 envelopes.

JAX-WS RI also supports binary encoding based on the Fast Infoset technology. The Fast Infoset specification (ITU-T Rec. X.891 | ISO/IEC 24824-1) defines a representation of an instance of the W3C XML Information Set using binary encodings. These binary encodings are specified using the ASN.1 notation and the ASN.1 Encoding Control Notation (ECN). In simple terms, this means that FI can be used to encode XML documents in a binary format. Fast Infoset documents are usually faster to serialize and parse and are smaller in size than the equivalent XML documents. Thus, Fast Infoset documents may be used whenever the size and processing time of XML documents is an issue. The Java platform bundles Fast Infoset parsers and serializers that support SAX, StAX, and the DOM APIs.

Fast Infoset uses tables and indexes to compress many of the strings present in the XML infoset. Recurring strings may be replaced with an index (an integer value) that points to a string in a table. A serializer adds the first occurrence of a common string to the string table, and then, on the next occurrence of that string, refers to it using an index into the table. This compression results in Fast Infoset documents being smaller in size compared to the equivalent XML documents. The size of Fast Infoset documents is related to the number of repeating information in the XML document. Small XML documents tend to have less amount of repeating information and hence the size of the Fast Infoset document will only be slightly smaller than the XML document. Larger XML documents may result in better size reduction because there is more chance of repeating information (for example, a large invoice document may have several line items). Our experiments showed a wide variation in size reduction depending on the size and type of XML document. For large invoice documents, the Fast Infoset document size was about 20% of the XML document size.

JAX-WS RI supports the Fast Infoset technology that improves Web services performance. At the service endpoint, Fast Infoset processors are initiated for content types declared as `application/fastinfoset`, and no application level modifications are necessary to harness the performance benefits of using Fast Infoset payloads. However, clients need to be configured to use Fast Infoset by setting the following system property to one of the values shown in Table 11-6.

Table 11.6 Fast Infoset Client Content Negotiation Properties

System Property	Comments
`com.sun.xml.ws.client.` `ContentNegotiation=none`	Disables Fast Infoset
`com.sun.xml.ws.client.` `ContentNegotiation=optimistic`	Enables Fast Infoset
`com.sun.xml.ws.client.Content` `Negotiation=pessimistic`	Client negotiates with server (see details below)

Setting the property to `pessimistic` allows the client to auto-negotiate with the server and use it only if the server supports Fast Infoset. The client sends the first request as XML with `application/fastinfoset` defined as one of the accepted types. The server responds with a binary message for clients that accept Fast Infoset or an XML message for others. Once the handshake is completed, the negotiated mode is used for all further communications between the client and the server. By default, the content negotiation attribute is set to pessimistic.

Since Fast Infoset parser and serializer are faster than their XML counterparts, the overall performance of the Web service is improved with the use of Fast Infoset. Figure 11-19 shows the performance of echoing invoice documents of various sizes with and without using Fast Infoset. A throughput ratio greater than one indicates that the performance of the Fast Infoset based Web service is better than the one not using Fast Infoset. Enabling Fast Infoset increases the throughput by about 60% for the small document, and the performance benefits increase as the size of the payload increases.

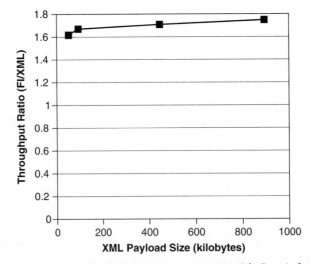

Figure 11-19 Performance improvements with Fast Infoset

There are limitations to how much performance improvement Fast Infoset can provide, since it improves the performance of only the parsing layer, which is just one part of the overall Web service processing. The performance improvements may be smaller for documents with limited repeating elements as well as for documents that have much higher binding cost compared to the parsing expense (e.g., documents based on complex nested schemas).

The major limitation of Fast Infoset is the lack of interoperability with other services since it is not a widely implemented standard. However, in intranet applications where interoperability with other systems is not a consideration, the performance of the service can be improved by using Fast Infoset.

> **Tip**
>
> Using Fast Infoset improves Web services performance. Since Fast Infoset documents are smaller in size compared to XML documents, Fast Infoset based Web services are ideally suited for devices with low network bandwidth. Enabling the auto-negotiation feature allows the service to communicate with both Fast Infoset and non-Fast Infoset based clients.

HTTP Compression

Web services that use HTTP binding can use data compression at the transport level to decrease the size of the transmitted data. HTTP compression reduces the size of the payload, which results in smaller data transmission costs. However, use of compression increases the CPU load on both the client and the server. Compression is useful for clients with limited network bandwidth. JAX-WS clients use HTTP compression by setting up appropriate HTTP headers using the `RequestContext` object available through the `BindingProxy`.

A client can inform the server that it is capable of receiving compressed messages by setting the `Accept-Encoding` header as follows. This does not cause any side effects even if the server does not support compression, in which case the server responds with uncompressed data.

```
Map<String, List<String> httpHeaders = new HashMap<String,
List<String>>();
httpHeaders.put("Accept-Encoding", Collections.singletonList("gzip"));
Map<String, Object> reqContext =
((bindingProvider)proxy).getRequestContext(); requestContext.
put(MessageContext.HTTP_REQUEST_HEADERS, httpHeaders);
```

The client can send and receive compressed data if it is known that the server supports compression (GlassFish supports it) by setting up the additional header, `Content-Encoding`.

```
Map<String, List<String> httpHeaders = new HashMap<String,
List<String>>();
httpHeaders.put("Content-Encoding", Collections.singletonList ("gzip"));
httpHeaders.put("Accept-Encoding", Collections.singletonList ("gzip"));
Map<String, Object> reqContext =
((bindingProvider)proxy).getRequestContext(); requestContext.
put(MessageContext.HTTP_REQUEST_HEADERS, httpHeaders);
```

Web Service Client Performance

The clients access the Web service using the client proxy. Client applications can either create a new proxy for each request or create a single proxy and reuse it for subsequent requests. The creation of the service and getting the Port steps involved in setting up the proxy are expensive operations including the access of remotely deployed WSDL, so it is important to reuse an existing proxy for optimal performance. For the most part, the proxy within JAX-WS RI is thread-safe and can be used concurrently from multiple threads. However, it should be noted that the Request Context object within the proxy is shared among the different threads. So the only limitation in reusing proxies is if the RequestContext object needs to be modified in a thread specific manner.

> **Tip**
>
> It is a good performance practice to create the client proxy once and reuse it for subsequent requests.

As mentioned earlier, creation of the client proxy involves the access of WSDL/Schema documents deployed on a remote server. For performance reasons, it may sometimes be preferable to eliminate this network access and use a local copy of the artifacts bundled with the application. As in the case of XML Entity resolvers, using an XML Catalog is the best way to achieve this. A sample Catalog file, jax-ws-catalog. xml file follows.

```
<catalog xmlns="rn:oasis:names:tc:entity:xmlns:xml:catalog" prefix="system>
    <system systemId="http://javaperf.sun.com/wstest?wsdl"
uri="DocumentService.wsdl"/>
</catalog>
```

The JAX-WS runtime locates the catalog files as follows:

- **Servlet based endpoints or JSR 109 based Web module.** WEB-INF/ jax-ws-catalog.xml

- **JSR 109 based EJB modules.**   META-INF/jax-ws-catalog.xml
- **Client.**   META-INF/jax-ws-catalog.xml picked up from the classpath

When working with large payloads, performance can be improved by enabling HTTP chunking at the client. HTTP chunking allows the connection to send the data in chunks thus avoiding the need to buffer the entire message in memory. The "Sending XML Document as Attachment Using MTOM" section earlier in the chapter details how to enable HTTP chunking at the client.

Bibliography

Litani, Elena, and Michael Glavassevich. "Improve performance in your XML applications, Part 1." http://www.ibm.com/developerworks/xml/library/x-perfap1.html.

JAXB Architecture. http://download.oracle.com/docs/cd/E17802_01/webservices/webservices/docs/1.5/tutorial/doc/JAXBWorks2.html.

Sandoz, Paul, Alessando Triglia, and Santiago Pericas-Geertsen. "FastInfoset." http://java.sun.com/developer/technicalArticles/xml/fastinfoset/.

"Java Web Services Performance Analysis and Benefits of Fast Infoset." http://java.sun.com/performance/reference/whitepapers/Java_FastInfoset.pdf.

"XML Processing Performance in Java and .NET." http://java.sun.com/performance/reference/whitepapers/XML_Test-1_0.pdf.

Mundlapudi, Bharath. "Implementing High Performance Web Services Using JAX-WS 2.0." http://www.oracle.com/technetwork/articles/javase/high-performance-142343.html.

12

Java Persistence and Enterprise Java Beans Performance

Enterprise Java Beans (EJB) is a component-based architecture for large scale, distributed, transaction-oriented enterprise applications. Enterprise beans are the server side components in this architecture that run within an EJB container of the application server. Some of the salient characteristics of the enterprise bean instances are they are created and managed at runtime by the EJB container, can be customized at deployment time, are portable across EJB compliant containers, can make use of container provided services such as security and transactions, which can be specified separately from the business logic, and their access is mediated by the container.

The EJB container provides certain fundamental and commonly used services needed by enterprise applications such as bean life cycle management, transaction management, security, object persistence, and messaging. These services enable a developer to quickly build and deploy enterprise beans. The services are exposed by the runtime through standard hooks defined in the EJB specification, and any enterprise bean that makes use of the services exposed in this manner is portable across containers that are EJB specification compliant. EJB containers may also provide additional services with vendor-specific extensions. The vendor-specific extensions are not portable across different containers, and hence it is a good programming practice to limit their use.

The EJB specification defines three kinds of components: session beans, message driven beans, and persistent entities. (Note: The JPA specification is a separate specification referenced in the EJB 3.0 specification.) Session beans usually implement the core business logic of an enterprise application and represent the interactive session between a client and a server. Even though session bean implementations are shared between clients, at any point session beans can represent only one client. There are two kinds of session beans: stateless session beans and stateful session beans. Stateless session beans provide synchronous stateless services and optionally can also implement a Web services endpoint. Stateful session beans provide synchronous stateful services and in addition also maintain conversational state between client invocations. Persistent entities embody the persistent state of business objects and through object-relational mapping in annotations or in deployment descriptors map to relational databases. Clients usually interact with persistent entities through session beans. Message driven beans provide asynchronous stateless services and are driven by the arrival of messages and expose no client interfaces. In the following discussions, references to client interfaces implicitly apply only to entity and session beans.

As of the writing of this book, the EJB specification is in its third version, and the programming model has changed significantly between EJB 2.1 and EJB 3.0. Access to session beans has been simplified considerably in EJB 3.0; enterprise bean attributes along with their interactions with the container can be customized through annotations in addition to deployment descriptors. Arcane interfaces for using persistent entities have been removed, creating a simplified Plain Old Java Object (POJO) based persistence model. The performance aspects of two programming models are discussed separately in the following sections. In spite of all the changes in the EJB specification, remember that the changes are essentially in the access and use of these enterprise components; under the covers enterprise beans still essentially work to provide the same services as before. A choice between the two different EJB versions should be based on a preference for a programming model and not performance. However, with a much simplified programming model in EJB 3.0, it would seem more pragmatic to choose EJB 3.X over EJB 2.1. The examples in this book have been written for EJB 2.1/EJB 3.0 running on GlassFish Server Open Source Edition V2.1 (also referred to as GlassFish hereafter). The performance characteristics of EJB 3.1 included with the JavaEE 6 specification is similar to that of EJB 3.0 described here.

EJB Programming Model

An EJB 2.1 component has a Home interface, a Business interface, and a bean implementation. This is true for both session and entity beans, whereas message driven beans have only the bean implementation. A Home interface is used by a client to create an instance of a bean implementation. The Business interface represents the available business methods in the bean implementation. When a client creates an instance of a bean using the Home interface, it is returned an instance of the Business interface by the EJB container. The client then invokes the business method on this implementation of the Business interface.

The Enterprise JavaBeans 3.0 specification is a revision of the Enterprise Java-Beans 2.1 specification. The EJB 3.0 specification simplifies the EJB 2.1 programming model by

- Using metadata annotations to reduce the amount of code needed to interact with container services and eliminate the need for deployment descriptors
- Following a "configuration by exception" approach, by specifying programmatic defaults for the most common scenarios
- Eliminating the need for EJB component interfaces and reducing the need for checked exceptions
- Simplifying entity persistence by using a Plain Old Java Object (POJO) model (discussed in more detail in the "Best Practices from EJB 2.1" section of the chapter)

The Java Persistence API and Its Reference Implementation

The Java Persistence API (JPA) specification defines object/relational database mapping for applications using a Java domain model to interact with relational databases. The JPA specification is a simplification over the EJB 2.1 persistent entity programming model. It does so through the elimination of required interfaces for entities and also by following the "configuration by exception" model through the extensive use of programmatic defaults.

The JPA 1.0 specification defines certain important concepts in the following manner. It defines an `Entity`, as a lightweight persistent domain object. The entity is the primary programming artifact in the JPA programming model. An `EntityManager` instance is used to manage the life cycle of entities within a persistence context. A persistence context is essentially a set of persistent entities being managed by an entity manager instance, such that given an entity identity, there's only one instance of the entity in the persistent context. The persistent context in the JPA implementation is conceptually similar to a level one (L1) cache.

A cache keeps in memory copies of entities stored in the database to expedite entity access. A persistent context (L1 cache) is an integral part of the JPA specification. A persistent context can be transactional or extended. A transactional persistent context's lifetime spans the life cycle of a transaction, whereas an extended persistent context's lifetime may span multiple transactions.

Starting with GlassFish V3, EclipseLink (http://www.eclipse.org/eclipselink/jpa.php) is the Reference Implementation of the JPA 2.0 specification. Although ToplinkEssentials is the Reference Implementation of JPA 1.0 in previous versions of GlassFish, starting with GlassFish V2.1 EclipseLink can be used in a seamless manner. EclipseLink is the JPA implementation discussed in the following section.

Level Two Cache

While the JPA 1.0 specification does not require an implementation to provide a second level cache (L2 cache), most JPA implementations, including EclipseLink, provide one. In EclipseLink the L2 cache is referred to as the session cache. A single instance deployment of an enterprise application usually has one L1 cache per client session and one L2 cache shared across client sessions on the same JVM. Each client session works with its own persistent context when executing a business operation and at the time transaction commit changes made to entities are committed to the database and written to the shared L2 cache. Figure 12-1 shows the interaction between the persistence context and the session cache.

The size of the L2 cache can affect the performance of an application. While an L2 cache can significantly improve access to entities because it stores in memory copies of objects retrieved from the database, it can also lead to a large number of in-memory objects in a heavily used application. This in turn can force the JVM to do frequent garbage collections to reclaim unused memory, leading to large pause times and severely degrading the application performance, negating any performance boost from using caches. On the other hand an underallocated cache may result in objects being evicted from the cache more often and leading to more trips to the database, providing little or no benefit from caching. Thus it is important to understand how to configure the L2 cache for a JPA implementation.

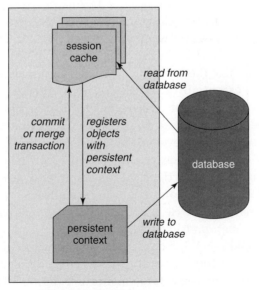

EclipseLink Session

Figure 12-1 JPA session cache

Configuring the cache correctly is an iterative process requiring a preliminary configuration, followed by one or more cycles of monitoring of cache hits and misses, and tweaking the configuration. Monitoring of JPA caches is discussed in the monitoring EclipseLink Session Cache section later in the chapter.

The following discussion covers the object cache in EclipseLink. This object cache is not to be confused with the JPS QL results cache, which is used for storing JPA QL query results. The query results cache is discussed in a later section.

EclipseLink provides options for the kind of cache to use and also to set the size of the cache. The cache is implemented using a `HashMap` and inherently satisfies the requirement of object identity (only one object per entity identity). The options available for cache type and examples for setting those options in the persistence. xml using EclipseLink's JPA extensions are given in the following list.

- **Full Identity Map.** Objects are never evicted from the cache unless they are deleted. This should be used only for applications that use a small number of persistent objects and have a large amount of memory allocated.

```
<properties>
    <property name="eclipselink.cache.type.default" value="Full"/>
</properties>
```

- **Weak Identity Map.** Objects are held in Weak References, which allows the JVM to garbage collect them when there are no other references from the application. This may not provide reliable caching across transactions, but provides a more efficient use of memory than the Full Identity Map option.

```
<properties>
    <property name="eclipselink.cache.type.default" value="Weak"/>
</properties>
```

- **Soft Identity Map.** Objects are held in Soft References, which allows the JVM to garbage collect them when memory is low. This provides all the benefits of the Weak Identity Map and in addition the JVM will garbage collect objects from the cache when the memory is low.

```
<properties>
    <property name="eclipselink.cache.type.default" value="Soft"/>
</properties>
```

- **Soft Cache Weak Identity Map.** Similar to the Weak Identity Map, but additionally this option maintains a most frequently used subcache in addition to the Identity Map cache. In this option, the subcache is a linked list of Soft References, and objects will be released when the JVM determines it is low on memory. The size of the subcache is fixed and equal to the size of the Identity Map cache initially. The Identity Map starts at the specified size and may grow based on application usage until the objects in the Identity Map are garbage collected. When the identity map is garbage collected, the application still benefits from caching as the objects in the fixed-size most frequently used subcache will be available until the JVM's free memory becomes low.

```
<properties>
  <property name="eclipselink.cache.type.default"
      value="SoftWeak"/>
</properties>
```

Tip

It is recommended to set the size of the cache to be at least as large as the number of objects of the same type used in a transaction.

- **Hard Cache Weak Identity Map.** Similar to the Weak Identity Map, but additionally, this option maintains a most frequently used subcache, which is a linked list with hard references. This is essentially similar to Soft Cache Weak Identity, but since some JVM implementations do not differentiate between weak and soft references, leading to the subcache being garbage collected with each GC, this option guarantees that the subcache exists and that the application benefits from caching.

```
<properties>
          <property name="eclipselink.cache.type.default"
              value="HardWeak"/>
</properties>
```

- **No Identity Map.** This option does not provide object caching or preserve identity. This is not a recommended option and is mentioned here only for completeness. If for any reason you do not want to use caching, use isolated caches in EclipseLink.

```
<properties>
  <property name="eclipselink.cache.type.default" value="None"/>
</properties>
```

The default cache type in EclipseLink is Soft Cache Weak Identity Map with a subcache size equal to the size specified for the Identity Map. The default size of the Weak Identity Map cache is 100. The default size can be overridden and specified explicitly. For example, the Weak Identity Map cache size can be explicitly set to a size of 1500. This implies that the last 1500 objects accessed by the application are stored in the subcache and the rest are in the IdentityMap until garbage is collected by the JVM. Explicit sizing of the cache size is configured with the following EclipseLink property in the persistence.xml file:

```
<properties>
  <property name="eclipselink.cache.size.default " value="1500"/>
</properties>
```

Recall previously that the default value is 100. This cache size additionally sets the overall cache size for all entities managed in the persistence unit. EclipseLink also provides the option for setting the cache size for individual entities. This allows for a more fine-grained control on the cache size.

```
<properties>
  <property name="eclipselink.cache.size.Order" value="1000"/>
</properties>
```

Monitoring and Tuning the EJB Container

Chapter 9, "Benchmarking Multitiered Applications," discussed how the various containers within an application server can be monitored to identify potential performance bottlenecks and use the observed values to tune the container for optimal performance. By tuning the containers appropriately, we hope to maximize the use of the resources. This section discusses the important parameters to monitor within the EJB container. The examples are based on the GlassFish application server, but the general principles should apply to other application servers as well. Refer to the "GlassFish Monitoring" section in Chapter 9 for how to enable monitoring of the different containers in GlassFish. Setting the monitoring level of the EJB container to HIGH can cause significant performance degradation (as much as 20% in our experiments). It is recommended that this level be used for debugging purposes and not on production systems. The examples in this section are based on the GlassFish V2.1 server, not on GlassFish V3.

Thread Pool

The thread pool used to process the business logic of an EJB instance depends on the invocation pattern. In the case of a local bean (for all bean types—stateless, stateful, or entity), the processing is executed on the thread that invokes the bean's method. Consider the example of a Web application, in which a servlet invokes a local bean's business method. The execution of the method including any database interaction is carried out on one of the HTTP processing threads. In this case, for optimal performance, the HTTP worker thread pool needs to be monitored and tuned. Refer to the "HTTP Listener" section of Chapter 10, "Web Application Performance," for more information regarding this.

Remote EJB invocations on the other hand, are handled by a different thread pool (ORB thread pool). On the arrival of a new request, one of the available threads in this pool is selected to process the request including database interactions if any, and commit the response to the client. The same thread pool is used for processing of the message driven beans, which are activated on the arrival of JMS messages. It is important to monitor and tune the ORB thread pool to achieve optimal application performance.

By default, the minimum threads in the ORB thread pool, specified by the attribute `min-thread-pool-size`, is set to zero, and the maximum threads (`max-thread-pool-size`) is set to 200. These values may need to be tuned depending on the application. Table 12-1 provides some general guidelines on setting up these values.

For GlassFish, these values can be inspected and changed using the Administration Console, or using the `asadmin` CLI.

```
asadmin get "server.thread-pools.thread-pool.thread-pool-1.*"
server.thread-pools.thread-pool.thread-pool-1.max-thread-pool-size = 8
server.thread-pools.thread-pool.thread-pool-1.min-thread-pool-size = 4
```

The minimum and maximum values can be changed using the `asadmin set` command. In most cases, these values need to be further tuned based on the characteristics of the application. Since database interactions are typical in EJBs, some of the threads may be waiting for the I/O operation to complete, thereby freeing up CPU resources for the processing of other requests. Monitoring of the runtime pool statistics allows for the determination of whether the size of the pool needs to be modified. The two

Table 12-1 Initial Thread Pool Settings

Attribute	Initial Value
Minimum Pool Size	Number of hardware threads or virtual processors
Maximum Pool Size	2X Number of hardware threads or virtual processors

important attributes to monitor are the `numberofavailablethreads-count` and `numberofworkitemsinqueue-current` as shown in the following example:

```
asadmin get -m "server.thread-pools.orb\.threadpool\.thread-pool-
1.numberofavailablethreads-count" "server.thread-
pools.orb\.threadpool\.thread-pool-1.numberofworkitemsinqueue-current"
server.thread-pools.orb\.threadpool\.thread-pool-
1.numberofavailablethreads-count = 0
server.thread-pools.orb\.threadpool\.thread-pool-
1.numberofworkitemsinqueue-current = 6
```

Table 12-2 shows a description of the attributes of interest along with some tuning hints.

Tip

Tuning the thread pool appropriately is essential for obtaining maximum performance. A good starting value for `max-thread-pool-size` is twice the number of cores (the number of virtual processors for SPARC T-series CPUs). Monitor the `numberofavailablethreads-count` value to verify the efficacy of the setting and make further changes as required.

GlassFish supports request partitioning through the use of dedicated thread pools for the processing of EJBs. Say that an application has two stateless session beans, one whose business methods are lightweight and are completed in a short time. The second one handles heavyweight transactions and take several seconds to complete. In the default case, both invocations are handled by a single thread pool. Under heavy load, a lightweight method invocation may be queued until a thread becomes

Table 12-2 Attributes to Monitor for Tuning Thread Pools

Attribute	Description	Tuning Hints
`numberofavailablethreads-count`	Number of threads available for request processing	If this value is consistently zero, it signifies that there is enough load on the system to keep the thread pool fully utilized.
`numberofworkitemsinqueue-current`	Number of requests waiting to be processed	A consistently high value indicates either a heavily loaded system or improper thread pool tuning. No tuning is necessary if the system can fully utilize the CPU resources. Increase the maximum pool size if CPU resources are available and there are no available processing threads.

available to process the request, which leads to a large response time for that invocation. The solution to this problem is to provide request partitioning in the container that allows beans to associate a particular thread pool for its processing. In our example, the user would create a separate thread pool for handling the lightweight bean and use the default thread pool for the other EJBs. The sample descriptor snippet shows how to associate a bean with a thread pool in the sun-ejb-jar.xml.

```
<ejb>
    <ejb-name>SimpleBean</ejb-name>
    <jndi-name>ejb/SimpleBean</jndi-name>
    <use-thread-pool-id>session-pool-1</use-thread-pool-id>
    <bean-cache>
        <max-cache-size>1000</max-cache-size>
        <resize-quantity>512</resize-quantity>
        <cache-idle-timeout-in-seconds>7200</cache-idle-timeout-in-seconds>
        <victim-selection-policy>nru</victim-selection-policy>
    </bean-cache>
</ejb>
```

As mentioned earlier, the default thread pool is also used for processing message driven beans. So thread pool partitioning is useful in allocating separate pools for the processing of remote EJBs and message driven beans.

Tip

Thread pool partitioning is an effective way to dedicate resources to handle requests of varying processing costs.

Bean Pools and Caches

The "EJB Programming Model" section discussed the various events associated with the creation and maintenance of different beans. The EJB container uses a variety of pools and caches to improve the performance of the server. The type of pools and caches used depends on the type of EJBs—stateless session, stateful session, entity, or MDB. It is important to make a distinction between the bean instances that are pooled and/or cached versus the bean references that the client obtains though resource injection, EJBHome.create, or JNDI (Java Naming and Directory Interface) lookup. All client interactions utilize a bean reference; the container intercepts the method calls, retrieves the appropriate bean instance from the pool and/or cache, executes the necessary business logic, and returns them to the pool (at the end of business method or at transaction commit/rollback). This section describes how the pools and caches can be tuned for optimal performance.

Bean Pools

There are multiple ways to configure the bean pool properties. The properties can be set at the EJB container level such that it applies to all deployed EJBs. The following `asadmin` command lists the different EJB container properties.

```
asadmin get server.ejb-container.*
```

Individual properties can then be modified using the `asadmin set` command.

EJBs within an application can choose to override the default behavior by specifying it in the sun-ejb-jar.xml deployment descriptor where EJB configurations can be specified individually. In this section, we describe the individual EJB configuration approach since it provides finer grain control over the cache settings.

Bean pools are used by stateless session, entity, and message driven beans. In the case of stateless session beans, on bean invocation, an instance of the bean is retrieved from the pool and used for executing the business method. At the completion of the method invocation, the bean is returned to the pool. In the case of message driven beans, an instance is retrieved from the pool at the arrival of a message, and the instance is returned to the pool at the completion of the `onMessage()` method. Entity bean pools contain instances of entity beans that are not associated with a primary key. The instances in this pool are typically used for executing finder methods.

Bean pool configuration is not very relevant for simple beans with relatively small creation and destruction cost. However, pooling can improve performance in some cases, for example, a bean that does a JNDI lookup of a resource and stores the reference for future use.

The properties of the bean pool can be specified using the sun-ejb-jar.xml deployment descriptor. Some of the important properties that can be tuned include `steady-pool-size`, `max-pool-size`, and `pool-idle-timeout-in-seconds`.

The `steady-pool-size` specifies the minimum number of instances maintained in the pool, whereas `max-pool-size` specifies the maximum number of beans in the pool. The element `pool-idle-timeout-in-seconds` specifies the maximum time that a stateless session bean or message driven bean is allowed to be idle in the pool. After this time, the bean is passivated to the backup store.

The monitoring framework in GlassFish allows inspection of the bean pool statistics as shown in the following sample.

```
asadmin get -m
server.applications.SPECjAppServer.mfg_jar.LargeOrderSes.bean-pool.*count
server.applications.SPECjAppServer.mfg_jar.LargeOrderSes.bean-
pool.totalbeanscreated-count = 5
server.applications.SPECjAppServer.mfg_jar.LargeOrderSes.bean-
pool.totalbeansdestroyed-count = 5
```

As specified earlier, the decision to tune the pool is based on the cost of instance creation and destruction. The primary tunings include increasing the `max-pool-size` and/or `pool-idle-timeout-in-seconds`. Use caution in increasing the size of the pool—pooling a large number of instances can reduce performance due to the increased memory pressure.

Bean Caches

In addition to the bean pools, the container also maintains several caches to hold bean instances. The two main caches visible to users are the stateful session bean cache and the entity bean cache.

The stateful session bean cache holds the bean instances used to maintain the data associated with stateful session beans. Once a stateful session bean has been created, its state is maintained either in the cache or in persistent storage until the bean is destroyed. The life cycle of the bean instances in the cache is as follows. When a new stateful session bean is created, a bean instance is created and added to the cache. Any subsequent method invocation on the bean causes the container to retrieve the bean instance from the cache, execute the method, and return the instance back to the cache.

While returning the instance back to the cache, if the number of instances has exceeded the maximum cache size, then one of the existing instances in the pool is evicted to make space for the returning instance (more details on the eviction policy are provided later). Eviction and reloading of stateful session bean instances from the cache are expensive operations and can affect the performance of the application. Eviction of an instance causes bean passivation resulting in serialization of the bean to persistent storage. Any method invocation on an evicted bean causes reloading of the bean from persistent storage resulting in a high response time for that interaction. Thus it is important to size the cache size of stateful session beans appropriately for optimal performance.

There are two types of caches for entity beans—*Transactional Cache* and *Ready Cache*. The Transactional Cache is an internal cache and is not visible to the user. The user can, however, monitor and tune the Ready Cache. The caching of entities depends on whether the request is part of a transaction and is explained in the following paragraphs.

The Transactional Cache is an intermediate cache where all entities involved in a particular transaction are stored. The key used to identify an instance in this cache is a tuple consisting of the transaction ID and the primary key of the entity. When a method in an entity bean is invoked as part of a transaction, the container first checks the Transactional Cache to see whether an instance of the bean exists in the cache. If it does, then the instance is used for further processing. If an instance is not found, the container checks the Ready Cache for the existence of an instance of this bean (the key in this case is the primary key of the entity). If a bean instance with that primary key is found, it is removed from the Ready Cache, `ejbLoad()` is called to refresh the bean from the database, and the bean is added to the Transaction Cache and used for further processing. In the absence of an entity bean with the specified primary key in the Ready Cache, the container removes a bean instance from the entity bean pool, calls `ejbLoad()`, adds the bean instance to the Transaction Cache, and uses it for further processing.

At the end of the transaction, the container removes the bean entities associated with that transaction from the Transactional Cache and adds them to the Ready Cache. If the Ready Cache is at maximum capacity, then one of the entities is evicted from the cache and passivated. Passivation is not an expensive operation for container managed beans, but that may not be the case for some bean managed entities.

If instances in the Ready Cache need to be synchronized with the database at the start of the transaction, then the question is what is the benefit of using a Ready Cache? If all requests to an entity are transactional, then there is no benefit in keeping an instance of that entity in the Ready Cache. In such cases, the use of commit option C allows Ready Cache to be bypassed, and the instance is returned to the bean pool rather than being cached. Another case for using commit option C is when an entity with a specified primary key is used only once, say, a new instance is created for every request and never used again. The commit option can be specified by setting the `commit-option` element to `C` under the `ejb` element in the sun-ejb-jar.xml (`<commit-option>C</commit-option>`).

> **Tip**
>
> For GlassFish, it is recommended that the deployer use commit option C for entity beans that are used only in transactions or used only once or twice (hence no benefit in caching the instances).

Ready Cache improves performance for entities that are invoked without transaction. In this case the container checks the Ready Cache and if a suitable instance is found, it is removed from the cache and used without any additional `ejbLoad()` call, thereby improving the performance. Absence of an instance in the cache results in the retrieval of an instance from the bean pool, followed by `ejbLoad()`.

As discussed earlier, when the cache is full, the container uses an eviction policy to select the bean instance to be removed. GlassFish supports three eviction policies: FIFO (first in first out), LRU (least recently used), and NRU (not recently used). The recommended option is NRU, which is an optimized selection policy similar to LRU that provides better performance, especially under high load. The eviction selection policy is specified using the element `victim-selection-policy` in the sun-ejb-jar.xml.

The individual bean caches can be monitored once the EJB container's monitoring level is set to LOW. The `asadmin list -m` command can be used to list all the different caches as shown in the following example (the sample application is SPEC-jAppServer2004 benchmark).

```
asadmin list -m "server*bean-cache*"
server.applications.SPECjAppServer.corp_jar.CustomerEnt.bean-cache
server.applications.SPECjAppServer.orders_jar.ItemBrowserSes.bean-cache
...
```

Statistics of individual bean caches can be obtained using `asadmin get -m <cache>.*` where cache is one of the listed caches as shown in the following example.

```
asadmin get -m
server.applications.SPECjAppServer.corp_jar.CustomerEnt.bean-cache.*
```

The first step in tuning the stateful session bean cache is to identify the number of active stateful session beans in use in the container. This can be achieved by inspecting the number of instance creations and removals as shown here.

```
asadmin get -m beanName.createcount-count beanName.removecount-count
```

where `beanName` is the name of the bean (obtained using the `list` command). An example follows:

```
asadmin get -m
server.applications.SPECjAppServer.orders_jar.ItemBrowserSes.createcount
-count
server.applications.SPECjAppServer.orders_jar.ItemBrowserSes.removecount
-count
server.applications.SPECjAppServer.orders_jar.ItemBrowserSes.createcount
-count = 20492
server.applications.SPECjAppServer.orders_jar.ItemBrowserSes.removecount
-count = 19087
```

Once the number of active stateful session beans has been determined, the next step is to look at the cache hit ratio and the number of passivations. This can be achieved by inspecting the bean cache as follows.

```
asadmin get -m
server.applications.SPECjAppServer.orders_jar.ItemBrowserSes.bean-cache.
cachehits-current
server.applications.SPECjAppServer.orders_jar.ItemBrowserSes.bean-cache.
cachemisses-current
server.applications.SPECjAppServer.orders_jar.ItemBrowserSes.bean-cache.
numpassivations-count
server.applications.SPECjAppServer.orders_jar.ItemBrowserSes.bean-cache.
numbeansincache-current
```

A high hit ratio suggests that the cache settings are working reasonably well. A high miss rate or a high number of passivations, on the other hand, indicates room for improvement. As mentioned earlier, active stateful session beans are stored in the cache, and they are passivated to persistent storage under one of the following conditions: the instance has been evicted to make room in the cache or the idle timeout has expired.

If the current size of the pool is close to the maximum size of the pool and the number of active stateful session beans is higher than the maximum pool size, then it is advisable to increase the size of the pool to at least the maximum number of active stateful session beans. On the other hand, if the number of instances in the pool is less than the maximum, then the passivations are due to the expiry of idle timeouts. In this case, one option to improve performance is to increase the idle timeout so that the instances are kept in cache longer.

As a general note, use caution when increasing the size of the pool. Setting it to very high values can degrade performance due to increased memory usage and the associated garbage collection cost.

Monitoring of entity bean caches is similar to the steps described earlier for stateful session beans. The primary attributes to monitor are the hit and miss rates. A high hit rate suggests that the cache is tuned well and also that the bean is accessed frequently. For such entities, it is worth investigating whether they can be specified as read only. Setting an entity bean to read only is described in further detail in the "Read Only Entity Beans" section later in the chapter.

A high miss rate could either mean that the cache is undersized or that the invocations involve new entities that are not available in the cache. As mentioned earlier, if the application uses an entity for only one or two invocations, it is better to use commit option C for such entities. For frequently used entities, a high miss rate results in degraded performance due to the cost of evicting an existing bean instance and the cost of activating the bean. In such cases, performance can be improved by increasing the size of the cache.

As in the case of stateful session beans, an instance is removed from the bean cache if the idle timeout for that instance has expired. It may be beneficial to change the idle timeout based on the usage pattern of the entities. Increase the idle timeout of frequently used beans thus allowing them to stay in the cache longer, thereby improving the hit rate, and decrease the timeout of infrequently used beans to reduce the cached instances of the bean.

EclipseLink Session Cache

EclipseLink, the reference implementation of the JPA 2.0 specification, has an L2 cache for caching entities and JPA QL query results. The purpose of the cache is to provide faster access to entities by eliminating access to the database for frequently accessed entities. However, if the cache is too big, the JVM spends a large amount of time doing garbage collection, and if the cache is too small EclipseLink may make trips to the database for a frequently used entity; both of these scenarios have a negative impact on the performance of an application. To tune the cache optimally, it is important to know the cache hit and miss statistics for an entity. EclipseLink provides a configuration in the persistence.xml to print out the cache statistics.

```
<property name="eclipselink.profiler" value="QueryMonitor"/>
```

The QueryMonitor configuration for the EclipseLink profiler tells the implementation to print out running statistics of the cache hits and misses per entity in the log at regular intervals. A sample output generated at the end of a benchmark run is as follows:

```
Cache Hits:[#{com.orangerepublic.entity.Customer-findByPrimaryKey=310,
com.orangerepublic.entity.Order-findByPrimaryKey=698}#] Cache
Misses:[#{com.orangerepublic.entity.Customer-
findByPrimaryKey=4510,com.orangerepublic.entity.Order-
findByPrimaryKey=2398}#]
```

From the preceding data we can conclude that for both the Customer and Order entity, the cache miss rate is significantly higher than the hit rate, and increasing the size of the cache would improve performance. The challenge is to identify the optimal cache size that balances increasing the hit rate without deteriorating the performance due to increased garbage collection times. Finding this optimal cache size often requires a series of experiments while monitoring cache and garbage collection statistics. Refer to Chapter 7, "Tuning the JVM, Step by Step," for more information on tuning the JVM.

To change the cache size of individual entities, modify the following property in persistence.xml.

```
<properties>
    <property name="eclipselink.cache.size.Order" value="1000"/>
</properties>
```

Modifying the preceding value sets the appropriate size of the Order entity cache.

Tip

Use the cache and garbage collection statistics to figure out the optimal size for the object and query results cache.

Transaction Isolation Level

Transaction isolation levels are specified to maintain data integrity during concurrent transactions. Usually databases allow for the following transaction isolation level, listed here in decreasing order of performance:

- READ_UNCOMMITED
- READ_COMMITED
- REPEATABLE_READ
- SERIALIZABLE

READ_UNCOMMITED allows a transaction to read data that can be changed or removed before the end of another transaction that is writing the data. This offers the best performance since it does not require any serialization, but may lead to dirty and ghost reads. READ_COMMITED requires that only committed data is read.

REPEATABLE_READ requires that within a transaction, multiple reads of the same entity return the data in the same state. This can be achieved through the use of pessimistic or optimistic locking. In pessimistic locking the corresponding database row is locked, blocking other transactions from accessing the row until the transaction completes. In optimistic locking, no lock is obtained on the entity, but data integrity is maintained through other means, such as version numbers. Stale data is detected if the version number in the database is greater than the version number in memory indicating that the entity's state was changed by another transaction; at this point the application can roll back its transaction, refresh the state of the entity from the database, and retry the transaction. Due to the cost associated with transaction rollbacks, optimistic locking may not be the best option for highly concurrent applications where the data is modified frequently. REPEATABLE_READ isolation level can have phantom reads.

SERIALIZABLE requires that all transactions in a system occur in isolation, as if executed serially. The database may choose to use an optimistic or pessimistic approach to ensure serializability. In the pessimistic approach this may require locking a range in a table or a table lock. In the optimistic approach it is required to detect a concurrent transaction that violates the serializability requirement.

Tip

An optimistic locking approach may provide better performance for applications where the data is seldom modified. However, the optimistic locking approach may not be the best option in highly concurrent applications with frequent data modification because of the cost associated with rollbacks, and in such cases the pessimistic locking approach may provide better performance.

Details about how to set transaction isolation levels for EJB and Java persistence are included in the remainder of this chapter covering performance best practices with EJBs and Java Persistence.

Best Practices in Enterprise Java Beans

This section describes some of the performance best practices for EJBs. But first, a short description is provided of the benchmark used to generate the data shown in this section.

EJB Benchmarking Benchmark Used for Illustration

A micro-benchmark modeling a manufacturer with an online ordering system was used to illustrate the best practices or performance differences in various approaches. The benchmarks for EJB 2.1 and EJB 3.0/JPA are somewhat different because of the inherently different programming models and also because slightly different use cases were considered for emphasizing different points.

In the EJB 2.1 benchmark there is one stateless session bean, `OrderSession Bean`, which is the primary client interface and implements the benchmark's business logic. There are two entity beans, `Order` and `OrderLine`, which represent the business data objects. The benchmark's driver client uses a servlet to interface with the server components and data access objects for transfer of entity state between the EJB container and Web container.

In the EJB 3.0/JPA benchmark there are two session beans, `OrderSessionBean`, which is the primary client interface, and a `ShippingSessionBean`, which is delegated various operations from the `OrderSessionBean`.

EJB 2.1

This section describes the best practices that are applicable to EJB 2.1. It is important to note that several of these practices are applicable to EJB 3.0 as well. EJB 2.1-specific tuning mechanisms are discussed here, and EJB 3 tunings are covered later in the chapter.

Container Managed Transaction Versus Bean Managed Transaction

In container managed transactions, the enterprise bean developer delegates the responsibility of managing transactions to the EJB container. The EJB container is responsible for starting, committing, and rolling back transactions. Enterprise bean developers can customize the transaction characteristics of the enterprise bean through predefined transaction attributes specified through deployment descriptors.

In bean managed transactions, the application is responsible for managing transactions, and the enterprise bean developer writes code to demarcate the transaction boundaries. The advantage of using bean managed transaction is that enterprise bean developers decide when to start and end a transaction. This is advantageous when dealing with large method implementations in which a transaction is required only for a small part or only if certain conditions are met. On the other hand, in container managed transactions the scope of the transaction is over the entire method without providing any mechanism to narrow the scope of the transaction.

Tip

Use bean managed transactions to limit the scope of a transaction or if a transaction is needed conditionally.

Choose Correct Transaction Attributes

Enterprise bean developers can customize transaction characteristics by using one of the six transaction attributes in the deployment descriptor.

- Required
- Requires New
- Mandatory
- Not Supported
- Supports
- Never

All EJBs default to the Required attribute when container managed transaction is specified. It is important to override the default transaction attribute if appropriate for improved performance. For example, if a transaction is not required, but is supported on a bean method, then mark the method with the Supports attribute; otherwise the container will needlessly start and end a transaction with each invocation of the method since the transaction attribute defaults to Required.

Tip

Avoid unnecessary transactions by choosing appropriate transaction attributes.

Control Serialization

The EJB container may need to temporarily transfer the state of an idle stateful session bean instance to secondary storage to efficiently manage the size of its pool of stateful session beans. This transfer of state to a secondary storage is called passivation and involves the serialization of the fields of the stateful session bean and also all the objects that can be reached from the stateful session bean through Java references. Serialization and deserialization are expensive operations, and any attribute that does not need to be passivated should be marked with the `transient` keyword to eliminate the unnecessary serialization/deserialization overhead. The following section provides an example regarding the use of `transient` for caching resource references.

Remote EJB invocation is another instance in which the bean is serialized. During an EJB invocation from the client, each object parameter in the call is serialized at the client side and deserialized at the server side. The same serialization and deserialization process is repeated for the returned object as well. As mentioned earlier, this includes all objects that are reachable through Java references from the parameter objects. As in the case of EJB passivation, when making remote calls it is important to mark the fields that don't need to be serialized as `transient`. The cost of serialization depends on the complexity and size of objects. The factors that affect serialization cost are discussed in the "Session Persistence" section of Chapter 10.

> **Tip**
>
> Mark member fields of a stateful session bean that don't need to be serialized as `transient`. Keep the size and complexity of the attributes that need to be serialized to a minimum.

Cache Static Resource References

An enterprise bean often has references to external resources such as a data source, a JMS (Java Message Service) destination, or to a session bean that are looked up through JNDI. Lookup of resources using JNDI is expensive and should be minimized if possible. Static resources thus should be looked up once and cached to improve performance. The resource references can be created in the session bean's `ejbCreate()` method, which is called once by the container before any business method is invoked.

In stateful session beans, the resource references should be cached as transient fields and should be released in their `ejbPassivate()` method. Marking the resource references as transient prevents these references from being passivated, which as mentioned earlier is expensive. The references should be looked up again in the `ejbActivate()` method. The following sample code demonstrates how to cache static database references. Resource references acquired and cached by an enterprise bean should eventually be released in the `ejbRemove()` method.

The following example demonstrates caching a `Handle` to the EJBObject instance of a remote stateless session bean in a stateful session bean.

```
public class CartSessionBean implements SessionBean{
    transient OrderSessionRemote session;
    transient OrderSessionHome sessionHome;
    javax.ejb.Handle handle;
    javax.ejb.HomeHandle homeHandle;
    SessionContext ctx;

    /**
     * Creates a bean.
     * @exception throws CreateException, RemoteException.
     */
    public void ejbCreate() throws CreateException {
        session=getOrderSession();
    }

    /**
     * Removes the bean. Required by EJB spec.
     */
    public void ejbRemove() {}

    /**
     * Loads the state of the bean from secondary storage.
     * Required by EJB spec.
     */
    public void ejbActivate() {
        session = getOrderSession();
    }

    /**
     * Keeps the state of the bean to secondary storage.
     * Required by EJB spec.
     */
    public void ejbPassivate() {}

    /**
     * Sets the session context. Required by EJB spec.
     * @param sc A SessionContext object.
     */
    public void setSessionContext(SessionContext sc) {
        this.ctx=sc;
    }

    private OrderSessionRemote getOrderSession() {
        try {
            if (sessionHome == null && homeHandle == null) {
                sessionHome = (OrderSessionHome) ctx.lookup(
                        "java:comp/env/ejb/OrderSession");
                homeHandle = sessionHome.getHomeHandle();
            } else if (sessionHome == null) {
                sessionHome =
                    (OrderSessionHome) homeHandle.getEJBHome();
            }
            if (session == null && handle == null) {
                session = sessionHome.create();
                handle = session.getHandle();
            } else if (session == null) {
                session = (OrderSessionRemote) handle.getEJBObject();
```

Continued

```
        }
        return session;
    } catch (Exception ex) {
        ex.printStackTrace();
        return null;
    }
  }
}
```

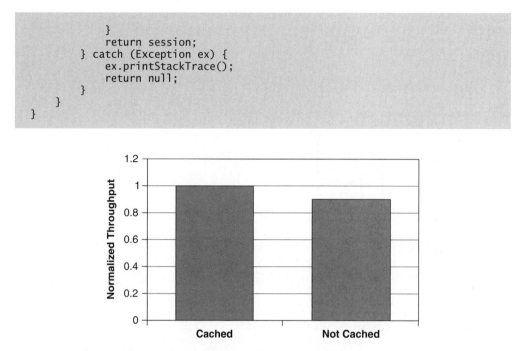

Figure 12-2 Performance benefit of caching resource reference

In the preceding example, the stateful session bean creates a reference to the `OrderSession` object in the bean's `ejbCreate()` method and caches a `Handle` to the `OrderSession` object. The `javax.ejb.Handle` is a serializable reference to the `EJBObject` acquired by a client. This `Handle`, used to uniquely identify an EJB object (session and entity bean), can be serialized to a persistent store and deserialized at a later time to get a reference to the same EJB object. However, in the case of session beans, if the EJB object is explicitly destroyed by invocation of the `remove()` API, is timed out, or the server crashes, the `Handle` becomes invalid as the server no longer has the bean object in memory. The `EJBHome` object also provides an API to obtain a serializable `Handle` (`javax.ejb.HomeHandle`) to the `EJBHome` object.

Figure 12-2 shows the performance benefit of caching a remote stateless session bean's `Handle`. There is a 10% difference between the throughput of the cached test case compared to the throughput of the noncached test case. This difference increases if more resources are looked up in each business method invocation.

Use Local Interfaces instead of Remote Interfaces

The EJB specification provides both remote and local interfaces to session and entity beans. All parameters to remote interfaces are pass-by-value, which involves argument copying, serialization, and deserialization, as well as the additional overhead of communicating to a server over the network. In contrast, parameters to local interfaces are pass-by-reference since method invocations are contained within the same JVM, and thus it is much faster. It is recommended to use local interfaces when making enterprise bean method invocations whenever possible.

In a Web application, the reference to a local interface is defined in the web.xml as in the following example.

```xml
<ejb-local-ref>
    <description>EJB Session</description>
    <ejb-ref-name>ejb/Session</ejb-ref-name>
    <ejb-ref-type>Session</ejb-ref-type>
    <local-home>
        com.orangerepublic.ejb.session.SessionLocalHome
    </local-home>
    <local>
        com.orangerepublic.ejb.session.SessionLocal
    </local>
    <ejb-link>SessionBean</ejb-link>
</ejb-local-ref>
```

The EJB module exposes the session bean's local interfaces with the following declaration in the ejb-jar.xml.

```xml
<enterprise-beans>
 <session>
    <ejb-name>SessionBean</ejb-name>
    <local-home>
        com.orangerepublic.ejb.session.SessionLocalHome
    </local-home>
    <local>
        com.orangerepublic.ejb.session.SessionLocal
    </local>
    <ejb-class>
        com.orangerepublic.ejb.session.SessionBeanImpl
    </ejb-class>
    <session-type>Stateless</session-type>
...
 </session>
</enterprise-beans>
```

The GlassFish application server provides an extension that allows parameters to a method call to be passed by reference, even if a client is invoking the remote interfaces on the enterprise beans, if the beans are co-located on the same JVM. This provides the same performance benefit as a local invocation. There are a couple of limitations to using this performance optimization. It should be used only if the called method does not modify the objects being passed as parameters, and this approach is not portable across application servers. Specifying pass-by-reference when invoking local interfaces on enterprise beans has no effect.

The pass-by-reference configuration is done for individual enterprise beans in the sun-ejb-jar.xml. For example, the `ServletDriver` invokes the remote method of `OrderSessionBean` enterprise bean co-located on the same JVM, and if we still wanted to pass parameters by-reference instead of by-value, we would use the following entry in the sun-ejb-jar.xml:

```
<ejb>
    <ejb-name>Session</ejb-name>
    <jndi-name>ejb/Session</jndi-name>
    <pass-by-reference>true</pass-by-reference>
    ....
</ejb>
```

This significantly improves the performance by avoiding the copying of parameter and return objects. In the test results shown in Figure 12-3, a session bean is used to look up and return an `Order` entity. In the Local scenario, a local session bean is used, and all parameters and the return value are pass-by-reference. In the Remote scenario, a remote session bean is used, and all parameters and return values are pass-by value. The `Order` entity has an average of 50 line items, and instances of all `OrderLine` objects that are referenced by the `Order` entity are also copied when using Remote interfaces. The test returned Data Access Objects instead of the `Order` or `OrderLine` entity instances to return the state of the corresponding `Order` and `OrderLine` entities; the reason for which is explained in the next section.

In the case shown in Figure 12-3 there was a 11% difference between the Local and Remote interface scenarios. The performance difference increases as the complexity and/or the number of parameters are increased.

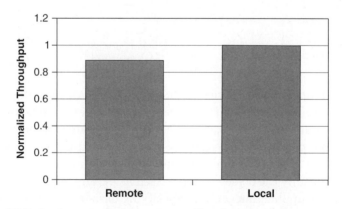

Figure 12-3 Performance comparison of local versus remote invocation

Coarse-Grained Access

The performance cost of making remote calls can be reduced by using a coarse grained access model when accessing session beans, which is more commonly known as the Session Façade design pattern. In the Session Façade design pattern, the server encapsulates multiple smaller tasks into one business operation. The client, instead of making multiple remote invocations makes one invocation to complete the business operation. The following code demonstrates the use of a coarse-grained access model.

```java
public interface CheckoutSessionLocal extends javax.ejb.EJBLocalObject {
    public void placeOrder(String cartID);
}

/**
 * Session Facade that encapsulates multiple smaller tasks
 * associated with placing an order
 */
public class CheckoutSession implements javax.ejb.SessionBean {
    public OrderDAO placeOrder(String cartID){
        ShoppingCart cart = getShoppingCart(cartID);
        //create the order from cart's content
        Order order = createOrder(cartID);
        //debit amount from bank
        charge(order.getTotal(), cart.getChargeDetails());

        //send order to warehouse & update inventory
        String whsID = scheduleWarehouseMessage(order);

        //arrange shippping
        ship(whsID);

        //update records in order history
        updateOrderHistory(order, cart.getPerson());

        //send confirmation email
        sendEmailConfirmation(order);

        //create data access object
        OrderDAO odao = createOrderDAO(order);

        //remove cart
        ...
        return odao;
    }
}
```

In the preceding example the `CheckoutSession` class implements a Session Façade design pattern. The `placeOrder()` business method encapsulates multiple operations so that the client can avoid making multiple method invocations to place an order. In this case it also simplifies the transaction management, since we would want to debit the bank account only if the order is successfully sent to the warehouse.

Another place where a coarse-grained access model can be applied is the access of entity bean fields. If an entity bean state is directly accessed from a client, each access to the entity's attribute would result in a remote invocation and the client would encounter unnecessary network latency as well as serialization and deserialization costs. The better approach to accessing the entity bean state is to access it through a Session Façade model, which returns the entity state in a Data Access Object (DAO). Since the DAO is not an enterprise bean, all access to its state is local. In the preceding example the `placeOrder()` API returns an `OrderDAO` object instance, which is a copy of the state of the `Order` entity bean.

Use Lazy Loading or Prefetching

Container-managed persistence (CMP) allows enterprise developers to define relationships between entity beans. Lazy loading is a strategy used by many persistence implementations to load a related entity only when it has been explicitly accessed. This approach allows the underlying persistence implementation to quickly create an entity bean instance that was requested by the application without having to create all the entity beans it is related to. Lazy loading in EJB 2.1 is specified through vendor-specific descriptors.

Prefetching, on the other hand, allows related entities to be fetched along with the parent entity. In GlassFish, prefetching or eager fetching can be enabled by specifying the Fetch Group of entities in the sun-cmp-mappings.xml deployment descriptor. Following is an example that specifies the fetch group in the sun-cmp-mappings.xml file.

```xml
<?xml version="1.0" encoding="UTF-8"?>
<sun-cmp-mappings>
  <sun-cmp-mapping>
    <schema>EJB21</schema>
    <entity-mapping>
      <ejb-name>Order</ejb-name>
      <table-name>ORORDER</table-name>
      ...
      <cmr-field-mapping>
        <cmr-field-name>lines</cmr-field-name>
        <column-pair>
          <column-name>ORORDER.ID</column-name>
          <column-name>ORDERLINE.ORDER_ID</column-name>
        </column-pair>
        <fetched-with>
          <default/>
        </fetched-with>
      </cmr-field-mapping>
      ...
  </sun-cmp-mapping>
</sun-cmp-mappings>
```

The preceding excerpt from sun-cmp-mappings.xml defines the mapping of the `Order` entity to the `ORORDER` database table and also the relationship between the `Order` entity and the `OrderLine` entity. The `<fetched-with>` subelement `<none/>` specifies that the `lines` field should be fetched lazily. The persistence implementation is allowed to create an instance of the `Order` entity bean with only a shell object for the related `OrderLine` instances, which will be populated only if an explicit access is made to those instances. This enables an implementation to create an entity bean instance without having to do multiple joins across tables for creating related entity beans that may not be accessed.

On the other hand, if the related entity beans are likely to be accessed when the entity bean is loaded, it should have the `<default/>` fetch group; otherwise, the implementation needs to make multiple JDBC (Java Database Connectivity) calls. In the preceding example, the `Order` entity bean has a one-to-many relationship with `OrderLine` entity bean, and since we expect the order's line items to be accessed when the `Order` entity is loaded, we specify a `default` fetch group, which results in the underlying CMP implementation to load the `Order` and `OrderLine` entity beans in a single SQL using a SQL Join.

Figure 12-4 shows the performance comparison of lazy versus eager fetching. In the lazy scenario, the Order-OrderLine relationship has a fetched-with subelement of `<none/>` so that the `OrderLines` are not fetched when the `Order` is looked up. In the eager scenario, the Order-OrderLine relationship has a fetched-with subelement of `<default/>` so that the `OrderLines` are fetched when the `Order` is looked up. The throughput of the eager scenario is 38% of the lazy scenario. So in the case when `OrderLine` entities are not accessed immediately after an `Order` entity is looked up, using the lazy fetch type provides a significant performance advantage.

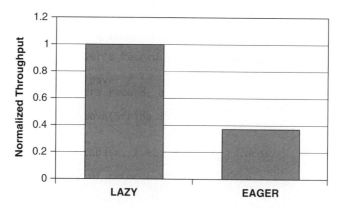

Figure 12-4 Performance comparison of eager versus lazy fetching

Tip

Use lazy loading of relationships if the related entity beans are not accessed when the parent entity is accessed. Conversely, use eager fetching if the related entity beans are accessed when the parent entity is accessed.

Choose Correct Database Locking Strategy

To ensure data integrity, you can choose from one of two commonly used strategies: optimistic locking or pessimistic locking. In pessimistic locking, the corresponding database row is locked, blocking other transactions from accessing the row until the transaction completes. Pessimistic locking assumes that modification data is likely and prevents concurrent access.

Optimistic locking, on the other hand, assumes that concurrent data modification is not likely and handles the case of data modification with an optimistic lock exception and a transaction rollback.

If your application has a large user load, then contrary to common belief, you may not benefit from optimistic locking if the accessed data is updated frequently. In such cases, optimistic locking may result in a large number of transaction rollbacks, which are expensive operations. In this situation, pessimistic locking may provide better performance than optimistic locking.

The locking strategy is specified in the vendor-specific deployment descriptor. Optimistic locking on an entity bean is implemented using version consistency in the GlassFish Application Server's CMP 2.1 implementation. In this approach, a version column is checked to determine whether an entity bean's state is stale, before it is flushed to the database.

To specify optimistic locking on an entity bean

1. Create a version column with numeric data type in the primary table representing the entity bean in the database.

2. Create triggers on the version column so that each time the database row is updated, the row's version column is incremented.

3. In the sun-cmp-mappings.xml file specify the following under the <consistency> element.

```
<entity-mapping>
    <ejb-name>Order</ejb-name>
    ....
    <consistency>
        <check-version-of-accessed-instances>
            <column-name>ORORDER.version</column-name>
        </check-version-of-accessed-instances>
    </consistency>
</entity-mapping>
```

Pessimistic locking in CMP 2.1 requires database support of row locking. Pessimistic locking can be specified in the following manner in the sun-cmp-mappings.xml.

```
<entity-mapping>
    <ejb-name>Order</ejb-name>
    ....
    <consistency>
        <lock-when-loaded/>
    </consistency>
</entity-mapping>
```

Tip

Use optimistic locking if data is not likely to be modified frequently by concurrent transactions. Use pessimistic locking if data is likely to be modified by concurrent transactions frequently.

EJB Query Language

EJB Query Language (QL) queries enable defining custom queries. In some situations EJB QL select queries are preferable over the use of findByPrimaryKey. Consider the following example, which given an `orderID` returns a collection (`ArrayList<OrderLines>`) of line items from an order that may have been marked as discounted.

```
public ArrayList<OrderLine> getDiscountedLines(String orderID);
```

The following code snippet shows an implementation using findByPrimaryKey:

```
public ArrayList<OrderLines> getDiscountedLines(String orderID){
    ArrayList<OrderLine> dLines = new ArrayList();
    try {
        InitialContext ic = new InitialContext();
        OrderHome oh =
            (OrderHome)ic.lookup("java:comp/env/ejb/local/Order");
        Order order = oh.findByPrimaryKey(orderID);
        ArrayList<OrderLine> lines = order.getLines();
        for (int i = 0; i < lines.size(); i++) {
            OrderLine ol = (OrderLine)lines.get(i);
            if(ol.getDiscount() > 0){
                dLines.add(ol);
            }
        }
    } catch (NamingException nex) {
        ....
    } catch (FinderException fex) {
        ...
    }
    return dLines;
}
```

In the preceding implementation, the `getLines()` brings all the order lines into memory, and the appropriate items are selected by applying the filter condition on each item. This in-memory filtering approach is both CPU and memory intensive. It would be more appropriate to delegate the selection process to the database which is optimized for handling such operations. EJB QL allows us to specify SQL to be executed by the database. So our alternate implementation will use the EJB Select query shown in the following listing.

```
public interface OrderLineLocalHome extends javax.ejb.EJBLocalHome {
    ...
    public Collection findByDiscountedLines(String id)
        throws javax.ejb.FinderException;
}
```

The ejb-jar.xml looks like the following:

```
<entity>
   <description/>
   <display-name>OrderLine</display-name>
   <ejb-name>OrderLine</ejb-name>
   ...
   <query>
       <description>Find discounted line items from order</description>
       <query-method>
               <method-name>findByDiscountedLines</method-name>
               <method-params>
                       <method-param>java.lang.String</method-param>
               </method-params>
       </query-method>
       <ejb-ql>
         SELECT OBJECT(1) FROM OrderLine AS 1 WHERE 1.discount > 0 AND
1.orderInfo.id = ?1
       </ejb-ql>
   </query>
   ...
</entity>
public ArrayList<OrderLine> getDiscountedLinesByQuery(String orderID){
    ArrayList<OrderLine> dLines = null;
    try {
        InitialContext ic = new InitialContext();
        OrderLineLocalHome olh = (OrderLineLocalHome) ic.lookup(
                "java:comp/env/ejb/OrderLine");

        Collection<OrderLine> lines = olh.findByDiscountedLines(orderID);

        if(lines==null){
            System.out.println("Lines: " + orderID+" is null!");
        }

        dLines = new ArrayList<OrderLine>(lines);
    }
```

```
        catch (NamingException nex) {
            nex.printStackTrace();
        }
        catch(FinderException fex){
            fex.printStackTrace();
        }
        return dLines;
    }
```

The preceding client code invokes the `findByDiscountedLines` method on the `OrderLine` entity to get a list of discounted line items in one SQL query.

Figure 12-5 compares the performance of using in-memory filtering versus the use of SQL to select the appropriate items. In this example, the throughput when using the findByPrimaryKey scenario is only 22% of using EJB QL.

Tip

The use of appropriate EJB QL queries can provide better performance than filtering items in memory.

Read-Only Entity Beans

For entity beans, every access to an entity's attribute, if in a separate transaction, triggers a database call. If the entity's corresponding row in the database table is not modified often or if the application can tolerate outdated data, this synchronization of the entity bean's instance state with the database is redundant and expensive. Most application servers including GlassFish allow configuring entity beans as read-only entities.

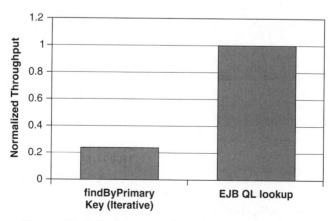

Figure 12-5 Performance benefit of using EJB QL

In CMP such read-only entities are read from the database only once, and every time the entity bean is used the cached data is copied. In Bean-managed persistence (BMP), the entities are read once, and every time an entity is used within a transaction its cached values are used. However, when used outside a transaction, every use of the entity bean triggers a reload of its state from the database. Thus CMP entities and in-transaction BMP entities get the maximum benefit of the read-only configuration. The following example shows configuring a rarely changing entity bean as read-only.

```
<sun-ejb-jar>
    <enterprise-beans>
    ...
    <ejb>
        <ejb-name>BookCatalog</ejb-name>
        <jndi-name>ejb/BookCatalog</jndi-name>
        <is-read-only-bean>true</is-read-only-bean>
        <refresh-period-in-seconds>600</refresh-period-in-seconds>
    </ejb>
    ...
    </enterprise-beans>
</sun-ejb-jar>
```

The `refresh-period-in-seconds` parameter is the number of seconds before the state of the entity instance is reloaded from the database. In the preceding example, the `BookCatalog` bean is marked as a read-only entity bean, and in transactions access to its attributes will not trigger access to the database; also the entity state will be considered stale after 600 seconds and refreshed.

> **Tip**
>
> For entities whose values do not change or where stale data can be tolerated, use read-only entity beans.

EJB 3.0

As noted in the previous section, both EJB 2.1 and EJB 3.0 share several optimization techniques. However, the implementation details vary between the two EJB types, which are covered first. This is followed by EJB 3.0 specific optimization techniques.

Best Practices from EJB 2.1

Though there has been a significant change in the programming models between EJB 2.1 and EJB 3.0, most best practices that apply to the EJB 2.1 also apply to EJB 3.0, but the ways to implement them have changed. These are discussed in this section.

The coarse-grained access best practice that relates to using DAOs is not relevant in EJB 3.0 since entities are essentially Plain Old Java Objects (POJO) and all access to their state on the client side is essentially local method invocations. On the other hand, coarse-grained access through the use of a Session Façade is still relevant for accessing enterprise beans through remote interfaces as it reduces network latency. As in EJB 2.1, wherever possible, it is recommended to make use of local interfaces instead of remote interfaces in EJB 3.0 as well.

> **Tip**
>
> As in the case of EJB 2.1, use local interfaces over remote interfaces whenever possible. If only remote interfaces are available, use pass-by-reference in co-located modules to avoid expensive copying of parameters.

EJB 3.0 allows for resource injection into enterprise beans, thus eliminating the need to do JNDI lookups. When resource injection is used, the container ensures that each time the resource is used a valid reference is available.

> **Tip**
>
> EJB 3.0 containers manage the life cycle of injected resources efficiently, and the developer does not have to explicitly cache resource references.

Persistence related best practices such as lazy loading and database locking strategy are discussed in the "Best Practices in Java Persistence" section later in the chapter.

Business Method Interceptors

Interceptors are enterprise bean developer defined methods that intercept a business method invocation. An interceptor method can be used for a variety of purposes including but not limited to validation and preprocessing of data. An interceptor method can be defined within the enterprise bean class itself or defined in a separate class. There can be only one interceptor method per class.

When defined within the bean class itself, by default the interceptor method is invoked for every method the enterprise bean exposes to its clients. This can be an unnecessary overhead for a frequently invoked enterprise bean method, especially if the interception is not required for every method and the interceptor method has expensive operations.

When defined in an external class, there are three levels at which an interceptor method can be bound to the enterprise bean class.

- **Default.** Default interceptor methods are invoked for all session bean invocations for all session beans in a deployment unit. Default interceptors can be specified through deployment descriptors only.

```
    <assembly-descriptor>
    <!-- Default interceptor-->
    <interceptor-binding>
     <ejb-name>*</ejb-name>
        <interceptor-class>
com.orangerepublic.ejb.session.interceptor.AuthorizationInterceptor
        </interceptor-class>
        <interceptor-class>
com.orangerepublic.ejb.session.interceptor.ValidationInterceptor
        </interceptor-class>
        <interceptor-class>
            com.orangerepublic.ejb.session.interceptor.AuditInterceptor
        </interceptor-class>
        <interceptor-class>
            com.orangerepublic.ejb.session.interceptor.LoggingInterceptor
        </interceptor-class>
    </interceptor-binding>
    .....
</assembly-descriptor>
```

- **Class level.** Class level interceptor methods are invoked for all method invocations on the session bean they are bound to. Class-level interceptors can be specified on the enterprise bean class or in the deployment descriptor.

```
@Stateless
@Interceptors({com.orangerepublic.ejb.session.interceptor.
AuthorizationInterceptor.class})
public class ShoppingCart{
    ...
}

<assembly-descriptor>
<!-- Class interceptor-->
    <interceptor-binding>
        <ejb-name>OrderSessionBean</ejb-name>
        <interceptor-class>

com.orangerepublic.ejb.session.interceptor.AuthorizationInterceptor
        </interceptor-class>
        <interceptor-class>

com.orangerepublic.ejb.session.interceptor.ValidationInterceptor
        </interceptor-class>
        <interceptor-class>
            com.orangerepublic.ejb.session.interceptor.AuditInterceptor
        </interceptor-class>
```

```
    <interceptor-class>
        com.orangerepublic.ejb.session.interceptor.LoggingInterceptor
    </interceptor-class>
  </interceptor-binding>
  ...
</assembly-descriptor>
```

- **Method level.** Method level interceptor methods are specified on the enterprise bean method and invoked when the method on the session bean is invoked.

```
@Interceptors({com.orangerepublic.ejb.session.interceptor.
AuthorizationInterceptor.class})
    public void getItem(){
        ...
    }

<assembly-descriptor>
  <!-- Method interceptor-->
  <interceptor-binding>
    <ejb-name>OrderSessionBean</ejb-name>
    <interceptor-class>
com.orangerepublic.ejb.session.interceptor.AuthorizationInterceptor
    </interceptor-class>
    <interceptor-class>
com.orangerepublic.ejb.session.interceptor.ValidationInterceptor
    </interceptor-class>
    <interceptor-class>
        com.orangerepublic.ejb.session.interceptor.AuditInterceptor
    </interceptor-class>
    <interceptor-class>
        com.orangerepublic.ejb.session.interceptor.LoggingInterceptor
    </interceptor-class>
    <method>
        <method-name>getItem</method-name>
    </method>
  </interceptor-binding>
  ...
</assembly-descriptor>
```

Using a default interceptor in cases where a class level or method level interceptor would suffice adds overhead. This is especially true for expensive interceptor methods. If only lightweight operations are included in the interceptor methods, the overall impact including the cost of Java reflection used to invoke the interceptor can be negligible.

The specification provides mechanisms to exclude a bean from the default interceptors or for some methods to be excluded from the class interceptors for the bean. This can be achieved via annotations or through the use of deployment descriptors.

To exclude the default interceptor, apply the @javax.ejb.ExcludeDefault Interceptors annotation to a bean class or a method. To avoid the invocation of a class interceptor on a bean method, use the @javax.ejb.ExcludeClass Interceptors annotation. The exclusion can also be specified in the deployment descriptor as follows:

```
<assembly-descriptor>
    <!-- Method interceptor-->
    <interceptor-binding>
        <ejb-name>OrderSessionBean</ejb-name>
        <exclude-default-interceptors>true</exclude-default-interceptors>
        <exclude-class-interceptors>true</exclude-class-interceptors>
        <method>
            <method-name>getItem</method-name>
        </method>
    </interceptor-binding>
    ...
</assembly-descriptor>
```

Tip

Use appropriate level of granularity when using interceptors. Inappropriate use of class and default interceptors can degrade application performance.

Best Practices in Java Persistence

This section discusses some of the best practices for the use of the Java Persistence APIs. Most of the best practices described in this section apply independently of the JPA implementation. The examples as well as the implementation discussions are based on the EclipseLink JPA implementation, which conforms to the JPA 1.0 specification. The newer version of the specification, JPA 2.0, is not covered here, and readers are encouraged to check it to see how some of the vendor-specific items discussed here can be done in a standardized way. The discussion also assumes a Java EE container environment, but the same concepts apply to EclipseLink in a Java SE environment.

JPA Query Language Queries

The JPA 1.0 specification defines the following kinds of queries:

- Named queries
- Named native queries

- Dynamic queries
- Native queries

Named queries are static JPA Query Language queries defined as part of an entity's metadata information. Since these queries do not change, most JPA implementations precompile the queries during deployment. These queries support parameter binding. The following example shows a `NamedQuery` used to look up an Order entity based on a Customer's id.

```
@NamedQuery(name="ordersByCustomer",
        query="SELECT o FROM OROrder o WHERE o.customer.id=:id")

Query q = em.createNamedQuery("ordersByCustomer");
q.setParameter("id", nid);
List<Order> o = q.getResultList();
```

Named native queries are static SQL queries defined as part of an entity's metadata information. These queries also support parameter binding, and additionally it is possible to map the result set to an entity. The following example shows a `Named NativeQuery` version of the preceding `NamedQuery` using a `resultClass` to map the returned result set to an Order entity. Alternatively, a `resultSetMapping` string, which contains the mapping between the database fields and the entity attributes, can also be used.

```
@NamedNativeQuery(name="ordersByCustomerNative",
    query="SELECT t1.ID, t1.DESCRIPTION, t1.TOTAL, t1.STATUS,"+
        "t1.CUSTOMER_ID FROM CUSTOMER t0, ORORDER t1 " +
        "WHERE ((t0.ID = t1.CUSTOMER_ID) AND (t0.ID = ?))",
        resultClass=Order.class)

Query q = em.createNamedQuery("ordersByCustomerNative");
q.setParameter(1, nid);
List<Order> o = q.getResultList();
```

Dynamic queries are JPA Language Queries created at runtime. These queries are compiled during runtime. However, some implementations, such as EclipseLink, keep a cached copy of the compiled query if it is parameterized and subsequent invocations of the same query do not result in compilation. The query shown previously is parameterized on the ID of the customer.

However, if a dynamic query is not parameterized, as shown in the following code snippet, the implementation has to compile the JPA QL query on each invocation.

```
Query q = em.createQuery(
        "SELECT o FROM OROrder o WHERE o.customer.id="+id);
List<Order> o = q.getResultList();
```

Since each query string is unique, each execution of the query requires the JPA implementation to recompile the query.

Since native SQL queries may be nonportable, their use should be limited to special cases when the use of JPA QL queries do not suffice. The following example illustrates a native SQL query with a `resultClass` to map the returned result set to the Order entity.

```java
public class Order {
    ...
    public static final String nativeQuery = "SELECT t1.ID, "+
        "t1.DESCRIPTION, t1.TOTAL, t1.STATUS, t1.CUSTOMER_ID"+
        "FROM CUSTOMER t0, ORORDER t1 " +
        "WHERE ((t0.ID = t1.CUSTOMER_ID) AND (t0.ID = ?))";
    ...

    }

    Query q = em.createNativeQuery(Order.nativeQuery,
                    com.orangerepublic.entity.Order.class);
    q.setParameter(1, nid);
    List<Order> o = q.getResultList();
    ...
}
```

Figure 12-6 shows the performance of named, named native, dynamic parameterized, and dynamic nonparameterized queries. There is a distinct advantage in using named queries or parameterized dynamic queries whenever possible, as the JPA provider can skip the compilation stage during runtime and uses the precompiled queries from its cache.

The JPA specification also supports pagination through the `javax.persistence.Query` API. This enables an application to control how much data is retrieved from

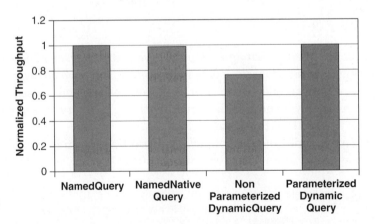

Figure 12-6 Performance comparison of different query types

the database and can significantly improve performance in cases where a large collection is retrieved from the database.

This can be done through the following Query apis:

```
//sets the maximum number of results to retrieve
public Query setMaxResults(int maxResult);

//sets the start position of the first result to retrieve
public Query setFirstResult(int startPosition);
```

Query Results Cache

Most JPA implementations support caching of named query results. If a named query is executed with the same parameters and the query results cache is enabled, the persistence provider returns the results from the query results cache, saving a trip to the database. If the query results cache is not enabled, EclipseLink still executes the query on the database, checks whether the objects in the result set already exist in its object cache, and, if they do, returns the cached object instead of recreating it. In EclipseLink a query results cache can be specified through the object relationship mapping file, orm.xml. Following is an example of configuring a query results cache for the Order entity in the orm.xml file.

```xml
<?xml version="1.0" encoding="UTF-8"?>
<entity-mappings xsi:schemaLocation="http://www.eclipse.org/eclipselink/
xsds/persistence/orm xsd/eclipselink_orm_1_0.xsd" xmlns="http://www.
eclipse.org/eclipselink/xsds/persistence/orm" xmlns:xsi="http://www.
w3.org/2001/XMLSchema-instance" version="1.0">

    <named-query name="findByStatus">
        <query>SELECT o FROM OROrder o WHERE o.status=:status</query>
        <hint name="eclipselink.query-results-cache" value="true"/>
        <hint name="eclipselink.query-results-cache.size" value="200"/>
    </named-query>

    <entity name="OROrder" class="com.orangerepublic.entity.Order"/>
</entity-mappings>
```

The orm.xml in the preceding example configures a query results cache for the query named "findByStatus", which stores the last 200 result sets of distinct parameters; the default is 100 result sets. The query results cache, even though it is a part of the session cache, is different from the EclipseLink object cache mentioned earlier, while the object cache is keyed on the object's primary key, the query results cache is keyed on the query and its parameters. The query results cache is maintained using hard references, so it is not garbage collected when the JVM is running low on memory as is the Soft Cache Weak Identity Map Object Cache.

While caching provides a boost to performance, cached data may become stale. EclipseLink provides for invalidation of cache using the following hints that can be specified as a subelement of the `query` element in the orm.xml:

```
<hint name="eclipselink.query-results-cache.expiry" value="1800000"/>
```

This expires the cache every 30 minutes and forces the query to execute on the database. By default, the results obtained by the query do not update the shared session cache in EclipseLink; to change this behavior consider using the following hint:

```
<hint name="eclipselink.query-results-cache.refreshOnlyIfNewer "
value="true"/>
```

This forces all queries that go to the database to refresh the cache only if the data received from the database by a query is newer than the data in the cache based on the optimistic locking field.

The preceding query hints can also be specified through the `Query` interface's `setHint(String hintName, Object value)` API.

> **Tip**
>
> It is a good performance practice to use named query whenever possible. Use pagination to restrict the number of entities retrieved from the database. Use a query results cache for named queries where applicable.

FetchType

`FetchType` specifies the data-fetching strategy used by a persistence provider to fetch data from the database. `FetchType` is used on the `@Basic` annotation, `@LOB` annotation, and relationship annotations such as `@OneToMany`, `@Many ToMany`, `@ManyToOne`, and `@OneToOne`. The default for `FetchType` is EAGER, except for many-to-many and one-to-many relationships, for which the default is LAZY. A `FetchType` of EAGER means that a persistence provider loads the attributes of an entity, whether basic or an entity relationship, when fetching an entity instance, whereas a `FetchType` of LAZY is a hint to the provider that the attribute need not be fetched along with the entity.

A `FetchType` of EAGER is a requirement on the persistence provider, whereas a `FetchType` of LAZY is only a hint. So even though you may specify the `FetchType` on an entity attribute to be LAZY, the persistence provider may choose to load the attribute eagerly. In EclipseLink, specifying a `FetchType` of LAZY loads the entity attribute lazily in the Java EE environment as bytecode enhancements are done

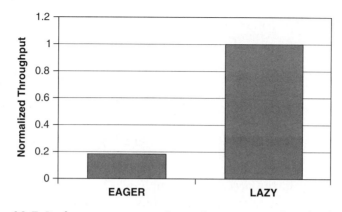

Figure 12-7 Performance comparison of eager versus lazy fetch types

on the deployed JPA entities. However, in the Java SE environment, by default, the FetchType of LAZY is ignored for the following types of annotations: @OneToOne, @ManyToOne, and @Basic.

A FetchType of LAZY benefits entities with one-to-many or many-to-many relationships, where the cardinality of the relationship is high, and the attributes are not accessed immediately after the entity is loaded. Figure 12-7 shows the performance of loading an Order entity with a 1:M relationship with OrderLine entity. The mean cardinality of the relationship is around 50.

The eager fetch relationship between the Order entity and the OrderLine entity is marked as follows:

```
@OneToMany(cascade=CascadeType.ALL, mappedBy="order",
fetch=FetchType.EAGER)
    private Collection<OrderLine> lines;
```

For the lazy fetchType, the relationship between the Order entity and the Order-Line entity is marked as follows:

```
@OneToMany(cascade=CascadeType.ALL, mappedBy="order",
fetch=FetchType.LAZY)
        private Collection<OrderLine> lines;
```

It is unlikely that a single fetchType on an entity relationship fits all use cases in an application. Even though in most cases lazy fetch may be a good option, for some cases, using eager fetch would be better. In such situations, it is best to specify a fetchType of LAZY on the relationship through the annotations or deployment descriptors so that a lazy fetch happens by default for the use cases that need a lazy fetch and to use a JPA join fetch query to do an eager fetch for the use cases that need an eager fetch.

```
@NamedQuery(name="selectByStatus",
       query="SELECT DISTINCT o FROM Order o LEFT JOIN FETCH o.lines
WHERE o.status = :status")
@Entity
@Table(name = "ORORDERS")
public class Order implements Serializable {
    ...
      @OneToMany(cascade=CascadeType.ALL, mappedBy="order")
      private Collection<OrderLine> lines;
      ...
}
```

The named query in the preceding example when executed fetches the related
`OrderLine` objects along with the `Order` object with a specific status. The LEFT
keyword specifies that an order should be fetched even if it doesn't contain any
related `OrderLine` objects

Tip

Select the `fetchType` based on the relationship. Use eager fetch for entities loaded together.
In cases where related entities may not be loaded together, use lazy fetch.

Connection Pooling

A JDBC connection pool allows a database client, EclipseLink in our case, to reuse
connections without having to go through the time-consuming process of creating
new connections to the database. Applications deployed in a Java EE container can
use the JDBC connection pool support provided by the container. For more information on monitoring and tuning JDBC connection pools, refer to the "Monitoring and
Tuning Resource Pools" section in Chapter 9.

In the Java SE environment, EclipseLink connection pooling can be configured
through the use of EclipseLink-specific JPA extensions in the persistence.xml. In
the Java EE environment, EclipseLink can make use of application server-provided
connection pooling through the use of a predefined `DataSource`. Following is an
example of setting up the `DataSource` in the persistence.xml for EclipseLink in a
Java EE environment.

```xml
<?xml version="1.0" encoding="UTF-8"?>
<persistence xmlns="http://java.sun.com/xml/ns/persistence"
xmlns:xsi="http://www.w3.org/2001/XMLSchema-instance" >
    <persistence-unit name="ejb30">
        <provider>org.eclipse.persistence.jpa.PersistenceProvider </provider>
        <jta-data-source>jdbc/ejb30</jta-data-source>
    </persistence-unit>
</persistence>
```

In this example, the `ejb30` persistence unit is configured with an EclipseLink provider and a JTA enabled `DataSource` with a JNDI name `jdbc/ejb30`. The `Data Source` makes use of a JDBC connection pool whose max pool size should be set to the number of request processing threads. In the case of an application that is purely Web-based, this would be the HTTP request processing threads. If the application is accessed through a direct client connection using the ORB such as in the case of a direct client connection to a session bean, and the session bean accesses the database, then the max connection pool size should also include the number of ORB threads.

Setting this value less than the number of request processing threads may force the JPA implementation to block for an available database connection, reducing the overall application throughput. To illustrate the effect of connection pool size, the named query in Figure 12-8 was executed with a connection pool size of 4 and a connection pool size of 12. The GlassFish application server was configured with 12 HTTP request processing threads.

As demonstrated in Figure 12-8, with a connection pool size of 4, the throughput is 76% of the throughput with a connection pool size of 12. This is because in the case of the connection pool of size 4, the request processing threads are waiting to get a connection from the connection pool.

Tip

Set your connection pool size to be at least as high as the number of request processing threads.

Refer to the "Application Server Monitoring" section of Chapter 9 for more details on how to monitor the JDBC connection pools in GlassFish.

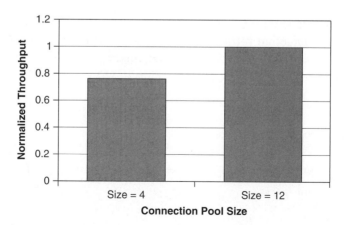

Figure 12-8 Performance impact of setting the connections pool size incorrectly

The JDBC driver used to access the database is typically provided by the database vendor. It is often the case that each driver has its own set of tuning parameters that provide the best performance. For example, when using the Oracle JDBC driver, it is important to enable statement caching as follows:

```
ImplicitCachingEnabled=true
MaxStatements=200
```

Tip

Apply appropriate JDBC driver specific tunings for best performance.

Bulk Updates

JPA QL allows bulk updates and deletes on entities of a single entity class and its subclasses. In a bulk update or delete only one abstract schema type can be specified. Executing a bulk update using a JPA QL query can reduce the number of SQL statements executed on the database. Consider the following example that cancels all orders belonging to a customer.

```
} public cancelOrder(String customerID){
    Query q = em.createQuery("ordersByCustomer");
    q.setParameter("customerID", customerID);
    Collection<Order> orders = q.getResultList();

    for(Order o:orders){
        o.setStatus(Order.OrderStatus.CANCELLED);
        em.merge(o);
    }
}
```

The preceding implementation would result in as many SQL statements as there are orders in the Collection returned by the query execution. Alternatively, we can write the same implementation with a JPA QL query that updates the status on the orders with a single SQL query.

```
@Entity(name="OROrder")
@NamedQueries(
    @NamedQuery(name="bulkUpdateStatus",
        query="UPDATE order c SET c.status = 'cancelled' WHERE
c.customer.id=:customerID"))
public class Order implements Serializable{
    ...
    public cancelOrder(String customerID){
    Query q = em.createQuery("bulkUpdateStatus");
    q.setParameter("customerID", customerID);
    q.executeUpdate();
}
```

Figure 12-9 shows the performance of iterative versus bulk update for a customer that has on average ten orders associated with it. The throughput of an iterative update is 20% of the throughput achievable through a JPA QL bulk update.

It is important to note that the persistence context is not synchronized with the result of a bulk update or delete, so bulk updates may result in inconsistencies between the database and the persistence context. In general a safe approach to bulk updates and deletes is to do it in a separate transaction or do it at the beginning of a transaction before entities whose state might be affected by such operations are accessed.

Choose Correct Database Locking Strategy

As mentioned in the EJB 2.1 section, optimistic locking is a good strategy for maintaining data consistency in applications without sacrificing performance but may not always give the best performance for applications where the data is modified often due to the cost of transaction rollbacks. In such cases pessimistic locking may provide better performance. In Java Persistence, optimistic locking is implemented using version consistency. Entities using this strategy are required to have a numeric version attribute with a corresponding version column in database table. The following example demonstrates how to configure optimistic locking.

```
public class Order implements Serializable {
    ...
    @Version(column="version")
    private Long version;

    public Long getVersion() {
        return version;
    }
}
```

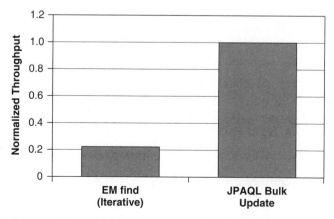

Figure 12-9 Performance benefit of using bulk update

Reads without Transactions

The Java Persistence specification allows for entity manager operations that are read-only to execute without a transaction. Nontransactional reads do not have the overhead of starting and stopping a transaction and should be preferred in cases where entity state is not being modified.

```
@TransactionAttribute(TransactionAttributeType.SUPPORTS)
public Order getOrder(String id) {
    return em.find(Order.class, id));
}
```

In the preceding example, if the client code does not invoke the `getOrder()` method in a transaction, the `em.find()` method looks up the appropriate `Order` instance without a transaction.

Inheritance

The Java Persistence specification allows for an entity to inherit from another entity or a nonentity. There are three strategies in the Java Persistence 1.0 specification for mapping inheritance hierarchy to database tables.

- **SINGLE_TABLE.** Uses one table for all classes and distinguishes between instance types by using a discriminator column.
- **JOINED.** Uses one table for the root class, and each subclass is represented by a table that contains attributes specific to the subclass.
- **TABLE_PER_CLASS.** Uses one table per concrete class; this is an optional strategy and is not required to be implemented by persistence providers.

The JOINED table strategy requires the use of SQL join operations on potentially one or more tables and would seem to be poor in performance. However, the JOINED inheritance strategy is not necessarily a bad choice with respect to performance. Typically a SQL join will perform worse compared to a single table lookup when the SQL join statement results in a table or index scan. As the cardinality of the join increases, the performance correspondingly decreases. However, in the case of inheritance using the JOINED strategy the cardinality of the relationship is always one, and looking up single records using the primary key across tables through indexes, which most databases automatically provide for records using their primary key, makes no perceptible difference in performance.

Bibliography

Enterprise JavaBean 3.0 Specification. http://jcp.org/aboutJava/communityprocess/final/jsr220/index.html.

Enterprise JavaBeans 2.1 Specification. http://jcp.org/en/jsr/detail?id=153.

Biswas, Rahul, and Ed Ort. "The Java Persistence API—A Simpler Programming Model for Entity Persistence." http://www.oracle.com/technetwork/articles/javaee/jpa-137156.html.

Java Persistence 2.0. http://jcp.org/aboutJava/communityprocess/final/jsr317/index.html.

EclipseLink. http://www.eclipse.org/eclipselink/.

"Oracle Database Concepts: Data Concurrency and Consistency." http://download.oracle.com/docs/cd/B28359_01/server.111/b28318/consist.htm.

Sucharitakul, Akara. "Seven Rules for Optimizing Entity Beans." http://java.sun.com/developer/technicalArticles/ebeans/sevenrules/.

Oaks, Scott, Eileen Loh, and Rahul Biswas. "Writing Performant EJB Beans in the Java EE 5 Platform (EJB 3.0) Using Annotations." http://java.sun.com/developer/technicalArticles/ebeans/ejb_30/.

Appendix A

HotSpot VM Command Line Options of Interest

This appendix contains a listing of Java HotSpot VM (also referred to as HotSpot here-after) command line options of performance interest and any mentioned within this book, along with a description of each option and when it is most applicable to use it.

Command line options that toggle on or off a feature or attribute of the HotSpot VM have the form `-XX:<+|->FeatureName` where + indicates enable the feature and − indicates disable the feature.

Command line options that require a numerical value have the form `-XX:FeatureName=<n>` where n is some numerical value. All command line options that require a numerical value that controls the size of some attribute in kilobytes, megabytes, or gigabytes accept the following suffixes: g, m, k. Other command line options require a numerical value to express a ratio or a percentage.

-client

Specifies that the HotSpot VM should optimize for client applications. At the present time, this option results in the use of the client JVM as the runtime environment. This command line option should be used when application startup time and small memory footprint are the most important performance criteria for the application, much more important than high throughput.

-server

Specifies that the HotSpot VM should optimize for server applications. At the present time, this option results in the use of the server JVM as the runtime environment. This command line option should be used when high application throughput is more important than startup time and small memory footprint.

-d64

Loads the 64-bit HotSpot VM instead of the default HotSpot 32-bit VM.

This command line option should be used when there is a need to use a larger Java heap size than is possible with a 32-bit HotSpot VM. `-XX:+UseCompressedOops` should also be used in conjunction with this command line option for `-Xmx` and `-Xms` values less than 32 gigabytes. HotSpot versions later than Java 6 Update 18 enable `-XX:+UseCompressedOops` by default.

Also see `-XX:+UseCompressedOops`.

-XX:+UseCompressedOops

Enables a feature called compressed oops. *Oops* stands for *ordinary object pointer,* which is the means by which the HotSpot VM represents a reference to a Java object internally.

64-bit JVMs come with a performance penalty due to an increase in the size of Java references from 32 bits to 64 bits. This increase in width results in fewer ordinary object pointers being available on a CPU cache line, and as a result decreases CPU cache efficiency. The decrease in CPU cache efficiency on 64-bit JVMs often results in about an 8% to 20% performance degradation compared to a 32-bit JVM.

`-XX:+UseCompressedOops` can yield 32-bit JVM performance with the benefit of larger 64-bit JVM heaps. Some Java applications realize better performance with a 64-bit HotSpot VM using compressed oops than with a 32-bit HotSpot VM. The performance improvement realized from compressed oops arises from being able to transform a 64-bit pointer into a 32-bit offset from a Java heap base address.

Useful when you want a Java heap larger than what can be specified for a 32-bit HotSpot VM but are not willing to sacrifice 32-bit VM performance. It should be used when specifying a Java heap up to 32 gigabytes (`-Xmx32g`), though best performance is realized up to about 26 gigabytes (`-Xmx26g`).

Also see `-d64`.

-Xms<n>[g|m|k]

The initial and minimum size of the Java heap, which includes the total size of the young generation space and old generation space. `<n>` is the size. `[g|m|k]` indicates whether the size should be interpreted as gigabytes, megabytes, or kilobytes. The Java heap will never be smaller than the value specified for `-Xms`.

When `-Xms` is smaller than `-Xmx`, the size of Java heap may grow or contract depending on the needs of the application. However, growing or contracting the Java heap requires a full garbage collection. Applications with a focus on latency or throughput performance tend to set `-Xms` and `-Xmx` to the same value.

-Xmx<n>[g|m|k]

The maximum size of the Java heap, which includes the total size of the young generation space and old generation space. `<n>` is the size. `[g|m|k]` indicates whether the size should be interpreted as gigabytes, megabytes, or kilobytes. The Java heap will never grow to more than the value specified for `-Xmx`.

When -Xmx is larger than -Xms, the size of Java heap may grow or contract depending on the needs of the application. However, growing or contracting the Java heap requires a full garbage collection. Applications with a focus on latency or throughput performance tend to set -Xms and -Xmx to the same value.

-XX:NewSize=<n>[g|m|k]

The initial and minimum size of the young generation space. <n> is the size. [g|m|k] indicates whether the size should be interpreted as gigabytes, megabytes, or kilobytes. The young generation space will never be smaller than the value specified.

When -XX:NewSize is smaller than -XX:MaxNewSize, the size of the young generation space may grow or contract depending on the needs of the application. However, growing or contracting the young generation space requires a full garbage collection. Applications with a focus on latency or throughput performance tend to set -XX:NewSize and -XX:MaxNewSize to the same value.

-XX:MaxNewSize=<n>[g|m|k]

The maximum size of the young generation space. <n> is the size. [g|m|k] indicates whether the size should be interpreted as gigabytes, megabytes, or kilobytes. The young generation space will never be larger than the value specified.

When -XX:MaxNewSize is larger than -XX:NewSize, the size of the young generation space may grow or contract depending on the needs of the application. However, growing or contracting the young generation space requires a full garbage collection. Applications with a focus on latency or throughput performance tend to set -XX:MaxNewSize and -XX:NewSize to the same value.

-Xmn<n>[g|m|k]

Sets the initial, minimum, and maximum size of the young generation space. <n> is the size. [g|m|k] indicates whether the size should be interpreted as gigabytes, megabytes, or kilobytes. The young generation space size will be set to the value specified.

A convenient shortcut command line option to use when it is desirable to set -XX:NewSize and -XX:MaxNewSize to the same value.

-XX:NewRatio=<n>

The ratio between the young generation space size and old generation space size. For example, if n is 3, then the ratio is 1:3, and the young generation space size is one-fourth of the total size of young generation space and old generation space. The ratio of the sizes of both young generation space and old generation space are maintained if the Java heap grows or contracts.

A convenient command line option when -Xms and -Xmx are different sizes and there is a desire to maintain the same ratio of space between young generation space and old generation space.

-XX:PermSize=<n>[g|m|k]

The initial and minimum size of the permanent generation space. <n> is the size. [g|m|k] indicates whether the size should be interpreted as gigabytes, megabytes, or kilobytes. The permanent generation space will never be smaller than the value specified.

When -XX:PermSize is smaller than -XX:MaxPermSize, the size of the permanent generation space may grow or contract depending on the needs of the application, in particular the need to load classes or store interned Strings. However, growing or contracting the permanent generation space requires a full garbage collection. Applications with a focus on latency or throughput performance tend to set -XX:PermSize and -XX:MaxPermSize to the same value.

-XX:MaxPermSize=<n>[g|m|k]

The maximum size of the permanent generation space. <n> is the size. [g|m|k] indicates whether the size should be interpreted as gigabytes, megabytes, or kilobytes. The permanent generation space will never be larger than the value specified.

When -XX:MaxPermSize is larger than -XX:PermSize, the size of the permanent generation space may grow or contract depending on the needs of the application, in particular the need to load classes or store interned Strings. However, growing or contracting the permanent generation space requires a full garbage collection. Applications with a focus on latency or throughput performance tend to set -XX:PermSize and -XX:MaxPermSize to the same value.

-XX:SurvivorRatio=<n>

The ratio of the size of each survivor space to the eden space size, where <n> is the ratio. The following equation can be used to determine the survivor space size for a ratio specified with -XX:SurvivorRatio=<n>:

survivor size = -Xmn<n>/(-XX:SurvivorRatio=<n> + 2) where -Xmn<n> is the size of the young generation space and -XX:SurvivorRatio=<n> is the value specified as the ratio. The reason for the + 2 in the equation is there are two survivor spaces. The larger the value specified as the ratio, the smaller the survivor space size.

-XX:SurvivorRatio=<n> should be used when you want to explicitly size survivor spaces to manipulate object aging with the concurrent garbage collector, or to manipulate object aging with the throughput garbage collector when adaptive sizing is disabled using the command line option -XX:-UseAdaptiveSizePolicy.

-XX:SurvivorRatio=<n> should not be used with the throughput collector with adaptive sizing enabled. By default adaptive sizing is enabled with the throughput garbage collector by -XX:+UseParallelGC or -XX:+UseParallelOldGC. If an initial survivor ratio is desired for the throughput garbage collector's adaptive sizing to begin with, then -XX:InitialSurvivorRatio=<n> should be used.

-XX:InitialSurvivorRatio=<n>

The initial survivor space ratio to use with the throughput garbage collector, where <n> is the ratio. It is only the initial survivor space ratio. This command line option is intended to be used with the throughput garbage collector with adaptive sizing enabled. Adaptive sizing resizes survivor spaces as the application behavior warrants.

The following equation can be used to determine the initial survivor space size for a ratio specified with -XX:InitialSurvivorRatio=<n>:

initial survivor size = -Xmn<n>/(-XX:InitialSurvivorRatio=<n> + 2) where -Xmn<n> is the size of the young generation space and -XX:Initial SurvivorRatio=<n> is the value specified as the ratio. The reason for the + 2 in the equation is there are two survivor spaces. The larger the value specified as the initial ratio, the smaller the initial survivor space size.

-XX:InitialSurvivorRatio=<n> should be used with the throughput collector with adaptive sizing enabled when there is a desire to specifically initially size survivor spaces. By default, adaptive sizing is enabled with the throughput garbage collector using -XX:+UseParallelGC or -XX:+UseParallelOldGC.

If adaptive sizing is disabled, or the concurrent collector is in use, the -XX:SurvivorRatio=<n> command line option should be used when you want to explicitly size survivor spaces to manipulate object aging for the entire execution of the application.

-XX:TargetSurvivorRatio=<percent>

The survivor space occupancy the HotSpot VM should attempt to target after a minor garbage collection. The value to specify is a percentage of the size of a survivor space, rather than a ratio. Its default value is 50%.

Tuning the target survivor occupancy is rarely required. Through extensive testing of a vast variety of different types of application workloads by the HotSpot VM engineering team, a 50% target survivor space occupancy tends to work best for most applications since it helps deal with spikes in surviving objects seen at minor garbage collections in many disparate types of Java applications.

If the application being fine-tuned has a relatively consistent object allocation rate, it is acceptable to raise the target survivor occupancy to something as high as -XX:TargetSurvivorRatio=80 or -XX:TargetSurvivorRatio=90. The advantage of being able to do so helps reduce the amount of survivor space needed to age objects. The challenge with setting -XX:TargetSurvivorRatio=<percent> higher is the HotSpot VM not being able to better adapt object aging in the presence of spikes in object allocation rates, which can lead to tenuring objects sooner than you would like. Tenuring objects too soon can contribute to increasing old generation space occupancy, which may lead to a higher probability of fragmentation since some of those promoted objects may not be long-lived objects and must be garbage collected in a future concurrent garbage collection cycle. Fragmentation is a situation to avoid since it contributes to the eventual likelihood of a full garbage collection.

-XX:+UseSerialGC

Enables the single threaded, stop-the-world, young generation, and old generation garbage collector. It is the oldest and most mature of the HotSpot VM garbage collectors.

Generally, -XX:+UseSerialGC should be used only for small Java heap sizes such as -Xmx256m or smaller. The throughput garbage collector or concurrent garbage collector should be used in favor of -XX:+UseSerialGC with larger heap sizes.

-XX:+UseParallelGC

Enables the HotSpot VM's multithreaded, stop-the-world throughput garbage collector. Only the young generation space utilizes a multithreaded garbage collector. The old generation space uses a single-threaded stop-the-world garbage collector.

If -XX:+UseParallelOldGC is supported by the version of the HotSpot VM in use, -XX:+UseParallelOldGC should be used in favor of -XX:+UseParallelGC.

Also see -XX:ParallelGCThreads.

-XX:+UseParallelOldGC

Enables the HotSpot VM's multithreaded, stop-the-world throughput garbage collector. Unlike -XX:+UseParallelGC, both a multithreaded young generation garbage collector and a multithreaded old generation garbage collector are used.

-XX:+UseParallelOldGC auto-enables -XX:+UseParallelGC.

If -XX:+UseParallelOldGC is not available in the HotSpot VM version in use, either migrate to a more recent version of the HotSpot VM or use -XX:+UseParallelGC.

Also see -XX:ParallelGCThreads.

-XX:-UseAdaptiveSizePolicy

Disables, (note the '–' after the –XX: and before UseAdaptiveSizePolicy), a feature called adaptive sizing of the young generation's eden and survivor spaces. Only the throughput garbage collector supports adaptive sizing. Enabling or disabling adaptive sizing with either the concurrent garbage collector or the serial garbage collector has no effect.

Specifying the throughout garbage collector via -XX:+UseParallelGC and -XX:+UseParallelOldGC auto-enables adaptive sizing.

Adaptive sizing should be disabled only in situations where there is a desire to achieve higher performance throughput than can be offered with adaptive sizing enabled.

Also see -XX:+PrintAdaptiveSizePolicy.

-XX:+UseConcMarkSweepGC

Enables the HotSpot VM's mostly concurrent garbage collector. It also auto-enables `-XX:+UseParNewGC` a multithreaded young generation garbage collector to use with the old generation concurrent garbage collector called CMS.

The concurrent garbage collector should be used when application latency requirements cannot be met by the throughput garbage collector. Fine-tuning of young generation size, survivor space size, and the initiating of the CMS garbage collection cycle are usually required when using the concurrent garbage collector.

-XX:+UseParNewGC

Enables a multithreaded, stop-the-world, young generation garbage collector that should be used with the mostly concurrent old generation garbage collector CMS.

`-XX:+UseParNewGC` is auto-enabled when `-XX:+UseConcMarkSweepGC` is specified.

Also see `-XX:ParallelGCThreads`.

-XX:ParallelGCThreads=\<n>

Controls the number for parallel garbage collection threads to run when the multithreaded garbage collectors \<n> is the number of threads to run.

\<n> defaults to the number returned by the Java API `Runtime.available Processors()` if the number returned is less than or equal to 8; otherwise, it defaults to 5/8 the number returned by `Runtime.availableProcessors()`.

In cases where multiple applications are running on the same system, it is advisable to explicitly set the number of parallel garbage collection threads with `-XX:ParallelGCThreads` to a number lower than the default chosen by the HotSpot VM. The total number of garbage collection threads running on a system should not exceed the value returned by `Runtime.availableProcessors()`.

-XX:MaxTenuringThreshold=\<n>

Sets the maximum tenuring threshold to \<n>.

Used by the HotSpot VM as the maximum object age threshold at which it should promote objects from the young generation space to the old generation space.

The `-XX:MaxTenuringThreshold` should be used when using the concurrent collector and fine-tuning the survivor spaces for effective object aging.

Also see `-XX:+PrintTenuringDistribution`.

-XX:CMSInitiatingOccupancyFraction=\<percent>

The percent of old generation space occupancy at which the first CMS garbage collection cycle should start. Subsequent starts of the CMS cycle are determined at a HotSpot ergonomically computed occupancy.

If `-XX:+UseCMSInitiatingOccupancyOnly` is also specified, it is the percent of old generation space occupancy at which all CMS garbage collection cycles should start.

Generally, it is advisable to use both -XX:CMSInitiatingOccupancyFraction=
<percent> and -XX:+UseCMSInitiatingOccupancyOnly.

-XX:+UseCMSInitiatingOccupancyOnly
Indicates all concurrent garbage collection CMS cycles should start based on the
value of the -XX:CMSInitiatingOccupancyFraction.

Generally, it is advisable to use both -XX:CMSInitiatingOccupancyFraction=
<percent> and -XX:+UseCMSInitiatingOccupancyOnly.

Also see -XX:CMSInitiatingPermOccupancyFraction and -XX:CMSInitiat
ingOccupancyFraction=<percent>.

-XX:CMSInitiatingPermOccupancyFraction=<percent>
The percent of permanent generation space occupancy at which the first CMS garbage collection cycle should start. Subsequent starts of the CMS cycle are determined
at a HotSpot ergonomically computed occupancy.

If -XX:+UseCMSInitiatingOccupancyOnly is also specified, it is the percent of
permanent generation space occupancy at which all CMS garbage collection cycles
should start.

Generally, it is advisable to use both -XX:CMSInitiatingPermOccupancy
Fraction=<percent> and -XX:+UseCMSInitiatingOccupancyOnly.

Also see -XX:+UseCMSInitiatingOccupancyOnly.

-XX:+CMSClassUnloadingEnabled
Enables concurrent garbage collection of permanent generation.

Use -XX:+CMSClassUnloadingEnabled when it is desirable for garbage collection of permanent generation to use CMS.

Use of the Java 6 Update 3 or earlier also requires the use of -XX:+CMSPermGen
SweepingEnabled.

-XX:+CMSPermGenSweepingEnabled
Enables permanent generation CMS garbage collection sweeping.

Only applicable for Java 6 Update 3 or earlier JDKs and when
-XX:+CMSClassLoadingEnabled is used.

-XX:+CMSScavengeBeforeRemark
Instructs the HotSpot VM to perform a minor garbage collection prior to executing
a CMS remark.

A minor garbage collection just prior to a CMS remark can minimize the amount of
work for the remark phase by reducing the number of objects that may be reachable
from the old generation space into the young generation space.

Useful when wanting to reduce the duration of time it takes to complete a CMS
cycle, especially a CMS remark.

Also see -XX:+UseConcMarkSweepGC.

-XX:+ScavengeBeforeFullGC

Instructs the HotSpot VM to garbage collect the young generation space before executing a full garbage collection.

This is the default behavior for the HotSpot VM.

It is generally not advisable to disable this option via -XX:-ScavengeBeforeFullGC since garbage collecting the young generation space before a full garbage collection can reduce the number of objects that may be reachable from the old generation space into the young generation space.

-XX:+ParallelRefProcEnabled

Enables multithreaded reference processing.

This option can shorten the amount of time it takes the HotSpot VM to process Reference objects and finalizers.

-XX:+ExplicitGCInvokesConcurrent

Requests the HotSpot VM to execute any explicit GCs, i.e., System.gc() calls, to invoke a CMS cycle rather than a stop-the-world GC.

Useful when it is desirable to avoid an explicit stop-the-world full garbage collection.

It is generally advisable to use -XX:+ExplicitGCInvokesConcurrentAndUn loadsClasses in favor of -XX:+ExplicitGCInvokesConcurrent.

Also see -XX:+ExplicitGCInvokesConcurrentAndUnloadsClasses.

-XX:+ExplicitGCInvokesConcurrentAndUnloadsClasses

Same as -XX:+ExplicitGCInvokesConcurrent with the addition of unloading of classes from the permanent generation space.

It is generally advisable to use the -XX:+ExplicitGCInvokesConcurrentAnd UnloadsClasses command line option over -XX:+ExplicitGCInvokesConcur rent.

-XX:+DisableExplicitGC

Disables full garbage collections invoked as a result of an explicit call to System. gc().

Useful in applications that explicitly call System.gc() without a known or justified reason to explicitly request a full garbage collection.

Also see -XX:+ExplicitGCInvokesConcurrentAndUnloadsClasses and -XX:+ExplicitGCInvokesConcurrent.

-XX:+CMSIncrementalMode

Enables the incremental CMS concurrent garbage collector in which the concurrent phases of CMS are done incrementally, periodically stopping the concurrent phase to yield back the processor to application threads.

Generally not recommended for multicore systems or large Java heaps.

-XX:+CMSIncrementalPacing

Enables automatic control of the amount of work the incremental CMS collector is allowed to do before giving up the processor, based on application behavior.

Use only with -XX:+CMSIncrementalMode.

-verbose:gc

Enables reporting of basic garbage collection information at each garbage collection.

Recommend using -XX:+PrintGCDetails over -verbose:gc.

-XX:+PrintGC

Enables reporting of basic garbage collection information at each garbage collection. Reports the same information as -verbose:gc.

Recommend using -XX:+PrintGCDetails over -XX:+PrintGC.

-Xloggc:<filename>

Enables reporting of garbage collection statistics to a file with the supplied name for <filename>.

A recommended practice is to capture to a log file with a minimum of the output of -XX:+PrintGCTimeStamps or -XX:+PrintGCDateStamps and -XX:+PrintGCDetails.

-XX:+PrintGCDetails

Enables detailed reporting of garbage collection statistics from young generation, old generation, and permanent generation space.

Recommended to use -XX:+PrintGCDetails over -verbose:gc and use -Xloggc:<filename> to capture the data in a log file.

-XX:+PrintGCTimeStamps

Enables the printing of a time stamp at each garbage collection indicating the amount of elapsed time since the JVM launched.

Recommended to use -XX:+PrintGCTimeStamps or -XX:+PrintGCDateStamps with -XX:+PrintGCDetails to provide a context of time when a garbage collection occurred.

-XX:+PrintGCDateStamps

Enables the printing of a localized date and time stamp at each garbage collection indicating the current date and time.

Use -XX:+PrintGCDateStamps over -XX:+PrintGCTimeStamps when it is desirable to see wall clock time over a time stamp representing the time since JVM launch.

Recommended to use -XX:+PrintGCTimeStamps or -XX:+PrintGCDateStamps with -XX:+PrintGCDetails to provide a context of time when a garbage collection occurred.

-XX:+PrintTenuringDistribution

Enables the reporting of object tenuring statistics including the desired occupancy of survivor spaces to avoid premature tenuring of objects from a survivor space into old generation space, the HotSpot VM's calculated tenuring threshold, the current maximum tenuring threshold, and an object age histogram showing object ages currently held in the survivor space.

Useful to obtain tenuring information and object age information when tuning the young generation's survivor spaces to control object aging or when objects are tenured to the old generation with the concurrent or serial garbage collector.

Advisable to use this option in applications emphasizing low latency and continuously fine-tuning object aging or when objects are promoted from survivor space to old generation space.

-XX:+PrintAdaptiveSizePolicy

Enables the reporting of detailed garbage collection statistics of the throughput garbage collector including information on the number of bytes that have survived a minor garbage collection, how many bytes have been promoted in a minor garbage collection, whether survivor space has overflowed, a time stamp of when the minor garbage collection started, the major cost, mutator cost, the throughput goal, the amount of live space bytes, amount of free space bytes, the previous promotion size, the previous eden size, the desired promotion size, the desired eden size, and the current survivor space sizes.

When adaptive sizing is disabled via -XX:-UseAdaptiveSizePolicy, reports only the number of bytes that have survived a minor garbage collection, how many bytes have been promoted in a minor garbage collection, and whether survivor space has overflowed.

Useful when disabling adaptive sizing, -XX:-UseAdaptiveSizePolicy. The statistics produced are useful when explicitly fine-tuning the sizes of young generation's eden and survivor spaces for effective object aging and tenuring of objects from survivor spaces to old generation space.

Also see -XX:-UseAdaptiveSizePolicy.

-XX:+PrintGCApplicationStoppedTime

Enables the printing of the amount of time application threads have been stopped as the result of an internal HotSpot VM operation including stop-the-world garbage collections, stop-the-world phases of the CMS garbage collector, and any other safepoint operations.

Useful in applications emphasizing low latency and wanting to correlate latency events to HotSpot VM induced latencies as the result of safepoint operations.

Also see -XX:+PrintGCApplicationConcurrentTime and -XX:+PrintSafe pointStatistics.

-XX:+PrintGCApplicationConcurrentTime

Enables the printing of the amount of time application threads have been executing concurrently with internal HotSpot VM threads. In other words, the amount of time application threads have been executing between HotSpot VM operations that caused application threads to be stopped.

Useful in an application emphasizing low latency and wanting to correlate latency events to HotSpot VM induced latencies as the result of safepoint operations.

Also see `-XX:+PrintGCApplicationStoppedTime` and `-XX:+PrintSafepoint Statistics`.

-XX:+PrintSafepointStatistics

Enables the printing of HotSpot VM safepoint operations that have occurred and when they occurred. The output is printed at VM exit time. The output contains a line of output for each safepoint that occurred. Each line contains the time since VM launch of the safepoint operation occurred, type of VM operation, current number of threads active in the VM, current number of threads, current number of threads initially running, current number of threads waiting to block, amount of time in milliseconds threads spent spinning, amount of time in milliseconds threads spent blocked, amount of time threads spent in milliseconds synchronizing, amount of time in milliseconds threads spent cleaning, amount of time in milliseconds spent in VM operations, and number of page traps.

A summary is printed at the end of the output summarizing the number of different safepoint operations along with a maximum synchronization time in milliseconds and the safepoint operation that took the maximum amount of time.

Useful for applications emphasizing low latency and wanting to correlate latency events to HotSpot VM induced latencies as the result of safepoint operations.

Also see `-XX:+PrintGCApplicationStoppedTime` and `-XX:+PrintGCAppli cationConcurrentTime`.

-XX:+BackgroundCompilation

Instructs the JIT compiler to run as a background task, running the method in interpreter mode until the background compilation is finished.

This option is enabled by default in HotSpot VMs.

When writing micro-benchmarks, it can be useful to disable background compilation, `-XX:-BackgroundCompilation`, in an attempt to produce more deterministic behavior of the JIT compiler and more deterministic results of the micro-benchmark.

`-XX:-BackgroundCompilation`, disabling background compilation, is also accomplished with `-Xbatch`.

Also see `-Xbatch`.

-Xbatch

Disables JIT compiler background compilation, equivalent to `-XX:-Background Compilation`. Normally the HotSpot VM compiles the method as a background task, running the method in interpreter mode until the background compilation is finished. `-XX:-BackgroundCompilation` and `-Xbatch` disable background compilation so that JIT compilation of methods proceeds as a foreground task until completed.

When writing micro-benchmarks, it can be useful to disable background compilation in an attempt to get more deterministic behavior of the JIT compiler and more deterministic results of the micro-benchmark.

`-Xbatch`, disabling background compilation, is also accomplished with `-XX:-BackgroundCompilation`.

Also see `-XX:+BackgroundCompilation`.

-XX:+TieredCompilation

Enables a JIT compilation policy to make initial quick JIT compilation decisions analogous to optimizations made by the HotSpot VM's `-client` runtime and then continue to make more sophisticated JIT compilation decisions similar to those made by the VM's `-server` runtime for frequently called Java methods in the program.

In short, it uses a combination of the best of both `-client` and `-server` runtimes, quick compilation along sophisticated optimizations for frequently called Java methods.

At the time of this writing, it is not recommended to use this command line option as a replacement for the `-server` runtime since the `-server` runtime offers better peak performance. This recommendation may change in the future as the tiered compilation feature is enhanced.

Client applications running Java 6 Update 25 or later may consider using this command line option with the `-server` runtime (`-server -XX:+TieredCompilation`) as an alternative to the `-client` runtime. It is recommended you measure application startup performance and application responsiveness to assess whether the `-server` runtime with `-XX:+TieredCompilation` is better suited for the application than the `-client` runtime.

-XX:+PrintCompilation

Enables the printing of JIT compilation information for each method optimized by the HotSpot VM's JIT compiler.

Useful when wanting to know more about JIT compilation activities and in the creation or evaluation of micro-benchmarks.

Description of the output produced is as follows:

```
<id> <type> <method name> [bci] <(# of bytes)>
```

where `id` is

    compile id, (uses at least three columns)

      `---` if compiled method is a native method

`type` is none or more of

    `%` – compile for on stack replacement (osr)

    `*` | `n` – compiled method is native
    `s` – compiled method is synchronized
    `!` – compiled method has exception handler
    `b` – interpreter blocked until compile completes
    `1` – compile without full optimization, tier 1 compilation
    `made not entrant` – method deoptimized
    `made zombie` – compiled method no longer valid
`method name` is
    method name without signature
`bci` is
    `@ ##` - for osr compiles, bytecode index of osr
`# of bytes` is
    `(## bytes)` - # of bytes of bytecodes in method

Additional information on "made not entrant" and "made zombie": "made not entrant" and "made zombie" are life cycle states of a JIT compiled method. Live JIT compiled methods are "made not entrant" as a result of executing an uncommon trap in the generated (machine) code. Uncommon traps are used to handle situations such as references to unloaded classes and to recover from some optimistic optimization that made assumptions that later turned out to be invalid. More formally, JIT compiled methods reported as "made not entrant" may still have live activations but are not allowed to run new activations. JIT compiled methods that are reported as "made zombie" are a later life cycle state. It means that there are no live activations of that compiled method. JIT compiled methods can go directly to the zombie state when a class is unloaded since it is known that all methods referencing that class are no longer live. JIT compiled methods reported as "made not entrant" transition to a reported "made zombie" state after the JIT compiler has detected that there no longer exists any live activations for that JIT compiled method. Once the JIT compiler is sure no other compiled method has references to a "made zombie" method, the "made zombie" method is freed. That is, it can be freed from the VM's code cache where generated code is stored.

It is possible the output from `-XX:+PrintCompilation` may suggest that a method that is known to be executed frequently by an application has been deoptimized, but the output does not reflect that the method has been reoptimized. This can occur as a side-effect of method inlining done by the JIT compiler. If a frequently executed method is reported as deoptimized and it had been inlined, it is possible the `-XX:+PrintCompilation` output may not report the method as having been reoptimized.

-XX:+PrintInlining

Reports methods that are inlined or attempted to be inlined along with method byte size in bytecode.

Use of `-XX:+PrintInlining` requires what is known as a HotSpot debug VM. Information from `-XX:+PrintInlining` can be used to fine-tune `-XX:MaxInlineSize=<n>`.

-XX:MaxInlineSize=<n>

Sets the maximum bytecode size beyond which a method is not inlined unless there is strong evidence that it should be inlined, such as profile information that suggests the method is a hot method.

It is not advisable to use this command line option. Rarely do applications benefit from explicitly setting `-XX:MaxInlineSize`.

This command line option is only included since it is mentioned in Chapter 8, "Benchmarking Java Applications," as part of illustrating unexpected observations in micro-benchmarks.

Also see `-XX:+PrintInlining`.

-XX:+PrintOptoAssembly

Reports optimization decisions made by the HotSpot Server JIT compiler including generated assembly.

Requires a HotSpot debug Server VM (works only with `-server` switch on HotSpot debug VMs).

Useful for understanding and evaluating optimization decisions made by the Server JIT compiler, especially in micro-benchmarks.

Generally, using a profiling tool such as Oracle Solaris Studio Performance Analyzer on Oracle Solaris or Linux offers a better way to observe compiler generated code for applications larger than a micro-benchmark. But, it does not offer any information on optimization decisions the compiler made in arriving at the generated assembly code shown in the Performance Analyzer.

-XX:+HeapDumpOnOutOfMemoryError

Enables the generation of a heap dump of the JVM's heap spaces when an OutOfMemoryError occurs.

The heap dump created in the directory where the JVM is launched having a filename of the form `java_pid<JVM process id>.hprof`, where `<JVM process id>` is the process id of the JVM process executing the Java application.

Useful when wanting to be able to perform memory usage analysis in the event an OutOfMemoryError occurs in a Java application.

Also see `-XX:HeapDumpPath=<path>`.

-XX:HeapDumpPath=<path>

Sets the directory path to where a heap dump file is created to the path specified as `<path>`.

Useful when wanting to direct the generation of a heap dump file to a specific directory location.

Also see `-XX:+HeapDumpOnOutOfMemoryError`.

`-XX:OnOutOfMemoryError=<command or set of commands>`

Enables the ability for a command or set of commands to be run when the HotSpot VM experiences an OutOfMemoryError.

Useful when specific commands or operations are desirable if an OutOfMemory-Error occurs.

Also see `-XX:+HeapDumpOnOutOfMemoryError` and `-XX:HeapDumpPath`.

`-XX:+ShowMessageBoxOnError`

Enables an ability to have the HotSpot VM, before it exits, to display a dialog (GUI) box saying it has experienced a fatal error.

This command line option essentially prevents the VM from exiting and provides the opportunity to attach a debugger to the VM to investigate the cause of the fatal error.

Useful when wanting to diagnose a VM before it exits as a result of a fatal error.

`-XX:OnError=<command or set of commands>`

Enables the ability to invoke a set of commands when the application experiences an unexpected HotSpot VM exit.

Useful when it is desirable to collect specific system information or invoke a debugger such as Oracle Solaris or Linux dbx or Window's Winddbg to immediately examine the unexpected VM exit.

`-Xcheck:jni`

Enables an alternative set of debugging interfaces to be used by a Java application using the Java Native Interface to help with debugging issues associated with or introduced by the use of native code in a Java application. The alternative Java Native Interface introduced with this command line option verifies arguments to Java Native Interface calls more stringently, as well as performing additional internal consistency checks.

Useful when wanting to confirm a JVM execution issue is not the result of an issue in how Java Native Interface methods are invoked.

`-XX:+AggressiveOpts`

Enables the latest HotSpot VM performance optimizations.

Useful for a Java application in need of all the performance it can find.

Performance optimizations when first introduced in the HotSpot VM usually come in under this command line option. After one or more releases, those optimizations are made the default.

For application's where stability or availability of the application is more important than performance, it is not suggested to use this command line option.

`-XX:+AggressiveHeap`

An encompassing command line option that enables a larger set of aggressive options including, but not limited to Java heap size and configuration or performance features.

It is recommended to use `-XX:+AggressiveOpts` in favor of using `-XX:+AggressiveHeap`.

Also see `-XX:+AggressiveOpts`.

`-XX:+UseBiasedLocking`

Enables biased locking feature.

Introduced in Java 5 HotSpot VMs; when enabled, it biases locking to the thread that previously held the lock. In uncontended lock situations, near lock free overhead can be realized.

In Java 5 HotSpot VMs `-XX:+UseBiasedLocking` must be explicitly enabled to use the feature. In Java 6 HotSpot VMs this feature is automatically enabled by default. It must be explicitly disabled, `-XX:-UseBiasedLocking`, if this feature is not desired with Java 6 HotSpot VMs.

Generally useful for most Java applications.

Applications that predominately utilize locks in a manner where the thread that acquires a lock is not the same as the thread that acquired it last. An example would be an application where locking activity is dominated by locking activity around worker thread pools and worker threads. In this family of Java applications, since a HotSpot VM safepoint operation is required to revoke bias, it may be beneficial to explicitly disable biased locking, `-XX:-UseBiasedLocking`.

`-XX:+DoEscapeAnalysis`

Enables escape analysis optimization feature. An object, after it is allocated by some executing thread "escapes" if some other thread can ever see the allocated object. If an object does not escape, the HotSpot VM Server JIT compiler may perform any or all of the following optimizations:

- Object explosion; allocate an object's fields in different places and potentially eliminate object allocations.
- Scalar replacement; store scalar fields in CPU registers.
- Thread stack allocation; store object fields in a stack frame.
- Eliminate synchronization.
- Eliminate garbage collection read/write barriers.

`-XX:+DoEscapeAnalysis` is automatically enabled with `-XX:+AggressiveOpts`, but otherwise disabled by default in Java 6 updates prior to Java 6 Update 23.

Introduced in Java 6 Update 14.

Also see `-XX:+AggressiveOpts`.

-XX:+UseLargePages

Enables use of large memory pages in the HotSpot VM.

Automatically enabled on Oracle Solaris platforms. Not automatically enabled on Linux or Windows platforms.

Use of -XX:+UseLargePages can reduce TLB (translation lookaside buffer) misses.

32-bit Intel and AMD x86 support 4 megabyte pages.

64-bit Intel and AMD x64 support 2 megabyte pages.

Recent 64-bit Intel and AMD x64 supports up to 1 gigabyte pages.

SPARC T-series supports up to 256 megabyte pages with recent T-series supporting up to 2 gigabyte pages.

Oracle Solaris pagesize -a command reports page sizes supported by the underlying hardware. Large page support on Oracle Solaris requires no additional operating system configuration changes.

Linux getconf PAGESIZE or getconf PAGE_SIZE reports the currently configured page size. Linux requires additional operating system setup and configuration. The modifications required can vary depending on the Linux distribution and Linux kernel. It is advisable to consult a Linux administrator or your Linux distribution documentation for the appropriate changes.

Windows requires additional operating system setup and configuration, see Chapter 7, Tuning the JVM, Step by Step for instructions. Not all Windows operating systems provide large page support.

Also see -XX:LargePageSizeInBytes and -XX:+AlwaysPreTouch.

-XX:LargePageSizeInBytes=<n>[g|m|k]

Enables use of large memory pages in the HotSpot VM with an explicit size. The underlying hardware platform must support the size <n>[g|m|k] page size. Otherwise, its use falls back to its default page size usage.

Useful when explicitly desiring a page size be used, i.e., 1 gigabyte pages on AMD or Intel platforms that support 1 gigabyte pages or 256 megabyte pages on SPARC T-series platforms or 2 gigabyte pages on recent SPARC T-series platforms.

Also see -XX:+UseLargePages and -XX:+AlwaysPreTouch.

-XX:+AlwaysPreTouch

Enables the touching of all memory pages used by the JVM heap spaces during initialization of the HotSpot VM, which commits all memory pages at initialization time. By default, pages are committed only as they are needed. In other words, pages are committed as JVM heap space fills.

A garbage collection that copies to survivor space or promotes objects to the old generation space, which necessitates a new page may result in a longer garbage collection pause as a result of zeroing and committing the new page. Note, this additional overhead only occurs the first time there is a need for that additional page.

If the HotSpot VM is using large pages in the absence of this command line option, the additional overhead of zeroing and committing the new page may be noticeable in garbage collection times. As a result it can be useful to use -XX:+AlwaysPreTouch when using large pages.

The enabling of -XX:+AlwaysPreTouch increases application startup time. But observing lengthier garbage collection pause times as a result of pages being zeroed and committed as JVM heap space is consumed is less likely.

Also see -XX:+UseLargePages and -XX:LargePageSizeInBytes.

-XX:+UseNUMA

Enables a JVM heap space allocation policy that helps overcome the time it takes to fetch data from memory by leveraging processor to memory node relationships by allocating objects in a memory node local to a processor on NUMA systems.

Introduced in Java 6 Update 2.

As of this writing, it is available with the throughput collector only, -XX:+UseParallelOldGC and -XX:+UseParallelGC.

On Oracle Solaris, with multiple JVM deployments that span more than one processor/memory node should also set lgrp_mem_pset_aware=1 in /etc/system.

Linux additionally requires use of the numactl command. Use numactl --interleave for single JVM deployments. For multiple JVM deployments where JVMs that span more than one processor/memory node, use numactl --cpubind=<node number> --memnode=<node number>.

Windows under AMD additionally requires enabling node-interleaving in the BIOS for single JVM deployments. All Windows multiple JVM deployments, where JVMs that span more than one processor/memory node should use processor affinity, use the SET AFFINITY [mask] command.

Useful in JVM deployments that span processor/memory nodes on a NUMA system.

-XX:+UseNUMA should not be used in JVM deployments where the JVM does not span processor/memory nodes.

-XX:+PrintCommandLineFlags

Enables the printing of ergonomically selected HotSpot VM settings based on the set of command line options explicitly specified.

Useful when wanting to know the ergonomic values set by the HotSpot VM such as JVM heap space sizes and garbage collector selected.

Also see -XX:+PrintFlagsFinal.

-XX:+PrintFlagsFinal

Enables the printing of all production HotSpot VM command line option names and their corresponding values as they are set by the HotSpot VM based on the command line options explicitly specified and HotSpot VM defaults for options not specified.

Introduced in Java 6 Update 19.

Useful when wanting to know the configuration of HotSpot VM options in use by a Java application.

In contrast to -XX:+PrintCommandLineFlags, -XX:+PrintFlagsFinal prints all HotSpot VM options and their corresponding values as set by the HotSpot VM, not just those that are ergonomically set.

Also see -XX:+PrintCommandLineFlags.

Appendix B

Profiling Tips and Tricks Example Source Code

This appendix contains the source code used in the examples for reducing lock contention, resizing Java collections, and increasing parallelism presented in Chapter 6, "Java Application Profiling Tips and Tricks."

The examples found in this appendix illustrate scalability issues. Since desktop systems are rarely configured with a large number of virtual processors, scalability issues may not be observed when attempting to run them on desktop systems. In addition, these example programs require at least two gigabyte of Java heap to execute reasonably well without experiencing a lot of garbage collections. Hence, to observe scalability issues with these examples, they should be run on a system with a large number of virtual processors and large amounts of memory. In general, the larger the number of virtual processors, the more likely it is to observe scalability issues.

Lock Contention First Implementation

The first implementation uses a synchronized HashMap.

```
BailoutMain.java
/**
 * An example program to illustrate lock contention.
 */
import java.text.DecimalFormat;
import java.text.NumberFormat;
import java.util.ArrayList;
```

Continued

```java
import java.util.HashSet;
import java.util.List;
import java.util.Random;
import java.util.Set;
import java.util.concurrent.Callable;
import java.util.concurrent.ExecutionException;
import java.util.concurrent.ExecutorService;
import java.util.concurrent.Executors;
import java.util.concurrent.Future;
import java.util.logging.Level;
import java.util.logging.Logger;

public class BailoutMain {

    final public static int TEST_TIME = 240 * 1000;
    final public static Random random =
            new Random(Thread.currentThread().getId());
    private static char[] alphabet = {'a', 'b', 'c', 'd', 'e', 'f',
        'g', 'h', 'i', 'j', 'k', 'l', 'm', 'n', 'o', 'p', 'q', 'r',
        's', 't', 'u', 'v', 'w', 'x',
        'y', 'z'};
    private static String[] states = {"Alabama", "Alaska", "Arizona",
        "Arkansas", "California", "Colorado", "Connecticut",
        "Delaware", "Florida", "Georgia", "Hawaii", "Idaho",
        "Illinois", "Indiana", "Iowa", "Kansas", "Kentucky",
        "Louisiana", "Maine", "Maryland", "Massachusetts", "Michigan",
        "Minnesota", "Mississippi", "Missouri", "Montana", "Nebraska",
        "Nevada", "New Hampshire", "New Jersey", "New Mexico",
        "New York", "North Carolina", "North Dakota", "Ohio",
        "Oklahoma", "Oregon", "Pennsylvania", "Rhode Island",
        "South Carolina", "South Dakota", "Tennessee", "Texas",
        "Utah", "Vermont", "Virginia", "Washington", "West Virginia",
        "Wisconsin", "Wyoming"};

    public static void main(String[] args) {
        final int numberOfThreads =
                        Runtime.getRuntime().availableProcessors();
        final int dbSize = TaxPayerBailoutDB.NUMBER_OF_RECORDS_DESIRED;
        final int taxPayerListSize = dbSize / numberOfThreads;

        System.out.println("Number of threads to run concurrently : " +
                        numberOfThreads);
        System.out.println("Tax payer database size: " + dbSize);

        // populate database with records
        System.out.println("Creating tax payer database ...");
        TaxPayerBailoutDB db = new TaxPayerBailoutDbImpl(dbSize);
        List<String>[] taxPayerList = new ArrayList[numberOfThreads];
        for (int i = 0; i < numberOfThreads; i++) {
            taxPayerList[i] = new ArrayList<String>(taxPayerListSize);
        }
        populateDatabase(db, taxPayerList, dbSize);
        System.out.println("\tTax payer database created.");

        System.out.println("Allocating (" + numberOfThreads +
                        ") threads ...");
```

```
// create a pool of executors to execute some Callables
ExecutorService pool =
        Executors.newFixedThreadPool(numberOfThreads);

Callable<BailoutFuture>[] callables =
        new TaxCallable[numberOfThreads];
for (int i = 0; i < callables.length; i++) {
    callables[i] = new TaxCallable(taxPayerList[i], db);
}

System.out.println("\tthreads allocated.");

// start all threads running
System.out.println("Starting (" + callables.length +
                    ") threads ...");
Set<Future<BailoutFuture>> set =
        new HashSet<Future<BailoutFuture>>();
for (int i = 0; i < callables.length; i++) {
    Callable<BailoutFuture> callable = callables[i];
    Future<BailoutFuture> future = pool.submit(callable);
    set.add(future);
}

System.out.println("\t(" + callables.length +
                    ") threads started.");
// block and wait for all Callables to finish their
System.out.println("Waiting for " + TEST_TIME / 1000 +
                    " seconds for (" + callables.length +
                    ") threads to complete ...");

double iterationsPerSecond = 0;
long recordsAdded = 0, recordsRemoved = 0;
long nullCounter = 0;  int counter = 1;
for (Future<BailoutFuture> future : set) {
    BailoutFuture result = null;
    try {
        result = future.get();
    } catch (InterruptedException ex) {
        Logger.getLogger(
            BailoutMain.class.getName()).log(
                Level.SEVERE, null, ex);
    } catch (ExecutionException ex) {
        Logger.getLogger(
            BailoutMain.class.getName()).log(
                Level.SEVERE, null, ex);
    }
    System.out.println("Iterations per second on thread[" +
                    counter++ + "] -> " +
                    result.getIterationsPerSecond());
    iterationsPerSecond += result.getIterationsPerSecond();
    recordsAdded += result.getRecordsAdded();
    recordsRemoved += result.getRecordsRemoved();
    nullCounter = result.getNullCounter();
}
```

Continued

```
        // print number of totals
        DecimalFormat df = new DecimalFormat("#.##");
        System.out.println("Total iterations per second -> " +
                        df.format(iterationsPerSecond));
        NumberFormat nf = NumberFormat.getInstance();
        System.out.println("Total records added ---------> " +
                        nf.format(recordsAdded));
        System.out.println("Total records removed -------> " +
                        nf.format(recordsRemoved));
        System.out.println("Total records in db ---------> " +
                        nf.format(db.size()));
        System.out.println("Total null records encountered: " +
                        nf.format(nullCounter));

        System.exit(0);
    }

    public static TaxPayerRecord makeTaxPayerRecord() {
        String firstName = getRandomName();
        String lastName = getRandomName();
        String ssn = getRandomSSN();
        String address = getRandomAddress();
        String city = getRandomCity();
        String state = getRandomState();
        return new TaxPayerRecord(firstName, lastName, ssn,
                address, city, state);
    }

    private static void populateDatabase(TaxPayerBailoutDB db,
                    List<String>[] taxPayerIdList, int dbSize) {
        for (int i = 0; i < dbSize; i++) {
            String key = getRandomTaxPayerId();
            TaxPayerRecord tpr = makeTaxPayerRecord();
            db.add(key, tpr);
            int index = i % taxPayerIdList.length;
            taxPayerIdList[index].add(key);
        }
    }

    public static String getRandomTaxPayerId() {
        StringBuilder sb = new StringBuilder();
        for (int i = 0; i < 20; i++) {
            int index = random.nextInt(alphabet.length);
            sb.append(alphabet[index]);
        }
        return sb.toString();
    }

    public static String getRandomName() {
        StringBuilder sb = new StringBuilder();
        int size = random.nextInt(8) + 5;
        for (int i = 0; i < size; i++) {
            int index = random.nextInt(alphabet.length);
            char c = alphabet[index];
            if (i == 0) {
                c = Character.toUpperCase(c);
            }
```

```
            sb.append(c);
        }
        return sb.toString();
    }

    public static String getRandomSSN() {
        StringBuilder sb = new StringBuilder();
        for (int i = 0; i < 11; i++) {
            if (i == 3 || i == 6) {
                sb.append('-');
            }
            int x = random.nextInt(9);
            sb.append(x);
        }
        return sb.toString();
    }

    public static String getRandomAddress() {
        StringBuilder sb = new StringBuilder();
        int size = random.nextInt(14) + 10;
        for (int i = 0; i < size; i++) {
            if (i < 5) {
                int x = random.nextInt(8);
                sb.append(x + 1);
            }
            int index = random.nextInt(alphabet.length);
            char c = alphabet[index];
            if (i == 5) {
                c = Character.toUpperCase(c);
            }
            sb.append(c);
        }
        return sb.toString();
    }

    public static String getRandomCity() {
        StringBuilder sb = new StringBuilder();
        int size = random.nextInt(5) + 6;
        for (int i = 0; i < size; i++) {
            int index = random.nextInt(alphabet.length);
            char c = alphabet[index];
            if (i == 0) {
                c = Character.toUpperCase(c);
            }
            sb.append(c);
        }
        return sb.toString();
    }

    public static String getRandomState() {
        int index = random.nextInt(states.length);
        return states[index];
    }
}
```

Continued

TaxPayerRecord.java

```java
import java.util.concurrent.atomic.AtomicLong;

public class TaxPayerRecord {
    private String firstName, lastName, ssn, address, city, state;
    private AtomicLong taxPaid;

    public TaxPayerRecord(String firstName, String lastName, String ssn,
                          String address, String city, String state) {
        this.firstName = firstName;
        this.lastName = lastName;
        this.ssn = ssn;
        this.address = address;
        this.city = city;
        this.state = state;
        this.taxPaid = new AtomicLong(0);
    }

    public String getFirstName() {
        return firstName;
    }

    public void setFirstName(String firstName) {
        this.firstName = firstName;
    }

    public String getLastName() {
        return lastName;
    }

    public void setLastName(String lastName) {
        this.lastName = lastName;
    }

    public String getSsn() {
        return ssn;
    }

    public void setSsn(String ssn) {
        this.ssn = ssn;
    }

    public String getAddress() {
        return address;
    }

    public void setAddress(String address) {
        this.address = address;
    }

    public String getCity() {
        return city;
    }

    public void setCity(String city) {
        this.city = city;
    }
```

```
    public String getState() {
        return state;
    }

    public void setState(String state) {
        this.state = state;
    }

    public void taxPaid(long amount) {
        taxPaid.addAndGet(amount);
    }

    public long getTaxPaid() {
        return taxPaid.get();
    }
}
```

TaxPayerBailoutDB.java

```
public interface TaxPayerBailoutDB {

    static final int NUMBER_OF_RECORDS_DESIRED = 2 * 1000000;

    /**
     * Get a tax payers record from the database based on his or her id.
     *
     * @param id - tax payers id
     * @return tax payers record
     */
    TaxPayerRecord get(String id);

    /**
     * Add new tax payers record in the database.
     *
     * @param id - tax payer's id
     * @param record - tax payer's record
     * @return taxPayersRecord just added to the database
     */
    TaxPayerRecord add(String id,  TaxPayerRecord record);

    /**
     * Remove a tax payer's record from the database.
     *
     * @param id - tax payer's id
     * @return tax payers record, or null if id not found in database
     */
    TaxPayerRecord remove(String id);

    /**
     * Size of the database, i.e. number of records
     *
     * @return number of records in the database
     */
    int size();
}
```

TaxPayerBailoutDbImpl.java

```java
import java.util.Collections;
import java.util.HashMap;
import java.util.Map;

public class TaxPayerBailoutDbImpl implements TaxPayerBailoutDB {
    private final Map<String,TaxPayerRecord> db;

    public TaxPayerBailoutDbImpl(int size) {
        db = Collections.synchronizedMap(
                new HashMap<String,TaxPayerRecord>(size));
    }

    @Override
    public TaxPayerRecord get(String id) {
        return db.get(id);
    }

    @Override
    public TaxPayerRecord add(String id, TaxPayerRecord record) {
        TaxPayerRecord old = db.put(id, record);
        if (old != null) {
            // restore old TaxPayerRecord
            old = db.put(id, old);
        }
        return old;
    }

    @Override
    public TaxPayerRecord remove(String id) {
        return db.remove(id);
    }

    @Override
    public int size() {
        return db.size();
    }
}
```

TaxCallable.java

```java
import java.util.List;
import java.util.Random;
import java.util.concurrent.Callable;

public class TaxCallable implements Callable<BailoutFuture> {

    private static long runTimeInMillis = BailoutMain.TEST_TIME;
    final private static Random generator = BailoutMain.random;
    private long nullCounter, recordsRemoved, newRecordsAdded;
    private int index;
    private String taxPayerId;
    final private List<String> taxPayerList;
```

```java
final private TaxPayerBailoutDB db;

public TaxCallable(List<String> taxPayerList,
                   TaxPayerBailoutDB db) {
    this.taxPayerList = taxPayerList;
    this.db = db;
    index = 0;
}

@Override
public BailoutFuture call() throws Exception {
    long iterations = 0L, elapsedTime = 0L;
    long startTime = System.currentTimeMillis();
    double iterationsPerSecond = 0;
    do {
        setTaxPayer();
        iterations++;
        TaxPayerRecord tpr = null;
        // Just in case there 'iterations' is about to overflow
        if (iterations == Long.MAX_VALUE) {
            long elapsed = System.currentTimeMillis() - startTime;
            iterationsPerSecond =
                    iterations / ((double) (elapsed / 1000));
            System.err.println(
                    "Iteration counter about to overflow ...");
            System.err.println(
                    "Calculating current operations per second ...");
            System.err.println(
                    "Iterations per second: " + iterationsPerSecond);
            iterations = 0L;
            startTime = System.currentTimeMillis();
            runTimeInMillis -= elapsed;
        }
        if (iterations % 1001 == 0) {
            tpr = addNewTaxPayer(tpr);
        } else if (iterations % 60195 == 0) {
            tpr = removeTaxPayer(tpr);
        } else {
            tpr = updateTaxPayer(iterations, tpr);
        }

        if (iterations % 1000 == 0) {
            elapsedTime = System.currentTimeMillis() - startTime;
        }
    } while (elapsedTime < runTimeInMillis);

    if (iterations >= 1000) {
        iterationsPerSecond =
                iterations / ((double) (elapsedTime / 1000));
    }
    BailoutFuture bailoutFuture =
            new BailoutFuture(iterationsPerSecond, newRecordsAdded,
                              recordsRemoved, nullCounter);
    return bailoutFuture;
}
```

Continued

```java
    private TaxPayerRecord updateTaxPayer(long iterations,
                                          TaxPayerRecord tpr) {
        if (iterations % 1001 == 0) {
            tpr = db.get(taxPayerId);
        } else {
            // update a TaxPayer's DB record
            tpr = db.get(taxPayerId);
            if (tpr != null) {
                long tax = generator.nextInt(10) + 15;
                tpr.taxPaid(tax);
            }
        }
        if (tpr == null) {
            nullCounter++;
        }
        return tpr;
    }

    private TaxPayerRecord removeTaxPayer(TaxPayerRecord tpr) {
        // remove a tax payer from DB
        tpr = db.remove(taxPayerId);
        if (tpr != null) {
            // remove record from TaxPayerList
            taxPayerList.remove(index);
            recordsRemoved++;
        }
        return tpr;
    }

    private TaxPayerRecord addNewTaxPayer(TaxPayerRecord tpr) {
        // add a new TaxPayer to the DB
        String tmpTaxPayerId = BailoutMain.getRandomTaxPayerId();
        tpr = BailoutMain.makeTaxPayerRecord();
        TaxPayerRecord old = db.add(tmpTaxPayerId, tpr);
        if (old == null) {
            // add to the (local) list
            taxPayerList.add(tmpTaxPayerId);
            newRecordsAdded++;
        }
        return tpr;
    }

    public void setTaxPayer() {
        if (++index >= taxPayerList.size()) {
            index = 0;
        }
        this.taxPayerId = taxPayerList.get(index);
    }
}
```

BailoutFuture.java

```java
public class BailoutFuture {
    private double iterationsPerSecond;
    private long recordsAdded, recordsRemoved, nullCounter;
```

```
        public BailoutFuture(double iterationsPerSecond, long recordsAdded,
                             long recordsRemoved, long nullCounter) {
            this.iterationsPerSecond = iterationsPerSecond;
            this.recordsAdded = recordsAdded;
            this.recordsRemoved = recordsRemoved;
            this.nullCounter = nullCounter;
        }

        public double getIterationsPerSecond() {
            return iterationsPerSecond;
        }

        public long getRecordsAdded() {
            return recordsAdded;
        }

        public long getRecordsRemoved() {
            return recordsRemoved;
        }

        public long getNullCounter() {
            return nullCounter;
        }
    }
```

Lock Contention Second Implementation

The second implementation replaces the use of a synchronized HashMap with a ConcurrentHashMap.

BailoutMain.java

```
/**
 * An example program to illustrate lock contention.
 */
import java.text.DecimalFormat;
import java.text.NumberFormat;
import java.util.ArrayList;
import java.util.HashSet;
import java.util.List;
import java.util.Random;
import java.util.Set;
import java.util.concurrent.Callable;
import java.util.concurrent.ExecutionException;
import java.util.concurrent.ExecutorService;
import java.util.concurrent.Executors;
import java.util.concurrent.Future;
import java.util.logging.Level;
import java.util.logging.Logger;

public class BailoutMain {
```

Continued

```java
final public static int TEST_TIME = 240 * 1000;
final public static Random random =
    new Random(Thread.currentThread().getId());
private static char[] alphabet = {'a', 'b', 'c', 'd', 'e', 'f',
    'g', 'h', 'i', 'j', 'k', 'l', 'm', 'n', 'o', 'p', 'q', 'r',
    's', 't', 'u', 'v', 'w', 'x',
    'y', 'z'};
private static String[] states = {"Alabama", "Alaska", "Arizona",
    "Arkansas", "California", "Colorado", "Connecticut",
    "Delaware", "Florida", "Georgia", "Hawaii", "Idaho",
    "Illinois", "Indiana", "Iowa", "Kansas", "Kentucky",
    "Louisiana", "Maine", "Maryland", "Massachusetts", "Michigan",
    "Minnesota", "Mississippi", "Missouri", "Montana", "Nebraska",
    "Nevada", "New Hampshire", "New Jersey", "New Mexico",
    "New York", "North Carolina", "North Dakota", "Ohio",
    "Oklahoma", "Oregon", "Pennsylvania", "Rhode Island",
    "South Carolina", "South Dakota", "Tennessee", "Texas",
    "Utah", "Vermont", "Virginia", "Washington", "West Virginia",
    "Wisconsin", "Wyoming"};

public static void main(String[] args) {
    final int numberOfThreads =
                Runtime.getRuntime().availableProcessors();
    final int dbSize = TaxPayerBailoutDB.NUMBER_OF_RECORDS_DESIRED;
    final int taxPayerListSize = dbSize / numberOfThreads;

    System.out.println("Number of threads to run concurrently : " +
                numberOfThreads);
    System.out.println("Tax payer database size: " + dbSize);

    // populate database with records
    System.out.println("Creating tax payer database ...");
    TaxPayerBailoutDB db = new TaxPayerBailoutDbImpl(dbSize);
    List<String>[] taxPayerList = new ArrayList[numberOfThreads];
    for (int i = 0; i < numberOfThreads; i++) {
        taxPayerList[i] = new ArrayList<String>(taxPayerListSize);
    }
    populateDatabase(db, taxPayerList, dbSize);
    System.out.println("\tTax payer database created.");

    System.out.println("Allocating (" + numberOfThreads +
                ") threads ...");

    // create a pool of executors to execute some Callables
    ExecutorService pool =
            Executors.newFixedThreadPool(numberOfThreads);

    Callable<BailoutFuture>[] callables =
            new TaxCallable[numberOfThreads];
    for (int i = 0; i < callables.length; i++) {
        callables[i] = new TaxCallable(taxPayerList[i], db);
    }

    System.out.println("\tthreads allocated.");

    // start all threads running
    System.out.println("Starting (" + callables.length +
                ") threads ...");
```

```
      Set<Future<BailoutFuture>> set =
            new HashSet<Future<BailoutFuture>>();
      for (int i = 0; i < callables.length; i++) {
          Callable<BailoutFuture> callable = callables[i];
          Future<BailoutFuture> future = pool.submit(callable);
          set.add(future);
      }

      System.out.println("\t(" + callables.length +
                          ") threads started.");
      // block and wait for all Callables to finish their
      System.out.println("Waiting for " + TEST_TIME / 1000 +
                          " seconds for (" + callables.length +
                          ") threads to complete ...");

      double iterationsPerSecond = 0;
      long recordsAdded = 0, recordsRemoved = 0;
      long nullCounter = 0;   int counter = 1;
      for (Future<BailoutFuture> future : set) {
          BailoutFuture result = null;
          try {
              result = future.get();
          } catch (InterruptedException ex) {
              Logger.getLogger(
                  BailoutMain.class.getName()).log(
                      Level.SEVERE, null, ex);
          } catch (ExecutionException ex) {
              Logger.getLogger(
                  BailoutMain.class.getName()).log(
                      Level.SEVERE, null, ex);
          }
          System.out.println("Iterations per second on thread[" +
                          counter++ + "] -> " +
                          result.getIterationsPerSecond());
          iterationsPerSecond += result.getIterationsPerSecond();
          recordsAdded += result.getRecordsAdded();
          recordsRemoved += result.getRecordsRemoved();
          nullCounter = result.getNullCounter();
      }

      // print number of totals
      DecimalFormat df = new DecimalFormat("#.##");
      System.out.println("Total iterations per second -> " +
                          df.format(iterationsPerSecond));
      NumberFormat nf = NumberFormat.getInstance();
      System.out.println("Total records added ---------> " +
                          nf.format(recordsAdded));
      System.out.println("Total records removed -------> " +
                          nf.format(recordsRemoved));
      System.out.println("Total records in db ---------> " +
                          nf.format(db.size()));
      System.out.println("Total null records encountered: " +
                          nf.format(nullCounter));

      System.exit(0);
  }
```

Continued

```java
public static TaxPayerRecord makeTaxPayerRecord() {
    String firstName = getRandomName();
    String lastName = getRandomName();
    String ssn = getRandomSSN();
    String address = getRandomAddress();
    String city = getRandomCity();
    String state = getRandomState();
    return new TaxPayerRecord(firstName, lastName, ssn,
            address, city, state);
}

private static void populateDatabase(TaxPayerBailoutDB db,
                List<String>[] taxPayerIdList, int dbSize) {
    for (int i = 0; i < dbSize; i++) {
        String key = getRandomTaxPayerId();
        TaxPayerRecord tpr = makeTaxPayerRecord();
        db.add(key, tpr);
        int index = i % taxPayerIdList.length;
        taxPayerIdList[index].add(key);
    }
}

public static String getRandomTaxPayerId() {
    StringBuilder sb = new StringBuilder();
    for (int i = 0; i < 20; i++) {
        int index = random.nextInt(alphabet.length);
        sb.append(alphabet[index]);
    }
    return sb.toString();
}

public static String getRandomName() {
    StringBuilder sb = new StringBuilder();
    int size = random.nextInt(8) + 5;
    for (int i = 0; i < size; i++) {
        int index = random.nextInt(alphabet.length);
        char c = alphabet[index];
        if (i == 0) {
            c = Character.toUpperCase(c);
        }
        sb.append(c);
    }
    return sb.toString();
}

public static String getRandomSSN() {
    StringBuilder sb = new StringBuilder();
    for (int i = 0; i < 11; i++) {
        if (i == 3 || i == 6) {
            sb.append('-');
        }
        int x = random.nextInt(9);
        sb.append(x);
    }
    return sb.toString();
}
```

```java
    public static String getRandomAddress() {
        StringBuilder sb = new StringBuilder();
        int size = random.nextInt(14) + 10;
        for (int i = 0; i < size; i++) {
            if (i < 5) {
                int x = random.nextInt(8);
                sb.append(x + 1);
            }
            int index = random.nextInt(alphabet.length);
            char c = alphabet[index];
            if (i == 5) {
                c = Character.toUpperCase(c);
            }
            sb.append(c);
        }
        return sb.toString();
    }

    public static String getRandomCity() {
        StringBuilder sb = new StringBuilder();
        int size = random.nextInt(5) + 6;
        for (int i = 0; i < size; i++) {
            int index = random.nextInt(alphabet.length);
            char c = alphabet[index];
            if (i == 0) {
                c = Character.toUpperCase(c);
            }
            sb.append(c);
        }
        return sb.toString();
    }

    public static String getRandomState() {
        int index = random.nextInt(states.length);
        return states[index];
    }
}
```

TaxPayerRecord.java

```java
import java.util.concurrent.atomic.AtomicLong;

public class TaxPayerRecord {
    private String firstName, lastName, ssn, address, city, state;
    private AtomicLong taxPaid;

    public TaxPayerRecord(String firstName, String lastName, String ssn,
                          String address, String city, String state) {
        this.firstName = firstName;
        this.lastName = lastName;
        this.ssn = ssn;
        this.address = address;
        this.city = city;
        this.state = state;
```

Continued

```java
        this.taxPaid = new AtomicLong(0);
    }

    public String getFirstName() {
        return firstName;
    }

    public void setFirstName(String firstName) {
        this.firstName = firstName;
    }

    public String getLastName() {
        return lastName;
    }

    public void setLastName(String lastName) {
        this.lastName = lastName;
    }

    public String getSsn() {
        return ssn;
    }

    public void setSsn(String ssn) {
        this.ssn = ssn;
    }

    public String getAddress() {
        return address;
    }

    public void setAddress(String address) {
        this.address = address;
    }

    public String getCity() {
        return city;
    }

    public void setCity(String city) {
        this.city = city;
    }

    public String getState() {
        return state;
    }

    public void setState(String state) {
        this.state = state;
    }

    public void taxPaid(long amount) {
        taxPaid.addAndGet(amount);
    }

    public long getTaxPaid() {
        return taxPaid.get();
    }
}
```

TaxPayerBailoutDB.java

```java
public interface TaxPayerBailoutDB {

    static final int NUMBER_OF_RECORDS_DESIRED = 2 * 1000000;

    /**
     * Get a tax payers record from the database based on his or her id.
     *
     * @param id - tax payers id
     * @return tax payers record
     */
    TaxPayerRecord get(String id);

    /**
     * Add new tax payers record in the database.
     *
     * @param id - tax payer's id
     * @param record - tax payer's record
     * @return taxPayersRecord just added to the database
     */
    TaxPayerRecord add(String id,  TaxPayerRecord record);

    /**
     * Remove a tax payer's record from the database.
     *
     * @param id - tax payer's id
     * @return tax payers record, or null if id not found in database
     */
    TaxPayerRecord remove(String id);

    /**
     * Size of the database, i.e. number of records
     *
     * @return number of records in the database
     */
    int size();
}
```

TaxPayerBailoutDbImpl.java

```java
import java.util.Map;
import java.util.concurrent.ConcurrentHashMap;

public class TaxPayerBailoutDbImpl implements TaxPayerBailoutDB {
    private final Map<String,TaxPayerRecord> db;

    public TaxPayerBailoutDbImpl(int size) {
        db = new ConcurrentHashMap<String,TaxPayerRecord>(size);
    }

    @Override
    public TaxPayerRecord get(String id) {
```

Continued

```
        return db.get(id);
    }

    @Override
    public TaxPayerRecord add(String id, TaxPayerRecord record) {
        TaxPayerRecord old = db.put(id, record);
        if (old != null) {
            // restore old TaxPayerRecord
            old = db.put(id, old);
        }
        return old;
    }

    @Override
    public TaxPayerRecord remove(String id) {
        return db.remove(id);
    }

    @Override
    public int size() {
        return db.size();
    }
}
```

TaxCallable.java

```java
import java.util.List;
import java.util.Random;
import java.util.concurrent.Callable;

public class TaxCallable implements Callable<BailoutFuture> {

    private static long runTimeInMillis = BailoutMain.TEST_TIME;
    final private static Random generator = BailoutMain.random;
    private long nullCounter, recordsRemoved, newRecordsAdded;
    private int index;
    private String taxPayerId;
    final private List<String> taxPayerList;
    final private TaxPayerBailoutDB db;

    public TaxCallable(List<String> taxPayerList,
                       TaxPayerBailoutDB db) {
        this.taxPayerList = taxPayerList;
        this.db = db;
        index = 0;
    }

    @Override
    public BailoutFuture call() throws Exception {
        long iterations = 0L, elapsedTime = 0L;
        long startTime = System.currentTimeMillis();
        double iterationsPerSecond = 0;
        do {
            setTaxPayer();
            iterations++;
```

```
            TaxPayerRecord tpr = null;
            // Just in case there 'iterations' is about to overflow
            if (iterations == Long.MAX_VALUE) {
                long elapsed = System.currentTimeMillis() - startTime;
                iterationsPerSecond =
                        iterations / ((double) (elapsed / 1000));
                System.err.println(
                        "Iteration counter about to overflow ...");
                System.err.println(
                        "Calculating current operations per second ...");
                System.err.println(
                        "Iterations per second: " + iterationsPerSecond);
                iterations = 0L;
                startTime = System.currentTimeMillis();
                runTimeInMillis -= elapsed;
            }
            if (iterations % 1001 == 0) {
                tpr = addNewTaxPayer(tpr);
            } else if (iterations % 60195 == 0) {
                tpr = removeTaxPayer(tpr);
            } else {
                tpr = updateTaxPayer(iterations, tpr);
            }

            if (iterations % 1000 == 0) {
                elapsedTime = System.currentTimeMillis() - startTime;
            }
        } while (elapsedTime < runTimeInMillis);

        if (iterations >= 1000) {
            iterationsPerSecond =
                    iterations / ((double) (elapsedTime / 1000));
        }
        BailoutFuture bailoutFuture =
                new BailoutFuture(iterationsPerSecond, newRecordsAdded,
                            recordsRemoved, nullCounter);
        return bailoutFuture;
    }

    private TaxPayerRecord updateTaxPayer(long iterations,
                                        TaxPayerRecord tpr) {
        if (iterations % 1001 == 0) {
            tpr = db.get(taxPayerId);
        } else {
            // update a TaxPayer's DB record
            tpr = db.get(taxPayerId);
            if (tpr != null) {
                long tax = generator.nextInt(10) + 15;
                tpr.taxPaid(tax);
            }
        }
        if (tpr == null) {
            nullCounter++;
        }
        return tpr;
    }
}
```

Continued

```java
    private TaxPayerRecord removeTaxPayer(TaxPayerRecord tpr) {
        // remove a tax payer from DB
        tpr = db.remove(taxPayerId);
        if (tpr != null) {
            // remove record from TaxPayerList
            taxPayerList.remove(index);
            recordsRemoved++;
        }
        return tpr;
    }

    private TaxPayerRecord addNewTaxPayer(TaxPayerRecord tpr) {
        // add a new TaxPayer to the DB
        String tmpTaxPayerId = BailoutMain.getRandomTaxPayerId();
        tpr = BailoutMain.makeTaxPayerRecord();
        TaxPayerRecord old = db.add(tmpTaxPayerId, tpr);
        if (old == null) {
            // add to the (local) list
            taxPayerList.add(tmpTaxPayerId);
            newRecordsAdded++;
        }
        return tpr;
    }

    public void setTaxPayer() {
        if (++index >= taxPayerList.size()) {
            index = 0;
        }
        this.taxPayerId = taxPayerList.get(index);
    }
}
```

BailoutFuture.java

```java
public class BailoutFuture {
    private double iterationsPerSecond;
    private long recordsAdded, recordsRemoved, nullCounter;

    public BailoutFuture(double iterationsPerSecond, long recordsAdded,
                         long recordsRemoved, long nullCounter) {
        this.iterationsPerSecond = iterationsPerSecond;
        this.recordsAdded = recordsAdded;
        this.recordsRemoved = recordsRemoved;
        this.nullCounter = nullCounter;
    }

    public double getIterationsPerSecond() {
        return iterationsPerSecond;
    }

    public long getRecordsAdded() {
        return recordsAdded;
    }
```

```
        public long getRecordsRemoved() {
            return recordsRemoved;
        }

        public long getNullCounter() {
            return nullCounter;
        }
    }
```

Lock Contention Third Implementation

The third implementation replaces the use of a static java.util.Random with a
ThreadLocal java.util.Random.

BailoutMain.java

```
/**
 * An example program to illustrate lock contention.
 */
import java.text.DecimalFormat;
import java.text.NumberFormat;
import java.util.ArrayList;
import java.util.HashSet;
import java.util.List;
import java.util.Random;
import java.util.Set;
import java.util.concurrent.Callable;
import java.util.concurrent.ExecutionException;
import java.util.concurrent.ExecutorService;
import java.util.concurrent.Executors;
import java.util.concurrent.Future;
import java.util.logging.Level;
import java.util.logging.Logger;

public class BailoutMain {

    final public static int TEST_TIME = 240 * 1000;
    final public static ThreadLocal<Random> threadLocalRandom =
            new ThreadLocal<Random>() {
                @Override
                protected Random initialValue() {
                    return new Random(Thread.currentThread().getId());
                }
            };
    private static char[] alphabet = {'a', 'b', 'c', 'd', 'e', 'f',
        'g', 'h', 'i', 'j', 'k', 'l', 'm', 'n', 'o', 'p', 'q', 'r',
        's', 't', 'u', 'v', 'w', 'x',
        'y', 'z'};
```

Continued

```java
static String[] states = {"Alabama", "Alaska", "Arizona",
    "Arkansas", "California", "Colorado", "Connecticut",
    "Delaware", "Florida", "Georgia", "Hawaii", "Idaho",
    "Illinois", "Indiana", "Iowa", "Kansas", "Kentucky",
    "Louisiana", "Maine", "Maryland", "Massachusetts", "Michigan",
    "Minnesota", "Mississippi", "Missouri", "Montana", "Nebraska",
    "Nevada", "New Hampshire", "New Jersey", "New Mexico",
    "New York", "North Carolina", "North Dakota", "Ohio",
    "Oklahoma", "Oregon", "Pennsylvania", "Rhode Island",
    "South Carolina", "South Dakota", "Tennessee", "Texas",
    "Utah", "Vermont", "Virginia", "Washington", "West Virginia",
    "Wisconsin", "Wyoming"};

public static void main(String[] args) {
    final long start = System.nanoTime();
    final int numberOfThreads =
                Runtime.getRuntime().availableProcessors();
    final int dbSize = TaxPayerBailoutDB.NUMBER_OF_RECORDS_DESIRED;
    final int taxPayerListSize = dbSize / numberOfThreads;

    System.out.println("Number of threads to run concurrently : " +
                numberOfThreads);
    System.out.println("Tax payer database size: " + dbSize);

    // populate database with records
    System.out.println("Creating tax payer database ...");
    TaxPayerBailoutDB db = new TaxPayerBailoutDbImpl(dbSize);
    List<String>[] taxPayerList = new ArrayList[numberOfThreads];
    for (int i = 0; i < numberOfThreads; i++) {
        taxPayerList[i] = new ArrayList<String>(taxPayerListSize);
    }
    populateDatabase(db, taxPayerList, dbSize);
    final long initDbTime = System.nanoTime() - start;
    System.out.println("\tTax payer database created & populated " +
                "in (" + initDbTime/(1000*1000) + ") ms.");

    System.out.println("Allocating (" + numberOfThreads +
                ") threads ...");
    // create a pool of executors to execute some Callables
    ExecutorService pool =
        Executors.newFixedThreadPool(numberOfThreads);

    Callable<BailoutFuture>[] callables =
        new TaxCallable[numberOfThreads];
    for (int i = 0; i < callables.length; i++) {
        callables[i] = new TaxCallable(taxPayerList[i], db);
    }

    System.out.println("\tthreads allocated.");

    // start all threads running
    System.out.println("Starting (" + callables.length +
                ") threads ...");
    Set<Future<BailoutFuture>> set =
        new HashSet<Future<BailoutFuture>>();
    for (int i = 0; i < callables.length; i++) {
        Callable<BailoutFuture> callable = callables[i];
```

```
                Future<BailoutFuture> future = pool.submit(callable);
                set.add(future);
            }

            System.out.println("\t(" + callables.length +
                            ") threads started.");
            // block and wait for all Callables to finish their
            System.out.println("Waiting for " + TEST_TIME / 1000 +
                            " seconds for (" + callables.length +
                            ") threads to complete ...");

            double iterationsPerSecond = 0;
            long recordsAdded = 0, recordsRemoved = 0, nullCounter = 0;
            int counter = 1;
            for (Future<BailoutFuture> future : set) {
                BailoutFuture result = null;
                try {
                    result = future.get();
                } catch (InterruptedException ex) {
                    Logger.getLogger(
                        BailoutMain.class.getName()).log(
                            Level.SEVERE, null, ex);
                } catch (ExecutionException ex) {
                    Logger.getLogger(
                        BailoutMain.class.getName()).log(
                            Level.SEVERE, null, ex);
                }
                System.out.println("Iterations per second on thread[" +
                            counter++ + "] -> " +
                            result.getIterationsPerSecond());
                iterationsPerSecond += result.getIterationsPerSecond();
                recordsAdded += result.getRecordsAdded();
                recordsRemoved += result.getRecordsRemoved();
                nullCounter = result.getNullCounter();
            }

            // print number of totals
            DecimalFormat df = new DecimalFormat("#.##");
            System.out.println("Total iterations per second --> " +
                            df.format(iterationsPerSecond));
            NumberFormat nf = NumberFormat.getInstance();
            System.out.println("Total records added ----------> " +
                            nf.format(recordsAdded));
            System.out.println("Total records removed --------> " +
                            nf.format(recordsRemoved));
            System.out.println("Total records in db ----------> " +
                            nf.format(db.size()));
            System.out.println("Total null records encountered: " +
                            nf.format(nullCounter));

            System.exit(0);
        }

    public static TaxPayerRecord makeTaxPayerRecord() {
        String firstName = getRandomName();
        String lastName = getRandomName();
```

Continued

```
        String ssn = getRandomSSN();
        String address = getRandomAddress();
        String city = getRandomCity();
        String state = getRandomState();
        return new TaxPayerRecord(firstName, lastName, ssn,
                address, city, state);
    }

    private static void populateDatabase(TaxPayerBailoutDB db,
            List<String>[] taxPayerIdList,
            int dbSize) {
        for (int i = 0; i < dbSize; i++) {
            String key = getRandomTaxPayerId();
            TaxPayerRecord tpr = makeTaxPayerRecord();
            db.add(key, tpr);
            int index = i % taxPayerIdList.length;
            taxPayerIdList[index].add(key);
        }
    }

    public static String getRandomTaxPayerId() {
        StringBuilder sb = new StringBuilder();
        for (int i = 0; i < 20; i++) {
            int index =
                threadLocalRandom.get().nextInt(alphabet.length);
            sb.append(alphabet[index]);
        }
        return sb.toString();
    }

    public static String getRandomName() {
        StringBuilder sb = new StringBuilder();
        int size = threadLocalRandom.get().nextInt(8) + 5;
        for (int i = 0; i < size; i++) {
            int index =
                threadLocalRandom.get().nextInt(alphabet.length);
            char c = alphabet[index];
            if (i == 0) {
                c = Character.toUpperCase(c);
            }
            sb.append(c);
        }
        return sb.toString();
    }

    public static String getRandomSSN() {
        StringBuilder sb = new StringBuilder();
        for (int i = 0; i < 11; i++) {
            if (i == 3 || i == 6) {
                sb.append('-');
            }
            int x = threadLocalRandom.get().nextInt(9);
            sb.append(x);
        }
        return sb.toString();
    }
```

```
    public static String getRandomAddress() {
        StringBuilder sb = new StringBuilder();
        int size = threadLocalRandom.get().nextInt(14) + 10;
        for (int i = 0; i < size; i++) {
            if (i < 5) {
                int x = threadLocalRandom.get().nextInt(8);
                sb.append(x + 1);
            }
            int index =
                threadLocalRandom.get().nextInt(alphabet.length);
            char c = alphabet[index];
            if (i == 5) {
                c = Character.toUpperCase(c);
            }
            sb.append(c);
        }
        return sb.toString();
    }

    public static String getRandomCity() {
        StringBuilder sb = new StringBuilder();
        int size = threadLocalRandom.get().nextInt(5) + 6;
        for (int i = 0; i < size; i++) {
            int index =
                threadLocalRandom.get().nextInt(alphabet.length);
            char c = alphabet[index];
            if (i == 0) {
                c = Character.toUpperCase(c);
            }
            sb.append(c);
        }
        return sb.toString();
    }

    public static String getRandomState() {
        int index = threadLocalRandom.get().nextInt(states.length);
        return states[index];
    }
}
```

TaxPayerRecord.java

```
import java.util.concurrent.atomic.AtomicLong;

public class TaxPayerRecord {
    private String firstName, lastName, ssn, address, city, state;
    private AtomicLong taxPaid;

    public TaxPayerRecord(String firstName, String lastName, String ssn,
                          String address, String city, String state) {
        this.firstName = firstName;
        this.lastName = lastName;
        this.ssn = ssn;
        this.address = address;
```

Continued

```java
            this.city = city;
            this.state = state;
            this.taxPaid = new AtomicLong(0);
    }

    public String getFirstName() {
        return firstName;
    }

    public void setFirstName(String firstName) {
        this.firstName = firstName;
    }

    public String getLastName() {
        return lastName;
    }

    public void setLastName(String lastName) {
        this.lastName = lastName;
    }

    public String getSsn() {
        return ssn;
    }

    public void setSsn(String ssn) {
        this.ssn = ssn;
    }

    public String getAddress() {
        return address;
    }

    public void setAddress(String address) {
        this.address = address;
    }

    public String getCity() {
        return city;
    }

    public void setCity(String city) {
        this.city = city;
    }

    public String getState() {
        return state;
    }

    public void setState(String state) {
        this.state = state;
    }

    public void taxPaid(long amount) {
        taxPaid.addAndGet(amount);
    }
```

```
      public long getTaxPaid() {
          return taxPaid.get();
      }
  }
```

TaxPayerBailoutDB.java

```java
public interface TaxPayerBailoutDB {

    static final int NUMBER_OF_RECORDS_DESIRED = 2 * 1000000;

    /**
     * Get a tax payers record from the database based on his or her id.
     *
     * @param id - tax payers id
     * @return tax payers record
     */
    TaxPayerRecord get(String id);

    /**
     * Add new tax payers record in the database.
     *
     * @param id - tax payer's id
     * @param record - tax payer's record
     * @return taxPayersRecord just added to the database
     */
    TaxPayerRecord add(String id,  TaxPayerRecord record);

    /**
     * Remove a tax payer's record from the database.
     *
     * @param id - tax payer's id
     * @return tax payers record, or null if id not found in database
     */
    TaxPayerRecord remove(String id);

    /**
     * Size of the database, i.e. number of records
     *
     * @return number of records in the database
     */
    int size();
}
```

TaxPayerBailoutDbImpl.java

```java
import java.util.Map;
import java.util.concurrent.ConcurrentHashMap;

public class TaxPayerBailoutDbImpl implements TaxPayerBailoutDB {
```

Continued

```java
    private final Map<String,TaxPayerRecord> db;

    public TaxPayerBailoutDbImpl(int size) {
        db = new ConcurrentHashMap<String,TaxPayerRecord>(size);
    }

    @Override
    public TaxPayerRecord get(String id) {
        return db.get(id);
    }

    @Override
    public TaxPayerRecord add(String id, TaxPayerRecord record) {
        TaxPayerRecord old = db.put(id, record);
        if (old != null) {
            // restore old TaxPayerRecord
            old = db.put(id, old);
        }
        return old;
    }

    @Override
    public TaxPayerRecord remove(String id) {
        return db.remove(id);
    }

    @Override
    public int size() {
        return db.size();
    }
}
```

TaxCallable.java

```java
import java.util.List;
import java.util.Random;
import java.util.concurrent.Callable;

public class TaxCallable implements Callable<BailoutFuture> {

    private static long runTimeInMillis = BailoutMain.TEST_TIME;
    final private static ThreadLocal<Random> generator =
            BailoutMain.threadLocalRandom;
    private long nullCounter, recordsRemoved, newRecordsAdded;
    private int index;
    private String taxPayerId;
    final private List<String> taxPayerList;
    final private TaxPayerBailoutDB db;

    public TaxCallable(List<String> taxPayerList,
                    TaxPayerBailoutDB db) {
        this.taxPayerList = taxPayerList;
        this.db = db;
        index = 0;
    }
```

```java
@Override
public BailoutFuture call() throws Exception {
    long iterations = 0L, elapsedTime = 0L;
    long startTime = System.currentTimeMillis();
    double iterationsPerSecond = 0;
    do {
        setTaxPayer();
        iterations++;
        TaxPayerRecord tpr = null;
        // Just in case there 'iterations' is about to overflow
        if (iterations == Long.MAX_VALUE) {
            long elapsed = System.currentTimeMillis() - startTime;
            iterationsPerSecond =
                    iterations / ((double) (elapsed / 1000));
            System.err.println(
                    "Iteration counter about to overflow ...");
            System.err.println(
                    "Calculating current operations per second ...");
            System.err.println(
                    "Iterations per second: " + iterationsPerSecond);
            iterations = 0L;
            startTime = System.currentTimeMillis();
            runTimeInMillis -= elapsed;
        }
        if (iterations % 1001 == 0) {
            tpr = addNewTaxPayer(tpr);
        } else if (iterations % 60195 == 0) {
            tpr = removeTaxPayer(tpr);
        } else {
            tpr = updateTaxPayer(iterations, tpr);
        }

        if (iterations % 1000 == 0) {
            elapsedTime = System.currentTimeMillis() - startTime;
        }
    } while (elapsedTime < runTimeInMillis);

    if (iterations >= 1000) {
        iterationsPerSecond =
                iterations / ((double) (elapsedTime / 1000));
    }
    BailoutFuture bailoutFuture =
            new BailoutFuture(iterationsPerSecond, newRecordsAdded,
                              recordsRemoved, nullCounter);
    return bailoutFuture;
}

private TaxPayerRecord updateTaxPayer(long iterations,
                                      TaxPayerRecord tpr) {
    if (iterations % 1001 == 0) {
        tpr = db.get(taxPayerId);
    } else {
        // update a TaxPayer's DB record
        tpr = db.get(taxPayerId);
```

Continued

```
            if (tpr != null) {
                long tax = generator.get().nextInt(10) + 15;
                tpr.taxPaid(tax);
            }
        }
        if (tpr == null) {
            nullCounter++;
        }
        return tpr;
    }

    private TaxPayerRecord removeTaxPayer(TaxPayerRecord tpr) {
        // remove a tax payer from DB
        tpr = db.remove(taxPayerId);
        if (tpr != null) {
            // remove record from TaxPayerList
            taxPayerList.remove(index);
            recordsRemoved++;
        }
        return tpr;
    }

    private TaxPayerRecord addNewTaxPayer(TaxPayerRecord tpr) {
        // add a new TaxPayer to the DB
        String tmpTaxPayerId = BailoutMain.getRandomTaxPayerId();
        tpr = BailoutMain.makeTaxPayerRecord();
        TaxPayerRecord old = db.add(tmpTaxPayerId, tpr);
        if (old == null) {
            // add to the (local) list
            taxPayerList.add(tmpTaxPayerId);
            newRecordsAdded++;
        }
        return tpr;
    }

    public void setTaxPayer() {
        if (++index >= taxPayerList.size()) {
            index = 0;
        }
        this.taxPayerId = taxPayerList.get(index);
    }
}
```

BailoutFuture.java

```
public class BailoutFuture {
    private double iterationsPerSecond;
    private long recordsAdded, recordsRemoved, nullCounter;

    public BailoutFuture(double iterationsPerSecond, long recordsAdded,
                        long recordsRemoved, long nullCounter) {
        this.iterationsPerSecond = iterationsPerSecond;
        this.recordsAdded = recordsAdded;
        this.recordsRemoved = recordsRemoved;
        this.nullCounter = nullCounter;
```

```
        }

        public double getIterationsPerSecond() {
            return iterationsPerSecond;
        }

        public long getRecordsAdded() {
            return recordsAdded;
        }

        public long getRecordsRemoved() {
            return recordsRemoved;
        }

        public long getNullCounter() {
            return nullCounter;
        }
    }
```

Lock Contention Fourth Implementation

The fourth implementation replaces the java.util.Random with a ThreadLocal java.util.Random and reverts back to using the synchronized HashMap.

BailoutMain.java

```java
/**
 * An example program to illustrate lock contention.
 */
import java.text.DecimalFormat;
import java.text.NumberFormat;
import java.util.ArrayList;
import java.util.HashSet;
import java.util.List;
import java.util.Random;
import java.util.Set;
import java.util.concurrent.Callable;
import java.util.concurrent.ExecutionException;
import java.util.concurrent.ExecutorService;
import java.util.concurrent.Executors;
import java.util.concurrent.Future;
import java.util.logging.Level;
import java.util.logging.Logger;

public class BailoutMain {
    final public static int TEST_TIME = 240 * 1000;
    final public static ThreadLocal<Random> threadLocalRandom =
            new ThreadLocal<Random>() {
                @Override
                protected Random initialValue() {
                    return new Random(Thread.currentThread().getId());
```

Continued

```
            }
        };
private static char[] alphabet = {'a', 'b', 'c', 'd', 'e', 'f',
    'g', 'h', 'i', 'j', 'k', 'l', 'm', 'n', 'o', 'p', 'q', 'r',
    's', 't', 'u', 'v', 'w', 'x',
    'y', 'z'};
private static String[] states = {"Alabama", "Alaska", "Arizona",
    "Arkansas", "California", "Colorado", "Connecticut",
    "Delaware", "Florida", "Georgia", "Hawaii", "Idaho",
    "Illinois", "Indiana", "Iowa", "Kansas", "Kentucky",
    "Louisiana", "Maine", "Maryland", "Massachusetts", "Michigan",
    "Minnesota", "Mississippi", "Missouri", "Montana", "Nebraska",
    "Nevada", "New Hampshire", "New Jersey", "New Mexico",
    "New York", "North Carolina", "North Dakota", "Ohio",
    "Oklahoma", "Oregon", "Pennsylvania", "Rhode Island",
    "South Carolina", "South Dakota", "Tennessee", "Texas",
    "Utah", "Vermont", "Virginia", "Washington", "West Virginia",
    "Wisconsin", "Wyoming"};

public static void main(String[] args) {
    final int numberOfThreads =
                Runtime.getRuntime().availableProcessors();
    final int dbSize = TaxPayerBailoutDB.NUMBER_OF_RECORDS_DESIRED;
    final int taxPayerListSize = dbSize / numberOfThreads;

    System.out.println("Number of threads to run concurrently : " +
                numberOfThreads);
    System.out.println("Tax payer database size: " + dbSize);

    // populate database with records
    System.out.println("Creating tax payer database ...");
    TaxPayerBailoutDB db = new TaxPayerBailoutDbImpl(dbSize);
    List<String>[] taxPayerList = new ArrayList[numberOfThreads];
    for (int i = 0; i < numberOfThreads; i++) {
        taxPayerList[i] = new ArrayList<String>(taxPayerListSize);
    }
    populateDatabase(db, taxPayerList, dbSize);
    System.out.println("\tTax payer database created.");

    System.out.println("Allocating (" + numberOfThreads +
                ") threads ...");

    // create a pool of executors to execute some Callables
    ExecutorService pool =
        Executors.newFixedThreadPool(numberOfThreads);

    Callable<BailoutFuture>[] callables =
        new TaxCallable[numberOfThreads];
    for (int i = 0; i < callables.length; i++) {
        callables[i] = new TaxCallable(taxPayerList[i], db);
    }

    System.out.println("\tthreads allocated.");

    // start all threads running
    System.out.println("Starting (" + callables.length +
                ") threads ...");
    Set<Future<BailoutFuture>> set =
```

```
                new HashSet<Future<BailoutFuture>>();
    for (int i = 0; i < callables.length; i++) {
        Callable<BailoutFuture> callable = callables[i];
        Future<BailoutFuture> future = pool.submit(callable);
        set.add(future);
    }

    System.out.println("\t(" + callables.length +
                       ") threads started.");
    // block and wait for all Callables to finish their
    System.out.println("Waiting for " + TEST_TIME / 1000 +
                       " seconds for (" + callables.length +
                       ") threads to complete ...");

    double iterationsPerSecond = 0;
    long recordsAdded = 0, recordsRemoved = 0, nullCounter = 0;
    int counter = 1;
    for (Future<BailoutFuture> future : set) {
        BailoutFuture result = null;
        try {
            result = future.get();
        } catch (InterruptedException ex) {
            Logger.getLogger(
                BailoutMain.class.getName()).log(
                    Level.SEVERE, null, ex);
        } catch (ExecutionException ex) {
            Logger.getLogger(
                BailoutMain.class.getName()).log(
                    Level.SEVERE, null, ex);
        }
        System.out.println("Iterations per second on thread[" +
                           counter++ + "] -> " +
                           result.getIterationsPerSecond());
        iterationsPerSecond += result.getIterationsPerSecond();
        recordsAdded += result.getRecordsAdded();
        recordsRemoved += result.getRecordsRemoved();
        nullCounter = result.getNullCounter();
    }

    // print number of totals
    DecimalFormat df = new DecimalFormat("#.##");
    System.out.println("Total iterations per second --> " +
                       df.format(iterationsPerSecond));
    NumberFormat nf = NumberFormat.getInstance();
    System.out.println("Total records added ----------> " +
                       nf.format(recordsAdded));
    System.out.println("Total records removed --------> " +
                       nf.format(recordsRemoved));
    System.out.println("Total records in db ----------> " +
                       nf.format(db.size()));
    System.out.println("Total null records encountered: " +
                       nf.format(nullCounter));

    System.exit(0);
}
```

Continued

```java
public static TaxPayerRecord makeTaxPayerRecord() {
    String firstName = getRandomName();
    String lastName = getRandomName();
    String ssn = getRandomSSN();
    String address = getRandomAddress();
    String city = getRandomCity();
    String state = getRandomState();
    return new TaxPayerRecord(firstName, lastName, ssn,
            address, city, state);
}

private static void populateDatabase(TaxPayerBailoutDB db,
            List<String>[] taxPayerIdList, int dbSize) {
    for (int i = 0; i < dbSize; i++) {
        String key = getRandomTaxPayerId();
        TaxPayerRecord tpr = makeTaxPayerRecord();
        db.add(key, tpr);
        int index = i % taxPayerIdList.length;
        taxPayerIdList[index].add(key);
    }
}

public static String getRandomTaxPayerId() {
    StringBuilder sb = new StringBuilder();
    for (int i = 0; i < 20; i++) {
        int index =
            threadLocalRandom.get().nextInt(alphabet.length);
        sb.append(alphabet[index]);
    }
    return sb.toString();
}

public static String getRandomName() {
    StringBuilder sb = new StringBuilder();
    int size = threadLocalRandom.get().nextInt(8) + 5;
    for (int i = 0; i < size; i++) {
        int index =
            threadLocalRandom.get().nextInt(alphabet.length);
        char c = alphabet[index];
        if (i == 0) {
            c = Character.toUpperCase(c);
        }
        sb.append(c);
    }
    return sb.toString();
}

public static String getRandomSSN() {
    StringBuilder sb = new StringBuilder();
    for (int i = 0; i < 11; i++) {
        if (i == 3 || i == 6) {
            sb.append('-');
        }
        int x = threadLocalRandom.get().nextInt(9);
        sb.append(x);
    }
    return sb.toString();
}
```

```
    public static String getRandomAddress() {
        StringBuilder sb = new StringBuilder();
        int size = threadLocalRandom.get().nextInt(14) + 10;
        for (int i = 0; i < size; i++) {
            if (i < 5) {
                int x = threadLocalRandom.get().nextInt(8);
                sb.append(x + 1);
            }
            int index =
                threadLocalRandom.get().nextInt(alphabet.length);
            char c = alphabet[index];
            if (i == 5) {
                c = Character.toUpperCase(c);
            }
            sb.append(c);
        }
        return sb.toString();
    }

    public static String getRandomCity() {
        StringBuilder sb = new StringBuilder();
        int size = threadLocalRandom.get().nextInt(5) + 6;
        for (int i = 0; i < size; i++) {
            int index =
                threadLocalRandom.get().nextInt(alphabet.length);
            char c = alphabet[index];
            if (i == 0) {
                c = Character.toUpperCase(c);
            }
            sb.append(c);
        }
        return sb.toString();
    }

    public static String getRandomState() {
        int index = threadLocalRandom.get().nextInt(states.length);
        return states[index];
    }
}
```

TaxPayerRecord.java

```
import java.util.concurrent.atomic.AtomicLong;

public class TaxPayerRecord {
    private String firstName, lastName, ssn, address, city, state;
    private AtomicLong taxPaid;

    public TaxPayerRecord(String firstName, String lastName, String ssn,
                          String address, String city, String state) {
        this.firstName = firstName;
        this.lastName = lastName;
        this.ssn = ssn;
```

Continued

```java
        this.address = address;
        this.city = city;
        this.state = state;
        this.taxPaid = new AtomicLong(0);
    }

    public String getFirstName() {
        return firstName;
    }

    public void setFirstName(String firstName) {
        this.firstName = firstName;
    }

    public String getLastName() {
        return lastName;
    }

    public void setLastName(String lastName) {
        this.lastName = lastName;
    }

    public String getSsn() {
        return ssn;
    }

    public void setSsn(String ssn) {
        this.ssn = ssn;
    }

    public String getAddress() {
        return address;
    }

    public void setAddress(String address) {
        this.address = address;
    }

    public String getCity() {
        return city;
    }

    public void setCity(String city) {
        this.city = city;
    }

    public String getState() {
        return state;
    }

    public void setState(String state) {
        this.state = state;
    }

    public void taxPaid(long amount) {
        taxPaid.addAndGet(amount);
    }
```

```
        public long getTaxPaid() {
            return taxPaid.get();
        }
    }
```

TaxPayerBailoutDB.java

```
public interface TaxPayerBailoutDB {

    static final int NUMBER_OF_RECORDS_DESIRED = 2 * 1000000;

    /**
     * Get a tax payers record from the database based on his or her id.
     *
     * @param id - tax payers id
     * @return tax payers record
     */
    TaxPayerRecord get(String id);

    /**
     * Add new tax payers record in the database.
     *
     * @param id - tax payer's id
     * @param record - tax payer's record
     * @return taxPayersRecord just added to the database
     */
    TaxPayerRecord add(String id,  TaxPayerRecord record);

    /**
     * Remove a tax payer's record from the database.
     *
     * @param id - tax payer's id
     * @return tax payers record, or null if id not found in database
     */
    TaxPayerRecord remove(String id);

    /**
     * Size of the database, i.e. number of records
     *
     * @return number of records in the database
     */
    int size();
}
```

TaxPayerBailoutDbImpl.java

```
import java.util.Collections;
import java.util.HashMap;
import java.util.Map;

public class TaxPayerBailoutDbImpl implements TaxPayerBailoutDB {
    private final Map<String,TaxPayerRecord> db;
```

Continued

```
    public TaxPayerBailoutDbImpl(int size) {
        db = Collections.synchronizedMap(
                new HashMap<String,TaxPayerRecord>(size));
    }

    @Override
    public TaxPayerRecord get(String id) {
        return db.get(id);
    }

    @Override
    public TaxPayerRecord add(String id, TaxPayerRecord record) {
        TaxPayerRecord old = db.put(id, record);
        if (old != null) {
            // restore old TaxPayerRecord
            old = db.put(id, old);
        }
        return old;
    }

    @Override
    public TaxPayerRecord remove(String id) {
        return db.remove(id);
    }

    @Override
    public int size() {
        return db.size();
    }
}
```

TaxCallable.java

```
import java.util.List;
import java.util.Random;
import java.util.concurrent.Callable;

public class TaxCallable implements Callable<BailoutFuture> {

    private static long runTimeInMillis = BailoutMain.TEST_TIME;
    final private static ThreadLocal<Random> generator =
                                    BailoutMain.threadLocalRandom;
    private long nullCounter, recordsRemoved, newRecordsAdded;
    private int index;
    private String taxPayerId;
    final private List<String> taxPayerList;
    final private TaxPayerBailoutDB db;

    public TaxCallable(List<String> taxPayerList,
                    TaxPayerBailoutDB db) {
        this.taxPayerList = taxPayerList;
        this.db = db;
        index = 0;
```

```
    }

    @Override
    public BailoutFuture call() throws Exception {
        long iterations = 0L, elapsedTime = 0L;
        long startTime = System.currentTimeMillis();
        double iterationsPerSecond = 0;
        do {
            setTaxPayer();
            iterations++;
            TaxPayerRecord tpr = null;
            // Just in case there 'iterations' is about to overflow
            if (iterations == Long.MAX_VALUE) {
                long elapsed = System.currentTimeMillis() - startTime;
                iterationsPerSecond =
                        iterations / ((double) (elapsed / 1000));
                System.err.println(
                        "Iteration counter about to overflow ...");
                System.err.println(
                        "Calculating current operations per second ...");
                System.err.println(
                        "Iterations per second: " + iterationsPerSecond);
                iterations = 0L;
                startTime = System.currentTimeMillis();
                runTimeInMillis -= elapsed;
            }
            if (iterations % 1001 == 0) {
                tpr = addNewTaxPayer(tpr);
            } else if (iterations % 60195 == 0) {
                tpr = removeTaxPayer(tpr);
            } else {
                tpr = updateTaxPayer(iterations, tpr);
            }

            if (iterations % 1000 == 0) {
                elapsedTime = System.currentTimeMillis() - startTime;
            }
        } while (elapsedTime < runTimeInMillis);

        if (iterations >= 1000) {
            iterationsPerSecond =
                    iterations / ((double) (elapsedTime / 1000));
        }
        BailoutFuture bailoutFuture =
                new BailoutFuture(iterationsPerSecond, newRecordsAdded,
                                  recordsRemoved, nullCounter);
        return bailoutFuture;
    }

    private TaxPayerRecord updateTaxPayer(long iterations,
                                          TaxPayerRecord tpr) {
        if (iterations % 1001 == 0) {
            tpr = db.get(taxPayerId);
        } else {
            // update a TaxPayer's DB record
            tpr = db.get(taxPayerId);
```

Continued

```
                if (tpr != null) {
                    long tax = generator.get().nextInt(10) + 15;
                    tpr.taxPaid(tax);
                }
            }
            if (tpr == null) {
                nullCounter++;
            }
            return tpr;
        }

        private TaxPayerRecord removeTaxPayer(TaxPayerRecord tpr) {
            // remove a tax payer from DB
            tpr = db.remove(taxPayerId);
            if (tpr != null) {
                // remove record from TaxPayerList
                taxPayerList.remove(index);
                recordsRemoved++;
            }
            return tpr;
        }

        private TaxPayerRecord addNewTaxPayer(TaxPayerRecord tpr) {
            // add a new TaxPayer to the DB
            String tmpTaxPayerId = BailoutMain.getRandomTaxPayerId();
            tpr = BailoutMain.makeTaxPayerRecord();
            TaxPayerRecord old = db.add(tmpTaxPayerId, tpr);
            if (old == null) {
                // add to the (local) list
                taxPayerList.add(tmpTaxPayerId);
                newRecordsAdded++;
            }
            return tpr;
        }

        public void setTaxPayer() {
            if (++index >= taxPayerList.size()) {
                index = 0;
            }
            this.taxPayerId = taxPayerList.get(index);
        }
    }
}
```

BailoutFuture.java

```
public class BailoutFuture {
    private double iterationsPerSecond;
    private long recordsAdded, recordsRemoved, nullCounter;

    public BailoutFuture(double iterationsPerSecond, long recordsAdded,
                         long recordsRemoved, long nullCounter) {
        this.iterationsPerSecond = iterationsPerSecond;
        this.recordsAdded = recordsAdded;
        this.recordsRemoved = recordsRemoved;
        this.nullCounter = nullCounter;
```

```
    }

    public double getIterationsPerSecond() {
        return iterationsPerSecond;
    }

    public long getRecordsAdded() {
        return recordsAdded;
    }

    public long getRecordsRemoved() {
        return recordsRemoved;
    }

    public long getNullCounter() {
        return nullCounter;
    }
}
```

Lock Contention Fifth Implementation

The fifth implementation partitions the taxpayer database into 50 HashMaps, one for each state, and also uses the ThreadLocal Random.

BailoutMain.java

```java
/**
 * An example program to illustrate lock contention for Java Performance
book.
 */
import java.text.DecimalFormat;
import java.text.NumberFormat;
import java.util.ArrayList;
import java.util.HashSet;
import java.util.List;
import java.util.Random;
import java.util.Set;
import java.util.concurrent.Callable;
import java.util.concurrent.ExecutionException;
import java.util.concurrent.ExecutorService;
import java.util.concurrent.Executors;
import java.util.concurrent.Future;
import java.util.logging.Level;
import java.util.logging.Logger;

public class BailoutMain {

    final public static int TEST_TIME = 240 * 1000;
    final public static ThreadLocal<Random> threadLocalRandom =
            new ThreadLocal<Random>() {
                @Override
```

Continued

```
                protected Random initialValue() {
                    return new Random(Thread.currentThread().getId());
                }
        };
    private static char[] alphabet = {'a', 'b', 'c', 'd', 'e', 'f',
                                      'g', 'h', 'i', 'j', 'k', 'l',
                                      'm', 'n', 'o', 'p', 'q', 'r',
                                      's', 't', 'u', 'v', 'w', 'x',
                                      'y', 'z'};
    static String[] states = {"Alabama", "Alaska", "Arizona",
        "Arkansas", "California", "Colorado", "Connecticut",
        "Delaware", "Florida", "Georgia", "Hawaii", "Idaho",
        "Illinois", "Indiana", "Iowa", "Kansas", "Kentucky",
        "Louisiana", "Maine", "Maryland", "Massachusetts", "Michigan",
        "Minnesota", "Mississippi", "Missouri", "Montana", "Nebraska",
        "Nevada", "New Hampshire", "New Jersey", "New Mexico",
        "New York", "North Carolina", "North Dakota", "Ohio",
        "Oklahoma", "Oregon", "Pennsylvania", "Rhode Island",
        "South Carolina", "South Dakota", "Tennessee", "Texas",
        "Utah", "Vermont", "Virginia", "Washington", "West Virginia",
        "Wisconsin", "Wyoming"};

    public static void main(String[] args) {
        final int numberOfThreads =
                Runtime.getRuntime().availableProcessors();
        final int dbSize =
                TaxPayerBailoutDB.NUMBER_OF_RECORDS_DESIRED;
        final int taxPayerListSize = dbSize / numberOfThreads;

        System.out.println("Number of threads to run concurrently : " +
                        numberOfThreads);
        System.out.println("Tax payer database size: " + dbSize);

        // populate database with records
        System.out.println("Creating tax payer database ...");
        TaxPayerBailoutDB db =
                new TaxPayerBailoutDbImpl(dbSize, states.length);
        List<StateAndId>[] taxPayerList =
                new ArrayList[numberOfThreads];
        for (int i = 0; i < numberOfThreads; i++) {
            taxPayerList[i] =
                    new ArrayList<StateAndId>(taxPayerListSize);
        }
        populateDatabase(db, taxPayerList, dbSize);
        System.out.println("\tTax payer database created.");

        System.out.println("Allocating (" + numberOfThreads +
                        ") threads ...");
        // create a pool of executors to execute some Callables
        ExecutorService pool =
                Executors.newFixedThreadPool(numberOfThreads);

        Callable<BailoutFuture>[] callables =
                new TaxCallable[numberOfThreads];
        for (int i = 0; i < callables.length; i++) {
            callables[i] = new TaxCallable(taxPayerList[i], db);
        }
```

```
System.out.println("\tthreads allocated.");

// start all threads running
System.out.println("Starting (" + callables.length +
                    ") threads ...");
Set<Future<BailoutFuture>> set =
        new HashSet<Future<BailoutFuture>>();
for (int i = 0; i < callables.length; i++) {
    Callable<BailoutFuture> callable = callables[i];
    Future<BailoutFuture> future = pool.submit(callable);
    set.add(future);
}

System.out.println("\t(" + callables.length +
                    ") threads started.");
// block and wait for all Callables to finish their
System.out.println("Waiting for " + TEST_TIME / 1000 +
                    " seconds for (" + callables.length +
                    ") threads to complete ...");

double iterationsPerSecond = 0;
long recordsAdded = 0, recordsRemoved = 0, nullCounter = 0;
int counter = 1;
for (Future<BailoutFuture> future : set) {
    BailoutFuture result = null;
    try {
        result = future.get();
    } catch (InterruptedException ex) {
        Logger.getLogger(
            BailoutMain.class.getName()).log(
                        Level.SEVERE, null, ex);
    } catch (ExecutionException ex) {
        Logger.getLogger(
            BailoutMain.class.getName()).log(
                        Level.SEVERE, null, ex);
    }
    System.out.println("Iterations per second on thread[" +
                    counter++ + "] -> " +
                    result.getIterationsPerSecond());
    iterationsPerSecond += result.getIterationsPerSecond();
    recordsAdded += result.getRecordsAdded();
    recordsRemoved += result.getRecordsRemoved();
    nullCounter = result.getNullCounter();
}

// print number of totals
DecimalFormat df = new DecimalFormat("#.##");
System.out.println("Total iterations per second --> " +
                    df.format(iterationsPerSecond));
NumberFormat nf = NumberFormat.getInstance();
System.out.println("Total records added ----------> " +
                    nf.format(recordsAdded));
System.out.println("Total records removed --------> " +
                    nf.format(recordsRemoved));
```

Continued

```java
        System.out.println("Total records in db ----------> " +
                        nf.format(db.size()));
        System.out.println("Total null records encountered: " +
                        nf.format(nullCounter));

        System.exit(0);
    }

    public static TaxPayerRecord makeTaxPayerRecord() {
        String firstName = getRandomName();
        String lastName = getRandomName();
        String ssn = getRandomSSN();
        String address = getRandomAddress();
        String city = getRandomCity();
        String state = getRandomState();
        return new TaxPayerRecord(firstName, lastName, ssn,
                address, city, state);
    }

    private static void populateDatabase(TaxPayerBailoutDB db,
                            List<StateAndId>[] taxPayerList,
                                        int dbSize) {
        for (int i = 0; i < dbSize; i++) {
            String taxPayerId = getRandomTaxPayerId();
            TaxPayerRecord tpr = makeTaxPayerRecord();
            db.add(taxPayerId, tpr);
            StateAndId stateAndId =
                    new StateAndId(taxPayerId, tpr.getState());
            int index = i % taxPayerList.length;
            taxPayerList[index].add(stateAndId);
        }
    }

    public static String getRandomTaxPayerId() {
        StringBuilder sb = new StringBuilder();
        for (int i = 0; i < 20; i++) {
            int index =
                threadLocalRandom.get().nextInt(alphabet.length);
            sb.append(alphabet[index]);
        }
        return sb.toString();
    }

    public static String getRandomName() {
        StringBuilder sb = new StringBuilder();
        int size = threadLocalRandom.get().nextInt(8) + 5;
        for (int i = 0; i < size; i++) {
            int index =
                threadLocalRandom.get().nextInt(alphabet.length);
            char c = alphabet[index];
            if (i == 0) {
                c = Character.toUpperCase(c);
            }
            sb.append(c);
        }
        return sb.toString();
```

```
    }

    public static String getRandomSSN() {
        StringBuilder sb = new StringBuilder();
        for (int i = 0; i < 11; i++) {
            if (i == 3 || i == 6) {
                sb.append('-');
            }
            int x = threadLocalRandom.get().nextInt(9);
            sb.append(x);
        }
        return sb.toString();
    }

    public static String getRandomAddress() {
        StringBuilder sb = new StringBuilder();
        int size = threadLocalRandom.get().nextInt(14) + 10;
        for (int i = 0; i < size; i++) {
            if (i < 5) {
                int x = threadLocalRandom.get().nextInt(8);
                sb.append(x + 1);
            }
            int index =
                threadLocalRandom.get().nextInt(alphabet.length);
            char c = alphabet[index];
            if (i == 5) {
                c = Character.toUpperCase(c);
            }
            sb.append(c);
        }
        return sb.toString();
    }

    public static String getRandomCity() {
        StringBuilder sb = new StringBuilder();
        int size = threadLocalRandom.get().nextInt(5) + 6;
        for (int i = 0; i < size; i++) {
            int index =
                threadLocalRandom.get().nextInt(alphabet.length);
            char c = alphabet[index];
            if (i == 0) {
                c = Character.toUpperCase(c);
            }
            sb.append(c);
        }
        return sb.toString();
    }

    public static String getRandomState() {
        int index = threadLocalRandom.get().nextInt(states.length);
        return states[index];
    }
}
```

Continued

TaxPayerRecord.java

```java
import java.util.concurrent.atomic.AtomicLong;

public class TaxPayerRecord {
    private String firstName, lastName, ssn, address, city, state;
    private AtomicLong taxPaid;

    public TaxPayerRecord(String firstName, String lastName, String ssn,
                          String address, String city, String state) {
        this.firstName = firstName;
        this.lastName = lastName;
        this.ssn = ssn;
        this.address = address;
        this.city = city;
        this.state = state;
        this.taxPaid = new AtomicLong(0);
    }

    public String getFirstName() {
        return firstName;
    }

    public void setFirstName(String firstName) {
        this.firstName = firstName;
    }

    public String getLastName() {
        return lastName;
    }

    public void setLastName(String lastName) {
        this.lastName = lastName;
    }

    public String getSsn() {
        return ssn;
    }

    public void setSsn(String ssn) {
        this.ssn = ssn;
    }

    public String getAddress() {
        return address;
    }

    public void setAddress(String address) {
        this.address = address;
    }

    public String getCity() {
        return city;
    }

    public void setCity(String city) {
        this.city = city;
    }

    public String getState() {
```

```
            return state;
    }

    public void setState(String state) {
        this.state = state;
    }

    public void taxPaid(long amount) {
        taxPaid.addAndGet(amount);
    }

    public long getTaxPaid() {
        return taxPaid.get();
    }
}
```

TaxPayerBailoutDB.java

```java
public interface TaxPayerBailoutDB {

    static final int NUMBER_OF_RECORDS_DESIRED = 2 * 1000000;

    /**
     * Get a tax payers record from the database based on his or her id.
     *
     * @param taxPayersId - tax payers id
     * @param state - tax payers home state
     * @return tax payers record
     */
    TaxPayerRecord get(String id, String state);

    /**
     * Add new tax payers record in the database.
     *
     * @param id - tax payer's id
     * @param record - tax payer's record
     * @return taxPayersRecord just added to the database
     */
    TaxPayerRecord add(String id, TaxPayerRecord record);

    /**
     * Remove a tax payer's record from the database.
     *
     * @param taxPayersId - tax payer's id
     * @param taxPayersState - tax payer's state
     * @return tax payers record, or null if id not found in database
     */
    TaxPayerRecord remove(String id, String state);

    /**
     * Size of the database, i.e. number of records
     *
     * @return number of records in the database
     */
    int size();
}
```

Continued

TaxPayerBailoutDbImpl.java

```java
import java.util.Collections;
import java.util.HashMap;
import java.util.Iterator;
import java.util.Map;

public class TaxPayerBailoutDbImpl implements TaxPayerBailoutDB {
    private final Map<String, Map<String,TaxPayerRecord>> db;

    public TaxPayerBailoutDbImpl(int dbSize, int numberOfStates) {
        db = new HashMap<String,Map<String,TaxPayerRecord>>(dbSize);
        for (int i = 0; i < numberOfStates; i++) {
            Map<String,TaxPayerRecord> map =
                    Collections.synchronizedMap(
                        new HashMap<String,TaxPayerRecord>(
                            dbSize/numberOfStates));
            db.put(BailoutMain.states[i], map);
        }
    }

    @Override
    public TaxPayerRecord get(String id, String state) {
        Map<String,TaxPayerRecord> map = getStateMap(state);
        if (map == null) {
            System.out.println("Unable to find state: " + state);
        }
        return map.get(id);
    }

    @Override
    public TaxPayerRecord add(String id, TaxPayerRecord record) {
        Map<String,TaxPayerRecord> map = getStateMap(record.getState());
        // Update tax payer's record if found
        TaxPayerRecord old = map.put(id, record);
        if (old != null) {
            // not found, restore old TaxPayerRecord
            old = map.put(id, old);
        }
        return old;
    }

    @Override
    public TaxPayerRecord remove(String id, String state) {
        Map<String,TaxPayerRecord> map = getStateMap(state);
        TaxPayerRecord tmpRecord = null;
        if (map != null)
            tmpRecord = map.remove(id);
        return tmpRecord;
    }

    @Override
    public int size() {
        int size = 0;
        Iterator<Map<String,TaxPayerRecord>> itr =
                            db.values().iterator();
        while (itr.hasNext()) {
            Map<String,TaxPayerRecord> m = itr.next();
```

```
            if (m != null)
                size += m.size();
        }
        return size;
    }

    private Map<String, TaxPayerRecord> getStateMap(String state) {
        Map<String,TaxPayerRecord> map = db.get(state);
        if (map == null) {
            throw new UnsupportedOperationException(
                    "State (" + state + ") " +
                    "not found in tax payer database.");
        }
        return map;
    }
}
```

TaxCallable.java

```
import java.util.List;
import java.util.Random;
import java.util.concurrent.Callable;

public class TaxCallable implements Callable<BailoutFuture> {

    private static long runTimeInMillis = BailoutMain.TEST_TIME;
    final private static ThreadLocal<Random> generator =
                                    BailoutMain.threadLocalRandom;
    private long nullCounter, recordsRemoved, newRecordsAdded;
    private int index;
    private StateAndId stateAndId;
    final private List<StateAndId> taxPayerList;
    final private TaxPayerBailoutDB db;

    public TaxCallable(List<StateAndId> taxPayerList,
                    TaxPayerBailoutDB db) {
        this.taxPayerList = taxPayerList;
        this.db = db;
        index = 0;
    }

    @Override
    public BailoutFuture call() throws Exception {
        long iterations = 0L, elapsedTime = 0L;
        long startTime = System.currentTimeMillis();
        double iterationsPerSecond = 0;
        do {
            setTaxPayer();
            iterations++;
            TaxPayerRecord tpr = null;
            if (iterations == Long.MAX_VALUE) {
                long elapsed = System.currentTimeMillis() - startTime;
                iterationsPerSecond =
                        iterations / ((double) (elapsed / 1000));
```

Continued

```java
                System.err.
                    println("Iteration counter about to overflow ...");
                System.err.println(
                    "Calculating current operations per second ...");
                System.err.println("Iterations per second: " +
                                    iterationsPerSecond);
                iterations = 0L;
                startTime = System.currentTimeMillis();
                runTimeInMillis -= elapsed;
            }
            if (iterations % 1001 == 0) {
                tpr = addNewTaxPayer(tpr);
            } else if (iterations % 60195 == 0) {
                tpr = removeTaxPayer(tpr);
            } else {
                tpr = updateTaxPayer(iterations, tpr);
            }

            if (iterations % 1000 == 0) {
                elapsedTime = System.currentTimeMillis() - startTime;
            }
        } while (elapsedTime < runTimeInMillis);

        if (iterations >= 1000) {
            iterationsPerSecond =
                    iterations / ((double) (elapsedTime / 1000));
        }
        BailoutFuture bailoutFuture =
                new BailoutFuture(iterationsPerSecond, newRecordsAdded,
                                recordsRemoved, nullCounter);
        return bailoutFuture;
    }

    private TaxPayerRecord updateTaxPayer(long iterations,
                                        TaxPayerRecord tpr) {
        if (iterations % 1001 == 0) {
            tpr = db.get(stateAndId.getId(), stateAndId.getState());
        } else {
            // update a TaxPayer's DB record
            tpr = db.get(stateAndId.getId(), stateAndId.getState());
            if (tpr != null) {
                long tax = generator.get().nextInt(10) + 15;
                tpr.taxPaid(tax);
            }
        }
        if (tpr == null) {
            nullCounter++;
        }
        return tpr;
    }

    private TaxPayerRecord removeTaxPayer(TaxPayerRecord tpr) {
        // remove a TaxPayer from DB
        tpr = db.remove(stateAndId.getId(), stateAndId.getState());
        if (tpr != null) {
            // remove record from TaxPayerList
            taxPayerList.remove(index);
            recordsRemoved++;
        }
```

```
            return tpr;
        }

        private TaxPayerRecord addNewTaxPayer(TaxPayerRecord tpr) {
            // add a new TaxPayer to the DB
            String tmpTaxPayerId = BailoutMain.getRandomTaxPayerId();
            tpr = BailoutMain.makeTaxPayerRecord();
            TaxPayerRecord old = db.add(tmpTaxPayerId, tpr);
            if (old == null) {
                // add to the (local) list
                StateAndId sai =
                        new StateAndId(tmpTaxPayerId, tpr.getState());
                taxPayerList.add(sai);
                newRecordsAdded++;
            }
            return tpr;
        }

        private void setTaxPayer() {
            if (++index >= taxPayerList.size()) {
                index = 0;
            }
            this.stateAndId = taxPayerList.get(index);
        }
    }
}
```

BailoutFuture.java

```
public class BailoutFuture {
    private double iterationsPerSecond;
    private long recordsAdded, recordsRemoved, nullCounter;

    public BailoutFuture(double iterationsPerSecond, long recordsAdded,
                         long recordsRemoved, long nullCounter) {
        this.iterationsPerSecond = iterationsPerSecond;
        this.recordsAdded = recordsAdded;
        this.recordsRemoved = recordsRemoved;
        this.nullCounter = nullCounter;
    }

    public double getIterationsPerSecond() {
        return iterationsPerSecond;
    }

    public long getRecordsAdded() {
        return recordsAdded;
    }

    public long getRecordsRemoved() {
        return recordsRemoved;
    }

    public long getNullCounter() {
        return nullCounter;
    }
}
```

StateAndId.java

```java
final public class StateAndId {
    private String id;
    private String state;

    public StateAndId(String id, String state) {
        this.id = id; this.state = state;
    }

    public String getState() {
        return state;
    }

    public void setState(String state) {
        this.state = state;
    }

    public String getId() {
        return id;
    }

     public void setId(String id) {
        this.id = id;
    }
}
```

First Resizing Variant

This implementation is a slightly modified implementation of the previous "Fifth Implementation," which partitions the taxpayer database into 50 HashMaps, one for each state, and also uses the ThreadLocal Random and adds the calculating and reporting of the time it takes to allocate and create 2,000,000 records using the HashMap constructor using the default HashMap size.

BailoutMain.java

```java
/**
 * An example program to illustrate lock contention for Java Performance
book.
 */
import java.text.DecimalFormat;
import java.text.NumberFormat;
import java.util.ArrayList;
import java.util.HashSet;
import java.util.List;
import java.util.Random;
import java.util.Set;
import java.util.concurrent.Callable;
import java.util.concurrent.ExecutionException;
import java.util.concurrent.ExecutorService;
import java.util.concurrent.Executors;
```

```
import java.util.concurrent.Future;
import java.util.logging.Level;
import java.util.logging.Logger;

public class BailoutMain {

    final public static int TEST_TIME = 240 * 1000;
    final public static ThreadLocal<Random> threadLocalRandom =
            new ThreadLocal<Random>() {
                @Override
                protected Random initialValue() {
                    return new Random(Thread.currentThread().getId());
                }
            };
    private static char[] alphabet = {'a', 'b', 'c', 'd', 'e', 'f',
                                      'g', 'h', 'i', 'j', 'k', 'l',
                                      'm', 'n', 'o', 'p', 'q', 'r',
                                      's', 't', 'u', 'v', 'w', 'x',
                                      'y', 'z'};
    static String[] states = {"Alabama", "Alaska", "Arizona",
        "Arkansas", "California", "Colorado", "Connecticut",
        "Delaware", "Florida", "Georgia", "Hawaii", "Idaho",
        "Illinois", "Indiana", "Iowa", "Kansas", "Kentucky",
        "Louisiana", "Maine", "Maryland", "Massachusetts", "Michigan",
        "Minnesota", "Mississippi", "Missouri", "Montana", "Nebraska",
        "Nevada", "New Hampshire", "New Jersey", "New Mexico",
        "New York", "North Carolina", "North Dakota", "Ohio",
        "Oklahoma", "Oregon", "Pennsylvania", "Rhode Island",
        "South Carolina", "South Dakota", "Tennessee", "Texas",
        "Utah", "Vermont", "Virginia", "Washington", "West Virginia",
        "Wisconsin", "Wyoming"};

    public static void main(String[] args) {
        final long start = System.nanoTime();
        final int numberOfThreads =
                Runtime.getRuntime().availableProcessors();
        final int dbSize =
                TaxPayerBailoutDB.NUMBER_OF_RECORDS_DESIRED;
        final int taxPayerListSize = dbSize / numberOfThreads;

        System.out.println("Number of threads to run concurrently : " +
                    numberOfThreads);
        System.out.println("Tax payer database size: " + dbSize);

        // populate database with records
        System.out.println("Creating tax payer database ...");
        TaxPayerBailoutDB db =
                new TaxPayerBailoutDbImpl(dbSize, states.length);
        List<StateAndId>[] taxPayerList =
                new ArrayList[numberOfThreads];
        for (int i = 0; i < numberOfThreads; i++) {
            taxPayerList[i] =
                    new ArrayList<StateAndId>(taxPayerListSize);
        }
        populateDatabase(db, taxPayerList, dbSize);
        final long initDbTime = System.nanoTime() - start;
```

Continued

```java
System.out.println("\tTax payer database created & populated" +
                " in (" + initDbTime/(1000*1000) + ") ms.");

System.out.println("Allocating (" + numberOfThreads +
                ") threads ...");
// create a pool of executors to execute some Callables
ExecutorService pool =
        Executors.newFixedThreadPool(numberOfThreads);

Callable<BailoutFuture>[] callables =
        new TaxCallable[numberOfThreads];
for (int i = 0; i < callables.length; i++) {
    callables[i] = new TaxCallable(taxPayerList[i], db);
}

System.out.println("\tthreads allocated.");

// start all threads running
System.out.println("Starting (" + callables.length +
                ") threads ...");
Set<Future<BailoutFuture>> set =
        new HashSet<Future<BailoutFuture>>();
for (int i = 0; i < callables.length; i++) {
    Callable<BailoutFuture> callable = callables[i];
    Future<BailoutFuture> future = pool.submit(callable);
    set.add(future);
}

System.out.println("\t(" + callables.length +
                ") threads started.");
// block and wait for all Callables to finish their
System.out.println("Waiting for " + TEST_TIME / 1000 +
                " seconds for (" + callables.length +
                ") threads to complete ...");

double iterationsPerSecond = 0;
long recordsAdded = 0, recordsRemoved = 0, nullCounter = 0;
int counter = 1;
for (Future<BailoutFuture> future : set) {
    BailoutFuture result = null;
    try {
        result = future.get();
    } catch (InterruptedException ex) {
        Logger.getLogger(
            BailoutMain.class.getName()).log(
                        Level.SEVERE, null, ex);
    } catch (ExecutionException ex) {
        Logger.getLogger(
            BailoutMain.class.getName()).log(
                        Level.SEVERE, null, ex);
    }
    System.out.println("Iterations per second on thread[" +
                    counter++ + "] -> " +
                    result.getIterationsPerSecond());
    iterationsPerSecond += result.getIterationsPerSecond();
    recordsAdded += result.getRecordsAdded();
    recordsRemoved += result.getRecordsRemoved();
```

```
                    nullCounter = result.getNullCounter();
            }

            // print number of totals
            DecimalFormat df = new DecimalFormat("#.##");
            System.out.println("Total iterations per second --> " +
                            df.format(iterationsPerSecond));
            NumberFormat nf = NumberFormat.getInstance();
            System.out.println("Total records added ----------> " +
                            nf.format(recordsAdded));
            System.out.println("Total records removed --------> " +
                            nf.format(recordsRemoved));
            System.out.println("Total records in db ----------> " +
                            nf.format(db.size()));
            System.out.println("Total null records encountered: " +
                            nf.format(nullCounter));

            System.exit(0);
    }

    public static TaxPayerRecord makeTaxPayerRecord() {
        String firstName = getRandomName();
        String lastName = getRandomName();
        String ssn = getRandomSSN();
        String address = getRandomAddress();
        String city = getRandomCity();
        String state = getRandomState();
        return new TaxPayerRecord(firstName, lastName, ssn,
                address, city, state);
    }

    private static void populateDatabase(TaxPayerBailoutDB db,
                            List<StateAndId>[] taxPayerList,
                                        int dbSize) {
        for (int i = 0; i < dbSize; i++) {
            String taxPayerId = getRandomTaxPayerId();
            TaxPayerRecord tpr = makeTaxPayerRecord();
            db.add(taxPayerId, tpr);
            StateAndId stateAndId =
                    new StateAndId(taxPayerId, tpr.getState());
            int index = i % taxPayerList.length;
            taxPayerList[index].add(stateAndId);
        }
    }

    public static String getRandomTaxPayerId() {
        StringBuilder sb = new StringBuilder();
        for (int i = 0; i < 20; i++) {
            int index =
                threadLocalRandom.get().nextInt(alphabet.length);
            sb.append(alphabet[index]);
        }
        return sb.toString();
    }

    public static String getRandomName() {
```

Continued

```java
            StringBuilder sb = new StringBuilder();
            int size = threadLocalRandom.get().nextInt(8) + 5;
            for (int i = 0; i < size; i++) {
                int index =
                    threadLocalRandom.get().nextInt(alphabet.length);
                char c = alphabet[index];
                if (i == 0) {
                    c = Character.toUpperCase(c);
                }
                sb.append(c);
            }
            return sb.toString();
    }

    public static String getRandomSSN() {
            StringBuilder sb = new StringBuilder();
            for (int i = 0; i < 11; i++) {
                if (i == 3 || i == 6) {
                    sb.append('-');
                }
                int x = threadLocalRandom.get().nextInt(9);
                sb.append(x);
            }
            return sb.toString();
    }

    public static String getRandomAddress() {
            StringBuilder sb = new StringBuilder();
            int size = threadLocalRandom.get().nextInt(14) + 10;
            for (int i = 0; i < size; i++) {
                if (i < 5) {
                    int x = threadLocalRandom.get().nextInt(8);
                    sb.append(x + 1);
                }
                int index =
                    threadLocalRandom.get().nextInt(alphabet.length);
                char c = alphabet[index];
                if (i == 5) {
                    c = Character.toUpperCase(c);
                }
                sb.append(c);
            }
            return sb.toString();
    }

    public static String getRandomCity() {
            StringBuilder sb = new StringBuilder();
            int size = threadLocalRandom.get().nextInt(5) + 6;
            for (int i = 0; i < size; i++) {
                int index =
                    threadLocalRandom.get().nextInt(alphabet.length);
                char c = alphabet[index];
                if (i == 0) {
                    c = Character.toUpperCase(c);
                }
                sb.append(c);
            }
    }
```

```
            return sb.toString();
        }

    public static String getRandomState() {
        int index = threadLocalRandom.get().nextInt(states.length);
        return states[index];
    }
}
```

TaxPayerRecord.java

```java
import java.util.concurrent.atomic.AtomicLong;

public class TaxPayerRecord {
    private String firstName, lastName, ssn, address, city, state;
    private AtomicLong taxPaid;

    public TaxPayerRecord(String firstName, String lastName, String ssn,
                          String address, String city, String state) {
        this.firstName = firstName;
        this.lastName = lastName;
        this.ssn = ssn;
        this.address = address;
        this.city = city;
        this.state = state;
        this.taxPaid = new AtomicLong(0);
    }

    public String getFirstName() {
        return firstName;
    }

    public void setFirstName(String firstName) {
        this.firstName = firstName;
    }

    public String getLastName() {
        return lastName;
    }

    public void setLastName(String lastName) {
        this.lastName = lastName;
    }

    public String getSsn() {
        return ssn;
    }

    public void setSsn(String ssn) {
        this.ssn = ssn;
    }

    public String getAddress() {
        return address;
```

Continued

```
        }

        public void setAddress(String address) {
            this.address = address;
        }

        public String getCity() {
            return city;
        }

        public void setCity(String city) {
            this.city = city;
        }

        public String getState() {
            return state;
        }

        public void setState(String state) {
            this.state = state;
        }

        public void taxPaid(long amount) {
            taxPaid.addAndGet(amount);
        }

        public long getTaxPaid() {
            return taxPaid.get();
        }
    }
```

TaxPayerBailoutDB.java

```java
public interface TaxPayerBailoutDB {

    static final int NUMBER_OF_RECORDS_DESIRED = 2 * 1000000;

    /**
     * Get a tax payers record from the database based on his or her id.
     *
     * @param taxPayersId - tax payers id
     * @param state - tax payers home state
     * @return tax payers record
     */
    TaxPayerRecord get(String id, String state);

    /**
     * Add new tax payers record in the database.
     *
     * @param id - tax payer's id
     * @param record - tax payer's record
     * @return taxPayersRecord just added to the database
     */
    TaxPayerRecord add(String id,  TaxPayerRecord record);
```

```
    /**
     * Remove a tax payer's record from the database.
     *
     * @param taxPayersId - tax payer's id
     * @param taxPayersState - tax payer's state
     * @return tax payers record, or null if id not found in database
     */
    TaxPayerRecord remove(String id, String state);

    /**
     * Size of the database, i.e. number of records
     *
     * @return number of records in the database
     */
    int size();
}
```

TaxPayerBailoutDbImpl.java

```java
import java.util.Collections;
import java.util.HashMap;
import java.util.Iterator;
import java.util.Map;

public class TaxPayerBailoutDbImpl implements TaxPayerBailoutDB {
    private final Map<String, Map<String,TaxPayerRecord>> db;

    public TaxPayerBailoutDbImpl(int dbSize, int numberOfStates) {
        db = new HashMap<String,Map<String,TaxPayerRecord>>(dbSize);
        for (int i = 0; i < numberOfStates; i++) {
            Map<String,TaxPayerRecord> map =
                    Collections.synchronizedMap(
                        new HashMap<String,TaxPayerRecord>(
                            dbSize/numberOfStates));
            db.put(BailoutMain.states[i], map);
        }
    }

    @Override
    public TaxPayerRecord get(String id, String state) {
        Map<String,TaxPayerRecord> map = getStateMap(state);
        if (map == null) {
            System.out.println("Unable to find state: " + state);
        }
        return map.get(id);
    }

    @Override
    public TaxPayerRecord add(String id, TaxPayerRecord record) {
        Map<String,TaxPayerRecord> map = getStateMap(record.getState());
        // Update tax payer's record if found
        TaxPayerRecord old = map.put(id, record);
        if (old != null) {
            // not found, restore old TaxPayerRecord
```

Continued

```java
            old = map.put(id, old);
        }
        return old;
    }

    @Override
    public TaxPayerRecord remove(String id, String state) {
        Map<String,TaxPayerRecord> map = getStateMap(state);
        TaxPayerRecord tmpRecord = null;
        if (map != null)
            tmpRecord = map.remove(id);
        return tmpRecord;
    }

    @Override
    public int size() {
        int size = 0;
        Iterator<Map<String,TaxPayerRecord>> itr =
                            db.values().iterator();
        while (itr.hasNext()) {
            Map<String,TaxPayerRecord> m = itr.next();
            if (m != null)
                size += m.size();
        }
        return size;
    }

    private Map<String, TaxPayerRecord> getStateMap(String state) {
        Map<String,TaxPayerRecord> map = db.get(state);
        if (map == null) {
            throw new UnsupportedOperationException(
                    "State (" + state + ") " +
                    "not found in tax payer database.");
        }
        return map;
    }
}
```

TaxCallable.java

```java
import java.util.List;
import java.util.Random;
import java.util.concurrent.Callable;

public class TaxCallable implements Callable<BailoutFuture> {

    private static long runTimeInMillis = BailoutMain.TEST_TIME;
    final private static ThreadLocal<Random> generator =
                                BailoutMain.threadLocalRandom;
    private long nullCounter, recordsRemoved, newRecordsAdded;
    private int index;
    private StateAndId stateAndId;
    final private List<StateAndId> taxPayerList;
    final private TaxPayerBailoutDB db;
```

```java
        public TaxCallable(List<StateAndId> taxPayerList,
                        TaxPayerBailoutDB db) {
            this.taxPayerList = taxPayerList;
            this.db = db;
            index = 0;
        }

        @Override
        public BailoutFuture call() throws Exception {
            long iterations = 0L, elapsedTime = 0L;
            long startTime = System.currentTimeMillis();
            double iterationsPerSecond = 0;
            do {
                setTaxPayer();
                iterations++;
                TaxPayerRecord tpr = null;
                if (iterations == Long.MAX_VALUE) {
                    long elapsed = System.currentTimeMillis() - startTime;
                    iterationsPerSecond =
                            iterations / ((double) (elapsed / 1000));
                    System.err.
                        println("Iteration counter about to overflow ...");
                    System.err.println(
                            "Calculating current operations per second ...");
                    System.err.println("Iterations per second: " +
                                        iterationsPerSecond);
                    iterations = 0L;
                    startTime = System.currentTimeMillis();
                    runTimeInMillis -= elapsed;
                }
                if (iterations % 1001 == 0) {
                    tpr = addNewTaxPayer(tpr);
                } else if (iterations % 60195 == 0) {
                    tpr = removeTaxPayer(tpr);
                } else {
                    tpr = updateTaxPayer(iterations, tpr);
                }

                if (iterations % 1000 == 0) {
                    elapsedTime = System.currentTimeMillis() - startTime;
                }
            } while (elapsedTime < runTimeInMillis);

            if (iterations >= 1000) {
                iterationsPerSecond =
                        iterations / ((double) (elapsedTime / 1000));
            }
            BailoutFuture bailoutFuture =
                    new BailoutFuture(iterationsPerSecond, newRecordsAdded,
                                    recordsRemoved, nullCounter);
            return bailoutFuture;
        }

        private TaxPayerRecord updateTaxPayer(long iterations,
                                        TaxPayerRecord tpr) {
```

Continued

```
            if (iterations % 1001 == 0) {
                tpr = db.get(stateAndId.getId(), stateAndId.getState());
            } else {
                // update a TaxPayer's DB record
                tpr = db.get(stateAndId.getId(), stateAndId.getState());
                if (tpr != null) {
                    long tax = generator.get().nextInt(10) + 15;
                    tpr.taxPaid(tax);
                }
            }
            if (tpr == null) {
                nullCounter++;
            }
            return tpr;
        }

        private TaxPayerRecord removeTaxPayer(TaxPayerRecord tpr) {
            // remove a TaxPayer from DB
            tpr = db.remove(stateAndId.getId(), stateAndId.getState());
            if (tpr != null) {
                // remove record from TaxPayerList
                taxPayerList.remove(index);
                recordsRemoved++;
            }
            return tpr;
        }

        private TaxPayerRecord addNewTaxPayer(TaxPayerRecord tpr) {
            // add a new TaxPayer to the DB
            String tmpTaxPayerId = BailoutMain.getRandomTaxPayerId();
            tpr = BailoutMain.makeTaxPayerRecord();
            TaxPayerRecord old = db.add(tmpTaxPayerId, tpr);
            if (old == null) {
                // add to the (local) list
                StateAndId sai =
                        new StateAndId(tmpTaxPayerId, tpr.getState());
                taxPayerList.add(sai);
                newRecordsAdded++;
            }
            return tpr;
        }

        private void setTaxPayer() {
            if (++index >= taxPayerList.size()) {
                index = 0;
            }
            this.stateAndId = taxPayerList.get(index);
        }
    }
```

BailoutFuture.java

```
public class BailoutFuture {
    private double iterationsPerSecond;
```

```
        private long recordsAdded, recordsRemoved, nullCounter;

        public BailoutFuture(double iterationsPerSecond, long recordsAdded,
                             long recordsRemoved, long nullCounter) {
            this.iterationsPerSecond = iterationsPerSecond;
            this.recordsAdded = recordsAdded;
            this.recordsRemoved = recordsRemoved;
            this.nullCounter = nullCounter;
        }

        public double getIterationsPerSecond() {
            return iterationsPerSecond;
        }

        public long getRecordsAdded() {
            return recordsAdded;
        }

        public long getRecordsRemoved() {
            return recordsRemoved;
        }

        public long getNullCounter() {
            return nullCounter;
        }
    }
```

StateAndId.java

```
    final public class StateAndId {
        private String id, state;

        public StateAndId(String id, String state) {
            this.id = id; this.state = state;
        }

        public String getState() {
            return state;
        }

        public void setState(String state) {
            this.state = state;
        }

        public String getId() {
            return id;
        }

        public void setId(String id) {
            this.id = id;
        }
    }
```

Second Resizing Variant

This implementation is an update of the previous "First Resizing Variant" by using HashMap constructors taking explicit sizes where the HashMap exceed the default HashMap size of 16 and StringBuilder constructors taking explicit sizes where the String being assembled exceeds the default size of 16.

BailoutMain.java

```java
/**
 * An example program to illustrate performance impact of Java Collections
resizing for Java Performance book.
 */
import java.text.DecimalFormat;
import java.text.NumberFormat;
import java.util.ArrayList;
import java.util.HashSet;
import java.util.List;
import java.util.Random;
import java.util.Set;
import java.util.concurrent.Callable;
import java.util.concurrent.ExecutionException;
import java.util.concurrent.ExecutorService;
import java.util.concurrent.Executors;
import java.util.concurrent.Future;
import java.util.logging.Level;
import java.util.logging.Logger;

public class BailoutMain {
    final public static int TEST_TIME = 240 * 1000;
    final public static ThreadLocal<Random> threadLocalRandom =
            new ThreadLocal<Random>() {
                @Override
                protected Random initialValue() {
                    return new Random(Thread.currentThread().getId());
                }
            };
    private static char[] alphabet = {'a', 'b', 'c', 'd', 'e', 'f',
                                      'g', 'h', 'i', 'j', 'k', 'l',
                                      'm', 'n', 'o', 'p', 'q', 'r',
                                      's', 't', 'u', 'v', 'w', 'x',
                                      'y', 'z'};
    static String[] states = {"Alabama", "Alaska", "Arizona",
        "Arkansas", "California", "Colorado", "Connecticut",
        "Delaware", "Florida", "Georgia", "Hawaii", "Idaho",
        "Illinois", "Indiana", "Iowa", "Kansas", "Kentucky",
        "Louisiana", "Maine", "Maryland", "Massachusetts", "Michigan",
        "Minnesota", "Mississippi", "Missouri", "Montana", "Nebraska",
        "Nevada", "New Hampshire", "New Jersey", "New Mexico",
        "New York", "North Carolina", "North Dakota", "Ohio",
        "Oklahoma", "Oregon", "Pennsylvania", "Rhode Island",
        "South Carolina", "South Dakota", "Tennessee", "Texas",
        "Utah", "Vermont", "Virginia", "Washington", "West Virginia",
        "Wisconsin", "Wyoming"};
```

```
public static void main(String[] args) {
    final long start = System.nanoTime();
    final int numberOfThreads =
            Runtime.getRuntime().availableProcessors();
    final int dbSize =
            TaxPayerBailoutDB.NUMBER_OF_RECORDS_DESIRED;
    final int taxPayerListSize = dbSize / numberOfThreads;

    System.out.println("Number of threads to run concurrently : " +
                        numberOfThreads);
    System.out.println("Tax payer database size: " + dbSize);

    // populate database with records
    System.out.println("Creating tax payer database ...");
    TaxPayerBailoutDB db =
            new TaxPayerBailoutDbImpl(dbSize, states.length);
    List<StateAndId>[] taxPayerList =
            new ArrayList[numberOfThreads];
    for (int i = 0; i < numberOfThreads; i++) {
        taxPayerList[i] =
                new ArrayList<StateAndId>(taxPayerListSize);
    }
    populateDatabase(db, taxPayerList, dbSize);
    final long initDbTime = System.nanoTime() - start;
    System.out.println("\tTax payer database created & " +
                        "populated in (" +
                        initDbTime/(1000*1000) + ") ms.");
    System.out.println("\tTax payer database created.");

    System.out.println("Allocating (" + numberOfThreads +
                        ") threads ...");
    // create a pool of executors to execute some Callables
    ExecutorService pool =
            Executors.newFixedThreadPool(numberOfThreads);

    Callable<BailoutFuture>[] callables =
            new TaxCallable[numberOfThreads];
    for (int i = 0; i < callables.length; i++) {
        callables[i] = new TaxCallable(taxPayerList[i], db);
    }

    System.out.println("\tthreads allocated.");

    // start all threads running
    System.out.println("Starting (" + callables.length +
                        ") threads ...");
    Set<Future<BailoutFuture>> set =
            new HashSet<Future<BailoutFuture>>();
    for (int i = 0; i < callables.length; i++) {
        Callable<BailoutFuture> callable = callables[i];
        Future<BailoutFuture> future = pool.submit(callable);
        set.add(future);
    }

    System.out.println("\t(" + callables.length +
                        ") threads started.");
```

Continued

```java
            // block and wait for all Callables to finish their
            System.out.println("Waiting for " + TEST_TIME / 1000 +
                               " seconds for (" + callables.length +
                               ") threads to complete ...");

            double iterationsPerSecond = 0;
            long recordsAdded = 0, recordsRemoved = 0, nullCounter = 0;
            int counter = 1;
            for (Future<BailoutFuture> future : set) {
                BailoutFuture result = null;
                try {
                    result = future.get();
                } catch (InterruptedException ex) {
                    Logger.getLogger(
                        BailoutMain.class.getName()).log(
                                    Level.SEVERE, null, ex);
                } catch (ExecutionException ex) {
                    Logger.getLogger(
                        BailoutMain.class.getName()).log(
                                    Level.SEVERE, null, ex);
                }
                System.out.println("Iterations per second on thread[" +
                                    counter++ + "] -> " +
                                    result.getIterationsPerSecond());
                iterationsPerSecond += result.getIterationsPerSecond();
                recordsAdded += result.getRecordsAdded();
                recordsRemoved += result.getRecordsRemoved();
                nullCounter = result.getNullCounter();
            }

            // print number of totals
            DecimalFormat df = new DecimalFormat("#.##");
            System.out.println("Total iterations per second --> " +
                                df.format(iterationsPerSecond));
            NumberFormat nf = NumberFormat.getInstance();
            System.out.println("Total records added ----------> " +
                                nf.format(recordsAdded));
            System.out.println("Total records removed --------> " +
                                nf.format(recordsRemoved));
            System.out.println("Total records in db ----------> " +
                                nf.format(db.size()));
            System.out.println("Total null records encountered: " +
                                nf.format(nullCounter));

            System.exit(0);
    }

    public static TaxPayerRecord makeTaxPayerRecord() {
        String firstName = getRandomName();
        String lastName = getRandomName();
        String ssn = getRandomSSN();
        String address = getRandomAddress();
        String city = getRandomCity();
        String state = getRandomState();
        return new TaxPayerRecord(firstName, lastName, ssn,
                address, city, state);
    }
```

```
    private static void populateDatabase(TaxPayerBailoutDB db,
                            List<StateAndId>[] taxPayerList,
                                            int dbSize) {
        for (int i = 0; i < dbSize; i++) {
            String taxPayerId = getRandomTaxPayerId();
            TaxPayerRecord tpr = makeTaxPayerRecord();
            db.add(taxPayerId, tpr);
            StateAndId stateAndId =
                    new StateAndId(taxPayerId, tpr.getState());
            int index = i % taxPayerList.length;
            taxPayerList[index].add(stateAndId);
        }
    }

    public static String getRandomTaxPayerId() {
        StringBuilder sb = new StringBuilder(20);
        for (int i = 0; i < 20; i++) {
            int index =
                threadLocalRandom.get().nextInt(alphabet.length);
            sb.append(alphabet[index]);
        }
        return sb.toString();
    }

    public static String getRandomName() {
        StringBuilder sb = new StringBuilder();
        int size = threadLocalRandom.get().nextInt(8) + 5;
        for (int i = 0; i < size; i++) {
            int index =
                threadLocalRandom.get().nextInt(alphabet.length);
            char c = alphabet[index];
            if (i == 0) {
                c = Character.toUpperCase(c);
            }
            sb.append(c);
        }
        return sb.toString();
    }

    public static String getRandomSSN() {
        StringBuilder sb = new StringBuilder();
        for (int i = 0; i < 11; i++) {
            if (i == 3 || i == 6) {
                sb.append('-');
            }
            int x = threadLocalRandom.get().nextInt(9);
            sb.append(x);
        }
        return sb.toString();
    }

    public static String getRandomAddress() {
        StringBuilder sb = new StringBuilder(24);
        int size = threadLocalRandom.get().nextInt(14) + 10;
        for (int i = 0; i < size; i++) {
```

Continued

```
                    if (i < 5) {
                        int x = threadLocalRandom.get().nextInt(8);
                        sb.append(x + 1);
                    }
                    int index =
                        threadLocalRandom.get().nextInt(alphabet.length);
                    char c = alphabet[index];
                    if (i == 5) {
                        c = Character.toUpperCase(c);
                    }
                    sb.append(c);
            }
            return sb.toString();
        }

        public static String getRandomCity() {
            StringBuilder sb = new StringBuilder();
            int size = threadLocalRandom.get().nextInt(5) + 6;
            for (int i = 0; i < size; i++) {
                int index =
                    threadLocalRandom.get().nextInt(alphabet.length);
                char c = alphabet[index];
                if (i == 0) {
                    c = Character.toUpperCase(c);
                }
                sb.append(c);
            }
            return sb.toString();
        }

        public static String getRandomState() {
            int index = threadLocalRandom.get().nextInt(states.length);
            return states[index];
        }
    }
}
```

TaxPayerRecord.java

```
import java.util.concurrent.atomic.AtomicLong;

public class TaxPayerRecord {
    private String firstName, lastName, ssn, address, city, state;
    private AtomicLong taxPaid;

    public TaxPayerRecord(String firstName, String lastName, String ssn,
                          String address, String city, String state) {
        this.firstName = firstName;
        this.lastName = lastName;
        this.ssn = ssn;
        this.address = address;
        this.city = city;
        this.state = state;
        this.taxPaid = new AtomicLong(0);
```

```java
        }
        public String getFirstName() {
            return firstName;
        }

        public void setFirstName(String firstName) {
            this.firstName = firstName;
        }

        public String getLastName() {
            return lastName;
        }

        public void setLastName(String lastName) {
            this.lastName = lastName;
        }

        public String getSsn() {
            return ssn;
        }

        public void setSsn(String ssn) {
            this.ssn = ssn;
        }

        public String getAddress() {
            return address;
        }

        public void setAddress(String address) {
            this.address = address;
        }

        public String getCity() {
            return city;
        }

        public void setCity(String city) {
            this.city = city;
        }

        public String getState() {
            return state;
        }

        public void setState(String state) {
            this.state = state;
        }

        public void taxPaid(long amount) {
            taxPaid.addAndGet(amount);
        }

        public long getTaxPaid() {
            return taxPaid.get();
        }
    }
}
```

TaxPayerBailoutDB.java

```java
public interface TaxPayerBailoutDB {

    static final int NUMBER_OF_RECORDS_DESIRED = 2 * 1000000;

    /**
     * Get a tax payers record from the database based on his or her id.
     *
     * @param taxPayersId - tax payers id
     * @param state - tax payers home state
     * @return tax payers record
     */
    TaxPayerRecord get(String id, String state);

    /**
     * Add new tax payers record in the database.
     *
     * @param id - tax payer's id
     * @param record - tax payer's record
     * @return taxPayersRecord just added to the database
     */
    TaxPayerRecord add(String id, TaxPayerRecord record);

    /**
     * Remove a tax payer's record from the database.
     *
     * @param taxPayersId - tax payer's id
     * @param taxPayersState - tax payer's state
     * @return tax payers record, or null if id not found in database
     */
    TaxPayerRecord remove(String id, String state);

    /**
     * Size of the database, i.e. number of records
     *
     * @return number of records in the database
     */
    int size();
}
```

TaxPayerBailoutDBImpl.java

```java
import java.util.Collections;
import java.util.HashMap;
import java.util.Iterator;
import java.util.Map;

public class TaxPayerBailoutDbImpl implements TaxPayerBailoutDB {
    private final Map<String, Map<String,TaxPayerRecord>> db;

    public TaxPayerBailoutDbImpl(int dbSize, int numberOfStates) {
        final int outerMapSize = (int) Math.ceil(numberOfStates / .75);
        final int innerMapSize =
```

```
                    (int) (Math.ceil((dbSize / numberOfStates) / .75));
        db =
         new HashMap<String,Map<String,TaxPayerRecord>>(outerMapSize);
        for (int i = 0; i < numberOfStates; i++) {
            Map<String,TaxPayerRecord> map =
                Collections.synchronizedMap(
                    new HashMap<String,TaxPayerRecord>(innerMapSize));
            db.put(BailoutMain.states[i], map);
        }
    }

    @Override
    public TaxPayerRecord get(String id, String state) {
        Map<String,TaxPayerRecord> map = getStateMap(state);
        if (map == null) {
            System.out.println("Unable to find state: " + state);
        }
        return map.get(id);
    }

    @Override
    public TaxPayerRecord add(String id, TaxPayerRecord record) {
        Map<String,TaxPayerRecord> map = getStateMap(record.getState());
        // Update tax payer's record if found
        TaxPayerRecord old = map.put(id, record);
        if (old != null) {
            // not found, restore old TaxPayerRecord
            old = map.put(id, old);
        }
        return old;
    }

    @Override
    public TaxPayerRecord remove(String id, String state) {
        Map<String,TaxPayerRecord> map = getStateMap(state);
        TaxPayerRecord tmpRecord = null;
        if (map != null)
            tmpRecord = map.remove(id);
        return tmpRecord;
    }

    @Override
    public int size() {
        int size = 0;
        Iterator<Map<String,TaxPayerRecord>> itr =
                            db.values().iterator();
        while (itr.hasNext()) {
            Map<String,TaxPayerRecord> m = itr.next();
            if (m != null)
                size += m.size();
        }
        return size;
    }

    private Map<String, TaxPayerRecord> getStateMap(String state) {
        Map<String,TaxPayerRecord> map = db.get(state);
```

Continued

```
            if (map == null) {
                throw new UnsupportedOperationException(
                        "State (" + state + ") " +
                        "not found in tax payer database.");
            }
            return map;
        }
}
```

TaxCallable.java

```java
import java.util.List;
import java.util.Random;
import java.util.concurrent.Callable;

public class TaxCallable implements Callable<BailoutFuture> {

    private static long runTimeInMillis = BailoutMain.TEST_TIME;
    final private static ThreadLocal<Random> generator =
                                BailoutMain.threadLocalRandom;
    private long nullCounter, recordsRemoved, newRecordsAdded;
    private int index;
    private StateAndId stateAndId;
    final private List<StateAndId> taxPayerList;
    final private TaxPayerBailoutDB db;

    public TaxCallable(List<StateAndId> taxPayerList,
                    TaxPayerBailoutDB db) {
        this.taxPayerList = taxPayerList;
        this.db = db;
        index = 0;
    }

    @Override
    public BailoutFuture call() throws Exception {
        long iterations = 0L, elapsedTime = 0L;
        long startTime = System.currentTimeMillis();
        double iterationsPerSecond = 0;
        do {
            setTaxPayer();
            iterations++;
            TaxPayerRecord tpr = null;
            if (iterations == Long.MAX_VALUE) {
                long elapsed = System.currentTimeMillis() - startTime;
                iterationsPerSecond =
                        iterations / ((double) (elapsed / 1000));
                System.err.
                    println("Iteration counter about to overflow ...");
                System.err.println(
                        "Calculating current operations per second ...");
                System.err.println("Iterations per second: " +
                                iterationsPerSecond);
                iterations = 0L;
                startTime = System.currentTimeMillis();
```

```
                    runTimeInMillis -= elapsed;
            }
            if (iterations % 1001 == 0) {
                tpr = addNewTaxPayer(tpr);
            } else if (iterations % 60195 == 0) {
                tpr = removeTaxPayer(tpr);
            } else {
                tpr = updateTaxPayer(iterations, tpr);
            }

            if (iterations % 1000 == 0) {
                elapsedTime = System.currentTimeMillis() - startTime;
            }
        } while (elapsedTime < runTimeInMillis);

        if (iterations >= 1000) {
            iterationsPerSecond =
                    iterations / ((double) (elapsedTime / 1000));
        }
        BailoutFuture bailoutFuture =
                new BailoutFuture(iterationsPerSecond, newRecordsAdded,
                                  recordsRemoved, nullCounter);
        return bailoutFuture;
    }

    private TaxPayerRecord updateTaxPayer(long iterations,
                                          TaxPayerRecord tpr) {
        if (iterations % 1001 == 0) {
            tpr = db.get(stateAndId.getId(), stateAndId.getState());
        } else {
            // update a TaxPayer's DB record
            tpr = db.get(stateAndId.getId(), stateAndId.getState());
            if (tpr != null) {
                long tax = generator.get().nextInt(10) + 15;
                tpr.taxPaid(tax);
            }
        }
        if (tpr == null) {
            nullCounter++;
        }
        return tpr;
    }

    private TaxPayerRecord removeTaxPayer(TaxPayerRecord tpr) {
        // remove a TaxPayer from DB
        tpr = db.remove(stateAndId.getId(), stateAndId.getState());
        if (tpr != null) {
            // remove record from TaxPayerList
            taxPayerList.remove(index);
            recordsRemoved++;
        }
        return tpr;
    }

    private TaxPayerRecord addNewTaxPayer(TaxPayerRecord tpr) {
```

Continued

```
        // add a new TaxPayer to the DB
        String tmpTaxPayerId = BailoutMain.getRandomTaxPayerId();
        tpr = BailoutMain.makeTaxPayerRecord();
        TaxPayerRecord old = db.add(tmpTaxPayerId, tpr);
        if (old == null) {
            // add to the (local) list
            StateAndId sai =
                    new StateAndId(tmpTaxPayerId, tpr.getState());
            taxPayerList.add(sai);
            newRecordsAdded++;
        }
        return tpr;
    }

    private void setTaxPayer() {
        if (++index >= taxPayerList.size()) {
            index = 0;
        }
        this.stateAndId = taxPayerList.get(index);
    }
}
```

BailoutFuture.java

```
public class BailoutFuture {
    private double iterationsPerSecond;
    private long recordsAdded, recordsRemoved, nullCounter;

    public BailoutFuture(double iterationsPerSecond, long recordsAdded,
                         long recordsRemoved, long nullCounter) {
        this.iterationsPerSecond = iterationsPerSecond;
        this.recordsAdded = recordsAdded;
        this.recordsRemoved = recordsRemoved;
        this.nullCounter = nullCounter;
    }

    public double getIterationsPerSecond() {
        return iterationsPerSecond;
    }

    public long getRecordsAdded() {
        return recordsAdded;
    }

    public long getRecordsRemoved() {
        return recordsRemoved;
    }

    public long getNullCounter() {
        return nullCounter;
    }
}
```

StateAndId.java

```java
final public class StateAndId {
    private String id, state;

    public StateAndId(String id, String state) {
        this.id = id; this.state = state;
    }

    public String getState() {
        return state;
    }

    public void setState(String state) {
        this.state = state;
    }

    public String getId() {
        return id;
    }

    public void setId(String id) {
        this.id = id;
    }
}
```

Increasing Parallelism Single-Threaded Implementation

This implementation is a copy of the "Lock Contention Third Implementation" seen earlier in this appendix with added instrumentation to report how long it takes to create the fictitious taxpayer records and add them to the database.

BailoutMain.java

```java
import java.text.DecimalFormat;
import java.text.NumberFormat;
import java.util.ArrayList;
import java.util.HashSet;
import java.util.List;
import java.util.Random;
import java.util.Set;
import java.util.concurrent.Callable;
import java.util.concurrent.ExecutionException;
import java.util.concurrent.ExecutorService;
import java.util.concurrent.Executors;
import java.util.concurrent.Future;
import java.util.logging.Level;
import java.util.logging.Logger;

public class BailoutMain {

    final public static int TEST_TIME = 240 * 1000;
```

Continued

```java
final public static ThreadLocal<Random> threadLocalRandom =
    new ThreadLocal<Random>() {
        @Override
        protected Random initialValue() {
            return new Random(Thread.currentThread().getId());
        }
    };
private static char[] alphabet = {'a', 'b', 'c', 'd', 'e', 'f',
    'g', 'h', 'i', 'j', 'k', 'l', 'm', 'n', 'o', 'p', 'q', 'r',
    's', 't', 'u', 'v', 'w', 'x', 'y', 'z'};
static String[] states = {"Alabama", "Alaska", "Arizona",
    "Arkansas", "California", "Colorado", "Connecticut",
    "Delaware", "Florida", "Georgia", "Hawaii", "Idaho",
    "Illinois", "Indiana", "Iowa", "Kansas", "Kentucky",
    "Louisiana", "Maine", "Maryland", "Massachusetts", "Michigan",
    "Minnesota", "Mississippi", "Missouri", "Montana", "Nebraska",
    "Nevada", "New Hampshire", "New Jersey", "New Mexico",
    "New York", "North Carolina", "North Dakota", "Ohio",
    "Oklahoma", "Oregon", "Pennsylvania", "Rhode Island",
    "South Carolina", "South Dakota", "Tennessee", "Texas",
    "Utah", "Vermont", "Virginia", "Washington", "West Virginia",
    "Wisconsin", "Wyoming"};

public static void main(String[] args) {
    final long start = System.nanoTime();
    final int numberOfThreads =
        Runtime.getRuntime().availableProcessors();
    final int dbSize =
        TaxPayerBailoutDB.NUMBER_OF_RECORDS_DESIRED;
    final int taxPayerListSize = dbSize / numberOfThreads;

    System.out.println("Number of threads to run concurrently : " +
                    numberOfThreads);
    System.out.println("Tax payer database size: " + dbSize);

    // populate database with records
    System.out.println("Creating tax payer database ...");
    TaxPayerBailoutDB db = new TaxPayerBailoutDbImpl(dbSize);
    List<String>[] taxPayerList = new ArrayList[numberOfThreads];
    for (int i = 0; i < numberOfThreads; i++) {
        taxPayerList[i] = new ArrayList<String>(taxPayerListSize);
    }
    populateDatabase(db, taxPayerList, dbSize);
    final long initDbTime = System.nanoTime() - start;
    System.out.println("\tDatabase created & populated in (" +
                    initDbTime/(1000*1000) + ") ms.");

    System.out.println("Allocating (" + numberOfThreads +
                    ") threads ...");
    // create a pool of executors to execute some Callables
    ExecutorService pool =
        Executors.newFixedThreadPool(numberOfThreads);

    Callable<BailoutFuture>[] callables =
        new TaxCallable[numberOfThreads];
    for (int i = 0; i < callables.length; i++) {
        callables[i] = new TaxCallable(taxPayerList[i], db);
    }
```

```java
System.out.println("\tthreads allocated.");

// start all threads running
System.out.println("Starting (" + callables.length +
                    ") threads ...");
Set<Future<BailoutFuture>> set =
    new HashSet<Future<BailoutFuture>>();
for (int i = 0; i < callables.length; i++) {
    Callable<BailoutFuture> callable = callables[i];
    Future<BailoutFuture> future = pool.submit(callable);
    set.add(future);
}

System.out.println("\t(" + callables.length +
                    ") threads started.");
// block and wait for all Callables to finish their
System.out.println("Waiting for " + TEST_TIME / 1000 +
                    " seconds for (" + callables.length +
                    ") threads to complete ...");

double iterationsPerSecond = 0;
long recordsAdded = 0, recordsRemoved = 0, nullCounter = 0;
int counter = 1;
for (Future<BailoutFuture> future : set) {
    BailoutFuture result = null;
    try {
        result = future.get();
    } catch (InterruptedException ex) {
        Logger.getLogger(BailoutMain.class.getName())
            .log(Level.SEVERE, null, ex);
    } catch (ExecutionException ex) {
        Logger.getLogger(BailoutMain.class.getName())
            .log(Level.SEVERE, null, ex);
    }
    System.out.println("Iterations per second on thread[" +
                    counter++ + "] -> " +
                    result.getIterationsPerSecond());
    iterationsPerSecond += result.getIterationsPerSecond();
    recordsAdded += result.getRecordsAdded();
    recordsRemoved += result.getRecordsRemoved();
    nullCounter = result.getNullCounter();
}

// print number of totals
DecimalFormat df = new DecimalFormat("#.##");
System.out.println("Total iterations per second --> " +
                    df.format(iterationsPerSecond));
NumberFormat nf = NumberFormat.getInstance();
System.out.println("Total records added ----------> " +
                    nf.format(recordsAdded));
System.out.println("Total records removed --------> " +
                    nf.format(recordsRemoved));
System.out.println("Total records in db ----------> " +
                    nf.format(db.size()));
System.out.println("Total null records encountered: " +
                    nf.format(nullCounter));
```

Continued

```java
        System.exit(0);
    }

    public static TaxPayerRecord makeTaxPayerRecord() {
        String firstName = getRandomName();
        String lastName = getRandomName();
        String ssn = getRandomSSN();
        String address = getRandomAddress();
        String city = getRandomCity();
        String state = getRandomState();
        return new TaxPayerRecord(firstName, lastName, ssn,
                address, city, state);
    }

    private static void populateDatabase(TaxPayerBailoutDB db,
                    List<String>[] taxPayerIdList, int dbSize) {
        for (int i = 0; i < dbSize; i++) {
            String key = getRandomTaxPayerId();
            TaxPayerRecord tpr = makeTaxPayerRecord();
            db.add(key, tpr);
            int index = i % taxPayerIdList.length;
            taxPayerIdList[index].add(key);
        }
    }

    public static String getRandomTaxPayerId() {
        StringBuilder sb = new StringBuilder(20);
        for (int i = 0; i < 20; i++) {
            int index =
                threadLocalRandom.get().nextInt(alphabet.length);
            sb.append(alphabet[index]);
        }
        return sb.toString();
    }

    public static String getRandomName() {
        StringBuilder sb = new StringBuilder();
        int size = threadLocalRandom.get().nextInt(8) + 5;
        for (int i = 0; i < size; i++) {
            int index =
                threadLocalRandom.get().nextInt(alphabet.length);
            char c = alphabet[index];
            if (i == 0) {
                c = Character.toUpperCase(c);
            }
            sb.append(c);
        }
        return sb.toString();
    }

    public static String getRandomSSN() {
        StringBuilder sb = new StringBuilder();
        for (int i = 0; i < 11; i++) {
            if (i == 3 || i == 6) {
                sb.append('-');
            }
            int x = threadLocalRandom.get().nextInt(9);
```

```java
            sb.append(x);
        }
        return sb.toString();
    }

    public static String getRandomAddress() {
        StringBuilder sb = new StringBuilder(24);
        int size = threadLocalRandom.get().nextInt(14) + 10;
        for (int i = 0; i < size; i++) {
            if (i < 5) {
                int x = threadLocalRandom.get().nextInt(8);
                sb.append(x + 1);
            }
            int index =
                threadLocalRandom.get().nextInt(alphabet.length);
            char c = alphabet[index];
            if (i == 5) {
                c = Character.toUpperCase(c);
            }
            sb.append(c);
        }
        return sb.toString();
    }

    public static String getRandomCity() {
        StringBuilder sb = new StringBuilder();
        int size = threadLocalRandom.get().nextInt(5) + 6;
        for (int i = 0; i < size; i++) {
            int index =
                threadLocalRandom.get().nextInt(alphabet.length);
            char c = alphabet[index];
            if (i == 0) {
                c = Character.toUpperCase(c);
            }
            sb.append(c);
        }
        return sb.toString();
    }

    public static String getRandomState() {
        int index = threadLocalRandom.get().nextInt(states.length);
        return states[index];
    }
}
```

TaxPayerRecord.java

```java
import java.util.concurrent.atomic.AtomicLong;

public class TaxPayerRecord {
    private String firstName, lastName, ssn, address, city, state;
    private AtomicLong taxPaid;

    public TaxPayerRecord(String firstName, String lastName, String ssn,
```

Continued

```
                          String address, String city, String state) {
    this.firstName = firstName;
    this.lastName = lastName;
    this.ssn = ssn;
    this.address = address;
    this.city = city;
    this.state = state;
    this.taxPaid = new AtomicLong(0);
}

public String getFirstName() {
    return firstName;
}

public void setFirstName(String firstName) {
    this.firstName = firstName;
}

public String getLastName() {
    return lastName;
}

public void setLastName(String lastName) {
    this.lastName = lastName;
}

public String getSsn() {
    return ssn;
}

public void setSsn(String ssn) {
    this.ssn = ssn;
}

public String getAddress() {
    return address;
}

public void setAddress(String address) {
    this.address = address;
}

public String getCity() {
    return city;
}

public void setCity(String city) {
    this.city = city;
}

public String getState() {
    return state;
}

public void setState(String state) {
    this.state = state;
}

public void taxPaid(long amount) {
```

```
            taxPaid.addAndGet(amount);
    }

    public long getTaxPaid() {
        return taxPaid.get();
    }
}
```

`TaxPayerBailoutDB.java`

```java
public interface TaxPayerBailoutDB {

    static final int NUMBER_OF_RECORDS_DESIRED = 2 * 1000000;

    /**
     * Get a tax payers record from the database based on his or her id.
     *
     * @param id - tax payers id
     * @return tax payers record
     */
    TaxPayerRecord get(String id);

    /**
     * Add new tax payers record in the database.
     *
     * @param id - tax payer's id
     * @param record - tax payer's record
     * @return taxPayersRecord just added to the database
     */
    TaxPayerRecord add(String id,  TaxPayerRecord record);

    /**
     * Remove a tax payer's record from the database.
     *
     * @param id - tax payer's id
     * @return tax payers record, or null if tax payer's id not found
     */
    TaxPayerRecord remove(String id);

    /**
     * Size of the database, i.e. number of records
     *
     * @return number of records in the database
     */
    int size();
}
```

`TaxPayerBailoutDbImpl.java`

```java
import java.util.Map;
import java.util.concurrent.ConcurrentHashMap;

public class TaxPayerBailoutDbImpl implements TaxPayerBailoutDB {
    private final Map<String,TaxPayerRecord> db;
```

Continued

```java
    public TaxPayerBailoutDbImpl(int size) {
        db = new ConcurrentHashMap<String,TaxPayerRecord>(size);
    }

    @Override
    public TaxPayerRecord get(String id) {
        return db.get(id);
    }

    @Override
    public TaxPayerRecord add(String id, TaxPayerRecord record) {
        TaxPayerRecord old = db.put(id, record);
        if (old != null) {
            // restore old TaxPayerRecord
            old = db.put(id, old);
        }
        return old;
    }

    @Override
    public TaxPayerRecord remove(String id) {
        return db.remove(id);
    }

    @Override
    public int size() {
        return db.size();
    }
}
```

TaxCallable.java

```java
import java.util.List;
import java.util.Random;
import java.util.concurrent.Callable;

public class TaxCallable implements Callable<BailoutFuture> {

    private static long runTimeInMillis = BailoutMain.TEST_TIME;
    final private static ThreadLocal<Random> generator =
                                    BailoutMain.threadLocalRandom;
    private long nullCounter, recordsRemoved, newRecordsAdded;
    private int index;
    private String taxPayerId;
    final private List<String> taxPayerList;
    final private TaxPayerBailoutDB db;

    public TaxCallable(List<String> taxPayerList, TaxPayerBailoutDB db){
        this.taxPayerList = taxPayerList;
        this.db = db;
        index = 0;
    }

    @Override
    public BailoutFuture call() throws Exception {
```

```
        long iterations = 0L, elapsedTime = 0L;
        long startTime = System.currentTimeMillis();
        double iterationsPerSecond = 0;
        do {
            setTaxPayer();
            iterations++;
            TaxPayerRecord tpr = null;
            if (iterations == Long.MAX_VALUE) {
                long elapsed = System.currentTimeMillis() - startTime;
                iterationsPerSecond = iterations /
                                        ((double) (elapsed / 1000));
                System.err.println("Iteration counter overflow ...");
                System.err.println("Calculating current ops per sec.");
                System.err.println("Iterations per second: " +
                                        iterationsPerSecond);
                iterations = 0L;
                startTime = System.currentTimeMillis();
                runTimeInMillis -= elapsed;
            }
            if (iterations % 1001 == 0) {
                tpr = addNewTaxPayer(tpr);
            } else if (iterations % 60195 == 0) {
                tpr = removeTaxPayer(tpr);
            } else {
                tpr = updateTaxPayer(iterations, tpr);
            }

            if (iterations % 1000 == 0) {
                elapsedTime = System.currentTimeMillis() - startTime;
            }
        } while (elapsedTime < runTimeInMillis);

        if (iterations >= 1000) {
            iterationsPerSecond = iterations /
                                ((double) (elapsedTime / 1000));
        }
        BailoutFuture bailoutFuture =
                new BailoutFuture(iterationsPerSecond, newRecordsAdded,
                                recordsRemoved, nullCounter);
        return bailoutFuture;
    }

    private TaxPayerRecord updateTaxPayer(long iterations,
                                        TaxPayerRecord tpr) {
        if (iterations % 1001 == 0) {
            tpr = db.get(taxPayerId);
        } else {
            // update a TaxPayer's DB record
            tpr = db.get(taxPayerId);
            if (tpr != null) {
                long tax = generator.get().nextInt(10) + 15;
                tpr.taxPaid(tax);
            }
        }
        if (tpr == null) {
            nullCounter++;
        }
```

Continued

```
        return tpr;
    }

    private TaxPayerRecord removeTaxPayer(TaxPayerRecord tpr) {
        // remove a TaxPayer from DB
        tpr = db.remove(taxPayerId);
        if (tpr != null) {
            // remove record from TaxPayerList
            taxPayerList.remove(index);
            recordsRemoved++;
        }
        return tpr;
    }

    private TaxPayerRecord addNewTaxPayer(TaxPayerRecord tpr) {
        // add a new TaxPayer to the DB
        String tmpTaxPayerId = BailoutMain.getRandomTaxPayerId();
        tpr = BailoutMain.makeTaxPayerRecord();
        TaxPayerRecord old = db.add(tmpTaxPayerId, tpr);
        if (old == null) {
            // add to the (local) list
            taxPayerList.add(tmpTaxPayerId);
            newRecordsAdded++;
        }
        return tpr;
    }

    public void setTaxPayer() {
        if (++index >= taxPayerList.size()) {
            index = 0;
        }
        this.taxPayerId = taxPayerList.get(index);
    }
}
```

BailoutFuture.java

```
public class BailoutFuture {
    private double iterationsPerSecond;
    private long recordsAdded, recordsRemoved, nullCounter;

    public BailoutFuture(double iterationsPerSecond, long recordsAdded,
                         long recordsRemoved, long nullCounter) {
        this.iterationsPerSecond = iterationsPerSecond;
        this.recordsAdded = recordsAdded;
        this.recordsRemoved = recordsRemoved;
        this.nullCounter = nullCounter;
    }

    public double getIterationsPerSecond() {
        return iterationsPerSecond;
    }

    public long getRecordsAdded() {
```

```
            return recordsAdded;
        }

        public long getRecordsRemoved() {
            return recordsRemoved;
        }

        public long getNullCounter() {
            return nullCounter;
        }
    }
```

Increasing Parallelism Multithreaded Implementation

This implementation is a refactored copy of the previous "Increasing Parallelism Single-Threaded Implementation." It multithreads the initialization of the taxpayer database.

BailoutMain.java

```java
import java.text.DecimalFormat;
import java.text.NumberFormat;
import java.util.ArrayList;
import java.util.Collections;
import java.util.HashSet;
import java.util.List;
import java.util.Random;
import java.util.Set;
import java.util.concurrent.Callable;
import java.util.concurrent.ExecutionException;
import java.util.concurrent.ExecutorService;
import java.util.concurrent.Executors;
import java.util.concurrent.Future;
import java.util.logging.Level;
import java.util.logging.Logger;

public class BailoutMain {
    final public static int TEST_TIME = 240 * 1000;
    final public static ThreadLocal<Random> threadLocalRandom =
            new ThreadLocal<Random>() {
                @Override
                protected Random initialValue() {
                    return new Random(Thread.currentThread().getId());
                }
            };
    private static char[] alphabet = {'a', 'b', 'c', 'd', 'e', 'f',
        'g', 'h', 'i', 'j', 'k', 'l', 'm', 'n', 'o', 'p', 'q', 'r',
        's', 't', 'u', 'v', 'w', 'x', 'y', 'z'};
    static String[] states = {"Alabama", "Alaska", "Arizona",
        "Arkansas", "California", "Colorado", "Connecticut",
        "Delaware", "Florida", "Georgia", "Hawaii", "Idaho",
```

Continued

```
       "Illinois", "Indiana", "Iowa", "Kansas", "Kentucky",
       "Louisiana", "Maine", "Maryland", "Massachusetts", "Michigan",
       "Minnesota", "Mississippi", "Missouri", "Montana", "Nebraska",
       "Nevada", "New Hampshire", "New Jersey", "New Mexico",
       "New York", "North Carolina", "North Dakota", "Ohio",
       "Oklahoma", "Oregon", "Pennsylvania", "Rhode Island",
       "South Carolina", "South Dakota", "Tennessee", "Texas", "Utah",
       "Vermont", "Virginia", "Washington", "West Virginia",
       "Wisconsin", "Wyoming"};

   public static void main(String[] args) {
       final long start = System.nanoTime();
       final int numberOfThreads =
           Runtime.getRuntime().availableProcessors();
       final int dbSize = TaxPayerBailoutDB.NUMBER_OF_RECORDS_DESIRED;
       final int taxPayerListSize = dbSize / numberOfThreads;

       System.out.println("Number of threads to run concurrently : " +
                       numberOfThreads);
       System.out.println("Tax payer database size: " + dbSize);

       // populate database with records
       System.out.println("Creating tax payer database ...");
       TaxPayerBailoutDB db = new TaxPayerBailoutDbImpl(dbSize);
       List<String>[] taxPayerList = new List[numberOfThreads];
       for (int i = 0; i < numberOfThreads; i++) {
           taxPayerList[i] =
                   Collections.synchronizedList(
                       new ArrayList<String>(taxPayerListSize));
       }

       System.out.println("Allocating thread pool and (" +
           numberOfThreads + ") db initializer threads ...");

       // create a pool of executors to execute some Callables
       ExecutorService pool =
           Executors.newFixedThreadPool(numberOfThreads);
       Callable<DbInitializerFuture>[] dbCallables =
           new DbInitializer[numberOfThreads];
       for (int i = 0; i < dbCallables.length; i++) {
           dbCallables[i] =
               new DbInitializer(db, taxPayerList,
                               dbSize/numberOfThreads);
       }

       System.out.println("\tThread pool & db threads allocated.");

       // start all db initializer threads running
       System.out.println("Starting (" + dbCallables.length +
                       ") db initializer threads ...");
       Set<Future<DbInitializerFuture>> dbSet =
           new HashSet<Future<DbInitializerFuture>>();
       for (int i = 0; i < dbCallables.length; i++) {
           Callable<DbInitializerFuture> callable = dbCallables[i];
           Future<DbInitializerFuture> future = pool.submit(callable);
           dbSet.add(future);
       }
```

```
int recordsCreated = 0;
for (Future<DbInitializerFuture> future : dbSet) {
    DbInitializerFuture result = null;
    try {
        result = future.get();
    } catch (InterruptedException ex) {
        Logger.getLogger(BailoutMain.class.getName())
                .log(Level.SEVERE, null, ex);
    } catch (ExecutionException ex) {
        Logger.getLogger(BailoutMain.class.getName())
                .log(Level.SEVERE, null, ex);
    }
    recordsCreated += result.getRecordsCreated();
}
final long initDbTime = System.nanoTime() - start;
System.out.println("\tDb initializer threads completed.");
System.out.println("\tTax payer db created & populated in (" +
                initDbTime/(1000*1000) + ") ms.");
System.out.println("\tCreated (" + recordsCreated +
                ") records ...");

System.out.println("Allocating threads, main processing ...");
Callable<BailoutFuture>[] callables =
    new TaxCallable[numberOfThreads];
for (int i = 0; i < callables.length; i++) {
    callables[i] = new TaxCallable(taxPayerList[i], db);
}

System.out.println("\tthreads allocated.");

// start all threads running
System.out.println("Starting (" + callables.length +
                ") threads ...");
Set<Future<BailoutFuture>> set =
    new HashSet<Future<BailoutFuture>>();
for (int i = 0; i < callables.length; i++) {
    Callable<BailoutFuture> callable = callables[i];
    Future<BailoutFuture> future = pool.submit(callable);
    set.add(future);
}

System.out.println("\t(" + callables.length +
                ") threads started.");
// block and wait for all Callables to finish their
System.out.println("Waiting for " + TEST_TIME / 1000 +
                " seconds for (" + callables.length +
                ") threads to complete ...");

double iterationsPerSecond = 0;
long recordsAdded = 0, recordsRemoved = 0, nullCounter = 0;
int counter = 1;
for (Future<BailoutFuture> future : set) {
    BailoutFuture result = null;
    try {
```

Continued

```
                    result = future.get();
            } catch (InterruptedException ex) {
                Logger.getLogger(BailoutMain.class.getName())
                    .log(Level.SEVERE, null, ex);
            } catch (ExecutionException ex) {
                Logger.getLogger(BailoutMain.class.getName())
                    .log(Level.SEVERE, null, ex);
            }
            System.out.println("Iterations per second on thread[" +
                counter++ + "] -> " + result.getIterationsPerSecond());
            iterationsPerSecond += result.getIterationsPerSecond();
            recordsAdded += result.getRecordsAdded();
            recordsRemoved += result.getRecordsRemoved();
            nullCounter = result.getNullCounter();
        }

        // print number of totals
        DecimalFormat df = new DecimalFormat("#.##");
        System.out.println("Total iterations per second --> " +
            df.format(iterationsPerSecond));
        NumberFormat nf = NumberFormat.getInstance();
        System.out.println("Total records added ----------> " +
            nf.format(recordsAdded));
        System.out.println("Total records removed --------> " +
            nf.format(recordsRemoved));
        System.out.println("Total records in db ----------> " +
            nf.format(db.size()));
        System.out.println("Total null records encountered: " +
            nf.format(nullCounter));

        System.exit(0);
    }

    public static TaxPayerRecord makeTaxPayerRecord() {
        String firstName = getRandomName();
        String lastName = getRandomName();
        String ssn = getRandomSSN();
        String address = getRandomAddress();
        String city = getRandomCity();
        String state = getRandomState();
        return new TaxPayerRecord(firstName, lastName, ssn,
                address, city, state);
    }

    static DbInitializerFuture populateDatabase(TaxPayerBailoutDB db,
                                    List<String>[] taxPayerIdList,
                                    int dbSize) {
        for (int i = 0; i < dbSize; i++) {
            String key = getRandomTaxPayerId();
            TaxPayerRecord tpr = makeTaxPayerRecord();
            db.add(key, tpr);
            int index = i % taxPayerIdList.length;
            taxPayerIdList[index].add(key);
        }
        DbInitializerFuture future = new DbInitializerFuture();
        future.addToRecordsCreated(dbSize);
```

```
        return future;
    }

    public static String getRandomTaxPayerId() {
        StringBuilder sb = new StringBuilder(20);
        for (int i = 0; i < 20; i++) {
            int index =
                threadLocalRandom.get().nextInt(alphabet.length);
            sb.append(alphabet[index]);
        }
        return sb.toString();
    }

    public static String getRandomName() {
        StringBuilder sb = new StringBuilder();
        int size = threadLocalRandom.get().nextInt(8) + 5;
        for (int i = 0; i < size; i++) {
            int index =
                threadLocalRandom.get().nextInt(alphabet.length);
            char c = alphabet[index];
            if (i == 0) {
                c = Character.toUpperCase(c);
            }
            sb.append(c);
        }
        return sb.toString();
    }

    public static String getRandomSSN() {
        StringBuilder sb = new StringBuilder();
        for (int i = 0; i < 11; i++) {
            if (i == 3 || i == 6) {
                sb.append('-');
            }
            int x = threadLocalRandom.get().nextInt(9);
            sb.append(x);
        }
        return sb.toString();
    }

    public static String getRandomAddress() {
        StringBuilder sb = new StringBuilder(24);
        int size = threadLocalRandom.get().nextInt(14) + 10;
        for (int i = 0; i < size; i++) {
            if (i < 5) {
                int x = threadLocalRandom.get().nextInt(8);
                sb.append(x + 1);
            }
            int index =
                threadLocalRandom.get().nextInt(alphabet.length);
            char c = alphabet[index];
            if (i == 5) {
                c = Character.toUpperCase(c);
            }
```

Continued

```
            sb.append(c);
        }
        return sb.toString();
    }

    public static String getRandomCity() {
        StringBuilder sb = new StringBuilder();
        int size = threadLocalRandom.get().nextInt(5) + 6;
        for (int i = 0; i < size; i++) {
            int index =
                threadLocalRandom.get().nextInt(alphabet.length);
            char c = alphabet[index];
            if (i == 0) {
                c = Character.toUpperCase(c);
            }
            sb.append(c);
        }
        return sb.toString();
    }

    public static String getRandomState() {
        int index = threadLocalRandom.get().nextInt(states.length);
        return states[index];
    }
}
```

DbInitializer.java

```java
import java.util.List;
import java.util.concurrent.Callable;

public class DbInitializer implements Callable<DbInitializerFuture> {

    private TaxPayerBailoutDB db;
    private List<String>[] taxPayerList;
    private int recordsToCreate;

    public DbInitializer(TaxPayerBailoutDB db,
                         List<String>[] taxPayerList,
                         int recordsToCreate) {
        this.db = db;
        this.taxPayerList = taxPayerList;
        this.recordsToCreate = recordsToCreate;
    }

    @Override
    public DbInitializerFuture call() throws Exception {
        return BailoutMain.populateDatabase(db, taxPayerList,
                                            recordsToCreate);
    }
}
```

DbInitializerFuture.java

```java
public class DbInitializerFuture {
    private int recordsCreated;

    public DbInitializerFuture() {}

    public void addToRecordsCreated(int value) {
        recordsCreated += value;
    }

    public int getRecordsCreated() {
        return recordsCreated;
    }
}
```

TaxPayerRecord.java

```java
import java.util.concurrent.atomic.AtomicLong;

public class TaxPayerRecord {
    private String firstName, lastName, ssn, address, city, state;
    private AtomicLong taxPaid;

    public TaxPayerRecord(String firstName, String lastName, String ssn,
                          String address, String city, String state) {
        this.firstName = firstName;
        this.lastName = lastName;
        this.ssn = ssn;
        this.address = address;
        this.city = city;
        this.state = state;
        this.taxPaid = new AtomicLong(0);
    }

    public String getFirstName() {
        return firstName;
    }

    public void setFirstName(String firstName) {
        this.firstName = firstName;
    }

    public String getLastName() {
        return lastName;
    }

    public void setLastName(String lastName) {
        this.lastName = lastName;
    }
```

Continued

```java
    public String getSsn() {
        return ssn;
    }

    public void setSsn(String ssn) {
        this.ssn = ssn;
    }

    public String getAddress() {
        return address;
    }

    public void setAddress(String address) {
        this.address = address;
    }

    public String getCity() {
        return city;
    }

    public void setCity(String city) {
        this.city = city;
    }

    public String getState() {
        return state;
    }

    public void setState(String state) {
        this.state = state;
    }

    public void taxPaid(long amount) {
        taxPaid.addAndGet(amount);
    }

    public long getTaxPaid() {
        return taxPaid.get();
    }
}
```

TaxPayerBailoutDB.java

```java
public interface TaxPayerBailoutDB {

    static final int NUMBER_OF_RECORDS_DESIRED = 2 * 1000000;

    /**
     * Get a tax payers record from the database based on his or her id.
     *
     * @param id - tax payers id
     * @return tax payers record
     */
    TaxPayerRecord get(String id);

    /**
```

```
         * Add new tax payers record in the database.
         *
         * @param id - tax payer's id
         * @param record - tax payer's record
         * @return taxPayersRecord just added to the database
         */
        TaxPayerRecord add(String id,  TaxPayerRecord record);

        /**
         * Remove a tax payer's record from the database.
         *
         * @param id - tax payer's id
         * @return tax payers record, or null if tax payer's id not found
         */
        TaxPayerRecord remove(String id);

        /**
         * Size of the database, i.e. number of records
         *
         * @return number of records in the database
         */
        int size();
}
```

TaxPayerBailoutDbImpl.java

```java
import java.util.Map;
import java.util.concurrent.ConcurrentHashMap;

public class TaxPayerBailoutDbImpl implements TaxPayerBailoutDB {
    private final Map<String,TaxPayerRecord> db;

    public TaxPayerBailoutDbImpl(int size) {
        db = new ConcurrentHashMap<String,TaxPayerRecord>(size);
    }

    @Override
    public TaxPayerRecord get(String id) {
        return db.get(id);
    }

    @Override
    public TaxPayerRecord add(String id, TaxPayerRecord record) {
        TaxPayerRecord old = db.put(id, record);
        if (old != null) {
            // restore old TaxPayerRecord
            old = db.put(id, old);
        }
        return old;
    }

    @Override
    public TaxPayerRecord remove(String id) {
```

Continued

```
            return db.remove(id);
    }

    @Override
    public int size() {
        return db.size();
    }
}
```

TaxCallable.java

```java
import java.util.List;
import java.util.Random;
import java.util.concurrent.Callable;

public class TaxCallable implements Callable<BailoutFuture> {

    private static long runTimeInMillis = BailoutMain.TEST_TIME;
    final private static ThreadLocal<Random> generator =
                                BailoutMain.threadLocalRandom;
    private long nullCounter, recordsRemoved, newRecordsAdded;
    private int index;
    private String taxPayerId;
    final private List<String> taxPayerList;
    final private TaxPayerBailoutDB db;

    public TaxCallable(List<String> taxPayerList, TaxPayerBailoutDB db){
        this.taxPayerList = taxPayerList;
        this.db = db;
        index = 0;
    }

    @Override
    public BailoutFuture call() throws Exception {
        long iterations = 0L, elapsedTime = 0L;
        long startTime = System.currentTimeMillis();
        double iterationsPerSecond = 0;
        do {
            setTaxPayer();
            iterations++;
            TaxPayerRecord tpr = null;
            if (iterations == Long.MAX_VALUE) {
                long elapsed = System.currentTimeMillis() - startTime;
                iterationsPerSecond = iterations /
                                        ((double) (elapsed / 1000));
                System.err.println("Iteration counter overflow ...");
                System.err.println("Calculating current ops per sec.");
                System.err.println("Iterations per second: " +
                                    iterationsPerSecond);
                iterations = 0L;
                startTime = System.currentTimeMillis();
                runTimeInMillis -= elapsed;
            }
```

```
            if (iterations % 1001 == 0) {
                tpr = addNewTaxPayer(tpr);
            } else if (iterations % 60195 == 0) {
                tpr = removeTaxPayer(tpr);
            } else {
                tpr = updateTaxPayer(iterations, tpr);
            }

            if (iterations % 1000 == 0) {
                elapsedTime = System.currentTimeMillis() - startTime;
            }
        } while (elapsedTime < runTimeInMillis);

        if (iterations >= 1000) {
            iterationsPerSecond = iterations /
                            ((double) (elapsedTime / 1000));
        }
        BailoutFuture bailoutFuture =
                new BailoutFuture(iterationsPerSecond, newRecordsAdded,
                            recordsRemoved, nullCounter);
        return bailoutFuture;
}

private TaxPayerRecord updateTaxPayer(long iterations,
                                    TaxPayerRecord tpr) {
    if (iterations % 1001 == 0) {
        tpr = db.get(taxPayerId);
    } else {
        // update a TaxPayer's DB record
        tpr = db.get(taxPayerId);
        if (tpr != null) {
            long tax = generator.get().nextInt(10) + 15;
            tpr.taxPaid(tax);
        }
    }
    if (tpr == null) {
        nullCounter++;
    }
    return tpr;
}

private TaxPayerRecord removeTaxPayer(TaxPayerRecord tpr) {
    // remove a TaxPayer from DB
    tpr = db.remove(taxPayerId);
    if (tpr != null) {
        // remove record from TaxPayerList
        taxPayerList.remove(index);
        recordsRemoved++;
    }
    return tpr;
}

private TaxPayerRecord addNewTaxPayer(TaxPayerRecord tpr) {
    // add a new TaxPayer to the DB
    String tmpTaxPayerId = BailoutMain.getRandomTaxPayerId();
```

Continued

```
            tpr = BailoutMain.makeTaxPayerRecord();
            TaxPayerRecord old = db.add(tmpTaxPayerId, tpr);
            if (old == null) {
                // add to the (local) list
                taxPayerList.add(tmpTaxPayerId);
                newRecordsAdded++;
            }
            return tpr;
        }

        public void setTaxPayer() {
            if (++index >= taxPayerList.size()) {
                index = 0;
            }
            this.taxPayerId = taxPayerList.get(index);
        }
    }
```

BailoutFuture.java

```
    public class BailoutFuture {
        private double iterationsPerSecond;
        private long recordsAdded, recordsRemoved, nullCounter;

        public BailoutFuture(double iterationsPerSecond, long recordsAdded,
                             long recordsRemoved, long nullCounter) {
            this.iterationsPerSecond = iterationsPerSecond;
            this.recordsAdded = recordsAdded;
            this.recordsRemoved = recordsRemoved;
            this.nullCounter = nullCounter;
        }

        public double getIterationsPerSecond() {
            return iterationsPerSecond;
        }

        public long getRecordsAdded() {
            return recordsAdded;
        }

        public long getRecordsRemoved() {
            return recordsRemoved;
        }

        public long getNullCounter() {
            return nullCounter;
        }
    }
```

Index